WOMEN IN AMERICAN SOCIETY

Women in American Society

An Introduction to Women's Studies

FOURTH EDITION

Virginia Sapiro

Sophonisba P. Breckinridge Professor of Political Science and Women's Studies
University of Wisconsin, Madison

Mayfield Publishing Company
Mountain View, California
London • Toronto

Library of Congress Cataloging-in-Publication Data
Sapiro, Virginia.
   Women in American society: an introduction to women's studies /
Virginia Sapiro—4th ed.
     p. cm.
   Includes bibliographical references and index.
   ISBN 1-55934-935-2
   1. Women—United States.   2. Women's studies—United States.
HQ1421.S27   1998
305.42'0973—dc21   98-9744
                                                   CIP

Manufactured in the United States of America
10 9 8 7 6 5 4 3 2 1

Mayfield Publishing Company
1280 Villa Street
Mountain View, California 94041

Sponsoring editor, Franklin C. Graham; production editor, Melissa Kreischer; manuscript editor, Shari Hatch; design manager, Jean Mailander; text designer, Joan Greenfield; cover designer, Amy Evans McClure; art manager, Robin Mouat; photo researcher, Brian Pecko; manufacturing manager, Randy Hurst. Cover: *Uncial,* 1967 by Lee Krasner, © 1998 Pollock-Krasner Foundation/Artists Rights Society (ARS), New York, image courtesy of Robert Miller Gallery, New York. The text was set in 10/12 Galliard by TBH Typecast, Inc. and printed on acid-free 45# Glatfelter Restorecote by Malloy Lithographing, Inc. Credits appear on page 553–554, which constitute an extension of the copyright page.

✺ This book is printed on recycled paper.

Contents

v

PART THREE

Choice and Control in Personal Life, the Family, and Work 321

Preface

About This Book

There are many ways to introduce the field of women's studies. *Women in American Society* emphasizes knowledge gained from the diverse approaches used by social scientists to understand the ways that gender structures the culture and society of the United States. This book is shaped by my roughly 25 years of teaching in women's studies and by the comments of many students, teachers, and scholars on earlier editions. It is designed to be a rigorous academic work, based on careful analysis of research, guided by feminist theory, but it is written to be interesting and accessible to those with no background in either women's studies or the social sciences.

Because this book is intended to *introduce* women's studies, I have traded depth for breadth in order to offer exposure to a wide variety of the interesting and important aspects of this field of study. Nevertheless, it cannot possibly cover everything. Writing this book required me to make many choices and solve many problems. My choices reflect my training, my research and teaching experience, and my disciplinary background.

Scope and Approach

Following are some of the choices I made in writing this book and their significance for those who read this book.

The United States in Comparative and International Perspective   *Women in American Society* focuses primarily on the United States, but it often views this nation from a comparative and international perspective. A *comparative perspective* places the United States in the contexts of both national and cross-national diversity. The context of *national diversity* refers to how the impact and experience of gender in the United States (or any other country) differs systematically, depending, for example, on one's class, race, or age, or on whether one lives in a big city or a rural area. The context of *cross-national diversity* refers to how gender-related social and cultural phenomena vary across nations, such that cross-national comparisons can enhance the understanding of these phenomenon within the United States.

This book also places the United States in *international perspective* because the dynamics of one society cannot be understood in isolation. This text shows how American women are affected by the global political economy and by events in other parts of the world, and how the gender basis of U.S. society affects people in other countries.

Women's Studies From a Social Science Perspective   This book is based in the social sciences. Among the disciplines from which it draws theory, approaches, and knowledge are anthropology, economics, education, history, law, mass communication, political science, psychology, social work, and sociology. Of course, this list of social science disciplines represents a diverse set of theories, methods, and approaches. The social science focus I adopt emphasizes the grounding of gender in *social institutions* and *institutionalized relationships*. This book discusses important aspects of human social life, such as cultural norms and values, psychological character, and interpersonal behavior, but it does so within the context of social structure and specific social institutions. The social-institutions approach also leads to a particularly strong emphasis on the legal and policy aspects of sex/gender systems.

My choice to limit myself primarily to social science does not suggest that this mode of theory and research is better than the distinctive approach offered by the humanities or that the humanities have little to contribute to the questions raised here. Each approach deserves careful and coherent interpretation. In recent years, women's studies has come to mirror the values of the surrounding academy. While the outside (mainstream) academic world undervalues the humanities and the social sciences in favor of the sciences, conventionally understood, women's studies has increasingly tended to undervalue social science approaches, focusing instead on the humanities. In contrast, this book highlights the kinds of problems the social sciences have addressed especially intelligently.

Methodology and the Process of Research and Interpretation   Most of the research described or analyzed in this book employs social science methods. These methods take many different forms, including survey, clinical, and experimental techniques; participant observation; and institutional, documentary, and content analysis. This work includes the use of some quantitative methods and some qualitative ones. *Women in American Society* treats social science methodology critically, but it is also shaped by social science methods.

Many students begin with at least some fear of or antagonism toward science-oriented writing, especially if it includes quantitative data analysis. Some women's studies scholars reinforce this anxiety by using the excellent feminist-theoretical literature on methodology and epistemology to attack quantitative analysis or to assert that some strategies, such as experimental or survey research, are incompatible with women's studies. *Women in American Society* is based on the assumption that systematically gathered and theoretically grounded empirical research not only can be done in a feminist mode and a manner that serves humane purposes, but also is central to the project of creating knowledge that enhances human life. Methods of research must fit the task. Some questions are best answered by one method and some by another, and the questions we consider are the ones social scientists happen to ask.

Much has been said by many different experts about the relationships among politics, human knowledge, scholarship, and education. For many years, women's studies has been at the center of debates about academic *political correctness*—the idea, among others, that researchers in this field evaluate research and knowledge only by whether it is ideologically appealing. At the same time, women's studies scholars engaging in the study of epistemology and the philosophy of knowledge and science remain deeply skeptical of scholarly claims of "objectivity," given the history of research on women and gender. Some scholars go very far in the direction of a radical constructivism that sees subjective narrative and fiction as little different from any other form of knowledge telling, except in its supposedly superior honesty. In this book, I promote the view that *knowledge,* the truth value of a statement, cannot be judged by how attractive it is, how much it feels right according to one's experience, or whether it has been asserted by a respected person, no matter how authoritative. It is crucial to have a critical understanding of the methods used to make a claim about how the social world, or some piece of it, works. Therefore, *Women in American Society* regularly discusses research methodology and its implications.

Historical Understanding   Although I focus primarily on contemporary society, I show how an understanding of historical developments places the current situation in context and enlightens us about the nature and processes of social change, both worldwide and in the United States. Many women's studies instructors have found their students sorely lacking in the historical background to discuss contemporary issues. The point is not just that many students lack knowledge of what life was like in the past. Rather, if students are to understand social phenomena in *any* historical period (including our own), they must understand something of the historical dynamics of these phenomena.

An Interdisciplinary Approach   The interdisciplinary approach used in this book interweaves the perspectives, methods, and findings of different social science disciplines and subfields to examine common themes and problems, rather than arranging the topics by discipline (the psychology of . . . , the sociology of . . . , the law on . . .). This integration is not easy to accomplish; the range of differences in assumptions, focus, language, method, and interpretation is enormous. Different fields use the same terminology to discuss different ideas, and different terminology to discuss the same ideas. It is especially difficult to achieve integration in a *rigorous* way; interdisciplinary research is not just a pastiche of bits selected from various disciplines.

The rewards of integration are great, however. Some social science disciplines are especially skilled in their analysis of individuals, others are much richer in their comprehension of communities or of social structure. Some consider human thought and behavior without explicitly recognizing the power of public law and policy; others investigate law and policy without examining their relationships to human thought and behavior. An integrated interdisciplinary approach promotes a more realistic understanding of human life.

Diversity Among Women   This book incorporates analysis of social diversity among women in a way that differs from many women's studies texts; it follows an integrated rather than a segregated approach. There is no special chapter on the unique situation of Black women, older women, lesbians, or any other subgroup of women often receiving such segregated treatment. The *segregated* approach often does less to encourage decentered, multiple perspectives than it appears to at first. This approach tends to emphasize a relatively few popular distinctive perspectives while ignoring others. In the U.S. context, for example, feminist work now usually emphasizes marginality based on race, age, sexuality, and class. It is not usually as cognizant of marginality based on region, urban–rural dimensions, or religion. The segregated approach tends to suggest to readers that unless otherwise specified, the text is about specific groups of women, such as those who are white (European American) and middle class. If multiple perspectives are fostered primarily by using special chapters on particular groups of women, the description of a few specific groups tends to overrun the larger theoretical, more comparative issues involved in the constitution of multiple versus singular perspectives.

The *integrated* approach is framed by two arguments: (1) Women's situations and experiences vary systematically because of differences in culture and in women's position in the social structure, and (2) the impact of gender for all women is partly dependent on or mediated by these other cultural and structural differences. Thus, this book continually considers the impact of social-group differences on the impact and experience of gender.

Where I do not name a specific group of women, the reader should not assume that I am referring to any specific group. I have worked to avoid making generalizations about women that systematically violate or ignore the experiences of particular groups of women. If social divisions, for example by race or age, make a difference in the gendered aspects of women's lives, the discussion of difference is integrated into the discussion of that aspect of gender. Nor is this book shaped only by looking for a boiled-down common denominator; indeed, it is partly the large variety of experiences of gender we see as we compare the situations of different groups that makes women's studies so fascinating.

What Is Basic in Women's Studies   This book reflects the state of the field of women's studies, but it is also a unique contribution to that field. The newness of the field means that conventional wisdom, accepted methodologies, and established models do not exist to the same degree as they do in other fields. Even so, women's studies has built up a core of shared views and commonly cited works. This book, however, does not take even these for granted; many of the observations and works commonly cited in women's studies are already out of date. In some cases, this means that old friends in the literature do not get the treatment to which they have grown accustomed, but change is inevitable as knowledge grows. In other cases I discuss works that are not widely known inside the women's studies community.

Study Aids   The text is largely devoted to discussion of the research literature and its theoretical and practical significance. I include extensive references and bibliographic comments, both to document the observations I make and to provide readers with the resources they will need to learn more. For the first time, I have also included references to many of the valuable resources available on websites throughout the Internet. I also offer my own Internet address: womaMsoc @polisci.wisc.edu.

Studies, bibliographic resources, and statistics are not all there is to learning this material, of course. At each turn, it is crucial for you to reflect on the material to decide how it does and does not fit with your own observations—and why. To assist in this process, I have provided study questions before each unit, asking you to "reflect before you read."

Feminist theory and women's studies offer diverse perspectives and interpretations. Sometimes, I present alternative theories and viewpoints without reaching a definitive conclusion about which is best. I have attempted to avoid the mind-numbing claim that knowledge and theories are all relative, while still leaving room for you to make your own theoretical and epistemological choices.

Revisions   This book has been thoroughly updated throughout since the previous edition, incorporating new insights and information gathered in recent years. Each revision of this work is enriched not only by the growth of general knowledge in the research and literature of women's studies scholars but also by the changes and events in the world at large. The point of studying this field is not just to learn the research field, but also to understand how to use this analysis and information to understand day-to-day life. Throughout the book, I have integrated examples and case studies from recent events; these should feel fresh even to the youngest readers.

The specific changes include the most up-to-date research available, gathered from the primary research reports of many different disciplines. An added source for this edition is extensive use of Internet-based resources, which includes many government databases. Although the Internet offers great opportunities for gathering research resources, two major problems confront prospective users: (1) The Internet is so rich in information that it is difficult to sort through the data, and (2) researchers must have clear standards by which to evaluate the information available there.

I have continued the practice of using a lot of illustrations, examples, and information from recent news. The *New York Times* is one of my main sources, but I have used many others as well.

Previous users of the book will find the chapters on women's studies (1), education (5), health (6), sexuality (11), reproduction (12), and the economy (13) most thoroughly rewritten. They are substantially reorganized and include a lot of theoretical and substantive updating.

The demands of the cybernetic era have led me to emphasize the process of gathering, sifting through, and interpreting evidence even more now than in the past. Most noticeably, Chapter 1 now includes a substantial focus on social science methods of research in women's studies. I have also placed this study of the United States even more fully in a global context than before. Chapter 2, which focuses on alternative theories of the development of sex/gender systems now begins with an overview of the comparison of women's status and situation around the globe. Chapter 9, on politics, includes a new section on gender and international politics.

Chapter 3, on alternative theories and approaches to understanding individual-level development of gender recasts and elaborates the section on discrimination to look at *institutional* approaches, which offer a good sociological contrast to the other more psychological theories. Chapter 14, on feminism and women's movements, includes more on current social-movement theory and research, which serves as the framework for analyzing women's movements.

In addition to these larger changes and many revisions in organization and clarity, this edition is marked by the events and issues of the 1990s, including the dramatic debates surrounding the integration of the Citadel and VMI military academies and the revelations about sexual harassment in the military; the debates about breast implants, mammography, and RU486; equity in sports; violence against abortion clinics and practitioners and relevant new legislation and court cases; welfare reform; and many others.

What Lies Ahead: Organization

Those familiar with women's studies may find this book's topical organization unique. I developed this structure after carefully considering problems of theory and pedagogy and the demands of working in a specifically interdisciplinary fashion. For example, rather than offering a particular chapter on violence against women, I have integrated it with the text in subsections of relevant chapters, such as those on health, the law, and relations between women and men. The main reason for this format is that I have used large complex social institutions as the main framework for organizing the analysis; thus, it is important to show how the different important aspects of gender and women's experience are shaped by each of these institutions. Nevertheless, I have divided the chapters into clearly marked subsections to facilitate restructuring it for reading assignments, as desired. The book is divided into four parts, corresponding to four of the most important themes in the field of women's studies: frameworks for study, societal institutions, choice and control, and feminism.

Part One, "Developing Frameworks for the Study of Gender and Society," introduces the field of women's studies and especially its underlying themes and theories. It provides the analytical framework for the remainder of the book. Chapter 1, "Women's Studies: An Introduction," outlines the scope, history, and point of women's studies as a field. This chapter begins the discussion of the process of research and theorizing in women's studies. Because theory is the framework that makes an otherwise shapeless set of facts and pieces of information coherent and useful, theory construction and evaluation are among the most important tasks of students in any field, including this one. Chapters 2 and 3 discuss a variety of theories that have been offered to explain the development and significance of *sex/gender systems,* the pattern of relationships between women and men in society. Many different theories have been used to explain sex/gender systems, and these two chapters outline and compare some of the main ones.

The difference between the theories presented in Chapter 2 and those in Chapter 3 lies in what the theories attempt to explain. The first type, discussed in Chapter 2, "Societal-Level Approaches to Understanding Women's Lives" seeks to explain how sex/gender systems, social structure, and culture come to be shaped as they are. These theories focus, as some disciplines would say, on the macrolevel questions. Chapter 3, "Individual-Level Approaches to Understanding Women's Lives," focuses on more microlevel phenomena. How can we explain the behavior and thinking of individuals within their given societies? How do individuals come to fit—or not—into the more general patterns found in their societies? Sometimes people argue about which level of explanation—societal or individual, macro or micro—is better. This question does not make much sense in the abstract. These two types of theories explain different things, equally important and equally incomplete on their own. Chapter 4, "Commonality and Difference Among Women," emphasizes the importance of differences among women in the dynamics of gender in society. It offers a variety of theories and approaches scholars have used to understand the relationship of social differences among women to the nature of gender and the impact of gender on women.

Part Two, "Gender-Defining Institutions," presents the second major theme of the book. There are many different kinds of power and control. One of the most important is *normative power*, the power to define the values and standards against which we measure ourselves and others. The words *norm, normal,* and *normative* are derived from the Latin *norma,* which is a carpenter's or mason's square, a tool used for measurement and setting patterns. Most major social institutions participate in setting, teaching, and enforcing values, standards, or norms related to gender; for some institutions, these gendered activities are a primary purpose. This book looks at the institutions of education (Chapter 5), health care (Chapter 6), religion (Chapter 7), communications media (Chapter 8), and government and politics (Chapter 9) to see how these institutions define and enforce norms of good and bad, normal and abnormal, healthy and sick, skilled and unskilled, important and unimportant, valuable and not valuable. You might notice that there is no single chapter in this section devoted solely to the family. In fact, however, hardly a page of this book fails to discuss some aspect of the family. Instead of looking at the family as simply one more institution, this book looks at different aspects of the family throughout. In addition, the family as an institution is most consistently and thoroughly discussed in Part Three.

Each chapter in Part Two follows a similar pattern. Together, these chapters show both how these institutions and their underlying values interrelate and how they shape and are shaped by gender norms. Part Two investigates these institutions as parts of a larger sex/gender system, considering both how their values control women's lives and how women have influenced these values and used these values to exert control over their own lives. Part Two also explores the development of current gender norms and the potential for change within each institution.

Part Three, "Choice and Control in Personal Life, the Family, and Work," examines some of the types of problems, decisions, and experiences most women constantly face in their adult lives, especially in the context of the family and work. How much choice do women have in life decisions and how do they make these choices? What are the impacts of the institutional settings in which most women live most of their lives? Chapter 10, "Gender, Communication, and Self-expression" suggests that there are many gender-related limitations on people—and especially women—even in what they say and how they act with other people.

Chapter 11, "Consenting Adults? Personal and Sexual Relationships," looks at another kind of social interaction and relationship: intimacy. This chapter focuses on different kinds of intimacy, including sexual and nonsexual, heterosexual and homosexual, heterosocial and homosocial relationships. This chapter looks at one of the most widespread structures of heterosexual relationship: marriage. It also examines some of the problems in distinguishing between sexual and nonsexual relationships and between sexuality and violence. Chapter 12, "Reproduction, Parenthood, and Child Care," focuses on the choices and decisions women make about whether to have children, under what circumstances women have children, and what women do about children when they have them. It also examines the effects of these experiences on women.

Chapter 13, "Work, Employment, and the Economics of Gender," includes discussions of many different types of work: paid and unpaid (for example, housework); professional, white collar, blue collar, and agricultural; traditionally female and traditionally male. It looks at the ways in which women attempt to exert influence over their work lives and economic situation. It also explores some sources of income other than paid labor and questions of women's poverty, wealth, and economic resources and strategies.

Part Four, "Feminism and the Global Context," explains women's movements of the past and present and makes some educated guesses about what the future holds. I end with a full-fledged discussion of feminism, feminist (and antifeminist) movements, and feminist theory per se. An introduction to women's studies must help the reader understand what feminist analysis is and how it differs from other kinds of study. My experience in introductory women's studies courses taught me that to discuss feminism as a social movement before describing and analyzing the situation of women is to put the cart before the horse. Therefore, questions of feminism are inseparably woven throughout the pages of this book, but explicit treatment of the topic is reserved for the finale.

Acknowledgments

Many people have helped me write this book. At the top of my list are my students, who are too numerous to mention individually; the many scholars in the field with whom I have talked and whose work I have read over the years; and those who have used the book and made comments and suggestions, particularly the following reviewers: Helen Bannan, Florida Atlantic University; Lisel Blash, Kansas State University; Jane Smith Boyd, San Jose State University; Sandra Coyner, Kansas State University; Mary Margaret Fonow, Ohio State University; Irene C. Goldman, Ball State University; Angela E. Hubler, Kansas State University; Audry T. McCluskey, Indiana University; Faye Plascak-Craig, Marian College; Kim Romenesko, University of Wisconsin, Milwaukee; and Judith Wishnia, State University of New York, Stony Brook.

The students in my various women's studies classes at the University of Wisconsin—Madison have been important in the writing of this book. They are my audience in writing, I see their faces while writing, much as I do when I lecture. When I lecture, I do not see an abstract student, but many different individuals in what some theorists like to call their "concrete situations." My students are women and men who come from many backgrounds and have many different interests. Their ages range from adolescence to senescence. Most are full-time students, but some are working people from the community, taking a single course because they are interested or because it relates to their work. Some come in as radical feminists; some are as skeptical and anxious as a student in this kind of course can be. Some are new to academic study; some are relatively advanced scholars in other fields who are investigating women's studies for the first time. This book has been written for all these people. I assume that my readers are even more diverse than the students I have already met.

In preparing this edition, I racked up more debts than usual for a variety of reasons. Lisa Levenstein, Alisa Rosenthal, Gwynn Thomas, Mimi Schippers, and Jennifer Becker provided very valuable assistance. I would like also to thank the National Science Foundation and the National Election Studies, not because they had anything directly to do with this book, but because whenever I thought finishing this was going to be difficult, I always had something even more daunting on my plate. And to Ziggy Zeos, Tilly TI, Lana Laserjet, and the rest of the crew, what can I say?

My greatest debts are to Graham Wilson and Adam Wilson—the former because, as always, he went beyond the call of duty and the latter for growing up so amazingly. The dedication in the first edition noted that Adam's impending arrival kept me writing. The dedication of the second edition noted that he could read his name on that page; the dedication of the third announced he could read the whole book. For this edition, he literally *pitched* in to help keep me sane—especially that no-hitter in the early all-stars game. Throughout his life, he has played a crucial role in my feminism and women's studies writing. Audre Lorde (1984) said it best:

> I am thankful that one of my children is male, since that helps to keep me honest. Every line I write shrieks there are no easy solutions.

To my family:
William and the memory of Florence,
Graham,
and Adam Ross Wilson, who teaches me much

Developing Frameworks
for the Study of Gender and Society

WHAT IS THE SITUATION of women in society, and how did it get that way? Over the centuries, many theorists and scholars have attempted to answer this question. In the process of seeking the answers, they have developed alternative theories or frameworks to organize an analysis and interpretation of the role of gender in society. In the past few decades, scholars interested in the study of women and gender have organized a field of inquiry known as "women's studies." This book introduces part of the field of women's studies, and this part of the book introduces many of the frameworks used by students of women's studies.

It begins with a look at the nature of women's studies as an academic field of study and then turns to an overview of the facts of life for women in the United States today. This section also considers some problems in *how* to study women in society. Chapters 2 through 4 then explore some of the theories and approaches used by women's studies scholars, especially in the social sciences, to understand women and gender in society. Chapter 2 focuses on theories used to explain how *societies* develop particular patterns of relationships between the sexes over historical time. These theories ask how to explain the development of particular *sex/gender systems,* social structures of gender. Chapter 3 focuses at a different level of explanation, looking at theories used to explain how *individuals* develop gender-related patterns of behavior in their individual lives, through their own experiences in the context of the larger society. These theories ask how to explain how individuals come to be the kinds of women and men they are. Finally, Chapter 4 offers ways of understanding women, that take full account of the fact that women do not constitute a homogeneous group; instead, women differ crucially in their personal history and life experiences, on the basis of such things as race, class, and religion, among many other characteristics. These approaches ask how to talk about *women* if *women* are so different from each other. In order to understand women's situation in society, it is necessary to understand all of these types of theories.

Reflect *Before* You Read

1. Some people say that men and women are very unequal in society today. Others acknowledge that there used to be inequality between the sexes, but they say that society has changed so that men and women now have equal opportunities to live the lives they choose. What position do you take? Why?

2. Women constitute a very small proportion of the people who have top positions in education, government, and business. Why? Does this minority status matter?

3. Construct a list of the five most important problems facing people like you today. Whom did you define as "people like you"? Why? What other choices might you have made in defining "people like you"? How many of the problems you selected truly affect women and men in the same way? What role can or does feminism play in the solutions to these problems?

4. Construct a list of the five most important problems facing women today. Now think about the relationship of these problems to different kinds of women. Do women of different classes face these problems in the same way? How about women of different races, ages, religions, or sexual orientations? How did your own personal situation and experiences affect the way you defined the problems of "women"?

1

❧

Women's Studies: An Introduction

Are there women, really?
Simone de Beauvoir (1952),
The Second Sex

Representing Women

Imagine a philosophy textbook beginning with the question "What is man?" What would you expect the book to be about? You would probably expect an exploration of how man differs from other animal species, or from angels, gods, and other celestial beings.

Now imagine a philosophy textbook beginning with the question "What is woman?" What would this book be about? You would probably anticipate not a discussion of women versus animals or gods, but rather an analysis of the similarities and differences between women and men.

Why would most people's expectations of these two books be so different? One answer is that *man* is often considered a generic term, but *woman* is not; in other words, *man* can refer to either one particular sex or to human beings as a species. Isn't this confusing? How do people know when *man* means males and females and when it means only males? Perhaps they can judge by the context. Unfortunately, the immediate context often does little to solve the ambiguity. To avoid such ambiguity in this book, from now on, *man* and *men* will refer only to males.

This remedy for confusion and ambiguity is simple enough, but the important issue remains. How did it happen that one word came to refer to both the whole of humanity and one specific half of it? Why does *man* represent both males and females, while *woman* refers very narrowly to females? This question recurs as a theme throughout this book. The answer suggested by many feminist theorists throughout the ages is that using *man* to represent human society as a whole reflects the societal tendency to view men as the central actors or characters in

3

human society and to consider "male" characteristics, manliness, or masculinity as the defining characteristics of human beings.

The term used to describe this situation is *androcentrism,* which literally means "centered on men." This word was used as long ago as 1911 by sociologist and feminist theorist Charlotte Perkins Gilman in *The Man-Made World: Our Androcentric Culture. Androcentric* has parallels in three words that are more widely used and understood: *egocentric, ethnocentric,* and *anthropocentric. Egocentric* refers to the tendency of individuals to see themselves as the center of the world, as though everything revolves around them. *Ethnocentric* refers to people's tendency to view their own culture as normal and to think of other cultures only as deviations from their own—better—way of life. *Anthropocentric* refers to the human tendency to view the human species as the most significant entity in the universe. *Androcentric,* then, refers to the tendency to think of men as the norm against which women are compared and to the view that men are the main actors in—the center of—the social world.

An analogy using the ideas of characters and actors illustrates the point. Consider one of the most famous plays in Western literature, William Shakespeare's *Hamlet.* Why is this play called *Hamlet?* The Danish prince is not the only person in the play; he is not even the only character who seems to have an interesting history, faces a tragedy, or dies. The title reflects the fact that the play is essentially about Hamlet and his role in the story. The events that occur in the play—even when Hamlet is absent—are significant in the eyes of the audience primarily for the ways they affect or are affected by the young prince. Although the perspectives of the other characters are significant, it is really Hamlet's perspective and problems that move the play and those who view it.

Nearly four centuries after Shakespeare wrote *Hamlet,* another English playwright, Tom Stoppard, took the same material and twisted it inside out. His play, *Rosencrantz and Guildenstern Are Dead,* presents the same set of events and the same characters, but from the point of view of two of the most minor characters in the original play. In Stoppard's version, Rosencrantz and Guildenstern, who cannot even remember themselves which one of them is which, become the central actors. The events, the characters, and Shakespeare's original words are suddenly transformed because of the change of perspective.

Just as all the other characters in *Hamlet* revolve around, support, and gain their significance from the central character, women are socially defined as revolving around, supporting, and gaining their significance from men. In *Hamlet,* we care that the prince is on a ship to England; it is less important to us that Rosencrantz, Guildenstern, and the ship's captain are there, as well. Likewise, the centrality of men in society leads observers of society and history to write, as did one eminent political scientist, "The analysis which this book contains is based on what might be called the storybook truth about American history: that America was settled by men who fled from the feudal and clerical oppressions of the Old World" (Hartz, 1955, 3). Some of us do not notice anything odd about this sentence, but some of us do: Surely American history would have been quite different had *men* been the only people to settle it. Acknowledging that women were also on the ship makes a great difference to understanding American history.

A well-known study by a group of psychologists in the 1960s shows that this "man–woman–human" question is not a mere matter of playing with words

(Broverman et al., 1970). These psychologists asked a number of mental-health clinicians to define the characteristics of a "healthy man," a "healthy woman," and a "healthy adult." The results showed that the clinicians defined the healthy adult and the healthy man in much the same way: rational, independent, ambitious, active, and so forth. Their healthy woman, however, had very different characteristics: She was emotional, dependent, and submissive. Thus, not only in the language but also in the eyes of those who define the standards of health, men are the real adults. To act like a healthy woman, one cannot act like a healthy adult. This situation persisted for many years (O'Malley and Richardson, 1985).

An example from a very different arena offers another perspective on how society defines women and men. A long-standing constitutional problem concerning women revolved around jury service. Americans are constitutionally guaranteed the right to a trial by a jury of their peers. Nonetheless, although the laws of different states varied, until the late 20th century, they tended to exclude women from serving on juries. Only in 1975 (*Taylor* v. *Louisiana*)[1] did the U.S. Supreme Court decide that women could not be systematically excluded from juries because of their sex. In an earlier case about juries, Supreme Court justice William O. Douglas considered the question of whether women and men were simply exchangeable puzzle pieces. Many people argued that they were exchangeable, but only in the sense that it did not matter whether men alone were on juries. A jury composed only of men was "as truly representative as if women were included." Douglas disagreed, offering the following problem for consideration:

> [It] is not enough to say that women when sitting as jurors neither act nor tend to act as a class. Men likewise do not act as a class. But, if the shoe were on the other foot, who would claim that a jury was truly representative of the community if all men were intentionally and systematically excluded from the [jury]? The truth is that the two sexes are not fungible; a community made up exclusively of one is different from a community composed of both; the subtle interplay of influence one on the other is among the imponderables. To insulate the courtroom from either may not in a given case make an iota of difference. Yet a flavor, a distinct quality is lost if either sex is excluded. (*Ballard* v. *U.S.*, 1946)

Douglas's point is clear. There are two alternative arguments on which to base a claim that men can fully represent women. The first is that women and men are in this context fully interchangeable persons, in which case it would make no difference whether juries (or, for that matter, Congress or almost any other organization) were composed entirely of men or entirely of women. Few people seem to worry that Congress is composed mostly of males, but would the same be true if Congress were suddenly to become composed mostly of females? The other argument is that men can adequately represent women, but women cannot adequately represent men because women are narrower creatures, more parochial, less competent, or, like children, dependent on the better judgment of men.

Notice what has happened in the discussion thus far. I began by talking about the meaning of words and by asking what real-life entities *man* and *woman* represent. It became clear that words, meanings, and definitions have a great deal to do with real-life issues of power and choice. I have gradually turned to this problem of representation: Who can represent whom in society? Can women's interests and needs be satisfied if men are invested with the power to act and make decisions for them? If men can act for women, why can't women act for men? If men and women are not precisely the same, as Douglas argued, what are the differences? What is the significance of these differences for the way people arrange important social, economic, and governmental institutions? These are some of the questions we probe throughout this book.

Justice Douglas had to face a series of important problems as he deliberated the jury case. Do men or women act as a "class"? That is, is there a set of orientations or types of behavior that are common to one sex and not to the other? How, if at all, would communities or organizations composed only of men, composed only of women, or composed of both differ? As Douglas suggested, differences could emerge because women and men act differently from each other or because people's behavior varies depending on whether they are in a single-sex or mixed-sex group. Above all, however, Douglas apparently felt he did not have enough knowledge to be able to argue that one sex or the other can be excluded from the important activities of society.

Two decades after Douglas rendered his opinion, in the 1960s, many students, scholars, and other people began to realize how little knowledge they had about women and men *as* women and men. There are at least three reasons for this ignorance:

1. Many aspects of women's lives are simply ignored or dismissed as unimportant, compared with most aspects of men's lives. Basic philosophy courses give great attention to what philosophers said about men and very little to what they said about women. History courses teach more about the changes in men's activities, strategies, and equipment in battle than about changes in childbirth. If an event in history caused great suffering only or primarily to men, we (justly) take great interest in how and why it happened, with the hope of avoiding similar suffering in the future. If an event caused great suffering only or primarily to women (for example, the European witch burnings, which led to the deaths of at least thousands of women), it does not seem quite as important to study.

2. Scholarship still tends to view men as "generic," as representative of everyone. Sometimes, people are almost fooled into thinking they have studied women when they have really only studied men. In psychology, a large proportion of general research involves males only but is discussed as though it applies to everyone (Holmes and Jorgensen, 1971). In sociology, scores of people who claim to study social status and how it is determined actually gather and look at evidence only about men.

3. When conventional courses and texts discuss women, they usually offer a very narrow perspective. They usually focus on women's roles, behavior, and significance as wives, mothers, lovers, or supporting muses. These roles are important but are not the only significant aspects of women. Such courses and texts provide only a limited and distorted view of women.

In most of the social sciences, women are discussed as though they are merely a component of "the family," a unit composed of an employed husband, a homemaking wife, and some number of dependent children who live at home. The woman who lives in such a family is probably most people's image of the "typical woman." In fact, this "typical woman" is very rare today. Excluding women who are unmarried or employed outside the home, who have no children or whose children are grown up and have left home, only 14% of women in the United States fit that "typical woman" image.

How can there be such disparity between image and reality? One answer is that women are seen as people want to see them: as comfortable, nurturing, always-available mothers. Another answer (which does not contradict the first) is that women are seen through stereotypes. Stereotypes allow people to deal with women without really having to pay close attention to them or to any contradictory evidence in the facts of women's lives.

French feminist Hélène Cixous (1976) has made a similar point in a different way. She has reminded us of the Greek myth of the Medusa, the snake-haired woman who would supposedly turn to stone anyone who looked directly at her. She could be viewed only indirectly, through a reflection. Cixous has argued that the myth is more dangerous than the woman herself. When we see the Medusa— or any woman—only indirectly, through the distorted reflections of cultural fears and stereotypes, we are harmed. The accepted "facts" (like the appearance of the "typical woman") are often wrong. Scholars of women's studies seek to look directly at women: at their roles in society, at their impact on society, and at the impact of social institutions and processes on them.

Women's Studies as a Field of Study

The field of study called "women's studies" was born soon after the reemergence of the women's movement in the late 1960s. At first, it consisted mainly of handfuls of students and instructors who met in often informal, unofficial study sessions. The participants spent much of their time in the early years trying to figure out what questions they needed to ask and searching for any information they could find on women's history and roles in society.[2] Those participants, mostly young women, seemed very radical to everyone else and, frankly, slightly obsessive and strange.

Women's studies has grown and changed since those early days. Most universities now have some women's studies courses, and many have programs or departments devoted to the field. There are undergraduate majors in women's studies, and M.A. and Ph.D. programs in the field. Thousands of instructors and students are involved, and they are a much more heterogeneous group than the group of early participants. Many women's studies students are motivated by their feminist activism, but many are just there to learn. There are as many reasons for taking a women's studies course as there are for taking a course in any other field.

What, then, is this field called "women's studies"? The answer might seem obvious at first. In economics, we study economics; in political science, we study politics; in women's studies, we study women. In fact, the definition is not that simple. Academic fields are defined not only by *what* they study but also by *how* they study it. For example, Gloria Naylor's novel *The Women of Brewster Place*

The role of women in American society has changed dramatically since this photo was taken in 1918.

(Naylor, 1982) could be assigned reading in a literature course or an urban politics course. However, the reasons for reading the book, the questions asked about it, and the lessons learned from it would be somewhat different in the two fields. Similarly, scholars of women's studies approach the study of women in a different way than do scholars in other fields; the women's studies approach frames this book.

Women's studies scholars look at the meanings that events, ideas, and social institutions have for women, as well as for men. They investigate experiences that only (or almost only) women have with the same care and attention that others use in examining experiences that only (or almost only) men have. They notice that even when men and women do the same sorts of things, they are often *interpreted* or *valued* differently. For example, when men tell each other stories about another man, such exchanges are called the "old boys' network," or "networking." When women do the same, it is called "gossip" or a "hen session."

It probably would not surprise anyone that women's studies focuses heavily on such aspects of life as the family, women's employment, abortion and contraception, and family and child-oriented issues because these are often thought of as *women's* issues. In addition, however, women's studies probes further and examines the full range of human concerns and realms of activity to examine their relationship to gender and the lives of women and men specifically *as* women and men. Studies of women that look only at areas of life conventionally associated with women miss an important point. Women's and men's roles in *most* social institutions are different, and most social institutions are structured in at least some ways along gender lines.

Women's studies focuses on understanding women, but it is impossible to learn about the female half of society without also learning something about the male half. In some cases, women's studies researchers *compare* the thoughts, behavior, and roles of men and women. At other times, these researchers look at the *interactions* between men and women, including how they think about and act toward each other and how they influence each other. By examining the lives of both sexes, women's studies offers a much wider and more profound understanding of society as a whole.

Perhaps the overriding difference between women's studies and other studies of women is the special kind of skepticism women's studies scholars bring to their studies. A good student in any field should be questioning, skeptical, and wary of easy answers. In addition, women's studies students are deeply skeptical of conventional wisdom about women, for the reasons already mentioned. Too often, such wisdom proves false or distorted when we consider systematic evidence. For example, have labor-saving devices in the home diminished the amount of effort women put into their housework over the course of the past century? Surprisingly, the answer is no, as Chapter 13 shows. What other people use as assumptions about women, women's studies scholars pose as questions.

Thus, women's studies is not just a simple matter of filling in gaps in information. It is a matter of reevaluating what we think we know. Women's studies considers some very basic questions: What is important enough to know? To whom is it important and in what ways? Women's studies involves constant critical evaluation of our own and other people's understanding of and reactions to women. Both women and men find that women's studies entails much learning and questioning about themselves.

Feminism shapes the practice of women's studies. Certainly many students in women's studies courses do not think of themselves as feminists, but women's studies is both a result and a part of the feminist movement. In the 1960s and early 1970s, women's movement activists realized they needed to know more about the social forces that shaped their lives. When they thought about what they had learned about women in the past, they realized they had been taught very little accurate information. Thinking, studying, and learning became an important part of feminist political and social action. Although there are many different types of feminism (discussed in the final chapter), these types share a central core of ideas and attitudes revolving around the desire to see women take control of and responsibility for their own lives and become participants and leaders in society.

Women's studies is not unique in the fact that it links academics and current political and social issues. Many traditional social science disciplines (sociology and political science, for example) were products of the social and political movements of their founding days. None of the social sciences is immune to pressing world problems. After World War II, many people began to study public opinion and the psychology of politics because they wanted to know how people came to tolerate (if not participate in), fascism and the Holocaust, in order to try to avoid a repeat performance. In the 1960s, many social scientists turned their attention to questions of poverty, urban life, and race relations because these were the problems that seemed most to need solving. In the 1980s, awareness of AIDS spurred social, as well as medical, research. Contrary to the "ivory tower" cliché, universities are indeed part of the real world, and relating scholarship to the real world has always been accepted practice in some—although not all—areas of the social sciences.

Only the rare student in women's studies courses never becomes angry, frustrated, anxious, or elated. The topics that are discussed, such as relations between parents and children or sexuality and violence between men and women, touch all of us very deeply. Scholars in some fields of study argue that feelings and personal experiences should play no role in academic efforts to discover truth. Women's studies scholars, even in the social sciences and other sciences, tend to argue that our personal understandings and experiences play important roles in learning. At the same time, however, if the personal nature of the subjects and themes of women's studies makes it difficult to think analytically or to comprehend and use unfamiliar or uncomfortable information, the ability to learn is substantially limited. This means that scholars of women's studies must maintain some skepticism about the immediate reactions we and other people feel, while still valuing those reactions.

Women's studies is *interdisciplinary;* that is, it draws on and weaves together theories, research, and insights from numerous fields throughout the humanities and the social and biological sciences. This interdisciplinary nature of women's studies grows in part out of necessity. Suppose that I, as a political scientist, deliver a lecture on why few women achieve high political office. Among the questions people usually ask me are the following: "Don't women's hormones make them less aggressive and competitive than men?" "Didn't this system grow out of a historical division of labor that goes all the way back to hunters and gatherers, with women staying close to home and men going out to hunt and fight?" "Isn't the division of labor, with women in the home and men out in society leading and working, functional and efficient? Doesn't this system exist because it works well and not because women are any less valued?" To answer these questions, I need to know something about biology, psychology, history, anthropology, sociology, and political economy. As a scholar, I can't just wing it; I have to *know* something about the research in these fields.

Just having some information from a lot of fields is not enough for really understanding human social life. Imagine a massive bag filled with the bits and pieces necessary to construct a Rolls Royce. The pieces are useful only if you know how to put them together, which in turn requires understanding the underlying principles of engineering and design. The bits of information obtained from a variety of different academic fields can be like the car pieces: a useless and confusing jumble of unlinked or incorrectly linked parts. In the social sciences, it is the *theories* that link the bits of fact, observation, and educated guesses together into a coherent whole.

Academic disciplines are at least as differentiated by their assumptions, theories, and methods as by the bits of information they provide. Thus, if we are to use interdisciplinary approaches for understanding women's situation, we must both learn about the methods and approaches of different kinds of research and develop the skills to integrate them coherently. For this reason, we pay attention not only to the *findings* of research on women (the bits of information such research has produced) but also to the *process* by which people have arrived at these findings and the *uses* to which the findings have been put.

Social Science Methods of Studying Women and Gender

This book is based on scholarly research in the social sciences. In order to be able to understand and evaluate this work, then, it is necessary to understand how social science research works. What are the methods used by those who approach the subject of women's studies through the social sciences? How do researchers in this area study their subject? On what grounds can we evaluate their work?

Social Science as Systematic Observation

The first thing to bear in mind is that there is no single social science method. Psychologists, economists, and anthropologists, for example, tend to go about their work very differently; even more to the point, they use different standards to define *good research*, done in a manner that gives them confidence in its conclusions. In fact, scholars in each discipline differ among themselves over how to do good research. This section focuses on some broad-stroke generalizations about the methods and problems of doing—and reading about—social science research on women and gender.

There are many excellent sources for studying important questions about the philosophy of knowledge, and the more ways in which we may approach people as a subject—through the social sciences, through philosophy, through the inventions of human creativity in the arts—the more understanding we may have. Here, however, we focus on the strategies used by social scientists in women's studies for doing *empirical research*, research that is based on systematically observing human beings engaged in the activities of interest to the researcher. There are many other ways of learning about human beings than doing empirical research, but for specialists in the social sciences, *systematic observation* is the key to finding the heart of the matter. Both terms are important to us here: *systematic* and *observation*. We consider them in reverse order.

Most social scientists are committed to the idea that one of the best ways to learn about human behavior is to watch people in action. If we want to know how people think, we should find a way of talking to them to find out, or we need to develop an alternative strategy to get at people's thoughts and feelings. Most forms of social science research, then, are based on (1) asking a question about some aspect of human life, (2) developing a strategy for observing people engaging in this slice of life, and then (3) analyzing the resulting observations to try to make sense of them and generate a coherent story about what we observed. We explore a range of these strategies in the next section of this chapter.

The idea of *systematic* observation is based on an important premise about human perception and social life. Any individual human being—including any social scientist—has very limited experiences in and perspectives on the world. People's perceptions are shaped by their own experiences and perspectives. Indeed, throughout this book, the impact of people's limited experiences and their beliefs, including their prejudices and stereotypes, are an important theme. The shaping and grounding of perceptions in experience, however, means that people have to go out of their way to invent means of stretching beyond the limitations of their experiences and prior beliefs to learn new things.

For example, if we want to learn about gender differences among infants, we could just watch them and see what we learn, or we could just sit and think about babies we have known and observed. Alternatively, we could go to the folks who have real everyday expertise and should know the most—parents—and ask them what they think are the gender differences among infants. Unfortunately, however, research shows that our memories of what we have seen can be shaped as much by our prior beliefs about gender differences as they are by what was there to observe. Research also shows that if you show a baby to parents and tell them it is a girl, or you show them the *same* baby and tell them it is a boy, the parents will see the baby differently, they will interpret its behavior differently, and they will treat it differently (Lyons and Serbin, 1986). Social scientists, then, devote a lot of effort to developing and refining research methodologies not only like the one just described, which measures the degree to which stereotypes shape young parents' perceptions of babies, but also others that may allow us to observe babies and figure out what the gender differences in babies' behavior actually are.

Therefore, social scientists tend to build two key elements into their research strategies. First, although most describe what they do as asking questions and answering them through research, most also describe what they do as *testing hypotheses*. A *hypothesis* is an educated guess, a tentative statement, about some aspect of the world, that the social scientist makes on the basis of prior reading, research, casual observation, logical analysis, flashes of insight, messages from outer space—anything that offers an idea about how the world works. The social scientist then tests the hypothesis or subjects the educated guess to a rigorous test of evidence. *Testing* is the operative term here; when social scientists are trained, they are drilled in the idea that they should not be trying to *prove* their hypothesis, which implies devoting their efforts to piling up as much evidence on its side as possible. Rather, to test a hypothesis, they follow procedures designed to prove it *wrong*.

In the case of the baby-study example, this would involve two steps. First, once I had developed the hypothesis that male babies are more independent than female babies, I would try to think of the factors that might keep that from being true, and I would try to think of the things that might account for those differences other than gender (such as the babies being treated differently while they are being observed) and enter them into my study to provide the strongest possible test for my hypothesis about gender. Second, the basic statistical tests social scientists use to determine whether two test groups are different are designed to tell me what the probability is that the two groups *are not the same*. In other words, the statistical tests in a sense assume that the groups are the same, and the burden is placed on the evidence to show that they are not.

In addition to hypothesis testing, the second major element of social science research is the tendency to prefer *systematic observation,* in which the researchers are as fully self-conscious as possible (that is, not casual about what they might see or miss) about collecting, analyzing, and interpreting evidence. For most social scientists, this means following these general steps.

1. As much as possible, specify the research questions or hypotheses in advance of conducting the study. The more carefully these questions are specified, the more possible it is to plan a research strategy that will yield the evidence needed to answer the questions. For example, if I were doing the gender-differences-in-babies research, I would find the question "What differences are there?" too broad to be helpful in planning my research. I would prepare by reading as much as I could about the research others have done, I would watch a lot of babies, and then I would narrow down and specify my questions. I might decide I want to test the hypothesis that boy babies are (a) more active, (b) more independent, or (c) slower to develop language skills than girl babies.

2. Plan a research strategy that is likely to provide all the evidence needed. *All* the evidence includes the idea that the design should help to eliminate as much systematic bias as possible, such as the kinds described in the baby experiment. This usually requires deciding the following in advance:

    a. I would determine the specific categories of actions or events I want to observe. For example, in order to study how independent babies are, I might look to see whether the babies demand to be fed or wait patiently for the parent to decide when they are to be fed.

    b. I would determine the definitions and boundaries of each category. Exactly what baby behavior will I look at to know when to say that the baby has been patient or demanding? How will I know it when I see it? How will I develop coding strategies and, if I'm using them, measuring strategies to make sure I treat each baby the same way?

    c. I would specify the other factors I need to take into account to make sure I am not confusing the effects of one phenomenon with another. If I am comparing boy and girl babies' fussing to decide whether boy babies are more independent than girl babies, I do not want to finish my observation and realize that I was observing some babies in a warmer room than others, or in a room that is much more full of interesting colors, objects, or people than others. I do not want to have to worry about whether some of the babies were not as healthy as others or had been up longer that day. Therefore, I will try to build into my research design ways of either *measuring* or *controlling for* the other factors I think might be relevant to the outcome. I might measure or gather information on such things as their body temperatures and how long the babies have been awake at the time I observe them, so I can take account of these differences when I compare the babies' fussiness. I would probably also control for some important factors artificially, for example, by observing all of the babies in the same setting, so even if the setting is not their natural one, it is the same for all babies.

    d. Applying techniques of observation and analysis helps one push against one's own parochial perceptions, and that might help convince other people (who don't necessarily agree with one's conclusions in the first place) that one might be right. There are many ways social scientists may try to do this. They strive for *replicability;* that is, they try to do their research in such a way that if other scientists did the same thing, they would come out with the same answer. They can say, "Don't take my word for it; *you* try it." Wherever possible they show the *reliability* of their measures and observations, for example by having different people code observations independently. They also *reveal their methods* as clearly as possible in their research reports because for most social scientists, it is not possible to evaluate the conclusions without knowing how the researchers reached those conclusions. If I can follow another researcher's methods, I can judge, for example, that I believe the observations were correct, but I do not necessarily buy that the categories mean what the researcher thought. (For instance, maybe I do not think that demanding to eat is a sign of independence.) Instead, maybe I notice an important factor that the researcher did not take into account. (Maybe the parents had very different socioeconomic class backgrounds, and the middle-class parents of boys made their sons fussy on the spot by prodding them excessively, to make sure the boys acted smart enough to get into Harvard some day.)

There are many other important aspects to doing systematic observation[3] in social science research. The key point, however, is that when social science researchers do their work, the basic rule of the game is to try to get it right by challenging their own hunches. They do so by using a research design aimed at clarity, explicitly considering alternative explanations, and recording their methods and observations in a manner that is so exacting that it is difficult to leave out the little bits that did not fit their theory—or that at least will help others to catch them if they do.

Some people confuse this commitment to struggling to transcend one's narrow perspective and not trusting too much to the authority of one's impressions and perceptions with a commitment to absolute objectivity as a standard in scientific work. Certainly, various theoretical traditions in the social sciences claim that objectivity is desirable and possible. Over the years, many feminist scholars grew weary of hearing the claims of objectivity from social scientists (and natural scientists) whose work was clearly based on stereotypes about women and even prejudices against them. These scholars have joined the many other observers of scholarly practices in attacking these claims to objectivity, undermining the idea that a person can be completely objective, and criticizing the idea that objectivity is even a desirable goal. These are interesting and important debates. Unfortunately, however, too few of the best-known feminist theorists of knowledge and research are trained or experienced enough in the practices of the scientific approaches to observe directly how most practicing social scientists actually do their work.[4]

One does not have to believe in objectivity in order to have a passion for at least certain aspects of scientific rigor. For many scholars who take scientific standards as their approach to learning, the heart of the excitement lies in the will to reach beyond what they already know and feel to be right, seeking the special kind of *intersubjectivity* (relationship and exchange among different selves with different perspectives) among scholars trying to make discoveries together, and the research ethic demanding that they act to prove their own hunches wrong rather than to prove them right (which is the essence of what it means to "test a hypothesis"). The *social* scientist, who applies these standards to the study of pressing social problems and issues, pursues science far from any notion of sterile distancing from humanity, often implied by critics of scientific approaches to knowledge.

Methods Women's Studies Researchers Use

Women's studies researchers have used most of the diverse social science strategies for their own purposes. These researchers often adapt and change these strategies because of their subject matter and, even more, because of the perspectives developed by feminist theory and women's studies research over time. This books draws on studies using most of these strategies. This section looks at some of the major types of research methods used by the scholars whose work is discussed in this book. Many other research designs and strategies useful in women's studies research are not listed here, but the strategies noted here are some that readers will encounter frequently in this book. Without this insight into the structure and process of the research it is very difficult to know how to evaluate it. While these methods are very different in some respects, they share an important goal: offering the researcher a way to try to understand women's lives in their many dimensions.[5]

This discussion begins with two ends of a research continuum. At one end is *ethnographic research,* in which evidence is collected in as natural a setting as possible, and at the other end is *laboratory experimental research,* in which scientists work to control and hold constant most of the things that would otherwise make a situation natural. The discussion then turns to a range of other methods that lie somewhere in between.[6]

Ethnography. Ethnography is more an approach involving various methods than it is a single method. The goal of ethnographic research is to understand some portion of human life in context. Researchers thus seek to observe the social phenomena of interest in as natural a setting as possible. This does not mean just hanging out and watching people; it is crucial for ethnographers, like other social scientists, to know a lot about what they are doing before they go into the field. They must also have clearly defined research questions and strategies, precisely because life in its natural setting *is* so complicated. Ethnography involves a painstaking and lengthy process of gathering as much diverse information as possible. Ethnographers are usually especially interested in seeking people's understanding of their own lives. At the same time, an ethnographer does not just present literal descriptions and verbatim transcripts of what their informants have done and said; the ethnographer also interprets and tries to come to an understanding that goes beyond what is manifest. Ethnography is most often associated with anthropology, but ethnographic methods are also common in sociology and political science, among other fields.

There are many variations in how ethnographic research is used. In the most common form, researchers go on site to observe the people they are interested in studying. For another version, *participation observation,* the researcher actually takes part or plays a role in the phenomenon she is studying. For example, many education researchers report on the dynamics of gender in classrooms in which they are the teachers. This means that the researcher very explicitly and directly becomes a subject of the research project. *Jane,* a moving example of a participant-observation study was written by a woman who has been a political activist and organizer her whole career. Jane was the underground abortion service that preceded the legalization of abortion in 1973 of which the author was a member (Kaplan, 1995). In her study of public harassment of women, Caroline Brooks Gardner (1995) clearly included herself as a subject of study.

The discussion of health care in Chapter 5 refers to a fascinating example of an ethnographic study of surgeons. Joan Cassell (1996) was interested in the significance of the fact that the vast majority of surgeons are men. She was especially struck by how *body-oriented* surgeons are, in a way that is similar to some other occupations, such as firefighting, waging war, race-car driving, and test piloting. Most of the people who do these jobs are men. More than that, however, these occupations involve profound bodily experiences and physical risks. Each confronts death. And each is not just male dominated, but a culture of male bonding, stereotypic masculinity, and distrust of women.

Cassell wanted to understand more about these *embodied* occupations and their connection with gender. She wanted to know what would happen if the body of the surgeon were female? What would that mean for the woman and for her male colleagues? How could people understand the relationship of male and female bodies to the way this occupation works? As she put it, "Is it possible to confront men's and women's bodies and perceive and explain difference without either denying its existence, arguing for an infinite and ultimately unconvincing plasticity, or, alternatively, subscribing to a vulgar mechanistic reductionism where bodily difference is believed to circumscribe our abilities, performance, and fate?" (Cassell, 1996, 43). The research strategy that made the most sense to her was to watch surgeons living and acting in their bodies, to see how they related to their bodies and related their bodies to their work, and to observe what happened when some of the bodies were female. She did a series of different observations in five geographic areas in eastern and midwestern North America. The results are intriguing.

Experiments.   Ethnographers do their fieldwork in settings that are as natural as possible, usually try to understand social phenomena from the perspective of the people they are studying, and analyze most of their evidence in a qualitative, often narrative form; in contrast, experimental researchers try to isolate and examine the phenomenon in which they are interested while controlling for and holding constant as many other factors as possible. When experimenters are interested in the points of view of the people they are studying, they usually seek to understand how different social forces shape, affect, or even manipulate those points of view; most experimentalists assume that under the right circumstances, experimental designs can reveal more about the nature of people's thoughts and behavior than we can usually learn by studying thoughts and behavior in natural settings. These experiments do not have to happen in a laboratory per se (and often do not); the point is that experimentalists want to hold constant as many confounding factors as possible in order to test the specific hypothesis of interest. Recall, for instance, the experiment for observing babies, in which some of the confounding factors to be controlled included whether some babies were in more stimulating environments and whether some were feverish. Psychologists are the most frequent practitioners of experimental research in social science.

Here is an example from my own research on citizens' use of gender stereotypes in evaluating political candidates (Sapiro, 1982b). It is notoriously difficult to study the use of stereotypes. If I do not hire a man to work in my child-care center because he does not seem nurturant enough to me, is it because he is not very nurturant or because I have a stereotype about men, which shapes my perception when I evaluate an individual man? Studies of prejudice and stereotype lend themselves very well to experimental research because of the kind of control the researcher can bring to bear on the situation. In my study, I was intrigued with the problem of why the public was failing to support women candidates for political office: Was it because of stereotypes about women, which kept voters from seeing the women candidates as competent? Public-opinion polls showed that many people believed that women generally lacked certain kinds of competence to run for office (for example, they were not aggressive enough or did not have enough experience in certain policy areas such as defense or foreign policy). No amount of ethnographic research on my part would convince the unconvinced that I had good evidence for my hypothesis that many citizens' perceptions of candidates were shaped by their gender stereotypes.

Instead, I found a typical speech that had been delivered in the U.S. Senate: It spoke of economic policy in broad, sweeping, and fairly vacuous terms. I duplicated this speech, adding an explanation that said I was studying how campaign speeches shaped people's images of candidates. I asked a large sample of undergraduates at my university to read the speech, telling them it was written by a candidate for the House of Representatives, and then I asked the respondents to answer a number of questions about the candidate and the speech. All the students received exactly the same speech and questions. The trick was that half of them received a speech labeled "Speech by John Leeds," and the other half received one labeled "Speech by Joan Leeds." The specific label each respondent received was chosen at random (that is, picked by chance). If the two samples were randomly drawn from the same classes, and they received the same speech and questions, any systematic differences in the responses of the two groups had to be due to the manipulation of the one pair of words: "John" and "Joan." Indeed, John appeared to have the more effective speech, and he seemed more competent at dealing with defense issues, crime, economics, and farm issues; Joan appeared more competent at dealing with health and education and maintaining honesty and integrity in government. The students who read John's speech judged him more likely to win than the students who judged Joan's speech evaluated her.

For another example, reported in Chapter 13, researchers sent African-American and White women and men to car dealers, prepared with a set script to use for bargaining to buy a car. By providing the same script, but varying the race and gender of the "buyer," the researchers were able to find out that car dealers quoted lower prices to White males than to either African-American or female buyers (Ayres and Siegelman, 1995).

Sometimes, researchers have an opportunity to analyze a *naturally occurring experiment,* in which a quasi-experimental condition exists in the real world without the researcher having to set one up. For example, many people have wondered about the different effects of going to a single-sex or a coeducational school. It is certainly possible simply to take a sample of schools with students of only one sex and a sample of coeducational schools and compare them. However, there may be *many* things that differ about these different types of schools, thus confounding the results. In contrast, a school that changed from being an all-women's college to being gender integrated served as an excellent case study in which to look at the effects of the two conditions in *one* school (Canada and Pringle, 1995).

Survey Research.   Probably the most frequently used form of research discussed in this book is survey research, in which researchers collect evidence by interviewing a sample of people. Survey research is especially effective for projects in which it would be useful to get responses to exactly the same questions from a lot of people, in order to analyze and compare their answers. Survey research is one of the most useful approaches for studying public opinion (for example, people's attitudes toward abortion or affirmative action), for getting people's reports of their own behavior (as in studies of sexual practices or voting), or for collecting information on people's experiences (such as employment histories, education, and salaries). Marketing experts interested in selling products or candidates use polls and surveys with increasing frequency (indeed, annoying frequency for those who are regularly called during dinner), but scholarly surveys are distinctive in a number of ways. The most important distinction is that as with other forms of social science research, the point of scholarly surveys is to subject the researcher's hypothesis to rigorous testing, which means taking great care with the design of the questions.

Useful surveys are based on some form of *random sampling;* that is, once the *population* of interest is chosen (for example, all Americans, first-time mothers, teenagers, or members of the National Organization for Women), a *sample* (subset of that population) is drawn for study in such a way that all the kinds of people we are targeting have the same chance of falling into the sample. Certain statistical procedures tell how large a sample we need to draw so that when we ask the people in the sample a question, their answers have a pretty high probability of reflecting the answers we would get if we asked the whole population the same question.[7]

One very common use of surveys in social science is to use statistics to make a summary of characteristics of the sample. For example, Table 13-1 in Chapter 13, on economics, shows the proportion of men and women from 1938 to the 1980s who thought it was appropriate for a married woman to earn a living if her husband could support her. As we would expect, the proportion has risen a lot over the years. Perhaps a little more surprisingly, those figures show that men's and women's attitudes are not greatly different from each other.

We can also use surveys to do more complicated statistical analysis that gives more than a snapshot of the characteristics of the sample (for example, in terms of averages and proportions). Surveys also allow us to analyze a lot of different information at once, to reach some conclusions about the effects of one *variable* (that is, measured phenomenon) on another. For example, Chapter 13 also reports on a study investigating the determinants of how much household labor men do. It would be impossible to analyze simultaneously in a precise and systematic way all of the variables the researchers wanted to take into account—the number of hours a man's wife works outside the household, how feminist the husband's attitudes are, the relative salary of the husband and wife, the occupational prestige of the wife, and a measure of the general dynamics of the relationship between the husband and wife—to explain husbands' domestic labor. There are well-known statistical procedures, however, that allow us to analyze all of these variables at once for a lot of people, to determine the relative impact of each variable. Also, if we wanted to and if we had the information, we could look separately at people of different socioeconomic class or race backgrounds, or at people who live in the country or in the city, to see whether the mix is different. Surveys are commonly used in most of the social sciences.

Depth Interviewing. Surveys allow researchers to ask a lot of people a lot of relatively brief questions in order to analyze a large breadth of information at once. Many times, however, researchers believe that the best research strategy is to interview people to get evidence, but rather than seeking *breadth* of information from many people, they might want much deeper and more detailed information from relatively fewer people. This is especially true when researchers want to understand more detailed nuances of how the subjects of their study think.

For example, when probing the causes of sexual violence, it is possible to do a survey to compare the characteristics of men who rape with those of men who do not. Diana Scully had a different idea, however: She wanted to know more about what went on in the minds of men who had raped. She therefore spent hours visiting a sample of convicted rapists in prison to ask them about their experiences and perspectives. Instead of finding out the general characteristics that distinguish rapists from men who do not rape, she learned how men who have raped think about and in many cases justify their acts (Scully, 1990). Another example of depth interviewing is Celia Kitzinger and Sue Wilkinson's study of women who made the change during adulthood from a heterosexual to a lesbian identity (Kitzinger and Wilkinson, 1995). The researchers in this project talked with the women for an average of an hour and a half each to find out how the woman experienced and understood the process of change.

Depth interviewing is used in many disciplines, although it is probably used most extensively in certain branches of psychology. Depth interviewing is also an important component of doing *oral histories*. Scholars are more likely to analyze the data gathered in depth interviewing through qualitative rather than quantitative methods, both because of the kinds of questions they are asking of the data, and because the number of cases tends to be relatively small, thus rendering useless many kinds of statistical techniques applied to survey findings.

Event or Institutional Case Studies. Many social scientists are especially interested in analyzing particular events or organizations because by studying these cases in particular, they might understand a larger social dynamic or a broader classification of events or organizations. The event or organization is interesting or important in and of itself, but the primary contribution of a case study is to fit a piece into a larger puzzle and either test a theory or help build one. For example, Elizabeth Kennedy and Madeline Davis's case study of a lesbian community in Buffalo, New York, was designed not only to learn about that community, but also to examine in depth a case that did not fit the general stereotype of a "gay community." This community was in a smaller city and was composed largely of working-class women, in an era before the rise of the gay and lesbian movement of the late 1960s and after (Kennedy and Davis, 1993).

A scholar might pick a particular event to study because it represents a turning point or an example of a larger phenomenon. Political scientists often use case studies to examine the development or application of particular public policies. Case studies usually involve gathering many different types of information, especially a combination of interviews with key players or observers, as well as a variety of documentary sources, such as newspaper articles, newsletters, and other documents from people and groups that were involved.

Julia Edwards and Linda McKie did a case study of a topic that a large proportion of women have found very important, at least at some point in their lives. Their question was, "Why is it that women invariably have to queue [line up] for the toilet in public places, whereas men do not?" (Edwards and McKie, 1996, 215). Although their research was not extensive, it used a variety of sources and points of access to explore the example of a campaign to make the number of public bathrooms available more adequate in Cardiff, Wales, for women, the elderly, and the disabled. It followed the actions by a number of individuals at the local and national level, aimed at better access. The study probed both the forces that cause the lack of women's facilities and those that slowed the progress toward success. This case study illustrates one of the beauties of a good case study (even one on this subject) it was designed and written to be worthwhile not just to people who have a special interest in toilets in Cardiff, or even the provision of public toilets as such, but to people interested in the forces that lead public facilities to be designed from a gendered point of view, and a distinctly inappropriate one at that.

Do institutional and event case studies use quantitative or qualitative methods? The answer depends on the problem and the data. If the relevant evidence that requires analysis involves a lot of different observations easily summarized in quantifiable form (e.g., dollars, populations or memberships, or numbers of events), then quantitative methods may be used.

Archival Research.   Most of the historical work we discuss in this book is based on archival research, in which scholars identify documents and other materials from which to gather appropriate evidence to answer their research questions, and then they study these documents systematically. One of the most difficult tasks in this kind of research is finding the right materials in the first place. Although a very few famous people have donated all their papers to a single archive or library, more often, the documents relevant to understanding a particular person's life, or an organization, or—even more often—a time period are scattered in many different places, sometimes where the documents are uncatalogued and unorganized. For this reason, feminist scholars are grateful for the special collections available that archive documents relevant to women's lives and history.

Content Analysis.   In many cases, the best way to answer a question is to do a systematic analysis of the content of particular documents or other kinds of texts. For example, many scholars interested in media treatment of women have taken a sample of mass-media outlets (e.g., prime-time television shows, newspaper articles or magazines, or advertisements during a particular period of time) and have recorded all of the instances of a particular kind of information about women. For instance, how many and what kinds of male and female characters appeared? How much news was announced about women? What types of descriptions does the medium use when it discusses women, as compared with men? Chapter 8, on the media, is filled with such examples.

Meta-analysis.   A very traditional form of research—one used by students of all levels all the time—involves reviewing as much of the research on a particular topic as possible to find out what the weight of the evidence of many studies concludes. *Reviewing the literature* is an essential first step in all research projects. (Scholars are ill-advised to go through all of the time and expense of designing their own research projects if they have not looked to see what others have done and learned first.) As anyone who has done a literature review can attest, however, it is not always easy to draw clear conclusions from the results of many different studies.

How do researchers draw clear conclusions from large bodies of literature, often using many different designs to answer almost but not quite the same question, while measuring the variables differently and taking somewhat different factors into account on samples that are of different sizes? In the 1970s, scholars developed a new technique for doing this work more systematically: *meta-analysis.* This method uses statistical procedures to develop summary conclusions that take these complicated differences into account.

A good example, partly because it stirred controversy over how to conduct meta-analysis, began with a study of gender differences in sexuality, that Mary Beth Oliver and Janet Shibley Hyde conducted (1993). They reviewed, coded, and analyzed 177 studies of sexual behavior and concluded that, overall, there is very little difference between men's and women's sexuality (except, for example, in frequency of masturbation and attitudes toward casual sex). Another pair of scholars, Bernard Whitley and Mary Kite (1995), used a slightly different method and came out with a different answer on 2 of the 21 different attitudes and behaviors Oliver and Hyde studied—specifically, two attitudes related to homosexuality. The exchange (concluded in Oliver and Hyde, 1995) is especially interesting because it shows how much each scholar's understanding and approaches to methodology help determine how each one identifies and interprets evidence relevant to her or his question.

Summary.   There is *much* more to learn about these research methods than appears here, and there are many other versions and varieties available from which researchers may choose. For the purposes of this discussion, however, it suffices to summarize with a few brief points.

1. Getting good training in research methodology is important for anyone who is going to do research and anyone who is planning on spending a lot of time reading or using research. (Of course, the type and amount of necessary training will differ depending on the field.) Trying to do good research without knowing what one is doing or what the likely result of one's actions will be is like doing anything else in life without knowing what one is doing. It might work, but it probably will not.

2. It is important to plan a research strategy as carefully and specifically as possible. Research is a complicated (and very interesting) enterprise. Not planning how one is going to do the research is like doing any other complicated task without planning. It might work, but it probably will not.

3. A research method is a strategy for problem solving—solving the problem of getting an answer to a question or testing a hypothesis. The method, therefore, should be chosen because it fits the problem. Unfortunately, too many researchers pick a particular method for a particular study just because it is the one they happened to learn, or it is the one that happens to be popular at the moment.

4. A lot of the best studies involve multiple methods; that is, a researcher chooses a variety of methods that use different kinds of evidence and offer different perspectives to answer a question.

5. A lot of silly things have been written about the differences between quantitative and qualitative research methods. As many astute students of methodology have written, there is less difference between *well done* quantitative research and qualitative research than many people think. Too often, proponents of one approach attack the other method by caricaturing it, often because they do not really know a lot of the details of how it works in practice. Good quantitative research does not just stick people in little boxes or objectify them (any more than bad qualitative research does); qualitative work does not involve just casually checking out the scene and making a few haphazard notes.

6. The choice of a method always involves trade-offs and problems. The choice of a method determines whether it will be easier or harder for me to summarize a lot of complex information, look at a case in depth, understand a problem from the inside, avoid mixing my own unexamined beliefs into my research, reach conclusions in a way that will be convincing to those who do not start out believing me, and most of all, learn something important and interesting.

Understanding and Interpreting Women's Lives

There was a popular elephant joke in the 1960s that went like this: Query—How do you make a sculpture of an elephant? Answer—Take a big piece of stone, and cut away everything that doesn't look like an elephant.

This is, in a sense, the way a lot of people think about what it means to study or know about women. Knowing about women is knowing how they are not like men. Not only is one of the most common ways to study women the identification of *gender differences;* it is also often framed in terms of how women are unlike (or

What do you know about these two children by knowing their sex? Are they different kinds of people? Will they lead different kinds of lives?

like) the male norm. The following discussion explores some of the problems of studying women, beginning with the gender-differences approach. It then turns to other considerations in understanding and interpreting women's lives.

When Is a Difference Really a Difference?

How different are women and men? This question arises repeatedly throughout this book. We consider differences in the life situations of women and men, differences in the treatment they receive, and differences in their personal characteristics, skills, interests, and beliefs. Before we study these differences, however, we have to answer some prior questions. What do we mean when we talk about gender *differences*? What makes a gender difference worth talking about? When is a difference really a difference? A number of problems make it difficult to answer these questions, such as vague or misleading language, imprecise or invalid measures, bias, or an overly narrow focus on gender alone.

The first problem we encounter in analyzing gender differences is the very language we use to express differences; also, the way we interpret the language used to describe gender differences is often imprecise, exaggerated, or otherwise misleading. Suppose that a test of mathematical skills were administered to 42 men and 42 women, and the distribution of scores on this particular test was as follows:

Grade	A	B	C	D	F	Average
Numerical grade	(4.0)	(3.0)	(2.0)	(1.0)	(0.0)	
Number of women	5	15	16	4	2	2.4
Number of men	6	17	15	3	1	2.6

How could we put these results into words? "Women demonstrate a lower level of mathematical skills than men"? "The average woman has a lower level of mathematical skills than the average man"? "Women are twice as likely to fail a particular test of mathematical skills as men"? "A majority of the people who got A's on a test of mathematical skill were men"? By reading these words without thinking carefully or looking at the evidence, you might be led to conclude that women are pretty poor indeed at mathematics. You might decide that a man would be a much better bet than a woman if you needed help with a mathematical problem. Look again at the actual numbers. Do the apparent sex differences in these scores really mean that you should look for a man to help you with your math problem? Would you rather have the advice of one of the five women who got A's than of the four men who got D's and F's? (To explore these concepts further, see Box 1-1.)

Words such as *average, most, more,* and *a majority* are summary terms for numbers, and it is impossible to understand their significance without knowing more about the numbers. Unfortunately, too many people think they can understand problems of difference without paying attention to precision. This much is clear: Saying that the *average* male or female possesses certain skills or personality traits almost never means that *all* members of one sex are better at the skill than all

---

BOX 1-1   See for Yourself: Interpreting Numerical Differences

After examining the preceding table, showing a hypothetical comparison of test results, try coming up with some examples for yourself:

1. Devise a plausible set of test grades that would result in the same gradepoint average for men and women but would also include having one gender group receive at least twice as many A's as the other group.

2. Create a plausible set of test grades that would result in one gender group having a higher grade-point average, while the *other* group has a higher proportion of A's.

3. Construct a plausible set of test grades that would result in one gender group having both a higher proportion of A's *and* a higher proportion of F's.

Review each of these sets of scores, and devise at least *two different* ways of summarizing the results verbally. What are the implications of each of these descriptions? What would be the most accurate and clear way of talking about differences?

BOX 1-2   See for Yourself: How Do You Know It When You See It?

One of the first tasks in research is to figure out how to define a concept *operationally*—that is, what practical definition to use so that the researcher knows what to observe to study the phenomenon.

Following are two personality characteristics often attributed to one sex more than the other. For each one, decide what test you would perform or what behavior you would look for to do research that would tell you whether there is a gender difference in this personality characteristic:

independent

emotional

Try the same thing with other personality characteristics for which you think there might be gender differences.

members of the other sex, or that all members of one sex display the trait and that members of the other sex do not. In fact, research usually shows much more variation *among* men and *among* women than there is *between* men and women. Also, contrary to what some people think, one does not necessarily avoid quantitative reasoning simply by avoiding statistics; one may still use quantitative concepts and analysis, but without adequate precision and clarity.

A second difficulty with interpretation of sex differences stems from the problems of constructing and analyzing appropriate measures of characteristics and skills. In this example, we wish to study mathematical skills. Before we can compare the abilities of the sexes, we need to devise a specific test or set of tests that we think provides a *valid* measure of mathematical skills, a test that actually measures what we want it to measure and only what we want it to measure.

Many of the widely circulated reports of sex differences are faulty because the tests used in the research did not measure only what the researchers claimed to be testing. There are many different ways of measuring any given skill, personality characteristic, attitude, or whatever, and differences in measures can make the results differ (see Box 1-2). Unfortunately many students find questions about research methods and statistics boring or intimidating and therefore do not pay attention to these important methodological problems.

A third difficulty in identifying gender differences, even if one is attempting to be precise, is the impact of bias on observation. As mentioned previously, researchers can be as prejudiced as anyone else, so two different researchers may observe the same situation or event and see different things happening, depending on their own expectations and stereotypes.

Finally, sometimes, the theory and methods we use make it more difficult to see the role gender plays in our lives because we have focused too narrowly on gender alone, without considering *other* aspects of human experience. This may seem strange to say, but think about this example: The family experiences of women of different races are different in some respects. If we fail to consider racial differences, we may miss gender differences that are not structured the same way for people of different races. In other words, in order to understand the role of gender in women's lives, it is also necessary to look at the role of race. Although being a woman or a man shapes people's lives regardless of race, it shapes their lives somewhat differently, depending on race. (The relationship between gender and other forms of social differentiation is discussed further in Chapter 4.)

When and Why Are Gender Differences Interesting?

As this book shows, gender-difference research is not the only way to learn about women's lives. Why and under what circumstances are gender differences of interest to us? What types of gender differences are worth our attention? The main reason to pay attention to certain types of differences is that we think they have some social relevance: They might make women's and men's lives and experiences different in some significant way. We pay little attention to the well-documented fact that older men, and not older women, may have visible hair in their ears. We pay considerably more attention to the more contentious assertions about gender differences in the ability to nurture or to fight.

Consider the case of skills. If we find that men and women differ in their visuospatial skills, we presumably have found out something about (a) the special abilities and limitations of each sex that might determine how they function in day-to-day life, and (b) the activities that might better suit women or men. Deriving the social significance of basic gender differences is not as simple as it might seem, however. If we find that on average, girls do better on one visuo-spatial skill test and boys do better on another, should we give boys and girls training only in the skill on which they do better? Should we base our occupational counseling on these results, sending girls and boys into different occupations? This might be an appropriate conclusion if *only* boys showed *any* talent on one skill and *only* girls showed *any* talent on the other, if these differences were entirely the result of innate sex differences, and if girls or boys could reach the full extent of their abilities with only a little training. However, none of these things is true.

Even if we found that there were indeed many more men than women with the particular skill needed for a certain job, we could not rule out all women from that job on the grounds that they are not as *likely* to be qualified. Some women will probably be as qualified as, and possibly even more qualified than, many men who happen to apply. This understanding of gender differences now forms part of the basis of American law on employment. After the passage of the 1964 Civil Rights Act, which (among other things) banned discrimination in employment on the basis of sex, the Equal Employment Opportunity Commission (EEOC) ruled that employers may not refuse jobs to women because of "assumptions of the comparative employment characteristics of women in general," or because of "stereotyped characterizations of the sexes."

> Such stereotypes include, for example, that men are less capable of assembling intricate equipment and that women are less capable of aggressive salesmanship. The principle of nondiscrimination requires that individuals be considered on the basis of individual capacities and not on the basis of any characteristics generally attributed to the group. (Goldstein, 1988, 500)

Thus, people must be considered on the basis of their individual merit, not on the basis of stereotypes about the social groups of which they are a part, even if the stereotype is true of a majority of the members of the group.

It is not even as simple as some people think to determine which human characteristics best enable a person to perform specific tasks or roles in society. For example, most people assume that a relatively high degree of competitiveness and aggression is required to be active in politics. They therefore assume that it is reasonable to compare women's and men's levels of competitiveness and aggression to help explain differences in male and female political participation. Is the initial assumption true, however? That is, *do* people need an extraordinarily high level of competitiveness and aggression to be active in politics? There is no clear indication that they do. True, a person who wishes to be elected to a political office must compete in an electoral contest, but this does not necessarily mean that the political candidate is especially competitive or particularly cares for competition. To argue otherwise would be like suggesting that to be a doctor, a person has to like taking tests because one has to take a lot of tests to become a doctor. Thus, the social significance of sex differences is rarely as obvious as it seems, and such determinations require careful thought and analysis.

There is another important issue in the language and method of gender differences. It is very easy to fall into a pattern of discussing gender differences that sets up one sex or the other as the norm. In traditionally male areas of life, for example, we tend to ask how women differ from men (taking men as the norm), whereas in traditionally female areas of life, we ask how men differ from women (taking women as the norm). These apparently little wording differences can have a lot of significance. For example, Chapter 9 shows that the "gender gap" in voting developed in the early 1980s, when women tended to vote more Democratic than men, and men voted more Republican than women. In observing this pattern, most journalists' natural tendency was to ask what happened to women to make them vote differently from the men. If there was a gap in voting, they presumed, it must be that men are the norm, and women are voting differently. Here's the problem: In fact, the gender gap was caused by a movement away from the Democratic Party on the part of some men who traditionally would have voted Democratic. To explain the gender gap, it was at least as important to figure out what had happened to men to make them move from their traditional partisan attachments as it was to explain why women did not change their behavior.

Above all, when looking at gender differences, it is important to bear in mind what is interesting about those differences and what questions we are asking. We cannot simply continue to use men as a representation of the norm and to ask how women differ from them. Exploring gender difference is a matter of asking how women and men are similar to and different from each other.

Finally, in women's studies, the differences between women and men are not the only area of interest. Scholars of women's studies are also interested in women's history and situation for its own sake. Similarly, if scholars were interested in the variety of forms women in the arts have used to express their understanding of womanhood, for example, they would probably focus on women alone and not on men at all. Understanding pregnancy and childbirth is a matter of looking not at gender *difference,* but rather at gendered *existence.* To understand the history of homemaking, scholars must consider more than simply gender *differences*. Many other examples appear throughout this book that require investigators to go beyond a narrow focus on gender differences.

Difference and Inequality

Many aspects of men's and women's lives are different from each other—their jobs, times spent with children, crime rates, hobbies, and clothing. *Difference,* however, is not the same as *inequality,* nor is *sameness* the same as *equality.* There is, as sociologists would say, a system of *differentiation* of women and men in the United States. However, are the two sexes differentiated in a way that gives them unequal value or power? That is, are they not only differentiated, but also *stratified?* Do women and men have not only different roles and activities, but also different statuses?

People can engage in different types of behavior without being unequal. For example, if I always have ice cream for dessert and you always have apple pie, or if I play piano as a hobby and you play basketball, there is no reason to believe that we are revealing a pattern of inequality. It is also possible for different people to engage in the same activities or to have the same resources and be regarded unequally. If a Black family and a White family with equal incomes try to buy the same house in the same neighborhood, they—and their money—may not be valued equally. A man who is smart and argumentative and a woman who is smart and argumentative will probably not be regarded equally positively. The meanings and measures of sameness and difference are related to but are not the same as the meanings and measures of equality and inequality. *How* they are related is determined by culture.

We can evaluate the degree of equality between women and men by asking several questions:

1. To what degree do women and men possess similar levels of valued resources?
2. To what degree do women and men have similar amounts, types, and ranges of life options?
3. To what degree are women and men and their major activities valued similarly?
4. To what degree do women's and men's psychological states—their mental health and degree of happiness or contentment—seem to indicate that their situations are satisfactory?

Women are economically poorer than men. They hold many fewer positions of authority in society, which means that they have considerably less control over the disposition of valuable resources, including time, labor, and deference, as well as tangible goods. Men have control over more valuable resources, which in turn expands the number of options they have. Men are in more positions of authority, which gives them control both over others and over themselves. Public officials, for example, make major decisions about the distribution of resources and about what people may and may not do in a community or nation, and that community or nation includes the public officials themselves. The very concept of democracy is based on the principle of self-government. Men are still vastly predominant among those who do the self-governing. In personal life and day-to-day decision making, women also seem to have—or at least to make—a much smaller range of choices. Nevertheless, readers must go considerably beyond the mere presentation of figures to understand the relative degree of choice women and men have. We attend to this task throughout the remainder of this book.

Money and power are not the only measures of worth, of course. Many people still value having a male child (an heir to carry on the family name) more than having a female child. *Who's Who* lists only a few women. Many women speak of their major day-to-day activity as being "just a housewife," thus devaluing their own work. To say that a woman writes or thinks "like a man" is supposed to be a compliment, but it indicates that the way women typically write or speak is viewed as less good. One of the points noted by many historians of women is that even when women have done remarkable and valued things, the women tend to be forgotten. Many other such examples appear later in this book.

Psychological states are also important to consider when discussing equality. When confronted with the degree to which men's and women's experiences and resources differ, many people argue that there really is not a problem because many women are happy and content with their segregated lives. Although a majority of people still think that women are happiest when they are devoting themselves to being mothers and homemakers, some surveys show that women in the traditional homemaking role are unhappier than employed women. Women in traditional roles also seem to have more psychological problems (including "middle-aged depression") than other women. (The relationship between gender roles and mental health is discussed further in Chapter 6.)

Simone de Beauvoir (1952) suggested an even more profound criticism of the "happiness and contentment" principle for evaluating the relative status of women and men. People can learn—or be taught—to be happy in all sorts of situations, including slavery and extreme poverty; the human population is amazingly varied. If we use only happiness and contentment as the criterion for judging whether a group has a problem, we could make wrongs right merely by convincing people to be happy with their lot. Some people are happiest when they save a life; others are happiest when they kill. Are all forms of human happiness morally equivalent? Is happiness the criterion we wish to use to evaluate human activity? Some suggest that it is; others say it is not. The measure that de Beauvoir uses, for example, is not contentment and happiness, but liberty.

We can conclude, even from the small amount of information we have examined thus far, that men's and women's lives and activities are not just different; they are unequal. Before we can probe more deeply into the ways this system of inequality works and how it can be changed, we must first find out how it came about. We turn to that question next.

Notes

1.   The full text of this Supreme Court case and most others cited in this book can be found in Goldstein (1988), in Kay (1996), and at the Cornell University Law School Legal Information Institute, http://www.law.cornell.edu/lii.table.html.

2. When I first agreed to teach a course on women and politics while I was a graduate student, the first thing I did was to go to the library and look under "W" in the card catalog to see what had been written on women.

3. There are many good basic texts on social science methods based in the various social sciences. One that is readable and interdisciplinary and has a lot of good examples is Sommer and Sommer (1997).

4. Some of the most interesting works in this field that might be accessible to a beginning student are Eichler (1980), Harding (1991), Keller (1985), and Smith (1987). An excellent book focusing specifically on research on sex and gender is Caplan and Caplan (1994).

5. An excellent source on methods of feminist research is Reinharz (1992), which has much more complete information on all of the methods listed here, plus others.

6. Experienced users of social science methods will see that not only is this discussion nontechnical, but it also leaves out many of the issues usually discussed in a basic methods overview of this sort. My purpose here is to offer the most basic, even common-sense understanding of how social science research works and of some of the varieties of research illustrated in this book. For a more complete, yet still elementary treatment, see Reinharz (1992) and the cases in Caplan and Caplan (1994).

7. This need for random sampling is why surveys based on having television viewers call a particular telephone number are useless. These nonrandom samples tell nothing about any population other than that the people who happen to watch the particular show have phones and take the time to call that particular station.

2

❦

Societal-Level Approaches to Understanding Women's Lives

THE WORLD IS MARKED by many variations in how women's lives are structured, and in the differences between women's and men's experiences. In this book, we focus specifically on the United States, but our understanding of the structure of gender relations, and especially of what might cause this particular structure to develop, must remain very limited if we do not place the United States in the larger global context. We therefore begin this chapter with a brief overview of cross-national variation. Then most of this chapter is devoted to looking at these crucial underlying questions: How can we explain how and why gender relations are structured in one or another general pattern in particular societies or at particular times? Why do women face a relatively egalitarian situation in some countries, and a much more inegalitarian situation in others? How does the structure of gender relations develop over time?

U.S. Women in Global Perspective

What is the status of women in the United States? How much gender equality is there? The most common way to answer these questions would be for us to focus on women in U.S. society and, especially, to compare them with men in the same society. That is how much of this book looks at the question. However, we can get a much clearer understanding of women's situation in one country by comparing it with that of others around the world. This gives us a better idea of the range of current possibilities, and it provides more information that might be useful in figuring out *why* women face the situations they do.

There are many excellent books on women in different countries, and some that compare women's situations cross-nationally. Here, we look briefly at a few clues about how to understand the situation American women face by viewing it in a comparative context. Specifically, we examine education, then marriage and reproduction, women's work, and women and the state.[1]

Literacy and Education

Experts on the status of women have long agreed that one of the most important indicators of women's status is how their level of education compares with men's. In almost all societies, education provides improved life chances for many reasons. It provides personal resources and credentials that help in the labor market. It provides knowledge and skills that assist people in coping with and even leading social change. Education also often confers a mark of status. For women in particular, education tends to raise the age at which women start bearing children, and it restricts their fertility over the course of their lifetime. Later in this chapter, a brief glimpse of global fertility patterns makes clear the importance of this effect.

In the United States, although many Americans either do not finish high school or do not go beyond that level, the average level of education is high, as is the proportion of people who get a college education; also, having at least some college education is important for earning a living wage in the United States. Therefore, the most obvious way of evaluating women's educational attainments is to compare the proportion of undergraduate and advanced degrees women and men receive. That kind of measure makes much less sense when turning to other countries, especially those in the economically poorer regions of the world.

Table 2-1 provides some measures of women's educational attainment that offer a useful picture on a world scale. That table and data elsewhere in this chapter show a sampling of nations around the world, classified by whether they are *advanced industrial countries,* those that are relatively wealthy and have fully developed industrial sectors, as well as substantial service sectors of the economy; *developing nations,* which includes the many poorer countries, with still relatively undeveloped industrial sectors, economies that tend to be low on technology, and, often, governmental systems that are relatively unstable, fragile, and dependent on nondemocratic rule; and the countries of the *former Soviet Union,* a set of countries sharing a recent communist and authoritarian past, but that vary a lot in how much their economies and new governmental systems have developed. None is yet a very wealthy nation.

There are four measures of education in Table 2-1. The first column shows the difference between women's illiteracy and men's illiteracy. Although it is important to know the overall levels of literacy, to investigate women's relative educational status, it makes more sense to see whether women's attainment of literacy is very different from men's. It is possible to have a relatively high level of literacy in a society but for women to be left behind men *in that context* of high literacy. This discrepancy appears in Belarus, where only 4.0% of women and 0.7% of men are illiterate. The overall literacy rate is extremely high—higher, overall, than in the United States—but women are nearly 6 times as likely to be illiterate as men are. Cuba is another example of a high-literacy country with a relatively big gender gap. Consider Haiti at the other end of the scale, where 76% of women and 69% of men are illiterate. In Haiti, although there is a gender difference, it pales in relation to the overwhelming illiteracy of the population as a whole.

The conclusion offered by the numbers is that at the very basic level of literacy, both the relatively wealthy advanced industrial nations and the less well-off countries of the former Soviet Union have high literacy rates and, for the most

TABLE 2-1
Women's Education

	% ♀ Illiterate – % ♂ Illiterate	♀ per 100 ♂ Enrolled: Secondary School	♀ per 100 ♂ Enrolled: Postsecondary School	% ♀ Among University Faculty
Advanced/New Industrials				
Australia	—	99	111	33
Canada	—	96	128	18
Denmark	—	96	104	—
France	—	102	113	28
Italy	2	96	91	—
Japan	—	97	63	11
Netherlands	—	93	80	21
Norway	—	99	113	21
Sweden	—	100	116	—
United Kingdom	—	98	91	19
United States	0✐	103	120	27
Developing				
Algeria	29✗✗✗✗	77	50	20
Argentina	1	107	88	35
Bangladesh	24✗✗✗✗	50	19	12
Brazil	3✗	116	110	41
Chile	1	105	80	20
China	31✗✗✗	73	50	30
Cuba	4	108	136	45
Egypt	28✗✗✗✗	79	59	29
El Salvador	12✗✗✗	102	49	21
Haiti	7✗✗✗✗	96	35	17
India	30✗✗✗✗	52	42	19
Iran	22✗✗✗	71	44	19
Ivory Coast	22✗✗✗✗	44	23	—
Kenya	28✗✗✗	69	45	—
Mexico	8✗	99	75	—
Morocco	26✗✗✗✗	68	57	19
Niger	10✗✗✗✗	42	18	11
Pakistan	21✗✗✗✗	41	22	17
Philippines	2	99	143	57
South Africa	4✗✗	116	87	29
Turkey	27✗✗	60	51	32
Uganda	30✗✗✗	53	38	18
Former Soviet or Soviet Bloc				
Belarus	3✐	104	111	—
Bulgaria	2✐	99	106	38
Czech Republic	—	99	123	29
Hungary	1✐	96	101	30
Poland	1✐	100	127	36
Russia	3✐	128	108	—
Ukraine	3✐	109	98	—

Note: ✐ ≤ 5% of the population is illiterate; ✗ ≥ 10% of women are illiterate; ✗✗ ≥ 25% of women are illiterate; ✗✗✗ ≥ 50% of women are illiterate; ✗✗✗✗ ≥ 75% of women are illiterate. A dash indicates that data were not available.

Source: UN (1995a, 99–103).

part, equivalent literacy levels among women and men. The poorer developing nations show a very different picture. There, especially in Africa and Asia, a pattern appears, showing both substantial levels of illiteracy and (often) large gaps between men and women in their levels of illiteracy.

Table 2-1 also shows how many women are enrolled in secondary school (high school) and postsecondary school for every 100 men enrolled in those schools.[2] Current levels of enrollment provide some sense of how egalitarian the distribution of education is for the younger generation now in school. Because there has been so much change in the levels of education in many countries, the *average* education of all women and men would include a substantial portion of many populations that were educated in an era when the gender gap in education was much greater than it is now. In addition to colleges and universities, postsecondary schools include many other kinds of educational institutions and programs, such as those offering professional and job training after completion of the equivalent of high school.

The table shows that in the United States, women are roughly as likely as men to be enrolled in secondary school, and they are somewhat more likely to be in postsecondary education. These figures are very close to the figures for a number of the other advanced industrial and former Soviet countries. There are certain exceptions: In the Netherlands and especially in Japan, women are much less well represented in postsecondary education than men are. Again, however, the situation is quite different in the developing nations. Certainly, in many Latin American countries, women are a slight majority of the secondary-school students, as in the advanced industrials and former Soviet nations. In much of the developing world, however, especially in Asia and in some parts of Africa, women drop out of school earlier. The figures in the developing world show remarkable variation in the presence of women in postsecondary education, again, with a tendency for many areas of Africa and Asia to show great gender differences. Consider how very small is the proportion of women at that level compared with that of men in Bangladesh, the Ivory Coast, Niger, or Haiti, in contrast to the high proportion of women in Brazil, Cuba, and the Philippines.

Finally, Table 2-1 also shows the proportion of university faculty members who are women. Of course, the number and quality of universities in the different countries vary widely, but these statistics can nevertheless provide a picture of the degree of gender equality in education at one of the highest levels of attainment: teaching in institutions of higher education. Here, the variation across countries, and especially across richer and poorer countries, flattens out. In the United States, for example, clearly less than one third of university faculty members are women, as is true of nearly every other country displayed here. Other than a couple of countries that stand out as having a relatively large proportion of women among the faculty—Brazil, Cuba, and the Philippines in particular—the proportion of women is remarkably similar across countries in its unimpressiveness.

Marriage and Reproduction

The vast majority of people in the world marry, and the vast majority of women give birth to at least one child. Also, while men's placement in their kinship organization helps determine men's status, roles, and experiences in many parts of the world (and in some classes or *parts* of the population in others), marriage and reproduction have a primary importance in women's lives in most societies, unmatched in men's. Nevertheless, the organization, experience, and meaning of marriage and reproduction differ cross-nationally in ways that are important to understand, both for seeing the larger picture and for being able to place the United States in a global context. These comparisons are especially interesting, given Americans' public focus on changing patterns of marriage and motherhood; for example, many Americans are concerned about single motherhood and its relationship to poverty or changed marital patterns and their relationship to morality and social stability.

By the early 1990s, the average age at first marriage for U.S. women was about 23 years. That is roughly the same as it was in the other major Western advanced industrial countries, although a little lower than in many. The worldwide variation is very large, however. In many African and some Asian countries, the average age at first marriage is less than 20 years; in some (e.g., Ethiopia, Mali, Niger, São Tomé and Principe, and Nepal), it is less than 18 years. In some countries, especially in the Caribbean, the average age at first marriage is 28 years or more (Réunion, Swaziland, the Bahamas, Grenada, Jamaica, Saint Kitts and Nevis, Saint Vincent and the Grenadines). The average age for women at first marriage is also relatively high in Japan.

Further clues about the differences in marriage patterns appear in Table 2-2, which shows the proportion of 15- to 19-year-old women who are currently married in a large sample of countries around the world. Research shows that all over the world, living in an urban area or having more education raises women's age at first marriage; unsurprisingly, therefore, many of the most urban societies, in which women are most highly educated—including the United States—show the lowest concentration of teenage marriages. Among the poorer countries, Latin American and former Soviet nations also tend to have relatively few women marrying before they are 20 years old. The picture is very different in the Arab world and in Africa, where a large proportion of women, the majority of them in some countries, are already married by the time they are 20 years old. Urbanicity and education cannot be the only factors that shape the age of marriage, however, given the very low early marriage rates in much of the Caribbean.

Many of the couples who are bound in long-term relationships within a single household are not formally married, and the rates of cohabitation and consensual union vary cross-nationally also. It is difficult to get good information on the frequency of cohabitation and other forms of consensual union because in many cultures, such as in the United States, these unions violate general social or moral norms or are even technically illegal. Although these unions are more widely accepted in other places, such as many countries in Latin America and the Caribbean and in Denmark, where a comparatively low proportion of couples marry, even there, official statistics do not reflect the reality very well. Figures from the late 1980s and early 1990s showed that more than one third of women in their late 20s were living in cohabiting relationships in Canada, Denmark, New Zealand, and Sweden.

Another way of gaining some insight into these patterns is to consider the proportion of women who have never married by the time they have reached 45 years

TABLE 2-2
Proportion of 15- to 19-Year-old Women Who Are Married

Proportion of 15- to 19-Year-Olds Currently Married	Countries
≤5%	Australia, Austria, Canada, China, France, Germany, Ireland, Italy, Japan, South Korea, Netherlands, New Zealand, Norway, Poland, Singapore, Spain, Sweden, Switzerland, Tunisia, United Kingdom, **United States**
5–9%	Algeria, Azerbaijan, Belarus, Belgium, Belize, Burundi, Czech Republic, Djibouti, Haiti, Hungary, Israel, Latvia, Lithuania, Malaysia, Portugal, South Africa, Sri Lanka
10–14%	Argentina, Bahrain, Bolivia, Brazil, Chile, Colombia, Greece, Kuwait, Myanmar, Panama, Paraguay, Peru, Philippines, Romania, Russia, Tajikistan, Ukraine, Uruguay
15–19%	Bulgaria, Costa Rica, Ecuador, Indonesia, Iraq, Lesotho, Mexico, Morocco, Thailand, Turkey, Venezuela
20–24%	Egypt, Guatemala, Jordan, Syria, Zimbabwe
25–29%	Cuba, Pakistan, Zambia
30–39%	Cameroon, Central African Republic, Iran, Tanzania
40–49%	Burkina Faso, Ethiopia, India, Ivory Coast, Malawi, Mali, Senegal
≥50%	Bangladesh, Gambia, Niger, Sierra Leone, United Arab Emirates

Source: UN (1995a, 33–37).

old. In the United States, that figure is about 5%. In many countries, especially in Muslim ones, the figure is much lower. In the Caribbean, however, a large proportion of women never marry—for example, more than 30% in Barbados, Dominica, French Guiana, Grenada, Saint Kitts and Nevis, and Saint Vincent and the Grenadines. More information about marriage and cohabitation may be found by considering patterns of reproduction, reported later in this chapter.

Of course, none of this information about rates and ages of marriage tells a lot about the differences in the ways marriage works or what the experience is like for married women in each country. Research shows that the distribution of power and resources within marriage varies a lot, as do the particular divisions of labor that are common. In some countries—such as Turkey, Spain, Nigeria, and Ireland—people who marry tend to be quite similar in their general outlook on life, while in others—such as Japan, Finland, and Russia—that is not true. The United States is among those in which married people show a relatively high level of similarity.[3] Even the degree to which marriage represents a stable bond between one man and one woman varies cross-nationally. Polygyny, for example, is still common in Sub-Saharan Africa (e.g., in Togo, Senegal, Mali, Cameroon, and Liberia, where more than 35% of women are in polygynous marriages), although in some countries, the practice is illegal even though still followed. (Polygyny was originally the normative practice among Mormons in the United States until it was made illegal; reports indicated for a long time after that the practice nevertheless continued in many families.) In countries where polygyny is practiced, it is more common among less educated women. Elsewhere, *serial* bonding and monogamy has increasingly become the norm. Half of all marriages end in divorce in Sweden, the United States, Liberia, and the Dominican Republic. Divorce is also very common in the Baltic states and in many parts of Africa, Latin America, and the Caribbean.

Relatively few women live their whole life without ever having a child. Women now have fewer children on average than they used to in most parts of the world, except in many parts of Africa, where economic conditions often worsened from the 1970s to the 1990s, and the fertility rate concomitantly increased. In the same period, the proportional reduction in childbirth was most notable in Catholic Europe, in Latin America, and in East Asia. Increasing education among women plays a large role in these changes, as do other economic changes and the availability of effective means of contraception and abortion. Fertility and the timing of children still vary widely around the world. Women in Sub-Saharan Africa and South Asia (India, Pakistan, Bangladesh) have much higher fertility rates than women in other parts of the world do, but much of the developed world does not even replace itself through reproduction. Women in Austria, Germany, Greece, Hong Kong, Italy, Portugal, Spain, and Singapore have fewer than 1.5 children on average. Other countries where women have fewer than 2 children on average are Australia, Belgium, Britain, Bulgaria, Canada, Cuba, Denmark, Finland, France, Hungary, Japan, Korea, the Netherlands, and Switzerland. In contrast, women in Angola, Benin, the Ivory Coast, Malawi, Mali, Niger, Rwanda, Uganda, and Yemen average more than 7 children per woman.[4]

One of the growing concerns in the United States has been the increasing number of very young and single women who have children. Table 2-3 shows the annual number of births for every 1,000 teenagers 15–19 years old in the early 1990s; clearly, the figure in the United States is indeed higher than in other advanced industrial nations. In the United States, teen births are especially heavily concentrated among the poor and among African-American and Hispanic-American mothers. Even among the other advanced industrial countries, however, the incidence of teenage births varies a lot; it is especially low in parts of East Asia and northern Europe. These figures are very small, however, compared with those in the developing world, especially in the parts of Asia and Africa where women marry young and where poverty and illiteracy among women is rampant. Those areas also have poor health care and nutrition, which means that maternal mortality rates are shockingly high. Just to offer a glimpse of the differences, in the late 1980s, the *maternal mortality rate* (i.e., the number of maternal deaths per 100,000 live births) was 26 in the developed areas of the world. In comparison, it was 160 in Central America, 220 in South America, 420 in Southeast Asia, 570 in South Asia, and 690 in Sub-Saharan Africa.

As Table 2-3 also shows, contraceptive use varies a lot from country to country, sometimes for cultural reasons, which usually emphasize birth control as a sin or

TABLE 2-3
Teen Births, Birth Control, and Abortion

	Reproduction		
Countries	Births per 1,000 15- to 19-Year-Olds	% Birth-Control Use, Married Women	Legal Abortion?
Advanced/New Industrials			
Australia	21	76	Yes
Canada	25	73	Yes
Denmark	11	78	Yes
France	12	81	Yes
Germany	17	75	No
Israel	23	—	No
Italy	10	78	Yes
Japan	4	64	Yes
Netherlands	6	76	Yes
Norway	20	76	Yes
Singapore	11	74	Yes
South Korea	6	79	No
Sweden	13	78	Yes
United Kingdom	34	81	Yes
United States	58	74	Yes
Former Soviet or Soviet Bloc			
Belarus	40	23	Yes
Bulgaria	72	76	Yes
Czech Republic	45	78	Yes
Hungary	44	73	Yes
Kazakhstan	48	30	Yes
Latvia	43	—	Yes
Lithuania	35	—	Yes
Poland	31	75	No
Romania	57	58	Yes
Russia	53	32	Yes
Ukraine	56	23	Yes

highlight a woman's duty to have children (but note the widespread use of contraception in Roman Catholic countries of the developed world). The larger issue, however, is the relative wealth of a nation, and whether effective means of birth control are available to those who would use it. In many parts of the world, especially in Latin America, a large proportion of women have had more children than they wanted to have. Abortion is also legal in most of the developed and the former communist world (including many Catholic nations), although the amount of restrictions varies, and access depends on the nature of the health-care systems. Poland, like all other communist countries, had had legal abortion but made abortion illegal under most circumstances in 1993, at the urging of the Roman Catholic Church.

TABLE 2-3 (continued)
Teen Births, Birth Control, and Abortion

Countries	Reproduction		
	Births per 1,000 15- to 19-Year-Olds	% Birth-Control Use, Married Women	Legal Abortion?
Developing			
Algeria	37	51	No
Bangladesh	149	40	No
Brazil	41	66	No
Chile	66	—	No
Costa Rica	93	70	No
Egypt	78	45	No
El Salvador	131	47	No
India	57	43	No
Iran	106	65	No
Ivory Coast	228	3	No
Jamaica	87	67	No
Jordan	61	35	No
Kenya	142	33	No
Kuwait	49	35	No
Mexico	88	53	No
Niger	239	4	No
Nigeria	176	6	No
Pakistan	64	12	No
Peru	68	59	No
South Africa	72	50	No
Sri Lanka	33	62	No
Tunisia	23	50	Yes
Turkey	56	63	Yes
Communist			
China	17	83	Yes
Cuba	82	70	Yes
North Korea	26	—	Yes

Source: UN (1995a, 28–32)

The problem of overpopulation and multiple births is so severe for women in developing countries that President Alberto Fujimori of Peru, a country where 90% of the population is Roman Catholic, defied the Vatican to speak in favor of abortion rights at the Fourth World Conference on Women in Beijing in 1994.[5] Although abortion is not legal in much of the developing world, it is widely practiced, often very unsafely. In many countries, birth control is used to control not just the total number of children a couple has, but also what kind of children. In many cultures, sons are still much more valued than daughters, and especially in societies in which people limit the number of children they have, abortion is sometimes used to get rid of female fetuses to make way for having a boy. Birth statistics reveal that this practice is widespread in many countries, such as China, India, and Korea. Even though this practice is illegal in South Korea, for example, about 30,000 fewer girls are born each year than would be born if there were no such differential abortions taking place.[6] In the early 1990s in India, only 874 girls were born for every 1,000 boys, a sure sign of a tremendous number of differential abortions.[7]

The bearing and rearing of children dominate the lives of millions of women around the world. It is common for women of the higher socioeconomic classes in the wealthy industrial nations to think about women's status in terms of how important it is for women to have alternative occupations and interests to child-rearing during their adult lives. Women in this social category generally expect to have an average of two or fewer children, usually with a partner sharing the load (at least by earning a high standard of living, if not by changing a lot of diapers), and they will spend a relatively small proportion of their adult lives with any small children around.

The perspectives and issues must be very different for a large proportion of the world's women, especially in the poorer countries and in the poorer segments of the wealthy countries. Women in many parts of Sub-Saharan Africa spend at least half of their reproductive years (ages 15 to 49) with at least one child less than 5 years old at home, and women in many Latin American countries spend more than one third of their reproductive years with small children. Consider, in contrast, the middle-class American, western European, or East Asian woman who has one or two children in her late 20s or even early 30s. She is likely to have been able to complete a high level of education and to enter a career before she has her first child; she will be unlikely to spend even one quarter of her reproductively active years with a child less than 5 years old. On the other hand, given the death rates in poorer populations, the divorce rates (and for consensual unions, the separation rates) around the world, and the rates of childbirth to single women, millions of women around the world care for their children and manage their families on their own. In the developed world, for example, there are at least seven countries (Belgium, Canada, Denmark, Estonia, Norway, Sweden, and the United States) in which more than 20% of families are headed by a single parent; the vast majority of those are headed by women.

Work and Economic Life

Of course, women do the majority of the domestic labor in the United States and everywhere else, but placing that fact in the wider global context helps to make more sense of what domestic labor means. Women who are used to cooking on clean electric or gas stoves—perhaps even those with delayed-action, self-cleaning, and other mechanisms—often fail to consider the cooking fuel used by women in many parts of the world. Wood, charcoal, and in some places dung are the basic fuels for many women around the world. Throughout rural Africa, South Asia, and parts of East Asia, most household energy is obtained from fuelwood, as is much of the household energy in parts of Latin America. The gathering of wood is generally women's work. Under the best of circumstances, this is difficult labor, but in areas with fuelwood scarcity, this task can occupy a significant portion of each day's work. Moreover, as women spend a lot of their time in contact with these inefficiently burning fuels, while cooking and otherwise going about their business, their direct exposure to air pollutants is extraordinarily high. Likewise, in the many areas of the world without domestic running water, especially those with little access to clean water, women's work includes many hours of collecting water, certainly between 4 and 10 hours in many countries much of the year; where conditions are especially bad, during the dry season, women spend many more hours than that. Thus, the meaning of "housework" and "domestic labor" depends on the larger economic context.

All over the world, women certainly work. An increasing number also work for pay. In many countries, it is especially difficult to determine exactly how much paid work women do because a lot of women's work is concentrated in the informal or black-market economic sector, which forms a considerable portion of many economies. In the United States, the type of informal-sector labor that is most familiar is undocumented personal services, such as housecleaning and child care, but also some proportion of industrial and other service labor (e.g., in the restaurant and hotel business) in some parts of the country. Moreover, in less developed regions and in subsistence economies, it is especially difficult to measure people's participation in agriculture, to which they contribute substantial labor. Nevertheless, it is clear that by adding together paid and unpaid labor, women *work* at least as much as men in many parts of the world, especially at some points in their lives, even if women are *employed* fewer hours and certainly for less pay. In the developed world, for example, women work at least 5 hours more per week than men do in Bulgaria, Hungary, Italy, Latvia, Lithuania, Poland, Spain, and the United Kingdom. These differences begin in childhood, when young girls are required to contribute to household labor more than their brothers are, and where child-labor laws are lax, girls are more likely to be put to work rather than kept in school. The United States is one of the few nations in which women do not spend more time working than men, on average.

As Figure 2-1 shows, there is wide variation in the employment rates of women around the world. The United States has relatively high employment rates among women, especially when they have young children. (One reason is that, as the following section [Table 2-5] shows, the United States has relatively stingy maternity-leave benefits.) Of course *what* work women do for pay also varies around the world; there is a relatively high degree of gender segregation in the U.S. labor market, compared with many others.

Women and the State

Many other points of comparison could be considered to put this investigation of the United States into context. Of those, I conclude with one general category: the relationship of women to the government and state. What role do women play as citizens and leaders of their own societies, and what kind of stance have the governments of the world taken toward women and their special problems?

Women and Political Power. By the middle of the 20th century, most of the nations on Earth, except many of the Islamic countries and Switzerland, had

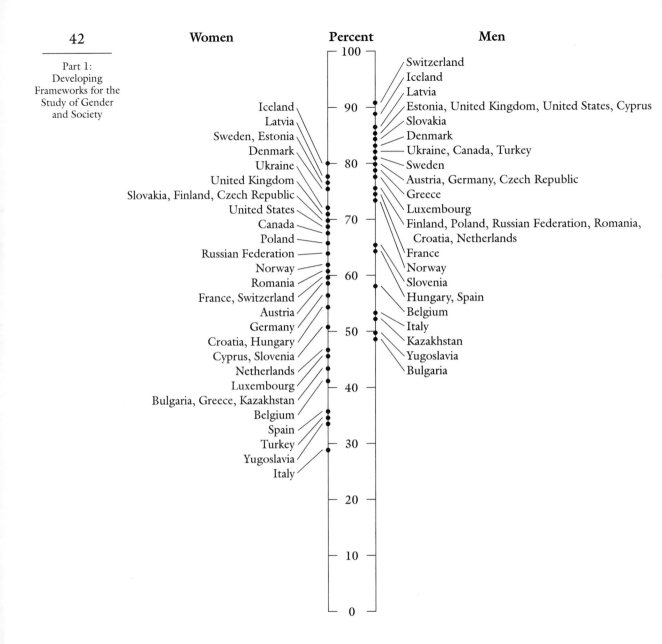

FIGURE 2-1
Employment of Women and Men, 1993

From United Nations (1995b). *Women and Men in Europe and North America, 1995.* p. 30.

TABLE 2-4
Women in National Legislatures, 1997

Country	% Female	Country	% Female
Sweden	40	Russia	10
Norway✔	39	Zambia	10
Finland	34	Syria	10
Denmark	33	United Kingdom✔	10
Netherlands	31	Dominica✔	9
New Zealand	29	Bangladesh✔	9
Austria	27	Malaysia	8
Germany	26	Chile	8
Iceland✔	25	Israel✔	8
Argentina✔	25	India✔	7
Mozambique	25	Brazil	7
South Africa	25	Bolivia✔	7
Spain	25	France✔	6
Cuba	23	Greece	6
China	21	Venezuela	6
Switzerland	21	Thailand	6
Luxembourg	20	Japan	5
Vietnam	19	Sri Lanka✔	5
Canada✔	18	Haiti✔	4
Costa Rica	16	South Korea	3
Australia	16	Egypt	2
Zimbabwe	15	Turkey✔	2
Mexico	14	Morocco	1
Ireland✔	14	Belau	0
Poland✔	13	Comoro Islands	0
Portugal✔	13	Djibouti	0
Indonesia	13	Kiribati	0
Belgium	12	Kuwait	0
Colombia	12	Micronesia	0
United States	12	Papua New Guinea	0
Italy	11	Saint Lucia	0
Nicaragua✔	11	Tonga	0
Philippines✔	11	United Arab Emirates	0

Note: ✔ Country that has had a woman prime minister or president.
Source: UN (1995a, 152), Inter-Parliamentary Union (1997).

granted women the basic citizenship right of voting (although in the many non-democratic countries, voting carried with it no real power of collective decision making). Women constituted only a tiny fraction of political leaders at any level. This has begun to change, although women are still a small minority of national leaders in most countries, and few women have led their countries. Table 2-4 shows the proportion of women in many of the world's national legislatures as of the beginning of 1997. A few countries stand out near the top, notably in

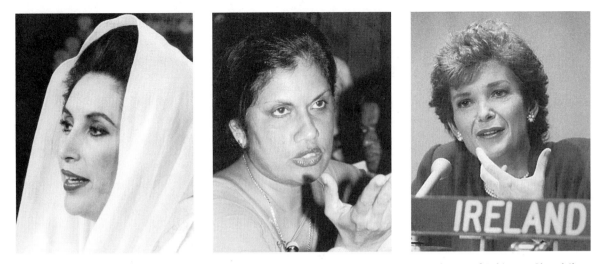

Women from around the world who have attained top leadership positions: Benazir Bhutto of Pakistan, Chandrika Kumaratunga of Sri Lanka, and Mary Robinson of Ireland.

Scandinavia and to some degree central Europe. Many Arab countries have no representation of women in the government. At the same time, countries with large Muslim populations are among those that have had women as heads of state, including Bangladesh, Pakistan, India, the Philippines, and Turkey.

Many countries and political parties have worked to facilitate the election of women to political office. In 6 countries (Argentina, Belgium, Brazil, North Korea, Nepal, and the Philippines), the law requires the national legislature to have a minimum number of women. In 36 countries, at least some political parties set rules committing themselves to a minimum number of women. Among these, many Norwegian and Swedish parties, the Austrian Greens, the Canadian New Democratic Party, the German Greens, and the British Labour Party at least aim for 50% representation of women. The Icelandic Women's Party, which has representation in the legislature, runs only women (Inter-Parliamentary Union, 1997, 67).

The number of women who successfully hold political office is not necessarily the best clue to how women are treated by the government. The configurations of law and policy specifically affecting women as women, their life chances, opportunities, and resources, are diverse around the globe. It is worthwhile to consider a number of different areas of law and policy.

Policies Affecting Women. The United States was the 20th nation to grant women the right to vote, but in the 1960s and 1970s, it became one of the early leaders in antidiscimination policy focusing on women in education and the workplace.[8] By the late 1970s, many European countries and the European Community (as it was then called) had also begun to develop antidiscrimination laws that were enforced to some serious degree.[9] One crucial set of policies affecting women's employment opportunities deals with the availability of maternity leave, allowing women (a) to take time off from their jobs for childbirth and early child

TABLE 2-5
Maternity Leave Required by Law, Amount of Time Off,
Proportion of Usual Wages Paid, and Who Pays

≥12 weeks off 100% of wages paid by employer **or** by government and employer	Bangladesh, Burkina Faso, Costa Rica, Djibouti, Dominican Republic, Ecuador, Haiti, Indonesia, Jamaica, Malta, Norway, Sri Lanka, Zambia
≥12 weeks off 90–100% of wages paid by government	Algeria, Benin, Brazil, Bulgaria, Cameroon, Chile, Colombia, Cuba, Germany, Greece, Hungary, Mexico, Morocco, the Netherlands, Peru, Poland, Portugal, Russia, Senegal, Sweden, United Kingdom, Uruguay, Venezuela, Vietnam
≥12 weeks off 60–89% of wages paid by government	Argentina, Belgium, El Salvador, Finland, France, Ireland, Israel, Italy, Japan, Nicaragua, Turkey
≥12 weeks off <60% of wages paid by government	Canada, Central African Republic, Chad, Niger, Paraguay
<12 weeks paid leave ≤50% of wages paid from any source	Bahamas, Bahrain, Bolivia, Egypt, Guatemala, Honduras, Iceland, Jordan, Lebanon, Libya, Liechtenstein, Malaysia, Mozambique, Nepal, Qatar, Saudi Arabia, Singapore, Switzerland, Syria, Tunisia, United Arab Republic, Yemen
≤12 weeks unpaid leave	New Zealand, **United States**

Source: UN (1995a, 137–139)

care without losing their jobs, and (b) to do this without losing their incomes. Table 2-5 shows the maternity-leave policies required by national law in a large sample of countries around the world as of 1995. The majority of developed countries, and many of the developing nations, require that women be able to take at least 12 weeks off from work around the time of having a baby without losing their jobs. In most of these countries the law requires that women be paid a majority of their usual wages (in many countries they must receive full pay), and in most countries the funds come out of national insurance, social security, or other public funds, or a mix of public funds and employer-provided benefits. The United States and New Zealand are the two developed countries of the world that provide for only unpaid leave, which gives women a choice of taking care of themselves and their new baby *or* earning an income. The U.S. policy came into effect only in 1993. Many feminists also think of public health-care coverage as a policy specifically affecting women as women because of the need most women face in getting prenatal-care and health-care assistance when they give birth and to help care for their infants. The United States is one of the few countries in the world in which basic health-care needs are not provided as a basic right, and that failure helps contribute to the relatively high rates of maternal, fetal, and infant mortality.

Another question is how the public and the government react to the harassment of women and to violence against them. It is, of course, very difficult to get reliable estimates of the amount of woman abuse and sexual assault, but surveys show this is a worldwide problem of massive proportions. Certain kinds of customary violence are concentrated especially in certain societies, cultures, times, and events, such as the widespread female genital mutilation practiced in Africa (see Chapter 6), the dowry deaths in India, the widespread use of children for sex tourism in Asia, the use of Filipinas and South Asian women as virtual house slaves in Kuwait, and the systematic rape, sexual abuse, or sexual exploitation that is often a part of war, and sometimes even a weapon of war, for example, during the 1990s Bosnian War, the Vietnam War, the "dirty war" in Argentina, the conflicts in Myanmar, and the Japanese invasion of China during World War II.

But violence against women is also an everyday affair for too many women around the world in their own homes and workplaces. Survey results show that between 25% and 40% of women have been physically assaulted by their spouses in countries as diverse as Belgium, Canada, the United States, Chile, Zambia, Ecuador, Guatemala, Korea, and Malaysia. The figures are even higher in other places. The problem of wife beating has become so great in Russia that an estimated 15,000 women were killed by their husbands in 1994.[10] Wife beating remains a widespread and acceptable practice in South Korea, where an estimated 42% of women say they have been beaten by their husbands at least once.[11]

Many international and national agencies have focused attention on domestic violence, but the responses to such attention have varied around the world. While many countries have implemented laws and policies seeking to combat domestic violence, the majority have yet to confront this problem as a problem. Many countries have no or few refuges or shelters for victims of domestic abuse. This problem has been acute, for example, in the Middle East, where the many women who face violence from their families have little recourse from the law and virtually no options for shelter. An office established for legal counsel for Palestinian women, for example, rarely even recommends the very few shelters available because women are so likely to suffer violence and even murder on their way to or from the shelter.[12] Many of the women killed as alleged informers during the Intifada (Palestinian uprising) were in fact the victims of "family-honor killings."[13] It is also impossible to document the number of rapes by husbands against their wives because in most of the countries of the world, there is no such thing as rape in marriage.

Sexual assault is also widespread, and many reports from around the world suggest that it has been on the rise. In many places in the world, it has not been regarded as a serious crime, and even where there have been laws against it, the justice systems have tended to treat the victim as the cause of the crime. Rape-reform laws have been passed in many countries, and in a few places (such as the United States), it is now legally possible for a woman who kills her attacker in self-defense to avoid being convicted herself for murder. But this is rare. Indeed, there are still countries in which a man who commits a "passion killing" of his wife if he finds her with another man will be let off, whereas a woman would be convicted of murder under the same circumstances. For the most part, however, it is still expected that good women are never raped.

Some violence is state sponsored or part of acts of war, such as the rapes in Bosnia and those committed by the World War II Japanese occupation forces, which coerced as many as 200,000 women into brothels. Most of the women were Korean, but some were also Filipina and Chinese, and a few were Dutch. In 1996, Japan issued an apology to these "comfort women" after great international pressure and pressure from women's groups within Japan, and established a fund to help some of the victims, now very aged. At the same time, it came out that as the American troops moved to occupy Japan at the end of the war, the Japanese authorities set up the "Recreation and Amusement Association," a front organization for brothels designed for the incoming American troops. The rationale was that the Japanese authorities feared that the occupying American troops would act as the occupying Japanese troops had, and they hoped the brothels would help protect the majority of Japanese women.[14]

When U.S. feminists began to discuss sexual harassment in the 1970s, and when such harassment was then treated as a civil wrong, even women in many other countries regarded this move at first as an example of typical American prudery. The movement against sexual harassment has spread, however, and there is an increasing tendency on the part of feminists and some legal experts to take the issue of harassment seriously. Companies in countries as different as Japan and Poland, for example, have faced sexual harassment charges from their employees.[15] Nevertheless, there is still a long way to go in most countries.

What can we conclude from this overly brief global tour? First, the variation in the experiences of women is quite wide. Second, the condition of women depends not just on attitudes toward women, but also on many features of the countries' situation, including especially the degree of economic development and wealth or poverty. Third, it is not possible to construct some simple notion of which countries are better or worse for women; that depends on the aspect of women's situation we are discussing. Fourth, placing the study of any *one* country in a comparative context provides important information and perspective on the subject. For example, the very unequal division of labor in the United States is serious, but it looks different if we place it in the context of the women of the world whose housework includes hauling water and firewood. For another example, the worry on the part of U.S. opponents of paid maternity leave that this is a luxury the public sector cannot afford looks different when considering that the United States is one of the few developed countries that does *not* provide such a benefit.

To learn more about the comparative situation of women would take more in-depth study, but even this glimpse raises some important questions: What accounts for variation in the societal-level situation of women? How do particular configurations of gender and power relationships develop? These questions are the subject of the following section.

Explaining Women's Situation at the Societal Level: Six Theoretical Approaches

Many different theories have been suggested over the centuries to explain why women's status and experiences are shaped as they are in different societies. Theory helps us make sense of the specific facts of women's experiences and social change; each theory is based on somewhat different kinds of evidence, looks at slightly different aspects of women's lives, and suggests different implications for the possibility of social change. In this section, we examine six theoretical approaches to sex differentiation and stratification: (1) explanations based in religion and theology; (2) biological explanations of women's status; (3) progress theories, emphasizing modernization and learning from one generation to the next, which results in inevitable change for the better; (4) functionalist evolutionary theories, which emphasize the development of efficient and harmonious social structure, especially in its divisions of labor; (5) economic or materialist theories, which focus on economic needs and structures as determinants of other aspects of society and change; and (6) sex-war theories, which identify conflicts of interest and power struggles between women and men as the key dynamic in understanding the structure of gender relations.

Four important themes or questions can be used to compare these alternative theories:

1. What assumptions do they make? What evidence do they employ?
2. How adequate is the theory for explaining women's situation and especially historical changes in women's situation? How well does the theory help to make sense of women's experiences now, of the differences we see across societies and cultures, and of the changes we have seen over time?
3. What is the historical context of each theory? Why was each theory developed when it was?
4. What are the political implications of each of these theories? How can each be used and how have they been used to justify different strategies for maintaining or changing the status of women and men?

The last question is especially important. Each of these frameworks suggests political points of view about that history and situation and about strategies for the future. Sometimes, the same general theory has been adapted by some people to show why gender inequality is good (or at least natural or normal) and by others to show why it must be overcome.

Women's God-Given Nature: The Eternal Feminine

Many theological interpretations of women's nature have provided explanations for sexual inequality. Within the Judeo-Christian tradition, the stories of creation and the expulsion from the Garden of Eden long served as the basis for ethical systems arguing for a God-given moral necessity of women's submission to men. In these stories, God the Father created women second, we are told, to be a helpmate to her husband. The influential Italian theologian St. Thomas Aquinas (1225–

1274) argued that God had a very specific type of helper in mind. "It was necessary for women to be made, as the Scripture says, as a helper to man; not indeed as a helpmate in other works, as some say, since man can be more efficiently helped by another man in other works; but as a helper in the work of generation" (1945, 880). He argued that women should be submissive to men because men had greater quantities of the active principle of reason. Women were created for the purpose of having babies so that men could carry on with God's work. In the order of life on Earth, men are answerable to God, and women are answerable to men.

Traditional Christian and Jewish theologians have often turned to the story of Eve to prove the need for female submission. Following Eve's disobedience to God when she ate fruit from the forbidden tree of knowledge, Genesis 3:16 states, "Unto the woman (God) said, I will greatly multiply thy sorrow and thy conception; in sorrow thou shall bring forth children; and thy desire shall be to thy husband, and he shall rule over thee." There have been some differences of interpretation of these words within Christianity and Judaism, but the most common interpretations include these arguments:

1. Eve's actions reveal women's moral weakness.
2. Adam's own weakness in accepting the fruit shows that women are dangerous temptresses who must be controlled if men are to be morally strong.
3. God ordained that there must be a division of labor by which women bear children (in sorrow and pain) and men produce the means of existence (by the sweat of their brow).
4. Men should rule over women.

Note that this theological view actually admits of the possibility for variation in male and female roles. It is *possible* for human beings not to follow some aspects of the divine order, just as it is possible for humans to violate most other divine laws. But, of course, the consequences of choosing to act against God's will are dire. (See Chapter 7 for more discussion of religion.)

Those who have called on religion to explain the status of women and its changes have generally constructed a very static view, incapable of explaining change and usually aimed at preserving gender difference and inequality. Calling on God or nature to understand the structure and history of relations between the sexes by no means necessitates taking either a static view or one that justifies inequality. Unfortunately, however, these have been the dominant views not just of the ancients, but also of many contemporary leaders. As late as 1972, for example, Senator Sam Ervin opposed passage of the Equal Rights Amendment on the grounds that, "when He created them, God made physiological and functional differences between men and women" (Sayers, 1982, 70).

Natural Woman and Man: The Role of Biology

The Greek philosopher Aristotle (384–322 B.C.) was the first influential theorist to use biological knowledge to explain sociopolitical differences between women and men. Using the biological knowledge of his day, Aristotle argued that the main difference between the sexes is that women are more passive. Because of their passivity and weakness, he argued, women may be regarded as a deformity, although a natural one.

Aristotle and many later theorists found evidence of women's passivity in two aspects of procreation. First, he argued that men are more active in courtship and sexual behavior, and they drew from this observation the conclusion that women are *in general* less active and more passive than men. (Some theorists even suggest that the fact that men are more likely to rape than women shows that women are more passive and, therefore, socially subordinate.) Second, Aristotle also believed that the male is the active principle in procreation itself: The male sperm *creates* a baby out of the female material in a woman's body, much as an artisan forms a candlestick out of passive brass.

Later sociobiologists derived their conception of female passivity from different misinformation—for example, that sperm fight their way upstream like so many (female) salmon and then compete with each other in a mad rush to conquer the demure, stationary egg.[16] The concept of natural passivity, even when derived from observing biological bits, has generally been one of the cornerstone arguments for explaining and justifying the inequality of males and females. Although both the methods and the findings of biological science have changed drastically from Aristotle's time to ours, the dominant conclusions derived from biological science remained largely the same for most of that time. Students of the history of science use this example to show how science is often shaped by cultural values and the perspectives of the scientists (Bleier, 1984).

Theorists have searched for many biological explanations for what they regard as women's weakness, especially of mind. People once thought that women's periodic cycles indicated that they were unduly influenced by the moon, which causes craziness or *lunacy,* a word derived from the Latin word for "moon." Later people argued that menstruation sapped the strength of women, leaving them weak. Many people now accept the "raging hormones" explanation of women's supposed instability and mental weakness. For a long time, people believed that the womb emitted vapors that caused instability. Others believed that the womb traveled around the body, sometimes causing women to faint. The word *hysteria* is derived from the Latin word for "womb." The conclusion is obvious: If women are hysterical lunatics, they are certainly not fit to take care of themselves, let alone others. (But why are women entrusted with the care of children?) These and other views of menstruation are discussed more fully in Chapter 6.

Biological arguments about the inevitability of inequality have also been grounded in women's reproductive capacities, suggesting that because of pregnancy and childbirth, women need a protector to watch over and act for them. This idea of women's natural need for protection has been used by governments to justify not only what is known as "protective labor legislation" (see Chapter 6) but also many restrictions on women's activities. In 1873, for example, a Supreme Court justice used the following argument to explain why a woman should not be allowed to practice law, even when she was qualified to do so (*Myra Bradwell* v. *State of Illinois*): "Civil law, *as well as nature herself,* has always recognized a wide difference in the respective spheres and destinies of man and woman. Man is, or should be, woman's protector and defender" (emphasis added).

Like the traditional theological arguments, these theories offer an unchanging view of the structure of relations between the sexes, based on "eternal" and "universal" characteristics of women, which allow neither equality nor similarity between men and women. They are useless in any real attempt to understand either the well-documented historical changes in relations between the sexes or possible future variation and change. Without arguing that biology has changed dramatically during recorded history or varies from culture to culture, these theories cannot possibly account for the fact that the structure of relations between the sexes has varied.

Biological theory need not be, and often is not, static in its understanding of women. It can also underscore the malleability or flexibility of human life. This discussion, however, began with the tradition of biological thinking that has been predominant in intellectual history. It is useful next to review some of the basic views of contemporary *empirical* biological science to assess the state of knowledge about sex differences and their potential for explaining the roles of women in society. To what degree does nature create the limits that structure the lives of women as women and men as men in society?[17]

The Genetic Basis of Sex.   Fertilized human egg cells, and thus human beings, normally contain 23 pairs of chromosomes. Sex is determined by a specific one of these pairs. The ovum, or egg, contributed by the mother to the sex-determining pair, contains only X chromosomes. Every human being therefore possesses at least one X chromosome, which contains genetic information affecting a wide range of physiological functions. The father, through the sperm, randomly contributes either another X or a Y chromosome to the egg. If it is an X chromosome, the baby will have an XX pair and be a girl. If it is a Y chromosome, the baby will have an XY pair and be a boy. This chromosome pair is the only sex difference in genetic structure. What is the effect of having an XX or an XY sex-determining pair of chromosomes?[18]

At first, there are no apparent sex differences among fetuses. At about the sixth week of fetal development, the genetic information on the sex-linked chromosomes begins to send out signals that turn one set of glands into either ovaries or testes, which will, in turn, produce *hormones,* powerful chemicals that aid further development. The same hormones are produced in both males and females, but the amounts of each hormone tell the body whether to develop a male or a female structure. Other than stimulating different levels of hormone production, what specifically genetically based sex differences are there? Males are prone to many more recessive genetically transmitted diseases and handicaps, such as hemophilia and color blindness. There is no conclusive evidence that the Y chromosome carries any other information that causes behavioral, cognitive, or personality differences between women and men. For this reason, scientists focus more attention on the hormonal basis of sex differences.

The Role of Hormones.   For ethical reasons, much of the research on the hormonal basis of sex differences uses animals other than human beings. Nevertheless, the discussion here is restricted to conclusions based on observations of human beings. I limit the discussion because this field is complicated enough to introductory readers, without the added problem of discussing findings not validated through research on human beings, rather than because research on other species is irrelevant to understanding human physiology.

Hormones are crucially important in determining physical existence as male or female. The hormones that play the most important role in sex differentiation are *testosterone,* produced in much greater quantities in males than in females, and *estrogen* and *progesterone,* produced in much greater quantities in females than in males. When these hormones begin to be released, they stimulate the body to develop a male or female structure. If the glands produce enough testosterone, the fetus becomes male; if not, the normal path of development is to become female. Male and female bodies are *analogues* of each other—shaped from the same basic form. One part of the body becomes either a clitoris or a penis; the breasts will either grow and eventually develop functioning mammary glands or remain small and functionless.

Females develop more quickly than males do. Some research suggests that testosterone is responsible for slowing down the process of physiological development, thus causing males to grow more slowly, develop coordination at a later stage, and reach puberty at an older age. How these differences affect the process of learning and eventual adult roles and behavior is unclear.

Male bodies develop a stronger muscular structure and more red blood cells, on average, than female bodies, although female bodies are more agile in certain ways. Sex differences in strength have been greatly exaggerated by the different types of training and opportunities males and females receive. Because of changes in training, the gender gap in some skills and sports has diminished considerably.

Although men and women may never compete with each other directly in sports that depend on strength, the larger social significance of strength differentials depends on the social construction of human tasks. Technological advances, for example, have decreased the importance of strength in many types of jobs. Protective labor legislation used to keep women out of jobs that required carrying loads "too heavy for women," but many of these limits were lower than the weights of the small children, grocery packages, and laundry baskets that women have commonly carried.

Sex hormones also have effects during adulthood. Although the evidence on their effects on human beings is still unclear, research has offered some clues. Research has linked elevated rates of testosterone in males with increased aggression and has tied raised rates of testosterone in women, at least under certain circumstances, with increased sex drive.

Hormonal changes stimulate and accompany puberty in males and females, as well as menopause in women. The balance of hormones in women shifts throughout the menstrual cycle. Many scientists have hypothesized that this shift causes mood and behavioral changes, some of which may have a great impact on women's capabilities and social activities. Of course, conventional wisdom has also long assumed that women are too unstable to do much work that is important or that requires skill because of mood swings—except, of course, raising children.

Early consensus has dissolved in the face of contradictory evidence and interpretation. Many of the symptoms conventionally associated with menstruation in one society do not commonly appear in others (Paige and Paige, 1981). Although researchers agree that women tend to experience mood changes in association with their menstrual cycles, the symptoms and timing vary considerably. Changes that seem to be associated with the menstrual cycle may not actually be caused by the hormonal changes themselves. In her research comparing women using birth-control pills (which affect hormone levels) and those not using them, Karen Paige found that negative psychological symptoms were related to the heaviness of menstrual flow. She also found that the degree of acceptance of traditional menstrual taboos and gender ideology was related to menstrual distress. Furthermore, as most women have found at one time or another, stress—which often causes mood changes—can affect a woman's normal cycle. Finally, many critics have pointed out that most of the research that finds a correlation between menstrual cycles and mood changes is not designed to rule out the possibility that negative reactions to menstruation might be caused by a socially constructed negative attitude toward menstruation and menstruating women. (For more discussion, see Chapter 6.)

These criticisms point to a problem that plagues the study of women and social science generally: Correlation does not necessarily indicate causation. In other words, just because two events happen at the same time, researchers cannot be sure, without further investigation, that one causes the other. Hormonal changes can affect moods, but moods can also induce hormonal changes. Hormonal changes bring on menstruation, and mood changes may be associated with the menstrual cycle, but something else—for example, a feeling that menstruation is embarrassing or that one's lover cannot abide sexual relations with a menstruating woman—may actually cause the mood changes.

Research has added a further twist to the study of hormonal fluctuations and cycles: Men have them, too (Doering et al., 1974). Men appear to have cycles in a variety of physiological and psychological respects. Whether these are related to fluctuations in sex hormones is still open to question. We do not yet know whether we should ground male pilots at "that time of the month." In any case, with regard to the basic question of what kind of sex differentiation is caused by hormones, we certainly see some important ones, including the basic functioning of our reproductive system. However, hormones do not seem to create as sweeping a set of basic personality differences between women and men as many people have thought.

The Structure of the Brain. One popular notion in the 19th century was that female brains were smaller than male brains, and that therefore women's cognitive capacities were more limited than men's. These observations led theorist and politician John Stuart Mill to remark that by the same logic, we should conclude that elephants are much smarter than people because of the relative sizes of elephant and human brains (e.g., see Rossi, 1970).

Current research focuses more on the *organization* of the brain and the functions of its components. A very interesting controversy concerns *brain lateralization* (that is, which hemisphere, or side—if any—is dominant in what functions) and its effects, especially on verbal and spatial abilities. Many brain researchers believe that each side of the brain is specialized for specific functions, and the degree to which functions are concentrated in one specific side of the brain makes a difference for how those functions are performed. Some argue that male and female brains are lateralized differently. Some think that the brains of women (and some men) are less lateralized than those of (most) men; that is, women's mental processing is less concentrated in one or the other half of the brain. Others argue that sex differences in lateralization occur only early in life, but that these differences have long-term effects in the development of cognitive skills, such as verbal or spatial ability. Yet others believe that young female brains are more lateralized than young male brains, but at later ages, male brains are more lateralized than female brains.

What difference would sex differences in lateralization make? When conventional wisdom and some research suggested there were broad differences between females and males in spatial, verbal, and mathematical ability, scientists thought that brain lateralization could explain these differences. Now that more systematic research shows no evidence of general differences in verbal ability (Hyde and Linn, 1988) or mathematical ability (Hyde, Fennema, and Lamon, 1990), and more limited differences in spatial ability than people formerly thought (Linn and Peterson, 1985), there is less cognitive difference to explain in the first place. Moreover, research scientists still do not agree as to whether brain-lateralization studies really distinguish between *innate* and *developed* brain capacity. Training and environmental factors not only enhance or limit capacity but also affect what part of the brain does what. It is possible that even some of the differences observed in young children are the result of the different types of games and activities undertaken with male and female children, just as some of the differences between left- and right-handed people could be caused by the common attempt to force left-handed children to become right-handed. It is possible, therefore, that gender differences in training could help shape gender differences not only in acquired skills (that is, how much of their potential they actually fulfill), but also in apparent biological potential.

Although the search for differences and the effects of brain structure remain an interesting and active field, for now, it has no *clear* results to offer those interested in understanding the sex differences that might structure societies, and especially how or why sex differences vary over time and across societies. For that, this discussion must turn elsewhere.

From Sex to Gender.   Biological research alone has not yet discovered a clear reason for the degree of gender differentiation and stratification in U.S. society, and it certainly has not accounted for the varying levels of differentiation and stratification *across* societies, although avenues for further investigation remain open. Scientists generally agree that human life and activity are products of an intriguing relationship between biology and society, nature and invention. In order to begin the task of thinking about sex differences and about the relationship between the impact of biology and society on the development of women and men *as* women and men, women's studies scholars have long emphasized the distinction between two related terms: *sex* and *gender.*

To state the point simply (although it will not remain simple as we proceed), *sex* is a physiological phenomenon, and *gender* also involves sociocultural aspects. Our search for the roots of distinctions between female and male in genetics, the hormonal system, and brain structure was an exercise in exploring *sex differences.* At the simplest level, we know that *sex* determines whether we can menstruate, bear children, and lactate, and it helps determine how much upper body strength we have. *Gender* involves these phenomena and much more. Sex does not determine whether it is socially acceptable to wear a dress or to train as a nurse or doctor. These, then, are *gender differences*. Even if biology determines the contribution women and men make to the physical reproduction of human beings, there is no clear evidence that it offers any distinctive guidelines on any other psychological or behavioral aspect relating to having children or being a parent. It sometimes seems that the more sophisticated biological research becomes, the less compelling is the evidence that nature provides us with very much guidance about how to be as females and males.

Gender is best understood as our sociocultural interpretation of the significance of *sex*. Gender roles are organized patterns of behavior we follow, based on our interpretations of the significance of sex. They structure our choices and guide our behavior in ways that are viewed as gender appropriate. Thus, gender roles lead people in many cultures to believe that men should be doctors and women nurses, or that menstruating women should not walk in agriculturally productive fields, or that if a child is sick, the mother rather than the father should be called home from work.

Many scholars' insistence that we make clear conceptual distinctions between *sex* and *gender* does not mean that in the real world, it is easy to tell what is a function of sex and what is a function of gender. In fact, it is difficult to make this determination for a number of reasons. First, our views tend to be colored by our own ideological preferences. Antifeminists, for instance, are often eager to label differences as biologically based and to view them as the major cause of the inequities we observe in society. On the other hand, some feminists are loath to see any influence of biology at all—unless it "favors women"—and are even suspicious of anyone who studies biology. Believing in sex differences that do not exist can have real effects on human beings: Such beliefs become the basis of sex discrimination. Rejecting the possibility of sex differences where they may actually exist does not make these differences any less real. In neither case is knowledge advanced.

Another reason it is difficult to distinguish between sex and gender is that one of the most powerful functions of gender is to tell what a particular culture regards as natural. People in some cultures, for example, believe that if a man has sexual intercourse with a menstruating woman, he will become impotent. Sure enough, many men who accept this belief do become at least temporarily impotent when they find that the woman with whom they wanted to have sexual relations has "the curse." Cultures also vary in how they view childbirth, and research shows that the physical experience of childbirth differs from culture to culture, depending on that view. If a society believes that women have no natural ability to be great artists and thus does not "waste" valuable resources training women, showing their work, or writing about their work, it will be easy to prove that women are not capable of being great artists.

It is also difficult to disentangle sex and gender because of the difficulty of determining causation: Which causes a person to act in a certain way—biology or society? In order to be absolutely sure whether an individual's personality is caused by nature or nurture, we would have to be capable of examining an individual totally removed from the context of society and any prior social training. Indeed, many scientists argue that biological and social factors have important interactive effects; to believe that important and complex aspects of human existence must be caused by *either* biology *or* society displays a primitive understanding of human nature and society (see, e.g., Bleier, 1984).

Most fascinating of all is the study of how human cultures and social life construct such complicated and nuanced systems of gender distinctions and gender-based rules of human behavior and interaction. Every member of each society becomes a willing or unwilling part of these interactions. Even when people reject traditional ideas of how women and men in their class and culture are supposed to act, they are usually still highly aware of those ideas and of their power. Everyone knows that women's and men's lives are just not the same; the more that researchers study the ways in which gender structures human life, the more impressive its power becomes.

Thus far, I have referred to the "structure of relations between the sexes" and to "systems of differentiation and stratification." These concepts are encompassed by the term *sex/gender system* (Rubin, 1974), the system or structure of roles, power, and activities predominant within a society that are based on the biological distinctions between males and females and further elaborated and interpreted through culturally defined gender norms. The remainder of this book uses this term to look at the role that different social institutions and processes play in taking the basic biological facts of male and female sex differentiation and turning these distinctions into one of the basic organizing principles of human culture and society. The questions now become, What accounts for the particular shape of a sex/gender system? How does research account for changes over time in the structure of such a system?

The Inevitable Progress of Enlightenment and Modernization

The 18th century witnessed the formulation of a new means for understanding social relations, based on Enlightenment philosophy, which continues to be the most widely accepted perspective in the West, especially in the United States. This philosophical outlook emphasizes that gradual progress of human society will result if—and only if—people can be free to learn from their collective mistakes and develop science and technology to improve their lives. This new approach to thinking about society, which formed part of the basis for both the American and the French revolutions, framed the liberal assault on the old feudal order of power relations in society and in government. It was quickly adopted by a number of early feminists as a means of understanding and criticizing inequalities between the sexes. Enlightenment or modernization theories are probably the most common basis for the way people think about how current sex/gender systems have evolved.

Foundations of Liberalism.   The liberal argument introduced by such people as John Locke (1672–1704) and Jean-Jacques Rousseau (1712–1778) opposed certain aspects of the patriarchal structure of political and economic power. *Patriarchy* means "rule of" (*arch*) "fathers" (*patri*). Most of the early critics of patriarchy did not, however, focus on the family as such. Rather, they attacked the rule by monarchs and the privileges of the aristocratic class of men over other men in

Patriarchy begins at home.

society. The logic of the patriarchal order was right, privilege, and power by birth. There were a number of different patriarchal views of society, but a good example is Jean Bodin's (1530–1596) observation that

> a family is like a state: there can be but one ruler, one master, one lord. A father . . . is the true image of God, our sovereign Lord, the Father of all things. . . . A father is obliged by nature to support his children while they are still weak and helpless, and to bring them up in honorable and virtuous ways. On the other hand, a child is obliged . . . to love, revere, serve, and support his father; to execute his commands in loyal obedience; to shield his infirmities; and never to spare his own life or property in order to save the life of him to whom he owes his own. (In Jones, 1963, 561)

The monarch and relations within the realm were analogous to the father and relationships within the family. Some writers went even further. Robert Filmer (1588–1653) argued, in his *Patriarcha* (Filmer, [1680]/1991), that royal authority is not only analogous to but also derived from the power God gave to fathers over the family. Kings, he claimed, derived their power through inheritance of the power the Father gave to the first father: Adam.

The liberal attack on patriarchalism is exemplified in the famous lines from the Declaration of Independence: "We hold these truths to be self-evident: that all men are created equal, that they are endowed by their Creator with certain inalienable rights, that among these are life, liberty, and the pursuit of happiness." What was so new and revolutionary about this view? First and foremost, it rejected the idea that only monarchs or certain classes of people were "endowed by their Creator" with rights and power. It argued that each individual White man (for at first, this notion was not applied to women or to men who were not White) had an equal birthright of fundamental or natural rights. These rights were "inalienable"; that is, in place of the patriarchal notion that all rights stem from or are granted by the king, Enlightenment theorists argued that individuals had certain autonomous rights that could not be taken away from them. The idea of the autonomy and independence of individuals was critical; men should not owe obedience to other men merely because of some condition of birth.

Liberalism and Women.   It did not take long for some people to extend these principles to cover the situation of women. The first person to undertake this task in a comprehensive way was Mary Wollstonecraft (1759–1797). In 1792, Wollstonecraft published her landmark treatise, *A Vindication of the Rights of Woman*, which argued that autocratic and patriarchal power relations between the sexes were as unjust and indefensible as those between monarch and subject. Much of the best-known and most influential feminist ideas on women's status, particularly in the United States and Western Europe, have been based solidly in this liberal tradition.

The liberal approach to explaining women's status revolved around the importance of *reason* in human development and the conditions of individual liberty that nurture reason. It argues that women, like men, should be considered free and equal at birth, with a virtually limitless potential for improvement. However, this potential can be developed only if society places no artificial constraints on their lives, so that women can be free to use their reason to discover what is good for them.

How do liberals explain the difference in status and roles of women and men? Wollstonecraft argued that the oppression of women, like the subjection of slaves to masters or people to an autocratic king, was the result of the artificial constraints of law and social institutions that stem from people's irrational prejudices (see Sapiro, 1992). If women appear very different from and inferior to men, it is because women have been made that way by social forces instituted by human beings who did not know any better. Such a system of inequity harms women because their rights are taken from them and they are denied the opportunity to develop reason and thus improve themselves. Men are also harmed, however, because, like kings and slave masters, they have been corrupted by holding excessive power over others. Indeed, society as a whole is harmed because inequities and the lack of freedom within it makes the entire society unjust, thereby impeding progress of the whole and its parts. Another important early liberal text on this problem was written by John Stuart Mill (1806–1873), in his *Subjection of Women* (1869; reprinted in Rossi, 1970). Mill claimed that the right of men over women was the last bastion of the bygone and unenlightened days when "might was right."

In liberal theory, the key to social change is that societies' gradual enlightenment by reason requires stripping away old blinding prejudices. Liberal feminists identified education as the primary instrument for progress. However, progress also involves tearing down the barriers that keep women from the freedom to develop themselves as individuals, including laws that barred women from doing certain kinds of jobs, voting, or, if they were married, owning property. This emphasis on enlightenment and progress is embedded in contemporary *modernization* theories used by many students of historical change. These theories argue that the growth of markets, technology, and science necessarily leads to other aspects of "progress," such as growing egalitarianism, including equality between the sexes.

The liberal view of social change is an optimistic one. It suggests that the ills of the past are irrelevant to today's world because people in the past simply did not know as much as we do now; past problems were caused by human stupidity and prejudice. Progress appears natural and almost inevitable, depending simply on increased education and technology and decreased governmental interference with our individual lives. Although widely accepted today, this perspective has some problems. As a theory of history, it is weak; indeed, some would argue that it offers no theory of historical changes at all, other than that society gets better.

A major fault from the point of view of women's history is that human history has not been a matter of slow and steady progress from less enlightened to more enlightened ages. Historians and anthropologists alike note that political and economic development, both in the United States and elsewhere, has often been marked by increasing gaps between women's and men's status, at least at the early stages of change. In the United States, women became increasingly *restricted* at the beginning of the 19th century. A similar phenomenon was noted immediately following World War II, when the idea of women's proper role at home was reestablished with renewed vigor. Students of African society and history have found that in many places, the sexes became less equal and the power of women was decreased by the impact of "enlightened" Western law and custom (e.g., Hafkin and Bay, 1976).

Modernization theory does little to help us understand why cultures differ in the arrangements of relations between the sexes, except for a vague notion that people in different cultures somehow have different ideas about what is right and proper. It suggests that all we have to do to achieve changes in the status of women is to change people's minds, or resocialize them. The matter is not as simple as that.

Finally, although the optimism of liberalism has spurred many people to action, it can also breed a kind of complacency. If we expect human beings to progress merely because we become smarter about ourselves as we gain experience in the world, we have little reason to do anything about the status of women other than go about the business of improving ourselves as individuals. It is interesting to see how often just this argument has been launched against feminism throughout the 20th century. It seems that each generation feels that the battles for equality have been won and that the only thing that holds women back is women's own lack of initiative. Unfortunately, good works by single individuals have rarely enabled any subordinate social group to achieve changes toward equality and liberty.[19]

Structural–Functionalist and Evolutionary Theories

The 19th century saw the emergence of two influential sets of explanations for the development of societal sex differentiation and stratification: evolutionary, structural–functionalist theories (discussed in this section) and economic and historical–materialist theories (discussed in the subsequent section). The theories of evolution grew out of the work of Charles Darwin (1809–1882) and Herbert Spencer (1820–1903) and sought to understand and link together the biological and social history of human life. These theories were among the first of many *structural–functionalist* theories of the structure of gender arrangements in society; that is, they explored the development of particular institutionalized gender relations to see how they function as means by which human beings assure their own survival as individuals, as societies, and as a species. Social arrangements that contribute to survival are functional; those that do not are dysfunctional. Although the earliest examples of this approach focused specifically on biological adaptation and evolution, later versions were more sociological in their emphasis. Most, although by no means all, of the theorists who have used evolutionary perspectives to explain the situation of women have concluded that both differentiation and stratification are inevitable, or at least desirable, if human life is to progress. This type of functionalist–evolutionary theory is often called "social Darwinism," although Darwin himself did not subscribe to it.

Foundations of Structural–Functionalist Thought.   Herbert Spencer believed that human society evolves through physiological adaptation to its surroundings in order to assure its own survival. Through the mechanism of the "survival of the fittest," those best adapted to the needs of human life will survive and reproduce their characteristics, while others will not survive. As human beings discover the social arrangements that are most *functional* (i.e., that contribute most to their ability to survive), these arrangements will become the order of society, and people will also develop and emphasize the characteristics best fitted to this order. Nature is naturally progressive; evolution is the path to survival. Spencer believed that the hallmark of progress in human life is the division of labor into specialized functions. Students of evolution noted that higher species were more specialized than lower species and argued that divisions of labor within human life were necessary for human survival and progress.

For Spencer and many others, the most important division of human labor is the one between men and women because it directly shapes the efficiency with which human life is reproduced and maintained. According to the early versions of evolutionary theory, as human life progresses, women become increasingly relieved of the burden of breadwinning and increasingly fitted to the exclusive tasks of childbearing and taking care of the home. The higher the level of society, the more differentiated women and men are. Some theorists noted that there was less differentiation between the sexes in the lower orders of society, by which they meant the working class, immigrants, and the poor. This only went to show, they said, that the more evolved human society is, the more distinctive men and women are. Of course, to accept this argument, followers also have to accept the idea that people in different classes or societies are on different rungs of the evolutionary

Spencer's biological arguments do not appear to have applied to pioneer women.

ladder: They are biologically different. Many people did just that, and social Darwinism became an important justification of racism, class exploitation, and imperialism.

Spencer argued that the sexes are not merely different but also necessarily unequal. Women have become increasingly well fitted to domestic duties but have had no need to become fit for anything else. Only men have evolved the characteristics necessary for other aspects of social, economic, and political life. Because it appears that men continue to evolve, while women do not, men must dominate women and reinforce gender inequalities if society is to continue to progress.

A century ago, many people used evolutionary–functionalist theory to argue that women should not be allowed to vote. Many proponents of this view of evolution have claimed that it is a mistake to make laws and policies designed to increase equality between women and men because these are doomed to fail; nature has not developed women and men for equality. Although many evolutionary theorists have claimed to trust evolution to move society in the direction of progress, they also seem to feel that only men know what that direction is.

Early Feminist Critiques.   Evolutionary theory was also adopted by some observers of the division of labor between the sexes who came to very different conclusions about the nature of inequality between women and men. Antoinette Brown Blackwell (1825–1921), an American feminist who began her career as a theologian, was very influenced by, but also critical of, the writings of Darwin and Spencer. Her book, *The Sexes Throughout Nature,* written in 1875, is a fascinating early discussion of bias in scientific research (for extensive excerpts from the text, see Rossi, 1988). She believed in evolution as the basis of human development, and she accepted the conclusions that the division of labor between the sexes was caused by evolution and that men's and women's personalities and abilities had evolved to be very different. However, she objected to the conservative conclusions about the natural dominance of women by men that the social Darwinists had drawn from evolution.

Blackwell thought that the sexes had developed different characteristics. But instead of arguing that the sexes were therefore naturally *unequal,* she claimed that they were *complementary;* men and women constituted two balanced halves of the whole of humanity. Therefore, she said, sex differentiation cannot give men grounds to restrict women or to declare them unfit to do anything but take care of children and the home. Male dominance of women and the exclusion of women from public life is dysfunctional—that is, it is contrary to the proper functioning of society. Both women and men must be free to contribute their special skills and attributes to society at all levels. Men could contribute the force and rationality necessary to society; women could contribute the gentleness and spirituality. Using the principles of evolution, therefore, Blackwell reached exactly the opposite conclusion from Spencer's. As she wrote, "No theory of unfitness . . . can have the right to suppress any excellence which Nature has seen fit to evolve. Men and women, in search of the same ends, must co-operate in as many . . . pursuits as the present development of the race enables them both to recognize and appreciate" (quoted in Rossi, 1988, 377). Many proponents of women's suffrage, such as the great social worker Jane Addams (1860–1935), made the similar argument that women's propensity for nurturance and their skills as housekeepers would upgrade the quality of politics and political decisions if they participated more in politics (see, for example, the selection in Rossi, 1988).

The sociologist Charlotte Perkins Gilman (1868–1935) offered quite a different feminist interpretation of functionalist–evolutionary theory. She also thought that divisions of labor between the sexes had developed through the struggle of human beings to survive (Gilman, 1966). At one time, when human life required both grueling labor for production and nearly constant attempts to reproduce simply to replace the current population, a relatively strict division of labor was functional—it made sense. However, many aspects of modernization meant that divisions of labor as they had existed in the past were no longer functional. In industrialized societies, work depended decreasingly on physical force and increasingly on intellectual and technical skills. Women did not need to become pregnant as often as they once did to ensure survival of the race. In her view, human beings had become "oversexed," by which she meant that they were exaggerating and overemphasizing differences between the sexes in a way that was becoming dangerous to the preservation and improvement of the human race.

Gilman (1966) thought that men could only hold themselves back if they continued to try to restrict women. Human society was wasting half its brainpower and turning the female half of society into useless parasites living off the work of others. It would be better, Gilman said, to advance useful divisions of labor based on skill, training, and efficiency and to do away with harmful ones, such as those based on sex. She thought that rather than having all women do cooking, cleaning, and child care in their individual homes, whether they were good at these things or not, such tasks should be done cooperatively by trained specialists outside the home whenever possible. Society had become dysfunctionally *androcentric;* that is, focused on and dominated by men.[20]

Current Views of Evolution and Sexual Differentiation.   Debates over the role of evolution in the development of sexual differentiation and stratification continue today. One influential theme among anthropologists and sociologists is this idea: In primitive times, social arrangements between the sexes developed into a functional division of labor between men the hunters and women the gatherers and nurturers, and the social arrangements since that time have continued to diverge from that original division. Encumbered by pregnancies and children, women could not travel far and in any case did not have the strength to engage in the hunt. Although women contributed considerably more than men to daily subsistence—some estimates suggest that at least 80% of the food consumed was the result of women's labor—men gained dominance and control in society as their hunting bands were transformed into warring bands and, ultimately, into governments. Sociobiologists such as E. O. Wilson (1975) have claimed that male dominance and divisions of labor have been reinforced by genetic differences through the evolution process. Sociobiologists disagree about how much equality is possible in the future, but almost all are deeply skeptical about the possibility of full equality.

Criticisms of sociobiological theories based on evolution stand on a number of points (e.g. Hrdy, 1981; Sayers, 1982; Sperling, 1991).

1. Contemporary research questions some of the assumptions often made about hunting and gathering societies. Female gatherers apparently traveled long distances to accomplish their tasks. Moreover, the division of labor was not always as rigid as many theories suggest; in some hunter–gatherer societies, men participated in what many people now think of as domestic tasks.

2. Sociobiologists tend to select examples to suit their arguments, choosing examples ranging from the most primitive times to modern, postindustrial societies, without any careful systematic historical analysis.

3. Sociobiologists often seem to confuse *human evolution* (changes in the physiological structure of the species) with *human history* (changes in culture, social structure, and human events). Some sociobiologists seem to accept the Lamarckian position suggesting that characteristics acquired during a person's life are passed on to that person's children through *biological* mechanisms.[21] Although social structures and culture have changed during recorded history and even during living memory, there is little, if any, evidence that relevant physiological and genetic characteristics have changed in significant ways during that time.

4. Even if sexual divisions of labor and dominance were once functional, Charlotte Perkins Gilman's question still arises: Are these divisions still functional, or should they be erased for better adaptation to contemporary needs?

Current biological research offers little support for the thesis that men and women have evolved into creatures that are well suited for the divisions of labor and dominance now seen in society. Although all known societies are marked by some division of labor between the sexes, the exact content of that division varies from one culture to another and from one historical period to another. Recent American history shows a tremendous shift in one aspect of the division of labor: Female civilian labor-force participation rose from about 18% in 1900 to 58% in 1990. On almost any personality or psychological test devised, most men and women reveal the same range of traits or characteristics. Biological science has failed to establish direct links between physiological characteristics and social roles and arrangements. Finally, if these divisions are natural, it is difficult to understand why people have had to work so hard to enforce and maintain them.

Structural–Functionalism in Twentieth-Century Social Theory. Structural–functional approaches gained new life in the 1940s and 1950s with the influence of the sociologist Talcott Parsons and his colleagues in their development of social-systems theory.[22] Structural–functional systems theory, which became one of the dominant approaches to social science, describes society as an integrated system of individuals interacting in their various social roles, which depend on their status or positions in society. These social roles are, in turn, embedded in social institutions that coordinate performance of the various functions of society. *Culture* is the set of underlying values and symbols that help lend coherent meaning to the whole and its parts. To the degree that personality is socialized or taught to the young, rather than being innate, personality can be seen as the internalized or learned aspects of culture that help individuals become motivated and able to carry out their part in this scheme. Thus, Parsons provides a picture of society as a system of coordinated, interlocking parts that contribute to the functioning of the whole.

Among the most important functions of society is reproduction and the nurturing and socialization of the young. Because of this, the family and family roles take on major significance in structural–functionalist social analysis. Within this tradition of research, the division of labor of males and females in and out of the family becomes an important determinant of the ability of societies to maintain themselves effectively.

Talcott Parsons outlined the basic argument in his 1942 essay, "Age and Sex in the Social Structure of the United States," in which he discussed how, from an early age, girls and boys are socialized into "feminine" and "masculine" personalities and work roles, so that they may become appropriately differentiated into their different adult roles to keep society working smoothly. Parsons wrote, for example, "It is of fundamental significance to the sex role structure of the adult age levels that the normal man has a 'job,' which is fundamental to his social status in general" (Parsons, 1954, 94). In contrast, "The woman's fundamental status is that of her husband's wife, the mother of his children, and traditionally the person responsible for a complex of activities in connection with the management of the household, care of children, etc." (Parsons, 1954, 95).

Parsons pointed out that while it is true that women might hold jobs, men might be unemployed, adults might not marry, or they might not even develop heterosexual orientations at all, these results are all dysfunctional. That is, they would cause disruption in the ability of society or its parts to work well. Thus, structural–functional approaches in the social sciences have tended to define gender divisions of labor and status as part of the support system of society, necessary for its functioning.

Economic and Historical-Materialist Theories

Another important set of theories stemming from the 19th century emphasizes the impact of economic structures and relations on the other aspects of society and culture. The most famous of the early theorists associated with this view were Karl Marx (1818–1883) and Friedrich Engels (1820–1895), whose writings became the source for the most influential materialist theory of social relations.

Marxist Foundations. The differences between the Marxist, historical–materialist analysis of society and the liberal, Enlightenment analysis can be approached through Marx and Engels's assertion in *The German Ideology* (1845–1846): "The first premise of all human history is, of course, the existence of living human individuals" (Marx and Engels, 1947, 7). This sentence may not appear remarkable at first, but the conclusions Marx and Engels drew from it make all the difference in the analytical world. They suggested that people may well argue that human beings "can be distinguished from animals by consciousness, by religion or anything else you like" (p. 7), but the first fact of human life is their physical existence and sustenance. "Life involves before everything else eating and drinking, a habitation, clothing and many other things" (p. 16). The key to seeing the impact of these ideas is to understand that "before everything else" refers not just to the historical fact that human beings learned to feed and clothe themselves before they learned to read and write, but also to the idea that the physical maintenance of life is primary in human social existence and substantially shapes people's consciousness and culture.

Marxists argue that consciousness, thought, language, religion, law, and other such manifestations of the human mind flow from and are shaped by material needs and the social and institutional arrangements, (i.e., economic production) through which people satisfy these needs. Language and the ideas it expresses are developed to help fulfill these needs and experiences of day-to-day life. Dominant thought systems (religion, theory, and so forth) reflect the interests of those in power and justify the economic, social, and political arrangements by which that power is maintained.

According to Marxist theories, the history of the world is "the history of class struggle." Divisions of labor within the economy do not simply mean that different people do different jobs. Within the divisions of labor that have developed under feudalism and later under capitalism, those in control of the means of production also control the products and the labor of those who actually make them.

Both labor power and therefore laborers themselves are exploited by capitalists in the following sense: It is in the capitalists' interest to get as much production out of workers for as little money as possible, just as it is in the workers' interest to get as much money for as little work as possible. The struggle between the two is far from even, however, because the capitalists control the material means of living and production and the ideology of society. Marxists argue that this struggle will only end with the workers retrieving control over their own labor, life situations, and consciousness, such that the capitalist system is replaced by one in which no single individual or class can own the means of production. Only by substantially rearranging economic institutions can political and social values and structures be truly altered.

How was this theory applied to understanding the condition of women? The earliest exposition of a Marxist analysis can be found in Friedrich Engels's *Origins of the Family, Private Property, and the State* (1884). Marx and Engels suggested that in subsistence economies, in which all individuals participate in the production process and provide for themselves with no significant amount of surplus, men and women are fairly equal because they have equal control over their labor and over the products of their labor. Women's subservience began with the development of private property. As agricultural production became more efficient, people created a surplus (more than they needed for immediate consumption) that could be exchanged for other products. Because men were the producers of goods with exchange value, they owned and controlled the production of surplus products. According to Marxist analysis, this is the key to power in exchange economies: The division of labor between men and women in the family paralleled the division in the larger society into capitalist and proletariat classes.

With the invention of private property, men sought to ensure that they could pass their property on to their own children (for reasons not entirely explained), giving them the motivation to control women in monogamous (at least for the woman) marriages, so men could be sure that their children *were* their children.

Property and family law were therefore designed by men to keep women under their control. For Marxists, the condition of women, like other social inequities and oppression, has its source in the class system—the structure of property ownership and production—found in capitalist societies. Thus, for orthodox Marxists, the liberation of women can occur only when working-class women participate with men in the overthrow of the capitalist economic structure that causes their oppression. Change will not simply happen because people become wiser and more modern from one generation to the next, because those in power will not usually choose to give up power. Marxists have also argued against having a distinct women's movement apart from the more general class struggle because it would only divert attention from the real source of women's oppression in the economy and class relations.

Contemporary Economic and Materialist Theories.   Although historical and anthropological research has long since contradicted many of Engels's assertions, several aspects of economic and materialist explanations of women's situation remain widely influential, even among people who are not Marxist. First, the divisions of labor and power between men and women, and the different value placed on men's and women's work, seem to depend at least partly on the structure of the economy as a whole. Research on many countries around the world, including the United States, shows that industrialization and the shift to a fully capitalist economy is often marked by an increasing gap between the power and value of men and that of women. As production moves out of the home, the divisions of labor between women and men leave men with the greater share of economic and other forms of power.

Many experts fear that this widening gap, due to the creation of a new capitalist economy, is occurring again, this time in Eastern Europe and the former Soviet Union, as those countries are restructuring their economies. In many of those countries, women are suffering greater unemployment, and social services that previously assisted mothers are disappearing or are threatened. A common belief among men in the former Soviet Union is this: One of the benefits of the new system is that women will stay home as homemakers and can now be kept out of the labor force. At the same time, some feminist theorists, especially those working in the formerly communist countries, argue that it is not capitalism per se that is causing the restructuring of gender relations because the working of the communist systems had also reinforced a culture of male dominance, even if those systems diminished many of the actual signs of gender inequality. Indeed, the reintroduction of increasingly severe gender inequality is *preceding* the establishment of new capitalist systems. Nonetheless, the upheavals in the economy, and the increasing emphasis on markets and market efficiency, seem to be having even more negative effects on women's work lives than on men's (Rosenberg, 1991).

These approaches to women's situations also emphasize that the structure of power within different major social institutions is interdependent across institutions. Although Marxist theory and its variants are not the only theories that make this point, this point is central to these theories. The relationships—and similarities —between divisions of labor inside the family and those outside it are so obvious that observers may sometimes forget how remarkable they are. Women's roles outside the family and the degree of social power women have depend on divisions of labor within the family. The jobs that are viewed as most appropriate for women to hold are those that seem most to resemble the tasks that women are supposed to undertake in the family. Even people who claim to desire equality for women in the marketplace tend to feel that women can seek employment only if their children are already taken care of, but they do not ask the same of men. Importantly, these theories pay close attention to the fact that *divisions* of labor usually mean more than different people doing different types of work. Divisions of labor often also entail division of power and control.

Consider the division of labor in marriage. Men are traditionally supposed to seek employment to support the family, while women are supposed to do most of the labor required for family upkeep. Some might argue that this division is simply a functional and efficient arrangement, not to mention (as some people would) a particularly nice one for women because they get to care for the people they love, while men are out working in competitive, alienating jobs. A closer look suggests that this division is no mere system of cooperation between equals, as the man's designation as "head of the household" suggests. Men in traditional marriages, who participate in the labor market and take home wages, gain added power and prestige over their wives.

Economic analyses of the structure of gender relations also emphasize that cultural definitions of women's and men's roles are grounded in the concrete, material aspects of life, and that they therefore are subject to great historical change as material conditions change. American history offers some clear examples. The idea of pregnancy as a glowing, happy time developed in the United States only after the facts of reproductive life had improved considerably. In the colonial era, for example, when one out of five reproductively active women died as a result of childbirth, and many babies did not survive their first year, women's views of pregnancy and motherhood had a lot more to do with resignation to possible death than with the joys of motherhood.

People are sometimes startled to realize how recent are the supposedly traditional ideologies of womanhood. In the early 19th century, as "productive labor" (and with it, men) moved increasingly out of the home, women began to be viewed as delicate, frail, and asexual keepers of the home fires to which men could return after a harrowing day in the world. This new ideological framework for understanding women, now known as the "cult of true womanhood" (Welter, 1966) could not make sense in an economy in which it is necessary for women and men to toil together. Moreover, it should not be surprising that this ideology was applied only to specific classes of women. Southern slaveholders did not apply the cult of true womanhood to the Black women they owned, and late-19th-century Boston Brahmins did not worry about the femininity and delicacy of their Irish maids.

More recent examples underscore the point that ideology often flows from institutional and social arrangements, rather than the reverse. During World War II, the figure of "Rosie the Riveter" had been used to convince women that armaments manufacturing was important and appropriately feminine work for women. After the war, how could women be convinced to give the jobs back to men? Freudian psychoanalysis became popular in the 1950s as one way to justify why an increasingly educated population of women—and women who had experienced employment during World War II—should feel happy staying at home making babies. Ideas about women's roles began to change again later, as the structure of the economy changed and masses of new auxiliary jobs (such as clerical work) opened up, education expanded dramatically, and more workers were needed in the "helping professions," such as nursing and social work.

Thus, many feminist theorists find Marxist and other materialist analyses of consciousness and ideology useful to explain the historical development of sex/gender systems. Materialists argue that people's social relationships and ideas about themselves reflect and justify the social arrangements and institutions that exist, especially the power relations within them. In short, ideologies support the power of the powerful. Dominant ideas of what is natural for women and of what women want may change over time, but these ideas support the existing arrangements and shape individuals' perceptions of people and events. Psychological research shows that these ideological constructions of men and women affect not just how men perceive and treat women, but also how women perceive and treat themselves, both as a group and as individuals.

If people's views of social arrangements are shaped by those arrangements themselves, how can change occur? At some times in history, some portion of the people in a subordinate group (in this case, women) become conscious of their situation—that is, something happens to make them understand that their situation is determined by their membership in a particular subordinated social group, and they begin to see through the cultural justifications of their subordination. Change, then, may occur as these women become active in a social movement to mobilize other women to gain the same recognition and to take political action based on this new group consciousness.

Consider the masses of women in recent decades who never thought they would have to earn their own living but found that they had to seek employment to support themselves and their families because of widowhood, divorce, or economic recession. Many women probably blamed themselves for their inabilities to earn enough money, explaining their situation by saying, "I don't have sufficient skills," "I didn't get enough training," or "I dropped out of school to support my husband and to have children." Group consciousness could lead such women to see that the fault is not theirs alone but is common to women because education and training are not considered to be as important for women as for men and because women are encouraged to get married and have babies at a young age and to drop out of school, if necessary for their families' well-being. Women without a group consciousness simply regret their personal fault for their situation and do whatever they can as individuals to better themselves. When the system is rigged against them, such solutions are doomed to failure. Women with a group consciousness work to change the situation of women as a group.

Sex War: The Struggle for Dominance

When one nation or class or people dominates another, most people assume that this situation was brought about and is maintained through competition and force. At first glance, men and women seem to pose the major exception to this rule. Could women and men have such opposing interests in society? If men and women were at war, they certainly would not choose to live with each other, would they?

The idea of a primeval struggle through which men have asserted their dominance over women is more deeply embedded in many cultures than might seem likely at first (Sanday, 1981a). Recall the story of the Medusa, discussed earlier, in which man must struggle to overcome woman or women's evil. A similar theme occurs in numerous myths and stories, such as the Greek myth of the Sirens, in which dangerous women drive sailors to self-destruction; the story of Eve, in which Eve seduces Adam from grace; and the Mozart opera *The Magic Flute*, in which the deceptive Queen of the Night is overcome by male rationality.[23] Many cultures have myths of an originally powerful goddess overthrown by men or a male god, who in turn put the world in proper order. Marx and Engels and numerous later theorists argued that there must have been a struggle for men to win control over women and property.

In fact, many theorists have suggested that the current configuration of power relations between the sexes results from a war between the sexes. Some theorists see struggles derived from conflicts of interest in the roles and personalities of women and men, and some point directly to sexuality as the battleground. Susan Faludi's (1991) book *Backlash* offers the influential argument that the 1980s witnessed the renewal of conflict in the rise of an "undeclared war against American women," in reaction to the gains that women were beginning to make. She has pointed to evidence in the mass media, the economic system, fashion, politics, and intellectual life.

Freud and the War Between the Sexes.   Sigmund Freud (1856–1939), the founder of modern psychoanalysis, was one of the first writers to try to understand the roots of antagonism between the sexes. Although Freud and, indeed, psychoanalysis are most discussed in relation to understanding *individual* development (as discussed in Chapter 3), they also provide a framework for examining social change and *historical* development. Freud's thoughts on history, culture, and society, including his story of the battle between the sexes, may be found in its most complete form in *Civilization and Its Discontents* ([1930] 1961).

According to Freud, the trauma of a girl's life is the discovery that she is not male, that she has no penis. (Some feminist theorists accept the outline of this argument but interpret the discovery symbolically. To them, the penis, or phallus, is simply the symbol of male power, which women lack.) This revelation causes her to grow hostile toward her mother, who made the daughter deficient like the mother herself, and to attach herself first to her father and later to potential fathers (of her own children). She also develops the need to acquire the missing penis, at least symbolically, by giving birth, particularly to a boy. She is thus set on the track toward heterosexuality; her choice of a love object is conditioned by her struggle for restitution of the penis.

Even getting married and having a son does not end a woman's struggle, however. She may place on her son all the ambitions she as a woman cannot or is not allowed to fulfill, which causes a struggle for autonomy between them. She will also try to achieve her ambitions through her husband. Although to remain attractive to him, she must seem passive and submissive, in fact, her insecurity leads her to strengthen her hold on him in marriage by turning her husband into her child and by acting as a mother to him.

Finally, according to Freud, the battle between men and women is carried to a broader field. Women's energies are focused on the home and family; men's energies are devoted to the larger society. As men increasingly turn their energies outward and away from the family and home, a struggle develops between men and women. Women resent men's lack of attention to them and battle against it, and they come to resent civilization itself, which stole men's attentions from them. Men are destined to win this battle, however, because, after all, they have what women want.

Some psychoanalytic scholars suggest that Freud may have been on the right track but that womb envy rather than penis envy is the main issue in dominance struggles between women and men. Men, they argue, resent the fact that only women can produce life from within their bodies and have spent most of their history trying both to control this powerful force and to make up for their own deficiencies (e.g., Horney, 1967). It is important to remember that the role of fathers in procreation is not readily apparent; women's power in reproduction is considerably more obvious.

Societal Stress and Cultural Strain.   Researchers in other scholarly traditions have also pondered the origins of dominance struggles between women and men. Anthropologist Peggy Reeves Sanday (1981a) explored evidence from more than 150 tribal societies from around the world to understand the sources and dynamics of *male dominance,* which she defined as "the exclusion of women from political and economic decision making," plus *male aggression against women,* defined as "the expectation that males should be tough, brave, and aggressive; the presence of men's houses or specific places where only men may congregate; frequent quarreling, fighting, or wife beating; the institutionalization or regular occurrence of rape; and raiding other groups for wives" (Sanday, 1981a, 164).

Sanday found that the degree of male dominance seemed to depend on other environmental and historical conditions, especially relatively recent migration, an undependable and fluctuating food supply, chronic hunger or protein deficiency, and chronic or endemic war. Her research led her to conclude that "the aggressive subjugation of women must be understood as part of a people's response to stress" (Sanday, 1981a, 184). Sanday has argued that men and women tend to respond differently to stress; men tend to respond with aggression although not always with domination, and not always with the subjugation of *women.* Under what stressful circumstances do men blame or turn against women?

She has argued for a complex interaction among the cultural meanings attached to male and female in a society, the specific stresses a society is undergoing, and the range of culturally possible solutions to societal problems. Sanday has pointed to circumstances in which life and death become threatening in such a way as to make male aggression and control of female fertility appear key to security. Women, she has argued, will not engage as a group in pitched battle against men, which makes it relatively easy for men to subjugate them. There are many historical examples in the past century of large-scale social struggles of men to control women, for example, in the context of the upheavals for creating new nations, such as those that occurred in many Islamic nations (Jayawardena, 1986; Kandiyoti, 1991; Sapiro, 1993a).

Writers from a wide spectrum of viewpoints suggest that even if no one knows how male dominance began, it is maintained through struggle and violence. As early as the end of the 18th century, Mary Wollstonecraft ([1792] 1975) argued that the division of power and labor between the sexes creates a constant war between men and women. Although the balance of power is on men's side, human nature leads women to pursue their own interests by using whatever power they might have over men. If men force women to be mere sex objects or objects of beauty, women will use their sexuality and beauty against men. If women are not allowed to be forceful and direct, they will be cunning, manipulative, and sly. The only way to end this battle, Wollstonecraft argued, is to grant both men and women the human dignity that comes through independence and equality.

Current Versions of Sex-War Theory.   Modern feminists have further developed the theme of sex war, finding different types of evidence to show the signs of struggle and antagonism. Although not all feminists are women, and not all antifeminists are men, the history of feminist movements is in part a struggle to gain rights and increased powers for women from governments, employers, and other male-dominated organizations. Women gained their new rights slowly, through considerable effort, and sometimes bloodshed.

Many feminists point not just to legal battles but also to what Kate Millett (1970) called the "sexual politics" of everyday life. Social psychologists and linguists have documented numerous ways in which men take control from women, even in normal conversation (see Chapter 10). Feminists point out that the battle is often violent and that rape and wife battery can be seen as means of physical control over women. Many contemporary feminists also agree with the liberal democratic theorist John Stuart Mill, who argued that men do everything in their power to make women "willing slaves" (for the text, see Rossi, 1970). Others point specifically to sexual control, the signs of which one can see in double standards of sexual morality and in the privileges women receive when they are associated with men, especially through marriage.[24] Whether the sex war is fought on the battleground of sexual politics or of sexual control, many argue that men have numerous privileges that they derive merely from being men and that they will not give up without a struggle.

Feminists are not the only observers of gender systems who see the condition of women as the result of a sex war. The conservative sociobiological theory of the "selfish gene" suggests that men seek to dominate women to be sure they reproduce themselves by passing on their genes to a new generation. Along similar lines, many sociobiologists argue that men have an instinct to control women sexually (and even have a natural tendency to rape) because they are driven to impregnate as many women as possible. Nor is the battle ended when pregnancy occurs. The man, having accomplished what he wanted, has little interest in the child he helped create, but the woman, who has made a significant investment in the child through her pregnancy, focuses her attention on the child.

Some sociobiologists see relations between the sexes as a continual battle in which each sex seeks to outwit and control the other; they argue that these relations are essentially mutually exploitative. Others argue that men dominate women because they are biologically capable of doing so; men are stronger and more aggressive. The conclusion these sociobiologists reach is that a battle between men and women is inevitable, and it is also inevitable that women must lose. These theories are currently very influential.

One of the most interesting antifeminist approaches to the sex-war theory is found in Helen Andelin's best-seller, *Fascinating Womanhood* (1974), a guide intended to help women improve their marriages. Andelin based her book on her antifeminist fundamentalist Christian principles. Women, Andelin argued, must be childlike and submissive to their husbands not because women are inferior or naturally submissive, but because men have such weak egos and insensitive and crude personalities that women must learn to manipulate them through coquettishness and apparent passivity. Andelin said that men and women have very different and basically antagonistic characters. Women are gentle, sensitive, religious, and nurturant, and men are insensitive, aggressive, and temperamental.

Andelin's advice to women was much like what many mothers used to pass on to their daughters: Never appear threatening. Never nag if your man is being bad (because men are like that). Never show that you are your man's equal, and certainly never take an obvious lead in sex or appear smarter or more skilled at anything than he is. Andelin also takes matters a step further. If a woman's husband beats or physically abuses her, Andelin says, the woman should pout, stamp her foot, shake her curls, perhaps pound weakly on his chest, and say, "How can such a big strong man hurt such a poor little girl?"

There are several important points to be drawn from the sex-war theories of male dominance.

1. These theories are not the sole property of feminists. The view that dominance grows out of sexual antagonism goes back in antifeminist thought at least to the time of Charles Darwin.
2. Different theories regarding the sex war have different implications for the future. Generally, antifeminist sex-war theories suggest that both antagonism and male dominance are inevitable. Most feminist theories argue that equality is possible, and, therefore, more harmonious relations between the sexes are also possible.
3. Acceptance of sex-war theories does not necessarily mean a belief that this war is a conscious conspiracy of nasty people. Sociobiological approaches generally assume that sex war is fostered by unconscious biological instincts and capabilities. Feminist theorists usually suggest that war is a natural outcome of inequity and therefore can be ended if inequity is defeated. As long as inequity exists, at least some members of the group with less power will fight for increased control over themselves, and at least some members of the group with power will try to justify their strength and will not willingly relinquish it.

Toward Understanding Social Change and Women's History

The six types of theories discussed here offer alternative ways to explain the development of particular sex/gender systems. They suggest somewhat different routes that societies may have followed to get where they are now, and they also suggest different possible futures. Although most of these theories have both positive and negative points, none is perfect, and all must be evaluated carefully in light of the evidence. With the exception of the very static versions of theological and nature theories, none is necessarily and exclusively feminist or antifeminist. People with a variety of political viewpoints have found something appealing in most of the theories outlined here. The difference lies in how the theories are formulated and applied and in how evidence is brought to bear on them.

The brief comparative overview of women's treatment around the world, presented earlier, suggests that at least a few of these theories can help to illuminate different aspects of women's situation and to make sense of it. The overwhelming evidence that the economic conditions of society have powerful effects on the sex/gender system suggests the utility of economic and materialist theories. Modernization theories are at least somewhat supported by the positive effects of education on women's life chances, and by the improvements for women's life expectancies through technological developments, that free them from carrying water and fuel, and that enable them to survive childbirth more often. Certainly, we have seen many eras of struggle between men and women over women's rights, and the fact that social tensions and war are often acted out to women's specific detriment also suggests that sex-war theories are worth some attention. The remainder of this book provides ample opportunity to evaluate these different perspectives in more detail.

Notes

1. Throughout this section, statistics are drawn from United Nations (1995b) unless otherwise specified, and they refer to the early 1990s.

2. Note that these figures show *ratios*, not *percentages*. For example, the table shows that in Sweden there were 100 women enrolled in secondary school for every 100 men. Clearly that does not mean that women were 100% of the people enrolled in secondary school; they were 50%. In the United States there were 120 women enrolled in postsecondary school for every 100 men enrolled, showing a ratio of 120 to 100, or (for those who remember their middle-school math) a ratio of 6/5 in favor of women. This means that women were 54.5% of the students in postsecondary school.

3. Nicholas D. Kritof, "Who Needs Love? In Japan, Many Couples Don't," *New York Times,* February 11, 1996.

4. Alan Cowell, "Legendary Big Italian Family Becoming a Thing of the Past," *New York Times,* August 28, 1993; Nicholas D. Kristof, "Baby May Make 3, but in Japan That's Not Enough," *New York Times,* October 6, 1996.

5. Patrick E. Tyler, "At Women's Forum, Peru's Leader Defies Church," *New York Times*, September 13, 1995.

6. Sheryl WuDunn, "Korean Women Still Feel Demands to Bear a Son," *New York Times*, January 14, 1997.

7. John F. Burns, "India Fights Abortion of Female Fetuses," *New York Times*, August 27, 1994.

8. These policies are covered in detail in Chapters 9 and 13.

9. It is very tricky, in fact, to judge when such laws were actually enforced. Many countries have had statutes and even clauses in their constitutions that barred discrimination but did not provide for any serious enforcement mechanisms. To say that these existed in the United States and Europe, for example, does not mean they were completely effective.

10. Helen Womack, "15,000 Women Killed by Husbands," *The Independent*, July 16, 1995.

11. Nicholas D. Kristof, "Do Korean Men Still Beat Their Wives? Definitely." *New York Times*, December 5, 1996.

12. Personal communication, Ramallah, West Bank, February 1997.

13. Karin Laub, "Arab Women Fight Back," *Wisconsin State Journal*, February 14, 1994.

14. Nicholas D. Kristof, "Fearing G.I. Occupiers, Japan Urged Women Into Brothels," *New York Times*, October 27, 1995; Nicholas D. Kristof, "Japanese Try to Reserve Fund for War's Comfort Women," *New York Times*, May 13, 1996; Andrew Pollack, "Japan Pays Some Women From War Brothels, but Many Refuse," *New York Times*, August 15, 1996.

15. David J. Morrow, "Sexual Harassment Complaints Rise in Japan," *Wisconsin State Journal*, October 24, 1993; Jane Perlez, "Central Europe Learns About Sex Harassment," *New York Times*, October 3, 1996.

16. Scientific research shows this widely held view of conception is mistaken. Sperm are moved along by the actions of the woman's body and the fluids within it.

17. This discussion of biology is very basic and nontechnical. A good basic text on female biology is Sloane (1993). Two important works on women's health also contain relevant information: *The Black Women's Health Book* (White, 1990) and *Our Bodies, Ourselves* (Boston Women's Health Book Collective, 1992).

18. In fact, human beings are not neatly divided into two sexes, female (XX) and male (XY). About 1 in 2,500 females is born with only one X chromosome, a condition known as "Turner's syndrome." As a result, they are relatively short, and their ovaries do not function. About 1 in 700 males is born with two X chromosomes and one Y, and the same proportion has two Y chromosomes and one X. "Normal" people can have quite a variety of combinations of X and Y chromosomes. Research has not identified clear personality or behavioral effects of these differing genetic structures.

19. For further discussion of liberal theory, see Eisenstein (1981) and Jaggar (1983).

20. For Gilman's theories, see especially her *Women and Economics* ([1898] 1966), *The Home* ([1903] 1972), and *The Man-Made World: Our Androcentric Culture* ([1911] 1970).

21. The most famous example of the Lamarckian principle is the suggestion that if the tail of a rat is cut off during its lifetime, its offspring will be tailless.

22. For the primary exposition of Parsons's work, especially as it concerns gender, see Parsons (1951, 1954) and Parsons and Bales (1955).

23. For Mozart fans (of which I am one), it is important to note that both Pamina and Tamino (the heroine and hero) are allowed to enter a condition of enlightenment.

24. By *privileges*, feminists mean the higher status and social respect women have when they are married or are at least associated with a man, and such benefits as the relatively greater degree of safety women have in traveling or even walking around their own communities when they are accompanied by a male protector (see, e.g., Rich, 1980).

3

⁂

Individual-Level Approaches to Understanding Women's Lives

> *Helen of Troy had a wandering glance*
> *Sappho's restriction was only the sky;*
> *Ninon was ever the chatter of France;*
> *But oh, what a good girl am I!*
>
> Dorothy Parker (1944), "Words of Comfort
> to Be Scratched on a Mirror"

IN THE STUDY OF WOMEN IN SOCIETY, one important set of questions focuses on the structure of sex/gender systems—that is, the overall patterns we see of the distribution of tangible and intangible resources between men and women, the cultural norms we use to define men and women, and the general patterns of interaction and divisions of labor between men and women. To understand change in sex/gender systems, we look at the history of those systems, to see how they change and are maintained. In the previous chapter, we looked at alternative theories that help account for the development and change in sex/gender systems.

Another important set of questions in the study of women and society focuses on individuals within the context of a particular sex/gender system. Consider the example of trying to understand the gender basis of work. The societal-level approaches discussed in Chapter 2 might help explain why and how the gender structure of work and occupations shifted in the United States from the 18th to the end of the 20th century, or why the gender-based structure of work and occupations is different in Japan and the United States. However, these approaches do not provide any direct help with understanding what forces shape the specific career paths of Jane and Bob, both born in the United States in 1980. What makes Jane become part of the statistics showing that women are more likely to become secretaries than men? What makes Bob appear to run counter to those general trends and enter a nursing program?

Even if general societal theories show that high levels of education are associated with lower fertility rates and higher ages at first marriage, how do these dynamics work in the lives of specific people in specific societies? How is it that although conventional wisdom says that men and women are very different in many respects, some men and women conform to these norms, and some do not? These are the questions addressed in this chapter. These questions require different kinds of evidence and methods. For example, the research and theories discussed in this chapter are based much more firmly in the field of psychology than are most of the research and theories discussed in the previous chapter.

In this chapter, we turn to an examination of research focusing on the role of gender in individual lives and life courses. In the previous chapter, we began with an overview of the general characteristics of sex/gender systems around the world; here, we begin with an overview of research on the gender basis of individual difference, especially in personality, basic skills, attitudes, and the other elements culturally defined as "femininity" and "masculinity." We then examine five alternative approaches for trying to explain the gender basis of individual difference.

What Difference Does a Person's Gender Make?

"Is it a boy or a girl?" Who cares? What difference does it make?

In fact, from the day of birth, girls and boys face different life chances and opportunities, as well as very different expectations about what kinds of people they will be and what they will do with their lives. Even in the most basic matters of life and death, being male or female seems to make a difference. The life expectancy of females at birth is higher than that for males in most countries, although *how* different the length of their life is expected to be differs from country to country. Life expectancy is much higher in the wealthier developed countries than among the poorer ones, and in much of the developed world, women live, on average, between 7 and 9 years longer than men. In some places, however, such as southern Asia, a boy and girl born in the early 1990s could expect to live roughly the same number of years. Even in a single country, many factors influence the life expectancy of men and women; in the United States, African-Americans have a lower life expectancy than White people because of differences in life situation and access to health care, and the gap between men and women is greater for them than among White people.

Differences in vulnerability and exposure to various kinds of diseases and violence also affect men and women and shape their lives differently. More males are born with genetically based diseases such as hemophilia and are more likely to die from infant diseases, heart disease, most forms of cancer, cirrhosis of the liver, AIDS, accidents, homicide, and suicide. Women, on the other hand, are more likely than men to die of cerebrovascular disease, diabetes, arteriosclerosis, breast cancer, genital cancer (except among people over age 65), and old age. Of course, most women give birth at some point in their lives, which takes a toll on their health in some ways but also ultimately benefits their health in others. Because women are more likely to spend a lot of time with children than men do, they are exposed to a lot of communicable diseases at that stage, but they also have the opportunity to build up resistances over time. Men seem to threaten their own lives more than women do in a variety of ways, both by being more likely to drink heavily or to smoke cigarettes, and also by being more likely to engage in physically risky behavior and violence.

Men, on average, spend more of their adult lives before old age living on their own, especially because women are more likely to live with their children than men are to live with theirs. Things change in old age, when women live alone much more frequently and for longer periods of their lives. This change occurs because men live shorter lives, on average, and it is culturally more acceptable and common for men than women to marry a younger partner.

As I discuss in much more depth throughout the book, women and men are educated somewhat differently, they enter different occupations, and they play somewhat different roles in most social institutions, from schools to the arts to government and the economy. Their crime rates are also different; so are their hobbies. As the discussion of gender differences in Chapter 1 pointed out, however, the similarities between women's and men's lives, on average, in the United States are much greater than the differences. This similarity occurs largely because the differences *among* women and *among* men are so large.

At the same time, Americans share a cultural view that there is something fundamentally distinct about women and men. Despite the increasing overlaps in the work we do and other aspects of the lives we lead, conventional wisdom tells us that our basic characters—our personalities, basic skills, interests, and attitudes—depend on whether we happen to be men or women. Many people say that women are nurturant, emotional, soft, weak, peaceful, and jealous; and men are aggressive, competitive, strong, and particularly good at mathematics and abstract reasoning. We even have general terms used to capture these composite portraits of difference: *femininity* and *masculinity*. These terms have meaning *because* we have such a strong cultural sense that there are different ways of being, depending on sex or gender. We now turn to both conventional wisdom and research on the relationship between gender and psychological characteristics. We begin with an investigation of the meanings of *femininity* and *masculinity*.

Masculinity, Femininity, and Character

The packages of psychological characteristics people tend to associate with one sex or the other are summarized by a pair of commonly used but often unexamined concepts: masculinity and femininity. What do these words mean? *Masculine*, the *Concise Oxford Dictionary* tells us, means "of men; manly, vigorous; (of women) having qualities appropriate to a man." *Webster's Tenth New Collegiate Dictionary* defines *feminine* as "appropriate or unique to women." Notice that these definitions turn not on whether men and women actually possess masculine or feminine qualities, but on whether we regard these qualities as appropriate for one sex or the other.

We can say that a woman is "not feminine" or that she is "masculine" and possesses "masculine characteristics." We can also say that a man is "not masculine" or that he is "effeminate" and possesses "feminine characteristics." These phrases imply that we consider certain characteristics to be more appropriate for one sex than the other and that a man or woman *should* have them. Of course, *masculine* and *feminine* are not used to describe just *people;* we can also describe many personality characteristics or behaviors as masculine or feminine, regardless of the sex of the person who has the characteristics or is engaging in the behavior. To regard particular personality traits as having a gender of their own is confusing, as the following example shows.

Suppose that I am interested in sex differences in nurturing behavior, and I think of nurturance as feminine, regardless of the sex of the person I am describing. I can regard my favorite male teacher, definitely a man, as nurturing, even though I regard nurturance as a feminine quality. Research on this characteristic provides conflicting evidence, but it offers little reason to believe that women and men, as groups, differ very much in the degree to which they have nurturing *personalities,* although women's roles in society involve them in more situations in which they can act out their nurturant propensities and develop their skills at caring for others.

What should we conclude? Should we say that women and men are roughly equivalent in their potential to nurture, although we regard this behavior as more appropriate for women? If so, we would then have to consider strategies for making sure men do not live up to their potentials so that they will not act inappropriately. Are we arguing, as some psychologists do, that nurturant men are "cross-sex typed" (behave in a way appropriate to the other sex)? This, too, suggests that there is something wrong with nurturant men. Also, if I know a woman who is very interesting and skilled, and even really nice to be around, but who does not happen to be nurturant, do I have to say that she is not acting appropriately for her sex—that there is something wrong with her? The problem is that the definitions of *masculine* and *feminine* are usually based on stereotypes, which means that a large proportion of us do not exactly fit all the characteristics we are supposed to have to be gender appropriate or normal.

Some people try to avoid the problem associated with the labels *masculine* and *feminine* by using the terms *androgyny* and *androgynous.* Some define an androgynous person as one whose personality comprises both "masculine" and "feminine" characteristics. Others go further and say that an androgynous person combines the best of both sexes, meaning the good characteristics stereotypically associated with males and females. (No one seems to have devised a term for a person who combines the worst characteristics of both sexes.) Still others define *androgyny* more in terms of flexibility, or the ability to call on a range of characteristics conventionally labeled masculine or feminine, depending on the given circumstances.

Many researchers have investigated masculinity, femininity, and androgyny, often by asking people how well each of a long list of personality characteristics describes them. A list of the traits they often use for this research appears in Table 3-1. The researchers then tally up the score to categorize the subjects as masculine (checking mostly stereotypically masculine traits), feminine (checking mostly stereotypically feminine traits), androgynous (scoring high on both stereotypically masculine and feminine traits), or undifferentiated (scoring low on both masculine and feminine traits). One of the most important things these studies show is how many people do not conform to traditional images of gender typing. Regardless of the method used, one common finding emerges: Most people do not describe themselves in anything like uniformly "gender-appropriate" terms (Cook, 1985). These findings cast even more doubt on the usefulness of the concepts *masculine* and *feminine.*

TABLE 3-1
Gender-Stereotypic Personality Traits

81

Chapter 3:
Individual-Level
Approaches to
Understanding
Women's Lives

The following terms describe different personality traits, most of which are widely viewed as "masculine" or "feminine." They have also been incorporated into tests used by psychologists to determine whether individual women and men are "masculine," "feminine," or "androgynous." Which of these terms are "masculine"? Which are "feminine"? Why did you choose the labels you selected?

affectionate	flatterable	self-sufficient
aggressive	forceful	sensitive to others'
ambitious	gentle	needs
analytical	gullible	shy
athletic	independent	soft-spoken
cheerful	individualistic	strong personality
childlike	leadership ability	sympathetic
compassionate	loves children	tender
competitive	loyal	theatrical
conceited	makes decisions easily	understanding
conscientious	reliable	warm
defends own beliefs	risk taker	willing to take a stand
dominant	self-reliant	yielding

Note: These items are derived from the Bem Sex-Role Inventory (BSRI). See Bem, 1974.

What difference does it make if a person fits the characteristics defined as masculine, feminine, or androgynous? To find out, researchers first have people complete these checklists so that they can be categorized. The researchers then give the subjects of their study a task to do or a problem to solve. They then analyze the data to see whether respondents who are self-identified as masculine, feminine, androgynous, or undifferentiated systematically do the tasks or solve the problems differently. Some researchers have found that "androgynous" people are more flexible in their ability to deal with different situations, but others (e.g., Jones, Chernovetz, and Hansson, 1978) have found that "masculinity" is associated with greater levels of flexibility. Other studies (e.g., Lamke, 1982) found that (a) "masculinity" is associated with higher levels of self-esteem among both adolescent females and adolescent males and (b) "androgynous" adolescents have higher self-esteem than "feminine" adolescents. The literature on androgyny is too large and varied to detail here, but much of the research literature suggests that androgyny is a healthy alternative to rigid sex typing because of the flexibility it implies. Psychological research gives no basis for arguing that people who conform to the stereotypes of masculinity and femininity are healthier, happier, or better adjusted (Cook, 1985).

These discussions do not change this fact, however: If we think of androgyny as the combination of "masculine" and "feminine" traits, we are still talking about how well individuals conform to stereotypes. *Stereotypes* may be defined as beliefs or expectations people have about members of particular social groups. When we say that a person views women through stereotypes, we are saying that he or she holds certain beliefs about the nature of women as a group (for example, that they are nurturant, passive, or emotional) and applies those beliefs to any given woman, regardless of her actual characteristics. To determine what is and is not a stereotype, it is necessary to review research on the psychological and personality characteristics of women and men.

Personality and Cognitive Skills

Consistent and conclusive evidence of psychological sex differences of any type is very rare. In article after article in professional psychology journals, the words "No sex differences were found" appear. The existence of differences between men and women has been exaggerated, partly because people pay more attention to the relatively few studies that find differences than to the vast number that do not.

Reviews of the literature on psychological differences almost uniformly lead to the same conclusion: Psychologists have not found significant sex differences in most personality characteristics or cognitive skills (e.g., Feingold, 1994; Hyde, 1991; Lips, 1993; Maccoby and Jacklin, 1974; Voyer, Voyer, and Bryden, 1995). In this section, we look briefly at cognitive skills, and then we turn to personality traits. In both cases, we rely for our conclusions primarily on published reviews of many research studies focusing on the actual behavior of women and men, rather than on individual studies or on people's stereotypes of how women and men act and think.[1]

Verbal, Mathematical, and Spatial Cognitive Skills.   Despite the stereotypes, research—especially the most recent studies—offers virtually no overall evidence of gender differences in verbal abilities (Hyde and Linn, 1988; Morisset, Barnard, and Booth, 1995). Males and females seem to develop slightly more strength in different kinds of perceptual skills relating to sight, hearing, and touch (Hyde, 1991; Lips, 1993). Males tend to outperform females on certain kinds of visuospatial tasks but not on others, and the differences depend on what test the researcher uses and the age of the subjects. In fact, gender differences in visuospatial tasks seem to be decreasing (Voyer, Voyer, and Bryden, 1995).

Of all the cognitive skills, mathematical ability has probably received the most attention from scholars, educators, and the public. The long-held stereotype is that boys and men are much better at math than are girls and women. This stereotype is probably also related to the conventional wisdom that females are less logical and analytical than males and cannot be as qualified for certain kinds of jobs and activities requiring those abilities.

Meta-analysis of the research in this area should put many of these stereotypes to rest. One group of researchers (Hyde, Fennema, and Lamon, 1990) meta-analyzed 100 different articles published between 1962 and 1988, representing research on 3 million people. Their results would surprise many people. Overall, females and males were virtually indistinguishable in mathematical ability. No gender differences appeared during elementary or middle school in understanding of mathematical concepts or problem solving, although girls showed slight superiority in computation. In high school and college, on the other hand, males performed better than females in mathematical problem solving. The conventionally expected male edge in mathematics performance is more likely to appear in specialized and selective settings (such as among those taking college-entrance exams) than in more general populations (such as students in high-school classrooms). Moreover, gender differences have declined over the years.

Many studies show that gender differences in mathematical performance are linked to aspects of students' family or school experiences, and the nature of the larger sex/gender system. Consider a study of the mathematics performance of more than 77,000 adolescents in 19 countries, showing that gender differences vary cross-culturally (always a good hint that the differences are not just the effects of native ability); these differences appear to relate to variation in the gender stratification of educational and occupational opportunities in the different countries. Certain aspects of school and family experience also are associated with the variation in gender differences, but they are less likely to make girls and boys perform differently in countries where women have more equal access to jobs and higher education—in other words, where there is a real incentive for girls to do as well as boys (Baker and Jones, 1993).

Another study helps explain the meta-analysis finding that gender differences appear in special high-end mathematics populations, rather than in general populations. A study of math reasoning among schoolchildren found that resources outside the home had more effect on boys' math reasoning than on girls'; therefore, boys' scores became more variable over time than did girls', with some boys really moving out ahead of others. By middle school, then, the boys at the high end outscored the girls, even though the means (averages) were about the same for girls and boys (Entwistle, Alexander, and Olson, 1994).

Some differences in mathematics achievement may also be due to an interaction of achievement with other kinds of gender differences in behavior. For example, one study confirmed a common result that girls are more anxious and less confident about mathematics than boys are, and girls tend to be somewhat more disciplined in class and want to be called on instead of volunteering (Levine, 1995). If teachers are not aware of this gender difference, and they respond especially positively to the (boy) students who seem eager, self-confident, and interested in volunteering, girls are less likely to become the outstanding achievers, even if, on average, they are doing every bit as well as the boys. (See Chapter 5 for more discussion of schools and education.)

Research results on different cognitive skills, therefore, reveal some gender differences on some skills, using some tests at some ages in some places. Nonetheless, these findings do not let us make broad generalizations about one sex or the other being better at broad categories of abilities such as "verbal skills," "mathematical skills," or "visuospatial perception." The differences we find appear stimulated and inhibited by many aspects of people's environment, training, opportunities, and motivations.

Personality Traits.   There is also little evidence to support the idea that men's and women's personalities are very different in most respects, although some differences arise consistently. Males exhibit more aggressiveness (especially in terms of physical rather than verbal aggressiveness) than females do, starting from an early age (Eagly and Steffen, 1986; Feingold, 1994; Hyde, 1984). Certainly, males seem to engage in more acts of antisocial aggression than females do, including all forms of crime, but especially crimes against persons. Men and adolescent boys are more assertive than women and girls (Feingold, 1994). Research also suggests that females and males use somewhat different means to get their way and to influence people (as discussed further in Chapter 10). Women appear more anxious than men (Feingold, 1994), but other research suggests that women (and probably men) are more cautious and risk averse when engaged in activities or settings that are *gender-typed* (stereotypically associated with the other sex). Women are not as cautious and risk averse when they are doing things women are generally expected to do well (Martinez, 1995).

Research regarding most other personality characteristics, including those that are most stereotypically masculine and feminine, shows scanty and often conflicting evidence of sex differences when females and males are given similar opportunities to display these characteristics. A review of 127 different studies found little difference in the activity levels of girls and boys (Eaton and Enns, 1986). Likewise, a review of the research on conformity and influenceability revealed only some tendency for females to be more easily influenced than males, and only under some circumstances—such as when men rather than women are the psychologists doing the research (Eagly and Carli, 1981). Although women are thought to be nurturant, research finds men more likely to engage in many forms of helping behavior (Eagly and Crowley, 1986). Meta-analyses also show no gender differences in self-esteem (Feingold, 1994). Females report themselves to be more empathetic than males report themselves to be, but research involving observation of behavior, rather than self-perception, has not revealed much in the way of gender differences (Eisenberg and Lennon, 1983).

The appearance of gender differences in personality depends on how they are measured. Consider three different ways we might probe the existence of gender differences in personality. First, we might look at *attributions*—that is, whether people say they think women and men have different traits. This is not a measure of gender differences per se, however; it is a measure of perceptions and stereotypes. Second, we might look at *personality scales,* sets of questions tapping people's reports about their own attitudes, beliefs, values, and even patterns of behavior. Third, we might look at *behavioral measures,* observations of how people act. Although researchers try to make personality scales and behavioral measures tap the same underlying personality traits, these measures yield different results. A good example is the study of *internal* and *external locus of control,* the degree to which particular individuals' feelings, thoughts, and actions are relatively independently guided from inside, like a human gyroscope, or to which they are more dependent on the views and expectations of others. A meta-analysis of many studies found that men appear to have more internal locus of control than women in studies using behavioral measures, but these gender differences disappear when using personality scales (Feingold, 1994).

Another example of how it helps to distinguish among different ways of measuring personality tendencies is John Moresque and Catherine Ross's (1995) work on gender differences in feeling distress. As they point out, research shows that women report being more distressed than men. Does this difference appear because women *feel* more distress, because they are more willing or able to *report* distress when they are asked about it, or because researchers tend to ask more about the kinds of distress women feel than, for example, anger, which is stereotypically associated with men as a form of negative emotion? (Remember that while women are stereotypically regarded as more emotional than men, men are typically more likely to get so angry that the best solution seems to be to kill people, as in crime or war.) Moresque and Ross (1995) found that indeed men do keep their emotions to themselves enough to make a difference in the research results; also, it is important to tap a wide range of emotions, but these factors together do not completely eliminate the gender differences in anger, sadness, anxiety, malaise, and aches.

Besides personality traits, many researchers have examined possible gender differences in the interests and social attitudes of men and women, and in the way they think about social and personal issues. This book examines evidence in many areas, but one of the most interesting areas revolves around gender differences in styles of moral thinking. Following the publication of Carol Gilligan's (1982) *In a Different Voice,* many researchers focused on possible differences between women and men in the way they understand and solve moral dilemmas. Many feminist writers have concluded, along with Gilligan, that women and men differ in this respect; women's approaches are more shaped by social connectedness and a stance of caring and relating to others, while men's are more shaped by more abstract and individualistic notions of rights and justice. (These questions are studied more closely later in this chapter.) There is little consistent evidence for gender differences in thinking about rights and justice, however, although women's thinking may be more embedded in social relations than is men's.

Summary of Psychological Differences.   We have only touched on a huge field of research discussing differences between women and men. By and large, however, this research suggests that the most fruitful approach to understanding the gender basis of human characteristics and behavior is not to focus on global, abstract skills and characteristics removed from their social context, but to discuss these skills and characteristics in the context of specific social institutions and organizations. When people ask whether women are happier, more anxious, more dependent, or more nurturant than men, the best answer is probably, "Under what circumstances? With regard to what situations?"

Human beings are very complex. We tend to respond in different ways to different situations. Although there may be people so thoroughly dominated by particular characteristics that they always act in the same manner, these people are a minority, comprising saints, devils, or people so out of touch with their surroundings and circumstances that they need protection from themselves. Personality characteristics depend very much on the context of behavior, and people's particular skills and motivations depend on their experiences. For this reason, we discuss psychological gender differences and the psychology of gender throughout the remainder of this book, but always in the context of specific social settings.

Explaining Women's Situation at the Individual Level: Five Approaches

A theory that explains how the social structure and culture of relations between women and men developed over historical time does not necessarily explain why, in a given society, individual women and men behave as they do. Marxist theories of social differences, for example, suggest that the relative status of women and men depends on historical changes in the structure of the economy. But how do individual people come to "fit into" this system? How do individuals acquire the beliefs, ideology, personality characteristics, or patterns of behavior that are appropriate to a given social or cultural system?

This chapter discusses five different approaches that scholars use to help explain how individuals come to adopt particular variations of gender norms. The first calls on *biology* for explanation, looking to genetic structures, the brain, or the hormonal system to understand why males become masculine and females become feminine. The second theory is *psychoanalytic theory*, especially that proposed by Sigmund Freud, who understood the development of gender and sexuality as a conflictual process involving psychological adaptation to the demands placed on the psyche by both biology and the environment. According to psychoanalysts, much of the work of becoming male or female is accomplished by reining in and giving culturally acceptable shape to unconscious drives.

The third theory, *cognitive development,* also defines gender as involving an interaction between biology and environment. Cognitive developmentalists believe that people progress through different stages of cognitive organization or structures of thinking. Thus, for cognitive developmentalists, the question of interest is how gender comes to shape and become part of the structure of thinking. The fourth approach involves *learning theories,* emphasizing the impact of the social and physical environment on individuals. In this perspective, people learn about gender through their experience in the world and especially the models it presents them, and they are influenced or conditioned to become male or female in specific ways because of the rewards and punishments they receive from others. After pausing to consider some attempts to synthesize the different learning and development theories, this section concludes with *institutional theories,* emphasizing the constraints that social institutions place on the behavior and opportunities of individuals, especially through discriminatory treatment based on gender. This approach suggests that the whole story of living a gendered life involves more than a description of how individuals learn or internalize gender norms. The institutional-discrimination model recognizes the possibility that individuals can be forced into gendered behavior against their will.

The Biological Basis of Female and Male

What makes men men and women women? The age-old hypothesis is that just as our secondary sex characteristics and reproductive capacities are determined by our biology, so are the aspects of our character and mental and emotional capabilities related to whether we are physiologically men or women. To what degree does nature bestow on each of us limits or capabilities that depend on whether we happen to be male or female? How much are our individual lives shaped by our sex?

Certainly, some broad, sweeping gender differences come from our biological makeup. Besides the secondary sex characteristics and the capability for different roles in reproduction (that is, the ability either to produce sperm or to give birth to a baby and to lactate), males and females have different average heights and weights, fat-to-muscle ratios, upper and lower body strengths, and degrees of stamina. As the previous chapter showed, however, what each society makes of these differences profoundly influences what difference these differences make.

What about our character and skills? As shown in Chapter 2, in the review of research on genetics, hormones, and the brain, biological research has offered very little in terms of evidence for general biologically based sex differences in what kinds of people we are. Clearly, if biology really differentiated our character and skills by sex very much, we would see more evidence of persistent, cross-cultural differences than we see.

That is not to say there is *no* sex distinction at all in these aspects of human life. Some research suggests, for example, that females mature faster, so girls and boys will show a difference in maturity until boys catch up. Other research suggests that higher rates of depression among women are due to chromosomal differences stemming from a mutant gene on the X chromosome (which women are therefore more likely to have). In this case, however, depression is not a normal feature of being female, but a relatively unusual feature that is more likely to occur in women (Nolen-Hoeksema, 1987). This may sound like verbal fast-footing, but it is not. In contrast to a condition due to a mutant gene on an X chromosome (of which men have one and women have two), having a womb is a normal condition of being female.

The research on sex differences is valuable and interesting, but it does not explain why women are so much more likely than men to choose to train to be elementary-school teachers, while so many more men seek Ph.D.s in engineering. To explain these phenomena requires a return to the idea of sex/gender systems and the construction of gender, rather than just the nature of sex and sex differences. Even the most obvious biologically based features of sex differences are *affected* by environmental conditions, and the social significance of these biological differences is *mediated* by social norms. Consider some athletic examples. Not only are men taller and stronger, on average, than women, but also the tallest and strongest 5% of men are taller and stronger than the tallest and strongest 5% of women. The average man can run faster and jump higher than the average woman, and as the history of track-and-field events and basketball shows, the tallest and strongest stratum of men can run faster and jump higher than the tallest and strongest stratum of women. Despite these distinctions, however, biological differences do not translate directly into athletic differences; training, nutrition, and many other factors intervene.

As a result, the history of running events in the Olympics during this century shows *linear* (that is, at a constant rate) improvements in speed among women and men in every running event, from the 200 meter to the marathon, from the beginning of the century to 1992. Human evolution has *not* occurred in such a short period; rather, social forces have shaped this change. In addition, comparing the improvement of men and women over this period of time, the *slope* or *rate* of change for women is double that of men. In other words, they are catching up with men over time. Also, probably because of the relative advantage women have in stamina, the rate of catching up is greater in the longer races than in the shorter ones. This does not mean that women and men will ever compete directly in most races (especially shorter ones), but it does show how many of the observed athletic differences are based on social forces. In this example, the biologically based differences are affected by social forces.

For another example, ever since the beginning of basketball, most people have agreed that the men's game is more interesting than the women's game. Early in the 20th century, physical education instructors altered the rules for women, to make sure it was a slower game. In any case, because men can run faster and jump higher, few people ever questioned the existence of men's but not women's professional basketball teams and associations, the better facilities for men's games on college campuses, and the creation of men's but not women's basketball as an income-generating sport. However, even if the best male basketball players are more likely to be able to dunk than the best female players, does this biologically based difference necessitate regarding men's basketball as interesting enough to pay to see and women's as a mere hobby? Until recently, American *cultural* norms distinguished the two sports in exactly this way. In the middle 1990s, however, the growth in women's athletics, facilitated partly by changes in the law, meant that one by one, many college basketball arenas began to fill when women's teams played. In 1997, professional women's basketball associations began. In this case, culture has *mediated* the social significance of biological differences through the fact that large numbers of people learned to think of women's basketball as interesting.

As we have seen, biological research has not been very successful in explaining how individuals in society come to be (or not be) part of the prevailing sex/gender system. We now turn to approaches that focus explicitly on the interaction between biological and environmental factors in human development, especially as it relates to "masculinity" and "femininity." In trying to understand how individuals come to be the kind of people they are, these theorists emphasize the degree of change that occurs in individuals' lives over time, especially the different phases or stages that occur during the course of individuals' development.

Psychoanalytic Theory: The Creation of Masculinity and Femininity

Throughout the 20th century, psychoanalytic theory was one of the most influential approaches to understanding human development. Although there are many different varieties of psychoanalytic theory, here we focus primarily on the most famous of all, developed by its major founder, Sigmund Freud. In Chapter 2, we looked at the role of conflict between women and men in Freud's psychoanalytic theory. Now we review his theories of psychosexual development.

Sex Similarity. The basic element of the human psyche is the psychic energy often called *drives* or *instincts*. Like other types of energy, these drives have no particular form or object other than self-gratification; they can be channeled to have any of several forms, objects, or effects. This is why a single feeling (for example, hatred of another person) can take on either a destructive form ("I'll kill him") or a constructive form ("I'll show him—I'll get this done faster and better than it's ever been done before").

According to Freud, human personalities and the structure of the human psyche are not sex differentiated at birth. The development of females and males is very similar for the first few years, when any observed "sexual differences are not . . . of great consequence: they can be outweighed by individual variations" ([1933] 1965, 118). This makes sense, given that psychic energy has no natural distinctive form, and that females and males are born essentially undifferentiated; a male baby and a female baby, he believed, are essentially the same creatures.

For this reason, newborn males and females are essentially bisexual (or, more accurately, pansexual). If the human drive for pleasure is unshaped or unchanneled, the infant does not care how that pleasure is achieved. A baby will try sucking on almost anything, it is happy to have almost any part of its anatomy stroked, and it feels no shock if a person of one sex or the other strokes it. The *libido* (pleasure-seeking drive) knows nothing of sex or gender, even if it is the source of sexuality and eroticism. For a human being to become heterosexual, which to Freud was central to appropriate sexual maturity and gender roles, this part of the human psyche has to be repressed and rechanneled.

How do these relatively undifferentiated masses of gurgles, cries, and burps acquire masculinity and femininity and develop particular psychosexual orientations? In Freudian theory, the process is posed as a series of stages through which people must pass to achieve maturity. Progress through these stages is easy; it might best be described as a hazardous struggle both *within* individuals and *between* individuals and the social world around them. Events in the child's environment or relationships between the child and others can make it go wrong at any stage.

The early stages of psychosexual development are similar for boys and girls. The first stage, the oral phase, is marked by the importance of the mouth in receiving pleasure. Sucking and feeding is the primary business of infants' lives. This focus changes when children face the first demand that they become self-conscious and exert control over themselves, during the anal phase, triggered by the experience of toilet training. This transition is very complex. The infant finds that he or she can please another person, but only under certain circumstances. The child can give a gift of properly deposited feces, but this act requires a certain amount of self-denial. Because of the role of self-denial (the first of many instances of self-denial to be learned), this stage is achieved only with resistance. The assault on the *id* (the unformed, unrestrained drives that occupy most of the psyche) by the *ego* (the "I," or potentially conscious or self-conscious self) has begun. The third phase, the phallic phase, is the time during which the child begins to learn about genital pleasure. Now the trouble begins.

Development of Difference.   The Freudian picture described thus far portrays girls and boys as relatively undifferentiated and unrestrained pleasure seekers. The pleasure drives have yet to be regulated; in other words, both the ego and the *superego* (literally, "over I") have yet to be developed. The superego is often described as the conscience, the (relatively small) part of our consciousness that flows from the world around us. It contains the moral rules and personal sense of right and wrong learned from parents and others who transmit cultural norms. The superego pushes the ego into battle against the dark unruly drives of the id, even though we repress and deny the presence of these impulses. The ego and superego have to learn what masculinity, femininity, and sexuality are about; the id can never learn and remains in conflict with the ego and superego throughout life.

Freud thought that this task is more difficult for females than for males because it takes females two extra steps to achieve the final goal of maturity. Both boys and girls originally derive their pleasure from the mother. This poses a special problem for girls. In finding his mother his primary erotic object (source of plea-sure), a boy is on the way to "mature masculinity." He will have to give up his mother as a consciously sexual object, but to become heterosexual, he merely has to turn to other women for erotic pleasure. This switch involves a struggle, but one not nearly as difficult as the task girls face to become mature heterosexual women, according to Freud. Girls must shift their focus of eroticism from women to men.

What could wrench girls' affections so completely that the original pleasurable feelings associated with physical relations with women are replaced with horror or profound anxiety in most women? For Freud, the answer lies in the female version of the castration complex. "After all, the anatomical distinction between the sexes must express itself in psychical consequences. It was, however, a surprise to learn from analyses that girls hold their mother responsible for their lack of a penis and do not forgive her for being thus put at a disadvantage" (Freud [1933] 1965, 124).

Like many people, Freud could not imagine that a woman's body could be regarded as complete. His standard and, he seemed to assume, everyone else's, for a complete human body is the male anatomy. According to Freud, one sight of a male's "superior equipment" ([1933] 1965, 126) and a girl is overcome with mortification for her own body, envy of the male's, and a need to place blame for her mutilation. She becomes hostile to her mother, who, she finds, is deformed like herself and is responsible for creating her without the essential organ. By gen-eralizing her view of herself and her mother, women become "debased in value for girls just as they are for boys" ([1933] 1965, 127). The girl is now on the road to maturity. She rejects women and turns to her father, who, after all, possesses a penis. She also begins to suppress her former feelings for her clitoris, or deficient penis, to pave the way for vaginal eroticism, which prepares her for heterosexuality and motherhood. This transfer of erotic feeling from one organ to another is the other major developmental step that girls, and not boys, must take.

When she discovers her castration, the girl begins a very difficult journey. According to Freud, she may take any of three roads:

1. She might develop "sexual inhibitions or neurosis," especially frigidity. This happens if the girl is so traumatized by her discoveries that she suppresses not only her "infantile" sexuality, but also all sexuality.
2. She might develop a "masculinity complex." In this case, she rebels against femininity and retains her more "infantile" form of sexuality, which means, among other things, homosexuality.

3. She might "renounce" infantile sexuality, which includes both women as love objects and her own clitoris as the focus of erotic pleasure to achieve "normal femininity."

Some feminists have pointed out that the idea of specifically vaginal orgasms—difficult to achieve because of the relative lack of nerve endings in the vagina, compared to the clitoris—is particularly convenient to a male-centered definition of sexuality and dangerous for women's senses of self-esteem. What about penis envy? For Freud, this envy becomes transformed into a desire for a child, and, if at all possible, a child with a penis. Notice that this theory accounts for considerable variation *among* women in their degrees of "femininity."

What differences between males and females develop as a result of this process? Freud believed that women become oriented toward home, husband, and child, and men turn their interests outward. Men also develop a stronger superego (conscience) than women do. To explain this, Freud turned to the castration complex and the child's feelings toward the mother and father. Boys continue to be sexually oriented toward their mothers and toward women in general. What force imposes itself against the id to keep boys from becoming literally incestuous? Boys compete with their fathers for the mothers' attention, but they also fear the power of their father and, especially the punishment of castration. (This psychic relationship with the father is called the "Oedipus complex.") This fear keeps males in line and strengthens their abilities to integrate societal rules into their psyches.

Women do not have to fear castration because it has already happened, and thus they have less reason to develop this social orientation. Rather than learning to be governed by societal rules, they become passively oriented toward men's will in order to achieve their goal of having a child. Notice that unlike other theorists who put women in "their place," Freud argued that women are not passive by nature. Rather, in the course of their psychosocial development, they "give preference to passive aims" (Freud, [1933] 1965, 115). Thus, for Freud, although it is normal for women to become passive, he did not believe that it is easy for women to accomplish passivity. They have to work on it.

Women's development has other effects that distinguish women from men, according to Freud. Their repression of their "masculinity" (especially their aggressiveness) makes them masochistic. Drives such as aggressiveness do not disappear when they are repressed (they are, after all, forms of energy) but remain alive in the id. Woman who achieve "normal femininity," therefore, turn their aggressive energy inward. Women also remain dominated by the envy sparked by their discovery of their castration. They therefore have less sense of social justice than men because social justice is incompatible with envy. They become more rigid than men and age more quickly, primarily because of the more arduous path they have taken. Freud thought that women appear tired out, spent, and aged by the time they reach 30 years of age, in comparison with men, who at this age are just reaching their peaks.

Evaluating the Psychoanalytic Perspective. The psychoanalytic perspective on the development of males and females offers a rich body of theories and observations. In its variety of interpretations and applications, it has been both celebrated and rejected from every point of view, from the radically antifeminist to the radically feminist. What are the sources of these reactions?

Many criticisms revolve around the research methods Freud and many of his followers used to reach conclusions. Critics point out that the subjects of Freud's study were his and his colleagues' patients. To accept Freud's arguments, followers must accept generalizations made on the basis of observing women who went to psychoanalysts' offices at the beginning of the 20th century, without any comparison to other populations.

The nature of both the clinical method (in-depth discussion with and observation and interpretation of one person by another) and psychoanalytic theory itself creates a problem for confirmation of the theory. Psychoanalytic method involves seeking the subjective meanings of people's perceptions and actions. As shown in the earlier example of how hatred can lead to either destructive *or* constructive activity, different acts can have the same meaning or motivation, and different people can engage in the same activity for very different reasons. Yet subjective and interpretive methods are favored in many areas of women's studies.

The psychoanalytic method is vulnerable to the charge that one can see whatever one *wants* to see. Consider penis envy. From the Freudian viewpoint, if a girl asks her mother why she cannot have a penis like her brother, she is displaying penis envy. If she suggests that it must be neat to be able to urinate standing up (or tries it), or if she playacts at having a penis, she is also expressing penis envy. On the other hand, what if, as many girls do, she expresses the feeling that having a penis must be strange or uncomfortable or that it might get in the way when one is riding a bicycle? The psychoanalyst might argue that this too is a sign of penis envy, expressed through her hostility toward the male body. Some psychoanalysts have gone further, regarding almost any of women's attempts to enter traditionally masculine domains as a sign of penis envy. In fact, attempts to confirm Freud's conclusions by using other methods, such as experimental evidence and even projective techniques, have found little confirmation for important cornerstones of Freud's theory, such as the universal existence of penis envy.

Some of Freud's critics, including feminist scholars, charge that Freud neglected the role of society and culture in his examination of female and male development. This is not true. First, much of the struggle in the development of the ego is fueled by the superego, formed by the individual's interaction with the social world. Because psychoanalytic theory regards the human psyche as shaped not exclusively by nature or by society but by the struggles between the two, it can encompass the effects of tangible reality, biology, and social relationships, myths and symbols, and the rational and the irrational. Many feminist theorists have found great potential in this aspect of psychoanalytic theory.

Freud argued that human suffering and unhappiness, both male and female, comes from three sources: "the superior power of nature, the feebleness of our own bodies and the inadequacy of the regulations which adjust the mutual relationships of human beings in the family, the state and society" ([1930] 1961, 33). A large part of the human struggle, therefore, is to civilize humanity and to remove the sources of suffering as much as possible. This observation has opened the way for feminist theorists such as Juliet Mitchell (1974) and Nancy Chodorow (1978) to suggest that Freudian theory can be used to explain the particular nature of suffering under patriarchal conditions and to point out how the restructuring of social institutions can have profound and positive effects on psychosexual development.

Nancy Chodorow has influentially argued that the arrangement of social institutions so that women do most of the child-rearing has gender-specific effects on the psychosocial development of children, which results in reproducing gender differentiation and inequality. She believes that women think more in terms of *connectedness* among people because of the continuities between themselves and their mothers. Males are more dominated by the task of *separation* because of the early need to distinguish themselves from their mothers in order to develop a masculine identity. The problem for males is that because men tend not to take a full share in nurturing children, they cannot gain the same sense of connection and continuity as girls, who are nurtured by their same-sex parent. Thus,

> because women are themselves mothered by women, they grow up with the relational capacities and needs, and psychological definition of self-in-relationship, which commits them to mothering. Men, because they are mothered by women, do not. Women mother daughters who, when they become women, mother. (Chodorow 1978, 209)

Chodorow has concluded that the institution of the family needs to be changed so that men develop the emotional structure that can equip them to expand their relational capacities and needs and that will equip women to develop greater autonomy.

Freud's discussion of the human drive toward civilization points to another key issue in the significance of psychoanalytic theory: its perspective on sexuality. Many feminists consider Freud a patriarchal, oppressive "Victorian" (a word many people use to mean "prudish"). In fact, his views are not so easily categorized. Civilization, he argued, is necessary to help people divert their self-destructive tendencies. It can help in the struggle between the id and the superego to channel destructive energies into creative social projects. However, "at the same time we have been careful not to fall in with the prejudice that civilization is synonymous with perfecting, that [civilization] is the road to perfection preordained for men [sic]" (Freud, [1930] 1961, 43). Civilization, Freud believed, is no friend of liberty, and civilization has rarely been based on justice.

Freud was dismayed at the degree of sexual repression he saw in society. "The requirement . . . that there shall be a single kind of sexual life for everyone, disregards the dissimilarities, whether innate or acquired, in the sexual constitution of human beings; it cuts off a fair number of them from sexual enjoyment, and so becomes the source of serious injustice" (p. 51). As mentioned previously, Freud thought that homosexuality was an infantile form of sexuality, but he did not think it dangerous or wrong and did not favor social or legal penalties for the homosexual. The man who pointed to the nature of the unconscious and the id, and who declared that human beings are naturally bisexual, not to mention incestuous, found little favor with the public or most of the medical establishment—and certainly the moral establishment—of his day.

Clearly, Freud and a great many of his influential followers were patriarchal and, in some cases, misogynistic. The great majority of Freudian psychoanalysts seem to have accepted the notion that the penis is superior equipment, and that women who achieve normal femininity are uncreative, jealous, unjust, and masochistic creatures. Psychoanalysis has been used to try to make women interpret their problems in light of penis envy and the need for a child. Psychoanalysis is one of the many modes of thought that view women's own perceptions as unreliable. In one of Freud's most famous cases, a woman traced her problems to a childhood experience of being raped by her father. Freud reinterpreted the woman's story as a fiction revealing an extreme case of normal childhood penis envy and father love. His evidence for concluding that the child only wished to have sex with her father was the father's claim that he had not raped his daughter.

Freudian orthodoxy has been extremely harmful to women in many respects. Many feminists, however, have begun to return to psychoanalysis and the theories of Freud and others, such as Karen Horney (1885–1952), a contemporary of Freud's. Some argue that men both fear women and, in a sense, "envy" the womb (Horney, 1967).[2] This envy, they argue, accounts for the male need to dominate women, in contrast to the Freudian idea that penis envy leads women to seek domination by men. Some argue that the general outline of Freudian theory is correct, although the substantive conclusions often reached have been shaped by androcentric ideology. They suggest that Freud's writing on women should not be taken as a theory of what *must* happen but as a description of what *does* happen in a patriarchal or androcentric society. One could argue that Freud's conclusions about normal femininity serve as an excellent guide to the pernicious nature of what society's ideal women should seek to attain.

Psychoanalytic theory is also one of the few theories that explicitly considers the importance of sexuality in social and cultural life and that suggests the important relationship between the social construction of sexuality and the social construction of gender. If one accepts Freud's argument that children's psyches are not naturally differentiated but are pressed to diverge because of the pursuit of what Freud calls "normal" sexuality, the theory begs a reconsideration of what is normal. Some feminists conclude that Freud's view of penis envy is also correct, but only within the context of a culture that perceives the phallus as a symbol of power, dominance, and liberty. If cultural conceptions of sex and gender were not "phallocentric," if the phallus were not a symbol of power, there would be little reason to be jealous of those who possess a penis. This interpretation has bolstered the argument that no change in society can occur until the social construction of sexuality is changed and the penis is regarded as merely an anatomical organ. In any case, psychoanalytic theory offers an excellent example of a theory that can have different and conflicting implications, depending on how it is interpreted and used.

Cognitive-Developmental Theories

Psychoanalytic theory is only one of a few approaches to understanding the differentiation of individual males and females that use the concept of stages of development. Cognitive developmentalists do also, but in a very different way.

Unlike psychoanalysts, cognitive developmentalists focus on the conscious part of the mind, especially the skills, structures, and styles of thought and reasoning. They are interested in the development of the frameworks people use to understand, analyze, and cope with questions of self-identity, social and physical relationships, and principles such as morality. Many (although not all) developmentalists have a more rigid notion than psychoanalysts regarding the succession or hierarchy of stages through which an individual passes. Most claim that once an individual has passed from one stage to the next (for example, from being able to add to being able to multiply), she or he will not return to a previous stage. Psychoanalysts make no such claims; in fact, the ideas of regression to previous stages and of constant tensions between earlier and later impulses figure very importantly in their views. The difference exists largely because psychoanalysts and cognitive developmentalists focus on different aspects of the mind. For the developmentalist focusing on the stages of learning specific problem-solving skills, a person would no more return to an earlier mode than he or she would forget how to ride a bicycle.

Becoming Boys and Girls. Most developmentalists see growth as a product of the interaction of the human organism with the environment. During the earliest stage of life, infants develop both basic physical capabilities, such as seeing and hearing, and the ability to manipulate physical objects purposefully. At this time, for example, babies learn the wonderful game of repeatedly throwing things on the floor during feeding time. During the next stage, they become capable of awareness of objects that are not physically present; that is, they show signs of imagination and memory. Whereas in the first stage, an object that is taken away from a baby ceases to exist for the child, in the next, it is not so easy to take candy from a baby.

More sophisticated cognitive abilities, such as the ability to classify objects and to understand the relationships among them, develop in the third stage. Children learn that not all fruits are apples, that apples and oranges are both fruits, and that although both apples and ice cream cones are edible, they are not both fruits. Finally, they reach an even more sophisticated stage, when they learn to solve more complex problems, requiring the ability to manipulate symbols and abstract ideas. They cannot reach this stage, however, until they have passed through the prior stages.

Cognitive developmentalists investigate many different aspects of human thought in this same way, including the development of gender identification: the first stages of learning to be girls and boys. Lawrence Kohlberg (1966, 82), one of the most important cognitive-development theorists, wrote, "[Basic] sexual attitudes are not patterned directly by either biological instincts or arbitrary cultural norms, but by the child's cognitive organization of his social world along sex role dimensions." Developing gender is a process of making sense of the world, including one's own body and its relationship to the environment and social context. Here, too, is one of the major distinctions between the psychoanalytic and the cognitive-developmental theories. "It is not the child's biological instincts, but rather his cognitive organization of social role concepts around universal physical dimensions, which accounts for the existence of universals in sex role attitudes," wrote Kohlberg (1966, 82). Cognitive developmentalists focus on the understanding, not on the unconscious.

According to Kohlberg, the process of gender development begins early in life, when little girls figure out that they are girls, and little boys figure out that they are boys; that is, they engage in cognitive self-categorization and acquire gender identity. It normally takes up to 3 years for this to happen. Children next learn that everyone has gender; everyone is a boy or a girl. Only after this do children begin to learn that gender does not change (if you are a girl, you are going to be a girl forever) and that gender has meaning. At this stage, children begin to recognize that girls and boys do different things, like different things, and have different amounts of power. They begin to learn about masculinity and femininity.

Learning about gender is one thing; learning to follow gender norms is another. How does this happen and why? Learning has both a *cognitive* (thinking and analysis) dimension and an *affective* (feelings and emotions) dimension. Children learn about themselves, but they also learn to value themselves and, through generalization, people like themselves. As children learn about their gender, they begin to value it. Boys want to do "boy" things, and girls want to do "girl" things. Once children develop a framework for understanding the world, ambiguities are painful until they acquire considerably more sophisticated analytical abilities. Young children thus not only become careful to uphold gender standards but also are often more rigid in their adherence to gender standards than are older children.

Research by Rebecca S. Bigler and Lynn S. Liben (1992) is a good example of cognitive-developmental research on this process. They were interested in the findings that young children seem especially rigid in their gender stereotyping. They hypothesized that this happens because most young children have not yet reached a cognitive level at which they can understand that one object can fall into more than one category; rigid stereotyping is, after all, partly a matter of making simple and inflexible gender categorizations. This rigid stereotyping can be self-reinforcing because children tend to remember gender-stereotype information better than information that contradicts stereotypes. Indeed, children with more advanced classification skills hold less rigid stereotypes.

Bigler and Liben studied a sample of White middle-class 5- to 10-year-olds. They investigated the children's level of occupation-related gender stereotyping and its relationship to their classification and verbal skills. Their findings support cognitive-developmental theory. Regardless of age or sex, the more advanced the children's multiple classification skills, the more *gender egalitarian* (the less rigidly stereotyped) they were. Among the younger children, if the experimenters taught the children skills in multiple classification using social examples (sorting people into categories), they became more egalitarian. Among the older children, if the experimenters taught skills in multiple classification using examples of sorting either people or physical objects into categories, the children became more egalitarian. This difference would occur because the older children, being more cognitively advanced, could generalize from a skill learned with respect to people or things, while the less sophisticated younger children have to learn about people to generalize to people. Children who became more flexible in gender stereotyping because of classification training with social examples also gained more memory for counterstereotypic stories; that is, they did not have as much trouble as other children remembering details of a story if a child was acting in a way that is stereo-typical for the *other* sex.

Why do children learn their gender lessons? Lawrence Kohlberg (1966) believed that boys and girls have different motivations for learning these lessons. As boys become acquainted with male social power and prestige, their desire to act like males increases. Boys identify with their fathers and want to act like them. They begin to want only to be with other boys and to avoid anything that seems girlish. If boys want to be boys because of male power and prestige, however, what motivates girls to become girls? Kohlberg thought girls also know that males have more power and prestige, and, like boys, girls define the male body as the basic body and the female's as the negative of the masculine, rather than as a positive entity. Nevertheless, he argued, girls also want to identify with and act like their same-sex parent. Why? Part of the answer, Kohlberg said, is that instead of power and prestige, girls value the "feminine" attributes of niceness and nurturance. These observations presumably help explain another one: Many studies show that girls are generally not as rigid in their gender stereotypes as boys are (e.g., Jessell and Beymer, 1992), and they are not as adamant about doing only "girl" things (witness the "tomboy") or about playing only with other girls. Within Kohlberg's view, the issue of power and privilege would make boys more eager to conform to gender norms.

More important, however, is the developmentalist's argument that people are very egocentric and have strong motives to value themselves and people like themselves. The higher prestige of males might reinforce their egocentric reasons for conformity, but children of both sexes tend to think their own sex is better. Some public-opinion polls undermine this view, however. In 1994, a sample of teenagers was asked about the attitudes boys and girls have about each other. The teens were asked whether they believed girls thought they were better than boys or boys thought they were better than girls. They were also asked whether there are more advantages to being a man or a woman. Table 3-2 shows their answers. Boys believed in roughly equal numbers that boys think they are better than girls, and girls think they are better than boys. Girls view the matter differently. They are, if anything, more likely to believe that boys think they are better than girls. But only a minority of girls believe that girls think they are better than boys. Also, girls were virtually no more likely than boys to believe that there are particular advantages to being a woman. The largest group of boys and girls thought the advantages of being male or female are roughly equal, and a large minority of both boys and girls thought there are more advantages to being a man than a woman. There must be another reason, then, for people—especially women—to identify with their own sex.

Kohlberg also believed that children tend to view physical and social regulari-ties in moral terms; that is, what exists is good. Kohlberg followed Jean Piaget's observation of a "tendency for the young child to view any deviation from the social order as bad or wrong, even if such a deviation would not be considered bad by adults. The child does not distinguish between conventional social expectations and moral laws and duties." Thus, Kohlberg argued, "The physical constancies underlying the child's concepts of gender identity tend to be identified with divine

TABLE 3-2
Teenagers' Opinions About Gender

	Females	*Males*
Do most boys think of girls as equals or do they think they are better than girls?		
Boys are better	63	59
Boys and girls are equal	34	39
Do most girls think of boys as equals, or do they think they are better than boys?		
Girls are better	42	56
Boys and girls are equal	57	41
All things considered, in our society today, do you think there are more advantages in being a man, or more advantages in being a woman, or that there are no more advantages in being one than the other?		
Advantages in being a man	37	32
Advantages in being a woman	8	6
The same	52	59

Source: New York Times Poll/CBS News Poll, May 26–June 1, 1994.

or moral law, and the need to adapt to the physical realities of one's identity are viewed as moral obligations" (1966, 122). This observation returns the discussion to cognitive-developmental paths and the relationship of gender identity to the ability to tolerate ambiguity and multiple classifications. Those who have not yet developed mature classification capabilities and the ability to tolerate ambiguity tend to have more rigid gender views than those whose cognitive abilities are more sophisticated.

Gender and Moral Development.   Besides these attempts to understand how children come to develop basic gender identity, cognitive-developmental theory has also opened up another train of research focusing on gender differences in the cognitive frameworks people use for analyzing moral questions. Kohlberg's research revolved around the answers people gave him when he asked them to solve moral dilemmas. A famous example is one about a man whose dying wife could be saved by a drug manufactured by a local pharmacist who was charging much more than the cost of producing the drug, so the man could not afford the drug. Should the husband steal the drug? Kohlberg's work did not focus on whether the final answer his subjects gave was to steal or not to steal. Rather, he was interested in the cognitive framework or reasoning they used to *reach* their answer. What reasoning did they use, regardless of what solution they gave? Did their answers refer to the need to obey rules? Avoid punishment? Gain other people's approval? Maintain order in society? Follow their consciences? Kohlberg and his colleagues argued that just as cognitive developmentalists believe that reasoning in math or physics problem solving follows certain stages of development, so does moral thinking. Thus, Kohlberg and his associates outlined a series of six stages of development, ranging from one displayed by most little children—choosing actions only to get rewards and avoid punishment—to one they argued very few adults ever reach as a *consistent* base of action: Using an abstract principle internalized in conscience, such as the Golden Rule.

There is little controversy over the earliest stages proposed by Kohlberg. The issue for gender development occurs at the middle and higher stages. Some of the early studies indicated that while most adults fall into the "middle" range, known as "conventional" morality, women tended to score lower than men. The women's answers were more likely to be framed in terms of the dynamics of social relationships within the stories, and the men's more in terms of rules of fairness. According to the original scale, this seemed to indicate that women had lower levels of moral development.

Psychologist Carol Gilligan launched an influential critique, *In a Different Voice* (1982), in which she argued that the original moralism scale was biased toward more "male" ways of thinking. She suggested that men's moral reasoning is based more on principles of individualism, rights, and justice, while women's is based more on caring, obligation, and responsibility to others. She attacked the notion, implicit in the conventional moral-development literature, that the "justice" mode of approaching morality demonstrates higher development than the "caring" mode. Her views are similar to Nancy Chodorow's (1978) interpretation of connectedness and separation in women's and men's lives. Along similar lines, Sara Ruddick (1982) argued that women use a form of thinking that she calls "maternal thinking," shaped by the caring work that women do in society.

None of these authors claims that these gender differences in thinking stem directly from biological differences; instead, they maintain that our ways of thinking are shaped by social practices or experiences, which tend to be gender differentiated. These arguments about women's and men's moral thinking have been very influential for many reasons. They are among the very few claims about psychological gender differences that appear to place women in as good or even better light than men.

Although many researchers continue to explore Gilligan's idea that the structure of female and male roles leads young women's development to be specially shaped by personal relationships of caring (Gilligan, Lyons, and Hanmer, 1990; Gilligan, Ward, and Taylor, 1988), these arguments have also been the target of considerable criticism (e.g., Kerber et al., 1986). Some writers are uncomfortable with the degree to which these arguments resemble and justify traditional stereotypes. In fact, systematic comparative research has not uncovered consistent gender differences in moral reasoning; rather, it suggests that women's and men's *reputation* for differences outstrips their *actual* differences in this regard (e.g., Brabeck, 1983; Ford and Lowery, 1986; Lifton, 1985; Walker, 1984). No research provides evidence that most men think differently from most women. Most suggests that women and men do not differ in their use of "justice" or "rights" frameworks in understanding moral and social dilemmas, although women *also* seem to use a "caring" framework more than men do. Although women's nurturance is supposed to make them more peace-oriented than men, analysis of

100

Part 1:
Developing
Frameworks for the
Study of Gender
and Society

public reactions to the Gulf War of 1991 shows that while American women were less supportive of military engagement in the Gulf before the war actually began, and they had more negative emotional reactions to it once it did occur, women supported and assessed the war in much the same way as men after it was over (Conover and Sapiro, 1993). No doubt, debates about gender and modes of thinking will continue.

Evaluating Cognitive-Developmental Theory.   Cognitive-developmental theory offers a handle on the growth of gender identity, its associated meanings, and the importance it plays in individual lives. This developmental approach regards the individual as struggling to adapt to or cope with the social and physical world (sometimes labeled *competence strivings*) and to develop and preserve a positive and stable self-image. This struggle leads children to develop gender identity, gender stereotypes, and provides them with a motive to become gender typed early in their lives. Many researchers find utility in the idea of gender as a framework through which people understand themselves and their social environment.

Other aspects of cognitive-developmental theory have been subject to greater attack. The idea of a relatively rigid and universal *stage-and-sequence* process of development is probably the most controversial aspect, and it prompts many important questions: Even if researchers find a general pattern of stage and sequence in development in some groups of people, is that pattern necessarily the same across cultures and classes? At minimum, might it be that the development of some cognitive skills follows a similar path cross-culturally but others do not? Certainly, the debates over moral development illustrate some of the problems in generalization.

Learning Theories

The most widely used approach to understanding how gender differentiation at the individual level occurs posits that people learn how to be male and female from their experiences. Children are *socialized* to become masculine or feminine; that is, they internalize norms from the culture around them, so that these norms become part of each person's identity, character, and patterns of action. Gender socialization occurs as children learn to imitate the models or examples they see in society, and as people reward children for behaving in gender-appropriate ways and punish them for acting otherwise. The social-learning approach to socialization leads researchers to investigate the ways in which *agents* of socialization—such as parents, peers, schools, and the mass media—encourage different types of behavior in males and females.

Development of Difference.   From the perspective of learning theories, the norms of femininity and masculinity originate in the larger culture and society into which a child is born. The child grows up observing these norms in action in the various institutions of society, and many agents of that larger society present in the child's life instill those norms in the developing child in conscious and unconscious ways.

101

Chapter 3:
Individual-Level
Approaches to
Understanding
Women's Lives

It is easy to see the ways in which the important people in children's lives design each child's world in a way that is likely to produce gender-appropriate behavior. From the moment of birth, girls and boys are treated differently, even by their parents. Parents interact with their male and female babies differently in how they respond to their crying, how much they handle and talk to them, and what tone of voice they use toward them. Parents treat baby girls as though they are more fragile than boys, and they treat baby boys as though they are more independent than baby girls. Of course, parents are not the only ones who do this; most other people do, too.

Could it be that parents treat baby girls and boys differently simply because they are different? Mothers and fathers certainly think that baby girls and boys act differently (Karraker, Vogel, and Lake, 1995; Rubin, Provenzano, and Luria, 1974). Research also shows that if a person is told that a baby is a girl or a boy, regardless of what the sex of the child really is, that person is likely to describe the child in "gender-appropriate" terms; that is, they perceive the baby as boyish or girlish, regardless of its real sex. Parents give female and male children different kinds of clothes, games, and books. As the children grow and are given more responsibility within the home, parents begin to teach them gender-appropriate tasks.

Often, this training for gender is neither conscious nor direct. Parents and other agents of socialization may give the child explicit gender messages: "Go and help your mother in the kitchen so when you grow up, you'll be a good mommy, too." "You don't want that toy—that's for girls!" "Don't sit like that —it's not ladylike!" "No, you may not phone Sam. A girl should wait for the boy to phone." More often, the teaching is not explicit or even conscious. Gender-typed toys simply appear. Toys are packaged in boxes depicting children playing with the toys in gender-typed ways. A study of mothers reading stories to their children found evidence that they unconsciously taught their children to think of the male as the norm. In 95% of the cases in which the sex of the character was indeterminant, the mothers referred to the character as a male (DeLoache, Cassidy, and Carpenter, 1987). Parents and other teachers set a constant example. If mommy and daddy are equally capable of driving, but mommy never drives if daddy is in the car, children learn who is supposed to drive the car.

These parental actions make a difference. Fathers' and mothers' own level of gender stereotyping, their preference for traditional family roles, and their encouragement of their children to play with gender-typed toys are associated with how well 2- and 3-year-olds recognize the gender of people in pictures they are shown, and how much the children's own thinking shows gender stereotyping (Fagot and Leinbach, 1989; Fagot, Leinbach, and O'Boyle, 1992; Weinraub et al., 1984). Parents of children who learn gender labeling earlier seem to care about gender typing more than parents of other children (Fagot and Leinbach, 1989). Modeling alone, without systematic reinforcement, may have only limited effect; research on children of gay and lesbian parents, for example, shows that these children do not differ from others in toy or television program preferences, in their relationships with peers, or in their own sexual preferences (Flaks, Ficher, and Masterpasqua, 1995; Patterson, 1992).

102

Part 1:
Developing
Frameworks for the
Study of Gender
and Society

Parents are only the first of many teachers of gender norms that children encounter. As later chapters show, schools, the mass media, the arts, religious institutions, and many others still transmit and enforce important messages about what constitutes appropriate behavior for females and males, both by the example of the people who act within those institutions and by the rules of the game of those institutions. Television still presents very gender-typed messages (Ferrante, Haynes, and Kingsley, 1988); therefore, it is not surprising that the more television children watch, the more gender stereotypic are their attitudes toward jobs (Signorielli and Lears, 1992). Chapter 5 offers many examples of how schools and teachers teach gender to children. A child's friends are also involved in the process of socialization; peer pressure is a very effective source of the enforcement of gender-appropriate behavior. In one study, researchers showed preadolescent boys a video of a boy playing either a masculine game with boys, a feminine game with girls, a neutral game with boys, or a neutral game with girls. The researchers first tested the boys to determine which ones they considered "masculine," "feminine," "androgynous," and "undifferentiated" (see p. 81). All four groups of subjects attributed stereotypically feminine traits and interests to the boy seen playing a feminine game with girls. All the boys except the ones who scored "feminine" on the screening test were most likely to like the boy playing a "masculine" game with a boy, and least likely to like the boy playing a "feminine" game with a girl. It is easy to imagine how the boy regarded as more feminine could be ostracized by the other boys (Lobel, 1994). In another study among elementary school children, boys gave higher friendship ratings to boys who were more male sex typed (Zucker, Wilson-Smith, and Kurita, 1995).

Adolescence is a time when gender learning and differentiation increase, probably because of the increasing physical differentiation of girls and boys as they reach puberty, and the increasing enforcement of difference because of the norms of conforming to idealizations of heterosexual roles at that time. (This change is discussed more in Chapter 11.) Even differentiation in math skills occurs in adolescence, for example. Research on gender-role differentiation in the family shows that children's household tasks become more differentiated in adolescence, and children's activities with the same-sex parent intensify at the same time, as though it is now time to get serious about recruiting girls and boys into the right gender (Crouter, Manke, and McHale, 1995).

Gender Learning After Childhood.   This process of socialization does not stop at the end of childhood. University and occupational training continues the task of gender-role teaching, as do family members and peers. Perhaps even more than during childhood, people expect different things from adult women and men, and they give rewards to people who act as expected and punish those who do not. Women who pursue nontraditional careers or activities often find that the only way they can succeed without tremendous opposition or disapproval is to make sure they also play their more "feminine" roles very carefully.

One study of young adults shows very clearly how the pressure of adult life continues to shape the enactment of gender roles. Even though large numbers of young women (and men) now think that they will follow less traditional, more egalitarian paths than earlier generations did, the pressure of day-to-day adult life still tends to shape their career decisions to reflect the older patterns in which the man's career takes precedence over the woman's (Foster, Wallston, and Berger, 1980; Machung, 1989).

Many women find that their adult family lives, their jobs, and their household commitments shape them in ways they did not expect. They may take a few years off to have children, only to find they never quite get back on track. Because the job market is still segregated, men and women spend their work lives in very different kinds of jobs. Thus, the socialization effects of employment can continue to create increased differentiation by gender. The obligations of child and household care—especially on top of a job—continue to push women away from doing things they might otherwise do.

Adulthood can also be a time in which people who have learned traditional gender and sexual orientations can experience a process of resocialization toward very new and different roles and identities. The feminist movement has been an important agent of socialization to new gender orientations (Sapiro, 1989). In their introduction to a collection of life stories of women in the arts and sciences, for example, Sara Ruddick and Pamela Daniels described the experience of a group of women "educated in the 1950s, at the height of the feminine mystique." This group of women "encountered the women's movement late, usually in [their] thirties" (Ruddick and Daniels, 1977, xxviii). As a result of contact with the women's movement,

All of us have had to relearn our pasts. We have had to reevaluate our purposes in working and review our commitments to our work and to those we love. Raised consciousness, whatever its ultimate value, has brought vulnerability and has invited risk. It has insisted on change. Our stories are the evidence that significant changes can and do occur in adult lives—after we are supposed to be "grown up" and "settled down." (Ruddick and Daniels, 1977, xxix)

In fact, certain influences are likely to have more impact at certain points in a person's life than at others. The women's movement, for example, seems to have had an effect on women of all ages, but it is especially potent when women are in their young adult years, just beginning to experience and formulate their adult ideas and choices (Duncan and Agronick, 1995; Sapiro, 1989).

The Complexity of Learning. The social-learning model of socialization has proven useful in providing insights about how gender differentiation and stratification are maintained from one generation to the next. It is not, however, without its problems. Girls and boys and women and men are not given only one message about how they are supposed to think, feel, and act. The social environment is complex and varied, offering many different values and patterns from which to choose. As parents know only too well, even carefully structuring a child's life so as to enforce certain values does not always work. Moreover, the world itself changes during the course of an individual's lifetime. The fact that no one in the 1930s or 1940s was encouraged to be an astronaut did not mean that no one was available in the late 1950s to fly in space rockets. In fact, one of the norms that children

103

Chapter 3:
Individual-Level
Approaches to
Understanding
Women's Lives

104

Part 1:
Developing
Frameworks for the
Study of Gender
and Society

learn in modern life is not only to expect change but also to participate in it. Young people anticipate that they will differ from their parents' generation in many ways, and they learn to be able to be different. The multiplicity of messages means that the outcome of gender socialization is less predictable than we may sometimes think. People sometimes excuse their behaviors by saying, "Well, I was socialized in this way," as though socialization precludes active, independent thought. It does not.

Perhaps the best caution against using socialization theory as an excuse to maintain the status quo is to review the findings regarding gender differences presented earlier. If social learning had produced unidimensionally "feminine" girls and "masculine" boys, we should be seeing many more differences between males and females in abilities, attitudes, personality characteristics, and behavior. Doubtless, the pressure to conform to gender stereotypes is quite strong, but there is still considerable room for variation. We must be careful to avoid painting a portrait of oversocialized, passive, conforming people.

Synthesizing Cognition and Learning: Gender-Schema Theory and Doing Gender

Some scholars have been trying to combine the insights of cognitive-developmental and social-learning theories to develop approaches that take account of both the internalization or learning of messages received and the useful understanding that cognitive psychologists offer about the ways that perception, mental framing, and memory work. A review of two of these approaches follows: gender schema theory and "doing gender."

Gender Schemas.   Sandra Bem, a leading theorist in this field, defines *schema* as a "network of associations that organizes and guides an individual's perception" (1983, 603); a *gender schema,* therefore, is a network of associations with the concepts of male and female (or masculinity and femininity) that organizes and guides an individual's perception. Bem has noted that these gender-related networks encompass

> not only those features directly related to female and male persons—such as anatomy, reproductive function, division of labor, and personality attributes— but also features more remotely or metaphorically related to sex, such as the angularity or roundedness of an abstract shape and the periodicity of the moon. (1983, 603)

As social-learning theorists argue, the content of the gender schema (the ideas found within it) is learned in large part from interaction with the social environment and the gender-linked practices of the social world. The gender schema is then used by the individual to process information by structuring and organizing perception and by helping the individual to evaluate incoming information (including information about the self) with regard to gender norms. The emphasis on cognitive frameworks and the active role of the mind in learning and processing information reflects cognitive-developmental theory.

105

Chapter 3:
Individual-Level
Approaches to
Understanding
Women's Lives

Consider some research that cognitive psychologists have done on emotions. Most of us feel that our emotions are *natural;* that is, they are our gut reactions, bypassing any real thinking. Most of us find the idea that we can be socialized how to *think* about things quite plausible, but are we also socialized to learn how to *feel?* Yes. Cognitive psychologists demonstrate that we learn frameworks for interpreting the sensations and emotions we feel, and in giving meaning to our emotions, the result is that our emotions are not just natural, but also learned.

One study, for example, investigated the possibility that women feel and report being more emotional because women are culturally expected to be more emotional than men. In this study, people who believed in this stereotype more actually followed the stereotype more. In another part of the same study, when men and women were given instructions leading them to believe that in a particular situation, men's and women's emotional experiences do not differ, no gender differences appeared between the men and the women. When their expectations told them that women should be emotional and men not, their emotions differed (Grossman and Wood, 1993). Research also suggests that men and women think about and explain the nature of certain emotions and emotional reactions differently, which also shows an important cognitive link to emotion. Women tend to understand aggression, for example, as a temporary loss of self-control, while men see it as an instrumental act of coercion (Campbell, Muncer, Guy, and Banim, 1996). If they understand emotion differently, they are likely to feel it and express it differently.

Children have already begun to learn the figurative or metaphorical meanings of gender by age 3 years. As one set of researchers concluded in a study in which very young children distributed toys in conventionally gender-appropriate ways, including giving bears to boys and cats to girls, children learn an underlying framework for understanding the nature of masculine and feminine that does not depend on the specific models having appeared in their environment. As they learn some basic information about gender, they become increasingly adept at generalizing it to different situations.

> Few men keep bears, and cats do not belong only to women. Rather, it appears that children, like the rest of us, make inferences on the basis of what they see or know about the nature of things. Children, even at these early ages, may have begun to connect certain qualities with males and other qualities with females. (Fagot, Leinbach, and Boyle, 1992, 229)

Even in childhood, these frameworks or schemas shape perception; highly gender-typed children cannot remember details of stories that are inconsistent with traditional gender stereotypes as well as other children can. In one study, not only could first-graders remember gender-typed information better, but they also tended to reconstruct the gender-inappropriate stories in memory to conform more closely to gender stereotypes, and their reconstruction of the story was even stronger when children talked about the stories 7 days later (Carlsson and Jaderquist, 1983). Other research shows that children have more trouble remembering materials that run against the stereotyping grain. Memory selectively recalls what we expected to see in the first place (Liben and Signorella, 1993).

106

Part 1:
Developing
Frameworks for the
Study of Gender
and Society

Selective memory and perception based on gender stereotype continues into adulthood, as Claudia Cohen's (1981) research on person perception and memory shows. After showing her subjects a short movie that identified the main character's occupation, including some details that conformed to their stereotypes and some that did not, she asked the subjects in her experiment to tell her what they remembered about the movie. She found that her subjects "were selectively more accurate in remembering those characteristics that fit their prototype than those features that were inconsistent with the target person's occupation" (1981, 447). These are only some examples of research showing that people remember gender-consistent information better than gender-inconsistent information. Men's gender expectations seem to bias their perceptions of other people more than women's do (Christenson and Rosenthal, 1982).

The degree to which people's mental frameworks for understanding the world are shaped by gender varies from person to person. As psychologists in this field say, people are not equally *gender schematic* or gender schematic under the same circumstances. Some people organize many of their thoughts, perceptions, and evaluations around concepts of male and female, masculine and feminine. These people, whom we might describe as highly gender-typed or gender schematic, see a wide variety of human characteristics, behavior, roles, and jobs as decidedly masculine or feminine and evaluate themselves and others according to how well each person conforms to gender norms and stereotypes.

Other people follow gender schemas less closely or not at all, such that psychologists would say they are *gender aschematic*. This does not necessarily mean that they lack what the highly gender-typed person might regard as appropriate masculine and feminine characteristics. Gender may simply not be the central means by which they organize their perceptions of themselves and the social world. Whereas the highly gender-typed person might immediately understand words such as *pink, nurturant, blushing, librarian,* and *curved* as "feminine," these words might not have any immediate gender connotation to the person without a gender schema.

People's level of gender schematicity affects how they see and treat other people. When preschoolers are trying to remember toys they have seen, those preschoolers who are high on gender schematicity cluster toys by gender associations more than do preschoolers low on gender schematicity (Levy, 1994). When adults are asked to remember a conversation, those who describe themselves in highly gender-schematic ways are more likely to make mistakes remembering which person of the other sex (as compared with their own sex) said what. Adults whose self-description does not conform to traditional male or female stereotypes were equally likely to make mistakes about people of their own or the other sex. The title of the research report said it all: "If you are gender schematic, all members of the opposite sex look alike" (Frable and Bem, 1985).[3]

Gender schemas are not just used to organize perception of and thinking about *other* people; people also use these schemas to integrate *self*-understanding (Markus, Crane, Bernstein, and Siladi, 1982). People differ not just in how they describe themselves, but also in the degree to which gender serves as one of the major frameworks for thinking about and evaluating themselves.

Doing Gender.   Discussion of gender schemas focuses our attention on the way we think about gender. It is clear, however, that gender is more than ideas and symbols. It involves action and interaction, behavior that displays and even asserts femininity, masculinity, or the rejection of these concepts. Recognition of the importance of action, interaction, and display has led Candace West and Don H. Zimmerman (1987) to write about "doing gender." They argue that "a person's gender is not simply an aspect of what one is, but, more fundamentally, it is something that one *does,* and does recurrently, in interaction with others" (140). Gender, they contend, is not just a matter of roles that have been learned and are repeated automatically; it involves continual work to reproduce gender in everyday behavior. Because gender is an important basis for social organization, doing gender, even while we are engaged in other activities, helps define our place and keep social relations orderly.

Women may be especially aware of doing gender while they are deciding how to dress for specific situations each day. How "feminine" should one appear at a job interview? At work? It depends on the job and the special circumstances. The same woman may highlight her gender much more forcefully when dressing to go to a party than when she goes to work. Sometimes, deciding how much to do gender takes very careful thought.

Gender-schema theory can be used to understand the meanings (and variability of meanings) of gender, while Zimmerman and West's notion of doing gender reminds us of the effort and activity it takes to learn and display (or refuse to display) our gender. The insights of cognitive-developmental theory can contribute to understanding the relationship between identity and gender meanings. This theory emphasizes that individuals actively participate in their own socialization and in their everyday maintenance or violation of gender expectations. Social-learning theory, on the other hand, focuses our attention on the social order and the means by which social interaction imposes rules and meaning.

A Summary of Learning Theories.   Learning theories of all sorts offer a way of connecting individuals into the larger sex/gender system. Agents and institutions of the larger society and culture transmit certain gender norms to the society's members. As this book shows repeatedly, however, just studying the apparent *messages* of a society does not give a full understanding of what people *learn*. As the multiplicity of different religions and denominations that use the same Bible shows, one text yields many messages (including what it says about gender), depending on the eye of the beholder. Students of human cognition and learning examine how this happens.

Research on most areas of human society suggest that the amount of gender inequality and, indeed, differentiation in the United States is at a historically low point, although it has far from disappeared. The American public is less prejudiced against women than it used to be, and people (especially women) hold fewer gender-based stereotypes than they used to hold. In fact, psychologist Janet Swim published a controversial study in which she compared meta-analyses of gender differences in personality with people's perceptions of gender differences. She concluded that *overall*, people have pretty accurate general perceptions of where there

107

Chapter 3:
Individual-Level
Approaches to
Understanding
Women's Lives

108

Part 1:
Developing
Frameworks for the
Study of Gender
and Society

are and are not gender differences in personality and of how strong those differences are (Swim, 1994). As mentioned previously, however, people have different levels of gender schematicity and different levels of gender-related prejudice. Most research suggests that people who are high in gender schematicity or gender prejudice will perceive gender differently from other people.

Indeed, Janet Swim (1994) and her colleagues have argued that because of historical changes, the nature of gender prejudice has changed. They argue that old-fashioned sexism—the kind that led people to claim that women should stay at home all their adult lives doing traditional feminine things, or to think that women were only good for being mommies or contestants in wet T-shirt contests—has declined over the years, although it has not disappeared. In its place, they see a modern sexism, which still functions as an antiwoman prejudice but does not necessarily endorse many of the traditional elements of sexism. Modern sexism, they argue, incorporates denial that women still face any discrimination, antagonism toward women's demands, and a lack of support for policies designed to help women overcome historical prejudices and discrimination.

Swim and her colleagues did an interesting study in which they compared what kinds of jobs their subjects thought women have, depending on whether the subjects displayed low or high modern sexism. The question was, What proportion of physicians, police officers, lawyers, engineers, architects, and airplane pilots, for example, are women? All of these are very heavily male-dominated fields, with positions ranging from only 2% of women among pilots and 8% among engineers, to 20% among physicians and 21% among lawyers. Both groups of subjects—those high and low in modern sexism—overestimated how many women were in these professions. They thought the world is more equal than it really is. However, the subjects who were high in modern sexism were even more likely to overestimate how equal is the situation that women face. They were also much less likely to believe that the reason for women's small numbers in these fields is prejudice; they were much more likely than the low-sexism subjects to ascribe women's situation to "tradition" (Swim, Aikin, Hall, and Hunter, 1995).

Institutional Theories and Discrimination

Up to this point, we have emphasized the ways in which individuals develop gendered character, cognitive frameworks, or styles of action and interaction through learning or internalizing cultural norms. Here, we explore another explanation: Men and women do not just *learn* to be different or *choose* to be different but are *forced* to be different. In the learning perspective, we might argue that because of their experiences in life, women learn to prefer and be better at some jobs, while men learn to prefer and be better at others. Thus, women and men enter different jobs because, for whatever reason, they choose to do so. According to the institutional approaches, women are forced either into or out of certain roles and activities because of the requirements they must meet in the various social institutions in which women operate, the rules of the game, and the treatment they receive, including discrimination that bars their way to certain goals.

The distinction between the learning theories and the more institutional approaches is important: If we argue that most differences between the lives of

109

Chapter 3:
Individual-Level
Approaches to
Understanding
Women's Lives

Supreme Court justice Ruth Bader Ginsburg and Senator Diane Feinstein have spent their careers fighting to end discrimination.

women and men develop because they have *learned* to choose different paths, we arrive at one set of solutions to the problem of gender differentiation and stratification; if we find that, regardless of what people have learned, they take different roles because they are *forced* to do so through discrimination, the solutions will have to be different.

The verb *discriminate* is derived from the Latin *discernere,* meaning "to distinguish between." Not all forms of discrimination are necessarily bad. In art and music, for example, we talk about the discriminating eye or ear. We discriminate between children and adults in meting out punishment. The type of discrimination with which we are concerned here, however, is not so commendable. Our use of the word refers to the act of singling out a person for special treatment, not on the basis of individual merit, but on the basis of prejudices about the group to which that person belongs. When a woman is barred from a job or receives relatively low pay because she happens to be a woman, not because she lacks ability, we say that she has been discriminated against on the basis of sex.

At one time, many graduate and professional schools explicitly required higher entrance qualifications from women than from men. Many employers announced their jobs as designed for men or women but not both. Now it is illegal to discriminate in jobs or education on the basis of sex. Still, many employers and

110

Part 1:
Developing
Frameworks for the
Study of Gender
and Society

schools or departments would prefer to rule out women in some areas on the grounds that few women are likely to be qualified. These people might claim that they are not discriminating; they are only looking for qualified people. As long as these employers automatically rule out women, however, and do not consider women on the basis of individual merit, these employers are discriminating, and according to the 1964 Civil Rights Act, they are engaging in an illegal activity.

A person does not have to be conscious of what he or she is doing to discriminate. Unconscious discrimination is more difficult to identify than conscious discrimination, however. None of us always sees people objectively; as the discussion of gender schemas suggested, our expectations of people affect how we see them. In other words, people apply the beliefs and attitudes they hold about a *group* of people to individual members of that group. These group-based beliefs or attitudes are *stereotypes*. They become the basis for discrimination when employers, for example, perceive a woman as not likely to be capable of strong leadership because she happens to be a woman and the employers believe that women in general are not capable of leadership.

As Chapter 1 pointed out, it is difficult to detect when discrimination is happening. If I am not hired for a job, how do I know the reason? In interpersonal relations, if someone treats me as though I tend to be overemotional and fly off the handle at unpredictable times, how do I know whether this is because (a) I fly off the handle unpredictably, (b) this person always treats everyone that way, or (c) this person treats women that way because of the stereotypes he has learned? Numerous studies have investigated the possibility that people see women and men and their qualifications differently even when they are objectively the same.

One of the most widely used research designs follows a model first used by Philip Goldberg in 1968: The subjects are asked to evaluate an essay, speech, job application, piece of artwork, or musical composition. All subjects are given the same work to evaluate, but some are told that a man created the work, and some are told that a woman did. Many of these experiments (although not including Goldberg's) found evidence of prejudice against women. A meta-analysis of 123 such studies concluded that the evidence does not show simply that women are evaluated more negatively than men because of the great differences in the results of these studies. The meta-analytic study concluded, "Gender-biased evaluations indeed occur, but the complexity of the conditions under which such evaluations occur and the flexibility of social perceivers' thinking must be taken into consideration" (Swim, Borgida, Maruyama, and Myers, 1989, 424).

These experiments suggest that people are more likely to be prejudiced in their evaluations if the situation or activity is stereotypically masculine. Also, the more information people are given about an individual, the less they rely on stereotypes (Swim, Borgida, Maruyama, and Myers, 1989). Discrimination is particularly likely to emerge in evaluations involved in hiring decisions (Glick, Zion, and Nelson, 1988). In addition, some research finds men more likely to be prejudiced against women than women are (e.g., Sapiro, 1982b).

These types of research suggest two things: (1) People who discriminate may not know they are doing so, and (2) it may be very difficult to identify cases in which discrimination has occurred. Considerable evidence suggests that there is sex discrimination in job and education counseling, letters of recommendation,

111

Chapter 3:
Individual-Level
Approaches to
Understanding
Women's Lives

BOX 3-1   See for Yourself:
How Do You Know When You Are Facing Discrimination?

Most people have some characteristic that makes them subject to some forms of stereotyping, prejudice, and discrimination under certain circumstances. You may be a woman. Or nonWhite in a White society. Or working class in a middle-class setting. You might be gay or a member of a religion that is not very common in your part of the country, or you might "have an accent" or be very overweight or short, much older than people doing what you do, or maybe you can't walk or have trouble hearing.

Has anyone ever discriminated against you? How do you know? Have you ever suspected someone was treating you in a prejudiced way? How did you sort through your impressions?

How much discrimination do you think there is against women? Against any of the groups mentioned above? How do you know?

and evaluations that affect the hiring, salary, and promotion of individuals. How much discrimination is there? As long as discrimination can occur unconsciously, and most of the important decisions about people are made confidentially, no one can know.

Feminists are sometimes criticized for blaming any women's lack of success on discrimination. Research on people's perception of discrimination against themselves and their reactions to facing discrimination shows that women have a psychological tendency *not* to perceive discrimination against themselves. Subjects in an experiment, for example, were given a task to do. Some were then told that the person judging their work always discriminates against women, while others were told that their judge sometimes discriminates (different subjects were given different probabilities). Finally, all were told that they were judged to have "failed" in the task. Those who had been told they almost certainly would face discrimination blamed discrimination for their failure. The others tended to blame themselves for their failure, and they limited the blame placed on discrimination. In other words, the women were not just using any excuse to blame discrimination for their failure. (See Box 3-1.) Further research showed that the reason women do not seem to go out of their way to attribute their problems to discrimination is that blaming discrimination places the control for outcomes in their lives in the hands of other people. If people look to themselves for reasons, they may find a way of controlling their own destiny (Ruggiero and Taylor, 1995).

Institutions have an impact on gender differentiation and inequality, not just through discrimination, but through the roles people are expected to play and the rules of the game they are expected to follow. Many scholars have argued that people's common patterns of behavior come not just from general norms they have learned, but from the demands of specific roles they play. Whether or not women happen to have particularly nurturant personalities to begin with, if they are put in the institutional position where it is their job, and not men's, to take care of children, the fact of the matter is that they *will nurture*. Further, in playing that role, they will act the part and, in fact, learn norms from their own behavior.

112

Part 1:
Developing
Frameworks for the
Study of Gender
and Society

One set of scholars had their subjects monitor themselves for 20 days and keep a diary of their behavior. The researchers sought to examine gender differences in *agency*—that is, acting instrumentally and individually, a trait usually ascribed as masculine—and *communion*—getting along with others and acting to support connections. Because a common way to emphasize communion is to be agreeable and nondominant, it is often ascribed especially as feminine. The research found that agency and communion are not just traits people carry around internally; these traits also have to do with the demand characteristics of particular roles and situations within a social or organizational structure. Thus, although women were more communal, regardless of their role (especially with other women), women and men both exhibited the most agency when they were with someone they supervised at work and the most communion when they were with their boss (Moskowitz, Suh, and Desualnier, 1994). If, because of the distribution of women within social institutions, women are more likely to spend more time with super-ordinates than with subordinates, they are more likely then to display more communion more often, regardless of their general psychological inclinations.

Finally, the effects of institutions may have simply to do with the rules the institutions enforce. Consider both formal and informal changes in the system of social welfare. Under what conditions can a poor mother get government assistance to feed her child? For most of this century, the cultural norm was that women should stay home with their children, and that one of the problems with poor mothers is that they needed to be more attentive to their children. The social program Aid to Families with Dependent Children (AFDC) therefore assumed that women should be helped to be with their children, and enforcement agents expected recipients generally not to be employed, or at least not employed for long hours. Norms have changed now, and women in U.S. society expect—and are generally expected—to hold jobs. At the same time, the public has become less sympathetic with the poor and more frustrated with the cost of government. In 1996, this normative shift caused a change in the AFDC program, which now requires women to be employed in order to receive their benefits; if they cannot find a paying job, they are put to work by government programs anyway, supposedly to earn their benefits. Thus, how poor women act out their gendered lives as mothers has changed not so much because they have been socialized any differently than before, but because the institutions of society have now established a different incentive structure, which makes them act differently.

Individual Development and Social Change

This chapter has described six broad approaches people use to explain the existence of differences between women and men at the individual level. Each is based on a different type of research and evidence, employs different assumptions, and comes to different conclusions. Which of these theories is "correct"? The answer is that no single theory completely explains the process of gender-role development and differentiation. Each has drawbacks, and each focuses on a slightly different aspect of the problem. These different approaches are by no means mutually exclusive; one can argue, for example, that psychoanalytic theories explain some aspects of gender development, cognitive-development theories others, and discrimination theories still others. These different theories can provide complementary insights that fill in the whole picture. The task for the student of gender development is to learn to evaluate and use these theories skillfully and appropriately. These theories of individual differences also need to be integrated with the theories of social differentiation and stratification reviewed in Chapter 2.

We began this chapter by observing the distinction between societal-level theories and individual-level theories. Thus, the theories used for explaining how a given society's sex/gender system evolves and is maintained do not necessarily tell us how individuals in the given society come to fit or not fit into that system. By the same token, theories that explain how individual gender development occurs do not tell us how the society as a whole comes to be structured in a particular way. The theories offered in this chapter may help us understand why so many young women today will become secretaries, rather than business executives. They do not, however, tell us why, in this century, secretaries have usually been women, although in the nineteenth century, they were usually men; nor do these theories tell why, since secretarial positions have come to be primarily female jobs, they have fewer promotion prospects than do lower-level business jobs held predominantly by men. Societal-level theories can help explain how and why the institution of marriage came to be based on patriarchal norms (and why those norms seem to be threatened now), and how the institution of marriage is linked to other social, political, and economic structures of society. Individual theories suggest some of the reasons why most women continue to participate in those arrangements, and why some do not. (For further explanation, see Chapter 10.)

Women's studies scholars are interested, therefore, in the insights offered by both the societal theories outlined in Chapter 2 and the individual theories outlined in this chapter because these scholars investigate both the historical development of sex/gender systems and the development of individuals within given societies. For this reason, each of the following chapters of this book includes discussion of both levels of analysis.

Notes

1. Many of these reviews are in the form of *meta-analyses,* in which researchers use statistical techniques to summarize the findings of many different specific studies.
2. This 1967 book is a compilation of papers Horney wrote between 1922 and 1936.
3. For purposes of this discussion, I am contrasting those who, on the BSRI scale used, were either gender-typed or cross-gender-typed, with those who are androgynous or aschematic.

113

Chapter 3:
Individual-Level
Approaches to
Understanding
Women's Lives

4

Commonality and Difference Among Women

At the end of the tour I purchased [General] Beauregard's biography and paid a dollar extra for a sheet detailing his family tree. The tour guide said, "You certainly asked a lot of questions, young lady. Do you have a particular interest in our general?" I responded, "Not exactly. It's the general who has an interest in me—a property interest. General Beauregard was my great-great-grandfather." The intake of breath was audible. "Those pictures of his children on the wall, those were only his White children. The general had Black children as well, including my maternal grandmother Susan," I said. . . . Our gracious guide did not even blink: "Well, we'd heard rumors that the general was like the other Southern gentlemen of his time. But we're not allowed to discuss it."

Adrien Katherine Wing (1997, 29–30)

THE MAJOR PREMISE OF WOMEN'S STUDIES—and of this book—is that we can use the concept of gender to organize important aspects of our knowledge of the social world. The idea of a sex/gender system leads us to suppose that whatever else also shapes social life, societies are structured in such a way as to make something of the sex into which people were born. We investigate the ways in which societies accommodate, build on, institutionalize, and give significance to biological sex. Thus, women's studies scholars tend to focus on differences between men's and women's character, thinking, and behavior, or the ways in which men and women are perceived, interpreted, and treated. The obvious implication of all this is that we can make meaningful generalizations about women (and also men) as groups. We have already explored claims about aspects of history and day-to-day social existence that affect women as women and men as men in specific, gendered ways.

This chapter considers the significance of an obvious but crucial fact of life for the study of gender: Almost anyone past the age of 6 could hypothetically divide most of the people on Earth into two groups, one labeled *women* and one labeled *men*. However, differences *among* the people labeled one way or the other are so profound and numerous that it seems difficult indeed to make any meaningful generalizations about either collectivity. Even when narrowing the focus to one nation or one community, a realistic look at gender and gender difference shows that they are crisscrossed and complicated by the simultaneous existence of other important structural bases of social life, such as race and ethnicity, class, age, and religion, to name just a few.

Are the differences between the lives of rich and poor women or Unitarians and fundamentalist Muslims or lesbians and heterosexual women so great that they render our concepts of *gender* and *women* useless? Or are these differences so trivial that we can talk about the "average" woman without wondering whether she is African-American, Hmong-American, or Swedish-American; whether she is the current women's title holder at Wimbledon or in an advanced stage of multiple sclerosis; whether she is just reaching puberty or long past menopause?

These and related questions discussed in this chapter have both *analytical* and *political* significance. The *analytical* question was just posed: Can we understand women, or the significance of gender in women's or men's lives if we do not also understand and take account of the other crucial bases of social life? The answer offered here is that sex/gender systems both depend on and shape other aspects of social structure and identity, such as race and ethnicity and class. The *political* significance of differences among women is related to the claims made by feminist and antifeminist political groups alike. Both feminists and nonfeminists claim that they can speak on behalf of women and their interests. However, this claim assumes that there is some underlying commonality of interest that can be represented. We must probe those commonalities and differences to have any idea what it means to act for or on behalf of women. This throws us back to the analytical question: For our understanding of gender, what difference does difference among women make?

Even though our primary focus is the nature of sex/gender systems, we have four reasons for analyzing these social divisions: (1) to recognize the variety of lives women lead, (2) to evaluate the different ways that sex/gender systems affect people, (3) to untangle the effects of different stratification systems on people, and (4) to understand the impact of the multiple contexts of people's lives. The remainder of this chapter looks at how the study of social divisions other than gender helps us to understand gender, sex/gender systems, and women's lives.

Recognizing Difference

The obvious truth is that women live many different kinds of lives, and to understand women, we must understand these differences. The more women's studies scholars think about how to do this, however, the more they find they have had to work hard to eliminate the blinders that make these differences and their significance difficult to see. Consider, for instance, the claim feminist scholars make about those whose perceptions of women are shaped by androcentric perspectives. We claim that group-based stereotypes distort the ability to understand women, partly by making it difficult to comprehend the variation in women's characters,

116

Part 1:
Developing
Frameworks for the
Study of Gender
and Society

abilities, and experiences. Indeed, psychological research shows that people who think of themselves in terms of gender stereotypes have trouble telling people of the other sex apart (Frable and Bem, 1985).

Critics charge that feminist scholars have *also* homogenized women, or over-generalized about them. Most traditional (nonfeminist) scholarship was blind to the experiences and perspectives of women, partly because women had little influence in the creation of that scholarship. Similarly, much of women's studies scholarship has been blind to the experiences of women other than middle-class, White women—that is, blind to the perspectives of the women who have had the least influence in the academy. Many scholars have detected pervasive race, class, and other biases in women's studies research (e.g., Hull et al., 1982; Spelman, 1988).

Is it strange that scholars who themselves put so much effort into thinking about equality are themselves subject to charges of prejudice and stereotype? Neither historical nor psychological research reveals any mechanism for assuring that someone who is consciously antisexist will necessarily be antiracist (or vice versa). Adrienne Rich has traced the unfortunate irony that leads many White feminists to reveal their racism just when they are trying to be antiracist (Rich, 1979). Feminists historically emphasize sisterhood and the commonalities of women's lives. Many White feminists have been so eager to emphasize their common womanhood and equality with Black women that they have ignored or denied race-based differences in their histories, experiences, and perspectives. In addition, this overgeneralization of commonality is usually framed in a very ethnocentric way; that is, the observer generalizes solely from her own perceptions, feelings, experiences, and aspirations. Whites in a White-dominated society do not usually experience themselves as having "race" or "color." In such a society, when a White person says she is "color blind," it usually seems to mean that she sees everyone as "White like me,"[1] rather like men who think it is a compliment to tell a woman she "thinks like a man."

Sensitivity to one kind of inequality simply does not naturally lead to sensitivity about any other kind. History offers many examples of racist and class-biased feminist movements, sexist and racist labor organizations, and sexist movements for racial or ethnic equality. Some White women's suffrage leaders made very racist statements in defense of the vote for native-born White women, claiming that these women could then help outvote the immigrant and the "colored" vote (Kraditor, 1965). Indeed, although the Ku Klux Klan (KKK) has not supported equality between White Protestant women and men, early in the 20th century, it claimed belief "in the purity of womanhood and in the fullest measure of freedom compatible with the highest type of womanhood including the suffrage" (Blee, 1991, 49).

Many national or ethnic liberation movements restricted women and their roles in the service of the apparent interests of the group as a whole (Enloe, 1989; Jayawardena, 1986; Sapiro, 1993a). Movements based on race, class, or ethnic solidarity face many pressures to appear and, indeed, to perceive themselves as completely unified and undivided. They often see women's movements as secondary or divisive and detrimental to the good of that group or of society. Workers' organizations historically have argued that separate women's organizations divide the working class, and that women's problems will be solved anyway when the problems of labor and capital are relieved. Some writers, such as E. Frances White (1990), worry that the particular way in which Black nationalism and African-

American social identity is being developed hinders the ability to see differences within the community and acts to the detriment of understanding women's problems. Many African-American leaders have argued that separate Black women's organizations are divisive to the organization of Blacks, and that Black women's problems will be solved anyway when Blacks as a group become free and equal to Whites. The same argument has been made within the Chicano movement (Mirandé and Enríquez, 1979). Leaders of primarily White and middle-class groups use similar arguments when they claim that the most important social ills are *human* problems, and that distinct organizations of women are divisive and misguided.

Many leaders of various movements argue that the "woman problem" may be a problem for *other* social groups—but not theirs. Middle-class representatives argue that working-class families suffer the most patriarchal norms, and working-class activists claim that the middle class foists the ideal of feminine fragility on women. Black activists have pointed to the long history of Black female employment and the image of the strong Black mother to show that feminism is a White problem. Chicano activists claim that behind the stereotype of machismo is veneration for the Chicana, who holds social life and the family together as the Anglo mother no longer does. Christians attempt to prove that theirs is the liberated group by pointing to the New Testament declaration that there is "neither male nor female," and Jews point out that because Judaism is a home-based religion, women's leadership in the home gives them a unique power and authority. Meanwhile, in none of these groups do women have the range of opportunities men have, and in none of them are women who are trying to support themselves and their families paid as much as men. These various groups seem to be able to agree about one thing: Women who try to organize women on behalf of their own quality of life are out of line.

Thus, analyzing and comparing women in different social groups can reveal important differences but also commonalities in women's lives that might otherwise be ignored. Just as conventional history has simply left women out of the picture, focusing only on men and on men's experiences, so it has often happened that women who are not part of dominant social groups are simply left out altogether. Women's historians, for example, have revealed the tremendous number of women involved in volunteer and public-service groups in the late 19th century, but for a long time, it seemed as though this was a White, middle-class phenomenon simply because historians had paid less attention to the participation by, for example, African-American and working-class White women. In fact, volunteer work was *not* just a middle-class White phenomenon (Knupfer, 1995). In any case, it is not possible to understand women's lives without considering these differences. For this reason, there has been a tremendous growth in research in many disciplines, focused on specific groups of women, and an increasing amount of research that offers comparisons among different groups of women.

The Differential Impact of Sex/Gender Systems

Studying difference among women gives us a more accurate picture of the experiences of women. In the preceding two chapters, however, we have been trying to probe a more theoretical or analytical question than this descriptive one. Rather than just describing what different women's lives look like, we are trying to understand what role gender plays in shaping women's lives. Looking at difference among women underscores a crucial point: Arguing that there is a sex/gender system that structures women's experiences does not imply that all women are affected by this system in the same way, any more than arguing that there is a political or economic system in a country means that it affects all social groups the same way. To understand how gender affects women's lives, we have to see how those effects are mediated by other social differences. To understand how a sex/gender system affects women, we have to see how it affects different women differently.

The View from the Dominant System

The structure of a sex/gender system is composed of the underlying rules and norms that determine how *male* and *female, masculinity* and *femininity* are defined; what expectations are made of men and women on the basis of their gender; and how they, their behavior, their work, and their ideas are treated. To begin, we imagine a very simple androcentric sex/gender system. In such a system, all women might be expected to be passive and submissive to men's will, feminine in the manner suggested by early 1960s situation comedies and family shows; these women would be required only to do as they are told, reproduce, and take care of the house. Any woman who deviated from this pattern would be punished and would never be allowed any benefits from the system. For example, if a woman were too sexually active, she would never be able to attract a husband, or at least not one who could offer her the rewards of the system.

Even under this very simple sex/gender system in which all women are judged by the same narrow standards, not all women will have the same experiences, and they will not be affected in the same way in their day-to-day lives. The most obvious point is that women who *will not* or *cannot* fulfill the expectations for femininity will be affected very differently from those who both will and can. The simple but important fact is that if women are rewarded for being dependent on and deferential toward men, both women who conform to that norm and women who do not are caught in that same system; they are treated differently and their experiences are different *because* of this one system. The prostitute and the traditional wife, the lesbian and the married heterosexual woman are judged by the same values. In fact, one of the social mechanisms for controlling the lives of traditionally married women is their fear of being treated like a lesbian or a prostitute if they violate the behavioral norms expected of them.

Thus, at minimum, the stereotypic images of women are double-sided: one image for women who fulfill the cultural ideal of proper womanhood, and one for those who do not—one for the good girls, and one for the bad girls. Feminist observers of Western society have long argued that a central double image of woman may be drawn from Christian imagery: On the one side is Mary, the asexual, self-sacrificing, moral mother, devoted to caring for her family, and on the other is Eve, the sexual, morally weak temptress responsible for the fall of man. There are many cultural variations on this theme, but the central point is that the more moral mother is the preferred ideal, while the sexual object deserves whatever bad consequences she gets. Although only one of these images is the *ideal* for women, both are culturally regarded as desirable to men, but for obviously different purposes. Thus, there is in fact pressure on women to conform both to the ideal and to its flip side.

Very few—if any—sex/gender systems are as simple as that just described. The norms of most human communities are complex, nuanced, and incomplete. Even those societies governed self-consciously by leaders attempting to enforce very narrowly specified gender norms for women, as in the more conservative Islamic countries, are more complicated than they appear to outsiders at first (MacLeod, 1991).

Closer inspection of recognizable and dominant sets of cultural norms defining male and female usually reveals contingencies based on situation, place, and other definers of social membership and status. These contingencies relate to the concept of "doing gender," discussed in Chapter 3. Any woman who attempts to fulfill cultural requirements of femininity knows that dress and demeanor are important aspects of doing gender properly. However, she also knows that she cannot appropriately "do gender" in exactly the same way in different settings. To display feminine dress and demeanor appropriately in different situations or settings in the course of a day, she must change her clothes and behavior. She is expected to be feminine, but the definition of *feminine* is contingent on the situation and the setting.

The norms and rules of sex/gender systems also include contingencies based on women's social identity and status. In the 19th century and the early 20th century United States, the cult of true womanhood, which idealized femininity in terms of passivity, delicacy, and moral superiority, could apply fully only to White women—and native-born, Protestant, middle- and upper-class White women at that. Dominant views of ideal femininity were in fact unattainable for *most* women, not just because only in wealthy families could women scorn hard labor and display the requisite frailty, but also because women who *were not* White northern European in origin were defined by those who *were* as being naturally incapable of achieving the ideal. Indeed, in the 19th century, working-class and poor women, even when they were White, northern European, and Protestant, were widely believed to be naturally inferior and incapable of attaining full ideal femininity.

Whites who were relatively progressive rejected these ideas of natural inferiority. Middle- and upper-class reformers throughout the country (for example, missionaries in the southern and western areas of the country) often tried to help nonWhite and immigrant women learn how to achieve the ideal. Two little-known examples include some schools for young Native American women (Trennert, 1988) and the efforts of German Jewish women to integrate newer Eastern European Jewish immigrant women into appropriate roles and character (Sinkoff, 1988). Of course, although these reform efforts were well-intentioned, they were often based on the idea that only one form of femininity—the reformers' own—was morally and socially acceptable. Thus, while hoping to free another group of women, those involved in reform movements often also helped perpetuate restricted views of femininity.

The fact that most 19th-century women could not live the life that some relatively wealthy White women led does not mean that they were unaffected by the cult of domesticity. The feminine image fostered by this view became an unreachable goal to which women often aspired, despite their circumstances. For those

120

Part 1:
Developing
Frameworks for the
Study of Gender
and Society

women, such as Black women, whose aspirations were futile because of racism, the image must have had especially devastating effects (hooks, 1981, 48; Perkins, 1983). Their attempts to fulfill the requirements of the predominant definition of femininity after emancipation were met by the racial hatred of Whites. As hooks has observed, "A Black woman dressed tidy and clean, carrying herself in a dignified manner, was usually the object of mudslinging by White men who ridiculed and mocked her self-improvement efforts" (p. 55). Aspiring women from most subordinate social groups were also chastised for reaching "above their station," or "putting on airs."

In complex societies marked by stratification and gender divisions of labor, the sex/gender system is composed of a *plurality of gender-based stereotypes* and expectations that depend on other aspects of social position and identity. As this chapter has shown, there may be a central, widely unattainable ideal that can be met only by women with the highest status, but the dominant society also develops stereotypes and expectations aimed specifically at women in different social positions. Despite the great variety of American Indian communities and the many different roles women play in those communities, White American society historically imagined Native American women either as silent, oppressed, laboring squaws or as romantic and noble princesses, described in the popular stories of Pocahontas (Clinton, 1985; Shoemaker, 1994; Tsosie, 1988). African-American women came to be characterized as either promiscuous, earthy women who could be used as beasts of burden, or as Mammy, a loyal member of a White household with a special knowledge of nature and children (Clinton, 1985). The late 20th century has added another African-American female figure: the welfare cheat, placing burdens on the system through having uncontrollable numbers of children for whom she cannot care or provide.

Esther Ngan-Ling Chow (1987) has offered further examples from the stereotyped views of Asian-American women, defined in a variety of closely related roles: Suzie Wong, geisha, picture bride, and sexpot. In each case, the definition of the Asian-American woman depends on both race and sex. These stereotypes often come together with colonialist myths, fostering male fantasies that serve as the basis of the frightening racialized sexual harassment that Asian-American women receive. As a result, Asian-American women find themselves victims of education and employment discrimination *despite* the popular image of being the model minority (Cho, 1997). Jewish women have their choice of stereotypes: the domineering, stifling "Jewish mother," or the bitchy, self-centered "Jewish princess."

Neither gender nor race nor ethnicity alone is sufficient to understand most women's situation. In each case, scholars have noted, the special characters of the stereotypes are not just accidents. These stereotypes serve the ideological needs of both an androcentric structure of power relations and the racial/ethnic structure of power by not just *describing* these power relations but *justifying* them. The cast of subculturally differentiated female characters could be extended indefinitely by turning to depictions based on other ethnic/racial groups or on socioeconomic class, sexuality, geographic region, or other aspects of sociocultural diversity. Lillian Faderman (1991) and Donna Penn (1991), among others, have written about the historical development of stereotypes of lesbian women during the 20th century, including the pervasive view that lesbians can either be categorized as "butch," in which case they are hypermasculine predators of other women, or "femme," the feminized victim who might be rescued from homosexuality if the right man came along. The construction of female (and male) gender is also partly determined by region, as in the case of the Southern belle (Clinton, 1985; Silber, 1989), the Boston "bluestocking," the "gentle tamer" of the West, the "madonna of the Plains," or the "tall woman" and the "mountain belle" of Appalachia (Mathews, 1987). Many of these variations are described later in this chapter and book.

Evelyn Nakano Glenn's (1992) research on service work offers an excellent example of the *institutionalization* of specific racial–ethnic norms of womanhood. She has reminded us that woman's central role has been defined as both physical and social reproduction, or the "creation and re-creation of people as cultural and social, as well as physical beings" (Glenn, 1992, 4). This role means having responsibility for the care of (but not the financial provision for) the household and the people within it.

Glenn has pointed out, however, an important contradiction in the expectations placed on women, which arose from the 19th-century cult of womanhood: Domestic labor is, in many respects, dirty, difficult, labor-intensive work, especially in a society without electricity. The image of the "domestic angel," therefore, is largely inconsistent with the actual domestic labor that is required to keep homes in the preferred domestic order. It should be no surprise, therefore, that in the era of industrial development, when labor was both plentiful and cheap, families of any means employed servants to do much of the domestic labor. First, the work was intensive enough that most women probably welcomed any help; only the most upper-class women tended to shift the entire burden of domestic labor to servants. Second, shifting the work to servants could reduce the contradiction within the gender role of the "lady" of the house.

This observation does not tell the whole story yet. This domestic labor was shifted from the hands of women to the hands of other women because it was gender-specified labor. Nonetheless, isn't there as much contradiction between the domestic-angel image and this dirty, laborious work for the women hired to do the labor as for the "lady" of the house? In the eyes of the employing class, there was not, because their gender norms depended not just on a woman's *gender*, but also on her *class* and *race/ethnicity*. Serving the domestic-labor needs of strangers is entirely consistent with dominant-culture definitions of appropriate womanhood for *some* types of women but not for others. As Glenn has pointed out, exactly which classification of women was supposed to perform these tasks changes historically and differs from geographic region to geographic region. In the northeastern United States at the turn of the century, recent European immigrants, especially Irish-American women, were thought to be specially fitted to doing domestic labor. White women in the South turned to African-American women; in the Southwest, Mexican-American women filled the service roles, as did Japanese-American women on the Pacific coast and in Hawaii.

These groups of women engaged in paid domestic service because they needed the money and they lived in those areas in large numbers. In each of these regions, however, these women came to be culturally reinterpreted as a servant

Society's definitions of appropriate roles for women depend on their race/ethnicity and class.

class *by nature,* marked out and determined by their gender and their race/ethnicity. Glenn (1992) has argued that in each case, the women, marked by their race/ethnicity, were understood to have inherent traits suiting them for service, and they were not perceived as mothers and wives in their own right, but rather as servants. Thus, Glenn has shown, in each region, young women were institutionally tracked into fulfilling their presumed natural destiny. She found examples of how Mexican girls in the Southwest and Japanese girls in Hawaii were blocked from school programs other than those that would lead to domestic service. Even in the job programs run by the federal Works Progress Administration (WPA) in the New Deal response to the Great Depression of the 1930s, Chicanas and African-American and Asian-American women were funneled into domestic service jobs and out of others.

The View From Different Groups of Women

We now add one further layer to this discussion of the differential impact of sex/gender systems on different women. As mentioned previously, a single sex/gender system, like an economic system or political system, contains a complex of norms and rules that place different expectations on people, depending on their situation and their group membership. In a complex society, however, the large sex/gender system contains a number of *subsystems,* the norms and rules of which are shaped not only by the larger national community, but also by the more specific communities defined, for example, by geography, race/ethnicity, religion, or class. From this perspective, we might say that the entire system is like a game with very complicated rules, but in which there are also a number of subgames with their own rules, which may be in conflict with the rules of the larger game. The players may thus be subject to differing sets of rules at the same time, some of which fit together coherently, and some of which do not.

Thus far, this chapter has focused on the perspective of the larger game in the United States—that is, the norms and rules of the dominant national sex/gender system. Within this system, any women who are not native-born White, middle- and upper-class and, in many areas, Protestant or of northern European extraction have historically been seen as incapable of fulfilling the ideal of femininity as presented in the cult of womanhood; instead, these women were offered another version of stereotypic femininity, which assumed that they were specially fitted to do female but dirty work or other families' domestic labor. At the same time, however, these second-class women—immigrants, racial minorities, those from working-class communities or from the urban slums or farming communities— developed their own understandings of gender because of the circumstances in which they lived and the cultures they carried with them from one historical era to the next.

Thus, women's actions can be—and are—interpreted simultaneously through the multiple perspectives contained within the system. Thus, when African-American, Hispanic-American, and Asian-American women went into domestic service in large numbers, from the perspective of the large game, these women were fulfilling the roles of second-class femininity; they were acting in gender- and race-appropriate ways. From their own points of view, many were being good mothers; they were struggling to help their families garner enough resources so that their daughters (they hoped) would not have to go into domestic service to support themselves (Glenn, 1992, 19).

For another example, consider the story of Pocahontas. To Euro-American society, the story of Pocahontas is a romantic tale of a beautiful Indian princess who falls in love with an Englishman, who generously marries her and takes her off to England, where she is the talk of the town. This story can be seen as symbolizing to the Euro-American the unique "marriage" of the civilized European with the wildness of nature on the new continent, with all living happily ever after as Indians and the wilderness are "tamed." American Indians are more likely to hear the rest of the story and, presumably, to take a different message from it. Pocahontas was offered to John Smith as part of a policy of alliance, much as European aristocrats and royalty intermarried to solidify international agreements. When she went to London, although she was displayed in society, neither her husband nor the society in which she was now isolated ever accepted her, and while longing to return home to America, she died before her 25th birthday.

Each of these subcultures, defined by race/ethnicity, class, and geography (among other things), has distinctive ways of understanding gender and different norms about how women and men should do gender to some degree. For communities defined by race/ethnicity, religion, or geography, distinctive rituals and practices, cultural figures, myths and stories, and graphic representations offer a way of understanding the specific subcultural constructions of male and female. The Navajo Changing Woman, for example, responsible for the growth of crops and the birth of new life, presents a model of the woman warrior and defender of

124

Part 1:
Developing
Frameworks for the
Study of Gender
and Society

her home that is a cultural ideal for Navajo women (Tsosie, 1988). Young Jewish girls dress up at Purim as Queen Esther, a savior of her people, as often as they might, like many other American children, appear as fairy princesses and witches at Halloween. Many Appalachian authors incorporate the locally well-known image of the "tall women," so named because of the saying that "a tall woman casts a long shadow." This image of "strong women, who can manage the household and children as well as milk the cows and cultivate the fields" served as a positive cultural image of femininity for Appalachian women for whom the image of the Southern belle must have seemed foreign (Mathews, 1987, 39). From one part of the country to another, where the different flow of seasons and the different cultural traditions shape women's and men's lives differently, the understanding of women as women and men as men varies.

The more closely women's lives are scrutinized, the more clear it becomes that there is immense variation in the ways that gender is shaped and represented in a complex sex/gender system. Nevertheless, they are not completely independent. They are linked through the common social institutions that tie them all together into the larger society, including, for example, the government, the mass media, and the school and health-care systems. Thus, women (and men) do gender within sex/gender systems that often simultaneously demand different and sometimes conflicting things of them, in order to act in gender-appropriate ways.

Untangling Oppressions

The subordination of women on the basis of their gender is one of the facts of life that women's studies seeks to understand. How prevalent is it? How does it work? How does it change? Chapters 2 and 3 looked at alternative theories that can be used to offer answers to these questions. Once researchers have accepted the idea that an understanding of sex/gender systems also requires an understanding of the structures of power based on other social markers, they are led to an obvious question: What are the relative effects of gender and, for example, race or class on social power structures? The literature on gender and social difference suggests four different general approaches people have used to understand the simultaneous dynamics of gender and other structures of social inequality: the parallel model, the distinct-components model, the complex model, and the hierarchical model.[2] This section looks briefly at each.

The Parallel Model

The parallel model is perhaps the most widely used way of thinking about oppression and inequality. This view does not attempt to *integrate* an understanding of gender with other forms of social inequality, although the parallel model does allow attempts to *compare* them. The parallel model views gender, age, class, and race (for example) as different principles of social structure and power, each of which has its own distinct effects. In social science research, scholars tend to study gender *or* race *or* class *or* age, but not to pay serious attention to all of these at once.

In the broader culture, our day-to-day thinking also shows evidence of parallel thinking. We often use the phrase "women and Blacks" in a way that suggests that these groups are not overlapping.[3] For example, discussions of post–Civil War movements to broaden the franchise often discuss the debates over whether reformers should fight to secure the vote for women as well as Blacks or just for Blacks; in the end, we are told, Blacks were given the legal right to vote. In fact, of course, not all Blacks were given the legal right to vote; technically, only the legal rights of Black men had changed. If we can account only for race or for gender at a given time, we gain little understanding of anyone if we assume that in a race- and gender-conscious society, all people's race *and* gender must play some role in shaping their experiences.

The parallel model often underlies the tendency for groups focusing on different forms of oppression to engage in what seems to be comparative measurement of oppression. There is little point in debating whose oppression hurts more; such debates tend to lead people almost to express pride in their oppression. The whose-oppression-is-greater debate defeats the whole purpose of comparing women's lives because it tends to lead the participants to reject or downplay the claims of other women. Moreover, attempts to rank oppressions are for many women an exercise in self-fragmentation. Individual women have many different social identities. How does a woman decide which bit of her is the source of her oppression? Cheryl Clarke, a Black radical feminist, arrived at perhaps the only sane response to women's self-fragmentation when she wrote, "So, all of us would do well to stop fighting each other for our space at the bottom, because there ain't no more room. We have spent so much time hating ourselves. Time to love ourselves" (1981, 137).

The Distinct-Components Model

The distinct-components model offers a widely used way of thinking about how different bases of social structure work together. The distinct-components model, very much like what Elizabeth V. Spelman (1988) and Evelyn Nakano Glenn (1992) call an "additive perspective," attempts to take account of the weight of different aspects of people's social identification in their overall experience. According to this view, to understand the whole of an individual's experience, we should attempt to parse it out into its various individual components of gender, race/ethnicity, class, and age. Spelman has correctly claimed that most feminist research and theory on racism falls into this category. Glenn has pointed out that the widespread view of research on women is that White women are oppressed by gender, while women of color are doubly subordinated. According to this perspective, "White women have only gender and women of color have gender plus race" (Glenn, 1992, 33). A distinct-components or additive model of oppression could also argue that all African-Americans are oppressed by racism, and some are further oppressed by sexism, or that all poor people are oppressed by class oppression, and some are further oppressed by ageism. In each of these cases, we imagine piles of distinct burdens that are added onto an individual.

Most social science research on gender, using statistical techniques for analyzing data such as those gathered from surveys, experiments, and censuses, take a

126

Part 1:
Developing
Frameworks for the
Study of Gender
and Society

distinct-components approach. Consider research on wealth and income. An economist who has access to data that includes information on people's income, job, education, family status, race, gender, age, and other characteristics can use statistical techniques to determine the relative weight of these different factors in determining someone's income. Within any given class or job, for example, research shows that, on average, people's salaries are lower if they are female, rather than male. Both Black and White women earn less than both Black and White men, even when controlling for their levels of education. Within each sex, Blacks earn less than Whites, although the gap is much wider among men than among women. The conclusion researchers draw from this work is that apart from education, training, and skill, both gender and race/ethnicity have *independent* effects on where people stand on the economic ladder. The effects of gender are slightly different for Blacks and Whites, and the effects of race and ethnicity are slightly different for women and men.

The distinct-components model has seemed very useful for trying to understand gender in relation to other aspects of social status. Nonetheless, it has also been widely criticized by scholars because while it may prove useful in some cases, such as the income problem just described, it is deeply flawed in dealing with questions of social identity. Such questions are crucial for trying to untangle the sources and effects of prejudice, discrimination, group-based violence, and other aspects of oppression.

Suppose that I fit the following description: I am female, Chinese-American, Roman Catholic, born and raised in San Francisco, a UCLA alumna, and I currently reside and am employed in Washington, D.C. A distinct-components model suggests not only that could I name these different aspects of my identity, but that they are identifiably distinct and independent components of my experience and sense of self, and that it would be possible to sort out the specific impact of each of these aspects of my identity independently.

Can I actually look at myself physically or psychologically and point out distinct parts of me that are, for example, Chinese-American, female, and urban? Is there an essential "Chinese-Americanness" that would not change at all if I were male instead of female, or rural born and raised instead of urban, or Unitarian instead of Catholic? Is there an essential "femaleness" that would not be different if I were Spanish-American rather than Chinese-American and Jewish rather than Catholic? As Spelman wrote,

> Selves are not made up of separable units of identity strung together to constitute a whole person. It is not as if there is a goddess somewhere who made a lot of little identical "woman" units and then, in order to spruce up the world a bit for herself, decided to put some of those units in Black bodies, some in White bodies, some in the bodies of kitchen maids in seventeenth-century France, some in the bodies of English, Israeli, and Indian prime ministers. (Spelman, 1988, 158)

Consistent with Spelman's point, there is no psychological theory of identity development or structure suggesting that an adequate theory can be based on the idea of distinct components of group identification.

This discussion should also raise another question: If we should try to understand gender by understanding it in relation to other aspects of social identity, which ones and how many should we consider at any given time? For many writers on this subject, race is central to this discussion. Others add class or sexual orientation or age. We can also argue that religion, language, region or locale, urbanicity, and any of a wide range of other factors are central in shaping human experience and—the relevant point for our purposes here—the meaning of gender and the way sex/gender systems are structured and affect people. For this reason, many scholars are turning to what we can call (for lack of a better term) a complex model of gender and difference in order to understand the dynamics of oppression.

The Complex Model

This view is based on the following observations. First, in the real world of human subjective experience, it is impossible for many purposes to make generalizations about women's experiences *as women*—that is, to imagine an abstract woman whose womanness is raceless, classless, ageless, and lacking any particular geography. This impossibility occurs largely because of a point repeated throughout the discussion thus far: Gender is a function not simply of biology, but also of culture and society. Gender is constructed through the arrangements of particular sex/gender systems, which are themselves complex. Thus, the definition of men's and women's gender is socially constructed in a way that makes it contingent on many aspects of a person's situation.

The second important point in a complex view of gender and difference is that the other markers of social identity, which are most important to take into account in understanding gender, also depend on the situation. It is not reasonable to expect that every discussion of the significance of gender must be placed explicitly in the context of race–ethnicity, religion, socioeconomic class, sexual orientation, language, region, urbanicity, health status, and any of the range of other aspects of social existence that may be important in defining identity and experience. However, the complex model does demand at least two things: First, any discussion of the structure or impact of sex/gender systems or the meaning of gender, or any attempt to explore the experiences of women, must specify both the particular women being discussed and the limitations constraining the range of women who may be encompassed by the descriptions. Second, it is important to understand that part of exploring the role of gender in people's lives is identifying the circumstances under which the role of gender is especially contingent on other specific aspects of social existence. The various types of social identification described previously are not equally and similarly relevant to gendered experience under all circumstances.

Hierarchies of Oppression

Some people have argued that not only are the meanings of different social statuses and identities interrelated and contingent, but they are also hierarchically related. This model assumes that certain kinds of oppression are, in a sense, master oppressions, and that some kinds of oppression are derivative of others. The classic

128

Part 1:
Developing
Frameworks for the
Study of Gender
and Society

example of this model is the traditional Marxist view of socioeconomic class divisions and class oppression. The basic social division is based on property relations and the division of labor and control between the workers and the owners; all other forms of oppression flow from that. Early Marxist theorists who expressed concern with women's condition argued that there was no distinct or particular social problem that afflicted women that did not flow from class relations, and therefore, solution of the class problem would lead to a solution for the women problem (Bebel, 1970). Traditional Marxist theorists also tried to explain race oppression as derived from the different class positions of the different races. As noted previously, 20th-century social movements have commonly declared one or another form of social division as primary and therefore prior to gender divisions.

In recent decades, some theorists have again posed the idea of a hierarchy of oppressions to understand gender.[4] Two well-known attempts to create such a hierarchy in the early stages of the contemporary women's movement are found in Kate Millet's (1970) *Sexual Politics* and Shulamith Firestone's (1970) *Dialectic of Sex*. Firestone took the family as the fundamental unit of society and therefore saw the basic form of oppression as *patriarchy*, the domination of women by men because of the domination of the father. For Firestone, racism was the domination of one race by another, in a manner that follows the logic of the primary form of oppression. Kate Millett likewise made an influential (among White women) argument that sexism is more fundamental than racism. These arguments have been widely criticized as being based in ignorance about the conditions of race and racism.

Some feminist theorists have argued that race should be understood as the primary social condition. Evelyn Brook Higginbotham, for example, has described race as a metalanguage with a "powerful, all-encompassing effect on the construction and representation of other social and power relations, namely, gender, class, and sexuality" (Higginbotham, 1992, 252). She has argued that race "subsumes" other sets of social relations. This formulation, like the traditional Marxist approach and Firestone's and Millett's arguments, is based in a worldview derived from a particular location in social and historical space, which oversimplifies social relations and ignores the dependence of social meaning on situation. Gender relations are not equally linked with race relations in all circumstances. Both race relations and gender relations (and, for that matter, class relations) have different importance and meaning in different historical, national, and cultural settings. Different societies do not even categorize races and classes in the same way, and the role of race and different races depends on what place is being discussed. It is certainly true that race can and often does serve as a metalanguage for social relations, just as gender sometimes does. However, neither race nor gender is the essential master language of oppression in all times, cultures, and circumstances.

Exemplifying Complexity:
Gender, Race, Sexuality, and Violence

To summarize the preceding models, theorists have used different perspectives to try to understand the social bases of oppression. This book is based on the complex model, assuming that (a) it is necessary to integrate an understanding of gender with other types of social relations, and (b) these relations are variable. Social phenomena that may seem at first glance to be entirely based on gender relations are in fact also based on other social divisions; those phenomena that may seem to be based on race or class are often also based on gender. This section briefly considers two examples: sexual violence and slavery.

Rape would seem at first to offer a clear example of a form of oppression or violence based solely on gender. Slavery would seem at first to offer a clear example of a form of oppression or violence based solely on race. In fact, however, for a complete understanding of rape, it is necessary to look beyond gender, and for a complete understanding of slavery, it is necessary to look beyond race.

Gender is a crucial determinant of the degree to which women are regarded and treated as objects of sex and rape, but their race, ethnicity, class, and status as recent immigrants or native-born Americans are also important. The lower a woman's status is by almost any measure, the more likely she is to be a target of sexual violence. Some examples of how this works follow.

bell hooks (1981) offered a powerful analysis of the intertwined effects of race and gender on sexual oppression. Rape was an integral part of the female slave experience, beginning with the sea voyage, during which the slavers did what they could to break the Africans' spirits and make them passive and compliant. For the women, this process included rape. Neither race nor gender alone accounts for the experience of slavery because "while racism was clearly the evil that had decreed Black people would be enslaved, it was sexism that determined that the lot of the Black female would be harsher, more brutal than that of the Black male slave" (hooks, 1981, 43; see also Jennings, 1990). Women were subjected to slavery because of their race, but they were also used as sexual objects and as breeders because of their sex. The same was true for the Native Americans held as slaves in the American Southwest (Mirandé and Enríquez, 1979). There are many other situations in which rape clearly depends not just on gender, but also on the race, ethnic, or class relations between perpetrator and victim. Susan Brownmiller's (1975) argument that rape has often been used as a tactic of war and imperialism depends on recognizing that rape does not occur just because of gender and sexual relations. A recent example in a long history may be found in the massive and systematic use of rape in Serbia against Muslim women in 1992–1993, during the civil war that followed the breakup of Yugoslavia.

Gender played other roles in differentiating the slave experience. For instance, bell hooks has pointed out that an important aspect of slavery in the United States was the requirement that women do labor regarded in America as men's work. Male slaves were less often subjected to the complementary treatment of being required to do women's work (1981, 20; Mann, 1989, 780).

Race and gender also combined to affect the experience of slave owners in 19th-century America. White men could own slaves because of their race and gender. Their sex gave them the right to own property (married women could not own property), and their race gave them the right to own human beings (very few nonWhites owned slaves [Schwendinger, 1990]). In one sense, this gender difference among Whites is little more than a technical point; White women had great power over their husbands' slaves. Moreover, during the Civil War, about three quarters of White Southern men were in the military, so their wives had to take

130

Part 1:
Developing
Frameworks for the
Study of Gender
and Society

over the management of plantations, including the slaves. Drew Gilpin Faust's historical analysis shows that many of these women were especially uncomfortable with this role and were caught in a web of conflicting social norms. They lived in a society based on violence, in which White people could hold Black people in bondage and enforce their power with violence against them; on the other hand, gender norms defined women as nurturant and nonviolent (Faust, 1992).

Gender distinguished among White slaveholders in one important respect: White women knew about their husbands', brothers', and sons' sexual treatment of their slaves. They knew that the children of some of the enslaved women were progeny of their "loved ones" through rape. This knowledge motivated some White women, such as the Grimké sisters, to become abolitionists, but many others simply stored their resentment or even blamed the victimized Black women. In addition, hooks has suggested another dimension to this complex picture of gender and race by speculating, "Surely it must have occurred to White women that were enslaved Black women not available to bear the brunt of such intense anti-woman male aggression, they themselves might have been the victims" (1981, 38). White society in general has tried to ignore the massive scale of the rapes that occurred.

Blaming the victim plays an important role in all forms of sexual- and gender-based violence. However, just as enslaved women were often held responsible for their own victimization, women of low-status groups, especially those perceived as alien, have often been regarded as excessively sexual (and even animal-like) and thus have become special targets for sexual violence and exploitation. As bell hooks has explained, by defining Black women as initiators of the sexual relationships that were in fact rapes, Whites reinforced a stereotype of Black women as sexual savages who, in effect, could not be raped (hooks, 1981, 52). The same principle applied to Hispanic and Native American women (Mirandé and Enríquez, 1979). Likewise, in the late 19th and early 20th centuries, native-born Whites often claimed that immigrant women—Irish, Italian, Jewish, or whatever—were especially promiscuous and likely to ruin the morals of innocent American men. Young immigrant women, especially those helping to support their families, were constantly subjected to sexual harassment and exploitation and then labeled promiscuous.

These examples demonstrate that the forms of gender-based oppression and exploitation people experience depend in part on their other social characteristics, and that racial/ethnic- or class-based forms of oppression and exploitation depend in part on gender (see also Hurtado, 1989; Mann, 1989). In fact, the exploitation of gender relations may often be seen as a means of enforcing other types of oppression. Some examples from the legal control of sexuality and marriage follow.

The state's control over marriage and sexual relations gives it leverage to pursue many different goals (see Chapter 11). Among these goals is the preservation of particular racial or ethnic hierarchies. In order to preserve a particular racial/ethnic social order, societies must ensure that different races or ethnic groups cannot intermarry or develop the mutual loyalty and commitment owed to intimates and family members. Thus, nations with an apartheid history, such as the United States and South Africa, declared *miscegenation,* racial intermarriage, illegal during those eras.

Laws against interracial sexual relations or marriage may seem to fall equally on the shoulders of women and men, and on those of different races or ethnic groups, but in fact, they do not. Higher-status men, however defined, tend to have sexual rights over lower-status women, or at least, they are not punished as severely as their partners in interracial sexual contact. In the American past, sexual relations between White women and nonWhite men were punished more severely than relations between White men and nonWhite women. The first American antimiscegenation law, passed in 1664 in Maryland, declared that a White woman who had sexual relations with an enslaved Black male must herself become a slave. No such law applied to White men.

These dynamics appear not just through law, but also in the way societies have often treated mixed-race, -ethnicity, or even -class couples and their babies. If a low-status female becomes pregnant by a high-status male, it has little effect on their relative status. Patriarchal ideology keeps the male in control; if the woman makes too many claims, he can abandon and reject her with relatively little social cost, partly because he can accuse her of promiscuity. A situation involving a low-status male and a high-status female is very different. For example, a baby of mixed-race parentage born to a White woman has been regarded as a pollution of the White race. Because women are regarded as the property of male protectors in a patriarchal society, a nonWhite male who has sexual relations with a White woman is ultimately seen as taking something from White men. The effects of this dual system of racial and sexual oppression lasted long after the end of slavery. The rape of a White woman by a nonWhite man has usually been treated by White society as the most serious type of heterosexual rape, whereas rape of a nonWhite woman by a White man has not often been regarded as rape at all. False charges that a Black man raped a White woman were often used as excuses for lynching Black men.

Almost a generation ago, women's studies researchers began to emphasize the need to take gender into account to understand important social issues. In recent years, they have been demanding yet more sophistication and argue that gender analysis is not complete without integrating it with an understanding of other structural bases of social life. Maxine Baca Zinn (1989) has offered a good example in her writing on the family and poverty. She has shown that efforts to understand and solve the problems of poverty are doomed to failure if researchers look only at culture or race and class structures or gender structures. Society and social relations are constructed of all of these elements.

Some Sketches of Unity and Diversity

This chapter has focused on general questions of comparison, commonality, and difference across different social groups. This section briefly looks at some problems raised in considering the relationship between gender and a few specific categories of social relations, including age, socioeconomic class, race/ethnicity, and geographic community. This discussion focuses on U.S. society; the dynamics of each of these categorizations would look different in other parts of the world. Among the social-group categorizations that are given more detailed attention later in the book are religion (see Chapter 7), sexual orientation (see Chapter 11), marital status (see Chapter 11), maternal status (see Chapter 12), and employment status (see Chapter 13). Once again, the point is not to *describe* different groups of women, but to underscore some of the analytical issues that pave the way to explore the commonalities and differences in women's lives later in the book.

132

Part 1:
Developing
Frameworks for the
Study of Gender
and Society

Age

When we study women, it is important to remember that many of the life experiences we are discussing have different relevance for women of different ages. Like the society around us, women's studies has tended both to devote more attention to the young than to the old and to engage unconsciously in age-specific generalizations. (After all, in women's studies classes, the average age of students is comparatively young and, indeed, so is the average age of women's studies instructors.) For example, in arguing that an important aspect of the way women are treated in society is that they are viewed by men as sex objects, we must also be aware of the severe age basis of cultural definitions of sexuality and beauty. There is not as booming a market for middle-aged or older models as there is for adolescents and women in their 20s.

Until recently, when social scientists turned to studying older women, the topics that seemed to come to mind were middle-aged depression, menopause, widowhood, the empty nest, and poverty. These are important topics, but not the only aspects of older women's lives. Older women's lives offer important illustrations of the workings of gender ideology because they do not fulfill dominant cultural definitions of femininity.[5] Older women are not treated as sex objects because American culture defines attractive females as young. Most older women have no dependent children. Their lives are much less likely than younger women's to revolve around men because of gender differences in life expectancy. Although the aged suffer from dependencies due to health and financial circumstances, in one sense, older women are among the most self-reliant of people; they are the Americans most likely to live on their own. Regardless of how women spend their younger adult years, there comes a time in most women's lives when they do not conform to some of the stereotypes of womanhood and femininity because these are built around age-specific norms.

Because older women do not easily fit into traditional definitions of womanhood, they are often viewed as though they are not real women but a kind of third sex or, worse, sexless. Many women react to menopause not just with the common anxiety most people feel when confronted with the realization of their aging and mortality, but also with depression over a loss of femininity. What does it mean that women are defined in such a way that any woman who lives out a normal life span will come to a point when she no longer feels that she is a real woman? A parallel problem affects men, although not to the same degree. For example, the term *old man* is used as an epithet to indicate that a man is weak and not in command—in other words, not masculine enough. Degrading treatment of older people is based primarily on age but also on gender norms.

Old age can release women from some of the problems they faced when younger. In some cultures, women gain respect and power only with age. Although the structure of American families has changed with geographic mobility, the family matriarch is still often the center of the extended kinship network and the person who defines and holds the family together. Women often feel that they gain some gender-based and sexual freedom as they grow older, sometimes finding that their sense of sexual enjoyment increases when they no longer need to worry about getting pregnant. The period of life often defined as the empty nest is also a time when women no longer have to balance their interests and pursuits against the demands of dependent children. Many women also readily admit, at least to each other, that they feel freer to act, speak, and dress as they wish because they feel less pressure to conform to the stereotypes of femininity.

Old-age interest groups such as the Gray Panthers, long led by Maggie Kuhn, and the women's movement in general have sought changes in the material and cultural conditions of older women. In recent decades, the material condition of older Americans has improved to some degree, at least relative to what has happened to younger people and children. There are still many issues that need to be resolved, however, especially with respect to health and housing. Some problems will become worse as the proportion of retired people in the population increases, thus increasing the financial burden on the young and the middle-aged. The even more difficult battle is against cultural stereotypes and social relations among people of different ages. It is not polite to refer to someone as an old woman or man because *old* has many negative connotations. When someone says "I am old," it is probably said in a tone of defeat. Instead, people use such euphemisms as *senior citizen, golden ager, mature,* or perhaps *aging* or *older.* It will take much work to make *old* a proud word.

Class

Assessing the effects of class on women's lives is difficult because most definitions of *class* are gender biased. People's *class background,* the class with which they are identified when they are children, is usually defined according to the status of their *father's* occupation. Class categorization in adulthood depends on gender. For men and for single women, we usually refer to the status of their occupation. There are several ways that jobs can be categorized; most analyses use a variation on the basic framework of blue-collar, white-collar, and professional or managerial occupations. But married women's class is usually defined by their husbands' occupations. Even if we wanted to define married women's class by their own occupations, the work that a very large proportion of women do—homemaking—is not defined as having a class ranking of its own. Moreover, because wives usually have lower-status, less-well-paid jobs than their husbands, does it make sense to say that in most families, women have lower class standing than their husbands? Instead, should we argue, as many have, that women's class standing is usually derivative of their fathers' or their husbands'? Should class be defined according to the structure of one's own labor? What kinds of arguments underpin the idea that we should use different definitions to identify women's and men's class standing?

These definitional problems highlight some important points about the nature of women's social roles and status. As Feldberg and Glenn (1979) have argued, whereas men's status and economic worth are defined largely by their work, women's are defined by their marital status and, if they are married, by their husbands' work. Women's employment is defined as secondary to their family roles, which is the reason a married woman's class status is often judged by her husband's work, even if she is employed. Women's domestic work is not defined as real work, or at least not the kind that shapes her place in socioeconomic and class relations.

Class designations are no more immune to gender effects if we focus on wealth and control over economic resources as the key to defining class, rather

134

Part 1:
Developing
Frameworks for the
Study of Gender
and Society

Maggie Kuhn (1905–1995), former leader of the Gray Panthers.

than occupation. Regardless of the wealth of the family in which women were raised, women are much more vulnerable to a descent into poverty than men are. Chapter 13 details this point and the related issue of the feminization of poverty. Responsibility for children and experiences after divorce have more effect on women's economic well-being than on men's.

The commonly used occupational categorizations of classes are, in any case, inadequate for information about the nature of women's work because they obscure some of the most important aspects of the structure of such work and its function in the economic system and economic relations. Traditional categorizations of class distinguish among farm, blue-collar, white-collar, business–managerial, and professional work, but they mask the gender-based divisions of labor *within* these categories. Many feminist scholars use a job category that crosses all the others to classify women's work: pink-collar or auxiliary service work. Unpaid housewives, blue-collar service workers, pink-collar clerical workers, and professionals in traditional women's occupations such as nursing and social work are included within these terms. Pink-collar workers are service workers of all classes. Pink-collar work dominates women's jobs, regardless of the women's class or race/ethnicity. These efforts to construct new definitions have provoked controversy (Abbott and Sapsford, 1988). Examining the concept of class as it applies to women reveals how important gender is in governing social and economic relations.

Despite these definitional difficulties, "class" is an important categorization for probing commonalities and differences in the gender-based experiences of women. Indeed, generalizations about women that are not class *conscious* are often class *biased*. Assertions that women are increasingly entering the labor market do not refer to the poorest women; they have always had to work for pay to survive, even if much of their work has been illegal (such as prostitution) or black-market labor. Women breaking into traditionally male middle-class jobs have received more attention than those in traditionally male working-class jobs, and less progress has been made in the latter than in the former.

Research by Theodore Caplow and Bruce A. Chadwick (1979) offers an interesting picture of class-based changes in women's roles during the 20th century. In 1929 and 1937, sociologists Robert and Helen Lynd published two very influential books based on studies of life in "Middletown," a fictional name for Muncie, Indiana. Caplow and Chadwick's research examined some of the differences between White working-class and middle-class women in Middletown in 1978 against the backdrop of the Lynds' findings in the 1920s. Caplow and Chadwick found that many changes had occurred in half a century, one of the most notable being the convergence in the lives of working-class and middle-class women.

Working-class women in the 1920s did much more domestic labor than middle-class women did. Middle-class women did very little washing and ironing, and they did less sewing, mending, and baking than working-class women did. In 1924, 95% of the working-class women but only 10% of the middle-class women had no paid help in the home; 33% of the middle-class women and none of the working-class women had full-time paid help.

The picture was very different 50 years later, largely because of the increase in the amount of domestic labor done by middle-class women. By 1978, working-

136

Part 1:
Developing
Frameworks for the
Study of Gender
and Society

class and middle-class women did essentially equivalent amounts of housework, including each of the tasks mentioned earlier. In the 1970s, women, especially middle-class women, did more laundry than they did earlier in the century, and they were more likely to bake bread than they were earlier. In 1978, 91% of working-class women and 83% of middle-class women had no paid domestic help; 1% of both middle-class and working-class women had full-time help. Caplow and Chadwick also found there was no longer any difference in the educational aspirations middle-class and working-class women had for their children. Surprisingly, perhaps, especially for those who romanticize the traditional family, both mothers and fathers reported spending more time with their children in 1978 than they did in the 1920s. Thus, understanding women's lives is not just a matter of studying how many well-educated middle-class women do or do not get to be partners in law firms.

Race and Ethnicity

It might seem that race is easier to analyze than class because it should be easier to define. Any appearance of simplicity, however, is a pernicious illusion. As Michael Banton (1983) has shown in his history of racial definition, different societies at different times vary considerably in how they define race. Race is not a biological classification, even though it is built around biological characteristics such as parentage or skin pigmentation. It is a social category defined by cultural norms.[6]

A few brief examples illustrate how elusive the concept of race is. Some cultures define Jews as a race; others do not. At one time, most Hispanic leaders in the United States objected to being categorized as a race distinguished from White, but by the late 1970s, many Hispanic leaders wished to be regarded as a distinct race. Even so, this demand is made only by some people of Latin American ancestry. A large proportion of African-Americans are descended from the union of White slave masters of European ancestry with Black slaves of African ancestry. The children of a Black–White union have generally been regarded as Black, even if their gene pools come from White parentage as much as (or sometimes more than) Black. As in other cases in which one race is regarded as inferior to another, it takes only a small fraction of the blood of the lower-status race for an individual to be treated as a part of that race. On the other hand, today there is a movement in some multiracial families to allow their children to define themselves as biracial or multiracial, rather than forcing them to identify with only one of their parents. Thus, the relevance of race to an individual's life is ultimately determined not by biology but by how societies and individuals deal with a clue that biology gives them.

Ethnicity is an even more subjective cultural concept than race, especially in a society in which there is a relatively high degree of intermarriage. Ethnicity is largely, although not entirely, defined by the nationality of one's forebears, often buttressed by differences in religion or language.

The history of African-American women is especially revealing of the nature of sex/gender systems in America because of the cross fire of demands based on the interplay of gender and racial politics they have faced. Their lives and experiences defy dominant stereotypes of femininity. They have worked at hard physical labor, and they have been the primary breadwinners in their families in larger proportions than is true for most other groups of American women, and they have done this work to support their children. These aspects of Black women's lives have often served as the basis for accusations that they emasculate Black men (Collins, 1989b).

As the realities of Black women's experiences are finally being examined more extensively, they are also serving as the basis for a new symbolism and mythology. Just as African-Americans have become the American symbol of poverty and oppression, in feminist and Black writing, the African-American woman has become the symbol of strength against odds, the wonder woman. Although pride in the history and strength of Black women has taken too long to arrive, turning Black women into romantic symbols has its dangers. For instance, bell hooks is wary of these romantic interpretations of Black women's history, claiming, "They ignore the reality that to be strong in the face of oppression is not the same as overcoming oppression, that endurance is not to be confused with transformation" (1981, 6). In addition, the romanticizing of any women's lives, and especially their oppression, can lead to complacency.

White women sometimes use Black women as symbols for their own purposes; hooks has pointed out an irony in this treatment:

> When the women's movement was at its peak and White women were rejecting the role of breeder, burden bearer, and sex object, Black women were celebrated for their unique devotion to the task of mothering; for their "innate" ability to bear tremendous burdens; and for their ever-increasing availability as sex objects. (1981, 6)

Also, hooks has pointed out that although White feminists have rarely devoted much effort to learning about or from Black women's lives, they have long used the analogy of Black oppression and struggle to underscore the oppression of women, sometimes to excess. "A White woman who has suffered physical abuse and assault from a husband or lover, who also suffers poverty, need not compare her lot to that of a suffering Black person to emphasize that she is in pain" (hooks, 1981, 142).

Women's experiences in America cannot be understood without reference to both race and sex. This necessarily includes understanding the role of race in White women's lives. Women who are not White have had to be more conscious of their race because in a White-dominant society those who are not White are defined more by their race. Indeed, even in scholarly books, it is rare to refer to an African-, Hispanic-, or Asian-American or Native American unless one means to say something about race. Whites are allowed to forget their race, but that does not mean that race is unimportant in their lives.

Geography and Culture

Any student of American history knows that one of the most important sources of division has been geography. American history is marked by economic and political struggles for power between different regions of the country and between urban and rural interests. Living in rural Nebraska and living in New York City are not the same. Despite great geographic mobility and the pervasiveness of the mass media, the regions of the country continue to differ considerably in economic structure, culture, and demography.

There is fascinating regional variation in American women's history. Some differences are obvious. The story of women under slavery is a story of the South; the story of 19th-century immigrant women working in sweatshops is a story primarily of the Northeast. Parts of the country found it in their interest to encourage women to be property holders, while other parts did not. The territory of Oregon, for example, offered single women settlers (but not single men) a large parcel of free farmland because it was thought that such an offer would encourage both men and women to settle and develop the territory. The Midwest was relatively quick to develop coeducational higher education, first at private colleges such as Oberlin in Ohio and Lawrence in Wisconsin, and then at the public land-grant colleges that are now state universities.

Observers sometimes exaggerate regional variation and sometimes minimize it. Life in the Old South (including gender norms) was undoubtedly different from that in other parts of the country. However, the stereotype of the White Southern belle is an overdrawn portrait that historians have labored to correct. Most White Southern women were not ladies of the manor; they were farm women struggling for existence. For most Southern White men, the ideal wife was not a delicate lady, but a woman who could carry her weight in helping to run farm and family (Hagler, 1980). Regardless of region, the ideal of the lady was a luxury only the wealthy could afford. In her history of Southern women, Anne Firor Scott (1970) focused on the much-neglected story of women who became involved in politics and struggles for change. Gerda Lerner's (1971) biography of the Grimké sisters, who devoted themselves to abolition and women's rights, shows the determination of these women to fight against a system their own family helped perpetuate. Nina Silber's fascinating history of the immediate post–Civil War era shows that Northern and Southern antagonisms were played out in highly gendered terms, in which Northerners redefined their images of the sexuality and gender of Southern men and women to "define their regional distinctiveness and, in the aftermath of the war, to establish their regional and political superiority" (Silber, 1989, 634). White Southerners' masculinity and femininity came to be seen as corrupt and dishonorable.

Most women's studies scholars now accept the charge that the field has been dominated by the experiences of middle-class White women. Less well recognized is a charge articulated by Southern scholars such as Jacquelyn Dowd Hall (1989): Women's studies is "New Englandized," or based largely on the experiences and perspectives of women from the Northeast. Hall has pointed out that the interpretive framework used most often for American women's history

> turned on the Industrial Revolution, which, beginning in the 1830s, severed work from life, the public from the private sphere, and transformed the household from a unit of production to a woman-dominated haven from a heartless world. Women lost their productive roles but gained access to education and a conviction of moral superiority. Above all they acquired the sense of grievance and group identity that would inspire them to form voluntary

associations, oppose slavery, and launch a movement for women's rights. (1989, 904)

This story is not exclusively of the Northeast, but it is certainly not an adequate rendition of conditions in the South of that period.

Comparing women in urban and rural settings offers another example of the way in which attention to commonalities and differences among women helps create a more complete picture of the meaning of gender in America. Certainly, the growth of cities and the development of suburbs changed the structure and effects of gender roles (Hayden, 1981). Experts in policy and planning are coming to realize that the structure and design of communities have a special impact on women because of their gender roles, and that women's needs must be given more attention in urban planning.

Although cities are often the base of progressive attitudes and social change, we should not exaggerate the differences between urban and rural settings. We have already seen that the 19th-century cult of domesticity, which counterposed the rough-and-tumble world of male commerce with the serene woman's domain of the home, or the Victorian-era image of the frail, swooning lady had little relevance to—indeed could provoke economic disaster in—the farmlands. Some of the almost entirely agricultural Midwestern states were among the first to grant women the right to vote.

One other type of cultural and geographic division among women should be considered. Although this book is about the United States, it is important to know whether the evidence provided by the American experience is similar to that found in other countries, and what aspects of the American experience are unique to this society. The question of how much change has occurred and how much change can occur is a relative one. How do the types and degrees of change that have occurred in the United States compare with those that have occurred elsewhere? It is impossible to make more than a few brief comments here, but these indicate directions for further inquiry.

This chapter has consistently emphasized two crucial points in considering diversity among women and the relationship between gender and other social divisions. First, it is crucial not to take the experience of some women and generalize to all women. Second, there is a tendency for people to generalize from their own experiences without realizing it. This is certainly the case with national differences. Throughout, this book offers comparisons with situations in other nations in order to help to understand the particular case being observed—the United States —more clearly.

The research literature on women in the various social sciences shows a noticeable tendency to overgeneralize. Sociologists studying specific American communities speak of "the" relationship between class or race and gender without noting that what they see is conditioned by the specific history and structure of the country they are studying. Psychologists are probably most likely of all to make no reference to the national setting of their research, assuming that if they conduct high-quality research, they can claim that their work is representative of people in general. History, social structures, the particular design of the state, and the place of that state in the global order make a difference in human meaning and social relations.

Conclusion: Learning From Difference

Doing good social science research on women involves two seemingly contradictory tasks. The first is to be able to make some nontrivial statements about women, their lives, and their experiences. The reason to look specifically at women is to claim there is something that makes them a collectivity, distinct from men, which implies some commonality among women. The second task, however, is to avoid seeking false commonality and, especially, to avoid comprehending women in such a way that makes some women represent all women. Recall the problem of representation that opened this book; the argument of feminists has long been that men have been taken to represent humanity as a whole. The problem here is to make sure that in the study of women in the United States, White, middle-class women (and perhaps those who are urban, Northern, and Christian) are not taken to represent American women as a whole.

People have a tendency to generalize from their own experience, so it is no surprise that scholarship dominated by one or another social group tends to generalize from its own standpoint. Psychologists also find that where social divisions exist, no matter how trivial, people tend (1) to exaggerate differences among the divided groups and (2) to see their own group as more complex and differentiated than the other group or groups. The tendency to generalize from our own experiences would tend to make us minimize differences from our own experience, and two other tendencies would lead us both to maximize differences between "us" and "them" and to trivialize differences among "them." We can see all of these effects in research on women and gender.

Writing on commonality and difference among women sometimes exaggerates commonality, sometimes difference. Certainly, the exact experiences of different groups of women differ greatly in detail, but as we have seen, there can be important parallels, or we can see where differences emerge because of a common rule that is being applied to them. Even now, as writers engage in what they see as sensitivity to difference, they can still overgeneralize. It is simply not adequate to generalize about gender relations in White, middle-class America, as though religion and ethnicity make no difference, for example. We cannot generalize about the gender relations among Native Americans; the different indigenous nations have different structures, cultures, and histories (Bonvillain, 1989). The labels "Hispanic" and "Asian American" mask large differences in national heritage. Similarly, we must not confound the historical inheritance and situation faced by African Americans whose families arrived recently from the West Indies with those of families from the slaveholding South, or of those raised in Southern rural versus Northern urban communities.

In recent years, women's studies writers have tended to emphasize difference among women, especially on the basis of race and sexuality. Many feminist theorists are now arguing that the dominance of "difference talk" threatens the very ability to say anything analytically or politically about women and gender (Gordon, 1991). To capture women's existence in all of its amazing variety and detail makes it difficult to say anything about women as a group. However, to capture women's existence only as undifferentiated women is to misunderstand the nature of the group.

Notes

1.   This phrase is a play on the title of an influential book and movie, *Black Like Me* (Griffin, 1961), in which a white man disguises himself as Black and learns how profound a difference race makes.

2.   I have made up these different names to distinguish among general tendencies that emerge from reading in this area; none of these are self-conscious schools of thought.

3.   For this reason, one of the first major books on Black women's studies was named *All the Women Are White, All the Blacks Are Men, But Some of Us Are Brave* (Hull, Scott, and Smith, 1982).

4.   Spelman (1988) embeds what I am calling a hierarchical model in her discussion of the additive model. The additive model does not logically imply a hierarchy of oppressions, however, so I discuss them separately.

5.   Older women are defined here as being at least 60 years old.

6.   Indeed, many writers routinely use the term *race* only with quotation marks.

Gender-Defining Institutions

PART TWO OFFERS A CLOSER LOOK at some social institutions and organizations whose primary function is defining *cultural norms,* the values through which we understand ourselves, other people, and the world in which we live. In this part, we focus on educational and health-care institutions, organized religion, the mass and cultural media of communication, and government.

Each chapter examines the ways in which these institutions define, create, maintain, and change gender norms and sex/gender systems. Chapter 5, on education, for example, shows how gender norms are taught in educational institutions, whereas Chapter 6, on health care, shows how definitions of health and health-care practices shape and are shaped by definitions of gender. All chapters explore how these institutions shape women's lives, and the influence women have had on these institutions. This examination of women's influence focuses not only on women's leadership positions within these institutions (as, for example, clergy, doctors, teachers, and government officials), but also on the kinds of influence women have had as community and family members. This investigation shows that although women's power has been limited by androcentric sex/gender systems, women have also had much more scope for shaping their own and other people's lives than is often realized.

Although the most important norm-defining institution, the family, is an underlying theme throughout this section, it does not have its own chapter in this section. Instead, because of the importance of understanding families as social institutions when studying gender, and especially women, each chapter devotes considerable attention to the family. Part Three focuses even more directly and intensively on women and the family.

Reflect *Before* You Read

1. Think about the education you have had up to this point, including, if applicable, your religious training. What did you learn about women? About men?

143

Did your education give you any hints or guidelines about what it should mean to you that you were born male or female? If you had been born the other sex, how might your education have been different?

2. Enjoy yourself this week. Watch television, go to the movies or a play, read a novel or a poem, listen to music on the radio, watch MTV, or go to a sporting event. What do you see women and men doing? What are their characteristics? What do these entertainments teach you about women and men, femininity and masculinity?

3. The vast majority of members of state legislatures, the U.S. House of Representatives, and the U.S. Senate are men. Why is this? What would it take for more women to get elected? Imagine for a moment that most of the members of these institutions were women. What difference would that change make? Why do so many people think that politics is men's business?

5

✿

Education:
Learning to Be Male and Female

EDUCATION HAS BEEN a central focus of women seeking to improve their condition and to raise their status for well over two centuries. Some of the reasons should be obvious. Education imparts skills that create options for individuals in economic, social, and political life. It is an instrument for attaining high-status positions. Education earns respect. But the education system is also one of the most important definers of gender norms and one of the most important institutional components of a sex/gender system. This chapter looks first at the historical evolution of women's education, then at the relationship between gender and the contemporary American educational system.

Historical Perspectives on Women's Education

We begin with three premises:

1. To think of education only as what happens in school buildings is to ignore much of what has constituted education, especially women's education, during most of history.
2. Both the substance and process of education impart far more than the three R's or even what we generally think of as school subjects. They also help shape people's values and ways of living in society.
3. Historically, education has been designed to help children find their place in society. Their place, and thus their education, has been defined partly by their gender.

Early Efforts

Relatively few people had any formal education until the 19th century. Most learned their trades and professions through apprenticeship or from parents or other relatives. Mothers and fathers passed their skills and knowledge to their

145

daughters and sons. Women taught women what they needed to know, and men taught men what they needed to know. For those who attained literacy, the only textbook was frequently the Bible, the only book people needed to read.

Formal education was largely restricted to the wealthy and well connected, generally men of the upper class. Formal education was considered irrelevant for most free citizens, dangerous for men of lower status and for women, and even illegal for enslaved black people. With few exceptions, education for upper-class women was confined to a bit of literature, music, and perhaps foreign language, all taught at home. The purpose of this education was to train women for their station.

The first real American battles over women's education revolved not around schooling per se but around *whether* women should write and speak and *what* they should write and say, especially with respect to religion. In colonial America, women were active as religious teachers, but they faced severe restrictions. In 1637, for example, "a synod of elders resolved that women might meet 'to pray and edify one another,' but when one woman 'in a prophetical way' resolved questions of doctrine and expounded Scripture, then the meeting was 'disorderly'"(Koehler, 1982, 41). Women could preach, but only to each other, and they could teach, but only thoughts derived from their husband's or minister's minds. Those who went too far posed a danger to social order and even to their own sanity. In 1645, Governor John Winthrop of Massachusetts wrote that Anne Hopkins, the wife of Connecticut's governor, had gone insane because she spent too much time writing and reading. Her sanity might have been saved had she "attended her household affairs, and such things as belong to a woman" (Koehler, 1982, 37).

The most famous dispute over women's education during the colonial period was waged between Anne Hutchinson and the religious authorities of the Massachusetts Bay Colony. Although the strict Massachusetts colony dealt harshly with all cases of suspected heresy, part of the reason offered by the authorities for Hutchinson's excommunication and banishment was that her teaching activities stepped beyond the bounds of women's proper role.

As Chapter 2 showed, Enlightenment theorists emphasized the development of rationality and knowledge as the keys to a better and more democratic future. To create a new kind of society based on reason, individual merit, independence, and achievement required creating individuals with the right kind of character and skills. But should women and men—*could* they—be educated in the same way?

The theoretical debates began in Europe. The very influential education theorist Jean-Jacques Rousseau (1712–1778) argued that men should be educated in reason and independence to enable them to carry on the major work of society. However, Rousseau and most others thought that extending this education to women would be counterproductive because women's tasks were to get married, be submissive and ornamental to their husbands, raise their children, and do or supervise the necessary domestic work. Mary Wollstonecraft in England and the Marquis de Condorcet (1743–1794) in France, among others, argued that the values of a liberal society must also extend to women. They agreed that most women would be primarily wives and mothers, but they could not imagine how women could even be proper companions to these "new men," or fit mothers to their children, if they themselves had not learned reason and independence of mind.

This debate also raged in the new American republic. What kinds of men and women would be needed in this new country? How should they be trained?

Liberal European ideas on education had great influence in America, and, as in Europe, some included and some excluded women. Many experts argued that it was "necessary that our ladies should be qualified to a certain degree by a peculiar and suitable education, to concur in instructing their sons in the principles of liberty and government," as Benjamin Rush (1745–1813) said in his address to the Young Ladies Academy, established in Philadelphia in 1786 as the first American school for girls (Kerber, 1982, 91). Women should be good "republican mothers" able to educate the sons of liberty, hardly a radical view in our eyes, but in the 1780s, it was a significant move forward.

That women should be educated for motherhood was not a new view, but the conception of what type of education would accomplish this was changing. An intellectual leader such as Rush probably knew that the verb *to educate* is derived from a word meaning *to rear*. He and most other educators certainly realized that all mothers are teachers and are involved in education regardless of their own schooling.

Some were more radical. Judith Sargent Murray (1751–1820), writing as "Constantia," was one of many women contending that as long as women's education was aimed at producing wives and mothers, it would create dependents, rather than the independent people required by the young republic. She was one of the first American feminists who insisted that females and males do not *naturally* have different characteristics but, rather, are *taught* to be different. In one of her most famous passages she asked her readers,

> Will it be said that the judgement of a male of two years old is more sage than that of a female's of the same age? I believe the reverse is generally observed to be true. But from that period on what partiality! how is the one exalted and the other depressed, by the contrary modes of education which are adopted! the one is taught to aspire, the other is early confined and limited! (Rossi, 1988, 19)

Others were even more direct. A speaker at the 1793 Young Ladies Academy graduation charged, "Our high and mighty Lords . . . have denied us the means of knowledge, and then reproached us for the want of it" (Kerber, 1982, 87).

Nevertheless, many women gained some formal education in those early days. They continued to teach each other and to learn informally at home and in church. That many women learned despite the lack of formal opportunities is evidenced by the number of women writers. Many women also submitted their writings to newspapers, often under assumed names (a practice also employed by men). We still read the poems of women such as Anne Bradstreet (1612–1672) and Phyllis Wheatly (1753?–1784), one of the first black American poets. Mercy Otis Warren (1728–1814) was the first historian of the American Revolution, and the letters of her friend Abigail Adams, wife of President John Adams, remain examples of the prolific writings of many early American women.

Expanding Access

Formal educational opportunities for women expanded in the 1830s and 1840s. As free public schools were founded, especially in the Northeast, girls joined boys in elementary school, although they were mostly excluded from higher levels until after the Civil War. When the first American colleges opened their doors in the

17th century (Harvard in 1636, William and Mary in 1693), all barred women. In 1821, Emma Willard (1787–1870) opened the Troy Female Seminary, offering a curriculum similar to that of men's colleges, although her main goal was to make her students good American mothers or teachers. Her school, which still exists as the Emma Willard School, fared better than one of the first schools for black girls, opened in 1833 by Prudence Crandall in Connecticut. Crandall was jailed on trumped-up charges, and her school was burned down.

The 1830s saw the beginnings of coeducational colleges. Oberlin College (Ohio) opened its doors to men and women, whites and blacks in 1832, followed in 1847 by Lawrence College (Wisconsin). Wheaton College was founded as the first real women's college in 1834, followed by Mount Holyoke in 1837. The New England Female Medical College was started in 1848, followed closely by the Philadelphia Women's Medical College in 1851. Only a tiny proportion of women went to these schools, but they had a major influence on American life. Among the earliest female college graduates were many leaders of the post–Civil War feminist movement, as well as the first formally trained female doctors, clergy, and other professionals.

These formal schools were not the only places where women taught and learned. Women sought other means to educate themselves and others. They organized study groups or seminars on many topics. Margaret Fuller (1810–1850), a member of the American Transcendentalist group (along with Emerson and Thoreau) and editor of their journal, *The Dial*, held "Conversations," or seminars, open only to women. She believed, as many feminists do today, that there must be at least some separate time and space in which women can learn among themselves, unimpeded by the hierarchical relations between the sexes.

While Fuller discussed philosophy, the classics, and other topics among relatively wealthy women, thousands of others across the country traded information and knowledge among themselves at quilting bees and other such gatherings. And women by no means restricted themselves to such safe, though revolutionary, activities. Although it was illegal to teach black slaves to read, many women did so; after the Civil War women organized missionary societies that sent women throughout the South to teach newly freed men and women. Others, organized by Catharine Beecher (Harriet Beecher Stowe's sister) in the late 1840s, went west to teach on the frontiers.

By 1873, 60% of all American secondary schools had mixed-sex classes. The number of coeducational colleges increased to 22 by 1867 and to 97 by 1872 (Leach, 1980, 72). Although opportunities for formal education increased during this period, women's education lagged behind men's in two respects: (1) Women still received less education than men, and (2) even if they went beyond the elementary level, their education continued to be oriented mostly toward producing good wives and mothers. Few educators thought females' education and males' education should be the same.

Increasing Leadership Roles

Women also gained some ground as teachers, administrators, and other shapers of education. In the early 19th century, the vast majority of teachers were men, but by the late 1880s, the majority (up to 90% in some cities) were women (Sklar,

1982, 146). Amazingly, perhaps up to one fifth of all New England women served as teachers at some point in their lives (Jones, 1980, 48). What caused this expansion? Kathryn Kish Sklar (1982) has argued that hiring women was a matter of practical finances: They were cheaper. Three arguments justified paying women teachers much less than men:

1. Women did not have to support families as men did.
2. Women deserved less pay because they would quit their jobs when they married.
3. Women's low salaries were merely determined by the free market; women would accept lower salaries, and so they got them.

Gender stereotypes and prejudices, then, served as mechanisms that helped allow mass education to grow cheaply in the United States. For women, the expansion of teaching jobs, even if they were poorly paid, meant the opening of a sector of jobs appropriate for a decent lady.

Women made less progress in entering administrative and policymaking roles, although these expanded somewhat, as well. Some women opened their own schools. Most of what became the "Seven Sisters" colleges (Mt. Holyoke, 1837; Vassar, 1861; Wellesley, 1870; Smith, 1871; Radcliffe, 1879; Bryn Mawr, 1880; and Barnard, 1889) were opened by women late in the last three decades of the 19th century. In 1904 Mary McLeod Bethune (1875–1955), a daughter of slaves and educated by missionaries, opened a small school for black youths in Daytona Beach, Florida. She began her school using charred splinters of wood as pencils and elderberry juice as ink; she eventually transformed the school into what is now Bethune–Cookman College (Bethune, [1941] 1982).

Even in women's schools, however, women remained constrained by restrictive views of their place. Emily James Putnam (1865–1944), dean of Barnard College, was threatened with the loss of her job when she married. Although she survived that round, when she became pregnant she was forced to leave: Employment and marriage did not mix well, and employment and motherhood was even worse. Until World War II, most school boards demanded that women resign when they married; some would not even let women wait until the end of the school year. These laws finally disappeared in the mid-1950s. Laws such as these, which applied only to women, were made illegal by the 1964 Civil Rights Act.

Women's roles in shaping education also grew in other ways through the 19th century. In 1837, property-owning (white) widows in Kentucky with children in school were allowed to vote in school-board elections. More places extended the school-board vote to women as education came to be viewed as an appropriate arena for women's action. The right to vote in school-board elections was followed by the right to run for school-board offices (first in Illinois in 1872). By the end of the 19th century, some women even served as school superintendents.

The number of women's clubs and organizations directed at improving education mushroomed. The 1870s saw the rise of "moral education," or "moral science," societies, groups of women who discussed among themselves topics such as sexuality, marriage, and birth control (Leach, 1980). Suffrage groups and others interested in women's roles in society held lectures, seminars, and other such meetings to educate women for citizenship.

Mary McLeod Bethune, educator and political activist, turned a small school into what is now Bethune–Cookman College.

The development of social science offered more scope for women's leadership. Proponents of this new field argued that the knowledge gained from the social science research could help make a better society. Women not only were active in the new American Social Science Association (ASSA) but also formed their own social science associations and clubs, beginning in the 1870s. As early as 1874, a leader in the ASSA argued, "The work of social science is literally women's work, and it is getting done by them more and more; but there is room for all sexes and ages in the field of social science" (Leach, 1980, 316). These women's groups, which later took leading roles in the politics of the Progressive era, lobbied for educational reforms.

Some groups took on radical issues, as demonstrated by Dr. Alice Stockham's 1878 address to the Illinois Social Science Association. She argued that "every child should get special instruction in procreation and reproduction. Let us see to it that no girl should go to the altar of marriage without being instructed in the physiological function of maternity" (Leach, 1980, 321). She was not alone in this view; by the early 20th century, a campaign advocating sex education in public schools was organized in an effort to combat venereal disease and prostitution (Trudell, 1993, 10). Margaret Sanger (1883–1960) brought education about reproductive issues to working-class women in the immigrant ghettos. Feminists were just as concerned as others about the quality of women's lives as wives and mothers, but their approach was then, as it is now, quite different from that of nonfeminists.

By the end of the 19th century, the education of immigrants and their children became a concern of school administrators, other government officials, and a variety of women's groups, including those in the new profession of social work. They believed that education should be designed to make immigrant women good American wives and mothers. Immigrant women needed English competency to run their households properly and to teach their children. They needed courses in household arts or home economics in order to make proper American homes and learn budgeting to avoid the discontent of poverty. They needed Americanization, enabling them to control their children and to ward off juvenile delinquency. They also needed to be taught appropriate trades for women, to avoid being drawn into the "white slave trade" (prostitution) before they got married. Many of the most popular and successful programs were run by (a) ethnic and cultural groups and churches themselves, such as the Polish Women's Alliance of America, the Union of Czech Women, the National Council of Jewish Women; (b) trade unions, such as the Ladies Waist Makers Union or the International Ladies Garment Workers Union (ILGWU); or (c) socialist groups (Seller, 1982). Of course, much more effort was devoted to educating immigrant men. Overcrowding, combined with traditional gender attitudes, meant that school officials were more willing to let girls drop out to create places for boys. The norm in the majority of immigrant families was that girls should leave school early to help support their families and to put their brothers through school.

New "women's" educational fields, such as home economics and domestic science, were developed in the early 20th century and introduced into secondary and college curricula to teach women how to be modern housewives. The *modern* housewife, experts claimed, needed more than her mother's recipes to be successful; she needed firm knowledge of nutrition, psychology, sociology, and even biology and organic chemistry to run her household scientifically. Mothers needed

TABLE 5-1
Proportion of All Degrees Awarded to Women, 1890–1990

Year	B.A.	M.A.	Ph.D.	Medicine (M.D.)	Dentistry (D.D.S.)	Law (L.L.D./J.D.)
1890	17	19	1			
1900	19	19	6			
1910	23	26	10			
1920	34	30	15			
1930	40	40	15			
1940	41	38	13			
1950	24	29	10	10	1	
1960	35	35	11	6	1	2
1970	42	40	13	8	1	5
1980	47	49	28	23	13	30
1990	53	53	36	34	31	42
2000 (proj)	55	51	40			

Source: U.S. Bureau of the Census (1982, 1997, 191).

some advanced mathematics and even physics to help their children with their homework. If a woman had to earn a living, she should have a career that (a) fit in with her "inevitable" family commitments and (b) could be dropped for a few years when her children needed her most. Motherhood was still woman's primary mission, but in modern times, it was a subject to be studied and pursued scientifically. (For further discussion of this topic, see Chapter 12.)

Achieving Higher Education

Women's education expanded in the 20th century, despite resistance and occasional slowdowns. Some experts worked hard to keep women back, often relying on "scientific" theories, such as one by Edward Clarke, who argued in the 1880s that if women became too educated, the energy that should go to their wombs would be diverted to their brains, leaving them too feeble to produce healthy children. By the middle of the 20th century, however, the question of whether women should be educated up to the secondary level had been resolved; the battle now focused more on facilitating women's access to university education, advanced degrees, and training programs in traditionally male fields such as business and industry.

Only in the 1980s did women and men reach parity in the number of B.A. and M.A. degrees they earn (see Table 5-1). These figures demonstrate that history has not provided steady progress for women. Notice, for example, the large dip in the proportion of degrees women received immediately after World War II, when large numbers of male veterans were assisted by the G.I. Bill, and women were discouraged from education and employment. The decline in the proportion of higher degrees gained by women occurred not because the absolute number of women fell, but because the number of men seeking these degrees rose so steeply in a time of massive discrimination against women. It took until the 1970s to recover women's portion. Progress in the traditionally male fields of medicine, dentistry, and law began in the 1970s and has been impressive since then. The period from 1980 through the 1990s witnessed substantial change, encouraged by (a) laws and public policies designed both to end discrimination and to encourage women's education, and (b) the actions of women's groups in promoting women's education.

Women's Education Today

The first clear legal or policy statement from the U.S. government supporting equal education and forbidding gender discrimination was written in Title IX of the Education Amendments Act of 1972: "No person in the United States shall, on the basis of sex, be excluded from participation in, be denied the benefits of, or be subjected to discrimination under any education program or activity receiving federal financial assistance." This act covers all public schools and many private ones. This crucial change in public policy has now been in place for over a quarter-century. Have Americans attained gender equity in education? One of the most important indications comes from a major report published in 1992 by the American Association of University Women (AAUW), the conclusions of which are clear from the report's title: *How Schools Shortchange Girls*. This section looks at that report and other evidence on women's education today.

How Much Education?

When asking how much education women need, two questions must be answered: (1) Do women and men get the same amount of education? (2) Do women get the amount of education they need? These are not different wordings of the same question. Even if men's and women's levels of education are similar, women may not necessarily be getting the amount of education they need. To earn the same amount of money as men, for example, women need more education than men.

The law requires that all children attend school from age 5 or 6 to age 16 years. Thus, let us look at gender comparisons in the amount of preschool education and of education after age 16, as well as of special education, where we might see gender differences. Education before first grade, such as nursery schools and kindergartens, has become increasingly popular since World War II, as more mothers sought employment, and antipoverty programs emphasized the importance of early education. Experts believe that roughly the same number of boys and girls are enrolled in such programs (AAUW, 1992, 18).

Boys outnumber girls in special-education programs for the mentally retarded, speech impaired, emotionally disturbed, and learning disabled by a very wide margin; about two thirds of students in special-education programs are boys. In 1990, girls constituted one third of special-education students.[1] Conventional wisdom has it that more boys suffer from these problems than girls, thus explaining enrollment differences. Research suggests that the real gender differences in *incidence* of these difficulties may be much smaller than the differences in enrollment would suggest. Teachers and others may be *diagnosing and treating* boys and girls with similar problems differently. Boys might more often be placed incorrectly in these classes because they are more likely to act out aggressively or in other noticeable ways, while girls who are in need of help are not as readily identified because they are not noticed (AAUW, 1992, 19–20).

The law does not require students to finish high school, and there are gender differences in dropout rates, but these depend on race. Government figures on 18- and 19-year-olds in 1995 showed no real gender differences in dropout rates among white students, but black men were somewhat more likely to drop out than black women (18% vs. 14%), and Hispanic women were more likely to drop out than Hispanic men (35% vs. 27%).[2] It is commonly believed that the main reason that girls leave school is because of pregnancy; in fact, 50–60% of female dropouts cite other reasons. Many more girls than boys cite other "family-related problems"; more boys than girls mention work as a reason for leaving (AAUW, 1992, 48). Because men are more likely to return for a *GED* (high school equivalency), ultimately, in the youngest generation, roughly the same proportion of men and women have a high school education. It is the *race* differences that tell a story of much greater inequality. In 1996, for example, among 25- to 29-year-olds, 93% of whites, 86% of African-Americans, and 63% of Hispanics had completed high school.[3]

The proportion of males and females going beyond high school changed dramatically over the course of the 20th century. As Table 5-1 shows, following the tremendous growth in the number of men who went to college after World War II, women and men reached parity in attaining B.A.s in the 1980s, when the women began to earn half the M.A.s. Although women now earn a slight majority of those degrees, they are still behind in attaining Ph.D.s and some advanced professional degrees. Even there, however, efforts to end discrimination and to attract women led to great strides in equality, especially after 1980. The changes in women's entry into professional and postgraduate programs, especially after Title IX of the 1972 Educational Amendments Acts, is remarkable. This law required schools to abandon their discriminatory policies, which often explicitly specified higher entrance requirements for women than for men.

Colleges and universities are not the only types of postsecondary education available; adults may also enroll in technical, vocational, business, and other kinds of training programs. Women are a majority of those enrolled in adult-education programs. They also get their adult education from different sources than do men. They are more likely to take courses from local schools and 2-year colleges, private tutors and instructors, or private community organizations. The courses men take are more likely to be provided by their own employers (U.S. Department of Education, 1992, 345).

> **BOX 5-1   See for Yourself: Women's Education in the Community**
>
> Explore the informal education system available to women in your community. Make a list or catalog of the educational opportunities women provide to themselves in your town or county. Don't forget to consider the following: lectures, workshops, classes, and demonstrations sponsored by women's groups, clubs, professional or service societies; events sponsored through churches and synagogues, hospitals and health clinics, parent–teacher organizations, senior citizen centers, neighborhood groups, commercial enterprises (such as cookware shops, bookstores, department stores, and shopping malls), and women's auxiliaries of men's groups. Look for media outlets aimed specifically at women, such as newspapers (or sections of the newspaper), radio shows, newsletters, and websites.
>
> How large is this education system? What are the characteristics of the women who are reached by it? What kind of education can women—do women—receive through this system? What is its relationship to the formal education system? How aware do you think most women are of what is available to them? Could women's access to this education system be expanded?

Women are also continuing their long tradition of educating themselves outside the school. (See Box 5-1.) Women's church groups, professional and labor organizations, and political and social clubs continue to hold lectures, meetings, courses, and training institutes for women to learn a wide range of subjects and skills. One of the most important functions of the new women's movement has been education. It has spawned innumerable lectures, seminars, and small informal discussion groups, as well as books, articles, newspapers, magazines, and publishing houses.

Thus far, this chapter has compared the amount of education males and females receive by looking at how many are sitting in what kinds of classrooms. Research provides evidence, however, that girls and boys receive different amounts of education even when they are in the same classrooms. These gender differences can occur in four different ways: (1) the amount of attention teachers pay to boys and girls, (2) the types of attention teachers pay, (3) the degree to which chosen teaching methods effectively reach girls and boys, and (4) the degree to which the subjects studied stretch and challenge girls and boys.

The AAUW report found differences as early as preschool, where teaching often focuses on competencies girls already have; thus, girls may receive less new education than boys. Some skills that boys tend to have developed by that time and in which girls need the most encouragement—large-motor skills—are regarded as "free play" and not directly incorporated to stretch girls' new learning in that area (AAUW, 1992, 18–20).

The amount of education children receive depends not just on the conscious choices of teachers and administrators, but also on the way the educators interact with students, in often unconscious ways. The influence of such interactions opens up more possibility for gender differences in educational experiences and in the impact of schools. Many studies suggest that teachers give more attention to boys than to girls (AAUW, 1992; Bailey, 1993). One often-cited study suggested that girls and boys have to act differently to get the same amount of attention from their teachers (Serbin et al., 1973). In that study, girls who were physically close to their teachers received more attention than did boys who were physically close, but boys who were aggressive received more attention than did girls who were aggressive. Perhaps that is why boys initiate more interactions with teachers than girls do (Irvine, 1986). Girls, indeed, may be either more disciplined or less confident in their classroom behavior and may wait to be called on, rather than volunteering as boys do, especially in subjects such as mathematics (Levine, 1995). It is important to emphasize that teachers' gender-based reactions are often not conscious or intentional. A study of preservice teachers' interactions and perceptions, for example, showed that while 71% judged their group dynamics to be equitable, in fact 55% of the men and only 28% of the women spoke (Lundeberg, 1997).

Teachers may structure classrooms in ways that advantage the participation of one sex over the other; for example, research has often demonstrated that boys respond better to competitive strategies of teaching than girls do, for example, in mathematics (Bailey, 1993). This observation should point out that giving all students exactly the same treatment does not necessarily create fairness and equitable education because people's needs may differ. The AAUW report shows that different teaching methods are sometimes differentially effective for girls and boys, but where this is the case, the method that is better for boys is more often used. Specialists interested in teaching computer science have found that males and females often use different routes to solve the same problems; thus, if computer instruction is done only one way, some students—usually the girls—will be disadvantaged (Kramer and Lehman, 1990; Turkel and Papert, 1990).

These patterns may also depend on the class *subject;* one study of second-graders showed that teachers made more contacts with girls during reading classes and with boys during mathematics classes (Leinhardt, Seewald, and Engel, 1979); other studies reinforce the idea that boys may get more attention in science classes, especially chemistry (Bailey, 1993). Certainly, not all boys benefit from these gender patterns; in fact, the differences may be accounted for by the attention received by a very few males, to the exclusion of most of the others (Eccles, 1989). Research comparing sexism in different subjects across different types of schools detected severe problems in chemistry, compared with the other subjects included in the study (calculus, English, history). In coeducational schools, chemistry classes accounted for 66% of all of the sexist incidents observed, revealing "the most blatant examples of male domination of discussions, of teachers favoring boys, and of the humiliation of girls" (Lee, Marks, and Byrd, 1994, 104).

Research also suggests that teachers may have different *kinds* of interactions with boys and girls. Some research concludes that boys get more negative treatment or criticism from teachers, although there is contradictory evidence as well (Bank, Biddle, and Good, 1980). Criticism in the classroom, of course, is not necessarily harmful to education. For example, boys may get more criticism from teachers, but they also may receive different kinds of criticism than girls do; research suggests that boys receive criticism for not trying hard enough to do well, which seems to assume that they could do better if they wanted, while girls are more likely to be criticized for their academic performance itself, which may be a less encouraging evaluation (Dweck et al., 1978).

Iona Dumitriu, the first woman to win the William Lowell Putnam Mathematical
Competition.

Race and gender interact to determine how teachers and students act with
each other. Teachers' behavior can be shaped by both gender and race perceptions
and biases. For example, when nearly 1,000 teachers were asked to rate 6- to 11-
year-old children, white teachers (regardless of gender) perceived white students
more positively than black students, and female teachers (regardless of race) perceived female students more positively. Black female teachers made no race distinctions in their ratings (Rong, 1996). Girls may generally get less feedback, but the
problem may be especially great for black girls (Irvine, 1986). Some research suggests that among girls, African-American children get more reinforcement for
good social behavior, while white girls may get more for good academic behavior
(Scott-Jones, and Clark, 1986).

We still need more research to untangle the effects of gender and race on classroom experiences. For example, one study based on interviews with African-
American students showed that the girls were twice as likely to say that teachers were
supportive of them, and when asked for examples, the girls named academic support
(e.g., helping when I don't understand), while the boys were more likely to name
social support (e.g., lets us get to know her, jokes around) (Pollard, 1993). Another
study, however, showed race differences but no gender differences in students' perceptions of their teachers' caring behavior (Hayes, Ryan, and Zseller, 1994).

Students' own interactions among themselves may also shape the amount of
education they receive, especially in the degree and types of interactions they have
in the classroom. Boys take more leadership roles for themselves among the children, and girls seem more willing to give boys help than the reverse (Bailey, 1993).

The balance of males and females in the classroom affects the degree to which they participate, for example, in asking questions or interacting with the teacher. A team of researchers observing college classrooms found that once males constitute even 30% of the students in a class, they dominate the discussion (Canada and Pringle, 1995).

What Did You Learn in School Today?

Schools and school curricula are designed in part to teach fundamental cultural values, including gender norms. Until recently, there was widespread consensus about the gender norms girls and boys should learn. To what degree do schools continue to teach gendered lessons?

Educators talk about two different types of curricula: the *overt curriculum,* the lessons teachers are consciously and explicitly trying to teach; and the *hidden curriculum,* things that may be taught consciously or unconsciously but are not part of the apparent lesson plan. Many critics of American education argue that the hidden curriculum still supports traditional gender roles and, more specifically, discourages girls who might otherwise stretch themselves beyond traditional gender boundaries in intellectual skills and interests. Others critics, however, worry that schools have become too involved in trying to change social values and are too critical of traditional family and gender roles.

Consider the content of textbooks. Even in the 19th century, some educational reformers realized that it was necessary to give girls examples of women who had achieved notability in a variety of fields in order to expand their ambitions and horizons (Leach, 1980). In the 1970s, a group of women published a study of 2,760 children's stories to demonstrate the lessons girls and boys learn about women's potential (Women on Words and Images, 1972). They found females notably absent from the world presented to children. There were 5 boy-centered stories for every 2 girl-centered stories, 3 adult male characters for every adult female character, and 6 biographies of males for every biography of a female. Although males were considerably more present than females, the word *mother* appeared more often than the word *father,* and the word *wife* appeared three times as often as the word *husband.* Similar findings have emerged from studies of textbooks at the primary and secondary levels (Weitzman, 1979). It does not look as though there has been much change since that time, although there has been some (AAUW, 1992, 62; Allen, Allen, and Sigler, 1993; Clark, Lennon, and Morris, 1993; Dellman-Jenkins, Florjancic, and Swadener, 1993). Nevertheless, many school districts have tried to introduce books that present more egalitarian gender roles.

Bias in schoolbooks is by no means limited to the primary and secondary levels. Reviews of college- and graduate-level textbooks show the same pattern. A review of medical textbooks, including those used in obstetrics and gynecology classes, shows that women are often presented in thoroughly negative terms and used gratuitously as sex objects in illustrations and examples (Elder, Humphreys, and Laskowski, 1988). Perhaps even more shocking, in regard to the possibilities for change in education, is Sadker and Sadker's (1980) content analysis of the most widely used education textbooks, which found the same pattern of bias.

Despite all the research on gender and sexism in education done in recent decades, only one book at which the Sadkers looked devoted even 0.5% of its space (1 page out of 200, for example) to issues of sexism. Another book discussed guidelines for nonsexist language but did not itself follow the guidelines. A review of introductory sociology textbooks published between 1982 and 1988 also found little material on women (Hall, 1988).

What difference does textbook bias make? Many psychologists emphasize the importance of role models in developing children's senses of identity and in giving them examples to follow. Two pieces of research show how textbooks affect what children learn and think. In one study, Ashby and Wittmaier (1978) read to fourth-grade girls either a story presenting women only in their traditional family roles or a story showing women in nontraditional activities. The girls were then asked to rate a series of jobs and characteristics, according to how appropriate they were for women. The girls who had heard the stories with the nontraditional themes for women rated traditionally male jobs and characteristics as appropriate for females more frequently than did the other girls.

In another study, researchers gave college students titles for chapters in a forthcoming general sociology textbook and asked them to select appropriate photographs for each of the chapters (Schneider and Hacker, 1973). Some of the students were given the chapter titles "Social Man," "Industrial Man," and "Political Man." The others were given chapter titles "Society," "Industrial Life," and "Political Behavior." The latter students chose pictures with a greater number of women in them. Apparently, the first set of titles supported images of a predominantly male world in the minds of the students.

Children already have a gender-typed understanding of historical human communities by middle school. When asked to illustrate textbooklike passages about history, fifth- and eighth-grade boys populated the world almost exclusively with men, and usually men fighting, while girls usually drew families. No child in the whole study ever drew two women together; there was always a man present (Fournier and Wineburg, 1997).

The gendered messages children receive are not simple; they are self-contradictory. On the one hand, they are told that in a democracy, all children are given an equal chance, and that math, science, and technology are important in the modern world. However, schools blunt these encouraging messages by offering conflicting ones to girls. Girls are still often subtly told that their most important role is that of wife and mother (even if she also studied physics) and that a girl should not sacrifice her femininity to pursue her education or a career.

Children learn very young that some subjects are masculine and some are feminine. For instance, as discussed previously, various gender-bias problems surround mathematics. Julia Sherman (1980) found that the degree to which high school girls considered mathematics a male domain affected their performance in the subject, and among eleventh-grade girls, it affected how much confidence they had in their abilities to learn math. Thus, a girl who thinks that mathematics is a masculine subject will not have much confidence in her ability to learn mathematics or will feel that it is better to avoid the subject for social reasons.

Labeling different subjects as *masculine* or *feminine* restricts both girls and boys. In the United States (although not in all countries), girls tend to be better than boys at reading in the younger grades. Carol Dwyer (1974) studied the problem and found that boys who did poorly in reading were more likely to consider reading to be a feminine occupation. Both boys and girls do well on school problems that are directly related to what they view as appropriate gender norms and poorly on those at odds with these norms (Christoplos and Borden, 1978). It is, of course, quite possible for young people to assert themselves against these norms, but that can take great determination and sometimes incurs ridicule. Teachers can also help, but first they must become aware of the problems.

Over the years, many researchers have investigated the ways in which schools contribute to driving girls away from science, technology, and mathematics. Parents, of course, contribute to their children's choices in school. A study of Scottish 16- to 18-year-olds, for example, showed that computer usage among males and females increased a lot between 1986 and 1995; by 1995, the vast majority (89% of men and 94% of women) used computers at school, but 59% of men and only 31% of women were using their own computers, which means that parents were more likely to provide their sons than their daughters with a computer (Durndell and Thomson, 1997). The same study found that women, who were less likely to take computer studies courses, were more likely to say that they were not qualified, would have difficulty getting a job with computer studies, or simply did not find it interesting.

Another study showed that middle-school girls were underrepresented in science activities outside the classroom, including going to science museums. The authors noted that while this might be viewed as a simple reflection of gender differences in interest, they believe that young people's tastes are strongly influenced by parents, and their participation in these activities is shaped by adults. "Adolescents very seldom decide all on their own to go to science (or any) museums; rather, their parents take them and their teachers urge them" (Lee and Burkam, 1996, 642). As this chapter has shown, the teaching strategies in these fields may be less encouraging for girls than for boys, and girls may face blatant sexism in these especially male fields.

A study of very highly qualified young scientists found that the vast majority of the women (73%) thought they had faced discrimination on the basis of their gender, while a small number of men (13%) thought they had faced discrimination on the basis of theirs (Sonnert and Holton, 1996). Discouragement may also come from the more subtle aspects of mentoring relationships. This same study of highly qualified young scientists found that women had experienced *less* research collaboration with partners of senior or equal rank than men, meaning they had less mentoring or collegial research relationships, but *more* collaborations with someone more junior, meaning that they were doing more mentoring (Sonnert and Holton, 1996). Providing more women mentors, however, may have only limited value, at least as science is currently structured. Men who had female advisors were less likely to drop out of their science programs than those with male advisors, but women who had female advisors were slightly more likely to leave. The reason many women gave was that they were put off by the kinds of sacrifices they saw that their female mentors had to make (Sonnert and Holton, 1996). In the end, whatever their abilities, women have less confidence in their own abilities in these traditionally male fields (Durndell and Thomson, 1997; Sonnert and

TABLE 5-2
Proportion of Degrees Awarded to Women, 1971 and 1993

Field	Bachelor's		Master's		Doctor's	
	(1971)	*1993*	*(1971)*	*1993*	*(1971)*	*1993*
Agricultural and natural resources	(4)	34	(6)	38	(3)	25
Biological/life sciences	(29)	51	(34)	51	(16)	40
Business and management	(9)	47	(4)	36	(3)	28
Communications	(35)	60	(35)	62	(13)	52
Computer and information sciences	(14)	28	(10)	27	(2)	14
Education	(75)	75	(56)	77	(21)	59
Engineering	(1)	14	(1)	15	(1)	10
English	(66)	66	(61)	66	(29)	59
Foreign languages	(74)	71	(64)	67	(35)	57
Health sciences	(77)	83	(55)	80	(17)	57
Home economics	(97)	89	(94)	83	(61)	72
Liberal studies	(34)	60	(45)	65	(31)	53
Library and archival science	(92)	89	(81)	80	(28)	66
Mathematics	(38)	47	(27)	40	(8)	24
Philosophy, religion, theology	(26)	31	(27)	38	(6)	17
Physical sciences	(14)	33	(13)	29	(6)	22
Psychology	(44)	73	(41)	72	(24)	61
Social sciences (not including psychology)	(37)	46	(29)	43	(14)	36
Visual and performing arts	(60)	61	(47)	57	(22)	46

Source: U.S. Bureau of the Census, 1997.

Holton, 1996). This gender difference appears relatively large among Latinos, and small among African-Americans (Catsambis, 1994), and it is larger among working-class children, who are likely to enter a more gender-segregated job market, than among middle-class children (Flanagan, 1993).

In any case, many academic fields remain dominated by one sex or the other, despite changes over recent decades. Table 5-2 shows the proportions of the recipients of undergraduate and graduate degrees in 1971 and 1993 who were women. This table reveals many different interesting patterns: the changes over time within

TABLE 5-3
Proportion of Social Science and History Degrees
Awarded to Women, 1990

Field	B.A.	M.A.	Ph.D.
Anthropology	64	58	52
Economics	31	25	20
History	38	38	33
Political Science	41	33	26
Social Work	86	81	70
Sociology	68	59	48

Source: U.S. Department of Education (1992, 246–252).

fields, the comparison of lower and higher degrees within fields, and the differences across fields. Some disciplines that were overwhelmingly male in 1971 have integrated to substantial extents, especially at the B.A. level: Agriculture and business are the best examples. Most formerly male fields have shown significant improvement. Psychology, which was formerly relatively balanced, has become female dominated. Fields that were female dominated at the lower levels, such as education, foreign languages, English, health science, and library science have stayed stable or have increased their proportion of men. In most fields, including some of the traditionally female ones, the rule of the higher, the fewer still holds, although perhaps not as much as it did in 1971.

Of course, the figures displayed in Table 5-2 mask more gender variation, which is revealed by looking at the various disciplines more finely broken down and distinguished. For example, Table 5-3 shows variation in gender balance across the different social sciences that are lumped together in Table 5-2. Table 5-3 shows the very big differences between, for example, sociology on the one side and economics on the other. The same is true in other categories listed in Table 5-2, such as in the visual and performing arts. In 1990, for example, 67% of undergraduate fine-arts majors were women, compared with 50% of music majors; 55% of the Ph.D.s awarded in the fine arts went to women, compared with 36% of those in music. When breaking each of these fields down further—for example, comparing physical anthropology with cultural anthropology, international relations with political philosophy, or music composition with music history—further differences become apparent.

Gender and Evaluation

Gender expectations help people explain their successes and failures. Experimental research shows that people tend to express male success and female failure in terms of possession or lack of skills and to explain male failure and female success in terms of other factors, often things out of their control. (For a review of this research, see Deaux, 1976.) In one study, for example, people were told about males or females who did well or poorly in school. They were then asked to make up stories to explain these successes and failures. The same pattern found in other studies emerged: In the stories the subjects composed, males did well because they were smart and poorly because they were unlucky. Females did well because the test was easy, because they tried harder, or even because they cheated; they did poorly because they were not smart. This pattern holds particularly for gender-inappropriate tasks, and for both African-American and white students. When African-American girls specifically do as well as white boys in school, teachers seem to attribute the equality to the black girls' hard work and the white boys' lack of trying. African-American girls have lower academic self-evaluations than African-American boys in some areas in which the girls' actual performance was as good as or even better than the boys' (AAUW, 1992, 71).

Perhaps the most disturbing aspect of this body of research is that males and females apply these different perceptions to *their own* experiences. Girls learn not to expect much from their own abilities, which leads many to underrate themselves. By the same token, males show a tendency to overrate their own work. Three studies provide examples. A study of third-grade and junior high school students in math showed that girls self-evaluated their abilities and expected lower grades in mathematics than boys did, and girls attributed their failures more to lack of ability and their successes less to high ability than did boys. Girls who did badly were more likely than boys to want to hide their papers from others. Among the junior high students (but not the fourth-graders), girls who had not expected to do well on a test continued to be pessimistic about their future math prospects, even just after they received good test results. Girls were less likely than boys to think that trying hard could guarantee doing well (Stipek and Gralinski, 1991). These kinds of results have been found consistently for other subjects and students of other ages.

In her investigation of British adolescents' self-evaluations, Michelle Stanworth (1983) found that when students and teachers ranked students according to how well they were doing academically, most of the students ranked themselves differently from the way the teacher ranked them. All the girls who differed from the teacher's evaluation underestimated their own ranking. All but one of the boys who differed from the teacher overestimated their own ranking. In most of these cases, the girls incorrectly ranked themselves lower than a boy, and the boys incorrectly ranked themselves higher than a girl.

Gender norms have direct effects on school performance. A study of groups of adolescent Hopi and African-American girls who were highly skilled at playing dodgeball found that the girls reduced their level of competitiveness—actually held back their own performances—when they played with boys, especially when they played with boys who were relatively unskilled. Further investigation showed that the girls were unaware of what they were doing (Weisfeld, Weisfeld, and Callaghan, 1982). Similar behavior in boys, playing girls, would be regarded as chivalrous, but because the girls' behavior is unacknowledged, the implication is different. It simply offers further, although mistaken, evidence to all involved that boys are better than girls.

Parents also assess their children's schoolwork and abilities on the basis of gender. A study of seventh-grade mathematics students found that among students of average ability, fathers (but not mothers) held lower achievement standards for daughters than for sons. Parents (especially mothers) attributed their daughters' math successes more to effort than they did their sons', and they attributed their sons' successes more to talent than they did their daughters' (Yee and Eccles, 1988).

Of course, much of the evaluation of students is based on tests. Do tests offer an "objective," unbiased means to assure fair evaluation of girls and boys? Both gender and race bias in testing has been the subject of debate for a long time. The AAUW report shows some evidence of continued gender bias in testing. For example, in the 1970s, test companies began efforts to balance gendered references in tests, by embedding math problems in stories about measuring lengths of fabric, as well as football fields. In the 1980s, however, many standardized tests, including the crucial SAT (Scholastic Aptitude Test) exams, found extreme bias in the number of references to males and females. The AAUW review shows that test structures can have great influence over the relative performance of girls and boys (AAUW, 1992, 55–57).

Segregation and Schooling

One of the oldest debates over women and education concerns the benefits and drawbacks of mixed- versus single-sex education. In some education traditions and subjects, gender segregation was long enforced. Many fields of study were available only to one sex. For example, women's training as artists was limited because they were not allowed into classes with (nude) life models. Medical training also posed problems because of the parts of the body that must be discussed and viewed. The very idea of women working on cadavers was considered indecent. As this book has shown, many fields remain gender segregated.

Many reformers of the 19th century advocated mixed-sex schools. As William Leach (1980, 78) noted, "At the heart of the coeducational rationale lay the conviction that everything 'one-sided' and dangerous happens in a segregated sexual world where everything is hidden." In her *Vindication of the Rights of Woman*, Mary Wollstonecraft ([1792] 1975) argued strongly for mixed-sex schools for these reasons. She was adamant about the "immodesty" and impropriety of behavior in single-sex boarding schools; no doubt one of the things she feared was exploration of homosexuality among the young. Also, however, she wondered how men and women could be good companions if they had never had a chance to get to know each other as ordinary human beings. In 1870, Elizabeth Cady Stanton wrote, "In opening all high schools and colleges to girls we are giving young men and women better opportunities of studying each others' tastes, sentiments, capacities, characters in the normal condition" (Leach, 1980, 80).

By the 20th century, most public schools were mixed, and as the century continued, so was an increasing proportion of colleges and universities, including most of the long-segregated "Seven Sisters" and "Ivy League" schools of the Northeast. The number of women's colleges declined from 228 in 1969 to 82 in 1997. Considerable sex segregation remained, however. Physical-education classes were (and are) rarely mixed, even in sports that could easily be played by mixed groups. Most schools segregated the sexes into special "gender-appropriate" classes until recently: Girls learned cooking and sewing, and boys learned metal- or woodworking or mechanical drawing. In sex-education classes, boys and girls are often segregated, giving boys, for example, no opportunity to learn about menstruation (AAUW, 1992, 77). Segregation increases as students move up the education ladder.

Debates over segregation in schools came to a head in the 1990s, when women agitated to enter the Virginia Military Institute (VMI), an elite public institution aimed at producing "citizen soldiers," and the Citadel (South Carolina), another all-male public military training college. (These are different from the official training academies of the U.S. military, which were integrated in 1976.) The staff, students, and alumni at these institutions bitterly opposed gender integration.

At the Citadel, Shannon Faulkner sued because she had been accepted when her application showed no signs of her gender, but her acceptance was revoked when the Citadel found out her sex. For 2½ years after she initiated her suit early in 1993, various courts offered different decisions regarding the attempts of the Citadel to block her entrance. A circuit court ruling, for example, would have let the Citadel off the hook if another program could offer an alternative program for women. (One did this.) Ultimately, the Supreme Court refused to support the Citadel. Faulkner entered the Citadel but soon withdrew, claiming that her 2½-year battle had left her exhausted and unable to withstand the training in 100° heat during "hell week." Two other women who later enrolled quit after a hazing that included setting their clothes on fire and spraying deodorant in their mouths.

After a woman was refused entry into VMI in 1989, the U.S. Justice Department sued on grounds of sex discrimination. VMI tried to avoid an integration order by establishing a women's program at nearby Mary Baldwin College. This case, too, received different treatment from different courts, some siding with the U.S. Justice Department's view of sex discrimination, some siding with VMI's claim that its unique mode of "adversarial" or "doubting" training is inappropriate for women, and thus admitting them would require a wholesale change in their program. This change was unnecessary, they argued, because an equivalent but appropriate program was available at Mary Baldwin. The final Supreme Court decision (*U.S.* v. *Virginia,* 1996) is important because it provides such a good test of whether an institution may respond to perceived differences between men and women, or whether it may exclude women on grounds of key features of the program, such as the traditional total lack of privacy accorded to "rats," first-year students at the academy. The Supreme Court's opinion, written by Justice Ruth Bader Ginsburg, agreed that changes would have to be made to accommodate women. However, the Court said, the point of this institution that must be preserved is its *ends* (producing citizen soldiers) not its *means,* thus if changes are necessary, they must be made. The first group of women entered in 1997.

Is segregation in education always bad? When segregation limits opportunities to learn, there is a problem. It is not conducive to learning to be the odd woman (or man) out in a classroom filled with people of the other sex. One of the things people learn in school is how to understand, work with, respect, and get along with others. Nonetheless, segregation may have benefits in certain circumstances. Advocates of women's colleges point out that when women at these schools take physics or chemistry classes, they cannot be discouraged by being in the minority; there is no peer pressure from male classmates not to be smart. When women at women's colleges take women's studies courses, men are not there to make fun of them. A study by Elizabeth Tidball (1980) shows that twice as many of the women who appear in *Who's Who of American Women* went to women's colleges as to coeducational colleges. Some educators in former women's colleges that have since become mixed or have merged with men's colleges regret the change. Sports serves as a good case in point. In many cases, men have become dominant in the traditionally male fields. In some cases, such as that of Harvard and Radcliffe, the schools have not merely been merged; the women's college has, for all intents and purposes, been swallowed up by the men's school.

Research on the educational implications of gender segregation and integration find that segregation does make a difference. One research team that studied the impact of transforming a formerly all-women's college into a coeducational institution concluded, "Simply, the shift from all-female to mixed-sex classrooms was accompanied by profound changes in the nature of the dynamic of classroom interaction" (Canada and Pringle, 1995, 179). Women professors' classrooms became somewhat less democratic, with the professor initiating more of the interaction. As the proportion of men increased, the women students became less likely to enter into sustained discussions with professors in class, while the men became more active.

Another research project investigated instances of sexism in 86 classrooms in 21 schools, some of which were boys', some girls', and some coeducational. Of course, domination of one sex by the other could occur only in the mixed schools, and it did, with boys dominating girls regularly. Gender stereotyping was *less* common in the mixed schools than in the single-sex schools. Explicit sexual incidents, for example, using sexualized pictures of girls, occurred only in the all-boys school (Lee, Marks, and Byrd, 1994). In both the all-male and the coeducational schools, male teachers attributed to themselves more control over school policies than female teachers attributed to themselves; only in girls' schools did women perceive themselves as more in control than men perceived themselves (Lee, Loeb, and Marks, 1995).

Some feminists look back at intellectual forebears such as Margaret Fuller, who felt that women needed to meet among themselves to learn from each other, and Virginia Woolf, who talked about a woman needing a "room of her own." Although most of these feminists do not suggest that all education should be segregated, they do argue that there are certain circumstances under which it should be. One example is segregating classes in traditionally male fields to help women gain confidence in themselves. Another is courses on topics directly relating to questions of gender and sexuality. Men often regard women's discussions of these topics as hostile, and men become antagonistic and defensive when women talk honestly about their perceptions and questions. Many women worry about hurting men's feelings if they discuss some important issues, such as violence against women, in front of men. Further, feminists point out that women have long been expected to learn about themselves through the opinions of male "experts." If

TABLE 5-4
Women as a Proportion of Precollege Educators

Education Degrees: Proportion Granted to Women, 1990

	B.A.	M.A.	Ph.D./Ed.D.
Preelementary	98	98	*
Elementary	93	91	77
Secondary	62	67	63
Education administration	*	59	51
All education fields	78	76	58

Elementary and Secondary Educators, 1990

Teacher aides	93
Prekindergarten and kindergarten	99
Elementary teachers	85
Secondary teachers	52

Educational Governance, 1990

School principals	28
School superintendents	5
School-board members	34
Chief state school officer	18
College chief executive officer	10

Note: * = fewer than 100 degrees total.

Source: U.S. Department of Education (1992), U.S. Department of Labor (1992), AAUW (1992).

women are to learn to think and talk independently and honestly, especially about gender and sexuality and the areas of life thus affected, there may be some times during which women must withdraw to work among themselves. Some male feminists make the same point, arguing that before men can deal honestly with women about questions of sexuality and parenthood, for example, men must be able to talk honestly among themselves.

Women as Educators

People often say that education is a woman's field—but is it? What proportion of the people responsible for shaping and dispensing education are women? As Table 5-4 shows, despite women's involvement in education, men clearly predominate at the highest levels. The higher the degree, the lower is women's share. The higher the teaching position, the lower is women's share. In every type of college or university, the higher the rank, the fewer the women. Men clearly hold the majority of positions of educational governance, although there has been improvement in this area. In 1994, 16% of college presidents were women, compared with 5% in 1975. Of those, 9% were African-American and 5% were Hispanic.[4]

TABLE 5-5
College Faculty Rank, by Race and Gender

Rank	Full Prof.	Associate Prof.	Assistant Prof.	Lecturer
White				
Female	14.3	24.7	36.0	53.4
Male	75.7	63.1	47.5	29.6
Asian				
Female	0.4	1.0	2.1	2.6
Male	4.5	3.6	5.0	3.9
Black				
Female	1.1	2.1	3.0	3.7
Male	2.1	2.9	2.8	2.6
Hispanic				
Female	0.3	0.8	1.2	1.1
Male	1.4	1.3	2.0	2.0
American Indian				
Female	0.1	0.1	0.2	1.1
Male	0.2	0.3	0.2	—
Total % Female	16.2	28.7	42.5	61.9
Total % Nonwhite	10.1	12.1	16.5	17.0
Total	100.1	99.9	100.0	100.0

Source: "Characteristics of Full-Time Faculty Members With Teaching Duties, Fall, 1992," *Chronicle of Higher Education*, http://chronicle.com/che-data/infobank.dire/almanac.dir/96alm.dir/facts.dir/fac4.htm.

What holds women back in the field of education? Many of the same problems exist in education that occur in other jobs (see Chapter 13 for a closer look at women and employment). Although certain parts of the field of education are considered especially appropriate for women, the more the job departs from traditional stereotypes of women's nature and interests, the more obstacles women face. Many people argue that women are naturally suited to be educators, but that does not necessarily mean that women should run the show. Many see women as nurturers fit for kindergartens, not scholars fit for universities. Often, contemporary attitudes are still like those in the 19th century, defining women as (a) less competent than men to teach in secondary schools, for fear that women cannot discipline older children, and (b) less qualified to be administrators because management has been believed to be a man's job (Strober and Tyack, 1980).

As any college student can readily see, women still lag behind in holding faculty positions, especially at higher levels. There are fewer women on the faculties of research universities than at 4-year colleges, and fewer at the 4-year campuses than at 2-year colleges. Table 5-5 shows the gender and race proportion at each faculty rank at American colleges and universities. *Lecturers* are teaching staff members, often without Ph.D.s, who usually have temporary teaching positions and do not hold any governance positions in the institution. Ordinarily, lecturers are not automatically promoted up the ranks. *Assistant professors* usually have Ph.D.s and are in the first 6 years of their teaching careers, before earning *tenure*, or job security. They hold relatively few governance roles in the institution. *Associate* and *full professors* are the more senior and influential faculty members. As Table 5-5 shows, about three quarters of the nation's full professors are white males, and they also constitute a majority of associate professors. The faculty is also overwhelmingly white at the other ranks, but the domination of males is not quite as great at the assistant-professor level, and women are the majority of lecturers. The proportion of teaching faculty who are not white is very small, especially at the higher levels. Looking across groups, however, much the same gender pattern holds, although to varying degrees. At the higher levels, males dominate, sometimes to substantial degrees. At the lower two ranks, there are many more African-American women than men. Among both Asian and Hispanic faculty, men dominate at all levels. There is progress for women in the younger generations, but it is limited among faculty who are not white, and we cannot predict the future exactly until we determine how equitably distributed promotions will be.

Are women held back because they possess lower academic qualifications than men? Even in the mid-1970s, a review of research on women as leaders in public education pointed out that about equal numbers of male and female teachers had the credentials needed to become administrators; however, women put in an average of 15 years and men put in an average of only 5 years in the classroom before they became elementary-school principals (Estler, 1975). Similar patterns emerge at the college and university levels. The amount a professor publishes is a better predictor of men's rank and salary than of women's; women's publications apparently do not guarantee women's promotion the same way that men's do (Unger, 1979, 439). Even student evaluations of teachers are gender biased, although males' evaluations show more evidence of bias than females' (Basow and Silberg, 1987; Kierstead, D'Agostino, and Dill, 1988; Martin, 1984; but see also Wheeless and Potorti, 1989). Women are evaluated less favorably on traditionally male characteristics.

Many women find that from the first days they enter the classroom as student teachers, they are subjected to the gender prejudices of their students and, for those teaching in high school especially, sexual harassment, including sexist comments, catcalls, and other signs of resentment. As the experience of one student teacher was described by a researcher, "During student teaching, she realized that the students saw her in ways she did not. Her image was of a serious English teacher; their image was of a pretty young girl" (Miller, 1997, 20). Another student teacher explained how she reacted when a male student challenged her in public by asking her whether she "engaged in premarital sex": "And afterwards I just was like, oh, God, what's the matter with me that they feel they have to do this?" (Miller, 1997, 22). Even in a traditionally female field, teachers can find themselves faced with discrimination so profound that it leads them to doubt themselves.

Organizations of women in science point to the special barriers that face them in pursuing their goals. In 1997, for example, only 7 of the 60 new scientists

While these Smith College students studied chemistry in 1889, some theorists argued that too much education was bad for women's health.

inducted into the National Academy of Sciences were women, a proportion only slightly higher than that of the preceding two decades. One of the new 1991 members, Dr. Jane Richardson of the Duke University Medical School, explained part of the problem: "It's an old club, elected by its own members. They're really trying hard, but still, you vote for somebody you know, and men just tend to know each other better than they do women."[5]

Others point out that at the higher levels, fields such as science are structured around the lives of people who have been left free to devote all of their attention to their work because someone else takes care of them and, if they have them, their children. Linda Wilson, a chemist and president of Radcliffe College, claims that women will not make greater entries into science until the culture of science changes so that it does not require excluding every other human activity. She considers the following dilemma for women: "Her critical scientific years, in which she is establishing her reputation, and her peak reproductive years coincide. This is a dirty trick." She and other education leaders ask whether science and other research areas must be structured as they are.[6]

Working conditions make a difference. As in any job, women face special difficulties in combining work and family. A study of the stresses faced by college faculty across the country found that women of five different ethnic/racial groups—American Indian, Asian-American, African-American, Latino, and white—were more likely than men to feel time pressures and a lack of personal time stressful.

Women in most of these groups were also more likely to feel stressed by household responsibilities and the need to care for elderly parents (Schneider, 1997, 12). Some colleges, like many corporations, are trying to find ways to help faculty and administrators balance work and family. A national study cited 29 colleges and universities as being especially family friendly because of offering benefits such as child-care centers, job-sharing opportunities, flextime, and programs to alter the tenure clock in response to family responsibilities.[7]

What difference would it make if more women entered the higher ranks of education? It certainly makes a difference to women wishing to pursue careers in education. Whether it would make a difference in the type of education people receive is more difficult to ascertain. It is not clear whether women would run their schools or school districts very differently than men do. At least the presence of more women at higher levels would provide more heterogeneous models for students to follow. In colleges and universities, women have certainly led the efforts to bring women into the curriculum, remove bias from evaluation procedures, and end sexual harassment on campus.

What difference does the gender of a teacher make in the classroom? Some research suggests that students benefit from contact with teachers of their own sex. One study found that children perform better on intelligence tests with an examiner of their own sex (Pedersen, Shinedling, and Johnson, 1968). Another concluded that students in science classes are more likely to consider science as a career for themselves if their teacher is of their own sex (Stake and Granger, 1978). There can be few female college and university professors who have not had small hordes of female students beating paths to their doors because they are women. (On the other hand, too many female college professors find an unusual number of both male and female students wanting to hand in papers late because they thought "a woman might be nicer than a man.")

Unfortunately, female teachers clearly participate in the hidden curriculum discussed in this chapter. This problem should not be surprising. Women grow up in the same sexist society, sit in the same classrooms, and read the same biased textbooks that men do. Many women become teachers because it is an occupation that is regarded as particularly appropriate for women. It will take considerably more than simply putting more women into positions of responsibility to eliminate the sexist bias of schools. Educators are becoming increasingly aware of the problem, however, and are beginning to seek solutions to it.

Education and the Future

It should be clear by now that certain problems need to be addressed for education to serve women and men better. This section reviews some of those problems.

The Question of Choice

Do girls and boys and women and men have the fullest possible opportunity to get the education they choose? Research suggests that they do not. Subtle and not-so-subtle messages still track students according to gender. Girls learn to devalue themselves in some fields in school.

Some questions affecting choice in education are especially difficult to tackle. Much of the sexism of people's attitudes and behavior is not conscious; teachers, for example, are often not aware that they treat female and male students differently. When female and male students make their choices in education, they are certainly not always aware of the pressures that have led them to their decisions. Much of the evaluation that goes on in schools and universities—test results, letters of recommendation, promotions, and committee meetings—is confidential, which means that it occurs in a secret way, which often does not allow the subjects to know how they were evaluated.

One of the clearest examples of unconscious or subtle sex discrimination in education is the process by which colleges and universities handle promotions among their faculty. When considering individuals for tenure or promotion, these institutions usually look for a complex combination of *scholarship* (generally, publication of original research), *teaching* (both how much and how well), and *service to the institution* (participation on committees and other decision-making bodies in the institution). Measuring these qualities and determining how well the individual will do in the future is immensely difficult. As in all of the other institutions analyzed in this book, these uncertainties and complexities of social life and social institutions provide an opportunity for prejudices and stereotypes of all sorts to enter the process unconsciously and often undetected.

Unfortunately, the appearance of choice is too often an illusion. How can the degree of choice be increased? Two common answers—"We must change people's minds or resocialize them to be less sexist," and "We should make laws against discrimination"—are inadequate. The first is too vague, and the second is too narrow, primarily because, for the most part, it has already been done and has not worked out as well as was hoped.

Education for What?

Until surprisingly recently, women's schooling was designed to prepare them for wifehood and motherhood. There is less gender-based tracking now than there was, but it has not disappeared. Some schools and school boards are unwilling to handle the problem of gender stereotyping directly within school curricula; few have made real strides in correcting gender biases in teaching methods and school curricula. In the early 1990s, a backlash developed in many areas of the country, which claimed schools had gone too far in teaching "alternative lifestyles" and in mixing up people's gender roles, thereby belittling women's traditional roles.

Ironically, many school officials who want their female students to grow up to be responsible wives and mothers balk at the idea that schools should teach students about sexuality and reproduction, and especially curricula that explicitly teach about sexuality. As a result, many American children still think that babies come from cabbages, storks, and supernatural acts or from parts of the body not connected to the reproductive system, while children in countries such as Sweden, where sex education is introduced in the first grade, understand the basic facts of life at an early age (Parsons, 1983). By the time many American schools get around to teaching sex education—late in high school if at all—up to one half of the students have already begun having sex, and many have accidentally found out where babies come from (Zellman and Goodchilds, 1983). The spread of AIDS has increased the need for education among adolescents. Most adolescents probably do not realize that about a third of women with AIDS were infected through heterosexual contact (AAUW, 1992, 78). Sex education is important; about 40% of 18-year-olds say they got "a lot" of information from these classes.[8]

Research shows repeatedly that education does not "pay off" for women in the same way it does for men. Because of discrimination and other barriers, some women become discouraged and curtail their studies even when they are fully qualified to continue them (Durio and Kildow, 1980). As Chapter 13 shows, women face discrimination in some fields even when they have had the appropriate training. Whereas at one time, women did not gain earning power from their education as much as men did, that is not true now, for the most part. Indeed, an added year of schooling boosts black and white women's earning power *more* than it helps white men's, especially at the lower levels. That is not the end of the story, however; among more educated people, men's added work experience increases their pay at a greater rate than it increases women's; in other words, well-educated women do face a glass ceiling (Duncan, 1996).[9]

Education for and About Women

Some progress has been made in including women in the world about which students learn. The most progress has been made in relatively ghettoized women's studies courses and programs in colleges and universities and, to a lesser extent, in high schools. For the most part, "women" are still a special topic, and women have to work hard to make their own space in existing schools. Many advocates of traditional education have criticized women's studies as being harmfully ideological and nonacademic, claiming that it refuses to acknowledge the value in studying "dead white males."[10] Female students have to work particularly hard to learn about themselves and to do what Adrienne Rich (1979) calls "claiming an education." Students themselves can take an active part in creating their own education by being watchful and demanding changes in their educational institutions when they see evidence of bias or closed opportunities. Most colleges and universities have women's groups or caucuses, and many high schools do, as well. Parents also have a role to play, either as individuals or through groups such as the Parent Teacher Association (PTA).

Teachers and school administrators also work to achieve change. There are women's groups within most professional societies and unions. These professional and labor organizations, as well as feminist groups such as the National Organization for Women (NOW), increasingly have special reports, programs, and training sessions designed to help teachers and administrators fight sexism in schools. Of course, most schools are paid for and regulated by a complex web of local, county, and state school boards and superintendents of schools; local, county, and state legislators; and the U.S. Congress and the U.S. Department of Education. Politics thus play a major role in education.

A case in point is the battle over implementation of Title IX of the 1972 Education Amendments, which bars discrimination in educational programs that receive federal funds. One of the most obvious traditionally discriminatory areas of education is sports. The National Collegiate Athletic Association (NCAA) originally fought intense legal battles to try to make sure that Title IX would not cover college athletics, even trying to claim that such coverage would be unconstitutional (Carpenter and Acosta, 1991). A 1990 survey of Division I members of the NCAA showed that women were 50% of the full-time undergraduates but only 31% of the athletes. Women received 30% of the athletic scholarship money, 23% of the operating expenditures, and 17% of the recruiting expenditures.[11]

Throughout the remainder of the 1990s, colleges and universities—especially NCAA Division I schools—struggled to figure out how to fulfill both requirements of Title IX: achieving gender equality in the amount of resources devoted to men's and women's sports without discriminating against the interests of particular groups of students, for example, by cancelling some men's sports to achieve equity. It is interesting to note that as much as Title IX has been heralded by supporters of women's equity in education, it has led to some losses for women. For example, while women's participation in college sports increased from 16,000 in 1966 to over 64,000 in 1991, there was a massive decline in the proportion of women's teams coached by women, from about 90% in 1972 to 47% in 1991 (Lirgg, DiBrezz, and Smith, 1994). In contrast, very few women coach men's teams. There are many possible explanations for this decline; one of the most likely is that as men's and women's sports programs were merged and integrated following Title IX, women's programs came under the authority of mostly male athletic directors, who are less likely to appoint women as coaches than women are.

Title IX is still in place, and lawsuits may be—and have been—launched against schools either by the Office of Civil Rights in the U.S. Department of Education or by private individuals. In addition to Title IX, numerous other laws and policies aim to equalize educational opportunities for women and men, although most observers argue that they are either not sufficient or not enforced rigorously enough. Other programs designed to bring gender equity into education under the 1974 Women's Educational Equity Act (WEEA) were developed to provide funds for new programs or research projects designed to promote women's education. Sex discrimination in employment, including employment in education, remains illegal under Title VII of the 1964 Civil Rights Act, and sex discrimination in pay is illegal under the Equal Pay Act of 1963. Experts, however, cite two particular problems in using legal means to redress sexism: (1) The laws are vague (Vladeck, 1981), and (2) the courts generally approach each case on the basis of its individual merit, thus making it difficult to focus the battle on the real issue, which is discrimination against a group of people (Abel, 1981).

Women have formed interest groups to combat sexism in education. Joyce Gelb and Marian Palley (1987) have reported that at least 60 different women's groups have been involved in Title IX battles. Some, such as the Women's Educational Action League (WEAL), NOW, and the National Women's Political Caucus (NWPC), are quite clearly associated with the feminist movement. Others, such as the League of Women Voters, the AAUW, and the Girl Scouts, are more traditional women's organizations. The National Council for Research on Women (NCRW), a federation of research centers on women, pursues issues of interest to research in this area. Alumnae groups sometimes also exert pressure on behalf of women. A group calling itself, "Committee for the Equality of Women at

Harvard" urged alumnae to escrow their donation funds rather than to donate them directly to Harvard until they increase the number of women faculty and pay more attention to Radcliffe and its alumnae.[12] There are now electronic-mail bulletin boards and networks, such as WMST-L, devoted to international discussion on women's studies concerns. Issues concerning education have often united women from diverse backgrounds and political perspectives, however, and these groups have joined to form the National Coalition for Women and Girls in Education.

Many people feel strongly that education must continue to change; the dilemma is how to create change and where to start. There probably cannot be major changes in the status and roles of women in society in general until education changes, but it is doubtful that education can undergo major changes until other social institutions change, as well.

Notes

1. U.S. Department of Education, "The Condition of Education 1995—Overview: Educational Progress of Women," http://www.ed.gov/pubs/CondOfEd_95/ovw3.html.

2. U.S. Department of Education, National Center for Education Statistics, "Digest of Education Statistics 1996, Table 102," http://www.ed.gov/NCES/pubs/D96/d96t102.html.

3. U.S. Department of Education, National Center for Education Statistics, "The Condition of Education, 1997, Supplemental Table 22-1," http://www.ed.gov/NCES/pubs/ce/C9722D01.html.

4. "New Report Shows More Women Are Leading Colleges," *Chronicle of Higher Education,* September 29, 1995, A23.

5. Natalie Angier, "Academy's Choices Don't Reflect the Number of Women in Science," *New York Times,* May 10, 1992.

6. Shirley M. Tilghman, "Science vs. Women—A Radical Solution," *New York Times,* January 26, 1993.

7. Robin Wilson, "A Report Praises 29 Colleges for 'Family Friendly' Policies," *Chronicle of Higher Education,* October 11, 1996.

8. Susan Fernandez, "Teen-agers Need More Education About Sex Topics," *Wisconsin State Journal,* June 25, 1996.

9. Also U.S. Department of Education, National Center for Education Statistics, "Education Indicators: Indicator 17. Education and Relative Earnings," http://www.ed.gov/NCES/pubs/eiip/eiipid17.html.

10. For a partial list of dead white males discussed in this book, look up the following names in the index: Aristotle, Jean Bodin, Charles Darwin, Sigmund Freud, John Stuart Mill, Talcott Parsons, Jean-Jacques Rousseau, and Benjamin Rush.

11. Douglas Lederman, "Men Outnumber Women and Get Most of Money in Big-Time Sports Programs," *Chronicle of Higher Education,* April 8, 1992.

12. "Boycott by Radcliffe Alumnae Denies Harvard $500,000 in Gifts," *Chronicle of Higher Education,* February 28, 1997, A32; and "Fund-Raising Report at Harvard Annoys Radcliffe Alumnae," *Chronicle of Higher Education,* May 23, 1997, A35.

6

❧

Normal Gender:
Health, Fitness, and Beauty

A pregnant woman chats with a friend during their lunch break. "Are you hoping for a boy or a girl?" her friend asks. "Oh, I don't care what sex it is—as long as it's a healthy, normal baby!" A student wakes up the first day of final exams and refuses the breakfast offered by her roommate. "I feel really ill," she explains, and both of them believe it but make no move to get her to a doctor because they know there is nothing physically wrong with her. A 95-year-old woman dies in her sleep, and her children comfort themselves by expressing happiness that she was "healthy and in good shape up to the end." An obviously robust male professional basketball player regularly appears in heavy makeup, women's clothes, and a feather boa. "He's really sick!" someone comments. Rising crime rates in parts of the country are regarded by some people as evidence of a "sick society." In 1973, the American Psychological Association, changing its collective mind, declared that homosexuality is not a sickness.

Words connoting health and sickness are among the most common and important we use to describe and evaluate people. Just what *is* good health, though? As this chapter shows, while scientific standards define health in many ways, our definitions of health and sickness actually depend on cultural and historical circumstances. What does not change, however, is the *evaluative* connotations of health and sickness. Health is good, and its absence bad. The absence of health (or the presence of sickness) should be corrected, if at all possible.

As the influential medical sociologist David Mechanic has argued, the concepts of *normal* and *abnormal* are central to our understanding of health. We (health professionals and laypeople alike) compare the way we feel or act to some standard of normality to determine whether we are healthy. "The concept of disease usually refers to some deviation from normal functioning which has undesirable consequences because it produces personal discomfort or adversely affects the individual's future health status" (Mechanic, 1978, 25). Standards of health or normality depend not only on the state of health institutions and health science, but also on the "social and cultural context within which human problems are defined" (Mechanic, 1978, 26).

Consider this simple health problem to see how flexible and contingent definitions of health are. The average temperature of human bodies is 98.6 degrees Fahrenheit. If my temperature is 99 degrees, is this a problem? Possibly not; some people's normal temperature is higher or lower than average. At what point has my temperature deviated enough from the norm to say that I am not healthy? Surely, the more complex the problem of physical, mental, or social health, the more complex are the problems of defining and dealing with health.

Like other fields of human science, medicine is an imperfect science, involving a lot of uncertainty. Even with limited and constantly changing information, however, doctors, nurses, and other health-care workers still try to help, relying if necessary on educated guesses. That subjective (although educated) guesswork leaves considerable room for the influence of ideology, including gender ideology. Procedures that represent the best guesses and the values of a given era may appear wrongheaded and even disgraceful at a later period. Observers generally agree that cultural and social values, especially those defining what is labeled as "normal" in human characteristics and behavior play large roles in health science and health care. Not surprisingly, gender, gender roles, and definitions of masculinity and femininity play roles in both health science and health care. In the process of teaching us how to be healthy, health professionals have often also taught us how to conform to gender norms. While restoring us to health and "normality," they have sometimes also restored us to "normal" masculinity and femininity.

Like the family and schools, health institutions define and enforce important social values. This chapter examines the relationship between gender and standards of health and health care, emphasizing the ways in which people and institutions charged with managing our health also manage gender. Because knowledge and decision making in health are linked in such important ways to science, this chapter also serves as a case study of the relationship between gender and science.

In this chapter, we look at how these problems are manifest in the health care of women. *Health* is used very broadly here and includes physical, mental, and social health. Although it is obvious that we should investigate institutions such as hospitals, clinics, and medical schools, this chapter also focuses on other, less obvious institutions that define health norms or that deliver health care, including families, schools, social-welfare agencies, the criminal-justice system, and the advertising and cosmetics industries, all of which can be considered, in a broad sense, part of the health-care system. This chapter emphasizes the social and institutional bases of health, and especially the interaction of science, attitudes and ideology, social behavior, and institutional structures and processes. For more information on the physiological aspects of health and on health-care advice, there are many other good sources.[1]

Gender-Based Norms in Women's Health Care

How are sex, gender, and women's gender roles related to definitions of health and illness? How have health *practitioners* viewed and treated women? How do health-care *institutions* treat women? We begin with medical views of women's anatomy and reproductive systems. We then turn to the relationship between women's health and their roles in the family and at work. Finally, we look at the relationship between women's health and conceptions of female beauty and fitness.

Anatomy and Health

A doctor addressing a medical society in 1870 noted that it seemed "as if the Almighty, in creating the female sex, had taken the uterus and built up a woman around it" (quoted in Ehrenreich and English, 1979, 108). The Bible claims that God began with a rib, but writers and practitioners of health care historically viewed women largely in terms of their reproductive organs, which have been seen not just as different from men's but also as the defining characteristics of women and their health potential. Unfortunately, women's ovaries, clitorises, wombs, and breasts have often been treated as special health hazards women would be better off not having. Today, many debates still have important bearing not just for women's health care, but also for a surprising range of public policy issues. This section reviews this history and the current situation briefly, to see how interpretations of these organs become part of the basis for how related social institutions function.

Ovaries. In the late 19th century, women's ovaries came to be regarded as dangers to mental health. Because of their link to women's periodicity, ovaries were assumed to control women's personalities, causing their apparent emotional instability. This "psychology of the ovary," as Ehrenreich and English (1979) have called it, had disastrous effects on women when doctors set their minds to figuring out how to care for women. Many advocated *ovariotomy,* surgical removal of the ovaries, to cure women of many problems, such as overeating, masturbation, "erotic tendencies," suicidal tendencies, and persecution manias (and no wonder!). In some cases, husbands brought their wives for this surgery, hoping to cure them of unruly behavior (Ehrenreich and English, 1979, 111–112). An estimated 150,000 women underwent the operation in 1906 alone. This practice has long since faded away.

Clitoris. Historically, women's sexual potential has often been seen as unhealthy. Although Victorians and many of their descendants commonly believed that women tolerated, rather than enjoyed, sex, many also thought women were dangerously insatiable. To control women's threatening sexuality, men have used various means, including chastity belts and segregation, the latter often mandated by religious authorities. In the mid–19th century, American doctors found a new cure for such problems as "nymphomania," masturbation, and other unruly feminine behavior: *clitoridectomy,* surgical removal of the clitoris. Again, some husbands at a loss to control unmanageable wives presented them to doctors for "female circumcision," as it is often mistakenly called. (The equivalent of clitoridectomy would be castration, not circumcision.)

This practice has disappeared among Western doctors, although it remains a widespread and important part of some cultures' female initiation rites, especially in many African countries. In some countries, a more radical and dangerous operation is performed: *infibulation,* in which the clitoris and external genitalia are removed, and then the raw edges of the labia are sewn or otherwise fastened together so that as they heal, scar tissue forms to close the vagina, leaving only a small hole for urination. In many places, these operations are performed in unsanitary conditions, without special surgical equipment and without anesthesia. In the societies in which clitoridectomy is practiced, women are often regarded as unmarriageable if they have not undergone this operation; thus, estimates are that in countries such as Djibouti, Ethiopia, Sierra Leone, and Somalia, virtually all women undergo a form of this operation, while in many others, such as Burkina Faso, Chad, Egypt, Kenya, and Nigeria, a majority of women do.

While feminist writers and activists have spread knowledge about these practices, health organizations from many countries, including most African countries, and international organizations such as the World Health Organization have mounted a worldwide campaign to eliminate clitoridectomy. These campaigns, and related political issues, raise many dilemmas for American women as they learn to relate to a global society. Anticlitoridectomy activists in societies that do not support this practice are often accused of imposing their cultural values on African and Mideastern societies. Is this accusation correct? Under what circumstances might the views of present-day U.S. feminists, for example, constitute just one set of cultural values imposed against others—for example, 19th-century American society or 20th-century African societies?

Consider the practical issues directly touching American women. Immigrants bring their valued cultural practices with them; this one is no exception. The Centers for Disease Control and Prevention (CDC) estimated in 1996 that 150,000 women and girls in the United States from families recently immigrated from Africa were subject to clitoridectomy. The U.S. Congress passed a law criminalizing the practice, but many families send their daughters out of the country to have it done.[2] Should the government and health authorities continue to suppress clitoridectomy, or is this a violation of another value supported by most feminist organizations—celebrating diversity? The issue heated up in 1994, when a 17-year-old woman fled Togo for fear of undergoing clitoridectomy and sought asylum in the United States. Immigration law allows refugee status only for those with reason to fear persecution on the basis of their race, nationality, religion, political views, or group membership. After the Immigration and Naturalization Service rejected her initial claim, in 1996, the Board of Immigration Appeals made a precedent-setting decision that fear of genital mutilation is a legitimate ground for granting asylum.[3] Is this decision a victory for the protection of women or an assault on Togo's cultural practices?

Uterus.   The womb has long been regarded as the cause of physical and emotional problems; in fact, *hysteria* is a word based on one meaning "womb." Before the 20th century, many experts thought the uterus traveled around the body, thereby causing grave danger. In the 20th century, hysterectomy became an important life-saving procedure, as it came to be used to save women from uterine cancer. However, many experts believe that hysterectomy, the second most common surgical procedure in the United States, is vastly overused; by the time women reach age 60 years, 1 out of every 3 of them will have had a hysterectomy, compared with 1 in 6 in Italy and 1 in 18 in France. In fact, cancer accounts for a very small (about 10%) proportion of hysterectomies. Many women's health experts claim that hysterectomies, which have negative effects on the body's endocrine system even after menopause, are vastly overdone because of a male-centered culture more willing to remove the uterus for various problems than, for example, the testicles and prostate gland for preventive medicine.[4] Older women are especially subject to high rates of hysterectomy; in these cases, age stereotypes combine with gender stereotypes to create problems for women.

Breasts.   In the 1880s, *radical mastectomy*—removal of the breast plus the underlying muscles and lymph nodes—was introduced to treat breast-cancer patients. Although this procedure greatly reduced breast-cancer-related deaths among women, experts have concluded that the *radical* mastectomy, like the hysterectomy, is overdone; too much surgery is done too often. Physicians now often prefer much less invasive forms of surgery. Radical mastectomy also seems especially likely to be overused on older women.

Women's health organizations, and now health organizations more generally, have worked hard to increase early detection of breast cancer, because in most cases, survival rates then should be very high. In the early 1990s, the American Cancer Society (ACS) launched an intensive campaign to convince women to do breast self-examinations and to get regular mammograms. Health consensus holds that women should begin regular breast self-examinations in adolescence[5] and that women over age 50 years should have annual mammograms. However, a number of controversies developed around preventive measures for breast cancer and the assumptions underlying those treatments.

The ACS underscored their arguments about health care with the statement that women face a one in nine chance of getting breast cancer. Critics argued that the ACS had greatly exaggerated the odds to scare women into preventive medicine. The ACS figure tells the cumulative probability that any given woman will develop breast cancer some time between birth and her 100th birthday. The odds that any given woman has undetected cancer at any given time (which therefore might be detected by a mammogram) are dramatically lower.[6] Who is right: The ACS, which points out that 70% of women are not getting mammograms and stand a chance of dying unnecessarily, or the critics who say that the campaign unnecessarily scares women about their bodies? Whatever the answer, all experts agree that breast cancer is a serious problem; at this point, more than 180,000 new cases are diagnosed each year, and around 44,000 women die from it annually.

Consider a related controversy: Who should get annual mammograms? Experts agree that unless symptoms suggest otherwise, most women should not begin annual mammograms until after they are in their 30s. However, debates have raged over whether the *National Institutes of Health* (*NIH*), the government agency for research and policy on health, should recommend that women begin annual mammograms in their 40s or 50s. Although some experts argue that the health and financial costs of the earlier annual diagnostics outweigh the likely benefits of prevention, a number of factors, including more recent research showing the benefit of regular screening (Smart, Henrick, Rutledge, and Smith, 1995) and the likelihood that many insurance companies would refuse to pay for annual mammograms for women in their 40s unless the NIH recommended them, led to a recommendation in 1997 that women begin annual mammograms in their 40s.

Because of these controversies and the seriousness of the problem, Congress established the National Breast and Cervical Cancer Early Detection Program in 1990, to assure that research and screening for breast and cervical cancer take place.[7] The CDC has implemented the program in partnership with many other government agencies and health organizations, as well as many American Indian/ Alaska Native organizations, and other organizations, such as the American Indian Healthcare Association; the National Caucus and Center on Black Aged, Inc.; the National Coalition of Hispanic Health and Human Service Organizations; the National Hispanic Council on Aging; and the National Center for Farmworkers Health, Inc. These groups play important roles because of the special problems of health-care knowledge and access among the poor, who are heavily represented among the groups these organizations represent. The Latino organizations are also especially important because of the impact of traditional Latino culture on women's access to information about their bodies. A study of Latina and Anglo women in California found that Latinas were much more likely to believe that breast cancer is caused by breast trauma or even breast fondling and were more poorly informed on preventive measures (Hubbell et al., 1996).

Summary. The organs of women's bodies that are most different from men's— those composing the reproductive system—have long been identified as sources of peculiar mental and physical health problems. Also, of course, real diseases afflict these organs, like any others in the body. Nonetheless, research on gender and health care suggests that people have been particularly willing to excise these organs (unlike men's, which are also subject to their own "peculiar" afflictions) because of the perception that these organs are extraneous in any case, especially for women who are past the age at which they are likely to bear children or to be culturally defined as attractive to men. Unnecessary radical surgery is not the only issue raised by a gendered perspective on women's health care, however. As the debates over clitoridectomy or breast health care show, cultural perceptions of women's bodies, gender ideology and stereotyping, and other cultural norms, such as views of aging, interact together with the uncertainties of science to create important issues for how to achieve the best health care for women.

Reproduction and Health

Like the organs themselves, the normal functions of women's reproductive organs have been seen as health problems. This section looks briefly at two examples: (1) menstruation and (2) pregnancy and childbirth.

Menstruation. Most cultures have some menstrual taboos, based on beliefs that menstrual blood can make crops fail, wine go sour, infants die, and men become impotent. In many cultures, men view sexual relations with a menstruating woman as disgusting, and many women find the idea embarrassing. Some religions, including Orthodox Judaism, ban sexual relations during menstrual periods and require women to undergo cleansing rituals following their periods.

Certainly, menstrual periods were once more unpleasant for most women than they are now. Modern hygiene practices, including regular bathing, are new. As recently as the middle of the 20th century, many people still believed that bathing or showering was dangerous for menstruating women. In fact, fresh menstrual blood is no more unhealthful than blood from any other part of the body.

The old menstrual ideology still persists, however, despite the availability of sanitary pads, tampons (invented in 1933), and sponges. The mass media portray women as crazed by their menstrual periods, and advertisements for "feminine hygiene products" imply that even menstruating women can be normal and feminine if they use the right products (Chrisler and Levy, 1990; Toth, 1980). In fact, however, the products labeled as offering "feminine hygiene" managed to create some real health dangers. The search for bigger tampons led to the distribution of tampons that increase the risks of toxic shock syndrome, a potentially fatal illness. Rather than wearing bigger tampons longer, women should change them more frequently.

The controversy over physical and psychological menstrual distress was discussed in Chapter 3. Many women suffer from problems associated with menstruation and menstrual cycles. For some women, these difficulties are caused by the physical functioning of their reproductive or hormonal systems. Some women experience physical and emotional difficulties at puberty and menopause. Both excessive bleeding and the lack of bleeding in women of reproductive age can be symptoms of other health problems. Uncomfortable amounts of weight gain and cramps are not just products of the mind, but what are the relationships among menstruation, menstrual cycles, and women's normal health and well-being?

Beginning especially with the work of Katarina Dalton (1964), many researchers, doctors, journalists, and the public seized on the idea of premenstrual syndrome (PMS) to explain women's apparent mood swings and erratic behavior. Medical researchers disagree about the definition, existence, or causes of PMS. They do not agree as to which psychological and physical correlates of menstruation are more generally caused by the *physiological* aspects of the menstrual cycle and which are caused by people's menstrual *beliefs* or expectations or by the way menstruating women are treated. Indeed, experts do not agree over what the psychological and behavioral correlates of menstrual cycles are or how many women might be affected (Walker, 1995). Some research shows that even when women believe they are being affected by PMS, their own behavior and performance does not necessarily show it (Richardson, 1989). Certainly, women's interpretations of their own menstrual cycles and menstrual symptoms are based on their bodily sensations. However, experimental research has shown that women who were told they were premenstrual on the basis of a (make-believe) "scientific test" detected more menstrual symptoms in themselves than women who were told, on the basis of the same test, that they were not premenstrual (Klebanov and Jemmett, 1992). Moreover, the symptoms of PMS seem to respond as much to placebos as to active preparations in experimental research (Richardson, 1995).

As early as the fifth grade, girls have clear ideas about what symptoms accompany menstruation. Interestingly, girls who had begun to menstruate reported *experiencing* less severe menstrual distress than those who had not yet begun *expected* to have. The more distress young girls expected, the more they felt when they actually reached menarche. Also, girls who had learned more about menstruation "from male sources rated menstruation as more debilitating and negative than those who learned less from male sources" (Brooks-Gunn and Ruble, 1982, p. 1576). Females who live in close proximity (e.g., in a dormitory room) often find that their menstrual cycles become more similar over time (McClintock, 1971). Thus, biology alone is not responsible for whether a menstruating woman feels good. Like many other physiological phenomena, it is partly shaped by culture and society (Buckley and Gottlieb, 1988; Delaney, Lupton, and Toth, 1988; Lander, 1988).

Nevertheless, both the institutions of health care and those of the mass media have fostered the idea that there is a clearly defined and common set of disturbing and dysfunctional correlates of menstruation. The 1987 edition of the *Diagnostic and Statistical Manual of Mental Disorders* (*DSM-III*) (APA, 1987) identified, for the first time, a disorder called "late luteal phase dysphoric disorder" (LLPDD), derived from research on PMS. According to the manual, a mental-health practitioner should look for the following symptoms (among others) in the week before and the first days after the onset of menses to determine whether a woman is suffering from this mental disorder: marked mood instability; persistent anger, irritability, anxiety, tension, or depression; decreased interest in usual activities; tiring easily; subjective sense of difficulty in concentrating; marked appetite change; insomnia; or physical symptoms such as breast tenderness, headaches, pain, or weight gain.[8]

Many experts object to this definition on the grounds that evidence is, at best, too contested to warrant such a designation (Caplan, McCurdy-Myers, and Gans, 1992; Parlee, 1992; Richardson, 1995). If the evidence is not good enough, why does the mental-health establishment treat this syndrome as if it is uncontested? Some experts argue that questionable ideas about PMS persist because they so comfortably fit the sexist ideology of much of the public and the medical researchers (Nicolson, 1995). Others point out that the creation of particular diagnostic categories is in large part a cultural activity that is related to the structure and needs of particular institutions. Once designations such as PMS become formally recognized diagnostic categories, different health professionals are in a position to compete over who should handle these cases. Parlee thinks it is "quite comprehensible as a claim [mental health professionals] make to advance their case as they compete with gynaecologists for a 'new' (medically insured) patient population—women who 'have' PMS/LLPDD" (Parlee, 1992, 107). The evidence must be reviewed carefully to reach a well-grounded opinion, and even then, it is not a simple matter to know how to *interpret* the results. "On the one hand, feminists acknowledge the importance of women's complaints receiving medical attention so that women's reported discomforts are seen as legitimate and not as a product of their imaginations," wrote Susan Markens. "On the other hand, there is fear that if the syndrome gains legitimacy, women will be seen as emotional, irrational and unreliable, victims of their own biology, and once again will be reduced to their 'raging hormones'" (Markens, 1996, 42).

Menopause is also a subject of scientific and therefore health-care controversy. The majority of women experience some symptoms, such as hot flashes, and perhaps 5–15% of women seek medical attention for menopause-related symptoms. Once again, it is hard to separate conventional wisdom from knowledge well-grounded in research. A review of the literature, for example, shows that there is not good scientific evidence to confirm that menopause causes depression (Nicol-Smith, 1996). Until recently, there had been little research on this subject because doctors did not regard women's menopause-related complaints as serious. However, as women began to demand more attention to their health needs, and potential treatment strategies such as hormone-replacement therapy became more widely known, a major 10-year study was initiated in the early 1990s, which should offer some needed answers.[9]

Pregnancy and Childbirth.   While childbirth is a "natural" act, it is also one that is organized and experienced through a historically shaped state of scientific knowledge, cultural practices, and social conditions. For much of women's history, childbirth was dangerous because of the general state of women's physical health and the way women were treated during pregnancy and childbirth. Because of women's low status in the family, women used to eat considerably less (and often less nourishing) food than their husbands, which placed them at increased risk of malnutrition. Women's status affects their nutrition and thus their bone and muscle quality, for example, which in turn affects their reproductive health (Das Gupta, 1995).

Childbirth practices have changed dramatically over the past two centuries. This section addresses some of these changes in relation to women's health.[10]

At one time, doctors considered delivering babies beneath their dignity. In the late 17th and the 18th centuries, however, they began to compete with midwives, especially in cities, where people had the money to pay for medical delivery. The doctors then charged that midwives were incompetent. Most research shows something quite different; midwives were at least as competent as doctors, and trained urban midwives were even more competent than other midwives and, therefore, probably better than the average doctor.

The innovations doctors brought to childbirth included new technology and surgical skills. The forceps were invented by barber–surgeon Peter Chamberlin in the early 17th century and remained a family secret for many years until other doctors began to use them. Forceps are appropriately used only in problem deliveries and only under certain circumstances. Unfortunately, they were too often used incompetently, and after the 1920s, doctors began to use forceps with increasing frequency. Forceps deliveries have declined, partly because so many doctors have turned instead to birth by surgery (cesarean section), a much safer procedure for the baby.

Two forms of surgery have become common in connection with childbirth. The first, *episiotomy,* is designed to enlarge the opening to the vagina by cutting the tissue at its base. If an episiotomy is not done in some cases, this tissue may be torn (perhaps dangerously) by the emerging infant's head. Episiotomies have become routine; they are performed in 70–80% of births in North America.[11] They are much more common in hospital than in home births (Rothman, 1982). A

Margaret Sanger, birth-control activist.

large Canadian study concluded that there is no justification for using episiotomy routinely; it does not usually help avoid the problems it is supposed to prevent, such as tearing, and in first-time mothers, it often *creates* these problems (Klein et al., 1994).

The other now-common surgical procedure is the *cesarean section,* surgical delivery of the baby through the abdomen. Cesareans were used in emergencies (usually unsuccessfully) as early as the 16th century. Although they became much safer at the end of the 19th century, they were rarely used in the United States until recently. The rate of cesareans increased from an average of 6% of births in 1970 to 25% in 1987.[12] Cesareans are more frequent in private than in public hospitals, suggesting that finances play an important role in decision making, along with health considerations. Some observers suggest that the high rate of cesarean sections is caused partly by hospital staff choosing the delivery time according to their own convenience. Also, however, cesarean sections are routine, relatively safe procedures, which many doctors and women prefer over riskier procedures, including lengthy and difficult labors.

Most babies were born at home until World War II; the proportion of hospital births rose from 37% in 1935 to 79% in 1945 and 99% by the end of the 1970s

(Shorter, 1982, 157). Midwives delivered about half the children born in the United States at the turn of the century; after 1910, the majority of women were assisted by male doctors. The use of the *lithotomy position* for birthing (back down, feet up; named after the operation used to remove gallstones) accompanied the anesthetized deliveries that became prevalent after the middle of the 19th century. Before that, women gave birth lying on their sides, squatting, standing, or sitting. Experts debate the relative benefits of the different positions. Medical personnel often prefer the lithotomy position for birth because it makes it easier for doctors to monitor the fetus and to deliver the baby, but it also makes it harder for women to give birth, by increasing the risk of tearing and having women work against gravity, thus rendering it more difficult for women to push because their feet are elevated. When women are ordered to stay immobile in bed, rather than walking around, labor lengthens. To compensate for these problems, some doctors do episiotomies, use more drugs to decrease the added pain, and induce births or perform cesarean sections ("c-sections") to shorten labor.

The invention of anesthesia in 1847 made pain relief during childbirth possible and increased the feasibility of procedures such as c-sections and episiotomy. Far from being restricted to cases of extraordinary pain or emergency, however, tranquilizers and anesthetics became routine parts of childbirth. Many women have been grateful for the relief, of course, but anesthesia has drawbacks. It diminishes women's ability to use their voluntary muscles, making it difficult for them to participate actively in childbirth and making surgery more likely. Also, if the mother is drugged, so is the fetus. Women are not given much information about what drugs they are receiving and why. One study of women who were described as having "normal vaginal deliveries" found that the average woman was exposed to 11 different drugs during pregnancy and 7 different drug administrations during childbirth (McManus et al., 1982).

What conclusions can be drawn about the institutional organization of reproduction-related health care? The history of childbirth in the West, especially the United States, is marked by the growing influence of the *medical model* of pregnancy and childbirth. As Barbara Rothman described it, "[Within] the medical model the body is seen as a machine, and the male body is taken as the norm. Pregnancy and birth are at best complications, stresses on the system. At worst, they are disease like states. In either case, in that model, they need treatment, medical management" (1982, 24). Pregnant women are transformed into "patients" and are treated, and expected to act, as though they are sick people—that is, not normal. Many medical definitions of what is normal during pregnancy are based on norms for nonpregnant women (considered a more normal state), which means that doctors end up attempting to cure women of abnormalities that are actually normal in pregnant women (Rothman, 1982, 141–157).

Women have learned to accept this medical model. They have also learned to think of pain as the most salient feature of childbirth. Most doctors and women prefer hospital births "just in case"—that is, because medical technology, drugs, and specialists are available in hospitals. In the hospital, however, "just in case" procedures may be routine. Further, as Judith Leavitt (1983) has pointed out, when birthing women began to use hospitals rather than delivering at home, they lost control over the process. (This point is addressed further later in this chapter.)

Research in the Netherlands, comparing planned hospital and home births among low-risk pregnancies, showed no difference in successful outcomes for first-time mothers and better outcomes in home births for women who had had children before (Wiegers et al., 1996). A study of the impact of physicians' style in caring for about 3,000 low-income pregnant women in the United States showed that where doctors tended to use aggressive fetal testing, there were more negative outcomes, including low birth weight, preterm delivery, and c-sections (Helfand and Zimmer-Gembeck, 1997).

Pregnancy and childbirth have become safer for women and babies in recent history, largely because of advances in medicine. On the other hand, infant and maternal mortality rates are not as low in the United States as they are in much of Western Europe, which tends to use approaches involving less intervention and less technology. In 1989, there were about 6 maternal deaths for every 1,000 live births, an improvement from 1970, when there were 14 maternal deaths for a comparable number of live births, but among the other nations that have lower maternal death rates than the United States are Luxembourg, Iceland, Ireland, Denmark, Belgium, Norway, Switzerland, Sweden, and Spain (Snyder, 1992, 396). Why? Perhaps, after a certain point, the value added by extra technology and intervention is not very great. Indeed, as noted previously, the medical and technological models of dealing with pregnancy and childbirth result in losses, as well as gains. Many women and health-care practitioners are beginning to seek more healthful alternatives.

Many experts agree, however, that the other reason for the unimpressive standing of the United States is the degree of poverty in this country and the relative lack of universal provision of health care for pregnant women. Despite skepticism in some circles about the medical model of childbirth and the overdependence on health care, regular prenatal health care is essential to having healthy babies and mothers. Although the United States spends more on health care than (almost) any other country, it has one of the most restrictive health-care systems in the industrial world. Over a quarter of women of reproductive age have no health insurance, and the health insurance of another 9% does not cover maternity care (Muller, 1990, 189). A study of a West Virginia community in the mid-1980s, which had a free prenatal health-care program for a 2-year period, showed significant improvement in fetal death rates during the period the program was in operation (Foster, Guzick, and Pulliam, 1992). The repercussions of the effects of poverty and the structure of the health-care system mean also that there are shocking race differences in reproductive health. In 1989, for example, 6 White and 18 Black women died because of pregnancy or childbirth for every 1,000 live births. This is probably partly due to the fact that African-American, Native American, and Hispanic women are much less likely than White women to receive any prenatal health care early in their pregnancies.

Families, Family Roles, and Health

In 1963, Betty Friedan published *The Feminine Mystique,* which helped spur the rise of the new women's movement. Friedan took a second look at the presumably happy, hopeful world of post–World War II suburbia and found a problem among homemakers that was widespread but had no name. In her book, she offered some doctors' views of the problem:

> [One] found, surprisingly, that his patients suffering from "housewife's fatigue," slept more than an adult needed to sleep—as much as ten hours a day—and that the actual energy they spent on housework did not tax their capacity. The real problem must be something else, he decided—perhaps boredom. Some doctors told their women patients they must get out of the house for a day, treat themselves to a movie in town. Others prescribed tranquilizers. Many suburban housewives were taking tranquilizers like cough drops. "You wake up in the morning, and you feel as if there's no point in going on another day like this. So you take a tranquilizer because it makes you not care so much that it's pointless."

Many began to wonder: Is it possible that family life was not as healthy for women as people had thought?

Scholarly research since then has compiled evidence that family life as it is commonly constructed creates special health problems for women. The influential sociologist Jessie Bernard (1972) introduced the idea that when men and women marry, most traditionally do not really enter into the same situation; they enter what she calls "his" and "hers" marriages, with different roles, stresses, and benefits. When feminist scholars first analyzed the situation, the most obvious difference between married men's and married women's situations was that most men's time and energy was dominated by paid employment, and most women's by caring for their homes and families. Even now, however, with most married women employed, their situations are different. Married women still tend to shoulder most of the care-taking responsibilities in the household; the husband is, among other things, another person within the family needing care. Besides doing domestic labor, a "good" wife is supposed to provide emotional support to the husband. Husbands' jobs are still often regarded as more important than wives', and his job-related problems take precedence. A full-time homemaker is supposed to be understanding and helpful when her husband comes home from work, regardless of what her day was like. Arlie Hochschild struck a chord in many households when she published her book *The Second Shift,* on the stressful results of this division of labor (Hochschild, 1989). Women with children face tremendous burdens when their marriages break up, but they are also left with one less person to manage.

Of course, men and women share many problems, especially in the approximately 20% of dual-career married couples in which the husband and wife share the domestic responsibilities (i.e., the "second shift"). For the majority of married couples, however, the "his" and "hers" marriage model still has some negative health implications for women in particular. Some mental-health research suggests that there are gender differences in the relationship between marital status and mental health. Married women have higher rates of mental disorder than do married men, but single, divorced, and widowed women have lower rates of mental disorder than do similarly situated men (Gove, Style, and Hughes, 1990).

During the 1990s, however, research has also shown that family experiences affect men and women very similarly, for the most part (Erickson, 1995). Overall, marriage tends to have positive effects on women and men, as does employment. Married men and women have lower death rates than unmarried men and women, although the reasons may be different; among women but not men, the apparent explanation is the greater financial security of married women, compared with unmarried women (Lillard and Waite, 1995).

When children arrive, the stresses on the marriage and the gender divisions of physical and psychological labor have different effects on men and women (McLanahan and Adams, 1987). Because a large minority of women but not men with small children withdraw from the labor force for some period of time, these women are more likely than men to be socially isolated and to spend much more of their day without any adult contact. Such social isolation is related to both depression and loneliness. Consider the research showing that 6 hours is the maximum contact with children that child-care workers can tolerate before their abilities to function are diminished (Seiden, 1976). Full-time homemakers spend much more than 6 hours per day in contact with children. One study (Shaver and Freedman, 1976) found that the more hours women spent alone with children, the more lonely they felt, and the more television they watched, the more worthless they felt. As one newspaper reporter said in her article on her return from maternity leave, "Let's face it. Being a full-time mom can beat out any desk job for stress, fatigue, unpredictable predicaments and tense moments. Besides, if working at home were so easy, men would be lining up to do it."[13]

Divorce also has different health implications for men and women. Married men still have less responsibility, on average, for their own or their families' day-to-day maintenance, such as cooking, cleaning, or shopping (Hochschild, 1989). While at work, they are not held as responsible for the care and supervision of their children as married women are when they are at work. Men who find themselves on their own must manage these things themselves. Given their socialization and lack of experience, this new set of tasks can be very difficult indeed. Some studies show that after divorce, fathers often find interacting with their children very stressful because they have not developed child-care skills, even with their own children.

Domestic Violence as a Health Issue

In recent years, increasing attention has been paid to another family health hazard: domestic violence. Estimates are that about 3.8% of American children ages 3 to 17 years—2 million children—are abused each year, and some violence between spouses occurs in approximately 16% of couples (Gelles, 1980). Most research agrees that even where both partners engage in violence, men tend to be the primary perpetrators (women's violence is more likely to be a response to violence), and women suffer greater injuries. At least 20% of women treated in hospital emergency rooms are injured by domestic violence. The AMA estimates that domestic violence is the single largest cause of injury to women in the United States, more common than automobile accidents, muggings, and rape combined. Domestic violence is responsible for more than one third of the visits women make to hospital emergency rooms (ERs); it creates 30,000 ER visits, 100,000 days of hospitalization, and 40,000 trips to doctors' offices every year.[14]

The Federal Bureau of Investigation (FBI) claims that in 1990, about 30% of women murdered in the United States were killed by their boyfriends or husbands.[15] A study of all homicides of women in New Mexico from 1990 to 1993 showed that a male intimate partner was the perpetrator in 46% of the cases. Guns were twice as likely to be used in the domestic violence (DV) cases, and evidence of old injuries was found much more often in the DV cases, meaning that these women had probably been victimized by DV multiple times. In this study, the rate of DV homicide was much higher among American Indians than among Latinas or Anglo women (Arbuckle et al., 1996).

Wini Breines and Linda Gordon (1983) have pointed out that there are two apparently contradictory images of the family: the "peaceful haven" and the "cradle of violence." Some of the aspects of the family that make it a peaceful haven, such as the intimacies, dependencies, and high expectations, sometimes also transform it into a cradle of violence. Certainly, stress of various sorts may trigger family violence, but stress alone is not the cause of violence. Millions of people face the stresses of crying babies, poverty and strained resources, time conflicts, intrafamilial disagreement, or other tensions without engaging in violence against partners, parents, or children. Something must lead individuals to turn their stress into violence against their family members and especially against women. Research in many fields suggests that gender ideology and the gender-based structure of families helps shape the amount and type of violence.

The likelihood that stress will be transformed into family violence increases under two circumstances: (1) perceived lack of alternative coping mechanisms, and (2) cultural views of family violence. First, individuals under stress may lack or feel unable to pursue alternative coping mechanisms. The isolation of mothers of young children, discussed previously, is an example. For instance, one study compared two groups of women: a group of women at a clinic for mothers who had abused their children and a control group of mothers who had not abused their children; the main difference between the two groups was that the abusive mothers were under more stress and were more socially isolated. They were pressed for time, often because besides taking care of small children, they were employed or in school, and they had smaller social networks, especially fewer adult friends (Salzinger, Kaplan, and Artmeyeff, 1983).

Why is so much domestic violence directed against family members, and against women and children in particular? One answer may be the differential use of violence by women and men in the family. Women and men generally tend to express distress differently; whereas women exhibit distress through such symptoms as depression and anxiety, thus turning their distress inward, men are more likely to exhibit distress through either aggressive behavior or substance use, which can then lead to aggressive behavior (Aneshensel, Rutter, and Lachenbruch, 1991). The fact that men are more likely than women to turn stress outward may help account for men's relatively high use of violence in the family, compared with women's. Also, of course, women are likely to be smaller than men and more physically vulnerable, thus making violence less likely as a coping strategy for women.

Another reason for the prevalence of domestic violence must lie largely in whether domestic violence is considered a normal or justifiable part of family life and intimate relations. To what degree is violence against women *or* children considered more normal, more justifiable, and less unhealthy than other kinds of violence? Consider the norms uncovered in a national study of family violence, which found that 63% of Americans admitted to having pushed, shoved, slapped, or thrown something at their children. Almost 82% thought that slapping a 12-year-old child is necessary, normal, or good; and 65% thought that slapping a 12-year-old child is necessary, normal, *and* good. A majority of the U.S. population, in other words, considers some level of violence by parents against their children a normal, presumably healthy part of family life (Dibble and Straus, 1980). It is no wonder that it is so difficult to define child abuse; where do people draw the line?

Evidence shows that a certain amount of gender-based violence against women is still widely considered normal, acceptable, and justifiable. *Gender-based violence* refers not just to any violence between women and men, but to violence that is understood and justified, in part, by people's understanding of the gendered character of men and women or of men's and women's appropriate relative roles and relationships to each other (Sapiro, 1993b). For example, until the 1970s, nowhere did the law recognize that a man could rape his wife. A woman's marriage was taken as a legal sign that she had given consent to having sexual relations with him. Thus, instead of regarding it as abnormal or unhealthy for a man to force an unwilling woman to have sex with him if they were married to each other, the law suggested that a woman who, at any time, did not want to have sex with her husband should be regarded as abnormal or unhealthy.[16] The law also used to regard some degree of wife battery as healthy and normal.[17] Many people still think it is necessary for men to hit their wives from time to time. In observations of staged street fights, psychologists found that male passersby would aid a man attacked by another man or a woman, and a woman attacked by a woman, but not a woman being attacked by a man. Why? A man attacking a woman might be her husband, which means that the violence is a "private matter" (cited in Rohrbaugh, 1980, 351).

Thus, the sex/gender system can make the family an unhealthy breeding ground for violence against women if it is based on patriarchal and androcentric ideas about the appropriate relationship between women and men in their families. The risk of violence between spouses is particularly high when there is a great status difference between husband and wife, especially when the wife's occupation is of higher status than the husband's (Hornung, McCullough, and Sugimoto, 1981). It is very stressful for some men to have wives with higher-status occupations because the men have learned that they are supposed to be superior to their wives.

People learn these ideas about violence as children. A national sample survey study (Ulbrich and Huber, 1981) shows that childhood observation of intraspousal violence helps men come to accept violence against women as normal, even when they do not engage in violence against women themselves. Men who had seen their fathers hit their mothers were more likely to think that violence against women can be justified than those who had not. In contrast, women who had seen their fathers hit their mothers were less likely to think that violence against women can be justified. Both men and women were more likely to find justification for violence against women if they saw their mothers hit their fathers. There is no inevitable cycle of violence, especially given new health, counseling, and relief agencies designed to help both the perpetrators and the victims of family violence, but this research shows that when children live with violence against women, those early experiences can help socialize men to accept that violence.

Work and Health

In the late 19th century, many psychologists and medical practitioners were disturbed to see more women seeking education and employment. As Ehrenreich and English (1979, 114) have argued, "Medical men saw the body as a miniature economic system, with the various parts—like classes or interest groups—competing for a limited supply of resources." If women used either their brains or their brawn to study or to work, they would deplete the energies needed to bear and raise children. There was also apparent proof: Female college graduates were less likely to marry and thus had fewer children than other women (Ehrenreich and English, 1979, 115). This is still true. This theory has long since lost its popularity, but the relationships between employment and women's health, especially reproductive and mental health, is an important theme in women's economic history.

What is the relationship between mental health and women's employment? The evidence is mixed. Some studies find employed women healthier than full-time homemakers, while others do not. Not surprisingly, health depends on the combination of *burdens* people shoulder. A national study of mental health found that among married women who were not employed, the presence of children was associated with increased depression, while among married women who *were* employed, depression was not affected by children per se, but by the level of difficulty they had in arranging child care and whether their husbands participated in child care. Employed mothers who had sole responsibility for children and difficulty in arranging child care showed the highest levels of depression. Neither the presence of children nor the availability of child care affected husbands' levels of depression (Ross and Mirowsky, 1988). Another study showed that for both homemakers and employed women, the degree of social support offered by husbands, friends, supervisors, and coworkers was important in determining their levels of stress and psychosocial strain (Houston, Cates, and Kelly, 1992).

Women's experience of combining roles also depends on their *attitudes* toward those roles. Consider a study of first-time mothers with babies 5 to 9 months old, who had left the labor force to care for their children. The study compared women who had been very involved with their work before the birth with those who had not. Those who had previously been very involved in their work showed greater irritability, decreased marital intimacy, greater depression, and lower self-esteem, and they perceived higher costs of motherhood than did mothers who had not been so involved in work before their babies were born (Pistrang, 1984).

Probably the most important health issue concerning gender and work is occupational health and safety; that is, women's health is most affected by the impact of the job itself and the work environment, not just the impact of the simple fact of being employed. At the turn into the 20th century, many groups pressed for legislation that would offer special protections to women workers—for example, to restrict their hours or the amount of weight they could lift. This "protective labor legislation" assumed that certain jobs involve tasks or situations that are more dangerous to women than to men.

Until 1908, the Supreme Court remained antagonistic to the idea of protective labor legislation, not because the justices were worried about sex discrimination but because, as they said in an earlier case (*Lochner* v. *New* York, 1905), protective legislation for workers (regardless of sex) constituted interference with the right to enter freely into a contract. The Court changed its mind in 1908 and allowed a maximum-hours law applying only to women, a case that pleased organized labor because it might be used to open the door for legislation to help workers in general. The Court, however, focused narrowly on *women*, and its argument contains the classic argument for restricting women's employment:

> That women's physical structure and the performance of maternal functions place her at a disadvantage in the struggle for subsistence is obvious. This is especially true when the burdens of motherhood are upon her. Even when they are not, by abundant testimony of the medical fraternity continuance for a long time on her feet at work, repeating this from day to day, tends to injurious effects upon the body, and *as healthy mothers are essential to vigorous offspring, the physical well-being of woman becomes an object of public interest and care* in order to preserve the strength and vigor of the race. (*Muller* v. *Oregon*, 1908, emphasis added)

In effect, the Court said that regardless of whether any particular woman was pregnant or a mother, she should be treated as though she were. The law has a special interest in protecting women's health because "her physical structure and a proper discharge of her maternal functions—having in view not merely her own health, but the well-being of the race—justify legislation to protect her from the greed as well as the passion of man." The restrictions "are not imposed solely for her benefit, but also largely for the benefit of all," said the Court.

Most special protective labor legislation for women has disappeared because it conflicts with laws barring discrimination on the basis of race and sex, such as Title VII of the 1964 Civil Rights Act. Research shows that some of the original fears were unfounded; for example, all other things equal, the degree of physical exertion at work (and, indeed, the degree of physical exertion at work combined with the amount at home) has no significant effect on spontaneous abortion rates (Fenster et al., 1997). Nonetheless, employment-related protection of women's reproductive systems continues to spark controversy. Many employers have tried to protect women, especially pregnant women, from substances considered hazardous to reproductive health. They usually do this by barring pregnant women or women of childbearing age from doing jobs that would bring them in contact with these substances. Employers fear lawsuits by women who may not have known they were pregnant when exposed to substances dangerous to the fetus's health. Critics charge that rules selectively protecting women's health at work have often been roadblocks selectively placed in the path of women's advancement, resulting in inequitable treatment of women and men. Many occupational health and safety dangers are hazardous to *both* sexes, but only women are barred from the affected jobs, while men's health is left at risk.[18] Some protective labor practices have been applied less rigorously in traditionally female jobs than in traditionally male jobs, so that weight-lifting restrictions did not apply to laundresses, and night-work restrictions did not apply to waitresses. More effort is expended to protect women from hazardous "male" jobs than from hazardous "female" jobs, revealing the gender ideology underlying the policies.

It is difficult to disentangle the issues of *women's* occupational safety and health from occupational safety and health in general. What choices should we make about controlling workplace conditions? Women now have more choices, but as Vibiana Andrade has said, such choices also give women the opportunity to pay with their own flesh (1981, 78). Women face a range of health hazards at work that we are only now beginning to understand. Stress is one of these; not only are women entering more stressful jobs, but also they are doing so without the same sort of help at home that men receive. Women are also entering fields in which they are likely to encounter discrimination and sexual harassment, which also has effects on women's health by adding to their levels of stress. Although old-style protective labor legislation is not the answer, some means must be found to deal with the specific health issues that women in the workforce face.

Beauty, Fitness, and Health

Physical fitness has become increasingly important for both men and women. At the same time, ideas about health have become more strongly linked to ideas about beauty and appearance. Consider the trends in advertisements; cleansers and cosmetics are now guaranteed to make our hair and skin not just beautiful but also "healthy looking." Women athletes are increasingly used for promoting clothes and beauty products. This situation stands in stark contrast to the recent times when women and girls were discouraged from athletics and other activities that might promote health but were thought to make women unattractive and unfeminine. Standards of feminine beauty have often been remarkably detrimental to women's health. Shifting health and beauty standards certainly affect both sexes, but women have had to endure more than men in the pursuit of beauty. Only rarely has the natural shape, color, or smell of the female body been promoted as attractive. This section looks at some of the relationships among beauty, fitness, and health.

The Ideal Size and Shape: Rubens Woman, Hourglass, California Girl, or Heroin Chic?   The image of ideal feminine beauty has changed many times over history, and it varies widely across different cultures. Consider changes in the ideal weight and shape of women's bodies. In the 19th century, the "consumptive look"—that is, the thin and fragile look of tuberculosis—was the beauty ideal of White, middle- and upper-class women. To make their waists appear tiny, women wore such tight corsets that over time, the corsets could change the structure and shape of the body, cramping and moving vital internal organs in the process, much as foot-binding did in the upper classes of Chinese women at one time. Corsets

How to achieve the "classic" hourglass figure: with a stiff corset.

could exert 28 pounds of pressure (in extreme cases, considerably more) on internal organs. Women's clothing was very heavy; street clothing averaged 37 pounds in the winter, 19 of which were suspended from the waist (Ehrenreich and English, 1979, 98). Swooning became a fashionable show of delicacy, but no wonder, given the effects of women's clothing.

Early in the 20th century, weight standards rose for women (look at the robust chorus girls in early movies), and then fell dramatically again after the 1960s. The women who serve as models are 9% taller and 16% thinner than the average woman.[19] Although with the fitness craze, the size of ideal women's bodies is once again rising, in the 1990s, some of the most popular models used for advertising clothes have looked emaciated.

Although one of the main definitions of beauty and fitness revolves around *overall* size and weight, women are also judged explicitly by the size and shape of an astonishing number of individual parts of the body. Because of concerns ranging from having "nicely turned ankles" (which might have a double meaning, given the structure of women's shoes historically) to worries about crows'-feet, women have subjected themselves to many techniques designed to alter the shape or size of their eyes, eyelashes, noses, lips, cheeks, fingernails, abdomens, buttocks, and thighs. In the post–World War II era, surgery and other invasive techniques were increasingly used to alter bodies. Face-lifts, nose jobs, *liposuction* (operations to remove layers of fat), and tummy tucks are all available to wealthy women who want to make their bodies conform more to the ideal.[20] Female models have even had their back teeth removed to give them hollow cheeks and the appearance of high cheekbones. Perhaps the greatest body-altering attention has been paid to women's breasts, which, at various times in the past century, have been bound to make them look small, raised by stiff brassieres to make them look large, exaggerated with padding, enlarged by implants, and even colored and pierced.

By 1990, at least 150,000 women a year were having breast implants inserted. Although many of these women had medically related reasons for implants, such as previous mastectomies, about 80% were for nonmedical reasons.[21] By the late 1980s, reports of implant-caused problems, such as scar tissue buildups, and even autoimmune diseases began to filter into the news. In 1991, widely publicized lawsuits awarded women with damages, and although the major manufacturer of the targeted silicone-gel-filled implants, Dow Corning Wright, argued that no scientific evidence showed that these caused autoimmune diseases,[22] the company offered to pay the cost for any woman who wished to have her implant removed. In 1992, the Food and Drug Administration (FDA) imposed a moratorium on the use of silicone-gel implants (still allowing saline-filled implants), and it initiated a study to determine the safety of breast implants.[23] As of 1997, the research had shown no large increased risk of traditional autoimmune disease, but women who receive implants are required to sign a consent form listing what the FDA designates as "known" risks (including hardening of the breast due to scar tissue, leaking and rupture, temporary or permanent change or loss of sensation in the nipple or breast, calcium deposits in surrounding tissues, shifting, and interference with mammography readings) and "possible" risks, including autoimmune disorders and *fibrositis*—pain, tenderness, and stiffness of muscles, tendons, and ligaments. Nevertheless, the cost in money and the potential cost in health risk offer a case study in the lengths to which women can be convinced to go to "look better."

Weight.   It is no wonder that research consistently shows that girls and women are more discontented with their bodies than men are and spend more time dieting and engaging in other efforts to make their bodies conform to ideal standards (Jackson, 1992). Weight is an important component of this discontent. Weight standards, practices, and results vary across different ethnic and racial groups (Dawson, 1988). For example, rates of obesity among African-American women are about twice the rates in White women, and these differences are also tied to many health problems among African-American women (Kumanyika, Wilson, and Guilford-Davenport, 1993). One study finds that overweight African-American women maintain a relatively positive body image, which is consistent with other work suggesting that Black women are not as devoted to thinness as an ideal as White women are (Harris, 1994). Other research finds that African-American and

BOX 6-1   See for Yourself:
What Do Clothing Stores Teach About Size?

Go to a local department store. First, examine the layout. Are different-sized clothes featured in different departments? Are there special departments for "petites" or for larger women? What do they call large women? What sizes are included in each of these designations? Where are the departments located, and what do they look like? Construct a basic wardrobe for three women: One wears size 6, one wears size 12, and one wears size 18.

Try the exercise in another clothing store that is more upscale or downscale than the original store you chose.

Try the exercise again, using different mail-order catalogs.

White women are similarly discontented with their own body size, although White women are more likely to think that their "overweight" will actually have negative repercussions in the way men treat them (Thomas and James, 1988).

A study of pregnant women and maternity clothes reveals an interesting aspect of women's reactions to weight gain, especially how their self-evaluations are mediated by external forces and social class. A survey of department stores found that the location of the maternity clothes was related to the socioeconomic class of the store (Horgan, 1983) (see Box 6-1). In more expensive stores, maternity clothes were near the lingerie department. In stores aimed at working-class women, maternity clothes were located near the large women's department and uniforms. (Why, in any case, do "large" women—usually meaning women size 16 and over—need a segregated section of department stores?) The same study found that wealthier pregnant women felt sexier and more attractive than other women, and the less wealthy and working-class pregnant women felt fatter and more unattractive.

Overweight people face prejudice and discrimination (Jackson, 1992; Rothblum, 1992). In fact, women hold more negative stereotypes of the obese than men do (Jackson, 1992, 166). Esther Rothblum (1992) has written that while observers have often explained the often-noted connection between poverty and obesity by looking for the conditions of poverty that lead to obesity (such as the types of available food), she believes that discrimination against the obese helps cause poverty.

Weight is an important part of fitness; obesity is associated with a number of health-threatening conditions, including especially high blood pressure. However, the focus on weight as a measure of women's beauty pushes many women to dangerous limits, with constant and obsessive attention to dieting. Those concerned with women's health have focused increasingly on related *eating disorders* found principally among women: *anorexia nervosa* (self-starvation) and *bulimia* (binge eating, alternated with self-induced vomiting and fasting). Both are serious illnesses, not just cases of going too far in attempts to lose weight. They involve compulsive and dangerous behaviors, often hidden from family and friends until they are well advanced, and they result in emaciation, other physical symptoms, and in some severe cases death. The death rate among anorexics is more than 12

Is this an appropriate grown-up's image of beauty—or a child's?

times higher per year than the normal death rate among females ages 15–24 years, and more than twice the rate for female psychiatric inpatients 10–39 years old (Sullivan, 1995). The anorexic continues to regard herself as fat and ugly, even after she has lost a dangerous amount of weight.

From 85% to 95% of all anorexics and bulimics are women (Jackson, 1992). There are small numbers of eating-disordered men, however, and their symptoms are much like women's, although research suggests that they are more likely to have been abused as children (Olivardia, Pope, Mangweth, and Hudson, 1995). Anorexia seems to strike at the time when major changes are occurring in a young woman's life—as she prepares to go to college or to get married. Most research suggests that the majority of afflicted women are in their late teens and early 20s and are somewhat overweight, although not necessarily extraordinarily so. At first, most research suggested that they tend to have well-educated parents, be from affluent homes, and be under pressure to succeed. Other research is beginning to suggest that this portrait may be due to bias in research. For example, a study of Chippewa women showed that the majority in the sample were trying to diet, and the majority of them were using unhealthy methods (reported in Jackson, 1992, 185). There is a widespread problem of eating disorders among women of color, and it seems to be increasing (Jackson, 1992).

Many theories have been advanced to explain the causes of eating disorders. Most agree that eating disorders are linked to gender roles and sexual pressures on young women but disagree about the precise cause and meaning of these problems. Some argue that anorexia is a flight from femininity. Others consider it an attempt to fulfill norms of femininity and feminine beauty run amok. Others argue that anorexia is based on feelings of dependency and unworthiness. One study of the life histories of Latina, African-American, and White women found in each group that many women who were survivors of sexual abuse also suffered from eating disorders, and many made an explicit connection in their minds between the abuse and eating (Thompson, 1992). Many described the eating in terms of a numbing hatred of their own bodies or a means of protecting it. In these cases, it may not be obsession with the way the women's bodies look that triggers eating disorders, but the act of eating.

Exercise. All other things being equal, body weight and tone depend on both diet *and* exercise, yet females have tended to diet and males to exercise to control their weight, partly because until recently, girls have been discouraged from most forms of exercise that would strengthen and tone their bodies. In the United States, debate about women, exercise, and athletics began in the 19th century, when some people shunned exercise for women on health and aesthetic grounds, and some reformers advocated more exercise for women for health reasons.[24] Because menstruating and pregnant women were considered disabled, until the past few years, exercise was considered especially bad for them. Attitudes are changing, however, and the current health consensus is that moderate exercise is an important part of a healthy lifestyle for many reasons besides weight control, including cardiovascular health, reducing the risk of breast cancer,[25] and stimulating the development of bone mass.[26] Pregnant women are now also encouraged to exercise.

The issues and debate surrounding Title IX and sports in schools (see Chapter 5) point to the degree to which organized sports have been institutionalized as a male domain. Indeed, some sports now regarded as traditionally male were quite popular among women early in the 20th century, including baseball and especially basketball. As these sports became more institutionalized and lucrative, however, women were increasingly excluded. Now that women have entered into the world

Ice hockey *is* a women's game.

of sport more and more, their performance is also improving—and in ways that once seemed biologically impossible (see Chapter 3). Perhaps the most bizarre example of how women's bodies are still regarded as inappropriate for sport occurred in 1997, when a 12-year-old girl who had played catcher for 2 years in her local Babe Ruth League was barred from the game because she refused to wear the jock strap and protective cup that is required of catchers in that league. In fact, she later found, there is a little-known female version: briefs with a padded crotch.[27]

As important as exercise is to women, and as much as women can be proud of their athletic accomplishments, excessive exercise, like excessive dieting, takes its toll on women. The *Journal of the American Medical Association* notes the growth of a "female athletic triad" of risk among women who sacrifice their health for sport. The quest for maintaining the right body weight and fitness leads many women athletes to exercise too much and to eat too little, which can lead to a disordered pattern of eating and put them at risk of *osteoporosis* (loss of bone mass) and *amenorrhea* (ceased menstrual periods). An epidemiologist at the CDC has estimated that in some sports, up to two thirds of women athletes have disordered eating patterns, resulting in amenorrhea, which in turn leads to osteoporosis and other problems. Some college athletes have bone-mass equivalents that would be more appropriate for 50- to 60-year-olds; when their menses return, however, their bone mass improves ("Female Athletic Triad," 1993). Some experts estimate that up to half of all top women athletes and 20% of all women who exercise vigorously do not menstruate (Ilknoian, 1993).

Skin Color. Over the centuries, women have used countless forms of coloring on their faces and other parts of their bodies to change their overall color or the color of some parts of their bodies, to decorate their bodies, or to create illusions of different sizes and shapes. Sometimes, women are even told to use cosmetics on their faces so that they can look natural (i.e., as though they are not artificially altered).

In the 19th century, White women were supposed to remain as pale as possible, which required them to avoid the sun and fresh air. Not only did these women *look* consumptive, but also their behavior contributed to large rates of tuberculosis among women. In the 20th century, standards changed; White women began to bake themselves mercilessly in the sun, go to "tanning spas," or use chemicals to simulate a tan. Now, medical experts warn that this pursuit of a tan has created a skin-cancer epidemic, as well as premature aging of women's skin. Women have been urged to be more careful about protecting their skin from the sun. A study of African-American women found that most believed that African-American men prefer lighter-skinned women, and "the lighter the skin color standards that subjects believed Black men held, the lighter the women viewed themselves relative to judges' ratings" (Bond and Cash, 1992, 883). The women in this study (especially the lightest and darkest women) were generally satisfied with their own skin color, but those who were dissatisfied (especially medium-toned women) generally wanted to be lighter.

Summary: Health and Beauty. Feminists raise five criticisms about these "beauty" practices. First is the *double standard of beauty*. Physical attractiveness simply makes more difference for the way women are perceived and treated than it does for men (Jackson, 1992). Why should women require so much ornamentation and alteration—and so much more than men—to be considered attractive? The second is *cost*. These practices require a considerable investment and, many argue, waste of women's time and money.

The third criticism is *choice and control*. Standards of beauty are established and guided in large part by the pharmaceutical, fashion, and cosmetic industries, through advertising and by the commercial entertainment media, such as television and motion pictures. Although women have choices, tremendous resources are marshaled into convincing them to follow industry-created and -directed beauty standards. To what degree do women look the way they want to look, and to what degree do they look the way other people want them to look?

The fourth and most important criticism feminists launch against beauty standards and practices revolves around the *physical and mental-health effects* on women. Many of these beauty practices put women's health at risk, and some are downright dangerous. Some women's cosmetics and toiletries are harmful, and many beauty and weight-loss aids do not do what their manufacturers claim, or they do so in an unhealthy way.[28] Women's clothes are often not designed with comfort, safety, or ability to be active in mind. Consider the historical parade of high spindly heels, pointed cramped toes, and high platforms, given that the primary function of feet is transportation. It is no wonder that dress reform has been a major goal of feminist movements since the 1840s. As shown in the case of eating disorders, some women literally kill themselves in the pursuit of beauty. The effects on women's mental health are also serious. Many critics charge that the contradictory and, for most women, unattainable beauty standards help lead women to low self-esteem and self-devaluation.

Fifth, gender-based beauty standards are also mediated by and help to maintain other forms of *inequality,* especially on the basis of class, race, and age. Of course, relatively few women could actually pursue traditional ideals of female delicacy and beauty. Working-class and agricultural women, regardless of race, and women of color of all classes were considered *naturally* stronger and hardier than other women; they were fit to be workhorses, not swooning feminine ideals. Standards of beauty also tend to be defined in terms of youth. Television commercials show relatively young women fretting about how to remove ugly wrinkles they are unlikely to develop in any case for decades. The fashion industry emphasizes clothes for the young, and many designers do not produce clothes that can fit more mature bodies. As this chapter has shown, the pursuit of beauty and fitness usually requires substantial amounts of money and time—resources that many women, especially those who are not wealthy, do not have.

Certainly, to the degree that beauty standards are based on norms defining appropriate skin or hair color, body shape, or hair texture, they also support racial and ethnic stereotypes and inequality. Even in the late 1990s, as globalism became fashionable in the clothing industry, many of the images projected in related advertising campaigns still perpetuated stereotypes. As Amy Spindler has reported, nonWhite models are presented as "exotic" and are less likely than White models, for example, to be pictured in everyday situations. The images often employ specific ethnic stereotypes, frequently not by placing women in ethnically or culturally coherent settings, but by drawing out ethnic clichés in sometimes patronizing ways.[29]

Practice of Health Care:
Are Men and Women Treated Differently?

Thus far, we have looked at the way women's health is shaped and defined by different social institutions and practices. We now look specifically at the health-care system, to reach some general conclusions about women's health care. To what degree do we find evidence of androcentrism or sexism in health-care institutions and practices?

Perceptions of Women and Men. A long train of studies suggests that mental-health clinicians define health in men and women differently. A well-known study by Inge Broverman and her colleagues, published in 1970, found that mental-health clinicians described a "healthy male" and a "healthy adult" in roughly the same way, but they used other terms to characterize a "healthy female." Later research obtained similar results (Aslin, 1977; Kravetz and Jones, 1981; O'Malley and Richardson, 1985). Other studies also show that judgments of health among patients and clients may be based on gender ideology. In one study, when hypothetical female patients expressed conventionally male attitudes, evaluators judged them as more disturbed than when they expressed attitudes or preferences conventionally considered neutral or feminine. The same statements did not affect evaluators' views when they were made by males (Zeldow, 1976). In another study, counselors listening to tapes of either a man or a woman expressing the same concerns about work rated the woman as more masculine than they rated the man, possibly because these concerns, apparently normal in a man, seem abnormal in a woman (Hayes and Wolleat, 1978). Another study found that counselors had more complete memory of what male clients had said than they did of what female clients had said (Buczek, 1981). The degree of sexism in the perceptions of health-care professionals has probably declined considerably, however (Smith, 1980).

Class and race interact with gender in perceptions of patients in health care. One study found that the higher the social class of a male patient, the more favorably the clinical psychologist viewed him, but the higher the social class of a female patient, the less favorably the therapist viewed her. Assuming that patients of higher social class are more articulate (which does not mean smarter), less deferential, and apparently less dependent, class and gender may interact to produce this result. The males of higher social class would be acting in ways therapists find preferable in males, and females of the lower social class would be acting in ways therapists find preferable in females (Settin and Bramel, 1981). When psychiatrists were presented with similar case histories, they tended to diagnose patients differently, depending on their gender and race. The same symptoms led them to diagnose White women as having histrionic personality disorders and Black women as having paranoid personality disorders. Male clinicians were especially likely to perceive women as being depressed (Loring and Powell, 1988).

Some research suggests that clinicians' attitudes have changed over time, so that the problem is less that they see women and men differently per se, and more that they define the *situations* in which they expect to find women and men differently. These clinicians defined mental-health characteristics differently for people in the home and at work. Appropriate characteristics for people in the home were the ones traditionally regarded as feminine, while appropriate characteristics for people at work were those traditionally regarded as masculine (Poole and Tapley, 1988). Of course, the result will continue to be differential evaluation of women and men if the clinicians think of women at home and men at work.

Treatment. Research also suggests that male and female patients are treated differently. An interview study of 253 physicians found doctors more likely to consider emotional factors important in diagnosing a woman's problems and more likely to expect a psychosomatic diagnosis of a woman's problem. These differences were especially evident among patients who did not, during the course of the medical interview, mention experiencing any personal problems (Bernstein and Kane, 1981). On the other hand, both psychotic and neurotic males are kept in mental hospitals longer than females with similar disorders are, and psychotic males are channeled into psychiatric treatment more quickly than are females (Tudor, Tudor, and Gove, 1977). Thus, it seems, "Standards of normality for females are reported to be lower than standards for males, and females are apparently less stigmatized for symptoms of mental incompetence" (Tudor, Tudor, and Gove, 1977, 101), demonstrating again that from the medical point of view, a normal female is not quite as healthy as a normal male, or that an unhealthy female is more normal than an unhealthy male.

Although, in the United States, the majority of HIV-positive (having human immunodeficiency virus) people are men (in 1987, men were 80% of the AIDS [acquired immune deficiency syndrome] population), AIDS is the third leading cause of death among women ages 25–44 years and the *leading* cause among African-American women of that age. AIDS education programs have been aimed primarily at men because the epidemic grew earliest and most noticeably among gay men, and strong support networks have developed within the gay male community. By the mid-1990s, it became clear that afflicted women were not receiving as much education, treatment, or support as men. Women and men are equally likely to be helped by available treatments if they receive them, but women are much less likely to receive them and more likely to face delays, which means that they become extremely sick and die faster than men. Women with AIDS are also more likely to be impoverished, isolated, and responsible for the care of a child.[30]

More psychotropic drugs are prescribed for women than for men, especially among older people, although the differences are greater for some kinds, such as antidepressants, than for others, such as antipsychotics (Hansen and Osborne, 1995). Interviews with physicians reveal a variety of reasons for the prescription differences, including beliefs that women are more vulnerable and need drugs more, that men are reluctant to use drugs, and that women have the kinds of stress that can be alleviated by these drugs. Both women and doctors are likely to understand women's problems in psychological, rather than purely physical, terms. Some doctors believe that the side effects of psychotropic drugs are less troublesome to women because women do not have to be as alert as men do (Prather and Fidell, 1975).

Drug advertisements play an important role in helping doctors to match drugs with patients and symptoms. Content analysis of drug ads shows that they tend to associate psychoactive drugs with women and nonpsychoactive drugs with men. Men in these advertisements have more specific or work-related problems, and women have more diffuse anxieties and tensions and are shown as difficult patients (Prather and Fidell, 1975). Some drug advertisements have suggested that a woman's reluctance or inability to do housework was a sign of mental illness, recalling Betty Friedan's picture of tranquilizer-popping housewives in the 1950s (Seidenberg, 1971). A comparison of drug advertisements in the *American Journal of Psychiatry* and the *American Family Physician* showed that the ratio of females to males was 5:1 in the psychiatric journal and 10:0 in the general medical journal. Thus, general practitioners, who are less specifically trained in mental health, but who prescribe a very high proportion of these drugs, are more exposed to gender-based (and age-based) images of who should be drugged (Hansen and Osborne, 1995). (For more discussion of commercials and advertisements, see Chapter 8.)

Older women face special problems in health care. They often face demoralizing situations of medical personnel using baby talk with them. Physicians—especially male physicians—do not seem as vigilant in keeping older patients current on their Pap tests and mammograms. Doctors are less aggressive in using high-technology treatments for heart disease with women than with men, and they rarely offer treatment for incontinence. Few physicians have any specific training in gerontology (Sharpe, 1995).

Several factors combine to create problems for women in the health-care system. If a culture is sexist or androcentric, health-care practitioners and patients alike assimilate these attitudes and perceptions. Moreover, women may be especially hesitant to question their treatment. Doctors and patients are unequal in status, and a female patient and a male doctor are even more so. Although consumer movements in health care have grown recently, a doctor's orders are still commanding, particularly for women who, because of gender ideology, feel incompetent to question males in what is regarded as a male field.

These problems are exacerbated by the training of health-care professionals and the organizations in which they work. Textbooks and teaching methods used in medical schools reinforce sexist views of women. One doctor, for example, reported that during her first day at medical school, the lab instructor told the students to cut off the female cadaver's breasts and discard them, as though there were nothing a doctor could learn from them, despite the near-epidemic of breast cancer.[31] Feminist critics have expressed dismay at the ignorance of women in medical research and technology. Health problems of special concern to women, including menstruation and menopause and osteoporosis, have received little serious research attention until recently. Heart disease has been treated much less aggressively in women than in men, and the instruments used in heart surgery are designed for men's bigger bodies.[32]

Many experts point to the shocking lack of research on women's bodies and health as one of the most serious health-care problems for women. Lots of medical research, including drug testing, was long done only on men because researchers worried about the effect of "abnormalities" of women's bodies, such as menstrual cycles and pregnancy, and because women do not die as young as men, so their problems are not seen as being as serious as men's. As Shumaker and Smith have said, in thinking about the degree to which White men have been identified as the normal population in medical research, "The possibility that a clinical trial would ever be conducted on an all female or African-American population, . . . and the findings extrapolated to White men, is unimaginable" (Shumaker and Smith, 1994, 191). Yet findings from White men are extrapolated to women and African-Americans all the time. Therefore, no one knows enough about gender (or race) differences in the effects of drugs. Adequate research on breast cancer is lacking, and much of the research on cardiovascular health has focused on men. In the early 1990s, it became clear that because most of the AIDS attention and research had focused on men, experts had not caught on to the fact that the AIDS-causing HIV may have different effects on women's and men's bodies, thus leaving many HIV-positive women undetected. It is no wonder that many feminist health professionals are discussing the possible development of a formal medical specialty in women's health. Would such a move ghettoize women's health concerns? This is a topic for serious debate.[33]

These problems were so great that women's health activists in and out of government began to press for change. In 1996, the Women's Health Equity Act was introduced by six senators, including five women; this act had as its chief goals the establishment of research programs designed to study breast cancer, women and AIDS, and women's cardiovascular disease and the expansion of women's scientific employment in health fields. This followed the establishment in 1993 of the Office of Research on Women's Health, a department within the NIH, mandated to work within that important agency to promote more research on women and to make sure women are included in more clinical research. The NIH also launched the Women's Health Initiative, a major planned 15-year study of the major causes of death, disability, and frailty in postmenopausal women, a group that had been neglected previously. With these and related efforts, knowledge of women's health should increase dramatically over the coming years.[34]

Medical definitions of femininity are changing, and increasing health activism among women is bringing pressure on the health-care system to be more responsive to women. In many communities, medical personnel and hospitals have become more favorable toward having women take more control of childbirth. Doctors increasingly expect women to take birth-preparation courses, such as Lamaze classes. Fitness among women is emphasized as it never was before. Women who do not conform to traditional female roles appear less likely to be suspected of being psychologically unhealthy.

Health care is expensive in the United States. Unlike those of most other industrialized nations, the U.S. health-care system has long been based on the principle that except under certain circumstances, the person receiving health care should be responsible for paying the bill. The fact that women are poorer than men, care for more children, and live longer makes the economics of health care particularly relevant to women. This situation presents special problems to the self-employed, employees of small companies, and part-time workers, who do not usually get health-coverage benefits through their work, and to homeless women, who have difficulties of access to care and whose homelessness exacerbates their health problems (Burg, 1995). Probably 9 million women of childbearing age lack health insurance.[35] This also means that health-care decisions in the U.S. system are made by the insurance companies that control health-care provision. For example, insurance companies routinely refused coverage to battered wives because of the high cost incurred by the companies until the industry and government moved against this practice.[36] A growing consumer movement and the women's movement have argued that the public must be more active in shaping health care. The following section turns directly to the question of women's influence on health-care systems.

Women's Roles in Shaping Health Care

Women provide most of the world's health care. However, as the study of women in society repeatedly shows, constituting a numerical majority by no means guarantees power and control. What contributions have women made to health care? We begin by looking at the people whose primary job it is to provide health care: health professionals and other workers. We then turn to health activists and social movements and organizations that attempt to influence health-care institutions and practices. Next, we consider one of the largest group of health-care providers: mothers. We conclude with the largest group of all: patients and other health-care consumers.

Healers, Doctors, and Other Health-Care Professionals

Professional medical training is a recent phenomenon. Many of the same midwives who delivered the babies also served as healers, employing herbal remedies and other means to manage people's health. Although many of their remedies were at best useless and at worst harmful (as were the strategies of male doctors of the same eras), many were also very helpful. In fact, medicine has recently been returning to some of these "natural" remedies. Until the 17th century, doctors trained in academies concentrated their study primarily on philosophy, theology, and perhaps astrology. Certainly, some of the women's herbs were at least as good as the men's stars and prayers. Surgery was a relatively low-status occupation, performed by men who doubled as barbers; the red-and-white barber pole, symbolizing a bloody rag, is a reminder of the dual role barbers once played. Most medical knowledge, including that of the healers and midwives, was learned on the job, from those who were more experienced.

As late as the 1840s, about 70% of all male physicians in the United States had no formal training, and for those who had it, it tended to be very theoretical, with little hands-on professional training of the sort that was more widely available in Europe. The first woman to finish formal medical training in the United States was Elizabeth Blackwell, in 1849. As Mary Roth Walsh has written, however, Blackwell "was recognized as the first woman medical doctor because she was the first woman who earned a degree from a medical college, a criterion which, if applied to her male colleagues, would have sharply reduced their numbers" (Walsh, 1979, 448).

Competition and antagonism between female healers and male doctors (and other male-dominated institutions) developed as early as the 14th century and was well established by the 15th and 16th centuries. This growing antagonism was manifested in part in the witch hunts of the late medieval period, when, it is estimated, thousands of people were executed as witches, about 85% of whom were women (Ehrenreich and English, 1979, 31). Among the charges leveled against the women were the crimes of healing, using drugs to ease pain, and assisting with contraception and abortion.

Although in early American history, women continued to serve as healers and midwives, their activities became increasingly restricted during the 19th and 20th centuries, as medicine became professionalized—and more lucrative. Medicine came under increasingly strict licensing requirements and eventually required training that excluded women. Women's medical colleges began to open in the 1840s, and other medical schools began to admit women in the 1870s. By 1900, there were about 5,000 trained women doctors, but at about that time, the co-educational medical colleges that admitted women began to impose quotas restricting the number of women. Those women who did gain admission were often harassed by their male colleagues. Medical schools explicitly imposed tougher entry standards on women than on men until the 1970s, when such actions became illegal. As soon as women were required only to be as good as men, rather than better than, to get into medical school, the proportion of women in medical schools rose dramatically. The powerful professional organization and interest group the American Medical Association (AMA) admitted women to full membership only in 1951, 104 years after it was founded.

The late 19th and early 20th centuries saw the rise of a number of other health-care fields, such as nursing, social work, and mental health, many of which became predominantly female. Nursing makes a fascinating case study of women health professionals. At first, nurses were generally trained on the job, as ward workers in hospitals and clinics, for example. The first training school for nurses was established at Bellevue Hospital in New York City in 1873. Nursing education expanded and was gradually professionalized, although it was not regulated and licensed until after World War II. Since then, nursing organizations have worked to foster more professional images and treatment of nurses, who have often been portrayed in popular culture as cocktail waitresses, maids, or governesses in white. In the 20th century, especially in the recent era of rapid technological and scientific development in medicine and health care, the number of female technicians and laboratory workers has also grown.

Men continue to hold higher proportions of the high-status roles in health-care organizations. In 1988, only about 20% of the nation's physicians and 9% of the dentists were women. Among the female-dominated health jobs in 1991, women constituted 99% of the dental assistants, 98% of the dental hygienists, 96% of the practical nurses, 95% of the registered nurses, and 94% of the dietitians (U.S. Bureau of the Census, 1992). Women physicians have tended to go into fields with high patient interaction and, often, relatively low pay and status, such as general practice, psychiatry, and pediatrics, although these patterns are now changing.

Women's experiences in medical training and practice are different from men's. Women face gender discrimination and sexual harassment during training (Cook, 1996). Men are less likely to encourage women to pursue certain specialties, such as surgery (Dresler et al., 1996). A study in Sweden, one of the most gender-egalitarian countries in the world, looked at the evaluations of research doctors and objective measures of their research impact and concluded that women have to be 2.5 times more productive than men to get the same peer-review ratings (Motluck, 1997). Many women feel that discrimination has hindered their careers (Dresler et al., 1996).

Some evidence shows that patients and clients tend to prefer male health-care practitioners in some fields, although not in others, yet they are more satisfied with women doctors (Bensing, van den Brink-Muinen, and de Bakker, 1993; Chesler, 1971; Delgado, Lopez-Fernandez, and De Dios Luna, 1993; Mandelbaum, 1978; Tanney and Birk, 1976). This finding is particularly intriguing because most people come into much more contact with female than with male practitioners in mental-health clinics. Many women prefer women as health-care practitioners, particularly, one might suspect, as gynecologists and obstetricians and, as Tanney and Birk (1976) have shown, as therapists for personal and social problems. A Norwegian study showed that women who prefer a doctor to have a democratic stance toward patients prefer women physicians, while those who want a more dominating style prefer a man (Elstad, 1994).

Some research explores whether women and men perform differently as health-care practitioners. An AMA survey found women more likely to report that they systematically review patients' health practices and counsel them on unhealthy behavior, especially with regard to the most sensitive behaviors such as drug use and sexual behavior (Frank and Harvey, 1996). Women are also more likely to recommend estrogen-replacement therapy for older women (Seto et al., 1996). One study showed that female doctors are more likely than male doctors to let their patients talk (West, 1984). In hospitals staffed by women doctors, there are fewer operative deliveries of babies and lower maternal mortality rates. It is certainly true that women do most of the feminist research in health-care fields. In some health-care areas, gender differences in medical behavior may be mostly due to generational, rather than gender, differences in approach, with younger and more recently trained doctors more sensitive to gender issues and women's health.

In some cases, however, research suggests that gender norms are more directly responsible. Anthropologist Joan Cassell (1996) studied surgeons, whom she has described as participating in one of a number of body-oriented occupations. "Embodied occupations such as surgery, firefighting, waging war, race car driving, and test piloting focus on one pole of a set of cultural oppositions. Practitioners describe themselves and their comrades as active, strong, decisive, brave, aggressive" (Cassell, 1996, 42). In these occupations, she has argued, there is a high degree of male bonding and a profound distrust of women's participation. Thus, in these arenas, either women tend to be excluded, or their existence as real women is questioned. "Women who possess the wrong body in the wrong place must not be 'real' women to place themselves in that situation"; the women often find it difficult to be understood both as a surgeon and as a woman at the same time (Cassell, 1996, 44).

Health-Care Activists

One of the most striking aspects of the history of women's organizations and feminist movements is the degree to which they have been historically trying to improve the quality and quantity of health care in America. Women were active in the health-care reform movements of the 1820s, 1830s, and later periods. Throughout the 19th century, feminists were committed to and involved in ideas of "preventive hygiene," which included not just medical treatment, but what we now call environmental health, fitness, mental health, and social health. It is no coincidence that numerous suffragists and other feminists were active in the temperance movement. Their motivation was, by and large, the protection of the health of women and children who suffered at the hands of drunken husbands.

These health activists often linked individual health to morality, equality, justice, and the "health of society." Jane Addams and her colleagues at Chicago's Hull House emphasized the needs of immigrants; Margaret Sanger, Emma Goldman, and activists in the birth-control movement focused on working-class women; and Ellen Richards and others who developed the field of home economics (endorsed in 1899 by the AMA) were motivated in part by a concern for the health of individuals and of society as a whole and the potential of domestic science to improve the health of the nation and its children.

As the 19th century came to a close, women pushed to have government directly involved in assuring the health of society through regulation and improvement of sanitation facilities, hospitals, parks, and prisons. By the end of the 19th century, women, including many feminists, were actively involved in state and city politics and government and the agencies that managed sanitation, health, and health education in schools. They found allies in the Progressive Movement, an early-20th-century movement dedicated to these and related social and political reforms. Today, these same concerns remain prominent in the feminist movement and in women's social and political activity more generally.

Many groups are involved in educating women on health issues of concern to them. Since 1971, the Boston Women's Health Book Collective (1992) has published a valuable book, written in lay language, now titled *The New Our Bodies Ourselves*. The National Black Women's Health Project, begun in 1981, focuses especially on the health needs of African-American women. The Native American Women's Health Education Resource Center, founded in 1987, offers information on Native American women's health, and the National Latina Health Organization, founded in 1986, focuses on many issues, including especially reproductive choice. The National Women's Health Network is an umbrella organization, including a membership of more than 20,000 individuals and organizations.[37]

As the discussion of the new government health initiatives shows, the health care of women became a goal of public policy in the 1990s. How long those efforts will last, and how well funded they will remain, will depend on the continued vigilance of health-care activist groups.

Mothers and Daughters as Health-Care Providers

One relatively unchanged aspect of the role of wife and mother is caring for the family's health, by creating a healthful home, by dispensing most of the immediate health care, and by making sure that members of the family who need treatment from professionals receive it. As Eugenia S. Carpenter has noted, "Women are the principal brokers or arrangers of health services for their children and spouses" (1980, 1214). This responsibility of women for family health care entails certain problems.

David Spiegel (1982), among others, has argued that this responsibility is in many ways a burden. "Because we have been willing to believe that mothers do something special for their children—something that cannot be replaced by anyone other than the mother—mothers have been given an inequitable share of the responsibility for child care and undue blame for the mental illness of their children" (p. 105). This burden becomes greater when a woman is employed for much of the day outside the home, without any major change in the division of labor at home. "Both the monetary and nonmonetary costs women incur in fulfilling their family responsibilities for health care of other family members are increasing" (Carpenter, 1980, 1215).

Mothers have more responsibility and take more blame than fathers in family health matters because they are given more responsibility in general for family care. Even beyond this, however, people tend to blame parents for gender-linked problems in their children (Kellerman, 1974). For example, a child's problems may be blamed on a "domineering mother" or a "henpecked father," both of which imply pejorative judgments of women.

The role of mothers and daughters is in fact *increasing* because of changes in the American political economy resulting in the "downsizing" of public and private agencies alike. As Nona Glazer said, in her fascinating study of women's paid and unpaid labor in health care and retailing, as health-care institutions have become strapped for resources, they have both squeezed more work out of their staff and passed much work previously done by paid labor back onto patients and their families, usually mothers and, for the elderly, daughters. Certainly, the self-help movement of the 1960s and after served as an important basis for this shift, as the public wanted to be freed from some of the control of experts and to participate more in health-related decision making themselves.

New home-health-care policies have not empowered the public as much as burdened them, however. "Home care was packaged by legislators, hospital administrators, and discharge planners as a benefit to patients: as assuring privacy, home comforts, and community and family support. Presumably it is highly moral because it shifts responsibility from institutions to the family, and it is sound psychologically because it lessens patient dependency and decreases the disorientation that the frail elderly may experience in hospitals" (Glazer, 1993, 202–203). However, the new system has tended to be stripped of supports for those in need, placing more burden on mothers and daughters caring for their children and their parents. By the middle of the 1990s, insurance companies were trying not to pay for more than the most minimal of hospital stays, beginning a round of criticism of "drive-by deliveries." "Demands were not for home health care with minimal support services, the system that has emerged in the 1990s," Glazer wrote (1993, 202). The weakness of the economy was being paid for—not for the first time—by the voluntary labor of women.

The Influence of Women as Health-Care Consumers

It is all too easy to think of health-care consumers as passive patients whose only real source of power in health care is to pick a doctor wisely. Much feminist writing about women and health emphasizes women's role as passive victims of health-care institutions. In fact, new research into the history of health and medicine points out that health-care consumers do not have to be passive recipients and that they never have been devoid of power as a group. They have provided much of their own training and passed on their knowledge, often disparagingly referred to as "old wives' tales."

Women visit doctors and dentists more than men do, and they spend more days in hospitals. Of course, a lot of the difference between men and women is concentrated on the childbearing years. Women have also often taken a strong hand in determining what treatment they received (Leavitt, 1980, 1983; Leavitt and Walton, 1982; Smith-Rosenberg, 1975). Childbirth is a good example. Birth was a cooperative effort among women before the widespread use of physicians or hospitals, including the mother, a midwife, and various female relations and friends. That control did not disappear suddenly; medical science did not simply appear at the door, forcing unwilling women to accept new models and practices and shipping women off to hospitals. Women continued to exert considerable control as long as birth occurred in their territory: the home. A doctor could be thrown out of the birthing room by a woman who disapproved of the doctor's methods. Doctors found themselves without patients if they were known to engage in practices women did not like. Judith Walzer Leavitt has cited the advice one doctor gave to others about attempting to shave a woman's pubic area before birthing: "In about three seconds after the doctor has made the first rake with his safety [razor], he will find himself on his back out in the yard with the imprint of a woman's bare foot emblazoned on his manly chest, the window sash round his neck. . . . Tell him not to try to shave 'em" (1983, 294). Taking control was no easy task for the doctor.

Women have often staunchly searched for and demanded the best treatment they thought they could obtain, including trained doctors in preference to midwives and state-of-the-art procedures and drugs. Old-fashioned practitioners who refused to use new procedures often found themselves rejected in favor of those who were deemed more modern. Eventually, women began to seek hospital rather than home care for childbirth. Once they left their own territory, however, they also lost their control over birth. Increasing numbers are now trying to regain that control.

In their everyday lives, the two chief ways in which women govern and influence health care are (1) how they take care of themselves, and (2) how they interact with others in the health-care system. For example, lifestyle choices (e.g., patterns of eating, exercise, sexual activity, or alcohol and other drug use) are also *health-care* choices; they have to do with what care women give their bodies. Men tend to engage in more risky behavior. They smoke and drink more than women, but research suggests that after taking account of body fluid (which determines the impact of alcohol), women do *not* drink much less than men ("Women Drinking Alcohol," 1995). In regard to issues of exercise and nutrition, women must fight gender ideologies that lead women to self-damaging extremes in pursuit of beauty or of what they think is men's ideal. In this sense, women's health depends on women's empowerment.

Toward a New Understanding of Women's Health

Throughout the 20th century, women have had longer life expectancies than men. A White male born in the United States in 1980 could expect to live 70 years, compared with 77 years for a White female; an African-American male born that year could expect to live to age 64, compared with age 73 for an African-American female. This apparent male fragility is attributable to a number of causes. More males are born with genetically based diseases, such as hemophilia, and they are more likely to die from infant diseases, heart disease, most forms of cancer, cirrhosis of the liver, AIDS, accidents, homicide, and suicide. Women, on the other hand, are more likely than men to die of cerebrovascular disease, diabetes, arteriosclerosis, breast cancer, genital cancer (except among people over age 65), complications of pregnancy and abortion, and old age. Understanding the nature of health and health care in any more detail requires not just expertise in the biological science, but also in the relationship of human beings to their environment and each other, and the way many health-related social institutions function.

Standards of normal health cover a wide range of human characteristics and activities and are intimately tied to definitions of gender and gender roles. Incomplete medical knowledge means that in the pursuit of high standards of health, gender ideology is likely to play a role in the development and application of health-care values and procedures. In any case, despite the tangible reality of physical states of body, a significant amount of how people think about health is socially constructed.

The study of women and health is highly charged and controversial. Some writers seem to suggest that women have been passive victims of medical professionals' purposeful attempts to destroy them; others suggest that medical science has single-mindedly saved women from their self-destructing bodies. The truth lies somewhere else. The practice of medicine and, more broadly, health care has saved women's lives and has improved the quality of their lives in gender-specific ways. It has also hurt women at times and not lived up to its potential for improving the quality of women's lives in other gender-specific ways. Women have been victims, sometimes passive victims. They have also often taken active charge of themselves and their health care and have struggled to increase their control, sometimes for better and sometimes for worse.

The health-care system in the United States has changed in recent decades, with respect to women's health care. There is considerably more organization on behalf of women. More and more hospitals and health maintenance organizations (HMOs) include designated women's centers or women's programs. The question is whether these centers are providing something fundamentally new or are simply repackaging and marketing something old. Perhaps most important of all, even where these special organizations do not exist, women are beginning to take their health and fitness more seriously.

Notes

1. See, for example, Sloane (1993); the Boston Women's Health Book Collective (1992); and the websites listed in these notes.

2. Celia W. Dugger, "Tug of Taboos: African Genital Rite vs. U.S. Law," *New York Times,* December 28, 1996.

3. Celia W. Dugger, "U.S. Grants Asylum to Woman Fleeing Genital Mutilation Rite," *New York Times,* June 15, 1996.

4. Natalie Angier, "In a Culture of Hysterectomies, Many Question Their Necessity," *New York Times,* February 17, 1997.

5. This is a very simple procedure of carefully feeling each part of the breast regularly to be able to detect new irregularities. Most women's health books contain detailed information on how to do this, and any doctor, nurse, or health-care clinic can offer information and help.

6. Sandra Blakeslee, "Faulty Math Heightens Fears of Breast Cancer," *New York Times,* March 15, 1992.

7. Information on this program may be found at http://www.cdc.gov/nccdphp/dcpc/

8. This is only a partial list. Mental-health practitioners attempting to diagnose LLPDD would look for a combination of symptoms that were consistent over an extended period of time. Do not try to diagnose yourself on the basis of this list!

9. Jane E. Brody, "Can Drugs 'Treat' Menopause?" *New York Times,* May 19, 1992.

10. For more on the history of childbirth, see Leavitt, 1986. For information on many aspects of childbirth, see "Childbirth.org," at http://www.childbirth.org/

11. "Study Faults Surgery on Women Giving Birth," *New York Times,* July 2, 1992.

12. Warren E. Leary, "Alternative to Cesarean Grows More Popular," *New York Times,* August 29, 1991.

13. Cindy Skrzycki, "Maternity Leave Is No Vacation," *Washington Post,* October 5, 1992.

14. American Medical Association, "Women's Health Overview," http://www.ama-assn.org/mem-data/Wmmed/Wmhealth/overview/html

15. Don Terry, "Stabbing Death at Door of Justice Sends Alert on Domestic Violence," *New York Times,* March 17, 1992.

16. For more discussion of the legal and social issues, see Chapter 11.

17. See further discussion in Chapter 9.

18. For more discussion of occupational safety and health, see Chavkin, 1984.

19. Lena Williams, "Girl's Self-image Is Mother of the Woman," *New York Times,* February 6, 1992.

20. For an informative list of the procedures one might have done, see the homepage on "Cosmetic Trends" available from plastic surgeons at http://cosmetic-trends.com/

21. Lena Williams, "Girl's Self-image Is Mother of the Woman," *New York Times,* February 6, 1992.

22. Tamar Lewin, "As Silicone Issue Grows, Women Take Agony and Anger to Court," *New York Times,* January 19, 1992.

23. Felicity Barringer, "First Steps Taken in Revived Use of Breast Implants," *New York Times,* May 3, 1992.

24. For some histories of women, exercise, and sport, see Berlage, 1994; and Cahn, 1994.

25. Gina Kolata, "Study Bolsters Idea That Exercise Cuts Breast Cancer Risk," *New York Times,* May 1, 1997.

26. "Gymnastics May Toughen Women's Bones," *New York Times,* November 25, 1994.

27. John Pacenti, "Girls Who Won't Wear Cup Punished by Baseball League," *Detroit Free Press,* May 22, 1997.

28. For an excellent compendium of information on the safety of cosmetics and other beauty aids, and on the efficacy of the claims of many beauty aids ("This will make your skin look younger!") and weight-loss aids ("Lose 10 pounds quickly!"), go to the FDA website homepage (http://www.fda.gov), and click on "Cosmetics."

29. Amy M. Spindler, "Taking Stereotyping to a New Level in Fashion," *New York Times,* June 3, 1997.

30. Sheryl Gay Stolberg, "The Better Half Got the Worse End," *New York Times,* July 20, 1997.

31. Tamar Lewin, "Doctors Consider a Specialty Focusing on Women's Health," *New York Times,* November 7, 1992.

32. Tamar Lewin, "Doctors Consider a Specialty Focusing on Women's Health," *New York Times,* November 7, 1992.

33. Tamar Lewin, "Doctors Consider a Specialty Focusing on Women's Health," *New York Times,* November 7, 1992.

34. To find out more about the Women's Health Initiative, see http://www.odp.od.nih.gov/whi/

35. See Note 14.

36. "Officials' Panel Moves to Aid Abused Wives on Insurance," *New York Times,* March 19, 1995.

37. National Black Women's Health Project, 1237 Ralph David Abernathy Blvd., SW, Atlanta, Georgia 30310. National Latina Health Organization, P.O. Box 7567, Oakland, CA 94601. National Women's Health Network, 1325 G. Street, NW, Washington, DC 20005. Native American Women's Health Education Resource Center, P.O. Box 572, Lake Andes, South Dakota 57358.

7

Women and Religion

In the Heavens are parents single?
No. The thought makes reason stare.
Truth is reason. Truth eternal
Tells me I've a Mother there.

Eliza Snow, 1843, in a popular
Mormon hymn, "Oh, My Father"

IN 1780, JUDITH SARGENT MURRAY, an American writer and daughter of a minister, argued against interpretations of Scripture presenting women as dangerous and as inferior to men. In 1837, the English social observer Harriet Martineau claimed that American women's morals were crushed by the repressive teachings of religion. In 1848, the participants at the Seneca Falls convention, a meeting often described as the beginning of the American feminist movement, denounced the treatment of women by organized churches. In the 1880s, Elizabeth Cady Stanton, Matilda Joslyn Gage, and many other feminists published attacks on church teachings about women. Emma Goldman declared organized religion to be one of the most vile oppressors of both men and women. In the 1970s, Mary Daly, then a professor of theology at a Roman Catholic college, argued that male religious authorities were guilty of *gynocide*—murder of women—physically, psychologically, and morally.[1]

American feminists have long criticized organized religion for its oppression of women. American feminist history also includes, however, uncountable figures, such as Sarah and Angelina Grimké, Lucretia Mott, and Elizabeth Cady Stanton, who derived their political principles, strength, and bravery and their speaking and organizing skills from their religions. Many women have fought from the inside to transform their religions and have demanded the opportunity to become religious leaders and authorities. Others have sought alternative forms of religion more suited to their principles of equality and freedom.

216

Organized religion is one of the most powerful institutions involved in shaping people's beliefs, attitudes, values, and behavior. Gender is such an important part of the theology, cultural precepts, ceremonies, and rituals of most religions that we could not understand the institutional roots of sex/gender systems without analyzing the role of religion. To do this, we look first at teachings about women, gender, and sexuality in the major American religions. We then turn to the role of women in shaping religion and the ways in which women have influenced society through their religious activities. Before we examine these issues, however, we must first consider some of the difficulties involved in any discussion of religion.

Organized religion is not a single, homogeneous entity. Even within a single family of religions such as Christianity, various denominations show substantial differences. Quakers and Roman Catholics are both Christians, both believe in a single deity that sent a son to Earth, and both use the Old and New Testaments of the Bible as their chief texts, but beyond these similarities, they diverge widely, especially on issues of gender. Nevertheless, this chapter cannot consider all American religions in detail because there are scores of them, ranging from those with millions of members to those with a few thousand or fewer. This discussion is limited to considering the denominations that have had the most widespread influence on American society and values, because of either their size or their distinctive roles.

The study of religion in American society poses some unique problems and questions. Unlike many other countries, the United States does not have an established or national religion. Even more important, the principles of American law call for a wall of separation between religion and government. Despite this wall, foreign observers are often amazed by the central role religion plays, not only in the personal life of Americans, but also in American public life. Surveys in the mid-1970s showed that 58% of all Americans considered their religious beliefs very important, compared with 36% each of Italians and Canadians, 23% of Britons, 22% of French citizens, and 17% of Germans (Benson, 1981). As Table 7-1 shows, the majority of Americans find religion a very important part of their lives, and almost half derive day-to-day guidance from religion. That table also shows that, at least on some questions, women express greater religiosity than men. Women are more likely to find religion important in their lives, to pray regularly, and to read the Bible. More women than men interpret the Bible as the literal word of God.

Americans do not just find their religions personally important; many also believe that religion should play a large role in guiding culture and politics. The wall separating church and state is in fact very porous and flexible in practice. Thus, it is especially important to understand how religion shapes gender norms and behavior.

Although the long history of each religion is important for understanding its contemporary ideas and practices, in this chapter, we look primarily at the American religious experience. We do not ask what Jesus or his disciple Paul really said or meant but what American Christians have thought they said and meant, and how these interpretations affect American life. We do not ask about the forms that patriarchal principles took among the ancient Israelites, but we do explore the norms of American Jews.[2]

TABLE 7-1
Religious Orientations, by Gender

	Men	Women
Religion is an important part of my life.	70	79*
Religion provides a great deal of guidance in my day-to-day life.	46	48
Prays at least once a day.	38	57*
Never reads the Bible.	40	28*
Believes the Bible is the actual word of God and is to be taken literally.	43	52
Attends religious services.	66	64
Goes to services almost weekly or weekly.	40	39
Born again (% of Christians).	38	42

Note: Numbers show proportion of people in each religion category who agreed with the statement to the left. Based on $N = 467$. *Gender differences are statistically significant, $p < .05$.

Source: 1991 American National Election Study Pilot Study, analysis by author.

Religious Teachings About Women and Gender

Religion offers guidelines for moral behavior and thought, but some doctrines are rules that believers must follow, for fear of punishment. Religious institutions are like other social institutions in an important way: They provide both explicit rules and more generalized norms that people internalize and enforce on themselves.

The Bible is an important source of moral norms for both Christians and Jews. It is important to remember that different denominations find very different messages in this same text. Mormons, for example, referred to the biblical patriarchs to support the institution of polygamy until polygamy was made illegal by an act of the U.S. Congress. Other Christians and Jews, revering the same patriarchs in the same Bible, have regarded polygamy as uncivilized and sinful or contrary to God's law. Orthodox and many Conservative Jews still follow the laws on female pollution found in Leviticus, which define a woman's natural bodily functions as unclean and prescribe purification rituals. Other denominations, including many that claim to accept literal biblical dictates, do not enforce these biblical laws, even if they still think that menstruating women are unclean. Muslims base their beliefs on a different book, the Koran, but its words are also interpreted in diverse ways by various believers.

Despite these differences, there are some remarkable similarities among various denominations' traditional views on gender. Among these are the beliefs that (1) women and men have different missions and different standards of behavior;

and (2) although women and men are equal in the eyes of the deity, women are to some degree subordinated to men. This section explores in more detail various religious definitions of gender and some of the changes now taking place. It begins with a discussion of images of God and then turns to religious prescriptions for everyday life and morality for women. This section ends with a look at some new and alternative views of women.

God Talk: Is It Male?

God the Father. God the King and Lord. The Father, the Son, and the Holy Ghost. The words used in Judaism, Christianity, and Islam describe God, the deity, as male. Some people argue that the use of *He* to refer to God is a generic term, but it is difficult to say the same of *Father, Lord,* and *King.* To see the importance of "he" words in religion, try taking a religious text or prayer and substituting female-gender words. Think about your reactions as you hear yourself refer to God as *She, the Queen,* or *my Lady.* Adults are not supposed to make the childish error of anthropomorphism—that is, seeing God as a human being. Even theological sophistication, however, is not a sufficiently powerful force to eliminate what might be called "andromorphism." God may not be human, but "he" is still male.

The gender images of Jesus in Christian theology and tradition are especially interesting. Whereas the character attributed to God has generally been unambiguously masculine, the character of Jesus is considerably more androgynous. God's compassion is often described as *fatherly,* a term that seems less appropriate to describe the compassion of Jesus. Although Jesus was male, many of his characteristics are usually regarded as feminine, such as his unfailing gentleness, humility, simplicity, and nonviolence; his healing qualities and immediately forgiving nature; and his suffering for others. Nevertheless, the fact that Jesus and the disciples were male has often been used to argue that women should not have positions of highest religious authority. Many leaders in the Anglican and Episcopal Churches used this view to argue against the installation of the first female bishop in the Episcopal Church in 1989. Roman Catholics generally regard this as the major stumbling block to uniting their churches.

Religious language helps define our conception of God, authority, goodness, and holiness. If God is a Father but not a Mother, that says something not just about our conception of God but also about our conceptions of fathers and mothers and, by extension, men and women. Religious language and thought teaches us not just about our religions, but also about other aspects of life. If we look at American history, we can see the crucial role religion has played in defining the roles of women in American life and culture.

Defining Male and Female

Religion played a crucial role in the formation of American ideology on gender, as well as on other aspects of life, during the colonial and early postrevolutionary eras. Although the Anglican colonials of the South had a somewhat less stern outlook than the Puritans of the North, a literal reading of the Bible and a patriarchal view of God and society were important bases of thought in both cases. When people learned to read, their text was the Bible; even if they could not read, they learned their lessons in church each Sunday or, if they were farther from civilization, from the traveling preacher.

The Puritans based their views of women on the Old Testament and their interpretation of the patriarchal ancient Hebrew values. Woman's purpose was to be a helpmate for her husband, to be fruitful, and to multiply. Both men and women must fear God and Satan (although in different ways), but women should also be submissive to their husbands, the moral authority of the household. Women's work, especially the pain of childbirth, was viewed by Christians as a punishment for Eve's insubordination: "I will increase your labor and your pain, and in labor you shall bear children. You shall be eager for your husband, and he shall be your master" (Gen. 3:16).[3]

Puritans and others found more warnings for women to submit themselves to their husbands in the New Testament: "For man did not originally spring from woman, but woman was made out of man; and man was not created for woman's sake, but woman for the sake of man" (1 Cor. 11:8–10). Women should be silent in church and should learn from their husbands (1 Cor. 14:34–35, 1 Tim. 2:9–15). "Wives, be subject to your husbands as to the Lord; for the man is the head of the woman, just as Christ also is the head of the Church. Christ is, indeed, the Savior of the body; but just as the church is subject to Christ, so must women be to their husbands in everything" (Eph. 5:22–24). Although more egalitarian than other denominations in matters concerning public speaking, even the gentle Friends ("Quakers") accepted the patriarchal view that man is to woman what Christ is to humans (Frost, 1973).

Religion and the Bible provided examples of the female character who served as lessons for all, particularly in the persons of Eve and Jesus's mother, Mary. Religious people found proof in Genesis that woman was created as man's auxiliary and also that woman is likely both to sin and to tempt men to sin if left to her own devices. The main lesson of this story has been that if women are not controlled, they will reenact the fall from God's grace. Rather than providing a maternal image (as the mother of us all), Eve has come to represent woman's treachery. Although Jews interpret the story of the Garden of Eden somewhat differently than Christians (neither the Fall nor original sin are part of Jewish theology), women and men are customarily separated in Orthodox synagogues because of the belief that women would otherwise distract men from their piety. In Islam, this separation is achieved through veiling and *purdah.*

Within the Christian tradition (especially among Roman Catholics), the primary contrasting female image to Eve is Mary, who, according to some Catholic traditions, was conceived *without sin* (that is, without her mother's recourse to sexual relations) and who most Christians believe conceived Jesus "without sin." She is the ideal woman and, most important for understanding religious norms of womanhood, an unattainable ideal. Although the cult of the Virgin has perhaps never taken hold in the United States to the same degree that it has elsewhere, Mary is nonetheless a powerful model in American Christian life (Warner, 1976).

Biblical stories are interpreted differently by different people and traditions. Many Jewish and Christian feminists have reinterpreted the story of Eve; they see her as the person responsible for making humans capable of knowing about good and evil. Jewish feminists have rehabilitated Vashti in the book of Esther in the Apocrypha. Vashti was rejected as a wife by King Ahasuerus in favor of Esther because Vashti refused to dance before her husband and his drunken friends at a party. The feminist intention is not to diminish Esther's accomplishments, but rather to reject the assumption that women who do not unquestioningly submit to their husband are bad. Other commentators point to additional female religious models, such as Deborah, the judge, or Ruth and Naomi.

Despite these alternative stories and interpretations, the predominant message of most religions is that women and men have very different roles and characters, that religious authority speaks mostly in a male voice, and that woman's primary role is to accept that authority and to bear and raise children. It is important to understand how religions presumably dedicated to holiness and justice support such a system of inequality and submission. Many religious authorities of different denominations have argued that the enforcement of these differences does not create or enforce inequality. They say that although men and women are *different*, they are *equal* in value in the eyes of God. For denominations with a concept of heaven, religious teachings claim that by fulfilling their different duties, women and men earn equal places in heaven. Some religions simply believe that God designed women as inferior beings. Changes in the texts and practices of many denominations over the past century show that the religious principles of female inferiority are being abandoned.

Religious teachings also have direct effects on gender ideology and attitudes toward women. Historically, theologians have elaborated on the theme of separate spheres and characters for women and men and have equated preservation of women's place with preservation of morality and of a civilized (and American) way of life. A sermon delivered in 1837 by a Presbyterian minister demonstrates the degree to which regulation of women's sphere, Christian morality, and attitudes toward civilization were intricately intertwined. The preservation of the moral order, he argued, depended on the preservation of distinct spheres for men and women. Women were responsible for determining whether civilization would rise or fall. Addressing women, he said,

> Yours it is to decide, under God, whether we shall be a nation of refined and high-minded Christians, or whether, rejecting the civilities of life, and throwing off the restraints of morality and purity, we should become a fierce race of semi-barbarians, before whom neither order, nor honor, nor chastity can stand. (Quoted in Kraditor, 1968, 50.)

The morality of separate spheres for the sexes, with women's spheres subordinate to men's, has remained an important religious theme. Many examples of politicians calling on God to reinforce their policies for limiting women ornament U.S. history. In 1887, Senator George Vest of Missouri argued against women's suffrage on the floor of the Senate by saying, "I do not believe that the Great Intelligence ever intended [women] to invade the sphere of work given to men, tearing down and destroying all the best influences for which God has intended them" (quoted in Kraditor, 1968, 195). Making a similar point at the turn of the century, President Grover Cleveland stated, "I believe that trust in Divine

Wisdom, and ungrudging submission to divine purposes, will enable dutiful men and women to know the places assigned to them, and will incite them to act well in their parts in the sight of God" (quoted in Kraditor, 1968, 200). As quoted previously, in the 1970s, Senator Sam Ervin called God into battle against the Equal Rights Amendment. During the national discussion of "family values" surrounding the 1992 election and throughout the 1990s, many representatives of the religious political right emphasized that recent changes in women's roles have threatened the destruction of the country's moral fiber.

The predominant message of most religious denominations has been that women and men are both to be carefully restricted to their distinct spheres, and that women's roles on Earth are to be good wives and mothers and to preserve traditional moral values, especially the modesty and domesticity of women. The punishments of religious women who transgressed the boundaries of these spheres have been enormous, including death (during colonial times, for witchcraft and homosexuality), damnation to hell, separation (banishment or excommunication) from the religious community, and charges of responsibility for the downfall of a religion or of civilization as a whole.

Because of these views, religious organizations and clergy have often played active roles in resisting feminism. In the 19th century, for example, many church leaders criticized women for publicly speaking on behalf of reform movements. Citing the biblical injunction, "suffer women not to speak," some wrote, "We cannot . . . but regret the mistaken conduct of those who encourage females to bear an obtrusive and ostentatious part in measures of reform, and countenance any of that sex who so forget themselves as to itinerate in the character of public lecturers and teachers" (quoted in Rossi, 1988, 305–306).

If public speaking was unfeminine, for many church leaders, the idea of women's suffrage was even worse. In 1869, an American Transcendentalist leader said, "The conclusive objection to the political enfranchisement is, that it would weaken and finally break up and destroy the Christian family" (quoted in Kraditor, 1968, 192). "Let the hand which rocks the cradle teach the coming young men and women of America the Lord's Prayer and the Ten Commandments," said a New York politician in 1894, "and you will do more for your emancipation . . . than you can do with both hands full of white ballots" (p. 198).

Religious organizations have been leading opponents of divorce reform, liberalization of birth-control and abortion policies, educational policies that would reform gender messages in textbooks and make sex education part of the curriculum, legislation supporting civil rights for homosexuals, and the Equal Rights Amendment. In the first decades of the 20th century, some religious organizations opposed the reforms urged by feminist and progressive groups on the grounds that they were socialist and therefore antireligious. Contemporary studies of antifeminist activist groups show that participants in those groups tend to be especially attached to religion (Burris, 1983; Conover and Gray, 1983; Mueller and Dimieri, 1982). An Arkansas Baptist church closed its child-care center, saying that working mothers neglect their children, damage their marriages, and set a bad example; "God intended for the home to be the center of a mother's world," the church's announcement letter noted.[4] The shift to more traditional views in the

Sonia Johnson, feminist activist and political candidate, was excommunicated by the Mormon Church for her support of the Equal Rights Amendment.

late 1990s is evident in a 1997 ruling by an Orthodox Jewish rabbinical board in New York that women's prayer groups violate Jewish tradition.[5]

Numerous politically and socially active women have been individually punished or reprimanded by their churches—for instance, Anne Hutchinson was banished for heresy (see Chapter 5), and Lucy Stone (1818–1893) was expelled from the Congregational Church for her abolitionist activity. In the 1980s, the Church of Jesus Christ of Latter-day Saints (Mormons) excommunicated Sonia Johnson for her support of the Equal Rights Amendment. More recently, in 1993, the Mormons excommunicated or took other severe action against a group of scholars and feminists, partly for their call to open the priesthood to women. Although 12-year-old boys can be deacons, and at 16, they can baptize others, and by their early 20s, they typically become bishops, women are allowed none of these religious roles. One woman who was disciplined was head of the Mormon Women's Forum, which claimed 2,000 members. A church leader said that feminists posed a serious threat to faith, along with homosexuals and "so-called intellectuals and scholars."[6]

Other religious groups have imposed similar sanctions. In 1983, the Catholic Church gave Agnes Mary Mansour the choice of resigning her post as director of social services in Michigan or dismissal from her order of nuns for tolerating the

TABLE 7-2

Attitudes Toward Gender Equality,
by Religious Fundamentalism and Personal Importance of Religion, 1991

	Religion Has Moderate/ Little Importance		Religion Has Great Importance	
	Not Fundamentalist	Fundamentalist	Not Fundamentalist	Fundamentalist
Men should have more power and influence than women in government and politics.	8	20	21	41
Men should have more power and influence than women in business and industry.	11	22	25	34
Men should have more power and influence than women in the family.	3	16	11	28

Note: People who said that religion provides "a great deal of guidance" in their day-to-day lives are in the "Religion has great importance" category. Those who agree that "The Bible is God's word and all it says is true" are categorized as fundamentalists. The numbers show the proportion of people in each religion category who agreed with the statement to the left. Based on $N =$ 467. All differences between fundamentalists and nonfundamentalists (holding guidance constant) and between those finding moderate/low and high guidance from religion (holding level of fundamentalism constant) are statistically significant, $p < .05$.

Source: 1991 American National Election Study Pilot Study, analysis by author.

use of federal funds for abortions. She left the order (Briggs, 1983). In many cases, these women were rebuked precisely because they claimed to derive their deviant views from their religious values; in these cases, they were punished for coming to their own conclusions about spirituality and religiosity.

Research continues to show that religious beliefs help shape people's views of gender and women's roles. Consider the evidence in Table 7-2, which looks at the relationships among fundamentalist beliefs, religiosity, and attitudes toward gender equality in government, the economy, and the family. It shows that *fundamentalists,* those who see the Bible as the literal word of God, are more likely than other people to think that men should have more power than women in government, the economy, and the family. It also shows that people who claim that they find a great deal of guidance from religion in their day-to-day lives are also more likely to believe in male dominance. The combined effects of these different aspects of religious belief offer substantial support for male dominance among religious fundamentalists.

On the other hand, religious organizations have also helped foster women's activism and even, at times, feminism. Many of the 19th-century suffragists were very involved in their religious communities. In recent decades, women have been actively involved in religion-based feminism. Nonetheless, the power of women to define their own terms, goals, and activities in conventional religious institutions has usually been limited; if their message provided too clear an alternative to traditional religious teachings, they found themselves opposed by the higher, male authorities.

Morality, Sexuality, and Gender

Religious authority regulates sexual morality in ways that have profound effects on women and men and that help further define gender and gender difference. Most denominations regard marriage as the cornerstone of the sexual, moral, and, therefore, social order. Marital law is based very heavily on traditional religious views and law (see Chapter 11). Although their specific views of sexuality and sexual practices vary, most religions agree that sexual relations may appropriately and rightfully take place only within marriage between a man and a woman. Many—probably most—believe that the primary, if not sole, purpose of sexual relations is reproduction. Two of the Ten Commandments serve as authority here: One forbids adultery, and one forbids a man to covet his neighbor's wife, house, slaves, or other possessions. Notice that the latter not only defines proper sexual relations but also reinforces the idea that women are men's (sexual) property. For some denominations, such as the Roman Catholic Church, reproduction is the sole moral reason for sexual activity.

This moral link between sexuality and reproduction has had two important implications. The first is that if only sexual acts that could result in conception are natural and good, sexual acts that could not result in offspring are unnatural and bad. Christians and Jews alike have used religious authority to forbid homosexuality (Lev. 18:22, 1 Cor. 6:9–11), although church authorities have been more vigilant in their suppression of homosexuality during some historical periods (e.g., the 12th, 13th, and 19th centuries) than in others (Weeks, 1977). American laws against sodomy were based directly on religious teaching and sometimes used the language of the Bible. Although sodomy laws are usually discussed in reference to homosexual activities, they applied (and were originally enforced) against heterosexual acts that could not result in conception, as well. These laws were serious in their consequences; early in American history, some homosexual acts were punishable by death. The Bible has also been used to declare masturbation (Gen. 38: 3–10) and transvestism (Deut. 22:5) sinful and wrong.

Among the mainstream Christian denominations, only the United Church of Christ fully accepts homosexual ministers. Events within the Presbyterian Church exemplify the kinds of debates and conflicts that have taken place in many denominations in recent years. In 1991, a task force report argued that the Presbyterian Church should not condemn sexual acts outside marriage—regardless of whether they involved two people of the same sex—if the acts were mutual and caring. Later the same year, the Human Sexuality Committee successfully recommended that the Presbyterian General Assembly reject the task force report.[7] In 1992, the highest court of the Presbyterian Church nullified the hiring of a lesbian pastor by one church, although it said that if she were celibate, she could be hired. At the same time, it said that an "unrepentant homosexual" could not be ordained.[8] That same year, the generally liberal National Council of Churches decided in a divided vote not to give "observer status" to the mostly gay and lesbian Universal Fellowship of Metropolitan Churches, a denomination with about 50,000 members. The most active opposition came from the Eastern Orthodox churches, some of the African-American denominations, and the Korean Presbyterian Church.[9]

The second implication of basing sexual morality on reproductive function is that the practice of birth control is considered wrong. Roman Catholic authorities remain adamant that any form of "artificial" birth control is sinful. Most Protestant denominations and Jews, however, officially leave the decision about whether to conceive to individual choice, although many religious authorities informally discourage the use of contraception. Unitarian churches, on the other hand, have often taken very strong stands in favor of birth control.

Abortion is an even more difficult issue than birth control because it involves terminating life that has already begun. Historically, theologians and the common law generally viewed abortion as murder only after *quickening* of the fetus took place (i.e., when the mother felt the fetus move), and abortion was generally tolerated within the first 40 days after conception. In 1869, Pope Pius IX changed the position of the Catholic Church, declaring almost all abortions murder and therefore sinful. According to Catholic doctrine, it is not acceptable to terminate a life purposely, even to save another life. The Church has remained firm on its stands on both birth control and abortion, although there is widespread controversy within the Church, and some Catholics have felt particularly alienated from their religion because of its stands on these matters. Catholics can even be found in the highest ranks of the National Abortion Rights League, an interest group dedicated to reproductive choice for women.

Religions further regulate sexuality and social relations by dictating who may and may not get married. The Bible enumerates forbidden marriages, such as those considered incestuous. Many religious authorities do not allow interfaith marriage within their communities unless the outsider agrees to convert or unless the outsider agrees to raise the children in the insider's religion. God's law has been used to bar sexual relations and marriage between people of different races (miscegenation), as this quotation from a Virginia court case in the 1960s shows: "Almighty God created the races white, black, yellow, malay, and red, and he placed them on separate continents. And but for the interference with his arrangement there would be no cause for such marriages. The fact that he separated the races shows that he did not intend for the races to mix."[10]

Most denominations have long supported the idea of personal choice with respect to divorce, at least to some degree, although the Eastern Orthodox, Episcopal, Mormon, and Roman Catholic Churches have generally held that marriages are indissoluble. Many denominations do not permit divorce except on strict grounds of adultery or desertion; many religious authorities will not remarry a divorced person unless that person was the presumed innocent party in the divorce or the ex-spouse is dead. Some denominations (e.g., Congregationalists, Christian Scientists, Jews, and Unitarians) leave the question of divorce to the conscience of the individuals involved; others (e.g., Baptists and Disciples of Christ) leave it to the conscience of the minister.

The impact of sexually repressive religious teachings on people's behavior should not be overestimated. Historians have found ample evidence of "prematurely conceived" (as opposed to prematurely born) babies throughout American history. Indeed, even among the sterner of American clerics, attitudes toward sexuality were not necessarily as repressive as they are sometimes painted. Some Puritan ministers carefully pointed out that they differed from Roman Catholics by not extolling the virtues of virginity to the same degree, even while they condemned sex outside of marriage. Historian Edmund Morgan ([1944] 1978, 364) found that "the Puritans were not ascetics; they never wished to prevent the enjoyment of earthly delights. They merely demanded that the pleasures of the flesh be subordinated to the greater glory of God: husband and wife must not become 'so transported with affection, that they look at no higher end than marriage itself.'" Morgan even found evidence that a church expelled one of its male members for denying "congiugall fellowship unto his wife for the space of 2 years."

Nevertheless, the conflict between being holy and experiencing sexual feelings is an important theme throughout the history of sexuality and religion. Witness, for example, the sentiments expressed in a love letter the feminist Quaker Angelina Grimké wrote to her husband-to-be in 1838:

Ought God to be all in all to us on earth? I tho't so, and am frightened to find that He is not, that is, I feel something else is necessary to my happiness. I laid awake thinking why it was that my heart longed and panted and reached after you as it does. Why my Savior and my God is not enough to satisfy me. Am I sinning, am I ungrateful, am I an IDOLATOR? (Rossi, 1988, 289)

The Roman Catholic Church further emphasizes a conflict between sexuality and holiness by maintaining that those who dedicate their lives to God by becoming priests or nuns must remain celibate. This rule of celibacy has somewhat different connotations for women and men. Nuns wear wedding rings to symbolize their marriage to Christ. Priests, of course, are not married to Christ; such a relationship, even if spiritual, would imply the sin of homosexuality. It is interesting to note the importance of sexuality and marriage in images of women. While nuns are married to Christ, women who were persecuted for witchcraft were said to be married to or to have sexual relations with the devil. Thus, even in images of profound goodness or profound evil, women are defined by their relations to male authority.[11]

Contemporary sociological studies show that people's religious orientations do shape their sexual views and behavior. In their study of American couples (which included married and unmarried homosexual and heterosexual couples), Philip Blumstein and Pepper Schwartz (1983) found that regular church attenders were more conservative about sexual matters than those who were not as overtly religious. Religious heterosexuals are more opposed to civil rights for homosexuals, for example, than are less religious heterosexuals. Most research (e.g., Hare-Mustin, Bennett, and Broderick, 1983) found that Catholics have a more conservative reproductive ideology than do other people. James Robbins's (1980) study of Black women who had had abortions found that the more involved these women were with religion, the less happy they were with their own decisions to have abortions.

Blumstein and Schwartz found that, although there may be differences in attitudes,

> there is very little difference between religious and nonreligious people when it comes to how they act. They have the same amount of sex. They are just as satisfied. They have no more and no less conflict about sex. And they are just as traditional about the woman's right to initiate it. But perhaps the most startling finding is that religious people are as nonmonogamous as anyone else. However attached people may be to religious institutions, they do not seem to be insulated from the temptations of the flesh. (1983, 285)

It is not entirely clear whether religious messages about morality have more impact in shaping people's attitudes and behavior, or simply their feelings of guilt about doing the same things other people do.

Feminist Alternatives and the Women's Spirituality Movement

A few examples show the types of alternatives many feminists have posed to the more orthodox views of their religious organizations. Two of the best-known feminist religious thinkers of the 19th century were the Quaker sisters Sarah (1792–1873) and Angelina (1805–1876) Grimké. In Angelina Grimké's most famous work, her 1836 "Appeal to the Christian Women of the South,"[12] she urged women to be instrumental in ending slavery, even if their actions brought them suffering, because they had to follow what they knew to be God's will, rather than sinful and oppressive laws created by men. Drawing on the New Testament statement that "there is neither male nor female," the Grimké sisters believed that enforcing separate spheres for women and men and withholding religious and political rights for women were un-Christian acts. Their work, like the work of many other feminist religious activists, shows that the same texts and basic ideas can be interpreted in a variety of ways, with very different effects.

Certainly many feminist critics of religion have offered attacks on what they have regarded as misogynist or androcentric theology and practices. Among these are Matilda Joslyn Gage, Elizabeth Cady Stanton, and a committee of other feminists who wrote *The Woman's Bible* (Stanton, [1895] 1974), an exegesis and criticism of the Bible, which they regarded as a man-made, error-filled document. A more contemporary example is Mary Daly, whose series of critiques and "revisions," have argued that our understanding of God and religion must be "exorcised" to root out the androcentrism of religion, much as the evil influence of Satan was exorcised by traditional Catholic ritual (Daly, 1973).

Today, many writers also stand in the tradition of the Grimkés in working not just to criticize their religions, but also to reconstruct them in a more feminist direction. Among the most well known of these are Rosemary Ruether, Carol Christ, Judith Plaskow, and Elizabeth Schüssler Fiorenza.[13] These and other thinkers and activists focus on both the substance and the practices of their religions to consider possibilities for change. Their work revolves around two different strategies: (1) to remove gender-specific content or rituals, and (2) to incorporate more woman-centered language and rituals. Following are examples of each.

A common strategy to "degenderize" religion is to focus on removing gender differences from liturgy and ritual. Formerly gender-segregated rituals are integrated. For example, the important Jewish initiation rite of *Bar Mitzvah* (son of the Commandments) historically was a male ritual, but for several decades, Reform Jews have celebrated the same ritual for girls, the *Bat Mitzvah* (Daughter of the Commandments). Traditional Jewish law does not count women among the 10 adults whose presence is required to say certain prayers; in more progressive Jewish communities, women are counted. Traditionally, only Jewish men wore prayer shawls and *yarmulkes* (skullcaps); in more progressive communities, many women do so, as well. Also, women are no longer barred from the rabbinate except among the Orthodox.

One of the most well known efforts to remove sexist differences within Christianity, other than allowing women into the clergy, occurred in 1983, when the National Council of Churches began publishing new translations of biblical passages under the title of *Inclusive Language Lectionary*, amidst considerable controversy. The lectionary refers to God as "the Father and Mother" or "Sovereign," rather than as "Father" or "Lord," and it refers to Jesus as the "Child" rather than as the "Son" of God, to reduce the emphasis on male religious imagery. Some churches gave the lectionary a warm reception, and others have attacked it as "tampering with the word of God."

While many efforts have focused on removing gender difference from religion as a means toward eliminating the subordination of women, other efforts have revised religious texts and traditions to incorporate more woman-centered aspects emphasizing a specifically female religious and spiritual experience. Here, the intention is largely to empower women, often by rediscovering women-created ideas and rituals and female figures that have been forgotten. Many feminist religious activists also work to create new practices and liturgy focused on women's specific experiences, history, and relationship to religion, morality, and spirituality.

Many such feminists, notably those in the women's spirituality movement, emphasize the symbol of the Goddess, a female conceptualization of the deity. Through Goddess symbolism, these feminists try to emphasize a changed conception of God, which affirms those parts of the universe more traditionally associated with feminine rather than masculine character. Thus, rather than thinking of God primarily as the "King," "Ruler," and "Judge," providing the constancy of the rule of law, the women's spirituality movement emphasizes the life-giving and -sustaining power, and the constant fluidity and change found in the life course throughout nature and the change of seasons.[14]

Another branch of feminist spiritualism has turned to witchcraft to find a tradition. This witchcraft has nothing to do with the Oz's Wicked Witch of the West or even Glenda the Good Witch, but rather the tradition of witchcraft (which comes from the word *wicce,* meaning "wise ones") that has been the general name for female priestesses, healers, and sages throughout the ages, many of whom have been punished only because they knew how to use medicinal herbs to help people. If women have rejected the long tradition of the *wicce,* they argue, it is not because the tradition is itself bad, but because men have feared and therefore punished it, generally by execution. Sometimes, in our eagerness to reject the violence of these men's actions, we have forgotten that many women have practiced witchcraft, although that practice bears little resemblance to the descriptions in the more orthodox religious texts.

These movements for change involve religious authorities, clergy, and members of traditional religious organizations, as well as people outside these organizations who are attempting to create their own spirituality. Although all these people have different points of view, they are linked by these convictions: (1) Religious organizations are among the most forceful institutions that shape and define sex/gender systems; (2) women have had very little control over these powers; and (3) religion should free the human spirit, rather than keep it in bondage. Although these movements for change have had wide impact, organized religion has also resisted change very strongly.[15]

Women's Religious Activities and Influences

Thus far, we have looked at some of the ways that religious teachings help to define gender, sexuality, and women's roles. We now look more directly at women's religious activity. What roles have women played in American religious life and religious organizations? How have their activities in religious organizations helped them shape their own and other people's lives? To what degree have women's activities influenced religious and spiritual life in the United States?

Everyday Life as Religious Activity

In "The Cult of True Womanhood," historian Barbara Welter has identified the central historical role that White women were expected to play in American religious life:

> The 19th-century American man was a busy builder of bridges and railroads, at work long hours in a materialist society. The religious values of his forebears were neglected in practice if not in intent, and he occasionally felt some guilt that he had turned this new land, this temple of the chosen people, into one vast countinghouse. But he could salve his conscience by reflecting that he had left behind a hostage, not only to fortune, but to all the values which he held so dear and treated so lightly. (1966, 21)

That hostage was woman. Although a good woman was supposed to be submissive to her husband, and her Lord, she was also supposed to create a religious home. She was responsible for guarding the spiritual life of her family, which sometimes meant acting outside the home and becoming, in effect, the backbone of church organizations and the occasional upsurges in religious activity.

Historians point out that women were central in the second "Great Awakening" of the 1820s in the East, the remarkable growth in evangelical Protestantism, with its famous revival meetings, which attracted large numbers of women and drew women into a view of everyday life as a moral mission. In her study of women's roles in the frontier West, Julie Roy Jeffrey found that many of the newly gathered congregations of the mid–19th century were composed primarily of women. "Women not only swelled membership rolls but were quickly recognized as recruiters and forcibly reminded of their responsibilities [by ministers]" (1979, 96). Jeffrey also found evidence that women often gave solace and encouragement to the struggling missionary ministers who were depressed and frustrated by their apparent failures to bring God's word to the frontier. What role might religion play in American life today were it not for the women who populated churches and supported their ministers a century ago?

When we look at women's roles historically, it is nearly impossible to separate women's specifically *religious* activities and duties from their other activities. Women's family roles have often been understood as expressions of their religious values and the primary means for enforcing women's piety. Consider, for example, the argument made by Catharine Beecher in her 1841 manual for the homemaker, *A Treatise on Domestic Economy* ([1841] 1977). She set her advice on topics as diverse as nutrition, clothing, charity, exercise, and flower cultivation within a deeper philosophical and religious context. She began by arguing that "the democratic institutions of this country are in reality no other than the principles of Christianity carried into operation" (p. 10). She then argued that "the success of democratic institutions (and therefore, by logical extension, Christian institutions) . . . depends upon the intellectual and moral character of the mass of the people" (p. 13). According to Beecher, the responsibility for securing this character depends on the woman. "The mother writes the character of the future man; the sister beds the fibers that after are the forest tree; the wife sways the heart, whose energies may turn for good or for evil the destinies of a nation" (p. 13). Because every detail of a household must be arranged according to important basic principles. "These general principles are to be based on Christianity" (p. 145). Thus, the activities of household management became expressions of religious duty and participation.

Similar beliefs are held in other religions. A central tenet of Jewish life is that the wife and mother is responsible for creating a Jewish home; she is thereby responsible for maintaining Jewish life and Judaism itself. Every meal that is eaten in the home of an Orthodox Jewish family is a reminder of religion and woman's role in it; the woman must carefully follow the laws of *kashruth* (kosher dietary laws) in buying, preparing, and serving food, thereby enforcing Jewish law and custom within her family. The conflation of women's religious activity and domestic obligation is especially apparent in Judaism because many important rituals and celebrations take place in the home, rather than in the synagogue. The Sabbath meal is itself a religious service and includes traditional foods and the lighting of the Sabbath candles by the woman. Passover, one of the most important Jewish festivals, is celebrated entirely in the home. Much of the woman's work during Passover week is regulated by the fact that it is Passover; her very domestic labor is a ritual act.

For women who are the wives of clergy and missionaries, wifehood is itself a religious occupation. The ministry is one of the many male-dominated jobs in which the wife has special tasks that are unpaid extensions of the husband's job; in fact, the husband's job creates nearly a full-time job for his untrained, unsalaried wife. The job of a minister's wife varies from denomination to denomination and from congregation to congregation. Generally, however, she is expected to attend most religious functions (or at least those that allow women), regardless of her own interests. She is expected to serve on committees, especially those that revolve around "women's concerns," such as education and entertainment. When the minister entertains congregants, visiting ministers, and others in his line of duty, she does the work. Above all, the minister's wife is the highly visible representative of her husband and his religious values. Ministers' wives, like the wives of other highly visible authorities, are subject to constant criticism and gossip if their homes, children, clothes, and smiles are not perfect or appropriate for the values of the congregation. The importance of this job is evidenced by the controversy surrounding ministers' wives who choose to pursue independent careers and therefore do not have the time or the inclination to serve their husbands' congregations full-time.

It is easy to underestimate the religious work and influence of ministers' wives, both historically and today. In the 19th century, missionaries sent to the frontier West to *civilize* (i.e., to Christianize) the new communities were urged to bring wives for the help and support they would need. Julie Jeffrey (1979) found that most of the wives thought of themselves as missionaries (as well they might have, given the work they did), even if their husbands and churches regarded them only as helpmates. As Jeffrey pointed out, however, "Few anticipated the potential conflict between [the roles of wife and missionary]. Nor did their religious enthusiasm and lofty idealism prepare them for the reality of missionary work" (1979, 100).

These women performed the hard duties of frontier women, plus many of the difficult duties of missionary work. They recruited women, taught, organized social events, and were responsible for fund-raising—often through their own labor, rather than through collections—so that their husbands could tend to more spiritual needs. They were shuffled from one place to another as their husbands were called to new missions. The toll on these women and their families was often great. It is unfortunate that these hard-working women are often either forgotten altogether or remembered only as the wives of the men who tamed the West.

Making a home is regarded as a religious activity of central importance; for many people, this is proof enough that women are highly regarded by their religions and are free to pursue a full life within their religious communities and to be influential in them. For many other women—including, of course, those who are not wives and mothers, as well as those who simply see wider horizons—this role is not enough.

Women's Service Outside the Home

Women have always constituted a substantial portion of the people who have practiced their religious values through public or community service, volunteer work, charity, or philanthropy. For many women bound even by the most traditional domestic values, these service activities and the religious organizations that undertake them have often provided the primary or even sole channel for extrafamilial public action and personal development. Religious organizations have provided ways for women to have an impact on their communities and society, which they could not achieve in the male-dominated worlds of politics and the professions.

The 19th century witnessed the development of a religiously based gender ideology that regarded charity and service work a necessary part of a homemaker's life, especially but not exclusively among middle-class women (Ginzberg, 1990; Scott, 1984; Shaw, 1991). As Catharine Beecher observed, "It is also one of the plainest requirements of Christianity, that we devote some of our time and efforts to the comfort and improvement of others" ([1841] 1977, 145–146). Such activities were especially appropriate because the focus of women's lives within their families was the comfort and improvement of others. Beecher included service work in her advice to women on how to schedule their time wisely: "The leisure of two afternoons and evenings could be devoted to religious and benevolent objects, such as religious meetings, charitable associations, Sunday school visiting, and attention to the sick and poor" (p. 147).

The impact of women who express the social implications of their religious concerns through organized activities is immeasurable. The number of people who have been fed, clothed, housed, educated, and otherwise comforted by religious organizations of women is uncountable. Through these organizations, women have pressed social and political concerns at all ends of the political spectrum and all levels of politics. Indeed, this work became part of the basis on which public-welfare policies were constructed. Throughout the 20th century, representatives of women's religious organizations have testified frequently before local and state legislatures, as well as before congressional committees. The social issues and concerns of churches are often manifest largely in the work of women.

Women's religiously based service work is important to understand not only because it has had a great impact on American women and on U.S. society more broadly, but also because it offers a good example of the complexities of developing a feminist analysis of the gender basis of social institutions. As Lori Ginzberg wrote in her study of 19th-century women's benevolent work, "Ideologies about gender serve broader purposes than either describing or enforcing supposed differences between women and men. It is necessary . . . to understand the uses to which those ideologies are put" (Ginzberg, 1990, 216). Women's influence and power in service work stems from a gender ideology of difference. Women were supposed to have moral influence because of their natural moral difference from and superiority over men.

> Women or, more accurately, the belief in women's moral superiority perfectly fit the requirement that charitable endeavors appear unmotivated by self- or class interest. As members of a group that seemed to be defined exclusively by gender, women could have no interest other than to fulfill their benevolent destiny; they could be applauded and recognized without calling into question the purity of their motives. (Ginzberg, 1990, 216)

Charity *did* serve class interests for the middle-class and business-owning-class women who were so very active in late-19th-century charity work. As Ginzberg has pointed out, charity played an important role in economic development by mediating "the most blatant harshness and dislocation of 19th-century capitalism and urbanization" and helping to foster a moral culture that was supportive of that form of industrial capitalism. Thus, the structure of gender relations had an impact on the structure of class relations.

Another important complexity in understanding the significance of the gender ideology of difference underpinning the ideal of female benevolence is its dual effect on the charitable women themselves. On the one hand, it provided an outlet for public and communal activity and, indeed, a base for them to exert a considerable degree of influence over their communities and even over government. Ann Douglas (1977) has claimed that women thus were powerful agents in the creation of 19th-century American culture, especially in helping it to forsake the harsh Calvinist character of the earlier century in favor of Victorian sentimentalism. Sara Evans has argued that women's activities helped forge a new meaning of public and domestic life, in which the moral mission of homemakers reached outward to public works; public life, these women asserted, should function to care for people and sustain them morally (Evans, 1989). Moreover, this notion of the unique spiritual character of women gave them grounds for collective identity, viewing themselves as sisters, and created the potential for collective action, including the creation of a feminist movement. On the other hand, this gender ideology reinforced the idea of separate spheres, in which women and men had different and, in fact, unequal places. It was an ideology with both a radical and a deeply conservative potential.

Religious organizations continue to provide a means through which women make contributions to others in their communities. Besides the continuing charitable efforts of churches, synagogues, and other religious organizations, many women have participated in efforts to create new forms of spirituality that emphasize a religious basis for accepting public and even political responsibility for justice and social welfare. These women reject what Judith Plaskow has called the "institutionalized separation of spirituality and politics."

> The assigned guardian of spirituality has been religion, which is itself relegated to the margins of society and expected to limit its interests to Saturday or Sunday mornings. As spirituality minds its otherworldly business, transformation of social structures is left to the often dirty work of politics, which catches us up in a realm of compromise, power seeking, struggle over what have been defined as limited resources, and confrontation with the distortions and disease in our social system. (Plaskow, 1990, 212–213)

Plaskow and others want to go beyond the traditional bounds of female benevolence and charity to argue for a spiritualism that is itself committed to transformational politics. She has underscored the idea of *tikkun olam*—the responsibility to participate in the restoration of the world to its wholeness—just as others, such as Pamela Couture (1991), emphasize the idea of "shared responsibility" grounded in Christianity. Likewise, many women became involved in new formulations of the political responsibilities of spirituality in the early 1980s in the "sanctuary movement," a religion-based movement to give sanctuary to the victims of government violence in El Salvador. At the time, El Salvador was ruled by a

U.S.-backed regime that tortured and killed its opponents, including religious workers (Lorentzen, 1991).

These notions of responsibility erase the difference between religion and politics. In these cases, religious activists are attempting to link spirituality, feminism, and a progressive political commitment to communal responsibility in the material, as well as the spiritual, world. These more liberal and progressive thinkers are not alone in their arguments for linking spirituality and political action. Those on the right have also done so, for example in antiabortion and "rescue" movements, which they also define as being based in social justice and social commitments (Ginsburg, 1989).

Women as Religious Authorities and Leaders

We have already seen that with some exceptions, most Judeo-Christian religions explicitly reserve leadership and positions of authority for men. Nevertheless, women have assumed a variety of leadership roles, and they are pressing for more.[16] Women have been the founders of a number of American Christian denominations. Among the most important and well known are Ellen White, who founded the Seventh Day Adventist Church and led it for 50 years; Aimee Semple McPherson, a charismatic evangelist who founded the Church of the Foursquare Gospel; and Mary Baker Eddy (1821–1910), who founded the Church of Christ, Scientist, best known for the beliefs that the spirit and the mind are the central facts of life and that illness, disease, and death are mere illusions that can be overcome by spirituality.

Another church founder was Ann Lee (1736–1784), an immigrant from England who, as a young woman, belonged to a religious group known as the "Shaking Quakers" because of members' behavior while praying. While imprisoned in England for heresy and accusations of witchcraft, she experienced what she considered divine revelations. Once freed, she led a small group of followers, who believed her to be a messenger of Christ, to New York, where she established the first Shaker community. The Shakers believed that only through celibacy could a person achieve the highest spirituality; the growth of the community thus depended on new converts. The Shaker community was based on sharing and hard work, and it is noted for its well-crafted furniture. By the middle of the 20th century, only a handful of old women were left in the community. These women decided to let the Shaker community die a natural death and sought no more converts.

Much attention has been focused on the issue of the ordination of women. Antoinette Brown Blackwell (1825–1921) was the first American woman to be ordained as a minister and to have her own congregation. At least three Protestant denominations have ordained women for a century or more, including the United Church of Christ, the American Baptist Churches, and the Disciples of Christ. Change has come much more recently in most denominations, however. Sally Priesand became the first woman ordained as a (Reform) rabbi, in 1972. In 1989, Barbara Harris became the first female Episcopal bishop, an event that caused great consternation in some sectors of the worldwide Anglican Church. Orthodox Jews still do not ordain women, women still may not become Roman Catholic

Mary Baker Eddy, who founded and for many years directed Christian Science.

priests, and some conservative Protestant denominations remain opposed to female ordination. Although women are still a small fraction of all ministers, the numbers are likely to change as more women train for the ministry. In 1989, the National Council of Churches found that of 172 denominations for which information was available, 84 ordained women, 82 did not, and 6 did not have ordained clergy. It also reported that women constituted about 8% of the clergy in denominations that ordained women.[17]

A survey of male and female Protestant clerics showed that their experiences and motivations differed to some degree (Carroll, Hargrove, and Lummis, 1981). Women were more likely to have upper-middle-class backgrounds, highly educated parents, and mothers who were employed. Men were more likely to have attended denominational colleges, partly reflecting the fact that women made their decisions to enter the ministry later than did men. Men were also more likely to feel that their families and pastors supported their decisions to enter the ministry in the first place. Women entering the ministry tended to have better academic records than did men. More women than men said their motivation in seeking clerical training was personal spiritual growth or service to Christ; more men than women said they pursued religious studies to become parish ministers.

The researchers also uncovered other differences. Men were more likely than women to feel that the ordained ministry carried with it particularly high "prestige

Episcopal bishop Barbara Harris became the first female
bishop in the worldwide Anglican Church in 1989.

and dignity." More women than men felt it was very important to "change the
sexist nature of the church." Most of the female ministers revealed strongly feminist attitudes toward women in the church, compared with only 24% of the men.
Clerical attitudes toward women's roles in the church vary from denomination to
denomination. While 39% of the United Church of Christ ministers expressed
strongly feminist attitudes, only 15% of the Episcopal clergy did so.

Women in the ministry face some segregation and discrimination, just as
women do in other jobs. Men find it easier to become ordained after attending the
seminary, although this varies by denomination. Ordained women tend to be
placed in smaller churches with older members, and their salaries are lower than
men's. As might be expected, the congregants in women's churches tend to be less
conservative than those in men's, although surveys show that in most denominations, lay leaders tend to be more conservative on gender issues than are the clergy
themselves.

As with other jobs, the fact that some women are now working in this male-
dominated profession does not mean that their day-to-day experiences are the
same as men's. Women and men feel themselves to be especially competent at different aspects of the job (see Box 7-1). Carroll, Hargrove, and Lummis (1981)
found that women felt more confident about their abilities to preach, lead worship, and teach children, and men felt more confident about their abilities to manage the church budget. Women and men both felt they got on well with different

BOX 7-1   See for Yourself: Women as Religious Leaders

What roles of religious leadership do women play in your community? Survey the formal religious institutions—churches, synagogues, mosques, or meetinghouses. In which of them do women serve as leaders? In what capacity? How would you explain the patterns of where women serve as religious leaders and where they do not?

age and gender groups within their congregations. Most of the female ministers thought their gender played a role in conflicts or difficulties they encountered in their jobs; 27% thought that their gender was a very important factor.

Studies suggest that women change the ministry and its imagery merely by pursuing their vocations. They have somewhat different attitudes than their male colleagues; for instance, women could not believe that church authority is necessarily masculine and remain in the career they have chosen. Women in the ministry have become increasingly aware of the problems of women, partly through their own experiences. Carroll, Hargrove, and Lummis (1981) found that clergywomen are somewhat more likely than clergymen to think that their congregations should get involved in social and political issues, including the rights of women and minorities.

There is also growing evidence that women have a different effect on their congregants than men have. Rabbi Laura Geller (1983, 210), for example, reported on the following reactions of two of her congregants:

> Rabbi, I can't tell you how different I felt about services because you are a woman. I found myself feeling that if you can be a rabbi, then maybe I could be a rabbi too. For the first time in my life I felt as though I could learn those prayers, I could study Torah, I could lead this service, I could do anything you could do. Knowing that made me feel much more involved in the service —much more involved with Judaism. Also, it made me think about God in a different way. I'm not sure why. (a middle-aged woman)

> Rabbi, I realized that if you could be a rabbi, then certainly I could be a rabbi. Knowing that made the service somehow more accessible to me. I didn't need you to "do it" for me. I could "do it," be involved with Jewish tradition, without depending on you. (a young man)

It seems to be an almost universal religious theme that negative aspects of the world can be lessons for the good. Geller's experience might be an object lesson of exactly this sort.

The relatively low status of the female rabbi, at least in these cases, brought people closer to their own spirituality. These two people were reacting in part to women's lower status, to the jarring image of a female leader in a masculine world, to their stereotypes of women. However, as Geller (1983, 210) noted, "The lessening of social distance and the reduction of the attribution of power and status leads to the breakdown of hierarchy within a religious institution." In this case, the breakdown of gender hierarchies did indeed seem to lead to a breakdown of religious institutional hierarchy because the two are interdependent; they mutually reinforce each other. This is, of course, precisely what conservative leaders fear will be the result of the entrance of women into traditionally male leadership roles. However, as these quotations also suggest, many people find a new spirituality and a renewed sense of religious affiliation and purpose when the hierarchy of religious institutions is weakened. Geller (1983) noted that a female friend of hers, who was an Episcopal minister, had a similar experience. "When she offers the Eucharist people take it from her differently from the way they would take it from a male priest, even though she follows the identical ritual. People experience her as less foreign, and so the experience is more natural, less mysterious" (p. 211).

Women take many other leadership roles in religious organizations. Many denominations have long allowed women to be deaconesses, and the Roman Catholic, Eastern Orthodox, and Episcopal churches have orders of nuns. In some cases, these women have been instrumental in changing the status of women. Many Roman Catholic sisters have worked for changes within the Church. Most people are aware that many orders of nuns no longer wear habits. In addition, however, the size and character of the community of Roman Catholic sisters have been changing over the years. First, it is considerably smaller than it once was: In 1968, there were more than 176,000 nuns in the United States, but by 1992, the figure was a little over 99,000. Far fewer women enter as novitiates each year. In addition, the women who enter are different. Today, a substantial portion of women who become nuns are much older than used to be the case; often, they are women who have raised families and have had careers, sometimes well-paid professional careers. Indeed, many religious orders now discourage younger women from joining, in favor of older women with skills and experiences that can benefit the group and its work.[18] At the same time, this trend is likely to exacerbate the discontent of nuns who are already frustrated with the limits placed on them by the male Church hierarchy.

Most denominations also allow women to fulfill other organizational leadership roles, such as committee work and leadership in religious education, some of which are designed only for women, and some of which are open to both women and men. The impact women have had in these various roles should not be underestimated, but many of these roles are limited by very specific boundaries, which also limit women's potential impact on religious life. Women who want to reach further within their religious organizations are still forced, for the most part, to ask permission from male authorities, to curb their own spiritual needs, or to leave.

Religion and Society

Few subjects stir up as much controversy and passion as the relationship between religion and gender norms. Often, those on opposing sides of the debate do agree about one point: Organized religion has been one of the most powerful human institutions for defining and controlling gender, sexuality, and woman's place in society. There is strong disagreement, however, about what can and should be done about this power. The solutions offered are wide ranging.

Religious institutions, like the other institutions discussed in this book, are not isolated enclaves; they are integrally linked to the wider society and its values. They both influence and are influenced by that society. They are powerful producers and enforcers of gender norms, but they are also affected by changes in these norms in other social institutions. Many aspects of religious teachings and structures depend on specific conceptions of women and their roles; when these begin to change outside of religious institutions, the religious institutions are also affected.

Religions have promoted inequality between women and men and have supported great violence against women—and men—who step out of their assigned gender and sexual roles. Because women have been assigned the subordinate place they have been especially subjected to punishments for gender-specific reasons. For example, the crime of the thousands of women accused of witchcraft was not only that they were heretics, but also that they had engaged in activities, such as healing, that were part of the province of men. In modern times, many religious organizations have formally and officially resisted changes in the status of women, even outside the institutions themselves.

The story of religious institutions is not a simple history of the victimization of women. Denominations differ in their treatment of women, and most have changed to some degree in recent years. Millions of women have found strength and inspiration in their religions, which have sometimes allowed them to battle their own religious institutions and to transform themselves and women's roles in subtle ways. A delicate balancing act is required to recognize both the religious power and influence of women, especially when it is often so subtle, and the very real gender-specific limits that have been placed on women in almost all their religious activities.

Many women have sought to create a spiritual bond among women through a feminist approach to religion that values women as a group. While this has been an active and important aspect of feminism, the feminist spirituality movement has also made many women more conscious of divisions among women, based in their religious beliefs and practices. These divisions arise not just because denominations disagree in their beliefs and differ in their practices. The conflict among women in the women's spirituality movement is related to some of the problems of difference discussed in Chapter 4. The remainder of this chapter considers two brief examples: relations between African-American and White Christians and between Christians and Jews.

Many Christian feminist writers have begun to identify a number of problems in developing a feminist theology or spirituality that does not deal specifically with race (Gilkes, 1987; Grant, 1989; Thistlethwaite, 1989). Just as the sexism inside organized religion both reflects and shapes the sexism in other social institutions, so does its racism. In most communities, African-Americans have no more been welcomed by Whites into their churches than they have been welcomed into White-dominated neighborhoods and schools. Despite the apparent welcome accorded the Whoopi Goldberg character in the movie *Sister Act*, African-American nuns face discrimination.[19]

Ethnic and other aspects of cultural heritage become woven together with religious practices; thus, for example, even within the same denominations, worship styles can differ dramatically in White and Black churches.[20] In addition, other intellectual and theological differences can cause race-based conflict in the effort to claim a "women's" Christian spirituality. Among these differences is the problem of freedom and free will, which looks different, depending on which side of slavery and other forms of institutionalized oppression shapes one's history. African-American and White views of religious claims of universality and the unity of human beings are also shaped by the realities of relationships of subordination. Another important point of difference is evident in the discussion of *Christology*, debates over the nature and place of Jesus in religious thought, including dealing seriously with the significance of Jesus' race and gender. Each of these is an important and emotional issue. These conflicts call to mind the problem of the false sense of universalism that comes from not recognizing differences, discussed in Chapter 4.

Many thinkers have also dealt with issues that divide Christians and Jews within the feminist spirituality movement. Judith Plaskow (1990) has written influential works on the problem of feminist anti-Judaism, especially in the context of apparently ecumenical discussions of spirituality. She has referred to more than *cultural anti-Judaism,* reflecting norms in the wider society, although she includes that aspect, as well. Rather, she has highlighted a fundamental source of anti-Judaism in Christian theology, especially the versions favored by feminists, which emphasize the "feminism" and "femaleness" of Jesus. Historically, part of the forcefulness of the Jesus story is its backdrop—the figures with whom Jesus is compared, and the significance of that comparison. The Jesus story depends heavily on what, to Jewish eyes, are the anti-Jewish caricatures found in Christian images of rabbis, Pharisees, and Jewish life and religion generally. This observation led Plaskow to write about the "psychological reality that Christians need Jews in a way that Jews do not need Christians" (Plaskow, 1990, 101). She has noted that in ecumenical dialogue, Christians are always asking Jews what they think of Jesus, and why they reject Jesus as the Messiah. As she wrote, "Christians seem to find it almost impossible to hear that Jews *don't* think about Jesus— except when Christian questions and a Christian culture force them to do so—and that they do not reject Jesus, they are simply not interested in him" (Plaskow, 1990, 101). She has argued that, contrary to the spiritualist urges toward universalism, Christians should take Judaism seriously as an independent religion on its own terms.

One of the most striking aspects of the study of women and religion is the degree to which given rituals and texts can offer different messages to different people. The same Bible has proven to some people that women and men are equal and that women should take full leadership roles in religions and society, while proving to others that women are inferior, periodically unclean, dangerous, and subordinate to men. Some people take religious prescriptions for women's domestic roles as a sign of the high esteem in which women are held; others find them the primary indications of women's subordination and even enslavement. Despite these distinctions and contradictions, various religions and denominations often take their own unique aspects to be *the* truth, and the potential source for universalism. These variations and similarities are sources of both the stability and resilience of religious institutions and the potential for their change, as well as sources of their possibilities for oppression and for liberation.

Notes

1. To read some of these women's writings, see Rossi (1988), which includes essays by Murray, Martineau, Stanton, and Goldman; see also Stanton ([1895] 1974), Gage ([1900] 1972), and Daly (1973, 1975, 1978).

2. For more reading on women and specific religions and denominations, see Ammerman and Roof (1995), Fishman (1995), and Hamington (1995).

3. All biblical quotations are from the *New English Bible with the Apocrypha* (New York: Oxford University Press, 1970).

4. Paisley Dodds, "Parents Furious After Church Cites Bible in Shutting Day Care," *Detroit Free Press,* April 5, 1997.

5. Gustav Niebuhr, "A Shift to Rigorous Tradition Gains Influence in Judaism," *New York Times,* May 1, 1997.

6. Dirk Johnson, "Growing Mormon Church Faces Dissent by Women and Scholars," *New York Times,* October 2, 1993.

7. Peter Steinfels, "Presbyterian Panel Rejects Sexuality Report," *New York Times,* June 9, 1991.

8. Ari L. Goldman, "Top Presbyterian Tribunal Bars Homosexual Minister," *New York Times,* November 5, 1992.

9. Dennis Hevesi, "Gay Church Again Rejected by National Council Group," *New York Times,* November 15, 1992.

10. This is a quotation from the 1967 Supreme Court case *Loving* v. *Virginia,* which invalidated the Virginia law against miscegenation.

11. The most important Christian book defining witchcraft is *Malleus Maleficarum,* written in 1486 by two Dominican friars; see Kramer and Sprenger (1928).

12. This is reprinted in Rossi (1988).

13. For some of the most basic works, see Christ and Plaskow (1979); Fiorenza (1984, 1992); Heschel (1983); Plaskow (1990); Ruether (1974, 1983).

14. For some influential writing about Goddess religion, see Starhawk (1979) and Christ (1987).

15. For an example of a blistering attack on the women's spirituality movement and on feminism more broadly, especially within Roman Catholicism, see Steichen (1991).

16. For more reading on women as clergy and religious leaders, see Lehman (1993), McNamara (1996), Purvis (1995), and Weissinger (1993).

17. "Women in Full Ministry Doubles," *Wisconsin State Journal,* May 27, 1989.

18. Jennifer Steinhauer, "Older and More Skilled, New Nuns Are Assuming Wider Roles," *New York Times,* December 27, 1992.

19. Steinhauer, "Older and More Skilled, New Nuns Are Assuming Wider Roles."

20. Steinhauer, "Older and More Skilled, New Nuns Are Assuming Wider Roles."

8

⊷❧⊶

Gender and the Institutional Media of Communication

Females constitute 27.7% of the U.S. population. Half of them are teenagers or in their 20s. They wear revealing outfits, jiggle a lot, but don't do much else. More than a third are unemployed or without any identifiable pursuit or purpose. Most others are students, secretaries, homemakers, household workers, or nurses.

Portrait of American women as presented on television[1]

MOST OF THE INFORMATION we receive about the world around us does not come from direct experience. Our knowledge about human life is gained secondhand from the mass media of communication—radio, television, newspapers, and magazines—or from the artistic media of communication, such as the performing, graphic, and literary arts. For this reason, the collective normative power of the people and organizations who manage these media is enormous.

The description that begins this chapter tells what the world looked like to people watching television in the 1970s. It is no wonder that feminists in the field of communications and media studies began to focus their attention on how the tremendous normative power of the media could distort the image of women in society. This chapter pursues the following questions: What images of women do the institutional media of communication offer, and why? What is the process by which these images appear? What impact do the media have on the construction of gender? To what degree and how do they foster and inhibit social change? What impact do women have on the media?

We begin by looking at the mass media, including radio, television, newspapers, and magazines, followed by a brief examination of the new electronic media. We then turn to advertising as a special form of communication that shapes and is shaped by gender. Finally, we consider the arts as an institutionalized medium of communication that plays an important role in sex/gender systems.

The mass media of communication both reflect and help create and alter social and cultural values. Although the mass media are often blamed for the problems of modern society (ironically, people usually communicate these criticisms through the mass media), they are not monolithic and do not present a solitary message. Indeed, while they are powerful agents in reinforcing dominant cultural norms, they are also among the most important channels for achieving social change. This complexity makes the study of the mass media especially important for anyone interested in the social meanings of gender and the position of women. To look at the issues more closely, we turn first to women's roles in the print (newspapers and magazines) and electronic (radio and television) media. We then consider the gender-related content of the media and its impact on the way people think and act.

Women in the News

Because one of the most important and long-standing functions of the mass media is to inform people about the news of society, this review of women's roles in the media focuses on women's changing contributions to journalism and the news. Before the advent of the electronic media of radio and television, other than town criers, the post, and the gossip of all sorts of travelers, newspapers and magazines served as the main means for people to know what was going on around them.

Print Media.   Although men have clearly dominated institutionalized media of communication, women are by no means newcomers.[2] Women were influential in the print media from its beginning in America; in fact, the first printing press was imported and installed by a woman in 1638. There were at least 14 female printers by the time of the American Revolution. The print shop was a crucial place in early American life; it was a center of all sorts of printed information, images, and other documents. Elizabeth Timothy became the first female editor–publisher in 1738, with the publication of the *South Carolina Gazette*. Political pamphlets, broadsides, and propaganda pieces, perhaps more important than newspapers in the early days of this country, were often written or published by women; at least 16 of the 78 colonial newspapers were edited by women (Heinemann, 1996, 190). It was a woman who first printed the Declaration of Independence, complete with the names of all signers (Beasley and Gibbons, 1993, 51; Marzolf, 1977).

Print shops were often family businesses and, as in many family businesses, women were important contributors. Many early female printers are invisible because history books tend to focus on the male members of printing (and other business) families. Consider the Franklin family, including Deborah, who ran the print shop when her famous husband Benjamin was away; Ann, Benjamin's sister-in-law, the state printer of Rhode Island in 1736 and a newspaper publisher in her own right; and Margaret H. Bache, also a newspaper publisher and the wife of Benjamin's grandson (de Pauw, 1975, 35).

As the importance of the public press increased in the 19th century, women continued to exert a clear if restricted influence. By 1831, there were at least 1,297 printers, about 30% of whom were women. Women and boys received about one third the average wages of men (Marzolf, 1977, 9). By 1850, about 16% of news-paper compositors were women. The tasks they were allowed to do were limited, and their pay was less than that of similarly occupied men, but women earned more as printers than they could doing most "women's" work (DuBois, 1978, 129). Print unions did not accept women as full members until 1873, which helped to restrict the number of women involved in the trade, although some women organized their own union for a time (DuBois, 1978).

Even if the number of women in the print media was low, some observers, such as Ann Douglas (1977), have argued that women writers helped shape important aspects of 19th-century American culture through their contributions to the periodical press at a time when it was first becoming a *mass* medium. Douglas believes that women were successful in attracting mass readership and gained "power through the exploitation of their feminine identity as their society defined it" (p. 7) by influencing the 19th-century culture of moralism. Douglas's argument underscores the complexity of both the mass media and the sex/gender systems. The "cult of true womanhood" was oppressive, but some women also found a way to bend it to their needs. By the mid–19th century, women's influence in all aspects of periodical production was sufficient to provoke resistance by men, who thought women were feminizing culture too much.

These 19th-century women submitted individual stories, poems, and religious pieces to newspapers and magazines, and some became regular contributors. Some were even editors, including Margaret Fuller, who edited the Transcendentalist magazine, *The Dial*. She also published some of her own important feminist writing through that journal. Most remarkable, however, was the rise of the women's magazines and other periodicals. Among the most famous was one of the first truly popular mass-circulation magazines, *Godey's Lady's Book* (1837–1897), edited by Sara Josepha Hale (1788–1879).[3] Widely remembered chiefly for its color fashion plates, which are now expensive collectors' items, *Godey's* was an arbiter of taste, voraciously devoured by women across the country. *Godey's* was only one of many women's magazines, but its circulation outstripped most of the others'. The first magazine designed explicitly for African-American women was Juli Ringwood Coston's *Ringwood's Afro-American Journal of Fashion*, begun in 1891.

The number of these women's magazines increased dramatically during the late 19th and early 20th centuries. Most "ladies'" magazines were not explicitly feminist, but they usually did favor expansion of women's rights and influence. Indeed, although at first glance, they might seem trivial to the untrained modern eye, not only were many prosuffrage, but they also gave women a rare opportunity for breaking into professional careers and having an influence on women across the country (Jolliffe, 1994).

The middle and late 19th century also witnessed an impressive growth in what would now be called a "*feminist press,*" periodicals established by and for women to further the cause of women's rights and change in women's roles. Many of these periodicals were quite radical in their politics (Russo and Kramarae, 1991). Among those periodicals aimed at women and promoting women's new interest and involvement in political and social issues were the *Free Enquirer*, established in 1828 by Frances Wright, as the first reform periodical published solely by women; Amelia Bloomer's *Lily* (1849–1859); Pauline Wright Davis's *Una* (1854–1856);

Elizabeth Cady Stanton and Susan B. Anthony's *The Revolution* (1868–1871); Lucy Stone's *Women's Journal* (1870–1917); Josephine St. Pierre Ruffin's *The Woman's Era* (1894–?), which focused on the African-American women's club movement; and Isidra T. Cárdenas's *La voz de la mujer* (1907–?) These publications were important links in the 19th-century women's movements.

The popularity of women's magazines did not go unnoticed by the rest of the press, which increasingly paid attention to women as an audience. Many newspapers began to include columns or series devoted to women and women's rights, such as Elizabeth Smith's 1850 series on women's rights in the *New York Tribune*. In 1859, Jane Croly (1829–1901) began the first women's page—actually a newspaper column—in a mass-circulation newspaper, the *New York World*. Most other newspapers followed suit, institutionalizing a segregated portion designed to appeal specifically to women, or at least to a stereotyped view of them. As newspapers and magazines began to use advertising to support themselves, fashion and consumer items related to women's domestic roles were also used to appeal to women.

The last half of the 19th century and the beginning of the 20th century witnessed the rise of the female reporter. Newspapers showcased two well-known types of female reporters, popularly known as the "stunt girls" and the "sob sisters" (Marzolf, 1977). The "stunt girls" performed great, or at least curious, feats and wrote about them. Elizabeth Cochrane, writing under the penname "Nellie Bly," for example, drew on Jules Verne's popular *Around the World in Eighty Days* and beat Phileas Fogg's fictional record by circling the globe in 72 days, 6 hours, and 11 minutes in 1889–1890. The "sob sisters" focused on crime, often painting the details in lurid colors (Abramson, 1990). Many of these early reporters later went into other types of journalism and resented the trivializing title they had been given.

Indeed, the traditional dismissal of the stunt girls and the sob sisters does trivialize the remarkable contributions women made to the development of journalism at the turn into the 20th century. Many of the "stunts," for example, were important contributions to the growth of serious investigative journalism. When Cochrane was 22 years old, she feigned insanity to investigate conditions in insane asylums and later published the resulting articles as a book, *Ten Days in a Madhouse*, in 1887. She also reported on a sweatshop from the inside, posing as a worker there. One of the most important investigative journalists in history was Ida B. Wells (1862–1931), the African-American editor and part owner of the *Memphis Free Speech*, who, in the early 1890s, published an exposé of lynchings that served as the focal point for agitation against these vicious acts. Ida M. Tarbell (1857–1944), who exposed the monopolistic practices of Standard Oil for *McClure's Magazine*, was another major contributor to the history of investigative reporting. The articles Genevieve Forbes wrote in the *Chicago Tribune* after she disguised herself as an immigrant in 1921 to investigate conditions on Ellis Island provoked a congressional investigation.

Women's roles in journalism expanded further after the late 19th century. In 1890, women constituted 14% of the people involved in printing and publishing, and in 1905, they were 20%. They held 24% of the editing and reporting jobs in the early 1920s, 32% in 1950, 37% in 1960, and about 50% by 1990. Women had to fight for what they gained, however. As mentioned previously, women printers faced resistance by male printers' unions, and they received relatively low pay. Women journalists also faced many roadblocks in their work. When women became eligible for membership in the Capitol Press Gallery, their numbers there rose from 4 in 1870 to 20 in 1879, but then women were virtually eliminated from membership by a new rule barring part-time reporters and limiting news organizations to one reporter each. (If a newspaper was only going to have one reporter in the Capitol Press Gallery, it was *not* going to be a woman.) In 1919, only 10 of the 110 reporters accredited to cover the U.S. Congress were women. During World War II, the number of accredited women rose to 98, but it fell to 30 right after the war.

Women in many fields complain that their profession seems like a "men's club"; in journalism, that complaint was literally true. The National Press Club, founded in the 19th century, did not admit women until 1971. This exclusion prompted women to form their own clubs, such as Sorosis, the Women's National Press Association (1885), and the Women's National Press Club (1919). The prestigious Gridiron Club admitted its first woman, Helen Thomas, in 1975, after she had already become the first woman head of the United Press International White House Bureau, and the first woman head of the White House press corps (Heinemann, 1996, 301). In 1992, when 11 of the club's 60 members were women, Thomas became the Gridiron's first female president, a mere 108 years after its founding. Although women journalists had earned Pulitzer Prizes since Anne O'Hare McCormick became the first woman to win it in 1937, no women served as jurors for the prize until 1972. Women often used only their initials or pen names for their articles to avoid the stigma of being identified as females.

Many women became prominent journalists in the years between the two world wars and especially during World War II. First Lady Eleanor Roosevelt helped promote women journalists by allowing only women at her morning press conferences, thus giving good opportunities to such women as Lorena Hickock of the Associated Press and May Craig, who later became a regular interviewer on television's prestigious *Meet the Press* show. Some editors had to keep women on staff only because otherwise their papers would be excluded from this weekly White House event (Heinemann, 1996, 295). These women differed in their views of women and gender, although some were feminist activists and wrote on feminism (Marzolf, 1977; Sochen, 1973, 1981).

A handful of individual women became powerful figures in journalism as editors and publishers, including Lila Bell Acheson Wallace, cofounder of the *Reader's Digest* with her husband in 1922; Freda Kirchwey, who became managing editor of the *Nation* in 1922, then editor (1933) and finally owner (1937); Eleanor Medill, who began editing the *Washington Herald* in 1930 and then in 1939 bought the *Herald* and the *Washington Times* and merged them into the *Washington Times-Herald;* Anne O'Hare McCormick, who became the first woman on the *New York Times* editorial board in 1936; Dorothy Day, founder of the influential radical periodical *The Catholic Worker* in 1933; Dorothy Schiff, who became publisher of the *New York Post* in 1942; and Alicia Patterson, who began editing and publishing *Newsday,* Long Island's (N.Y.) largest daily, in 1940.

World War II and the Spanish Civil War also saw many women reporters rising in the very risky and certainly nontraditional field of war and foreign correspondence, including Freda Kirchwey, Martha Gelhorn, and Dorothy Thompson (Wagner, 1989). Women made their mark in many other specialty fields of journalism and newspaper writing, including Sylvia Porter's financial writing, Elda Furry's ("Hedda Hopper") and Louella Parsons's gossip columns, and Dorothy Kilgallen's coverage of Broadway.

Women's influence in journalism rose during World War II and then stalled for some time after the war. The numerical presence of women in journalism did not decline, but women's roles became more limited. Many women complained that they were relegated to reporting traditional women's issues, and young women seeking entry into journalism were encouraged to stick to these. The pay and status gap between men and women remained large. Despite the impressive contributions of women journalists in the early and midcentury period, many editors claimed that some stories were just too dangerous for women to handle. Two distinct innovations of the 1950s included the new advice column Esther Lederer began in the *Chicago Sun-Times* in 1955 under the name Ann Landers and the first major lesbian magazine, *The Ladder*, published by the Daughters of Bilitis a year later.

The treatment of women in print journalism has grown again substantially during the last quarter of the 20th century, largely because of women's political and feminist activism. The year 1970 was a turning point, when women staged a sit-in at *Ladies' Home Journal* to protest its portrayal of women, and women staff members at *Time* and *Newsweek* filed suits against their employers for sex discrimination. The women at *Newsweek* charged the magazine with violating Title VII of the 1964 Civil Rights Act by its practice of designating news writing as almost exclusively a male domain and news researching (which was at that time given no byline) as almost exclusively a female domain. In 1974, the Equal Employment Opportunity Commission found that the *Washington Post* engaged in illegal employment practices.

In 1974, discrimination charges were filed against *The New York Times;* the plaintiffs won their case in 1978 after filing 90 charges of discrimination against that paper. Grace Glueck, an art news reporter, explained how the complaint developed:

> In the beginning, even as a group, we had on our white gloves and party manners. How we got started was that in 1972 Grace Lichtenstein was kvetching about the fact that the *Times* would not permit the use of the title "Ms." in the paper. Several of us, including Grace, got to thinking that this style rigidity was symptomatic of more basic problems. And so we began what you might call a group grope, meeting several times before drawing up a petition to the publisher and his board members. We pointed out the inequities of male–female salaries, the total absence of women in management jobs, and the stringent patterns of our nonpromotion. The managing editor then took it upon himself to call us troublemakers into his office and complain that our action was divisive.[4]

When the women did not receive satisfaction, they filed a lawsuit against the paper. Times changed at the *Times,* including acceptance of the term *Ms.* in 1986.[5]

Efforts to achieve equality in the journalism field continue, aided by women's press organizations and women's own publications, such as the *Media Report to Women*. Although some changes have taken place, much is left to be done, however. Female bylines (named authorship of articles) in the *New York Times,* for example, rose from 12% in 1974 to 24% in 1992.[6] Another study showed that women had 34% of newspaper bylines.[7] Even with their increasing numbers, women face many of the same problems experienced in other lines of work, including sexual harassment on the job.[8]

Electronic Media. The history of women in radio and television broadcasting parallels their involvement in print media.[9] The electronic media are also managed by gender-segregated, male-dominated organizations in which men hold the majority of visible, high-status positions, and women hold primarily auxiliary and lower-status jobs. Radio and television include a wide variety of programming, especially since the introduction of cable services, including channels devoted entirely to a specific genre, such as music videos, movies, travel documentaries, news, and even weather reports. This discussion of *electronic journalism* is instructive because unlike most other programming on radio and television, which has clear male and female parts, broadcast journalism's claim to neutrality offers a good test of how gender structures social institutions and how much change there has been.

The first female *radio news* commentator was Kathryn Cravens, who in 1934 launched her program "News Through a Woman's Eye" in St. Louis. In 1936, she became the first woman whose radio show was broadcast across the country (by CBS). Pauline Frederick joined the American Broadcasting Company (ABC) radio network in 1948 and for 12 years was the only woman hard-news commentator on radio and television (Marzolf, 1977). One of the justifications used by mass-media organizations for the small number of women commentators was that people did not like the sound of women's voices: They were too soft and shrill (that is, high pitched), and they lacked authority. Thus, "Singing and acting and, later, giving cleaning tips and recipes and reading commercials were a woman's place in radio's first decades. Changing that role took a war, an act of Congress [the 1964 Civil Rights Act], and a domestic revolution" (Hoseley and Yamada, 1987, 1).

The past 25 years have witnessed a dramatic increase in the presence of women in the main radio broadcast journalist positions. National Public Radio (NPR) has been a leader, with its extraordinary prominence of women on its news staff; by 1984, nearly half of NPR reporters were women (Heinemann, 1996, 303). Among its very impressive cast of women have been Susan Stamberg, who in 1972 became the first woman news anchor in radio, for the new show *All Things Considered;* Cokie Roberts, one of the few female congressional reporters; and Nina Totenberg, the legal correspondent who became directly embroiled in the Clarence Thomas–Anita Hill hearings in the early 1990s.

Women have also become more prominent in *television journalism* over the years, following a slow start. Nancy Hanschmann (Dickerson) became the first female news correspondent for CBS. Marlene Sanders served as the first evening news anchor, but only as a substitute, in an incident described later in this section. Joan Murray was the first African-American woman journalist hired by a major television station, in 1965. Other women who made prominent contributions were Barbara Walters, who led the way in television anchoring in 1976;[10] Marlene Sanders, who, having recovered from her brief anchoring stint, became the first vice president of a television network in 1976; Jane Pauley, who moved from NBC's *Today* show to other news and newsmagazine shows; Connie Chung, the first Asian-American woman on national network news; and Charlayne Hunter-Gault, who began her career as a newsmaker when she became part of the first group of African-American students to attend the University of Mississippi and who eventually became a news reporter on public television's *MacNeil/Lehrer News Hour.* Now, fortunately, the number of women involved in broadcast news is too large to list.

By the beginning of the 1980s, some improvements were evident, although women in local affiliate and cable news channels did somewhat better than those on the higher-status network news, reflecting the usual rule of "the higher the fewer." Similarly, a high proportion of stories reported by women were aired on weekends, a lower-status and less-visible slot for reporters (Sanders and Rock, 1988, 113). By 1992, women were still only 14% of the network broadcast correspondents, and a study of a month of newscasts that year showed that 14% of the news stories were reported by women.[11]

Women's experiences as news anchors offer good insight into the status of women in broadcast journalism. Marlene Sanders, involved in television broadcasting since its earliest years, has provided this illustrative passage from a *New York Times* article reacting to her appearance in 1964 as a temporary replacement for a news anchor who was ill:

> The masculine evening news line up received a temporary female replacement last night . . . when Marlene Sanders stepped in at 6:45 P.M. . . . People who should know report that never before has a distaff reporter conducted on her very own a news broadcast in prime time. For the record, then, the courageous young woman with a Vassar smile was crisp and businesslike and obviously the sort who wouldn't put up with any nonsense, from anyone. Her 15 minute show was not spellbinding, but that could have been because her delivery was terribly straightforward and her copy somewhat dull.

Sanders's reaction at the time was to wonder how one could deliver news other than in a straightforward manner. She was surprised at the suggestion that news anchors were usually "spellbinding" (Sanders and Rock, 1988, 49–50).

Women news anchors are much more common now, especially since both morning newsmagazines and evening local news shows have developed a "Ken and Barbie" formula, as some put it: a male and female pair (Paisner, 1989, 32). The fact that anchoring is an area of special progress should be understood partly as a function of the difference between anchoring and other broadcast news positions. Although most news anchors are drawn from the ranks of television journalists, they usually do not research or write the news stories themselves. They are not reporters. They are performers selected largely for their public appeal as personalities. As anchor Jane Pauley put it, "My daughter aspires now to have four children and be a broadcaster with NBC when she grows up. While I'm flattered . . . I hope she does something more productive with her life." She continued,

What's wrong with these pictures? Is the resemblance between Joan Lunden and her replacement on "Good Morning America" (Lisa McCree) a coincidence?

> It gives me the creeps when I hear . . . young women aspire to be an anchor-woman. You don't aspire to be an anchorwoman. I mean, that's like aspiring to be a Vanna White, a letter turner or something. You aspire to be a journal-ist. (Paisner, 1989, 74)

Other journalists agree.

This distinction between reporter and performer was highlighted in 1983 when Christine Craft, a former reporter serving as local anchorwoman, sued her station because she was demoted on the grounds that she was "unattractive, too old, and not deferential to men."[12] The station rebutted, saying that news anchors must be attractive to their audiences if the station is going to keep its audience, and market research showed that audiences regarded Craft as lacking warmth, too casual in her dress, and too opinionated. Craft's lawyers later claimed that the methods used to solicit audience reaction to Craft were discriminatory because they encouraged people to respond in a stereotypic way. Two juries found in favor of Craft, but she lost her case on appeal. Only Justice Sandra Day O'Connor voted to hear the case when Craft appealed to the U.S. Supreme Court.

Many female news anchors and journalists contend that higher standards for appearance are set for women on camera than for men, and that women are also judged on how well they conform to gender stereotypes. Many also believe that there is a double standard with respect to aging. As men get older, they are viewed as authoritative and perhaps avuncular, whereas aging women are simply judged less attractive (Paisner, 1989, 205–213). Is the problem sexist audiences or sexist media organizations? It is hard to tell, but as early as 1976, one study (Whittaker and Whittaker, 1976) found that audiences judged male and female news broadcasters equally acceptable, believable, and effective.

Even the most successful and prominent women in broadcast journalism have experienced some form of discrimination or sexual harassment. Mary Alice Williams has recalled a job interview in 1971 when, following an interview focusing mostly on her looks, the executive said, "We don't have anything right now, but we could probably arrange something. Do you fuck?" (Paisner, 1989, 179–180). Pauley found, during her time on the *Today* show, that all of the interviews were given to her male on-camera partner (Paisner, 1989, 176). When Lesley Stahl visited a set being designed for a prime-time broadcast in 1974, she found the participating journalists' positions labeled, respectively, "CRONKITE," "RATHER," "MUDD," "WALLACE," and "FEMALE" (Paisner, 1989, 17–18). Like leading women in many fields, women journalists find that they are not rid of this aspect of their lives once they become famous.

Some areas are more difficult than others, as women sportswriters have found out. Mary Schmitt, a sportswriter for the *Cleveland Plain Dealer*, has told about her experiences when she first covered men's sports in the late 1980s. The Minnesota Timberwolves at first wore their fancy robes when Schmitt came in for an interview, but after a while, many of the players became comfortable enough that they just wore towels, or nothing.[13]

> Now this was a conundrum. In an odd way, losing the robes and towels was a signal that they had accepted my presence in the locker room. Though I certainly would have been more comfortable had they elected to continue wearing them, I was hesitant to bring this up since I would be calling attention to the fact that this was an uncomfortable situation. . . . By careful positioning and peripheral vision not to mention that woman sportswriter's trick of carrying a really big notebook to blot out anything you don't want to see I could tell who was and wasn't dressed and I'd wait until a player was sufficiently clothed so that neither of us would be embarrassed during an interview.

Schmitt reported that her situation was easy, compared with that of her predecessors, who either were locked out of the locker room and got their interviews only after the male reporters were finished and the players were dressed and ready to go home or were viciously harassed.

CNN anchor and senior correspondent Judy Woodruff has observed that women reporters, like women in other professions, face other kinds of limitations, given the continuing divisions of labor between men and women at home. The proportion of women who have important assignments, such as traveling with a presidential campaign, has risen steeply over the years. In 1972, there were roughly eight women who traveled with the candidates at all. In 1996, more than one third of the reporters covering candidates Dole and Clinton were women. "The women covering the Dole campaign . . . discovered that the only parents on their plane were men with someone staying close to home for the children."[14] Women reporters are more welcome now than they were previously, but women reporters with responsibility for children tend to turn down plum assignments in a

TABLE 8-1
Broadcast News Workforce, 1992, by Gender and Race

	TV News		Radio News	
	Staff	*Directors*	*Staff*	*Directors*
White				
Women	27	14	23	24
Men	56	77	65	67
Black				
Women	4	<0.5	4	2
Men	6	2	3	1
Hispanic				
Women	2	1	1	2
Men	3	3	1	1
Asian				
Women	1	1	1	2
Men	1	<0.5	<0.5	<0.5
Native American				
Women	<0.5	<0.5	<0.5	1
Men	<0.5	1	1	2
Total % Women	34	17	30	29
Number	23,100	745	16,900	5,800

Note: Numbers are precentages; columns do not sum to 100%, due to rounding error.

Source: Media Report to Women, vol. 20 (Fall 1992), pp. 4–5.

way that is not true of men. Women are less likely to have someone who can cover for them at home or are less likely to ask that of someone.

It has been more difficult for women to establish themselves behind the scenes in the production and business aspects of the electronic media. In the early 1970s, women were a tiny fraction of the executive and production staff. CBS, for example, had no female directors and only one female crew member (U.S. Commission on Civil Rights, 1979). Like women in the print media, those in the electronic media began to turn to the courts for help. As a result, women's situation has improved, as Table 8-1 shows. Women overall constitute about 34% of the television news staff members and 30% of radio news staff members. They fare much worse as television directors. The organizations that bring us broadcast news remain disproportionately male and White.

Many women have been important on camera in television shows other than news broadcasts, and some have also been influential in shaping the medium. Women entertainers, such as Lucille Ball, Mary Tyler Moore, and others, made their mark not just as performers but as shapers of situation comedy as a genre. The role of women in the performing arts is discussed in the following section.

Gender and the Message of the Media

What image of women and norms about gender do the mass media offer people? Very influential analysis in the 1970s argued that media portrayal of women amounts to *symbolic annihilation* of women by systematically ignoring, trivializing, and distorting them (Tuchman, Daniels, and Benet, 1978). George Gerbner (1978) has argued that the media are major instruments of cultural resistance to changes in the roles and status of women. He has said that this happens in three ways:

1. Women and the women's movement are discredited by the media, which focus on the bizarre and the threatening.
2. Women are isolated or segregated and ghettoized. They are shown in special places (for example, the kitchen) and on special shows.
3. Television shows depict the exploitation and victimization of women as common, routine, and entertaining.

Mass-media research suggests that while there have been some improvements, these charges still have too much truth in them.

Empirical studies of the images of women on television agree: Women appear much less often than men on most kinds of television programs. Indeed, in all types of programming except soap operas, men outnumber women in proportions that would spell demographic disaster in real life. Research also shows that the images of women who do appear on television are highly stereotypical (Vest, 1992). Programming for children and adults underestimates the proportion of women in the labor force and shows women mostly in stereotypical roles (Butsch, 1992; Signorielli and Lears, 1992; Vande Berg and Streckfuss, 1992; Vest, 1992). This stereotyping is also true in the newer genres, such as the music videos on MTV, which perpetuate gender stereotypes among both Black and White characters (Seidman, 1992). A review of top-rated television shows in 1996 showed that 41% of men and 28% of women were shown working. (The same was true of 60% of men in movies and 35% of women.)[15]

Television representations are also class biased. A review of more than 40 years of situation comedies showed that portrayals of middle-class families usually imply that "father knows best," whereas in portrayals of the working class, *men* are characterized by "ineptitude, immaturity, stupidity, lack of good sense, or emotional outburst, traits that have been culturally defined as feminine or childlike" (Butsch, 1992, 390). Age stereotypes also play an important role. Old women rarely appear in television programs, and when they do, they are usually either comic characters lacking both brains and beauty or nasty and bothersome mothers-in-law. Not until the late 1980s did a television show (*Golden Girls*) begin to ask viewers to laugh with, rather than at, older women.

Representations of African-American women are constructed of both gender and race stereotypes (Rhodes, 1991). In the 1950s, the few African-American women who appeared on television played maids, mostly in the character of the friendly Mammy. From 1968 to 1971, actress Diahann Carroll starred as a nurse in *Julia,* the first show that avoided this stereotype entirely. Nevertheless, throughout the 1960s and 1970s, although the number of shows with African-American characters rose, most were situation comedies in which many of the men played some variety of the Stepin' Fetchitt character, and women portrayed a "cocky but nurturing mammy." By the late 1980s and early 1990s, changes in African-American women's television roles seemed to follow those of African-American men almost literally; an increasing proportion of African-American female characters on television served little dramatic purpose other than appearing as romantic interests for African-American male characters.

Despite the overall pattern, there has been some change in the kinds of characters portrayed by women on television. In the early days of television, we saw only homemakers and the occasional teacher (*Our Miss Brooks*), secretary (*The Lucy Show, Perry Mason*), saloon keeper (*Gunsmoke*), or supernatural (*I Dream of Jeannie, Bewitched*). From the 1980s on, women played a much wider range of roles. Many (although not all) of prime-time women's lives are more complicated and realistic than they were in past decades, even when the women have relatively traditional occupations.

Prime-time television dramas and situation comedies used to avoid dealing with politics. The few exceptions, such as the 1970s comedies *Maude* and *All in the Family,* were considered daring. Feminism was avoided or treated as funny. By the early 1990s, many shows wove political themes into their plots, and although the committed feminist character was rare, more prime-time characters—like those in real life—revealed their anger about violence against women and about discrimination and showed their frustration with characters who trivialized women and feminism. Some prime-time shows dealt explicitly with violence against women from the women's point of view, instead of the more usual "sexploitation" approach of violent television. Even situation-comedy characters now occasionally react to the news of the day, sometimes seriously.

The most famous incident in the early 1990s involving prime-time women was surely Vice President Quayle's attack on *Murphy Brown* for its presumed immorality and its role in undermining "family values" when the main character had a baby out of wedlock. The attack became the subject of national controversy (and international amusement as the world witnessed the vice president appearing to enter a debate with a fictional character), and the show was written to respond to the vice president. The incident led to some constructive discussion about "family values," but mostly it benefited the show: Its ratings and advertising price rose as a result.[16]

Many people have commented on the gender messages aimed at women in newspapers and especially magazines. Many—if not most—magazines are aimed at gender-segregated markets. Among these are the women's service magazines known as the "seven sisters": *Better Homes and Gardens, Family Circle, Good Housekeeping, Ladies' Home Journal, McCalls, Redbook,* and *Woman's Day,* which target women in general and emphasize women's roles as homemakers. Fashion and style magazines such as *Cosmopolitan, Glamour, Bazaar,* and *Vogue* also target women, as do those with special themes, such as home decoration, weddings, parenthood, and weight watching. *Essence* is a style magazine aimed especially at

African-American women. *Seventeen* is a style magazine for teenagers, founded in 1944.

Betty Friedan was one of the first to analyze the image of women presented by women's magazines. Friedan, who wrote for women's magazines in the 1950s, documented a postwar change in the portrayal of women in fiction and nonfiction in her book *The Feminine Mystique* (1963). Good fiction, she claimed, left the pages of women's magazines, as did nonfiction that was not concerned with women's stereotypic roles. By the end of the 1950s, women were portrayed almost exclusively as mindless but attentive homemakers. "In 1958, and again in 1959, I went through issue after issue of the major women's magazines . . . without finding a single heroine who had a career, a commitment to any work, art, profession, or mission in the world, other than 'Occupation: housewife'" (p. 38). This change in content was paralleled by a change in format: "The very size of [the women's magazines'] print is raised until it looks like a first-grade primer" (p. 58).

Many systematic studies of magazine content have documented changes over the years. A study of *Seventeen* magazine in 1951, 1971, and 1991 shows that the theme of beauty accounts for roughly one third of the content over time, while political themes ranged from a low of 2% in 1951 to 7% in 1971. A closer look at the political and social content of the magazine in those years reveals that a focus on "women's issues" went from about 39% in 1951 to 44% in 1971 to 34% in 1991. Even these figures do not tell the whole story; in 1971, a substantial part of the "women's issues" focus was in advertisements; in 1991, although there was less content, these issues appeared in the editorial content rather than being limited to messages about liberated women using one or another feminine hygiene product. A focus on minorities went from 30% in 1950 to 9% in 1971 to 24% in 1991 (Budgeon and Currie, 1995). A study of the content of the *Ladies' Home Journal* and *Good Housekeeping* from 1954 to 1982 shows a decline in the proportion of content on women as wives and homemakers and an increase in the focus on social, political, and economic themes. Nevertheless, traditional themes still dominated throughout this period (Demarest and Garner, 1992).[17]

In the 1970s, the world of women's magazines began to change in two respects. First, new magazines were founded that were aimed at employed women or that assumed that women had more interests in, for example, economics and public affairs than the traditional magazines indicated. These new magazines include *Essence,* launched in 1970 for Black women; *New Woman* (1971); and *Working Woman* (1976). In 1971, Gloria Steinem founded the major mass-market feminist magazine, *Ms.* In 1988, Frances Lear founded *Lear's,* she claimed, "for women who weren't born yesterday." Both of the latter efforts folded eventually; although *Ms.* especially had a passionate following, it was not able to achieve the popularity of the traditional women's magazines. Its circulation, for example, never exceeded 380,000, while *Family Circle* has had a circulation of about 8 million. Beginning in the 1970s, women founded hundreds of academic and nonacademic feminist periodicals other than *Ms.* Among the best-known nonacademic journals still available[18] are *Kalliope: A Journal of Women's Art* (1979); *The Lesbian Review of Books* (1994); *Lilith* (Jewish perspective, 1976); *Off Our Backs* (1970, the oldest continuing feminist journal); *Sinister Wisdom: A Journal for the Lesbian Imagination in the Arts and Politics* (1976); and *The Women's Review of*

Books (1983). There are also local feminist newspapers and periodicals in many areas.

Change also began to arrive at the traditional women's magazines in the 1970s. While they were never uniformly devoid of political and social content, including some support for women's rights, agitation by the women's movement and the reality of a growing trend for the women in their audience to be in the workforce led the traditional women's magazines to incorporate some of these new views into their content. Some changed their editorial policies, supplementing articles on domestic and fashion concerns with articles on other aspects of women's lives. Certainly, many changes have taken place. *The Ladies' Home Journal* instituted a monthly news column in cooperation with CNN. *Family Circle* won a National Magazine Award for public service in 1991 for examination of toxic contamination. *Glamour* won a National Magazine Award in 1992 for public interest for its articles on teen pregnancy and abortion.

Despite many changes, however, the most popular women's magazines continue to be shaped by—and to sell—views of women based on gender, race, and class stereotypes, as Ellen McCracken's excellent study of women's magazines in the 1980s shows (McCracken, 1993). Another study found that women's magazines "serve up a confusing hodge-podge of self-loathing attitudes and empowering opinion" (Doner, 1993, 37). Advertisers require the content of women's style magazines to serve their needs (see Box 8-1). Most, then, emphasize striving for a standard of beauty that is impossible for most women and, given the requirement that models look anorexic (which generally requires that they *be* anorexic), an unhealthy standard as well. Women's magazines, especially their advertisements, make a large proportion of women feel fat and ugly. Nevertheless, women's magazines tend also to support certain feminist perspectives, including not blaming the victim in rape and in woman battering (Doner, 1993). More of the editors of women's magazines are women than used to be the case, but having a woman editor does not reduce the amount of stereotypical material in the magazines. Women editors do increase the amount of positive portrayals of women, however (Jolliffe, 1994).

Recent decades have also witnessed struggles over the gender content of *newspapers*. For many years, most newspapers have had a segregated "women's page." The content of this section of the newspaper has undergone changes paralleling those in women's magazines. During and just before World War II, women were presented as relatively heterogeneous creatures. In the 1950s, however, they were viewed almost exclusively as homemakers. Most news about women was put on the women's page, thus casting stories about women as "soft" (peripheral) rather than "hard" (important) news, thereby trivializing significant events described therein:

In 1965 [the *New York Times* women's page] ran a brief story in which Betty Friedan announced the formation of N.O.W. Placed between a recipe for turkey stuffing and an article announcing that Pierre Henri was returning to Saks Fifth Avenue, the article clearly indicated that Friedan had been interviewed at least several days before. The founding of N.O.W. was treated as soft news. (Tuchman, 1978, 201–202)

BOX 8-1   See for Yourself:
What Are Women's Magazines Telling You?

Take a look at the same month's issue of a selection of any of the popular women's magazines, including the "seven sisters" magazines, *Better Homes and Gardens, Family Circle, Good Housekeeping, Ladies' Home Journal, McCalls, Redbook,* and *Woman's Day,* or other women's style and beauty magazines, such as *Bazaar, Cosmopolitan, Essence, Glamour, Mademoiselle, Seventeen,* and *Vogue.*

Make a chart that compares these magazines, answering the following questions:

1. TARGET AUDIENCE. Judging from the relative price of the magazine, its look, where it is sold, and what it contains, what is the target audience? To whom are the editors trying to appeal? (Consider such demographic markers as age, race/ ethnicity, class and wealth, region, occupation, and urban or rural residence.)

2. PICTURED COVER STORIES. The first thing you are likely to notice is the cover graphic. What story is highlighted by the cover picture? Is the picture of a person who is a subject of a story? Why was she picked? How is she posed? Is the picture of a thing that is the subject of a story (e.g., a particular kind of cake)? Instead, is the picture or graphic a generic representation—for example, an unnamed model representing an image?

3. OTHER COVER STORIES. What are the other cover stories? Taken as a whole, what themes, questions, problems, issues, or anxieties are the editors using to draw you into the magazine? How likely is this cover to draw *you* in? Why?

4. EXEMPLARY WOMEN. What real women are featured in the magazine? How well does this sample represent the range of women the editors might have told you about?

5. SOLVING PROBLEMS. Many magazine articles implicitly or explicitly offer advice on how to solve problems. What problems do the editors think their readers are or should be worried about? How does the magazine advise women to handle these problems—implicitly or explicitly?

6. ADVERTISEMENTS. Who advertises in this magazine? What messages do these ads promote? How are the ads related to the specific content of this issue of the magazine?

Some women journalists especially point out that there was always serious business in the "women's pages," or "society," "tempo," or "style" pages, as they came to be known in the 1970s, in an apparent response to the women's movement newspapers. Koky Dishon, former society editor at the *Milwaukee Journal* and the first woman on the masthead of the *Chicago Tribune,* has reported changes she observed in the women's pages. When she first went to the *Milwaukee Journal,* "slide-rule editing, based on Old Family and wealth, governed the size of photos and stories for weddings," but that changed when the newspaper ran side-by-side equal stories under one heading about the wedding of a CEO's daughter and the daughter of a factory worker in the same company.[19] Dishon has argued that the society pages were one place where a new breed of women professionals

Especially these days . . .
a man needs a good meal

I N PEACETIME, you owe it to yourself and your family to eat well-balanced, nourishing meals. In critical times like these, it's a patriotic duty.

The food you eat is the fuel which your body turns into *energy* — the energy needed for everything you do, physical and mental.

Your food supplies your body with the materials which *build it* and *keep it in repair*.

From your food, your body also gets the elements which help to *protect it from disease* and *keep it running smoothly*.

Everyone — desk worker, industrial worker, home worker — needs each day a varied selection of the right foods: milk, vegetables, fruits, eggs, meat or fish or poultry, cereals and breads, and fats. From these foods your body can obtain the nourishment it requires. Naturally, the amount of food you require varies with your activity. If your work is hard you can eat more of the foods high in energy value — bread, cereals, potatoes, fats, cheese and dried beans.

Nourishing meals not only help you feel better — they help you do better work and do it more easily. Even your spirits improve and you get more fun from leisure hours. Better eating habits can also build up your resistance to the illnesses which may become more widespread in times of war.

Housewives can do much to see that the members of their families get the nourishing meals they need. Where workers are on night shifts, it is important to arrange meals so that both the workers and the family have nutritious, satisfying meals at the right times. Try to arrange at least one meal so that the whole family may eat together.

To help you select the right amounts of the right foods, Metropolitan will send you on request a free booklet, 92-N, "Your Food — How Does It Rate For Health?"

World War II magazine advertisements showed women how they could contribute to the war effort. This example is from a 1942 *National Geographic*.

did make a difference, such as when the *Detroit Free Press* women's page editor ran a study of Detroit prostitutes on the women's page in 1967. The *Washington Post*'s "Style" section is well known for running sharp news stories. Even if the society pages (neé women's pages) have often run solid news stories, however, part of the problem has been that it is often the *only* part of the newspaper paying attention to women. According to Dishon, partly because the other news offices now work with those women-centered news ideas, and partly because of the retrenched climate of the 1990s, the women's/style pages have gone through some bad times more recently.

Even when news about women is not segregated, it is treated differently than news about men. Coverage of women has been more likely to mention personal appearance ("the petite blonde lawyer"), marital status, spouses, and children (Foreit et al., 1980). It is also more likely to mention the subject's sex explicitly. Few, if any, newspapers feel compelled to write about the "male police officer." Judging by the text and the pictures in newspapers, women are relatively few in number and of little importance. When they appear, they are usually either isolated as though they are a parochial special-interest group or pictured stereotypically.

After years of seeing trivializing coverage of female politicians in the press, a study of the coverage of women who entered the U.S. Congress as a result of the 1992 elections found it very good and unbiased on the whole (Carroll and Schreiber, 1997). On the other hand, an intriguing study of press treatment of male and female heads of state (e.g., Indira Gandhi and Rajiv Gandhi of India, Margaret Thatcher and John Major of Britain, Gro Harlem Brundtland and Jan Syse of Norway) found that women are less visible in the news. Also, while the media did not display simple stereotypes, they tended to frame news on women leaders through a very few themes: breakthroughs for women leaders, women leaders as outsiders, and women leaders as agents of change (Norris, 1997).

It is difficult for women to gain serious recognition for their accomplishments if the press does not cover them properly. Take the case of women's sports. On average, about 8% of the editorial and pictorial coverage in *Sports Illustrated* is about girls and women. An examination of all *Sports Illustrated* issues in 1989 showed a total of 644 photographs of females. Of those women, only 253—not even 40%—were athletes. The coverage of female athletes was concentrated into a very few sports, including especially tennis. Of the nonathletes, 36% were models in the annual swimsuit issue, 27% were male athletes' wives and girlfriends, 8% were male athletes' mothers, and 8% were other family members of male athletes. Models, especially those pictured purely for men to ogle, are more prevalent than athletes among the women who appear in the pages of the highest-circulation sports magazine in the country. In addition, the circulation of that magazine doubles every February for the annual swimsuit issue. Research also shows bias in television coverage of women's sports; for example, the camera tends to zoom in on body parts, simulating the eye of the ogling man—or adolescent boy (Daddario, 1992).

One continuing problem has been the trivializing and biased treatment of the women's movement. The mass media were quick to pick up on the image of feminists as "bra-burning libbers" and have often given less-than-serious, thorough coverage to the women's movement and women's political activities. Indeed, the media have tended to preserve the term *feminists* for a handful of prominent activists, helping to divorce the idea of feminism from the mainstream. The press covered different aspects of the women's movement differently, partly because of the editorial attitudes of the press, but partly because of the media strategies of different parts of the women's movement. Coverage does not just happen; as the

Women Pack Swedish Parliament

By Katarina Bjarvall
Associated Press

STOCKHOLM, Sweden — As Sweden's government shakes out following national elections, the biggest winners are turning out to be women. With 41 percent of the seats in parliament, they will hold more political power than in any other Western country.

"It's wonderful," Nalin Baksi, a 27-year-old Social Democrat, said Monday. Following Sunday's elections, she and more than 140 other women — many very young and taking office for the first time — will sit in the 349-seat Parliament.

After a campaign dominated by economic issues, Swedish voters dumped the conservative govern-

outside remains to be seen, said Olaf Ruin, a political scientist at Stockholm University

"I've always been skeptical about saying there is any fundamental difference between men and women in politics," Ruin said. "But probably so-called soft issues might be a little more emphasized."

While 41 percent of Parliament will be women — the exact number of seats is still not determined — they will hold half the Social Democrats' seats. Party leader Ingvar Carlsson has said he will appoint women to half the Cabinet posts.

"Men always want to calculate everything, and investigate, investigate," Baksi said. "We feel!"

This headline says that women *packed* the Parliament. How many women does it take to *pack* a legislature? How many men would it take?

large number of press agents and "spin doctors" employed today can attest, news coverage also depends on the strategies of the news subjects. In the early days of the women's movement, the part consisting of somewhat older, more publicly experienced women, for example, in NOW and the Women's Equity Action League (WEAL), pursued relations with the press that would lead to the coverage they wanted. Even if they were not as successful as they would have liked, they had more coverage and more serious coverage than the members of the younger, more radical wing of the movement, who were more skeptical about establishing links with traditional institutions (Barker-Plummer, 1995).

Reports on woman abuse, especially by men, tend to be written in a way that avoids assigning responsibility to men (Lamb and Keon, 1995). Research on coverage of abortion politics reveals bias in the mass media in general. A yearlong study of the four networks plus three major news magazines, beginning in mid-1991, shows that most of the stories were covered by men, and men's and women's coverage differed. Men's stories quoted antiabortion sources by a 65–35 margin, while women cited prochoice sources by a 56–44 margin.[20] Tiffany Devitt pointed out, when the *Los Angeles Times* published a lengthy article titled "Can Women Reporters Write Objectively on Abortion?" they never asked whether men can.[21]

Change is occurring. NPR reporter Sylvia Poggioli, especially well known for her superb reporting throughout the conflicts in the areas of former Yugoslavia, was one of the many women reporters from that region who helped make the world aware of the degree to which rape had become a systematic part of the so-called ethnic-cleansing campaigns. She thought that it was important that such a large proportion of the reporters in the area were women. "For centuries, rape has been treated sort of as a sideshow in wars. Usually, stories had always been done by men, for men. And women were very marginal."[22]

The Impact of the Mass Media

Demonstrating that the mass media present an androcentric or distorted view of women is not the same thing as demonstrating that they have an impact on the way people think about women. Millions of people watch the same television shows, but they do not think alike. What impact do the media have on people's views of women? How is this impact achieved?

Individuals do not receive the images and information transmitted through the media as clay receives thumbprints. People choose to attend to some messages or media and not others; if we are not interested in women's politics, we will not read articles on this topic even if they are in the paper. Psychologists refer to this process as *selective exposure*. Because of the less conscious process of *selective perception,* we tend to notice, highlight, or exaggerate certain details from among everything presented to us while ignoring or diminishing others. Perception of media images may depend on characteristics of the perceiver; as we saw in Chapter 3, people who are highly gender schematic see gender difference and stereotypes more readily than other people do. Perception also depends on context, including the social context in which someone is attending to the media. Thus, different people can interpret the same picture or text differently. Hence, assessing the impact of the medium is not a simple matter of decoding the message by looking at what is transmitted; we have to study the people exposed to the media messages also. Here, we turn first to research looking at media impact on children, then the impact on adults.

By the time children enter school, they have already spent more hours watching television than they will later spend in college classrooms. Most children spend more hours per week in front of the television than in school (Rickel and Grant, 1979). Children prefer to watch programs that contain characters of their own sex, and they watch more carefully and pay more attention when these characters act in gender-typed ways, almost as though they know what they are supposed to be learning (Sprafkin and Liebert, 1978). Gender-schematic boys pay more attention to males in televisions shows, and they watch programs with a higher proportion of males in them (Luecke-Aleksa, Anderson, and Collins, 1995). Children who watch a lot of television reflect more stereotypes in their gender views than those who watch little, and stereotyped views, especially those held by males, increase with age among heavy viewers (McGhee and Frueh, 1980; Signorielli and Lears, 1992).

In one study, some children saw a television show in which women appeared only in gender-typed roles, and other children saw one in which a woman was a police officer. Those who saw the latter show were more likely to think later that women really could be police officers. Similar studies yield similar results (Sprafkin and Liebert, 1978; Tuchman, 1978). In another study, children watched television advertisements portraying various toys as appropriate for one sex or the other. The children were then allowed to choose from a number of toys. Both girls and boys were more likely to pick toys that had been presented as gender appropriate than those that had been presented as gender inappropriate (Cobb, Stevens-Long, and Goldstein, 1982). These findings are not unusual.

Gender-based media messages also affect adults. People who watch more television are more stereotyped in their views, and they view themselves in more stereotyped terms (Ross, Anderson, and Wisocki, 1982). Sexist language and style in newspapers affect people's perception of female candidates for office. One study showed that sexist language and style in newspaper articles had a negative impact on readers' evaluations of the candidate for stereotypically masculine positions, such as sheriff, or relatively gender-neutral positions, but a positive effect on evaluations of female candidates for "feminine" offices, such as president of the League of Women Voters (Dayhoff, 1983). In other words, linguistic sexism highlights and exaggerates stereotypically feminine details, thus making the woman being described appear less appropriate for "masculine" or even "gender-neutral" positions and more appropriate for "feminine" positions. (Language and gender are discussed more extensively in Chapter 10.)

One of the problems in detecting media effects is the difficulty in gauging the effects of *absence*. In addition to the problem of seeing just stereotypes of themselves in the mass media, what does it mean to girls' and women's self-image not to see girls or women depicted at all? If women are rarely highlighted as important figures in world affairs or sports, where can women get the idea that they can excel? Alfred Kidwasser and Michelle Wolf (1992) have asked the same question with respect to gay and lesbian adolescents. Very few characters in prime-time television are described as gay. Kidwasser and Wolf ask what that means for gay and lesbian adolescents, who may not feel comfortable talking to anyone and can gain no self-image from television, other than invisibility.

The Commercial Media

The mass media are filled with messages aimed at selling us something. Public broadcasting is no exception; sponsors are mentioned not just to thank them for their support but also to show us they are nice companies to buy from. Everywhere, we see billboards, bumper stickers, and even T-shirts promoting various products. Our mailboxes—including sometimes our electronic mailboxes—are stuffed with advertisements and sometimes trial products. Advertisements fill the programs for concerts and plays. The packaging of food and other items in stores is designed to advertise the contents. Newsletters or surveys from our representatives in Congress or our state legislatures are also advertisements.

Women and gender have played important roles in the history of commercial communication—advertising. Advertising began to develop as serious business with the rise of industrialism in the 19th century. By the 1920s, it was professionalized, and later it became increasingly technical and scientific in its approach.

In his history of advertising in the United States, Stuart Ewen has argued that "the advertising which attempted to create the dependable mass of consumers required by modern industry often did so by playing upon the fears and frustrations evoked by mass society—offering mass produced visions of individualism by which people could extricate themselves from the mass" (1976, 45). The goal of advertising is to make people feel that they need or want a specific product. An advertisement for a particular brand of vaginal douche or cornflakes has to convince people, first, that they need the product, and second, that they want this brand, rather than others. Advertisers therefore transmit the message that without this product, potential customers will be less healthy, attractive, happy, secure, or caring than if they purchase the product. Advertisements are aimed at specific audiences, and the message is designed to fit the audience; these messages play on or even create the fears, needs, or desires of specific groups of people. Because of this power to shape emotions, they can have a profound influence on creating, or at least maintaining, specific gender and sexual norms.

Some of the first important efforts to direct advertising at women occurred in the late 19th century, as women took up the role of being the chief domestic consumers—fuel for the growing economy. Clothing manufacturers had to create markets for one of the most important new creations of late-19th-century production: ready-to-wear clothes. The clothing industry designed department stores—sometimes called "fashion palaces"—to convince women that they could be elegant and fashionable wearing "off the rack" clothing. These stores helped women by providing "experts" to help women make the right choices. As mentioned previously, women's magazines were filled with fashion plates showing women what they should wear. In such advertisements, the function of providing information merges with the sales pitch. Today, women still turn to magazine advertising to find out what the fashions are. In many women's magazines, almost all the pictures and many of the articles are in fact advertisements, even when they do not appear to be. Messages presented as "information" or "advice" are often actually advertisements (McCracken, 1993).

Although critics often underscore the impact of advertising on preserving traditional roles, both the creation of new products and industries' motivation to expand their markets often pushed advertisers in the direction of adapting traditional gender roles, even if they did so in limited ways. For instance, once the newly invented bicycle ceased to be a mere curiosity and showed promise of being a chic form of transportation, the bicycle industry squarely faced the rumor that women's bicycle riding violated their femininity and encouraged masturbation. The industry advertisers faced and reframed the practice in health terms, citing its beneficial effects on women's fitness (Garvey, 1995).

For advertising to sell products, it must reflect the social values of the time; it cannot create needs out of thin air. For instance, to convince people that bicycling promoted women's fitness depended on the existence of a growing view that women should be fit, at least for the purposes of being fit mothers. At the turn into the 20th century, when science and progress were the catchwords of the day, advertising directed at women began to play on these principles, especially the growing attraction of scientific home management, home economics. Since then, advertising has presented itself as a source of expert information about how women can keep their families healthy, their homes germ-free, and their households efficiently managed. The promotion of personal-hygiene products continues this tradition today, alerting women to germs and health hazards they never knew existed—indeed, health hazards that do not exist.

Part of the idea of scientific management, and certainly a desire on the part of women loaded down with domestic drudgery, is to lighten the burden of housework. The promotion of "labor-saving devices" for women—from gas stoves to electric appliances to fancy cleansing agents and Hamburger Helper—promises a healthier and more efficient household, as well as release from the drudgery of housework to spend more time (and happier, more relaxed time) with the family or in other activities. The promise that these devices will save labor remains unfulfilled, as many studies of time use and technology have shown (see, e.g., Robinson, 1980; Vanek, 1980). Homemakers today spend at least as much time on housework as housewives did in the 1920s. In his study in the mid-1970s, John Robinson (1980) found that so-called labor-saving devices make remarkably little difference in the time women spend on housework. Despite the claims of advertisers, a microwave oven reduces the average workday by only 10 minutes, a clothes dryer does so by only 5 minutes, and a vacuum cleaner by only 1 minute. A freezer *adds* 6 minutes to the working day, a washing machine adds 4 minutes, and a dishwasher and a sewing machine each add 1 minute.

If these figures seem implausible, consider the effects of these goods on a household. A woman with a washer and dryer does not wash the same amount of clothes in less time; she washes clothes more often in about the same time. Special new kitchen appliances, such as food processors, lead people to do different kinds of cooking from the type they did without them. Although Stuart Ewen is right in suggesting that, "rather than viewing the transformations in household work as labor-saving, it is perhaps more useful to view them as labor-changing" (1976, 163), the voice of the expert in advertisements convinces women otherwise.[23]

Advertising also incorporates political rhetoric and images in interesting ways. The 1920s witnessed the first generation of advertisement campaigns for diverse products incorporating feminist symbols and rhetoric and images of emancipated women. The infamous 1970s Virginia Slims campaign, "You've come a long way, baby," hearkens back to a 1929 campaign by the American Tobacco Company that attempted to convince women to smoke. In the early 1970s, women's style magazines incorporated feminist images to sell the products advertised in them (Budgeon and Currie, 1995).

During the two world wars, business subsumed patriotism into selling products by developing the theme that women's efforts could help win the wars. The promotional voice of the expert urged women to participate in programs to save resources needed for the war efforts. Advertisements showed women how to rearrange their household management to do their part and, incidentally, how this could be accomplished only by using Product X. Particularly during World War II, advertisements promoted the virtues of women working in nontraditional jobs for the sake of the war. They also showed how these good women used the right products; even Rosie the Riveter could keep her hands lovely and feminine by using special hand-care products. The images of working women increased in advertisements during World War II, although not to the same degree as these roles actually did expand in the economy. After the war, advertisements showed how happy women were to be back in the household caring for their families, and images of women in the workplace declined again (Lewis and Neville, 1995).

Commercial images remain gender typed. Television commercials directed at children include many more boys than girls, and girls play passive and gender-typed roles. Boys are more likely to be in fantasy settings or settings outside the home; girls are usually at home (Macklin and Kolbe, 1984; Smith, 1994). Women in television commercials generally play one of three roles: mother, housekeeper, or aesthetic interest (Mamay and Simpson, 1981). Women are usually pictured inside the house, especially in the kitchen or bathroom. Women also appear as sex objects in advertisements directed at men; they are draped over cars in revealing outfits, for example, as though for an extra price, they could be purchased as optional equipment, along with the air-conditioning. A content analysis of 1,480 television commercials revealed that although by the late 1980s, women were shown more frequently outside the home and in a wider range of occupations than they used to be, little else had changed (Ferrante, Haynes, and Kingsley, 1988).

A study of the content of advertising in magazines from the 1950s through the 1980s shows that advertisements in general-interest magazines depict women in employment roles more than women's magazines do. Men do not show up as much in advertisements in women's magazines as they do in general-interest magazines. The women portrayed in magazine ads are disproportionately very young and, of course, very thin. Changes brought about by the women's movement did not make advertisers reduce the degree to which women appear as decorative objects, but the reason for this lack of change is that so much advertising is devoted to beauty products. As researchers have noted, following the changes in the average woman's roles, "in advertising, she has exited the home and stepped up to the department store beauty counter" (Busby and Leichty, 1993, 259).

Advertising images, of course, do not play just on images of gender, but also on images of race. An analysis of cigarette and alcohol ads in magazines in the early 1990s showed similar use of erotic and romantic imagery to sell these products among African-Americans and Whites, but while White people were more often shown at work, African-Americans were more often shown at leisure. The advertisements with White models emphasized masculinity, while those with Black models emphasized femininity (Reid, King, and Kreshel, 1994). This may be because some cigarette companies consciously targeted young Black women as an undertapped market for their products.

The portrayal of expertise and authority in contemporary advertising is also gender based. The expert in television commercials (often the unseen voice-over) is usually a man, even in commercials aimed at women, and even when all visuals are of women (Mamay and Simpson, 1981). Expertise took an interesting twist with the rise of the women's movement and objections to commercial sexism. Many advertisements emphasized women's expertise, but this expertise was demonstrated in vignettes showing male incompetence at household work. In these portrayals, men rather than women were the objects of the jokes, but the underlying message was the same: Housework is for women.

Some changes in advertising were brought about by law. In the late 1960s, for example, it became illegal for "help wanted" columns in newspapers to categorize jobs as "male" or "female." Women's organizations have exerted pressure on companies with sexist advertisements by, for example, writing letters and urging boycotts. The underlying problem, however, is that companies would not use gender-typed techniques if they did not sell products. But they do, so they do.

The Cultural and Artistic Media

The mass and artistic media are not usually analyzed in the same context. However, the arts, like other media, are organized in social institutions structured partly by gender. Indeed, it is not always easy to distinguish between the mass media and the artistic media. The arts are often presented *through* the mass media. In addition to situation comedies, game and crime shows, news broadcasts, and self-help shows, television and radio also present theater, films, music, poetry readings, and art history. In addition to soap operas, television also may present the more classic genre of opera.[24] The recent spread of cable television has increased this overlap.

The important similarity, however is that the mass and artistic media are both media of communication. They are channels through which some people express themselves and their perceptions of events, people, ideas, and feelings and to which a much larger number of people turn to share, learn about, and possibly evaluate these perceptions. Both types of media are part of the cultural traffic of society, their appeal or utility based in part on the relationship of both form and content to surrounding cultural symbols, ideology, and social events. The arts, like the mass media, are often managed by large, bureaucratic organizations with a wide range of goals besides merely getting the message across. Under most circumstances, their products must sell or gain acceptance in the target audience.

Thus, publishing and movie houses, museums, theaters, and concert halls are all institutions that can be analyzed in terms of their relationship to the sex/gender system in much the same ways that other social institutions can be analyzed. The arts world has been gender segregated, and women have been valued less than men. The images reflected through the arts, especially the high-status arts, are often gender typed.

A full exposition of gender and the artistic and cultural media is beyond the scope of this book. Hence, this section only briefly analyzes some art and cultural forms, which emphasize important themes. The discussion focuses first on women's roles in the arts and then on some of the gender messages transmitted through the arts, taking examples from many different areas of artistic media.

Women as Artists

Anyone can participate in almost any of the arts as an amateur, but becoming recognized by others, participating in the great arts organizations, and certainly being able to make a living from the arts generally require access to training, the institutions of creation and distribution, and audiences. Historians of women in the arts suggest that access has been the greatest stumbling block for women. As Linda Nochlin (1971) has suggested, the often-asked question "Why are there no great women artists?" can be answered in several ways: (a) There have been, but they were not recognized; (b) there have been, but they have been forgotten; (c) there have been some, but not many because women were not allowed to be artists; and (d) there have been some, but not many because women are not able enough.

History offers ample evidence that women who might have developed their artistic talents were blocked in their efforts to seek the necessary training. For a long time, women were not admitted to the great academies for the graphic arts in most places. They were excluded from one of the most important aspects of art training: life drawing from a nude model, especially male nude models.[25] Aspiring female musicians were not allowed into many of the major music academies and courses. Schools of architecture were reluctant to admit women until recently, and from 1915 to 1942, aspiring female architects could train only at one gender-segregated institution. (Berlo, 1976). Although many great women writers have been well known, in the late 18th and early 19th centuries, many found it easier to be accepted if they used a male pen name.[26]

It is still relatively difficult for women to gain access to many artistic fields. Although about 50% of all contemporary graphic artists are women, women have more trouble getting their work reviewed in mainstream art magazines and newspapers. Women are also underrepresented among teachers at professional art schools, museum administrators, and artists shown in galleries and museums.

Women musicians have experienced a long history of discrimination, with some recent changes. Until the 20th century, orchestras generally refused to play music composed by women, to admit women instrumentalists, and, until very recently, to play under female conductors (Jepson, 1975–1976; Levy, 1983). Only certain instruments were regarded as acceptable for 19th-century women, including especially the keyboard, guitar, and harp. Women's posture was a key issue (once a stand was developed for the cello, women could play, as long as they "rode sidesaddle"), and ladies had to avoid instruments that required them to contort their faces. (The flute, requiring only a pout, was fine.) In any case, an 1895 issue of *Scientific American* declared that women did not have the stamina to be orchestral musicians (Macleod, 1993).

All-women orchestras gained in popularity between the 1880s and 1930s, although they usually lacked the instruments designated as unladylike (leaving the brass and reed sections a bit hollow). Even by the early 1970s, none of the 159 orchestras of the Symphony Orchestra League had a woman music director or

conductor. Sarah Caldwell and Margaret Hillis became regularly appointed conductors only by founding their own orchestras (Jepson, 1975–1976). The New
York Philharmonic Orchestra did not include a female instrumentalist until 1966.
In an infamous incident, the Vienna Philharmonic admitted a woman player—a
harpist—for the first time in 1997 and agreed that it would open auditions to
women even though it thought the musicians' maleness contributed to the orchestra's "special sound." In fact, the harpist had played with the Vienna Philharmonic
for years, but her name was not listed, and photographs of the orchestra always
excluded her.[27]

The lack of orchestra seats for women changed when orchestras introduced
blind auditions, in which the judges could not see the player. (In fact, blind auditions are often blind only in the early rounds because judges want to make sure the
performers have no distracting playing habits.) One study confirms that blind
auditions account for one third to one half of the increase in the rising proportion
of new female hires in orchestras between 1970 and 1996.[28] Nonetheless, blind
auditions could not change the fact that women still tend to be steered away from
some instruments (Macleod, 1993). Women are now roughly half the instrumentalists in metropolitan orchestras, although their numbers in the major orchestras
are much fewer.

As in other fields, "the higher the fewer" is still the case. Although women
constitute a large majority of music teachers of children, they are a minority on
university faculties in music and at the major academies. On the other hand,
although classical music composition has been dominated by men, women have
been particularly important in the blues, jazz, folk, and some other pop genres.
Even in the traditionally male-dominated fields, women are now achieving recognition. In 1983, for example, Ellen Taafe Zwillich became the first woman com-
poser to win the Pulitzer Prize in music.

Women have had a difficult time breaking into film direction. In 1990,
women were only 20% of the members of the Directors Guild of America, and
they directed only 5% of the feature films that year. Women's experience as television directors also demonstrates the principle of "the higher the fewer": Women
constituted 12% of the directors of half-hour shows, 9% of the directors of hour-
long shows, less than 3% of the directors of made-for-television movies, and none
of the directors of miniseries. On average, female directors earned a little more
than half of what male directors earned.[29] Women directors feel the subtle effects
of discrimination against them. Martha Coolidge (*Ramblin' Rose*), for example,
has said, "You have to look for it to see it, because it's around the corner. It's the
people who aren't interested in having a meeting with me or other women. It's
the producers who are friends or business associates who don't think of you for
something considered a man's piece of material. It's the look of hesitation that
comes across their faces when you suggest maybe they should."[30] Even actresses
may be implicated in the discrimination against women directors. Dyan Cannon,
an actress, recalled, "I remember once when I was doing a soap opera, I was upset
when a woman walked on the set to direct. I wanted a man to direct me, because
Daddy ran the house."[31]

Women also have difficulty rising through the ranks of the management of arts
industries. Again, consider the case of film. Film producer Lynda Obst (*The Fisher*

King) expressed the view of many women in the film industry when she said, "It is clearly the case for both women executives and producers that, reputation for reputation, experience for experience, we are not on the same levels as our male counterparts."[32] Women are not paid the same or given the same opportunities or clout. Only 2 out of 20 major entertainment companies could claim that 30% or more of their top executives were women. As in many other fields, women sometimes learn to devalue themselves and do not demand as much as men do. As one woman who runs an entertainment law firm said, "I have represented many women executives who find it so difficult to imagine that they deserve what they get paid. Women think they're so lucky. They're afraid someone will get angry if they ask for more." She thinks that "women have a hard time working as little as men do and taking the money as their due."[33]

Women's collective fortunes are better, of course, in fields such as acting and singing that specifically call for women artists. American dance is a field in which women such as Isadora Duncan, Martha Graham, and Twyla Tharp had a major impact; in fact, only in recent decades have men become as important as women in dance. We can single out names of successful women in most fields of art, but we cannot escape the conclusion that in many of the important fields, women have not been treated as seriously as men.

This observation leads to the question of how people judge women as artists. In many fields, opinion leaders have argued that women are incapable of greatness, by their nature. In music, it has been thought that women lack the physical strength to be great pianists, the strength of character to be conductors, and the imagination to be composers (Levy, 1983). Could a woman lead a performance of such masculine works as Beethoven's Fifth Symphony (Jepson, 1975–1976)? Many music professionals have thought that women do not have the mental capacity to teach music theory because it is so technical and mathematical. Architecture critics have worried about women's inferior spatial perception, as have painting and sculpture critics. Literary critics attack women's personalism, lack of strength, and inability to write like a man. Observers often interpret women's work through gender stereotypes: Regardless of the field, they notice its *interior* dimensions, *intuitiveness,* and *sensitivity*, and any links with other artists that might mark it as *derivative*. If the artist is a feminist, critics either notice the work's *shrillness* or compliment it for not being shrill, as though in the normal course of events, it must be.

Do the works of male and female artists differ? Because men's and women's experiences and training are different, it would make sense for their artistic expressions to be different. Portions of the art community go beyond this, however, and argue that differences exist and are rooted in the different sexual natures of men and women. Even people in the mainstream of the arts have used these differences as an argument for women's inferiority. Many radical feminists, especially those who argue for a special "women's aesthetic," also see differences springing from nature, but they place a positive value on "feminine art." Evidence of systematic differences has been elusive, especially where observers do gender-blind analysis of different works of art to see whether they can distinguish male from female (Melosh, 1991).

Many feminist artists and art critics have called for the art world to give more serious attention to the forms that have been the special domain of women, including quilting, embroidery, weaving, and certain kinds of pottery. These forms have been virtually excluded from art history courses, books, and museums, not because they have been designed and made by women but because they have been considered *crafts*, rather than fine arts. Crafts—and therefore much of women's artistic work—have lower status in the art world than the fine arts. The distinction turns on purpose and function: Crafts spring from the practical purposes of feeding, clothing, and sheltering, for example, and arts are "divorced from use, are 'useless' in any practical sense" (Hedges and Wendt, 1980, 2). In music, there is also a distinction between serious, high forms of music, and lower forms, such as folk, blues, rock, and pop. An investigation of women and the arts thus raises some of the most fundamental questions about the nature and role of the arts in society: What is the distinction among arts, crafts, and other forms of expression? What is a high form of art? What function do the arts play in society?

Pat Mainardi's classic essay on quilts passionately underscores the absurdity of excluding these beautiful creations from the scholarly and archival treatment given other art forms. Women's intricate quilts were "likely to be the only art that most of the populace saw, certainly the only art most of them possessed" (Mainardi, 1982, 337). She has also pointed out that historians have interpreted quilts through a set of sexist blinders. First, they are ignored or dismissed as arts, largely because they were functional, done by women of all social standing, from enslaved African-American women to wealthy upper-class women. Second, they are viewed not as the prize work of skilled individual artists, but as the anonymous production of collectivities, even when the artist's name was embroidered into the work. Mainardi has pointed out that "quilting bees" were, for the most part, occasions at which many women would assist the designer of the quilt; except for "album quilts," these were no more collective products than were the paintings designed and mostly executed by famous male painters and completed in detail by their assistants and apprentices. Finally, Mainardi has argued that while the materials used by the quilters are important, historians have looked at quilts more to learn about the technical aspects of the textiles, rather than as historical art pieces, which she has described as "somewhat akin to a work on Rembrandt which focuses on his paints and mediums while quickly passing over the paintings themselves" (Mainardi, 1982, 343). Women's crafts, like the other arts, have shared symbols, forms, and traditions and are manifest in unique displays of individual creativity and artistry.

Contemporary analysis casts into doubt the appropriateness of making such distinctions between art that is utilitarian and art that is for aesthetic pleasure alone. A review of the history of the arts and the social roles of the arts and artists suggests that these dichotomies are highly suspect. The fine arts are of utilitarian, as well as aesthetic, value in many senses. Humans need food and shelter, but they also need sensory stimulation. Studies of the effects of sensory deprivation on people show that sense stimulation is almost as necessary to survival as food and water. Some of the greatest fine music in the West originated as church music, designed to create a mood and help people praise, glorify, mourn, and celebrate. Do these utilitarian purposes diminish the value of Bach's cantatas, Beethoven's *Mass in B Minor*, or Verdi's *Requiem*? If not, how can one argue that women's lullabies and Native American women's healing songs are necessarily lower forms of music simply because they were composed for specific purposes (Jaskoski, 1981)? Is there such a thing as thoroughly useless art?

Women play crucial roles in the everyday life of the arts. They decorate their houses, sing lullabies, and tell stories to their children. In some fields—such as singing, dancing, acting, and writing poetry and novels—there have been many great and famous women. In other fields, it does not take long to uncover the names of women who should be remembered along with their famous male counterparts. Not all arts are the same; we probably do not want to rank the flower arrangement a woman puts on her dining room table with the sculpture of Barbara Hepworth. Nonetheless, the traditional sex/gender system is reinforced by the segregation of men and women into different artistic fields, the discriminatory treatment of women artists and women's arts, and the denigration of the functions of women's arts in the artistic and cultural media of communication.

Gender and Sexuality as Subjects of Art

The treatment of gender in the arts is related to the values, frustrations, and goals of the times. The sexual tensions and jokes and the dominant women present in Restoration comedies reflect that period of uncertainty and changing roles. In the 19th century, these formerly popular plays were considered too lewd and unsuitable for decent people. Cuckolding was a favorite theme of the Restoration, when everything generally worked out well in the end, but by the 19th century, the philandering woman became the fallen woman, and a fictional female who committed adultery usually died for her sins (often by her own hand), or at least went mad.

Although examples could be drawn from any art form, the 20th-century history of film demonstrates powerfully the connections between art and social history with respect to gender. In the earliest days of film, moving pictures were especially popular among urban immigrants. As Elizabeth Ewen (1980) has shown, movies were often about common people, and working-class immigrants flocked to neighborhood movie houses to see people acting out their own tensions and problems. Movies presented themes of gender and sexuality from both feminist and antifeminist perspectives. After World War I, the growing film industry increasingly reflected more middle-class views and perspectives. As the power of film was recognized, there was more pressure to consider the potential effects of them on audiences. Movies were considered to be potentially powerful tools of assimilation, for example, capable of teaching immigrant women how to be good American housewives.

An important shift in film images of women occurred between the late 1930s and the 1950s. In the late 1930s and early 1940s, there were many significant female parts, often showing women as strong, independent, employed, and even professional. After World War II, this began to change, as social values stressed women's return to the home and domestic values. In the 1950s, the strong women went home, became birdbrained sex objects, or both. In the immediate post–World War II era, the remaining strong women were often dangerous temptresses leading men astray in film noir.

Parallel historical shifts can also be seen in other art forms, both high and low, such as in the detective novel (Fritz and Hevener, 1979). Before the 1960s, women detectives in these novels were often not really detectives; they were amateurs who solved crimes, and they were usually unattractive or elderly and not employed. Now, most women detectives are employed, often as detectives or police officers, and they have become younger and more physically attractive.

Even traditional fairy tales are filled with androcentric norms in a form that can teach the young. After reviewing the lives of fairy-tale princesses, one writer concluded, "Nobody in her right mind could possibly want to be a fairy tale princess" (Waelti-Walters, 1979, 180). Most fairy-tale princesses are passive victims or merely decorative or must die in order to be loved. If they resist these roles, they are generally portrayed as evil or mad. Although there have been some improvements in children's literature, with publishers making conscious efforts to incorporate into their lists more active, positive representations of women and minority group members, not all is well. A study comparing the original Nancy Drew books of the 1920s and 1930s with those written more recently shows that poor Nancy is not what she was. Whereas in the early days, she was described only as "attractive," a more recent edition noted that "the tight jeans looked great on her long, slim legs, and the green sweater complemented her strawberry-blond hair." She is now a much more stereotypical character. Things she surely would have been able to do herself decades ago are now done for her by boys. She seems to require more help from them than used to be the case.[34]

One of the most interesting sites for investigating the relationship between gendered representations in art and the sociopolitical context in which they were created was the set of publicly funded art projects initiated through the New Deal programs of the 1930s, including especially the Section of Fine Arts, which sponsored sculpture and painting; the Federal Theater Project (FTP), which sponsored the writing and production of plays across the country; and the Federal Art Project, which was a public-relief program for artists. Barbara Melosh's (1991) gender analysis of the productions of the Section and FTP reveals fascinating dimensions to the depiction of gender in light of the political ideology of the New Deal. Farm families were often presented as "comradely" cooperation between strong men and women, while depictions of industrial work, projecting an image of "manly" labor, "consistently excluded and hence made invisible women's productive work, privileging the male domains of craft and heavy industry" (Melosh, 1991, 83). The antiwar art common in these projects rejected "the sentimental notion of the home as refuge" and "called women to the heroic role of pacifist mothers" (Melosh, 1991, 229). The radical aspects of the New Deal political vision often recast women's roles, while still subordinating them in certain settings, such as industrial labor and politics.

At times, the sexual and gender politics of art have erupted into major battles. One of the best-known of these controversies involved a massive work by Judy Chicago, titled *The Dinner Party,* consisting of a large, three-sided dinner table decorated with place settings constructed of various women's arts and crafts, representing 39 different well-known women. The names of 999 other women are embedded in the tablecloth and table base. Many viewers and critics have been disturbed by the distinctly vaginal form of much of the design. Whereas critics seem relatively undisturbed by phallic iconography and symbolism, the graphic themes of Chicago's work repulsed and even angered them. Established art critics are less likely to ask "Is it art?" of androcentric art, because androcentric art is considered normal. They ask "Is it art?" of gynocentric art, because gynocentric art is interpreted as political and therefore not artistic. The role of sexuality and feminism in the arts became extremely contentious in the 1980s and 1990s, when conservatives attacked the very notion of funding a National Endowment for the Arts, partly because of issues relating to gender and sexual politics.

One of the most contentious debates in feminist discussion of representations of women revolves around portrayals of sexuality and the erotic and their relationship to violence and pornography. Many feminist critics argue both that violence against women is central to dominant male definitions of the erotic and, especially, that pornography usually establishes dominance over or abuse of women as pleasurable, even to the victim. Advertisements for films often use an eroticized image of a terrified woman as the key selling image. In films, during incidents of terror against women, such as rape, the camera usually takes the *assailant's* viewpoint rather than the victim's; viewers watch the victim being terrified, rather than the assailant being terrifying. A study of a random sample of pornographic movies available in family video rental stores in southern California found that over half of the explicit sexual scenes were predominantly concerned with domination and exploitation (Cowan, Lee, Levy, and Snyder, 1988). A considerable amount of pornography involves children. In some films, women are literally mutilated or (in "snuff" films) killed.

What impact do these images of violence have on audiences? Many researchers have investigated the relationship between viewing violent pornography and engaging in violence against women, such as rape. The results are often contradictory. A meta-analysis of many of these studies found that pictorial nudity *reduces* aggression, and that viewing media depictions of nonviolent sexual interaction increases aggressive behavior, and media depictions of violent sexual activity increases aggression even more (Allen, D'Alessio, and Brezgel, 1995).

Why might this connection occur? One hypothesis, derived from social-learning theory, suggests that the violence effects are a matter of straightforward learning. If that were the case, however, why would increases in aggression occur from *non*violent depictions of sexual interactions? According to an alternative theory, called "excitation transfer," the point is not that viewers are simply learning or imitating violence, but that viewing the sexual depictions, especially if they are violent, puts viewers in an aroused or excited state (notice *aroused* and *excited* do not necessarily refer to pleasurable sensations here, just arousal), and those who are already predisposed to hostility will transfer that excitation into aggression. As described further in Chapter 11, many cognitive theories of sexuality emphasize the degree to which sexuality involves not just *feelings* but also the *interpretation* of feelings, which can make sense of the feelings in a variety of ways. According to the excitation-transfer theory, general predispositions or a particular context can lead to the transfer of a given episode of arousal from sexuality to aggression. Meta-analysis of research finds mixed results for both theories, suggesting elements of truth in both (Allen, D'Alessio, and Brezgel, 1995).

Although relatively few studies find conclusive evidence that pornographic images cause violence in a consistent direct way, many argue that they can be a contributing factor, especially in the long run. Research on long-term exposure to video violence against women found that as male viewers saw more such violence over time, their anxious and other negative reactions to it diminished, and they even perceived less violence in the videos than they had at first. The researchers concluded that exposure to violent (but not nonviolent) pornographic images desensitizes men to violence against women over the long haul (Donnerstein, Linz, and Penrod, 1987).[35] Also, depictions of violence against women have a direct effect on women: It heightens their feelings of disempowerment (Reid and Finchilescu, 1995).

The 1980s and 1990s witnessed a heated debate over what to do about artistic and mass-culture representations that devalue, objectify, and eroticize women and perhaps encourage violence against them. Feminists share broad agreement that both sexual objectification of women and sexual abuse of women are wrong and that societies need to seek means of eliminating these practices and of helping the victims. Feminists have also tended to agree that these representations and the industries that produce them are part of a larger system of oppression of women.[36] They do not, however, agree on what should be done about pornography. Some feminists, most notably Andrea Dworkin (1979) and Catherine MacKinnon (1979), have argued that pornography should be made illegal. Activists in many cities have worked to create ordinances that would ban pornography. One such ordinance was passed but vetoed in Minneapolis; another was enacted but overturned by a judge in Indianapolis.[37]

Many feminists have been opposed to this strategy for combating pornography, and some have questioned some claims of the antipornography activists (Burstyn, 1985; Segal and McIntosh, 1992; Vance, 1984). Although these feminists have proposed various questions, the main question has to do with issues of censorship, civil liberties, and freedom of expression. There is a long history of attempts to regulate representations of sexuality (Kendrick, 1987), most of which stem from conservative and moralistic views seeking to regulate people's expression and behavior according to a very limited, usually homophobic and sexist view. Many fear that defining the boundaries and limits of censorship of speech and other forms of expression is extremely difficult and dangerous once it has begun. The assaults on the National Endowment for the Arts in the late 1990s were rallied largely by reference to art that many people, especially religious conservatives, find entirely offensive and obscene.

Can people be sure of always knowing the difference between pornography and other depictions of sexuality? Is there an objective standard for identifying the demeaning? Consider the painting by Monica Sjoo, *God Giving Birth,* which pictures, in primitive style, an imposing standing female figure, surrounded by the heavens, with a head crowning from her vagina.[38] The artist was threatened with an obscenity charge. Indeed, many feminists and others have argued that those most likely to be hurt by censorship of the sort proposed are feminists, gay and lesbian artists and activists, and others who have traditionally fought against censorship.

Analysis of the nude female figure in painting offers important insights into both the relationship of art to the surrounding gender culture, including its androcentrism, and the difficulty—if not impossibility—of straightforward and undebatable interpretation. Feminist and mainstream analysis of the nude painting suggests that it is "a paradigm of Western high culture with its network of contingent values: civilization, edification, and aesthetic pleasure." However, it "is also a sign of those other, more hidden properties of patriarchal culture—that is, possession, power, and subordination" (Nead, 1992, 283). Different "nudes" will evoke these differing aspects to different degrees, even to the point that some may be regarded as high art but some as simply pornographic. The male nude is judged by different standards, especially since the invention of the stone fig leaf. As Nead (1992) has pointed out, however, these meanings are located not intrinsically in the nude, but in the larger cultural definitions that frame the way the nude is seen. In Melosh's discussion of New Deal art, she underscored the multiple views:

> Insiders viewed female nudes as part of a revered tradition of Western art, but the lay public sometimes saw them as pictures of naked women and an affront to public decency. In a few cases, . . . administrators defended nude figures even in the face of considerable public outcry; often, they chose to avert possible controversy by censoring nudity. (Melosh, 1991, 205)

In the federal art projects, the progressive view generally called for greater openness to representations of sexuality, although not, of course, violence and abuse.

The debate has sometimes become bitter. One such incident occurred in the course of a dispute among feminists surrounding the contents of an art exhibit displayed as part of a conference on prostitution, sponsored by the *Michigan Journal of Gender and Law* in 1992. In this dispute, Catherine MacKinnon summarized her view of the anticensorship argument, saying, "My real view . . . is that this is a witchhunt by First Amendment fundamentalists who are persecuting and blacklisting dissidents like Andrea Dworkin and myself as arts censors. I don't see it as a fight within feminism but a fight between those who wish to end male supremacy and those who wish to do better under it."[39] The dispute profoundly concerns the definition of art, sexuality, violence, and feminism.

At least at the margins, pornography and its power are in some ways in the eyes of the beholder, but the way in which those eyes *see* the pornography, its meaning, and its power depends on larger cultural definitions and on the institutional and power arrangements within which people view the pornography and the pornographers, their clients, and their victims. Carol Duncan (1992) reported on a fascinating experience in which she was trying to understand the nature of art museums in general and of New York's Museum of Modern Art (MoMA) in particular; she especially sought to understand how the structure of the museums' internal spaces and collections both reflects and maintains gender power structures. She began by sharing her curiosity about why modern art, so devoted to abstract forms, so often focuses on—even seems to obsess about—female bodies and parts of female bodies, all of them emphasizing the *female body,* abstracted from the women who might occupy them. "Why then has art history not accounted for this intense preoccupation with socially and sexually available female bodies? What, if anything, do nudes and whores have to do with modern art's heroic renunciation of representation?" (Duncan, 1992, 348).

Among the important paintings in the MoMA collection Duncan described, Willem de Kooning's *Woman I* and *II* have a very special place in the layout of the museum.[40] At about the time Duncan was thinking about this problem, she saw a large ad on a bus stop for *Penthouse* magazine. The image on the poster strongly reminded her of the images she had been considering in the art museum, except that someone had scrawled "For Pigs" on the *Penthouse* poster. Duncan had a camera with her and decided to photograph the poster, an act that made her feel uncomfortable, given that she was conspicuous on a street, photographing an ad for *pornography*. As she took the photo, a group of young boys jumped into the picture and let her know she should not be photographing that picture. Duncan reflected,

> Apparently, the same culture that had conditioned me to feel uneasy about what I was doing made *them* uneasy with it. Boys this age know very well what's in *Penthouse*. Knowing what's in *Penthouse* is knowing something for men to know. . . . I think these boys were trying to protect the capacity of the ad to empower them as men by preventing me from appropriating an image of it. (Duncan, 1992, 355, emphasis in original)

That even these young boys knew that the abstracted female body is for *them* to gaze at and possess, and not for a woman, made Duncan conclude that "in certain situations a female gaze can *pollute* pornography." In fact, their "harassment of [Duncan] constituted an attempt at gender policing, something adult men routinely do to women on city streets" (1992, 355).

This observation led Duncan's thoughts back to the art she saw in MoMA. The haunting similarity between the "high art" nudes, many of which make women large and threatening, and the "pornographic" versions, despite the fact that the high art versions are very abstracted, transformed the museum into a public place that "[affirms] to male viewers their membership in the more powerful gender group" and "[reminds] women that their status as members of the community, their right to its public space . . . is not quite the same" (Duncan, 1992, 356–357).

So what are the differences between high art and other cultural expressions? What is the difference between pornography and erotic images? What is woman's place in cultural expression?

Media of Change?

In this chapter, we have looked at three overlapping types of media of communication: mass media, commercial media (advertising), and artistic media. In each of these, we find evidence of the segregation of women, often into lower-status positions. In each, we find that the mainstream of the media often projects androcentric views of society and a lower status for women. At the same time, we can find women who have had a powerful impact on society through these media. We also find that women working in these fields have organized to look at women's roles in different ways and have worked to provide alternative visions and alternative forms.

Our observations of the relationship between gender and the media leave us with problems and questions that need to be solved. Growing numbers of people work in the media as writers, performers, publishers, market analysts, artists, journalists, and technical personnel. Those of us in these fields have a responsibility to understand how our work reflects or shapes gender roles and ideology. Mere understanding is not enough, however, and individual action is difficult. As individuals, we are constrained in our ability to bring about change—constrained by the organizations in which we work, by the demands and preferences of our audiences, and by the need to earn a living. Few people can afford to sacrifice their incomes for the principle of gender equality in media messages, particularly if the lack of compromise means losing the ability to speak through the media. On the other hand, few people aware of the problems of gender messages in the media can ignore these problems entirely in their work. What action can feminists who work in the media take?

Although only some of us work in the media, all of us are consumers. We also face important problems and questions as media consumers. We have a responsibility—to ourselves and, if we have them, to our children—to understand how the media reflect and shape gender roles and ideology. It takes effort and expense to identify and use the media that promote less androcentric views of the world, and it certainly takes effort to attempt to influence those who offer us an androcentric view. This, however, is what needs to be done.

Notes

1. U.S. Commission on Civil Rights, *Window Dressing on the Set: An Update* (1979), quoted in *Media Report to Women,* February 1, 1979, p. 1.

2. For histories of women in the print media, see Marzolf (1977), Russo and Kramarae (1991), and Shevelow (1989).

3. Copies of *Godey's Lady's Book* are available at http://www.history.rochester.edu/godeys compliments of the University of Rochester's Department of History.

4. "Grace Glueck Tribute to Attorney Harriet Rabb Recalls Beginning of Suit at 'Times,'" *Media Report to Women,* December 31, 1978, p. 2.

5. For an inside story of women at the *New York Times,* see Robertson (1992).

6. "Women Have Lost Ground in TV and Newspaper Coverage, Cal State Study Finds," *Media Report to Women,* vol. 20 (Summer 1992), p. 6. As I write this, I pick up two issues of the *New York Times* that happen to be in the house. In one, one of seven bylines on the front page is a woman's. In the other, three of seven front-page bylines are women's, including half the ones above the fold.

7. "Front Pages, Network Newscasts Still Overwhelmingly Male Dominated," *Media Report to Women,* vol. 20 (Summer 1992), p. 6.

8. "One-Third of Women Journalists Reported Sexual Harassment on the Job," *Media Report to Women,* vol. 21 (Winter 1993), pp. 2–3.

9. For some histories, see Hoseley and Yamada (1987).

10. She, unlike Marlene Sanders, was supposed to be permanent—or as permanent as anchors get in television—but she left 2 years later because of friction with her co-anchor, Harry Reasoner.

11. "Front Pages, Network Newscasts Still Overwhelmingly Male Dominated," *Media Report to Women,* vol. 20 (Summer 1992), p. 6.

12. *New York Times,* August 6, 1983.

13. Mary Schmitt, "Women Sportswriters—Business as Usual," *Media Studies Journal,* Spring 1997, http://www.mediastudies.org/define/schmitt.html.

14. Judy Woodruff, "Covering Politics—Is There a Female Difference?" *Media Studies Journal,* Spring 1997, http://www.mediastudies.org/define/woodruff.html.

15. Dinitia Smith, "Study Looks at Portrayal of Women in Media," *New York Times,* May 1, 1997.

16. *Media Report to Women,* vol. 20 (Fall 1992), p. 7.

17. For more on the *Ladies' Home Journal,* see Scanlon, 1995.

18. These are still available as of 1997.

19. Koky Dishon, "We've Come a Long Way—Maybe," *Media Studies Journal,* Spring 1977, http://www.mediastudies.org/define/dishon.html.

20. M. P. Taylor, "Abortion Coverage Reveals Bias," *Chicago Tribune,* September 1992.

21. Tiffany Devitt, "Abortion Coverage Leaves Women Out of the Picture," *Extra,* 1992, 18–19.

22. Sylvia Poggioli, "A Strategy of Rape in Bosnia," *Media Studies Journal,* Spring 1997, http://www.mediastudies.org/define/poggioli.html.

23. For further discussion of the history and impact of changes in domestic technology, see Cowan (1983).

24. One might argue that at least one opera that has been presented on television—Wagner's Ring Cycle, the story of everyday life among the gods—is a massive soap opera with music. It has love, hate, incest, illegitimacy, murder, identity and family crises, repetition, and everything else that makes a soap opera work.

25. A superb and moving essay on the 17th-century artist Artemisia Gentileschi, however, points out that while her nude women are marked by extraordinary naturalism for her time because she *did* have access to female nude models, men's nude women of the time have funny-looking molded breasts and fleshless skin because they did *not* have such access (Garrard, 1982).

26. But male romance writers have often used female pen names.

27. Jane Perlez, "Vienna Philharmonic Lets Women Join in Harmony," *New York Times,* February 28, 1997.

28. "Women More Likely to Get Orchestra Spots If Auditioning Sight Unseen," Women's Online Connection, http://www.womenconnect.com/channels/genderequity/mar10-1997.htm/.

29. Larry Rohter, "Are Women Directors an Endangered Species?" *New York Times,* March 17, 1991.

30. Rohter, "Are Women Directors an Endangered Species?"

31. Rohter, "Are Women Directors an Endangered Species?"

32. Anne Thompson, "Hollywood Is Taken to Task by Its Women," *New York Times,* January 17, 1993.

33. Thompson, "Hollywood Is Taken to Task by Its Women."

34. *Media Report to Women,* vol. 21 (Winter 1993), p. 3.

35. For further discussion about sexual violence, see Chapter 9 for legal issues, as well as Chapter 11.

36. For some of the most well known arguments on these points, see Dworkin (1979), Griffin (1981), and Lederer (1980).

37. For a history of these efforts, see Downs (1989).

38. See Chadwick (1990, 327).

39. Quoted in Tamar Lewin, "Furor on Exhibit at Law School Splits Feminists," *New York Times,* November 13, 1992.

40. If you do not live near enough New York to visit this amazing museum, try a visit to http://www.moma.org. This site does not have a reproduction of the paintings I discuss here, but it does have an illustrated essay on Willem de Kooning.

9

Law and Policy, Government, and the State

There are some who say there are so many women now on the floor of Congress, it looks like a mall.

Representative Henry Hyde[1]

O**F ALL THE INSTITUTIONS** that exert control over people's lives by teaching and enforcing values, those associated with government are the most powerful and authoritative. Government has the power to regulate all other social institutions and aspects of people's lives, at least to some degree. Even the decision that government may *not* regulate a particular aspect of life—for example, religion or private sexual behavior—is made by a governmental institution, such as the legislature or courts. After all, in a democracy, government is supposed to be the forum through which a people makes its authoritative decisions for itself. Government necessarily plays a large role in maintaining or changing the sex/gender system.

Many political scientists describe the workings of government as the "authoritative allocation of values." *Values* can refer to tangibles, such as goods and services, including health care, education, jobs, and wealth, but also less tangible items, such as power, legitimacy, and respect. One important difference between the institutions of government and the other social institutions discussed in this book is that when government supports or teaches particular values, including those related to gender, it does so with tremendous powers of enforcement and coercion.

The presumption underlying democratic politics is that government is a reflection of the needs, interests, and will of the citizenry as a whole; therefore, looking at the relationship between the *political system* and the *sex/gender system* leads us to ask fundamental questions about democracy. Are equal values accorded to women and men? Does government work in the equal interests of women and men? Do citizens share equivalent opportunities to shape government policy? Do we play equal roles in government and politics? If not, can we call the political system democratic? In this chapter, we seek answers to some of these questions. We begin

281

with a look at government definitions of women, as expressed through law and policy. We then turn to the special case of criminal justice. Finally, we consider the role women play in American politics as citizens and leaders.

Governmental Views of Women

The law and public policy are not a random package of legislation and court decisions. Law and policy are expressions of a political community's underlying set of values or ideology, and they are instruments for enforcing those values. Legal systems differ in their underlying views of rights, obligations, and relations among people and of the proper procedures for determining how laws should be interpreted and applied. This section of the chapter examines the American legal and policy tradition, to see its relationship to the ideology of the prevailing sex/gender system.

Protection of Rights

In 1776, a group of people (all men) meeting in Philadelphia wrote a document that read, "We hold these truths to be self-evident; that all men are created equal, that they are endowed by their creator with certain inalienable rights, that among these are life, liberty, and the pursuit of happiness." Their "Declaration of Independence" further argued that the purpose of government is to ensure these rights, and that if government does not do so, the people have a right to "alter or abolish" it.

Seventy-two years later, another group of people (mostly women), meeting in Seneca Falls, New York, rebuked the government by rewriting that same document, showing how men withheld from women the rights to which the women were entitled. Their "Declaration of Sentiments and Resolutions" included the passage, "We hold these truths to be self-evident: that all men and women are created equal."

In 1868, the Fourteenth Amendment to the U.S. Constitution was ratified. Since that day, the Constitution has asserted that no state shall "make or enforce any law which shall abridge the privileges or immunities of citizens of the United States, nor . . . deprive any person of life, liberty, or property without due process of law, nor deny to any person within its jurisdiction the equal protection of the laws." Unfortunately, another part of that same amendment seemed to imply that only men counted as citizens.

Between 1923 and the early 1980s, thousands, perhaps millions, of people worked hard to insert words such as the following into the Constitution, as well: "Equality of rights under the law shall not be denied or abridged by the United States or by any state on account of sex." This proposed amendment's supporters did not believe that the Fourteenth Amendment had been used rigorously enough to give women and men equal protection of the law. Indeed, until 1971, the U.S. Constitution was *never* used to stop discrimination against women; that was the first time the Supreme Court declared a law that discriminated against women unconstitutional. For well over a century now, feminists have been arguing that the government has not extended the same protection of the law to women as to men. Most go one step further and argue that law and policy have been based on androcentric and patriarchal norms and therefore maintain and enforce these norms. The law is part of the skeleton of a sex/gender system that privileges men over women.

The work to create *democracy* as a form of political system has taken a long time. The French and American Revolutions were crucial in the historical development of mass-based politics fed by the antipatriarchal ideas of Enlightenment political thinkers. Feminist thinkers have long argued that the transformation from a patriarchal to a democratic system took place more quickly for men than for women. Certainly, not all men were included equally—racism determined exclusion of African-American, Native American, and Asian-American men from American politics, for example—but in effect, all women, regardless of their race or class, retained subject status throughout much of American history, long after most Americans, including most women, *thought* of themselves as living in a democracy.

Founding Ideas.   What did the Founding Fathers have in mind for women when they began designing the American republic? The evidence of the stray words of Thomas Jefferson, John Adams, Benjamin Franklin, and others is that citizenship was not going to mean the same thing for women and men. Jefferson wrote, "Were the state a pure democracy there would still be excluded from our deliberation women, who, to prevent deprivation of morals and ambiguity of issues, should not mix promiscuously in gatherings of men" (quoted in Kay, 1996, 10). From the beginning, government and politics were regarded as a male domain.

In general, free women in the early republic could not vote, hold political office, or serve on juries.[2] Married women could not sue or be sued. They could not own property or make contracts and therefore could not seek employment without their husbands' permission. Husbands had nearly undisputed rights of control and custody over their children; women had no direct legal control over them. What rationale was used to deny women these rights in a self-proclaimed democratic republic?

The major justification is found in the common-law views of women, especially of married women. The *common law* is an English legal tradition, which was the basis for much of the structure of the law in the United States as it affected women.[3] As William Blackstone wrote in 1765 in the very important *Commentaries on the Law of England,* "By marriage, the husband and wife are one person in law: that is, the very being or legal existence of the woman is suspended during the marriage, or at least is incorporated and consolidated into that of the husband; under whose wing, protection, and cover she performs every thing" (quoted in Kay, 1996, 198).

Blackstone underscored repeatedly that the law cannot treat a woman as having an existence separate from her husband's. Upon marriage, they become one person, and the husband is her "baron, or lord," except, he pointed out, "there are some instances in which she is separately considered; as inferior to him, and acting by his compulsion." These instances are primarily in cases of crime. For the most part, however, a married woman was considered "civilly dead"; she had no separate existence apart from her husband.

Women's lack of rights, then, rested largely on the principle that in law, women did not exist apart from their husbands. A woman could not represent herself politically by voting because her husband was assumed to vote for the interests of the family; she could not have distinct political interests because she was a part of her husband. Further, women were considered not fully competent, rational, or responsible for themselves, particularly in politics, which was thought to be a man's world.

The 19th century added a new twist to these justifications as democratic reforms spread and it became even more difficult to justify the exclusion of women. The public and private worlds, epitomized by government and economy on the one hand and the family on the other, were increasingly seen as separate and even antagonistic but essential arenas of human life. The public domain was a man's world of competition, aggression, and rationality; and the private domain—the family—was a woman's world of compassion, tenderness, and loyalty. While more people acknowledged that it was *possible* for women to be active in the public world of politics, they argued that it would be destructive to human life and values—and femininity—if women actually did so. Women's even more important political role was to raise their sons to be good American citizens, a notion Linda Kerber (1986) calls "republican motherhood." Woman's role, political theorists argued, was of equal importance to man's, even if women were excluded from public leadership and decision making, because women were responsible for preserving the more human side of life.

Judicial Interpretations.   The official legal ideology regarding women and women's citizenship can be deciphered from the text of Supreme Court decisions.[4] The courts' job is to interpret the law when the practical meaning of a law is in dispute. The Supreme Court has the additional and critically important power of *judicial review,* meaning that it can nullify a law if it appears to contradict the spirit of the U.S. Constitution. This nullification is commonly known as "declaring a law unconstitutional." How did the Supreme Court view laws that discriminated between the sexes? Very few cases of sex discrimination reached the Court until the late 20th century, but when they did, the message was clear: Granting women fewer rights than men was consistent both with the Constitution and with democratic principles. Following are some examples of this judicial logic.

In the 1873 case *Bradwell* v. *Illinois,* the Court accepted Illinois's argument that it could prohibit women from admission to the bar because licensing lawyers was a state right with which the federal government could not interfere. One judge offered a different and famous justification for the same decision. He said that women and men have separate spheres and different personalities and that women's personalities naturally disqualify them from many jobs. Further, "man is, or should be, woman's protector and defender," which presumably means he has the right to protect her from unfeminine jobs. Finally, "the harmony, not to say identity, of interests and views which belong, or should belong, to the family institution is repugnant to the idea of a woman adopting a distinct and independent career from that of her husband." What about unmarried women? "The paramount destiny and mission of women are to fulfill the noble and benign offices of wife and mother. This is the law of the Creator. And the rules of society must be adapted to the general constitution of things, and cannot be based upon exceptional cases." In other words, women should be treated as though they are all wives and mothers because that is their natural role. This view was common in American culture.

The next sex-discrimination case was *Minor* v. *Happersett* (1874). Virginia Minor was part of a nationwide protest during the 1872 election, in which many women attempted to vote. They claimed that state laws forbidding women to vote were unconstitutional according to the Fourteenth Amendment because they denied women the rights of U.S. citizenship. The Supreme Court dismissed Minor's argument quickly, saying that people (e.g., women and children) could be citizens of the United States without being able to vote because states and not the federal government have the power to say who can vote. If the people (meaning men) want women to vote, they will say that through their elected representatives, who will pass appropriate laws.

An early-20th-century case marked a new departure for policies that maintained differences between women and men. In *Muller* v. *Oregon* (1908), the question was whether the law could bar women from jobs requiring more than 10 hours of work per day. The Court agreed that this law had the excellent purpose of protecting women from work that might harm their ability to be mothers (see also Chapter 6).

The Supreme Court had little else to say about women for the next six decades. Indeed, few courts in the United States did anything about women's roles and status until the 1960s and 1970s, other than to protect women in their roles as wives and mothers, usually by restricting their abilities to participate in activities outside the home.

Legislative Changes.   The history of legislation on women has been marked not by steady progress toward democracy and full citizenship for women, but by struggles that sometimes moved women forward and sometimes backward. One of the most important early legislative changes in the status of women occurred in the 1840s, when most states passed "Married Women's Property Acts," which gave (free) married women the right to own and manage property for the first time. This change, rarely noted in general history books, was one of the greatest democratizing reforms of the past few centuries. It probably resulted in more redistribution of wealth than any other single policy. It also made it possible for women to gain the numerous other rights that are based on property rights.

In the late 19th century, many states began to grant women the rights to vote and to hold public office, which, despite the 1874 argument of the Supreme Court, had already become one of the key symbols of full democratic citizenship. The Nineteenth Amendment to the Constitution, ratified in 1920, protected women's right to vote *throughout* the country.

Laws on abortion and contraception became more restrictive, however, and by the turn into the 20th century, abortion had become illegal across the country for the first time (Petchesky, 1984). (For further discussion of laws on contraception and abortion, see Chapter 12.) The turn of the century also witnessed the beginning of protective labor legislation, which primarily excluded women from certain jobs.

Also, beginning in the 1880s, Congress began to weaken women's tenuous grasp on citizenship by making their citizenship automatically follow from their husband's citizenship. Thus, if a foreign woman married an American citizen, she automatically became an American. If an American woman married a foreign man, she automatically lost her citizenship and became an alien, even if no other country in the world claimed her as a citizen. Some Congress members argued that this loss of American citizenship was no great loss to American women because they could not vote anyway. Some of the more disastrous implications of these laws became clear during World War I, when American women who had previously married Germans found that they were regarded by the American government not just as aliens but as enemy aliens, which meant that their property would be seized, among other things.

Once the Nineteenth Amendment was ratified, native-born American women who married foreigners found themselves stripped of their right to vote, merely because their husbands were not U.S. citizens. Congress began to give women back their citizenship in the 1920s. By the mid-1920s, women could keep their citizenship even if they married an alien, but only men could pass their citizenship on to their children. Congress finally equalized the laws of nationality in 1934 (Sapiro, 1984).

Each new step forward made it clear that large amounts of legal inequality remained. At every step, feminists found that legislators and judges tolerated, approved of, and even reinforced restrictions on women in jobs, education, and other aspects of life, usually asserting their belief that the restrictions protected women, their roles as mothers and wives, and their femininity.

The Late Twentieth Century.   The period of greatest legal progress occurred between the early 1960s and the end of the 1970s. Changes began before the rise of the new women's movement but were certainly spurred on by it once the movement developed. Some of the most important new federal laws focused on employment, including the 1963 Equal Pay Act, which required equal pay for women and men doing the same job; Title VII of the 1964 Civil Rights Act, which barred sex discrimination in hiring, firing, promotions, and working conditions; and the 1978 Pregnancy Discrimination Act, which declared that employers could not discriminate against pregnant women (see Chapter 13). Other important laws include Title IX of the 1972 Educational Amendments Act (see Chapter 5), which barred discrimination in education; and the 1974 Equal Credit Opportunity Act, which increased women's opportunities to get financial credit. In 1972, Congress finally passed the Equal Rights Amendment, after 50 years of consideration. The amendment did not, however, become part of the Constitution because it was not ratified by the required number of states within the time allowed.

The force of these laws depends on both the *interpretation* of courts when there are disputes and the degree to which agencies in the executive branch of government actually *enforce* the law. Title VII of the 1964 Civil Rights Act is a good example. Dozens of Supreme Court cases have refined the meaning of that statute. What exactly is sex discrimination? Under what circumstances is it illegal? Does discrimination have to be intentional to be illegal? Is the burden of proof on employers to prove that they did not discriminate or on employees and job candidates to prove that the employer did discriminate? The Supreme Court decided its first case involving Title VII in 1971 (*Phillips* v. *Martin Marietta*), when it signaled it was going to take the law seriously, and then it continued to use that law to make more and more inroads against discrimination through the end of the 20th century.

The executive branch of the government (i.e., the bureaucracy) also plays an important role in antidiscrimination policy, especially through the Equal Employment Opportunity Commission (EEOC), created to enforce the 1964 Civil Rights Act.[5] At first, the EEOC was given little real power, and therefore the act itself had little effect. Only in the 1970s, when the EEOC was given the power to sue on behalf of people who face discrimination, could Title VII be regarded as having any teeth. The force of law changed with the administration in office. Under President Ronald Reagan, for example, efforts to enforce antidiscrimination law slowed, whereas under President Bill Clinton, the efforts were reinforced.

The Supreme Court has shifted its position on the toleration of sex discrimination. As shown in this chapter, up through the 1960s, the Court generally saw no contradiction between democratic and constitutional principles and discrimination against women, even in the face of the Fourteenth Amendment guarantees of equal protection under the law. Not until 1971, the same year it first enforced the 1964 Civil Rights Act on behalf of women, did the Supreme Court declare a state law that discriminated on the basis of sex unconstitutional (*Reed* v. *Reed*). From then through the end of the 1980s, the Supreme Court took a very dim view of most forms of discrimination against women. The change came late in history, but it was substantial. The types of discrimination that were once considered natural are now rarely tolerated by U.S. courts.

Fulfillment of Obligations

Citizenship entails both rights, which governments guarantee, and obligations, which citizens owe to their political communities. Until recently, women have not had the same rights as men; they have also not had the same obligations as men. The three primary obligations citizens owe to the state are taxes, jury service, and military service. Have women had the same obligations as men? If not, why not? Can women share the same rights as men without sharing the same obligations?

Taxation.   Of the three forms of obligation individuals are said to owe the state, taxation is the one that women have historically shared with men. Indeed, if people pay taxes in exchange for guaranteeing that they receive rights, protection, and services from the state, women might be said to have given more than their due. Feminists might well have shouted the Revolutionary War cry, "Taxation without representation is tyranny!" as an appropriate slogan for their own social movement.

Jury Duty.   The situation is different in regard to jury duty. To ensure the constitutional right to a trial by a jury of peers, people are drafted to serve on juries. Moreover, the Supreme Court believes that "the requirement of a jury's being chosen from a fair cross section of the community is fundamental to the American system of justice" (*Taylor* v. *Louisiana*). Until long into this century, however, women were not well represented on juries. Many states barred women outright. Others said that women could serve if they wanted to, unlike men, who were drafted. Four important Supreme Court cases touched on this question.

The first, *Ballard* v. *U.S.* (1946), said that the systematic exclusion of women from *federal* juries "deprives the jury system of the broad base it was designed . . . to have in our democratic society." This case did not affect state courts, however, where most of the judicial action occurs.

The 1961 case of *Hoyt* v. *Florida* reflects the historical governmental view of women as jurors. Florida practiced affirmative registration for juries; that is, only women who specifically volunteered for jury duty could serve. Few people ever volunteer for service; thus women virtually never appeared on juries. The Supreme Court found this practice constitutional for the following reason:

> Despite the enlightened emancipation of women from the restrictions and protections of bygone years, and their entry into many parts of community life formerly considered to be reserved to men, woman is still regarded as the center of home and family life. We cannot say that it is constitutionally impermissible for a State, acting in pursuit of the general welfare, to conclude that a woman should be relieved from the civic duty of jury service unless she herself determines that such service is consistent with her own special responsibilities.

In other words, women are exempted from this obligation to the state because they have others—motherhood and homemaking—that come first. Only when those obligations are fulfilled need a woman participate in other acts of citizenship. Only in 1975 (*Taylor* v. *Louisiana*) did the Supreme Court change its opinion, declaring that the motherhood argument was not strong enough to relieve women of their civic responsibilities. Juries should be representative of the community, and the community includes women.

Just being *called* for jury service is not enough to guarantee that women and men *serve* equally, however. During the jury-selection phase of the trial process, lawyers for both parties to a dispute try to make sure that the jury will be as sympathetic to their side as possible, or at least not hostile. As they review the prospective jurors, they are allowed a limited number of *peremptory challenges,* which means, basically, that a juror can be dismissed from service with no reason given. Most legal experts see the basic system as a good one, but lawyers use all sorts of clues to decide whether a prospective juror is likely to be good or bad for their side. In 1986, the Supreme Court declared that juries could not be constructed on the basis of race, and in 1994, the Court declared, "We hold that gender, like race, is an unconstitutional proxy for juror competence and impartiality" (*J.E.B.* v. *Alabama*).

Military Service.   Military service is the third form of obligation citizens are supposed to owe the state because a government cannot provide defense for its citizens unless they join in that defense. As in the case of jury duty, the government assumes the right to draft people into military service. The role of women in the military raises many questions, but discussion here is limited to a comparison of

Veterans comforting each other near the memorial honoring women who served during the Vietnam War.

men's and women's obligation to serve and to the significance of the increasing attention to sexuality issues in the military.

Throughout most of American history, women were barred from military service except in auxiliary capacities, especially in the more "gender-appropriate" duties of nursing, cooking, cleaning, and prostitution. Although by World War I, the military included an auxiliary corps of nurses, women who served in this corps were not at first given formal military status. In World War II, a few women served as bomber pilots, but they were not given formal military status and privileges.[6]

In 1948, Congress formalized and integrated women's position in the military more thoroughly, but at the same time, it put a ceiling of 2% on the proportion of women in the military. After the end of the draft in the 1970s, when defense experts were afraid there were not enough people to fill the armed services, the ceiling was raised, and women were allowed into the military academies. When Congress reinstituted registration for the draft in 1980, the Carter administration's original intent to include women was dropped in the face of substantial resistance. For the next decade, military recruitment remained similar to the process that had been abandoned for jury service: Men were subject to conscription, and women could serve if they wished (up to a limit).

Even relatively early in the 20th century, it was clear that military service had important implications for the understanding of women's citizenship. Consider the 1929 Supreme Court case *U.S.* v. *Schwimmer.*[7] Rosika Schwimmer—a lecturer, writer, and pacifist—came to the United States from Hungary in 1921. She petitioned to become a U.S. citizen in 1926. During her citizenship interview, she was asked the usual question, "If necessary, are you willing to take up arms in defense of this country?" She replied that she could not because of her pacifism, adding that she would be ineligible anyway because of her sex and age. "I cannot see that a woman's refusal to take up arms is a contradiction to the oath of allegiance," she said.

Schwimmer's petition for naturalization was turned down because, the Court said, "That it is the duty of citizens by force of arms to defend our Government against all enemies whenever necessity arises, is a fundamental principle of the constitution." It concluded that "the fact that, by reason of sex, age, or other cause, they may be unfit to serve does not lessen their purposes or power to influence others." A willingness to serve in the armed forces was considered a crucial condition of citizenship, even for people barred from actually doing so.

That same year, another petitioner for citizenship, Martha Jane Graber, said she could go to the front in her profession as a nurse, but she could not bear arms because she was a pacifist. She said, "I could not bear arms; I could not kill; but I am willing to be sacrificed for this country." That was insufficient for the officials; they refused her naturalization. Thus, while claiming that bearing arms in defense of the country was central to the U.S. government, the government refused to allow women to do so.

If military service is an important condition of citizenship, why are women not required to serve when men are? This question was asked by a young man who refused his draft call to the Vietnam War and accused the government of sex discrimination because it did not draft women. A U.S. district court ruled against him in 1968, saying,

> Congress made a legislative judgment that men should be subject to involuntary induction but that women, presumably because they are "still regarded as the center of home and family life (*Hoyt* v. *State of Florida*)" should not. In providing for involuntary service for men and voluntary service for women, Congress followed the teaching of history that if a nation is to survive, men must provide the first line of defense while women keep the home fires burning (*U.S.* v. *St. Clair*).

Once again, and depending on the aforementioned jury-duty case, women's roles as citizens were held to revolve around their roles as mothers and wives, implying that family obligations *are* women's citizenship obligations.

By the 1980s, many feminists assumed that this different treatment of men and women would disappear. Even in 1981, however, the Supreme Court decided that a policy requiring men but not women to register for the draft was constitutional (*Rotsker* v. *Goldberg*). Congress had been divided over how to draft the law. A congressional subcommittee report stated that

> drafting women would place unprecedented strains on family life, whether in peacetime or in time of emergency. If such a draft occurred at a time of emergency, unpredictable reactions to the fact of female conscription would result. A decision which would result in a young mother being drafted and a young

father remaining home with the family . . . cannot be taken lightly, nor its broader implications ignored. (Quoted in Kay, 1988, 21)

The Supreme Court's acceptance of the inequality turned on a different point, however: Because women were not allowed to engage in combat and because the purpose of draft registration is to provide a pool of people who can be moved quickly into combat, Congress's decision not to require women to register was acceptable. Two justices dissented, arguing that it is "inconsistent with the Constitution's guarantee of equal protection of the laws."

Women were not allowed in combat jobs, but the proportion of women in the military continued to increase. They were 2.5% of active U.S. military forces in 1973, 9.3% in 1983, and 11.5% in 1993. The various branches of the military differed in their proportions of women, from a low of 4.5% of the Marines to a high of 14.7% of Army personnel on active duty.[8] A turning point in both public and governmental thinking about women in the military occurred during the early 1990s for three reasons: (1) a series of scandals about the harassment of women in the military, (2) women's performance during the 1991 Gulf War, and (3) the change of presidential administration.

Although there had long been reports about harassment of women in the military, reports became more spectacular by the end of the 1980s and beginning of the 1990s. A 1990 report identified rampant sexism at the Naval Academy, indicating that "low-level harassment can pass as normal operating procedure" among some people, and that "the negative attitudes and inappropriate actions of this minority exert such a disproportionate influence on the Naval Academy climate that most midshipmen readily acknowledge that women are not accepted as equals in the brigade."[9]

Even more dramatic was the 1991 annual convention of the Tailhook Association, an organization for top Navy fliers. The Tailhook conventions had long been rowdy stag parties, but in 1991, a scandal broke when four women sued the Tailhook Association and the hotel in which the convention was held because they had been sexually abused. The inspector general for the Defense Department issued a report in 1993, which described an atmosphere of abuse, including a gauntlet of men who assaulted women trying to walk down corridors and men wearing T-shirts proclaiming, "Women Are Property."

An admiral commenting on the report concluded, "Tailhook . . . brought to light the fact that we had an institutional problem in how we treated women. In that regard, it was a watershed event that has brought about institutional change."[10] Many of the men involved were punished, but in 1994, the Senate voted 54–43 to allow the Navy's top admiral to retire at four-star rank with full pension, despite the vigorous objections of the women senators and a demonstration held by the Democratic women of the House of Representatives. As the *New York Times* reported on part of Senator Dianne Feinstein's (D-Cal) participation in the debate,

"Do I believe he was there?" she said on the floor. "Yes. Do I believe he was protected by some of his flag staff around him? Yes. I recognize it wouldn't have been popular for Admiral Kelso to go in from the patio and say, 'Hey, guys, knock it off. This thing is at an end.'" But, she added, she feels that is what he should have done to end the age-old attitude in the military that "boys will be boys."[11]

More problems were yet to surface.

The Tailhook scandal attracted added attention because of women's participation in the Gulf War earlier in 1991. Five out of the 16 participating NATO nations sent women to the Persian Gulf, including the United States, the United Kingdom, Canada, Norway, and Denmark. Although none of the women were part of combat units—this was not allowed by the U.S. military at the time—women did come under fire.[12] In all, about 40,000 U.S. military women served in the Gulf in many roles, including as cargo-plane pilots; 16 of the military women died. The public was riveted by pictures of uniformed mothers kissing their children good-bye, their honorable service, and the news that 2 women had been taken prisoner of war.

Newspapers extensively covered the story of an Army flight surgeon taken prisoner when her plane was downed. She received no treatment for her broken arms until her third day in captivity, and she suffered sexual abuse during the 8 days she was held. Until that time, many people had argued that women should not be allowed in combat, precisely because they may be sexually abused if taken as prisoners. The flight surgeon reflected that while sexual abuse is serious, "everything that happens to you as a POW is non-consensual." She continued, "Compared to other things, being shot at, people threatening to shoot you in the back of the head, breaking your bones, it was a terribly insignificant event. Anyone who thinks I'm lying obviously never had those other things happen to them."[13]

Meanwhile, government officials and military leaders continued to debate whether women should be allowed in combat. A government panel studying the issue recommended in divided opinions that women should continue to be barred from ground combat and flying combat planes, although they might serve on warships. Some of the conservative members argued that it is wrong to allow women to kill, reflecting a continuing influence of a "separate spheres" argument.[14] A survey of military women, in contrast, showed a majority favored repealing of the ban on women in combat. In 1993, President Clinton's secretary of defense ordered the end of the combat exclusion. Most jobs in the Air Force and Navy are now open to women, but the Army and the Marines still bar women from the three main routes to senior leadership: armor, infantry, and field artilleries.[15]

After the demise of the combat exclusion, it became clear that women were still a problem for the military. In addition to the debates about whether women are *capable* of being good military personnel in their own right, issues relating to sex and sexuality in the military have stayed in the news throughout the 1990s. The military defines sexuality as an issue bearing on the degree to which the military can maintain "good order and discipline," including sustaining the appropriate hierarchy and trust among members of the military organization. It is clear that women have been getting in the way.

On a related note, the military has always levied harsh treatment on homosexuals. Although those known to have engaged in homosexual relations have always faced automatic dismissal (that is, after the days when they would have faced execution), military officials have also been aware that thousands of homosexual military personnel are simply not caught. The military discharged more than 15,000 people accused of homosexuality throughout the 1980s alone.[16] Why is homosexuality so bad for the military? General cultural norms remain highly homophobic, and these are translated as worries over discipline and order. In the debates about sexuality policy in the military, however, the worries often seemed much more related to personal anxieties, as one Marine Corps general illustrated when he tried to explain why having gays in the military would cause a problem:

> We were standing in this shower tent, naked, waiting in line for 35 minutes for a 5-minute shower. . . . Would I be comfortable knowing gays were there standing in line with us? No. It just introduces a tension you don't need.[17]

Whether he was worried about being attacked in line, or just being ogled in the way women experience every day, is unclear.

After much debate, the Clinton administration instituted a policy that pleased almost no one: "Don't ask, don't tell." Under this policy, homosexuals would still be discharged if they became known. A study released in 1997 showed that the number of discharges for homosexuality actually *rose* after the institution of this supposedly liberal policy, and that women constitute a disproportionately high number of these, especially in the Army, which is one of the two branches most hostile to having women in the military in the first place.[18]

A large proportion of military women have faced discriminatory and repressive treatment relating to sexuality, regardless of their own sexual orientation, because while lesbians are disproportionately likely to be discharged, women in general are subject to widespread and systematic sexual harassment from military men. As Timothy Egan of the *New York Times* has suggested, "the modern military is, by and large, a youth culture. As such, the job of [a supervising sergeant] can be like a traffic cop among colliding hormonal impulses."[19] More seriously, the military is a traditional male institution in which a large proportion of the male personnel have trouble coping with women as full equals, and in which women are considered sex objects and, occasionally, legitimate objects of violence. Defenders of the military tend to argue that sexual tension is unavoidable when women and men work closely together, and anyway, it is normal for men to be distracted and act like sexual predators. As long as women are in the military in close proximity to men, some argue, these things will happen.

A Pentagon study completed in 1996 found that more than half of the 47,000 women who responded said they had been subjected to some forms of sexual harassment within the year before the study; half of these women pointed the finger at superiors. A large proportion of women never report the abuse because they believe they would be subject to retaliation.[20] In that same year, women lodged a number of well-publicized accusations of rape and other sexual abuse against military superiors, beginning a new round of investigations. One of the best-known charges was leveled at an Army sergeant major assigned to help review the Army's sexual-harassment policies. His accuser said she could not stand silently watching that happen.[21]

All of these events were complemented by widespread accusations of sexual harassment within the military academies, especially at the Citadel, a state military college.[22] A 1997 Army report found widespread harassment and discrimination against women, stemming partly from a leadership that is not screened carefully enough; even wife beaters were not barred from being drill sergeants.[23] Women experience sexual abuse from their superiors, from their colleagues, and, occasionally, even from subordinates. Many women find they are especially likely to face distinctly sexual abuse during boot camp, when the license for superiors to abuse subordinates is great anyway.[24]

The problem is not just that sexual harassment and abuse seems so common within the military, but also that the system has protected such treatment for so long, the perpetrators include so many military leaders, and the reaction of so many people is to blame the victim. Rather than renewing efforts to figure out how women can become equal members with men in their country's defense forces, many offer the solution of cutting back on women in the military, or instituting more segregation—for example, during basic training. Indeed, a 3-year study by the Army Research Institute concluded that the training of men and women together improved women's performance but did not affect men's. Women have been trained together with men since 1976 in the Air Force, 1993 in the Army, and 1994 in the Navy.[25]

Summary.   This brief review of rights and obligations shows that women's and men's citizenship has not been treated the same way by government and that the exclusion of women from many of the activities, rights, and obligations expected of men has long been held to be consistent with the democratic principles in the U.S. Constitution. The reasons offered almost always refer to women's unique roles as mothers and wives or their natural condition as sexual objects. Women have not had full citizenship in the normal sense—that is, in the male sense—because their reproductive capacity and sexuality have gotten in the way.

Women's Policy Issues

The term *women's issues* is often used to refer to legal and policy issues thought to be especially relevant to women. Feminists have often claimed that without more women in government, women's issues will be ignored, or will not be solved in women's interests. What *are* women's particular interests? What makes an issue a *women's* issue?

The term *women's issues* usually refers to policies that relate specifically to traditional roles and activities with which women are stereotypically associated (e.g., the family and motherhood), or those aimed specifically at having an effect on women's lives. The most prominent women's policy issues in recent decades have been sex discrimination, especially in employment, education, and other financial questions; reproductive rights; family-welfare programs; violence against women; child care; and child support. These issues seem to be obvious candidates because they have profound implications for the quality of women's lives and the amount of control women have over their lives.

Nevertheless, there is a problem with using the term *women's issues*. Does this usage mean that these issues affect women *only*? Why is family policy or policy on children a *women's* issue? Don't these policies affect men also? The main reason why family policy strikes so many people as a women's issue is that the dominant ideology says that women are more central to families, and families are more central to women than to men.

Many family policies are implemented to affect men as little as possible. Consider the case of child care. In a family headed by a two-career married couple, child care is usually primarily the woman's responsibility. It is the woman, not the man, whose job is understood to create the need for child care. Child-care centers and baby-sitters are thought to be related to the structure of the woman's time and responsibilities, not men's. Because most child-care workers are women, even the vast growth in availability of child care may not alter the current structure of gender roles as much as expected. Women continue to have the main responsibility for child care, although more are paid for their work than in the past.

Of course, male-dominated political systems are slow to develop policies that benefit women because such policies often incur new costs to men. Similarly, some of the conditions that hurt women still benefit some men. If a society tolerates employment discrimination against women, men have easier access to employment. If family- and employment-related policies charge women with primary responsibility for child care, men have more freedom to engage in activities outside the home and to make their own independent decisions than they do under policies supporting egalitarian divisions of family labor. If women have more control over marital property, men have less. If the state is vigorous in its attempts to eradicate wife battery, many men have less power in their personal lives—indeed, many find themselves in prison.

Feminist policy experts have concluded that the usual way in which we think about women's issues is too limiting.[26] We should think more comprehensively about whether any given policy has gender-specific effects or implications. Many policies that are not stereotypically associated with women do in fact have gender-based significance. In an androcentric society, these gender-based implications may not even be noticed; therefore, policies can benefit men but not women through *unanticipated effects*. If we think about public policy this way, any public policy problem might be regarded as a women's issue if we attend to the gender-specific aspects of it. We should not assume gender neutrality where it may not exist. Consider a few examples:

1. An employment policy may cover a specific sector of the economy, such as heavy industry or clerical work, which is very gender segregated. An apparently gender-neutral policy giving a gender-segregated job or sector special treatment (e.g., higher wages or better benefits or working conditions or more power on the job) may well be discriminatory in reality.

2. Social-welfare policies affect women and men differently because women and men use different social services and benefits. Many benefits are aimed at children, who are usually the primary responsibility of women, or at older people, who are disproportionately female and often cared for by women family members. Because social services often involve labor that is otherwise done by

TABLE 9-1

Proportions of Women and Men Committing Specific Crimes, 1987

Most "Female" Crimes	Most "Male" Crimes
Prostitution and commercialized vice (65)	Forcible rape (99)
Juvenile runaways (57)	Weapons crimes (92)
Fraud (44)	Sex offenses (92)
Embezzlement (38)	Robbery (91)
Forgery, counterfeiting (34)	Drunkenness (91)
Curfew, loitering (25)	Motor-vehicle theft (90)

Note: Numbers in the female column show the percentage of women within the category; numbers in the male column show the percentage of men within the category.

Source: U.S. Bureau of the Census (1989, 173).

women for their families, there is often a direct trade-off between the availability of social services and the amount of unpaid labor women do.

3. General fiscal policy (policy on taxes) and monetary policy (policy on the money supply) affect how much money is available to individuals and families and therefore affect consumption patterns. There is a trade-off between certain kinds of consumption and women's labor: Below a certain threshold, women will mend clothes, rather than buy new ones; do more labor-intensive cooking, rather than buy more expensive convenience foods and restaurant meals; or spend more time directly caring for children and other dependents, rather than hire other people to do it.

The purpose of law and policy is to put into practice the values and goals of the government. Throughout most of American history, one of the government's stated purposes was to protect the traditional family and traditional family values. This underlying purpose resulted in the implementation of government policies confining women to wifehood, motherhood, and other functions that seemed especially consistent with those roles. Since the rise of the women's movement in the 1970s, policy increasingly treats women not just as wives and mothers but also as citizens whose rights need protection the same as men's. Even with the renewed support for "traditional family values" across the country, *most* law and policy have not reversed the advances made in gender-based aspects of law and policy since the 1960s.

Women, Crime, and Justice

One function of government is to help keep people secure in person and property and, in cases of crime, to dispense justice fairly and equitably. Is the justice system gender-neutral? Men commit more crimes, especially those involving violence. FBI crime figures certainly show some gender differences, as Table 9-1

Violence against women is a global issue. These people are protesting against rapes committed by U.S. servicemen.

shows. Women's crimes are concentrated into a few categories. In addition, women are especially likely to be the victims of some categories of crime, including especially sexual crimes. The question, then, is whether and how gender shapes the nature of crime and injustice, and the reaction of the justice system. This section begins by looking at the evidence relating first to women as victims of crime and second to women as criminals. To what degree is the disposition of justice determined by gender?

Women as Victims[27]

Two crimes are perpetrated primarily by men, primarily against women: domestic violence and rape. Examination of the reaction of the criminal-justice system to these forms of violence against women shows some of the special problems women face in gaining justice because of the large degree to which the criminal-justice system has institutionalized sexist assumptions and perceptions common in the larger sex/gender system. How does the treatment of these crimes compare with the treatment of other kinds of assault? In this chapter, discussion is restricted to a focus on the criminal justice system; Chapter 11 focuses more on the social dynamics of violence against women and the relationship between this violence and sexuality. (See also Chapter 6 for a discussion of family violence as a health issue.)

Both rape and wife battery are among the most underreported crimes that exist. The FBI estimates that about 72 out of every 100,000 females in the country were *reported* rape victims in a given year.[28] However, only about 1 in 4 rapes and 1 in 10 cases of serious wife battery are reported to the police. Only a tiny proportion of rape and wife-battery cases end in conviction and punishment of the offender. These are crimes in which the victim is especially likely to fear reprisals for pursuing justice; offenders are unlikely to be jailed, thus leaving them free to mete out reprisals. At the same time, convictions have increased dramatically in recent years. The number of sex offenders in prison climbed by almost 47% from 1987 to 1992, for example.[29]

Both rape and wife battery were tolerated by law and public opinion to a shocking degree until the 1980s. The main reasons were that (1) traditional sexual and gender ideology has limited women's autonomy, self-definition, and right to control their own bodies and sexual decisions; and (2) men have had proprietary rights over their wives and, indeed, over other women, thereby leaving women legally defenseless against attack, especially within the family. The following discussion explores how these reasons apply to criminal justice views of both rape and wife battery.

Domestic violence is a gender-based problem. About three quarters of its victims are women, and over 90% of reported spousal assault cases involve the husband as perpetrator and the wife as victim (Thomas, 1991, 313). In 1995, 26% of female murder victims were killed by their husbands or boyfriends; about 3% of male murder victims were killed by their wives or girlfriends,[30] and about 20% of women seeking help at hospital emergency rooms were there because of domestic violence.[31]

The legal view of domestic violence is also a gender-based problem. Under the common law, husbands were allowed to "chastise" their wives physically, as Blackstone wrote at the end of the 18th century, "in the same moderation that a man is allowed to correct his apprentices or children; for whom the master or parent is also liable in some cases to answer" (quoted in Kay, 1996, 199). Lawmakers tended to be reluctant to help women suing their husbands for intentional physical attacks because such suits might destroy the presumed peace and harmony of the home. Physical assault (except for rape) between spouses is now considered a crime throughout the country, so the problem now is the enforcement procedures.

The husband's proprietary rights are especially apparent in rape laws. The traditional definition of rape as "unlawful carnal knowledge of a woman without her consent" has been understood throughout the United States, until recently, to mean that there is no such thing as rape between marital partners. Sexual relations within marriage cannot be "unlawful,"[32] and the common-law tradition (and other traditions) has generally accepted the view that under the marital contract, the woman "hath given up herself in this kind to her husband, which she cannot retract" (Thomas, 1991, 338). In other words, she gave her irrevocable consent to sexual relations on her marriage day. Since the mid-1980s, some states have decided, along with the New Jersey Supreme Court, that this view is "offensive to our valued ideals of personal liberty" (*New Jersey* v. *Smith*, 1981), and they have limited or eliminated the spousal immunity. Nevertheless, neither lawmakers nor the public generally has wanted to interfere in what is viewed as a private matter between husband and wife.

Establishing a lack of consent is not just a problem for women who are married to their rapists. It is also very difficult for women to prove they did not consent to sexual relations even if they can establish that they said—or screamed— "no." Women's words alone are not enough when they are interpreted through a sexual culture believing that women are supposed to say "no" even when they mean "yes" and that men are supposed to try to make women's "no" become a "yes." In order to establish lack of consent, women traditionally had to make a "fresh complaint" (report quickly) and to prove physical resistance even to within an "inch of their lives." In other words, they had to show they suffered considerable brutality *other* than rape to get a rape conviction. The victim's past sexual history was routinely used by the defense to prove she was inclined toward sexual consent until the institution of the *rape shield laws* in the 1980s. Nevertheless, women who claim to have been raped often face grueling questions supposedly aimed at identifying consent, such as whether they had an orgasm.

Victims of wife battery also face questions about their consent to victimization. One of the most common questions asked about such women is "Why didn't they leave?" Many people cannot believe that women who do not abandon their husbands are truly victims of assault. This view shows ignorance about many features of domestic violence, not the least of which is that leaving a violent partner is not as simple as walking out the door. It entails abandoning one's own household, often suddenly, with all that involves if there are children. Moreover, leaving the household does not guarantee the end of domestic violence, which need not take place in one's home. In many cases, women need to ensure that their partners cannot find them, which has further implications for women and their children. A 1996 report estimated that there were about 60,000 cases of on-the-job violence that were extensions of domestic abuse. Some employers are now trying to help, especially because in some cases, employers can be held responsible if they know a person is subject to violence and she is killed or injured on the job.[33] Shelters for battered women also help, but women who leave violent partners and seek shelter must face total disruption of their family and of their personal and work lives.

Many of the difficulties women face in prosecuting their attackers in battery and rape cases revolve around perceptions of *victim precipitation*, the idea that the victim in some way provoked the attack against herself and that this provocation makes the perpetrator less guilty. Women's clothing or possible drunkenness has been used by police and courts to determine whether the woman caused the rape. Victims of battery often find that they are interrogated about what they did to cause the man's anger. The insensitive treatment of female victims at the hands of the criminal-justice system has often been labeled the second or double victimization of women: They are victimized first by the criminal and then by the criminal-justice system. One tragic effect of these legal and public views is that many victimized women actually feel guilty for what was done to them.

Prosecutors and police officers are very wary of both rape and domestic violence cases. These and other actors in the criminal-justice system often hold stereotypes about women that make them less helpful than they might be to those who have suffered violence and injustice. In addition, other aspects of these crimes affect police and prosecutors' behavior. Prosecutors worry about the credibility of rape and battery victims in the eyes of jurors. They worry about victims who drop their cases and leave the prosecutors with wasted time and records of unsuccessful cases (Stanko, 1982). For the police, domestic-disturbance calls are among those most likely to result in injury to the officers involved.

Until the 1970s and 1980s, explicit police policy usually stipulated that police officers should mediate domestic problems and avoid arresting anyone. It soon became clear that these policies were pushed to their limits. Sometimes, police officers refused to arrest violent husbands even when their wives requested it, and both they and the courts refused to enforce restraining orders against violent husbands. Eventually, some women sued police officers and court employees, on the grounds that, first, the women were being denied equal protection in comparison to people assaulted in places other than the home, and second, the "arrest avoidance policy was based on the broad and archaic sex-based assumptions that a man is privileged to punish his wife" (Woods, 1981, 43).

Many changes have occurred recently. Although old attitudes die hard, police forces often work closely with shelters for battered women and community-based rape crisis centers, and they sometimes employ specially trained police officers, often women, to deal with rape victims. Changes in the law have also helped. Rape shield laws bar courts from referring to a victim's prior sexual history. Some states have followed the example of Michigan, which in 1974 enacted a rape reform law that classified sexual offenses by degree, in categories ranging from sexual contact to penetration by force with a weapon involved. Many states allow battered women to get protective or temporary restraining orders (TROs) barring their attackers from contacting them. Some jurisdictions have instituted mandatory arrest policies in cases of domestic violence, which require the police to arrest the perpetrator. Women's organizations have worked hard to educate people about the remaining problems and to offer assistance to women who need it.

Both the federal government and states throughout the nation reacted vehemently—some say they overreacted—when in 1994 a young girl named Megan Kanka was raped and murdered by a convicted pedophile. All states now require that convicted sex offenders register with the police, at least during their time of parole or probation, and in at least a couple of states, as long as they live in the state. The federal government requires states to have public-notification programs to let people know about the existence of a convicted sex offender in the vicinity. Some states require hormone injections to reduce paroled offenders' sex drive. In 1997, the U.S. Supreme Court upheld a Kansas law allowing convicted sex criminals who are judged likely to commit a violent sex crime again to be committed involuntarily to a mental hospital.[34]

While some experts argue that these measures are necessary because of the high rates of recidivism among sex offenders, others claim that such measures actually punish criminals further by taking away their rights to privacy.[35] Some men who have already served their time for their crimes find themselves hounded out of towns and unable to get jobs. In fact, the FBI finds that within 3 years of release from prison, 41% of all violent offenders are arrested for new felonies, while only 20% of rapists are arrested for a new crime.[36] Of course, any inferences from these data must also take into account the low reporting, arrest, and conviction rates of sex criminals.

Change remains slow, and the criminal justice system is still at least partially based on a gender ideology that defines protection differently for women and men. Consider the case of a woman who lost her ability to prosecute her rapist successfully precisely because she was ingenious in finding a way to protect herself. In 1992, in Austin, Texas, a woman found an intruder with a knife demanding sex from her. She escaped to the bathroom and tried unsuccessfully to call 911 before he broke in. Facing the inevitability of rape, she tried to convince him to wear a condom. When he told her not to worry because he did not have AIDS, she asked, "How do you know I don't?" When he indicated he did not have any condoms with him, she gave him one she had in the house. Eventually, she fled naked to a neighbor's house. The city did not indict the man because the fact that she had provided a condom indicated consent. As she interpreted it, "The fact that I took extreme measures to protect my life means that I deserve to get raped."[37]

It is unfortunate, but perhaps not a surprise, that the number of women interested in buying guns doubled in the 1980s. Whereas in 1988, less than 5% of the students in the National Rifle Association's (NRA) introductory personal-protection courses were women, that figure was up to 75% by 1993.[38] The NRA has worked hard—and successfully—to recruit women, using newsletters, a web page, and a series of seminars called "Refuse to Be a Victim."[39]

Women as Criminals

Women constitute a very small proportion of the people arrested for crimes and an even smaller proportion of the prison population. Eighty percent of the people arrested in 1995 were male.[40] Women commit a particularly small proportion of the most serious and violent crimes and of the crimes involving use of a weapon. Like men, women commit the majority of crimes against others of their own sex, except in the case of murder: About 80% of both male and female murderers kill men (Wilbanks, 1982, 169). Women are less likely to use weapons, and when they do, the weapons are often kitchen knives and other household implements related to female roles (Parisi, 1982a, 118–119). Despite the general view that women tend either to be men's accomplices or to get men to commit crimes for them, research shows that, for the most part, they tend to work alone. If they work with someone else, they tend to work with women (Parisi, 1982a, 113). Thus, the crime world, like other domains of social life, is segregated by sex.

Women's crime rate, like men's, has increased in recent decades. Women's property crimes and, more recently, drug-related crimes constitute the bulk of the increase. The Justice Department estimates that one of every three women now in prison is there for a drug-related charge. Women are much more likely to be in prison on drug charges than are men.[41]

Like other women, female criminals have historically been interpreted through the prism of gender ideology. In their review of research on female criminality, Nicole Hahn Rafter and Elizabeth Anne Stanko (1982, 6–7) noted,

Nearly all traditional commentaries on female offenders, whether focused on the serious or the minor criminal, have been overwhelmingly concerned with violations of gender prescriptions. . . . [Theorists] have attributed . . . low arrest rates to the inherently law-abiding nature of women. Accordingly, they have assessed the female criminal by the fit of her crime to men's crime and the extent to which she violated her naturally law-abiding nature. Since crime was assumed to be a masculine phenomenon, women who committed crime were thought to do so either because they were too masculine (the evil women theory) or because they had been led astray (the bad little girl theory).

Such assumptions have clouded research on female criminality, including juvenile delinquency (Chesney-Lind and Shelden, 1992).

Some observers worry that women are now even more subject to gender-based regulation under criminal law because a new set of crimes revolving around pregnancy is being recognized (Humphries, 1993; Merlo, 1993; Reed, 1993; Sagatun, 1993). Because thousands—perhaps hundreds of thousands—of babies are born each year to mothers who used drugs such as crack and powder cocaine during pregnancy, efforts to tackle this problem have led to increased use of law enforcement against these women. Another 6,000 to 8,000 babies are born with fetal alcohol syndrome each year (Merlo, 1993). More states have now enacted fetal-abuse statutes that create a new form of female criminal offense.

To what degree is treatment of the female offender shaped by gender? Some states' statutes require indeterminate (and therefore maximum) sentences for women but not for men. Some experts argue that women should have longer sentences because women are more likely than men to benefit from rehabilitation while incarcerated. This idea is connected with the historical practice, stemming back to the establishment of the first separate women's prison in Indiana in 1869, to call women's prisons *reformatories*. Some researchers hypothesize that women receive often longer sentences for particularly "unfeminine" crimes—that is, for breaking the law *and* the gender norms.

Other observers argue that judges and prosecutors act chivalrously toward women by giving them lighter sentences. Some suggest that people find it difficult to believe that women can be as dangerous as men and therefore do not lock them away for as long. Women's responsibility for child care has also led to the notion that judges may be reluctant to create lengthy separation between mothers and children through incarceration. The evidence seems to suggest that women receive more lenient treatment than men in certain sentencing and parole situations, and "it occasionally appears that negative (punitive) treatment is accorded females for 'manly' crimes" (Parisi, 1982b, 215). In any case, it appears that women are now given longer prison sentences than used to be true (Rix, 1988, 304).

There are some differences between the prison experiences of men and women (Immarigeon and Chesney-Lind, 1993; Moyer, 1993; Muraskin, 1993). Because so few women are incarcerated, compared to men, women's prisons and prison programs are much neglected. They are underfunded and poorly equipped, even in comparison to men's prisons. On the other hand, the old reformatory model persists. Nicole Rafter has pointed out that this model is apparent in "its characteristically low security; its tendency to provide living quarters that (to the outsider, at least) resemble college dormitory rooms rather than cells; and in its paternalistic aspects, such as its tendency to treat female inmates as errant children" (1982, 256).

Prisons reinforce gender norms through their rehabilitation programs. Occupational training in women's facilities, for example, typically includes hairdressing and cosmetology, and women's programs traditionally worked to reinforce conventional notions of femininity. In recent years, however, some prisons have developed expanded notions of appropriate occupations and programs for women.

Although prisoners of both sexes may suffer from isolation from their families, mothers—and their children—particularly suffer from separation imposed by imprisonment. As one report indicated, "Male prisoners often have wives or girlfriends to bring children to visit them. Female inmates, more likely to be the child's sole support, often have no one."[42] About three quarters of the women in state and federal prisons are mothers, and roughly half of the children of prison inmates never see their mothers during the mothers' incarceration.[43] In most prisons, even mothers of infants and those who give birth while in prison are separated from their children. As difficult as the separation may be for the mothers, the implications for the development of the children are crucial. Many prisons and other organizations have developed programs to maintain contact and relations between mothers and their children.

Thus far, this chapter has discussed crime in general, without focusing on its specific forms. The remainder of this section briefly looks at two different types of crime to probe further into the relationship between criminal justice and gender. One is the primarily female crime of prostitution, and the other is the apparently gender-neutral crime of murder.

Prostitution.   Between 100,000 and 500,000 American women are working prostitutes. Prostitution is a women's crime, only because most of the people arrested for it are women. The male participants in women's prostitution, including the pimps and especially the clients, are relatively untouched by the law. The justice system often focuses on prostitutes as though it is only they and not the men who pay for their services who are the wrongdoers.

The state has long had an ambivalent attitude toward prostitution. Officials and other interested parties cannot seem to decide whether prostitution is a crime with victims, that must be eradicated; a victimless crime that should be contained and eliminated if possible; an unfortunate aspect of life that should be kept out of sight as much as possible; or an immoral but sometimes useful enterprise.

Does prostitution have victims? Those who are forced to take part in prostitution, as is true for many prostitutes, surely are. Research shows that prostitutes usually have histories of abuse; more than three quarters were raped before the age of 14 years, usually by a relative.[44] Those who become diseased or subject to other crimes because of prostitution are also victims; these include prostitutes, clients, and, in the case of disease, the families of either. Disease has become an even more vexing problem since the spread of AIDS in the 1980s. A very large proportion of prostitutes, including a majority who are intravenous drug users, become infected and are HIV-positive. The majority of prostitutes are also mothers, who will therefore leave their children orphaned. Prostitutes do the best they can to protect themselves from violence, but the nature of their jobs puts them in constant danger.

An influential study of prostitution concluded, "Looking at all the data, one cannot say that prostitution is a victimless crime. On the other hand, the data . . . suggest that prostitution victimizes society only in specific and limited ways" (Milman, 1980, 62). Certainly, prostitutes themselves are at least as victimized as anyone else.

The state has accepted and, in some cases, supported prostitution. Police officers have often turned a blind eye to prostitution, only occasionally hauling in women to beef up a lagging arrest rate. Some people claim that the system of charging and fining prostitutes from time to time constitutes a quasi-official license to practice. (This is not to say that prostitutes are not sent to jail. They are.) Police officers find prostitutes to be useful informers because the prostitutes know what is happening on the streets. In the early 1970s, President Nixon allowed prostitutes onto U.S. military bases in Vietnam to "help morale" among the troops. Even though these women were, in a sense, employees of the U.S. government, they were refused free medical treatment for the resulting venereal diseases and pregnancies.[45]

Milman (1980) has argued that if prostitution is more a moral and health problem than a crime problem, criminal sanctions are inappropriate. Many people now recommend alternative treatments of prostitution that do not put the full burden of punishment on the prostitute. Even if rehabilitative programs are more widely used for prostitutes, however, will the public support programs to rehabilitate the men who buy sex? Would most people even think that men who buy sex are in need of rehabilitation?

Homicide.   Whereas prostitution is regarded as a female crime, murder seems at first glance to be a gender-neutral crime. However, it also poses some interesting questions for the study of gender and law enforcement. As Table 9-2 shows, among Americans who die by violence, men are much more likely than women to die because of homicide. These figures also are shocking for their picture of African-American men's lives; their victimization by criminal violence is substantial.

Most homicides perpetrated by women involve men, especially family members, and tend to take place at home (Wilbanks, 1982). Female murderers are more often first offenders than are male murderers, and they tend to use as weapons any implements that are handy, rather than firearms. These points suggest that a large proportion of the murders committed by women may be done in self-defense, and the earlier discussion of the victimization of women points toward the reasons. The issues surrounding homicide committed by women in self-defense reveal gender-based aspects of criminal justice.

Until 1977, women who killed in self-defense against rape or battery almost always lost their cases in court. The reason for these losses was the combined effects of the legal definition of the self-defense plea, the characteristics of murder

TABLE 9-2
Death from Violence, by Race and Sex, 1989

	White		Black	
Cause of Death	*Men*	*Women*	*Men*	*Women*
Motor vehicle accident	27	12	28	9
Other accidents	25	13	37	15
Suicide	21	5	12	2
Homicide	8	3	61	13

Note: Figures show the number of deaths per 100,000 population.
Source: U.S. Bureau of the Census (1992, 89).

by females, and stereotyped views of women. Two criteria must be met to claim justifiable homicide on the grounds of self-defense:

1. The killer must have had a reasonable apprehension of danger and a reasonable perception of the immanence of that danger. In other words, the danger does not have to have been real, as determined by later investigation, but it must have appeared to be real to a reasonable person (traditionally, a "reasonable man"). Also, killing has to have appeared to be the only viable course of action.
2. Deadly force cannot be used against nondeadly force.

The problem for women who kill in self-defense is thus twofold: (1) Can their apprehension of danger be considered reasonable, and (2) what constitutes deadly force? As described previously, it is extremely difficult for women to convince the criminal-justice system that they have been victims of rape or battery. It is even more difficult for a given woman to convince a court that she had reason to believe she would have been killed, as well. The courts have usually denied that an unarmed man can be interpreted as using deadly force, ignoring the fact that if a relatively small woman is victimized—especially one who has not been trained in the use of physical force against others—an unarmed man may easily exert deadly force with no weapon but his body. Moreover, a self-defense plea must be buttressed by proof that the defendant attempted to flee, rather than kill.

In 1977, a state supreme court case marked the beginning of change in the treatment of women's self-defense claims (*State* v. *Wanrow*). This court argued that the courts tend to view women from an androcentric perspective and do not consider the perceptions and physical conditions of women. It also noted that "through the persistent use of the masculine gender," the instructions given to the jury about how to understand self-defense "leaves the jury with the impression the objective standard to be applied is that applicable to an altercation between two men." In other words, *he* is not a gender-neutral term. Since that case, many courts have moved toward a fairer consideration of women who kill in self-defense. This case represents a dramatic event in the history of criminal justice: a court's recognition that the legal system has been androcentric.

Women face the persistent lack of understanding of rape by the criminal-justice system. As one person said during the 1977 trial of Inez Garcia, a rape victim who killed her attacker, "you can't kill someone for trying to give you a good time." Only some states allow deadly force as self-defense in cases of rape against women. This stands in marked contrast to men's situation. The courts have generally acquitted men who use deadly force to protect themselves from rape by another man. These situations are not the only ones in which men have more rights to commit violence against people whom they perceive to be threatening their sexuality. The old "paramour" laws, which permitted murder in reaction to uncovering adultery, were based on similar norms. Men who found their wives in bed with another man could get away with murder; women who found husbands in bed with another woman could not.

Women in the Criminal Justice System

There is now considerably more awareness of issues relating to women and criminal justice than was the case only a few years ago. Much of the impetus for change has come from the women's movement and from women who became victims of crime and were politicized by the experiences they had, both during the crime itself and in the course of trying to seek help from the criminal justice system. Further impetus has come from women's increasing participation in occupations within the criminal justice system.

Until recently, women have had little hand in the formal enforcement and administration of justice. As late as 1987, no major city had a female police chief, although 11 smaller cities did. Also, only a small percentage of judges, even in municipal courts, have been women. In 1993, President Clinton appointed Janet Reno to be the first woman attorney general, the cabinet member who heads the Department of Justice and serves as the chief cop of the federal government. Evidence suggests that women have an impact when they become actors in the criminal-justice system.

The Defense Department investigation of the Tailhook convention offers telling related examples. Donald Mancuso, the inspector general, said that the female agents were especially valuable in establishing the facts for two reasons. First, the female victims—many of whom were wives, girlfriends, or relatives of the officers—were very reluctant to tell their stories and felt more comfortable talking to women investigators. Second, "officers were unable to make the impression with the female agents that this was just a guy thing. And the women put many of the men off balance. They weren't used to dealing with professional women who [were] older than they were."[46] Women do make a difference to women and to men, and this is only likely to be encouraged by the formation of women's groups such as the Committee on Women in Federal Law Enforcement and the International Association of Women Police.

A march for women's suffrage in New York City, 1912.

Women's Political Participation and Influence

It is commonly argued that women have been kept out of politics and government almost entirely, and that for a variety of reasons, women do not participate in politics. In fact, women have never been as fully absent from American political life as many people believe. There is no question, however, that women still have considerably *less* political power than men, and only a small fraction of governmental decision makers are women. To what extent do women participate in politics? How much influence do they have? Does it matter whether more women become active in politics or even obtain positions of political power?

Gender in Electoral Politics

Free elections and the right to vote are supposed to be crucial elements of a democratic polity. Women and men have died for this right. Yet after the long hard battle for women's suffrage was won, many activists were disappointed to find that women were not as likely to use their right to vote as men were. The gap eventually narrowed, and for many years now, there has been little difference between women's and men's voting rates. Indeed, in some elections, among people who are young, highly educated, or African-American, more women now tend to vote than men. Because male and female turnout rates fluctuate across elections, the size of the gender difference depends on the election. Women and men are also about evenly matched in other kinds of campaign activities, such as displaying buttons and bumper stickers, going to meetings and rallies, and doing campaign work. Women give less money to political campaigns than men do, but they also have less money than men do.

Women's electoral involvement should not be surprising. They have long been known as the backbone of the political parties—making phone calls, ringing doorbells, stuffing envelopes, compiling lists, and watching polls, as well as cooking and cleaning up for party and campaign picnics and other functions. Women were involved in these activities long before they had the right to vote.

Research suggests a number of reasons for the early gender differences in political involvement and the more recent achievement of parity. First, voting is a habit that most newly enfranchised groups, including immigrants and young people, take time to develop. Second, education and related socioeconomic factors determine how politically active people are; in general, the greater the gap in education, the greater the gap in electoral participation. Third, gender ideology and gender roles have had an impact. In the 1920s, many women did not vote because they did not think that their voting was appropriate. Women with an egalitarian gender ideology are still more likely to be active in elections than those who are more androcentric in their views of social and political roles (Sapiro, 1983). Women, especially single women, who are responsible for children are also less politically active than women without children.

At higher levels of politics, men's and women's involvement differs more markedly. The more powerful or authoritative, the better paid, or the more visible a political position is, the less likely it is that a woman holds it. Despite women's yeoman work in political parties, until recently, they have been a small minority of the delegates selected to participate in decision making at national nominating conventions. Relatively few women are among the major party decision makers. Until recently, women were not given many top decision-making roles in electoral campaigns, although this is changing. From 1988 on, women have been very prominent among the top levels of presidential campaign management, and many women are involved in the campaign business. Nonetheless, women still constitute a relatively small percentage of candidates for local, state, and national offices.

Why is this the case? If women are so active in politics at the mass level, why is there not gender parity in the number of candidates for office in a democratic system? Among the most common reasons cited by political scientists are (1) women are not motivated or lack ambitions for office, (2) they are not as qualified as men for office, and (3) discrimination and sexism have hindered women. This section looks at the evidence for each reason.

Many have said that women do not become political leaders because they are not interested in politics or do not want to be leaders. This reason is suspect; differences in interest and mass-level political activity are so marginal that they cannot explain the large gender imbalance in public officials. Studies of men and women who are already very active in politics—community activists and national nominating convention delegates, for example—show that women are less likely to want to hold a political office, but even by the 1970s, the difference was not large enough to explain the substantial gap in the proportion of male and female officeholders (Jennings and Farah, 1981; Sapiro and Farah, 1980).

Several reasons have been offered to explain the gender differences in political ambition. Some people argue that women are less competitive and aggressive, which causes them not to seek positions of political power and authority. Research suggests that the problem may be less a lack of competitiveness and more the fact that politically active women have lower expectations of success than men do (Jennings and Farah, 1981), and they anticipate encountering discouragement and discrimination from male colleagues in politics. Also, the juggling act politically active women must do among their political activities, jobs, and family life—assuming that women remain more responsible at home than men—can lead them to suppress their own political ambition. Research shows that women and men both feel that family and political roles can conflict, but that women tend to resolve these conflicts in favor of the family, and men make the opposite choice. This is why comparisons of male and female officeholders show that the women are less likely to be married or to have young children than the men are (Sapiro, 1982a).

Do women have the qualifications for office? Certainly, they have faced some disadvantages. Political leaders tend to be drawn from the ranks of people in certain occupations, such as the law, which have traditionally been segregated, male-dominated fields. One study, however, suggests that gender-segregated occupations do not account for the large differences in the numbers of male and female officeholders, nor are educational differences large enough to explain away the power differential (Welch, 1978).

A third major reason cited for the low numbers of women in positions of political leadership and authority is discrimination. Women in politics often testify about the discrimination they face in the political parties and other mixed-gender or male-dominated political organizations. There is plenty of evidence of institutionalized gender discrimination. A study of congressional races from 1916 to 1978 shows that women are put forward more often than men as candidates for seats their party is unlikely to win (Gertzog and Simard, 1980). Research disagrees over whether women face discrimination in gaining funding for their campaigns. Although studies of male and female candidates show little difference in the candidates' ability to attract money, some observers suggest that many women never get to be candidates because of the difficulty of attracting start-up funds. Now, many organizations are aimed specifically at raising money for female candidates. The most well known is Emily's List, run by Ellen Malcolm, founded in 1985, under the principle that *Early Money Is Like Yeast* (thus creating the acronym EMILY), which distributed about $6 million to female Democratic candidates in 1992.[47] Other such organizations include the bipartisan National Women's Political Caucus and the Women's Campaign Fund, and the Republican Wish List.

As in other cases, not all political discrimination against women is conscious. One researcher did an experiment in which she gave university students a speech to read that was supposedly given by a candidate for the House of Representatives (Sapiro, 1982b). Half the students were told that the speech was by Joan Leeds, and the other half were told that the speech was by John Leeds. Comparing the responses of the two groups showed that John's policy proposals were regarded as better than Joan's and that John was considered more likely to win. Men, but not women, judged John to be more competent than Joan at dealing with military, business, farm, and crime issues. Nevertheless, a large majority of Americans say they would vote for a qualified woman for office, and an increasing number actually do so.

There is one last explanation for the small numbers of women in public office, one that many scholars are convinced is the major roadblock women now face (Darcy, Welch, and Clark, 1994). Even if women's ambitions are high, they get the right training, they can manage their public and private roles, and discrimination continues to decrease, the increase in women's numbers in public office depends on certain structural opportunities. For instance, using the House of Representatives as an example, *incumbents* (current officeholders) are rarely defeated for reelection. A woman's best chance of getting elected to the House, thereby increasing the number of women, is to run for an open seat in a district dominated by her party. This fortunate confluence of events rarely occurs. At least one calculation taking into account such structural factors predicts that, at best, women may constitute about one third of the House members the decade after the turn of the century. Parity is much farther off (Darcy, Welch, and Clark, 1994).

The 1992 elections—defined by the press collectively as "The Year of the Woman"—offer a good example. That year, an unprecedented number of women ran for seats in the House of Representatives and the U.S. Senate. In all, 150 women ran for House seats; the highest previous numbers had been 70 in 1990 and 65 in 1984. The 20 female Senate candidates compared with 10 such candidates in 1984 and 8 in 1990. A combination of factors accounted for this dramatic increase. First, there was an unusual opportunity. For a variety of reasons, there were more open seats than there had been for a long time—in other words, more places to run and more possibility of winning. Second, opinion polls and the success of Ross Perot in attracting support indicated that the public wanted some newcomers in office. Women are symbolically the embodiment of newcomers. Finally, many women had become politically energized by the Senate hearings in which law professor Anita Hill accused Supreme Court nominee Clarence Thomas of committing sexual harassment. Indeed, it was clear that female candidates used images from these hearings to underscore the pitiful lack of women in office. Where women ran for Congress or governor, they even managed to energize women to be active in the *presidential* election (Sapiro and Conover, 1998). In 1996, the proportion of women continued to rise, but the jolt was not quite as strong.

Are women's campaigns different from men's? Are these campaigns treated differently? Research suggests that the answers to these questions have changed over time, as more women have entered politics, women's organizations have a larger influence, and the gender gap has emerged as a force in U.S. electoral politics. Certainly, most campaign strategists devote great effort to shaping the particular appeal of their candidates, male and female, to avoid alienating women, and women's campaigns in the 1990s have often traded heavily on the widespread desire among women—liberal and conservative—to see more women enter into political office. The most recent research suggests that although women and men now run their campaigns in very similar ways, women candidates tend to be somewhat more liberal than the men candidates of their own party, they focus on issues more (whereas men focus more on character), and they focus more on *social issues* —especially those generally regarded as women's issues—than men do (Kahn and

Gordon, 1997). One reason why they may emphasize these particular issues is that research also shows that female candidates gain a distinct advantage over male candidates when they do so; they garner no such advantage (but no disadvantage either) when they go head to head on other major issues (Iyengar, Valentino, Ansolabehere, and Simon, 1997).

One of the most important questions in electoral politics is whether women and men evaluate candidates, parties, and issues differently. Conventional wisdom has been that women are more conservative and moralistic than men in their political thinking and that they tend to oppose the use of force and violence and to support social-welfare programs. As usual, there has been more stereotype than systematic evidence on the subject. Although it is commonly argued that the supposed differences between women and men are due to their natures or to women's roles in the family, in fact, there have been few differences that are consistent over time or across countries. When gender differences in public opinion show up, they are usually relatively small.

Researchers have tracked gender differences in public opinion since the advent of widespread public opinion polling. In the 1950s, women were somewhat more likely than men to think of themselves as Republicans, and they were more supportive of the Republican candidates than men were in 1952 and 1956 (Eisenhower), and 1960 (Nixon). More recently, women have identified more with the Democratic Party and have cast a higher proportion of their votes for the Democrats than have men in 1964 (Johnson), 1968 (Humphrey), 1972 (McGovern), 1980 (Carter), 1984 (Mondale), 1988 (Dukakis), and 1992 and 1996 (Clinton). The differences are rarely very large, however, and the same candidate usually won among both women and men, although by different margins.

Only since about 1980 has there been a sizeable difference between men's and women's votes, and this was reflected only twice in the presidential election. Once was in the 1980 election, when Ronald Reagan was first elected, and men supported him more than women by about 9 percentage points. The other was in 1996, when it was clear that if it had been only up to men, Robert Dole would have won the presidential election. Many scholars and journalists have debated the reasons for this gap, and most try to figure out what it is about *women* that have led them to vote so Democratic. In fact, this is the wrong way to look at it. When the gender gap has emerged, it is more because many men who traditionally might have voted Democratic (especially White ethnics and young White men) abandoned that party for the Republicans. The reasons for this abandonment are various, but they chiefly have to do with men having been attracted to the Republican party because they blamed the country's economic problems on spending too much on welfare programs and because they believed that White men's job prospects were being hurt through affirmative action for African-Americans and women. In addition, in the early 1980s, men—especially young White men—were more attracted than women were to the hawkishness of the Reagan rhetoric, and they more strongly favored policies of cutting back on social-welfare programs than women did (Mueller, 1991).

One thing is certain: The existence and size of a gender gap in voting depend on the circumstances of the electoral season and the more general historical forces at work in politics. Gender differences in voting vary from election to election, and they exist in some elections in some countries and not in others. Are there any notable and stable gender differences of political opinion on political issues? There are not as many as people seem to think, and the differences tend to be small (Shapiro and Mahajan, 1986). More women than men oppose policies relying on or encouraging violence and tend to see violence as a last resort (Conover and Sapiro, 1993). Women are less hawkish on military and defense issues, more opposed to capital punishment, and more supportive of gun control than men. A survey of the foreign-policy opinions of American leaders shows similar results: Female leaders tended to oppose militarism and the use of the CIA to undermine governments and to support the use of international organizations such as the United Nations (Holsti and Rosenau, 1981).

Some studies show that women are more supportive than men of pro-environmental legislation. Women also have voiced more support for government policies to help the poor and to guarantee full employment. As a group, women's support of feminism and so-called women's issues is uneven. Women are more moralistic, in the traditional sense, on many issues, which may account for some of their ambivalence about feminist issues; more women than men support prayer in public schools, for example. Whereas women were once thought to be more trusting of government, however, polls now suggest that women have less confidence than men about the economic future of the United States and are more likely to feel that this country would get into a war. Nevertheless, on *most issues,* gender differences are trivial or nonexistent, and they change over time (Shapiro and Mahajan, 1986).

Nonelectoral Citizen Politics

Electoral participation is only one category of political participation. Women have long been noted for engaging in politics and community action through churches, clubs, and numerous other organizations (Scott, 1992). Indeed, government figures support this view, showing that women constitute a majority of the people involved in volunteer work (U.S. Bureau of the Census, 1992, 374). Women provide not just the troops for this work, but the leaders as well, even while they are not adequately recognized (Daniels, 1988). The importance of community and organization work in politics is underestimated because of the usual emphasis on elections. It is important to remember that a large part of public problem solving is done by people active in their own communities, where issues about education, land use, and the availability of other services are most focused.

The 19th century saw a dramatic growth in women's activity in formal and informal organizations of many sorts involving women of most classes, races, and religions. Some were organized for cultural activities and self-improvement, and others were organized for social philanthropy, or volunteer work and community service. Historians point out that even groups not organized explicitly for the purpose of participating in politics nevertheless often engaged women in politics or political discussion. Many women's clubs, for example, served as audiences for suffragists as they traveled across the country lecturing on women and the vote.

In 1890, many of these clubs joined together to form the General Federation of Women's Clubs (GFWC), which had over a million members by 1910. Many

GFWC affiliates were instrumental in establishing the early framework for public social-welfare programs through their work in health, education, poverty relief, and municipal reform (Skocpol, 1992). Club women were among the chief lobbyists for local and state government responsibility for social welfare. Interestingly, although these women thought it was crucial for women to be involved in "social housekeeping" and public affairs, the GFWC did not endorse the women's suffrage amendment to the U.S. Constitution until 1914 because many of its members thought that their own successes proved that women already had enough power in government, and they did not want women to become involved in "dirty" partisan politics. On the other hand, these same successes may have made it necessary for them to change their minds. As government increasingly took up their concerns with public policy and management, women found their continued involvement limited in those states that barred women from voting or holding office.

There is an unfortunate stereotype that women's organizational and grassroots political activity involved only middle-class White women. This is far from the truth. Although middle-class women historically have had more time to devote to these efforts (at least up until the 1930s, when they were unlikely to be employed and likely to have domestic servants), women of different classes and many ethnic and racial groups organized for community action and problem solving. For example, as early as the 1820s to 1840s, Black women organized literary societies that also helped needy Black women and gave financial assistance to Black newspapers (Giddings, 1984, 49). There was also a large Black women's club movement (Salem, 1990). White ethnic immigrant women also formed many organizations around the turn of the century. Part of the historical and current importance of women's community participation is that it is so embedded in the large variety of the circumstances of women's lives and their communities. Although *levels* and *types* of participation may differ, there are issues and organizations in which all types of women have participated from all the different communities of the United States.

Women have historically been active in many social movements and protest actions. (See also Chapter 14, which focuses on feminist movements.) Women's independent labor activity goes back at least to the 1820s (Foner, 1982; Kessler-Harris, 1982). In U.S. history, there are many instances of women organizing boycotts and other consumer-related political actions. A good example is the 1917 boycott that resulted in massive demonstrations among Jewish immigrant women living in New York's Lower East Side (Frank, 1985). There have been few major social movements in American history in which women were not involved in large numbers; among the more notable are the movements for abolition, temperance (Bordin, 1990), utopian communalism (Chmielewski, Kern, and Klee-Hartzell, 1993), health reform, peace (Alonso, 1993), progressivism and municipal reform, civil rights (Mills, 1993), and welfare rights (Pope, 1989). Examples of this activism in different arenas are described in most chapters of this book.

Women are now nearly as active as men in mass-level politics. Thanks in part to education and to changing gender-role ideology, more people than ever now think that political activity is appropriate for women. Unfortunately, however, it appears that girls are still socialized to express less interest in politics than boys are

(Owen and Dennis, 1988). Politics is still stereotypically regarded as a male domain.

Women's gender-related roles help shape the degree to which women become politically active, as well as the ways in which this activism is manifest. Motherhood has a greater impact on political activity than fatherhood; child-care responsibility can inhibit women's participation in some aspects of politics, especially for single women, but it can also push women, especially homemakers, into political activity in local and school affairs (Jennings, 1979; Sapiro, 1983). The mere fact that a woman is either employed or a housewife does not have as strong a relationship with political participation as some people think (McDonough, 1982; Sapiro, 1983). Employment can expand the number of contacts a woman has, and her occupation may help shape the kinds of interests she has. More important, however, may be the way a woman interprets her own roles and how compatible she thinks her roles are with political activism. It is important to remember that for a long time, Sojourner Truth's occupation was slavery and Elizabeth Cady Stanton's was homemaking; neither of them shied away from political activity.

Indeed, Nancy Burns, Kay Schlozman, and Sidney Verba (1997) found, in their nationwide survey of the political participation of married couples, that most people have been thinking about things the wrong way around, by emphasizing the degree to which women's roles might be limiting to their political participation. As these researchers have said, domestic arrangements affect both husbands and wives. In fact, they found that

> domestic hierarchies have greater implications for the political activity of husbands than of wives. The particular aspects of domestic inequality that matter for the political activity of husbands as individuals are his control over major financial decisions and his relative autonomy in using small amounts of time.

Whereas most scholars have thought the *lack* of these resources *depresses* women's political participation, Burns, Schlozman, and Verba found that an extra measure of these resources *boosts* men's participation. In addition, they found that beliefs about equality matter more for women. Women who believe in equality and have husbands who respect them gain an added lift to their political participation (Burns, Schlozman, and Verba, 1997).

The Impact of Women in Politics

What difference does women's participation in politics make? One way to answer this question is to determine whether women and men act differently or make different decisions when they hold positions of power and influence. Most studies of women legislators, judges, and bureaucrats suggest that most of the time, gender does not make much difference in how public officials view the issues. Studies of state legislators show women and men voting in similar ways and sponsoring the same number of pieces of legislation. Research on judges shows that, by and large, male and female judges make the same kinds of decisions (Gruhl, Spohn, and Welch, 1981). However, many women in politics claim that even when males and

⌇

BOX 9-1   See for Yourself: Women in Politics

Go to a meeting of your local city council, school board, or—if you are near a state capital—the state legislature. (An especially interesting kind of session to attend is a *hearing*, in which members of the public and interest groups testify about their views of a particular proposed ordinance, law, or policy.)

Do you see evidence of gender differences in behavior or interests?

females claim to support similar policies, it is the women in public office who generally do most of the work to put more egalitarian gender principles into practice.

Nevertheless, recent research sponsored by the Center for the American Woman and Politics at Rutgers points to many instances in which women now seem to be making more of a difference than they did.[48] It is not clear whether this increased influence occurs because the numbers of women in office had to pass a certain critical mass, which allowed the women to be more active, or because different kinds of women are now being elected. In either case, consider the findings from a national study of state legislators (Dodson and Carroll, 1991): The vast majority of men and women in state legislatures *think* that women make a difference. More women than men oppose prohibiting abortion, oppose parental consent for abortion, and oppose the death penalty and expansion of nuclear-power plants. Women are more likely to think that the private sector cannot solve most of our problems. Even within political parties, women legislators tend to be more supportive of liberal and feminist policies than their male colleagues. More women have worked on women's rights bills. Women and men have somewhat different ideas about qualities that are important for political leaders to have. Women are more likely to think political leaders should have a sense of mission and a concern for those affected by political decisions. Women think that men try to keep them out of leadership positions, but men disagree. (See Box 9-1.)

Sue Thomas's (1994) study of state legislators across the country found great overlap in the attitudes, roles, and activities of men and women. Her comparison of women legislators in the 1970s and the 1980s found the latter group much more integrated into their political institutions and much more similar to the men in education and occupation. The second group of women legislators seemed more resistant to discrimination and to being pigeonholed, although they still tended to gravitate toward the policy areas traditionally associated with women. As might be expected, the women in legislatures that had larger numbers of women could be braver and more nonconformist than women who were more isolated.

Even though we cannot yet know how many, which, and to what degree our policies would be different in a more sexually balanced government, some things would surely change. Our government would be more representative of society as a whole. Women would have more of a role in governing their own lives as citizens. Also, to the degree that our government is a model of our society's values, that model would show women as leaders and full participants.

Few individual countries were ever truly isolated in their politics and unaffected by the rest of the world. Nonetheless, the growing globalization of most aspects of human society makes it harder for the residents of any one country—including one as powerful as the United States—to maintain the myth that they are completely the shapers of their own destiny, unaffected by the world scene. It has become more important than ever to understand the significance of gender for international politics and, especially, to consider the impact of international politics on women and the role of women in international politics.

International politics shapes women's lives in many gender-differentiated ways. The globalization of the economy—especially the ease with which low technology, heavily labor-intensive employment such as textile work and electronics manufacture crosses borders—has a special impact on women's economic condition because they tend to be employed as a large, cheap pool of labor in these industries. International aid and development programs tend to be administered in a way that affects men and women differently; often, such programs reinforce traditional gender-based divisions of labor, but sometimes, such programs disrupt these divisions. Women's rights and the treatment of women were the focus of international debate many times during the 20th century, beginning with the idea, instigated in the 1930s, that women's rights had to be understood within the rubric of the developing concept of international human rights. Women's health, women's literacy, women's role in politics, violence against women, and female genital mutilation have all been the subject of international political campaigns involving both *national* and *international* organizations.[49] The series of "Women's Decade" activities sponsored by the United Nations (UN), as well as the UN's many committees, meetings, and international agreements relating to women's rights offer only one important set of examples.

Women have become increasingly active and influential in international politics. Of course, as a greater number of women become members of their countries' legislatures and heads of state, they take a greater hand in running international affairs. Some women heads of state have been very important on the world scene, such as India's Indira Gandhi, Britain's Margaret Thatcher, and Israel's Golda Meir, all of whom led their countries during times of war. The 1997 appointment of Madeleine Albright as the first woman secretary of state in the United States seemed to be greeted by remarkably little surprise at her gender. The appointment of Mary Robinson, the president of Ireland, as the UN's High Commissioner for Human Rights in 1997 was well received by women around the world.

The more women become aware of and involved in international politics, however, the more they find they hit the same barriers of discrimination and stereotype that they do at the national level. Women who work at the UN, for example, have complained for years about discrimination and sexual harassment. As Table 9-3 shows, few countries seem to go out of their way to make sure that women are represented among the professional staff members they send to work for the UN. Just as change is taking place in national politics around the world,

TABLE 9-3
Proportion of Women Among Professional United Nations Staffs, Selected Countries

0%	Bangladesh, Belarus, Mali, Mauritius, Poland
1–20%	Algeria, Burundi, Colombia, Egypt, Ethiopia, Finland, Ghana, Iraq, Ivory, Jordan, Kenya, Malawi, Malaysia, Netherlands, Nigeria, Russia, Tunisia, Ukraine, Uruguay, Zaire
21–40%	Argentina, Belgium, Brazil, Cameroon, Canada, Chile, China, Cuba, Denmark, Germany, India, Iran, Ireland, Israel, Italy, Jamaica, Morocco, Pakistan, Peru, Senegal, Sierra Leone, South Africa, Sweden, Switzerland, Tanzania, Turkey, Uganda, United Kingdom
41–60%	Australia, Austria, France, Greece, Guyana, Japan, Mexico, New Zealand, Norway, Philippines, Spain, Thailand, Trinidad and Tobago, **United States**
61–80%	Singapore

Note: This table includes countries with at least 10 professional staff members at the United Nations. Figures are the proportion of women in 1993.
Source: UN, 1995a, 171–175.

however, so it is in international politics. As Madeleine Albright said when she became secretary of state in 1997, "It used to be the only way a woman could truly make her foreign policy views felt was by marrying a diplomat and then pouring tea on an offending ambassador's lap. Today, women are engaged in every facet of global affairs."[50]

Women, Feminism, and Democracy

The people of the United States have long thought of their government as close to ideal in the principles and practice of democracy. American schoolchildren still learn that theirs is a government "of the people, by the people, and for the people." There is no question that this government is indeed one of the most democratic in the world. Has it been as democratic as Americans have claimed, however?

Throughout the history of this nation, feminists have argued that we have a long way to go before our democratic claims are truly fulfilled. Our standards for democracy have become tougher over the years; not so long ago, we described ourselves as democratic, even though at least half the adult population was barred by law from voting. Even now, many people find no contradiction between democratic principles and the low degree of governmental power that women share. Most people are unaware of how unequally law and policy affect women and men.

The central theme of democratic theory is the distribution of power in a political community: the degree to which people are free to share in making decisions about the community and, ultimately, themselves. The central theme of feminist theory is the distribution of power between women and men, especially the amount of power women have over themselves. Feminism, therefore, seeks to raise our standard of democracy.

The fall of many authoritarian governments in the late 1980s and early 1990s renewed worldwide attention to the meaning of democracy. Feminists in many of the countries of the former Soviet Union and Eastern Europe are learning the hard way that there are no simple solutions. Following the initial euphoria after the fall of the Berlin Wall and the toppling of dictators, members of those nations have been finding that the transition *to* democracy is more difficult than the fall *from* authoritarianism. Women especially are finding that in the shift toward democracy, they are often left behind, both losing the social-welfare assistance they had under the old system and being excluded and neglected to a large degree in the new one. In response to some of these fears, many feminists in the former Soviet Union adopted as the battle cry of their new movement, "Democracy minus women is not democracy." The United States is one of the many nations that stand to learn from this phrase.

Notes

1. Quoted in the *New York Times,* September 16, 1993.

2. Unless otherwise stated, the discussion of legal rights refers to the rights of free women (most of whom were White) under the law. Women held in slavery (most of whom were Black) did not have legal rights.

3. Because of colonial patterns, the French legal tradition also influences law in Louisiana, and the Spanish legal tradition has influence over much of the American Southwest.

4. The text of Supreme Court cases makes very interesting and important reading to understand the logic of the law; the cases are, in a way, *applied* political philosophy. Most of the cases mentioned here are in Kay (1996). All Supreme Court cases since 1990 and many other court cases can be found at the Cornell Institute for Legal Studies, http://www.law.cornell.edu/lii.table.html/.

5. Visit the EEOC at http://www.eeoc.gov/ and learn how to file a discrimination charge.

6. For very brief factual discussions of women's history in the military, see the links to the superb and witty homepage "American Women in Uniform, Veterans Too!" by Captain Barbara A. Wilson, USAF (Ret.), at http://userpages.aug.com/captbarb/index.html, or see the homepage of the Minerva Center, a nonprofit educational foundation supporting study of women in war and women in the military, http://208.8.220.10/MinervaCenter/. See also the Library of Congress exhibit on women journalists, photographers, and broadcasters who went to war at http://lcweb.loc.gov/exhibits/wcf/wcf0001.html/.

7. The House of Representatives held hearings on this and related cases. The report makes very interesting reading. See U.S. Congress (1930).

8. "Pentagon Plans to Allow Combat Flights by Women; Seeks to Drop Warship Ban," *New York Times,* April 28, 1993.

9. Felicity Barringer, "Four Reports Cite Naval Academy for Rife Sexism," *New York Times,* October 10, 1990.

10. Michael R. Gordon, "Pentagon Report Tells of Aviators' 'Debauchery,'" *New York Times,* April 24, 1993.

11. Maureen Dowd, "Senate Approves 4-Star Rank for Admiral in Tailhook Affair," *New York Times,* April 20, 1994.

12. William Tuohy, "Female NATO Officers Press for Wider Combat Roles," *Los Angeles Times,* May 25, 1992.

13. Mary Daniels, "Prisoner of War," *Chicago Tribune,* September 6, 1992.

14. Michael R. Gordon, "Panel Is Against Letting Women Fly in Combat," *New York Times,* November 4, 1992.

15. Eric Schmitt, "Army Allowing Women in 32,000 Combat Posts," *New York Times,* July 28, 1994.

16. John H. Cushman, Jr., "Top Military Officers Object to Lifting Homosexual Ban," *New York Times,* November 14, 1992.

17. Cushman, "Top Military Officers."

18. Philip Shenon, "New Study Faults Pentagon's Gay Policy," *New York Times,* February 26, 1997.

19. Timothy Egan, "Sexual Conflict in Army Can Be Undisciplined," *New York Times,* November 15, 1996.

20. Egan, "Sexual Conflict in Army."

21. Eric Schmitt, "Top Enlisted Man in the Army Stands Accused of Sex Assault," *New York Times,* February 4, 1997.

22. Adam Nossiter, "A Cadet Is Dismissed and 9 Others Are Punished in the Harassment of Women at the Citadel," *New York Times,* March 11, 1997.

23. Eric Schmitt, "Women in Army Face Wide Bias, 2 Inquiries Find," *New York Times,* July 31, 1997.

24. For more information on sexual abuse in the military, including both testimony from women and information on receiving assistance if one is or has been a victim of abuse, see the "American Women in Uniform" webpage listed in Note 6.

25. Eric Schmitt, "Bill Is Proposed to Segregate Sexes During Basic Training," *New York Times,* May 18, 1997.

26. To visit a feminist policy institute, go to the Institute for Women's Policy Research, http://www.iwpr.org/.

27. For information on violence against women, and help for those who need it, see The Feminist Majority's "911 for Women" at http://www.feminist.org/911/1-support.html/. This website can refer you to local resources also.

28. U.S. Department of Justice, Federal Bureau of Investigation, "Uniform Crime Reporting Program Press Release—10/13/96," http://www.fbi.gov/ucr/ucr95prs.htm/.

29. "Sex-Offender Registration Laws Pit Victims' Rights Against Civil Rights," *New York Times,* February 20, 1993.

30. See Note 27.

31. Don Terry, "Stabbing Death at Door of Justice Sends Alert on Domestic Violence," *New York Times,* March 17, 1992.

32. This is not strictly true because of the many states with antisodomy laws, which technically make such acts as oral or anal intercourse illegal. Thus, not all sexual relations within marriage are technically protected.

33. Barry Meir, "When Abuse Follows Women to Work," *New York Times,* March 10, 1996.

34. Matthew Purdy, "Wave of New Laws Seeks to Confine Sexual Offenders," *New York Times,* June 29, 1997.

35. "Sex-Offender Registration Laws Pit Victims' Rights Against Civil Rights," *New York Times,* February 20, 1993.

36. Purdy, "Wave of New Laws Seeks to Confine Sexual Offenders."

37. Ross E. Milloy, "Furor Over a Decision Not to Indict in a Rape Case," *New York Times,* October 25, 1992.

38. Mitchell Landsberg, "Women's Fears Lead to Gun Buys," *Wisconsin State Journal,* February 8, 1993.

39. Visit the fascinating NRA Women's Issues Department at http://www.nra.org/wi/wips2.html/.

40. See Note 27.

41. "Number of Women in Jail Rises," *New York Times,* March 24, 1996.

42. Peter Applebombe, "Holding Fragile Families Together When Mothers Are Inmates," *New York Times,* December 27, 1992.

43. Applebombe, "Holding Fragile Families Together When Mothers Are Inmates."

44. Barbara Goldsmith, "A Reporter at Large: Women on the Edge," *The New Yorker,* April 26, 1993, p. 65.

45. For further discussion of the military and prostitution, see Enloe (1983).

46. "Beating Wall of Silence by Navy Pilots."

47. Visit Emily's List at http://www.emilyslist.org:80/home.htm/.

48. Visit the Center for the American Woman and Politics at http://www.rci.rutgers.edu/~cawp/.

49. For more information on current international women's issues, see the Institute for Global Communications (IGC) WomensNet (http://www.igc.org/igc/womensnet/, which has excellent connections to information and organizations.

50. Bob Deans, "Albright's New Role an Historic Advance for Women," *Wisconsin State Journal,* January 21, 1997.

Choice and Control in Personal Life, the Family, and Work

ONE OF THE IMPORTANT THEMES in this book is the relationship between gender and power, control, and choice. Throughout Part Two we looked at the ways in which values that define individuals and their life choices are shaped by the gender norms embedded in the structures of social institutions. We have also looked at some of the ways in which women have influenced these institutions and attempted to expand their own options.

In Part Three, we look at the areas of life in which we are said most to express and to act on our own feelings, abilities, and desires as individuals: the way we talk, walk, and relate to others; our personal and intimate lives; and our family and work relationships. The question that unites these chapters is, To what extent does gender limit the control women have over their choices and experiences?

Reflect *Before* You Read

1. Imagine that tomorrow morning, you will wake up to find that you have become the other sex. Describe in detail what tomorrow will be like. How will you feel? What will you do? How will people treat you? What will you miss about your old sex? What will you like about your new one?
2. You have been restored to your current sex. Describe your adult life as it has been, as you imagine it will be, and as you hope it will be. How much of it—which of your choices, important experiences, major dilemmas, and turning points—is determined in any way by your gender? What would be different if you were of the other gender?
3. Think about the five people who are closest and most important to you. Imagine that they all suddenly changed their sex. Can you imagine them being just as they are now in all other respects? If not, what would be different? Would you feel differently about each of these people? Would you act differently? How? Why?

10

❧

Gender, Communication, and Self-Expression

In all acts words importing the masculine gender shall be deemed and taken to include females.

British Parliament, 1850

ONE OF THE MOST IMPORTANT TASKS we human beings undertake is to learn how to communicate with other people. Language provides the basis for our existence as both *social beings,* able to act and interact with other people, and *independent, autonomous beings,* capable of seeing ourselves as morally responsible social agents. Language is the means by which we know ourselves and others. By studying patterns of communication, we can better understand the delicate balance between the individual and social aspects of people's lives. Without communication, we are a collection of atomistic, unconnected individuals, not a society. Communication is the medium of which social structure is built because it is the medium by which values are transmitted and enforced. Social structure can be maintained relatively gently, through teaching young people culturally preferred values, or it might be maintained more forcefully by communicating severe threats to a population and using terror against deviants as a symbolic warning to others.

Communication, then, is the stuff of power and control. Power is not a lump of something that people possess; it is a characteristic of relationships among people. As such, an understanding of how sex/gender systems work requires investigating gendered aspects of language and communication.

Marx and Engels called language "practical consciousness"—that is, the means by which we categorize, recognize, or name tangible and intangible objects. When we cannot attach a word to an object, we call it "indescribable," something that cannot be identified, defined, or communicated to others. Objects or feelings we consider particularly dangerous or frightening we call "unmentionable" or "unspeakable," as though we could wipe them out of existence by excluding them from social discourse.

Language and *communication* encompass many kinds of nonverbal behavior, as well as acts of writing and speaking.[1] American Sign Language, for example, is a full language, based on gesture rather than the spoken word. In addition, however, almost all of us have a large vocabulary of gestures. We express ourselves regularly by smiling, shaking our heads, raising a hand, walking away, or hitting someone; often, these gestures are intertwined with spoken language to create meaning. Both verbal and nonverbal communication have vocabulary and grammar. That is, they are systems of sounds or gestures that symbolize or encode meaning understood by people within a specific language group when they are patterned in a certain way.

Analysis of language is complicated by the fact that there are many variations within any given natural language (such as English, French, or Hindi). Most people are familiar with regional dialects and similar language variations resulting from cultural factors, such as ethnicity, race, and religion. Language also varies by age, class, occupation, and gender. Sometimes, the differences are so great that people from one group unwittingly misinterpret or have difficulty understanding those from another group. That is the basis of the title of Deborah Tannen's (1990) popular book on gender and communication, *You Just Don't Understand*.

Situation and context strongly affect people's language use. Most people communicate differently with a stranger and a friend, a parent and a child, a superior and a subordinate, and a woman and a man. This often unconscious practice is due partly to subcultural variations among these groups, partly to the effects of status and hierarchy rankings among these groups, and partly to the different organizational and institutional positions that members of different social groups tend to occupy.

In the remainder of this chapter, we explore gender and language and communication behavior, beginning with the ways in which sex/gender systems are defined, maintained, and changed through the language people use to mark and refer to gender. We then examine how gender shapes communication behavior, including how we speak, carry ourselves, and interact with others. We also focus on the signs of gender-related differences in power and interaction in people's communication behavior. Finally, we consider the relationship between communication and social change.

Referring to Women, Men, and People

Most of us have had the experience of saying to someone, "Don't put words into my mouth," usually when someone interprets something we *said* in a way that conflicts with what we were *trying to say*. This misinterpretation can occur when we use a word or phrase that carries a connotation we had not recognized at the time, but which, nevertheless, is taken by the listener as part of the message. Many women's studies scholars (in fields such as linguistics, psychology, sociology, and philosophy) research the multiple connotations of words that refer to males and females. Not surprisingly, our gender language reflects the current nature of sex/gender systems and hierarchical social relationships, and it often incorporates values we might not recognize or intend. In the following section, we explore our gender vocabulary.

Gender-Specific Terms

Consider some words that most obviously refer to gender: *male* and *female*, *man* and *woman*, *girl* and *boy*, *feminine* and *masculine*. Each of these pairs consists of two words usually regarded as *antonyms*, opposites. Indeed, people often talk about "the opposite sex." Here is the first problem: Why are *male* and *female* antonyms? How are they "opposites"?

The answer might seem obvious. Among human beings, those who are not female are male, and those who are not male are female. Talk of "opposites" implies more than this segregation into mutually exclusive categories, however. *Male* and *female* are antonyms partly because they are linked to other pairs of antonyms culturally associated with males and females—the stereotypes discussed in Chapter 2. The opposition of *male* and *female* is linked to the opposition of other terms, such as logical/emotional, active/passive, independent/dependent, and rough/gentle. These are not simply words people use to describe men and women; they also reflect the deeper meanings people associate with these terms. Thus, *male* and *female* are opposite not just because human beings are divided into these two groups, but because *male* also incorporates connotations of *logical, strong, rational,* and *aggressive,* while *female* incorporates connotations of *emotional, weak, irrational,* and *passive.*

If one set of commonly used terms, such as *man* and *woman,* can drag along with it so many other connotations, do we not then face a problem in communication: Even if we choose our words carefully, will other people understand what we mean? Instead, might they pick up some of the culturally embedded connotations we do not mean? What is our power over our own gendered meanings?

We also have different terms to refer to roughly the same things. We often use *male* and *female* to refer generally to persons of one or the other sex, but we also use many other words to limit our meaning further to males or females of particular ages, marital status, or other characteristics. Some terms connote respect, some are informal, and some are derogatory. How and when these different words are used depend on what we mean and on the situation. Table 10-1 lists some of the words most commonly used to refer to males and females, as well as the other connotations of these words.

Clearly, one important aspect of these terms is that the male and female terms are often asymmetrical: Equivalent terms for both sexes are often lacking; certain statuses and situations are more important for defining one sex than the other; and females and males in the same situations are often regarded differently. This lack of equivalence implies that *male* and *female* are therefore not really antonyms or opposites, as framed by our language.[2] Some examples follow.

Although most of the words in Table 10-1 imply at least some age characteristic, there are four sets in which age is a very important part of the meaning: *woman/man, girl/boy, spinster/bachelor, matron/?*. There are some apparent analogues. *Woman* is to *man* as *girl* is to *boy* because the first pair constitutes the female and male adult analogues of the second pair, the terms for a female and a

TABLE 10-1
Gender Referents: Nouns and Titles

Female Referents	Male Referents	Additional Connotations
female	male	Generic* within gender
woman	man	Generic within gender—also implies age (adult); *man* is also used as generic "human"
girl	boy	Age (child)—*girl* is also used to refer to adult females, especially those in subordinate status to the speaker, such as a secretary or maid; *boy* has also been used to refer to adult Black males generically by Whites
dame, broad chick, cunt	?	Derogatory generic; this is a small selection; some are obscene
girl, gal	guy	Informal generic
lady	gentleman	Age and class—polite form
madam	sir	Age and class—polite form; *madam* also refers to a supervisor of prostitutes; *sir* is also a conferred title of rank in Britain
spinster	bachelor	Age and marital status
wife	husband	Marital status
bride	groom	Marital status and length of marriage; *bride* is also used for a young married woman; *groom* is used only on the wedding day; *bride* is often the object of a possessive noun ("John's bride"); *groom* is not ("Jane's groom")
housewife, homemaker	breadwinner (househusband)	Marital and occupational status
divorcée	?	Marital status

male child. *Woman* is to *girl* as *man* is to *boy* because the first pair comprises the terms for a female adult and child, and the second comprises the terms for a male adult and child.

A more careful look casts some doubt on this simplicity, however. These male and female terms are not precise analogues in common usage because of the extra baggage of meaning the terms carry. *Girl,* for example, is widely used to describe females of all ages, including adults, whereas the term *boy* for adult males is used under much more limited circumstances. Why is this the case? Some people claim that calling an adult woman a girl is a compliment because it suggests that the

TABLE 10-1 *(continued)*
Gender Referents: Nouns and Titles

327

Chapter 10:
Gender,
Communication,
and Self-Expression

Female Referents	Male Referents	Additional Connotations
matron	?	Marital status, age, social status (Note: *patron,* the apparent male opposite, means something else entirely.)
widow	widower	Marital status—*widow* is often the object of a possessive ("John's widow"); *widower* is not ("Jane's widower")
Ms.	Mr.	Generic title—*Ms.* is used less often than *Miss* or *Mrs.* and is probably chosen and interpreted as implying feminist attitudes
Miss, Mrs.	?, master	Title connoting marital status; masculine form rarely used
mistress	?	Marital status and heterosexual relationship
?	cuckold	Extramarital relationship of spouse
prostitute, whore, tramp, slut, hooker, nymphomaniac	lecher, stud	Heterosexual behavior outside marriage
lesbian, dyke, queer, gay, homo	queer, gay, fairy, pansy, fag, molly, homo, queen	Homosexuality
?	sissy, pansy, weak sister, mamma's boy	A very "feminine" person
tomboy, amazon, dyke, butch	stud, he-man, macho man	A very "masculine" person

Note: Words within parentheses are apparent equivalents that are rarely used or are completely different in meaning. *Generic* means that the term is generic *within* gender; that is, it can refer generally to males or females as a group.

woman is young. Why not, then, suggest that a man is young by calling him a boy? The reason has to do with definitions of both gender and aging. Calling a man a boy belittles his experience, competence, and manly attributes. This asymmetry coincides with the social view that aging in early and especially middle adulthood detracts more from women's attractiveness than from men's. *Girl* and *boy* do not refer to youth and vigor, but to childhood, a more desirable status for women than for men.[3]

Using childhood terms for some adults but not others reflects status differences. In U.S. society, the use of *boy* to refer to an adult male historically was a derogatory means for Whites to talk to or about black men. Calling a black man *boy* indicated his subordinate, servile status or "stripped him of his manhood." (Notice, at least in this case, the close ties between the politics of race and gender.) Abolishing this usage was an important symbolic issue during the civil rights movement of the 1960s, and within a generation, it virtually disappeared. The connotation of subordinate and servant status for women remains, however, and is easily detected when people use *girl* to refer to their female domestic help ("My girl is wonderful; she's absolutely devoted to the children") or to their female secretaries ("I'll have my girl phone your girl to make the arrangements").

Spinster/bachelor is another word pair with interesting age connotations, this time combined with an indication of marital status. *Spinster* and *bachelor* both refer to unmarried adults, but the words do not have parallel meanings. Consider the sentence, "They were always careful to have at least one attractive _____ at their parties." One could well imagine *bachelor* but not *spinster* filling in the blank. Indeed, one cannot imagine the circumstance under which someone would use the word *attractive* to modify the word *spinster*. People talk about a "confirmed bachelor"—that is, a man who chooses to be unmarried—but not a "confirmed spinster." Why is there no positive term to refer to an adult unmarried female?

Consider also the asymmetry in the titles assigned to women and men. The standard title for adult men, regardless of marital status, is *Mr.* Although the generic female title *Ms.* is available, most people continue to prefer a title for women that also indicates marital status: *Miss* or *Mrs.*[4] Marital status is a more important determinant of women's status than of men's.

Marital status is so important for defining women that most married women still change not only their title but also their personal identity tag: their names. The law used to force women to give up their surnames of birth and take their husband's, on the grounds that a married woman had no legal identity apart from her husband. Most state laws no longer make it difficult for women to retain their birth names, but if a woman gives up her birth name, it can be difficult and expensive to recover it legally. Even if the law does not require it, social pressure can be very strong. Soon after President Clinton's inauguration, considerable public attention focused on the fact that his wife used her birth name as her middle name and (even more shocking) had neglected to use his name at all when they were first married! As Table 10-2 shows, a married woman's name is very variable.

Some people argue that it is confusing for husband and wife (or, as the traditional marriage service has it, man and wife) to have different surnames. It is confusing only because people *expect* husbands and wives to share a surname. Parents and married daughters usually have different surnames, but they know they are related and so do others who need to know. The confusions faced by couples with different surnames does not compare with what happens to someone trying to find an old friend or business acquaintance who has married and changed her name. Many women add to this confusion by giving up both their first and last names, becoming "Mrs. John Smith." This identity tag tells us that it is more important to know her husband's name than to know hers.

TABLE 10-2
What's in a Name?

329

Chapter 10:
Gender,
Communication,
and Self-Expression

Lucy Stone Marries Henry Blackwell

While married, she might be addressed as:	*While married, he might be addressed as:*
Lucy Stone	Henry Blackwell
Ms. Lucy Stone	Mr. Henry Blackwell
Mrs. Lucy Stone	
Lucy Stone Blackwell	
Lucy Blackwell	
Mrs. Lucy Blackwell[a]	
Mrs. Henry Blackwell	
Miss Lucy Stone *and* Mrs. Henry Blackwell[b]	

[a] Many people regard this as correct only for a widow or a divorcée.
[b] Used by women who keep both a professional and a married name.

Research shows that there are many derogatory, or at least disrespectful, generic terms for women, but there are few for men generically. What is the male equivalent of *broads, bimbos,* or *chicks? Guys* is informal, but neither belittling nor derogatory. What social conditions create the need for so many derogatory terms to describe a particular social group?

It is also interesting to note the difference between the terms used to describe heterosexually active people who are male or female. *Lecher* or *stud* can be used in an admiring sense, but the female equivalents are clearly derogatory. A woman who likes a lot of sexual activity is a *slut* or a *tramp;* if she likes it "too much" (i.e., she wants to have intercourse more often than her partner), she is called a "nymphomaniac." What is the name for a man who likes sexual activity "too much"? The English language is considerably richer in the number of terms labeling a sexually permissive woman than in terms for a sexually permissive man. One researcher found 220 terms for the former, and only 22 for the latter (cited in Eakins and Eakins, 1978).

The admiration–derogation distinction vanishes when we look at the terms referring to homosexually active people. In this case, the words used for both men and women are generally taken as derogatory, and there are more derogatory terms for homosexual men than for lesbians. Likewise, there are more derogatory terms for an "effeminate" male than for a "masculine" female. Our language use seems to suggest that if a woman acts "too masculine" (or unfeminine), she is deviant, but at least she is emulating the superior sex; if a man acts "too feminine" (or unmasculine), there is something profoundly wrong with him.

Women notice gender-based modes of address and naming more than men do. For example, in a survey of New Jersey attorneys, although 61% of women claimed to have heard a judge speak to a female lawyer using her first name or a term of endearment while men were addressed by surname or title, 76% of men thought that they had *not* heard this happen (New Jersey Supreme Court Task Force, 1986). While 85% of the women had heard a male attorney use inappropriate forms of address to a woman attorney, only 45% of the men had. Many female attorneys also experience courts as being gender biased because of their perception of persistent patterns of linguistic discrimination. This is only one example of how language use can become part of an institutionalized system of inequity.

The politics of naming often becomes an important issue in the agenda of social movements. Many social movements have fought for awareness of the impact of using derogatory language against a social group. But some groups, instead, try to force a revaluation of names that have been applied to them. The 1960s black power movement declared, "Black is beautiful" because up to that time, *black* had always had culturally negative connotations. The gay movement used the slogan "Gay and Proud" to combat ideas of shamefulness because of homosexuality, and lesbians used a traditionally derogatory term, *dyke,* as a public symbol of pride. By the early 1990s, much of the gay movement had similarly adopted the traditional insult, *queer.*

Many words that are not initially about gender have been transformed to indicate gender. The most common examples are terms for occupations, especially gender-typed occupations. Nothing in the construction of the words *lawyer, poet, nurse, sculptor,* or *journalist* reveals the gender of the person being described, but many people seem to think it is important to modify these terms with a gender tag if the gender of the person being discussed is not in accord with the stereotype (e.g., lady lawyer, poetess, male nurse, sculptress, lady journalist), even when gender information is irrelevant or even redundant (Mary Jones, a lady lawyer).

Using the suffixes *-ess, -ette,* and *-ix* to denote female gender in these types of words conveys more than just the female gender. Note that they modify the *standard forms* of the words, suggesting that women are modifications of the standard or normal occupants of these positions. The generic forms, therefore, are transformed into male forms. This change is especially significant because most of the standard forms do not linguistically indicate gender in the first place. If *-er* or *-or* indicated male gender, we would have to say not just "waitress" or "sculptress" but also "workress," "professorix," and "stock brokerette." Members of the U.S. Senate might say, "I defer to my colleague from California, Senatress Dianne Feinstein."

The standard form of some occupational names does flag gender, such as *businessman, chairman, Congressman,* and *fireman.* For these terms, the standard practice used to be to use the *-man* form as a generic form or to refer to men, and to use either the *-man* form (as in "Madam Chairman") or the *-woman* form to refer to women. It is now common, however, to omit irrelevant gender connotations by substituting either *person* (as in *businessperson*) or a neutral alternative form—such as *chair* (for *chairman*), *firefighter,* and *representative* or *member* of Congress—for the gender-specific term.

Gender-Neutral Terms

Few controversies over language have aroused as much hostility as that over the use of generic, non-gender-bound terms. The dispute over the use of *man* alone has created considerable debate and innumerable snide jokes about "personhole covers" and the like. This book began with a consideration of the supposed generic uses of *man* and *he.* At the most practical level, such usage is ambiguous and confusing. Despite the claim that *man* and *he* can be generic terms, research shows that people receive a gender-bound meaning from them (Sniezek and Jazwinski, 1986). For example, using *man,* rather than gender-neutral terms, in chapter titles makes students think of males more often (Schneider and Hacker, 1973). Another study (Cole, Hill, and Daly, 1983) found that *man* is especially likely to bring males to mind when paired with the supposedly generic *he.* These researchers asked students to write a story flowing from the statement: (1) "In a large coeducational institution the average student will feel isolated in his introductory course," or (2) "In a large coeducational institution the average student will feel isolated in his or her introductory course." In the former case, 84% of the men and 52% of the women wrote about a male. In the latter case, 77% of the men and 22% of the women wrote about a male. The change in pronouns had very little effect on the men. It is significant, however, that only with gender-neutral terminology did women focus on their own sex about as often as men focused on theirs.

An ingenious study took real life as its model to study these language effects. The researchers had their subjects act as jurors for a murder trial in which a woman had killed her assailant. Some heard the judge's instructions defining self-defense in the traditional masculine "generic" way (e.g., "But he has no right to repel a threatened assailant . . . unless he believes. . . ."), and some heard it in a gender-neutral phrasing. The subjects who heard the gender-neutral phrasing were much more likely to think that the woman had acted in self-defense. This study reinforces the decision reached in the real case from which the model was drawn, *State v. Wanrow* 1977 (Hamilton, Hunter, and Smith, 1994).

Gender-neutral language is sometimes labeled "inclusive language," and research such as the Hamilton et al. study suggests why. Such language helps women feel that the world being described actually includes them. Not surprisingly, males both use more gender-biased pronouns and regard sexism as less relevant to language use than do females. In general, people who use gender-biased pronouns more hold stronger gender stereotypes about occupations and have less positive attitudes toward nontraditional women than do those who use more inclusive language (Matheson and Kristensen, 1987).[5]

The apparent gender neutrality of a word does not necessarily mean that it provokes a nonsexist image or has a nonsexist meaning. Claus Mueller has argued that the language people use encodes shared understandings of the surrounding social environment and reflects the structure of that environment. He wrote,

> Language, . . . or more precisely, the code a group shares, is context specific. The possibility of transcending the content of one's code is contingent upon accepting and learning other codes. Change from one code to another implies, therefore, not only a change of the language spoken but also a change of the social context. (1973, 14–15)

If the social context is one in which gender structures social roles and hierarchies, can even the most apparently gender-neutral terms still have gender-based meanings for people? There is considerable evidence that they can.

Consider these terms: *engineer, kindergarten teacher, army officer,* and *telephone operator.* Although all are technically gender-neutral, two of them probably conjure up specifically male images in readers' minds, and two probably conjure up specifically female images. The reason is not that the words are gender specific, but that the social reality and cultural expectations to which they refer are structured by gender. Not all engineers and army officers are male, and not all kindergarten teachers and telephone operators are female, but cultural expectations based especially on past social reality structures the mental image provoked by these words. People who do not conform to this image will seem out of place. Sociolinguists argue that language thus does not just reflect reality; it can help create or maintain it. Under normal circumstances, language changes more slowly than does social reality. Even stranger, the term *homosexual* calls up images of men in people's minds (once again, the generic is male), but the term actually refers to both males and females, so when the mass media use this term in news reports about AIDS transmission, some people conclude that lesbian sexual behavior puts women at the same risk for AIDS as does male homosexual behavior (Hamilton, 1988).

Research by Erica Wise and Janet Rafferty (1982) demonstrates how hard it is to find genuinely gender-neutral terms in a gender-structured society. Following up on earlier work about mental-health clinicians (Broverman et al., 1970), they asked students to define the characteristics of a healthy man, woman, and adult, and a healthy boy, girl, and child. As with the earlier research, they found that healthy males and females were defined differently. They also asked students to write about a healthy adult or child. Most of the students wrote about a male. In other words, the supposedly gender-neutral terms *healthy adult* and *healthy child* provoked male images on the parts of both men and women.

Many apparently gender-neutral words take on different meanings when they are applied to women versus men. Consider the words *selfish/generous* and *loving/unloving*. A stereotypical loving wife and mother bends her schedule around her family's needs, is proud to carry her husband's name, and is willing to uproot herself if her husband's job demands it. These things are generally not expected of a loving husband. Is a man considered unloving or selfish if his job usually takes priority in his household or if he refuses to assume his wife's name? Consider your responses to the exercise in Box 10-1. The definition of many words depends on whether a man or a woman is being described. Other examples might include the terms *aggression* and *success*.

The face values or dictionary meanings of words are not enough to tell how language maintains or changes the structure of gender. The influence of language on gender also involves the underlying meanings and associations in the contexts that drive those meanings. Sexism in language is not a trivial matter. Although change will not be effected simply by substituting *person* for *man,* the differences in terminology are not trivial, either.

Autonomy and Control in Communication

Research on gender and communication does not focus only on the gender content of words; it is also concerned with the ways women and men speak and interact. Scholars in this field agree that women's and men's communication patterns differ and that the way people communicate depends on the sex of their audience.

BOX 10-1   Is *Selfish* a Gender-Neutral Word?

The *Oxford English Dictionary* defines *selfish* as "devoted to or concerned with one's own advantage or welfare to the exclusion of regard for others." Imagine a scale like the following on which we might measure the amount of selfishness an individual displays in different situations:

1	2	3	4	5	6	7

Least   Average   Most
Selfish   Selfish

Using this scale, we would rate people who always go out of their way to help other people 1, least selfish, and people who always expect other people to drop what they are doing to serve them 7, most selfish.

For each of the following situations, where on the selfishness scale do you think *most people* would place the individuals involved? Where would *you* place these individuals?

Most People's
Rating   *My Rating*

_____ _____ A woman who does not want to entertain her husband's business associates because she finds them boring

_____ _____ A man who does not want to entertain his wife's business associates because he finds them boring

_____ _____ A woman who does not want to move to a new town where her husband has found a better job because her own job prospects would be diminished

_____ _____ A man who does not want to move to a new town where his wife has found a better job because his own job prospects would be diminished

_____ _____ A woman who refuses to bake cupcakes for her child's school party because she is preparing for an exam

_____ _____ A man who refuses to bake cupcakes for his child's school party because he is preparing for an exam

_____ _____ A woman who does most of the cooking and cleaning at home

_____ _____ A man who does most of the cooking and cleaning at home

_____ _____ A woman who does not spend much time caring for her children because she is busy with her job

_____ _____ A man who does not spend much time caring for his children because he is busy with his job

Scholars also agree that these patterns both reflect and help to maintain gender differences in status and power. While most people display at least some of these communication behavior patterns every day, they usually do so unconsciously. This section examines some of these important, but often unconscious, aspects of people's lives.

Male and Female Language

Some communications researchers argue that the gender differences in communication are so great that there are male and female dialects within the English language (Lakoff, 1975). Some emphasize that women's and men's language emanates from distinct cultures found among females and males (Tannen, 1990). Others claim that the differences flow from the effects of power relations between men and women (Henley and Kramarae, 1994). While the cultural explanation is a useful framework, it is incomplete without the power framework, which the following discussion explores. It also follows Penelope Eckert and Sally McConnell-Ginet's argument that language must be understood as embedded not just in individuals' behavior or even in the relationship among individuals, but also as "living social practices in local communities"—that is, as part of a larger social system in which people live (Eckert and McConnell-Ginet, 1994, 433). This view also supports the notion of language as "practical consciousness," discussed earlier.

Women and men use slightly different vocabularies.[6] Because of their different experiences and training, they use different specialized vocabularies. Women make finer distinctions in naming colors and, on the average, know and use more technical and precise words connected with clothing (especially words connected with sewing), food and cooking, and so on. Men use numbers more often and more precisely in ordinary conversation than women do. They also swear more and use more language generally regarded as obscene or aggressive. Many people also note differences in women's and men's descriptive vocabularies, especially in adjectives. For example, American men are less likely than American women to describe someone or something as "adorable," "darling," "marvelous," or "teeny-weeny."

Girls learn verbal language more quickly than boys do, but the differences even out by the age of 2 years (Huttenlocher, Haight, and Bryk, 1991). Among adults, women are more likely than men to use standard English (the type our English teachers wanted us to learn). Some researchers theorize that this is not because of differences in ability or even knowledge, but because of men's effort to show toughness and independence, and women's strategies to obtain higher status or respect (Adams and Ware, 1989, 476).[7]

In light of controversies over the use and teaching of Black English, it is interesting to note that these gender differences in the use of standard English appear among both African-Americans and Whites. Patricia C. Nichols (1978), for example, investigated gender differences in the use of a local African-American dialect in a rural southern area. In one locality, women were more likely than men to use this dialect rather than standard English; in another, the reverse was true. A deeper probe revealed that use of the more prestigious form was linked to economic differences between the two localities. In the second locality, women had more opportunity to have higher-status jobs that required standard language skills; in the first, men had greater opportunities. The same underlying principle probably explains gender differences in the use of prestigious language forms regardless of race. For people from working-class or poor families, women's job opportunities (for example, service work involving much social interaction or clerical work) are more likely to depend on language skills, and men's are more likely to depend on physical labor.

Researchers on gender differences in language often argue that women's language tends to be more self-deprecating than men's. In other words, women's speech suggests that they are more hesitant and doubt their own credibility more than men do. Some, although not all, research suggests that women are more likely to use the self-qualifying tag question, as in "That was a good movie, wasn't it?" Research also indicates that women are more likely to blunt or hedge their statements by adding personalizers ("In my opinion . . . ," or "Personally, I think . . .") or disclaimers ("I may be wrong, but . . ."), rather than simply stating opinions and observations straight out.

Women are also more likely to hedge their demands by phrasing them as requests or using long, complex sentences that blunt the request. To caricature the difference, the hedging form of the polite demand, "Please close the door," might be, "I hope you wouldn't mind terribly, but I would be ever so grateful if you would please close the door—that is, unless you want it open." Women also blunt their communication by using rising intonation as though asking questions or permission when they are making statements. For example, Bob asks his wife Sally when dinner will be ready; Sally, who knows exactly when it will be ready, answers, "In ten minutes?" as though asking for permission or confirmation. Thus, women are more polite (Holtgraves and Yang, 1992).

Men appear to use more words when describing objects (Eakins and Eakins, 1978, 25–29). Women often use a higher pitch and more breathy voice than is physiologically required, and they use more variation in intonation than men do (Eakins and Eakins, 1978). It is important, however, not to exaggerate the differences between female and male speech. As in most other things, there is considerably more gender similarity than difference. No single speech attribute distinguishes women from men, either consistently or dramatically.

Nevertheless, female and male styles differ, as research by Mulac and Lundell (1986) shows. The researchers taped 40 people describing the same photographs. Next, the researchers asked a group of observers to read the transcripts of the descriptions and to guess the sex of the speakers. The observers were not able to do this very well. The researchers then had the transcripts coded for the presence of the types of characteristics discussed in this section. They found that these characteristics did distinguish between female and male speakers in the ways that might be expected. "On the basis of the formula determined by [statistical analysis], 85% of the male transcripts could be accurately determined on the basis of the relative presence or absence of the 17 language features" (p. 90). Further analysis showed that the characteristics associated with male speech were viewed as more dynamic and those associated with female speech were viewed as more aesthetic. Even if an observer could not name the gender of the speaker, gender made a difference in the impact of the speech.

Communication is an interactive process, depending on both the social context and the people with whom one is communicating. If I speak in a hesitant manner, it may be because I always do this, because I am unsure of the particular topic I am discussing, or because the person to whom I am speaking makes me feel uncomfortable. Most investigators argue that the most important differences between female and male communication behavior are the result of the structure of power and authority relations between them.

The Right-of-Way: Gender and Status

We all follow many rules, usually unconsciously, when we communicate or interact with other people. Some of these are the rules of grammar that allow us to put together strings of words in a way that will transmit meaning clearly to others. (Would difficult understand be to if my message not were it correct grammatically through sentences transmitted.) Others are the rules of style that set the tone and indicate, for example, whether we are speaking formally or informally, as intimates or strangers, or as superior and subordinate. (I mean, like, it would be *really* distracting and might, like, screw up your studies really bad—and I, like, wouldn't want to do that!—if I wrote this whole book in this, y'know, kind of style. I mean, y'know what I mean?) Some of these rules may be regarded as the traffic rules we use to facilitate communication. These rules include the norms of politeness, which facilitate comfort and ease of communication and have the practical advantage, for example, of requiring people to take turns in conversations.

Communication rules depend on the status rankings of the people involved. Status and hierarchy rankings are reflected through communication behavior. When people break the traffic rules of interpersonal relations by not taking proper turns in speaking, they are not regarded as conversational bad drivers but as impolite or, if the infractions are major enough, crazy. When a subordinate violates communication traffic rules in relation to a superior, the subordinate is not just impolite. A subordinate's demand for equality in the traffic rules—for example, by taking even an equal speaking turn without the superior's permission—may be viewed as insubordination. Politeness is the act of granting the socially appropriate amount of respect to others, depending on their relative status. Indeed, power differences among people are even more important determinants of how polite men are in any given situation, largely because women tend to be more polite anyway (Holtgraves and Yang, 1992).

Gender differences in communication and social interaction reflect the existence of a hierarchical sex/gender system. These differences are governed in part by traffic rules calling for males to have the right-of-way, both in the use of social space and in conversation. Other hierarchical gender-related communication patterns also exist.

Right-of-Way in Space. Men take up more space than women do. This is not just because men are generally larger than women, but also because they occupy, use, and move through space differently than women do. Social psychologists and others have noticed that people of relatively high status act as though they have a

Law professor Anita Hill's testimony before an all-White male Senate Judiciary Committee reminded many women of the effects of communications rights-of-way on their ability to be heard, understood, and believed.

right to more space or territory than people of relatively low status. This pattern is reflected by men and women.[8]

Men sit and stand more expansively than women do, much more often spreading their arms and legs outward or sideways or sitting with their heads and trunks leaning backward and their legs spread out in front of them. American men tend to cross their legs in the ankle-over-knee position. Women position themselves as though to shrink themselves, with arms and legs closer to the body. The more submissive a woman is, the more she exhibits controlled body movements (Richards and McAlister, 1994). No matter how women sit, including when they cross their legs, their knees are closer together, and when they sit "properly" their knees touch, a position many find uncomfortable. These leg positions have sometimes been explained on grounds other than status. For example, some people suggest that women keep their legs close together when they wear skirts, so that their underwear will not show, or that men cannot sit with their legs together (for example, with legs crossed at the knee) because their genitals get in the way. However, women are likely to sit with their legs close together whether they are wearing short or long skirts or slacks, and there are cultural variations in the ways men cross their legs. French men, for example, cross their legs at the knees.

Certainly, gender differences in clothing help maintain some of these differences in demeanor and use of space. It is difficult to walk with long, free strides while wearing high heels. Skirts and some types of women's blouses also inhibit movement if women want to avoid displaying their underwear. Many popular dress-for-success guides of the early 1980s urged businesswomen to wear a female variety of the male business suit, precisely because such attire hides the body underneath. Even these outfits, however, which included a skirt and high-heel shoes, did not eliminate the need to sit and walk in a circumspect, modesty-conscious way.

Men have more *personal space* than women do, which is another characteristic of people with high status. Like other animals, we humans need a certain amount of territory. We become uncomfortable or even angry if the wrong people invade that space, for instance, by standing too close to us when conversing. Two people meeting under these circumstances tend to move in a kind of odd dance, with one person progressively moving backward to create more distance, and the other moving forward to diminish that space.

People's personal boundary spaces depend on their relationships to others in their vicinity. The more intimate and friendly a person is, the closer that person is allowed to approach. Status and relationship also determine people's rights with regard to others' personal space. High-status people assume a right to invade the personal space of lower-status people, whereas lower-status people must respect the personal space of superiors.

The gender-based differences in women's and men's behavior reflect these status-based right-of-way rules. Observers often remark on the relative absence of private places for women, as compared with men. It is common in households that can afford it for a man to have his own room or other place that no one else in the family may enter without permission. Even when the household cannot afford such a luxury, it is more common for a man to be allowed to hide behind his newspaper, surrounded by a symbolic "do not disturb" atmosphere, which is often enforced by his wife.

Women are less likely to own such private territory or to have such privacy. "Their" room, the kitchen, is one of the most public in a home. Likewise, secretaries are usually placed out in the open, with their tools and desks available to any passerby. Women's work or leisure, therefore, is regarded as less important than men's and more subject to interruption. Indeed, one could argue that one defining characteristic of women's work is that because women are supposed to be available, their space is designed to facilitate interruption.

Women's lack of real private space does not mean that they have no control over their surroundings. In the home, for example, women have a relatively large amount of control over the design of the physical environment through their responsibilities for decoration and cleaning. Bedrooms and bathrooms, for example, which are shared spaces, are generally decorated and furnished in what is regarded as conventionally feminine taste. The decoration and furnishing of a man's study or workroom often stand in stark contrast to those of the rest of the house. (For a parallel point, see the discussion in Chapter 6 regarding women's control of the at-home birthing room.)

Consider other evidence of the higher respect for men's personal space. People give men a wider berth on streets and sidewalks than they give women. This type of behavior can easily be observed in any library with narrow stacks. When a man or woman is sitting or standing in the middle of an aisle that is open at both ends, and another person wants to look at books at the other end of the aisle, women and men respond differently. Women tend to detour through another aisle, especially if the alternative is to brush close to a man, whereas men are more likely to walk straight through, especially if it is a woman who is blocking the aisle.

Although personal space is usually the privilege of high status, it takes more than measuring the distance among people to know how status relations are at work. Consider the anecdote told by Taunya Lovell Banks, about a day when she and four other well-dressed black women law professors entered the elevator in a luxury condominium.

> A few floors later, the door opened and a White woman in her late fifties peered in, let out a muffled cry of surprise, stepped back, and let the door close without getting on. Several floors later the elevator stopped again, and the doors opened to reveal yet another White middle-aged woman, who also decided not to get on. (Banks, 1997, 98)

Clearly these White women were not giving the black women "personal space" out of respect, but rather out of fear. Nevertheless, this geography of interpersonal relations was governed by status issues.

Touching behavior is also regulated by status relations. Higher-status people assume a right to touch and sometimes do not even notice what they are doing. Lower-status people, however, will arouse a reaction if they touch higher-status people. A male boss may greet a subordinate in the morning by slapping him on the back and saying, "How are you doing there, Sam?" Even if boss and subordinate are on a first-name basis, however, Sam would not be wise to greet his boss in the same way. Research shows that both men and women respond positively to being touched by someone of higher status than themselves. Research also shows that "when the toucher and the recipient are of equal or ambiguous relative status . . . women generally respond positively to being touched whereas men generally react neutrally or negatively, particularly if the toucher is female" (Major, 1981, 28).

In the occupational world, women such as secretaries or nurses are usually subordinate to men and are therefore touched regularly by people they themselves cannot touch, at least not without the contact being misinterpreted. (The misinterpretation problem is discussed further shortly.) This touching behavior is by no means limited to situations in which the male toucher is clearly of higher occupational status than the female being touched. Men in blue-collar jobs touch white-collar female secretaries as freely as men who are business executives. When receiving change, men of all statuses often prolong touching the hands of female sales clerks.[9]

The differences in touching behavior are also clearly observable in nonoccupational settings. A favorite game for boys of all ages is grazing against women's breasts or bottoms, supposedly accidentally. Even when men are not playing this type of sexual game, they are much more likely to touch women than women are to touch men. Women sometimes find strange men holding them by the back or shoulders as they move past in buses and aisles, or they find themselves pushed into small segments of bus seats because the man next to them is using his right-of-way to spread himself out. Men, much more than women, drape their arms across the backs of the chairs of the people sitting next to them.

One of the best-known observers of gender and nonverbal behavior, Nancy Henley, has written about an encounter she had with two high-status administrators at a university where she was working (1977, 95):

> After a large meeting one spring, the Vice Chancellor came over to me and took my upper arms in his two hands, saying he wanted to tell me something; he continued holding me in this restrictive fashion as he proceeded to talk with me. After he finished, and he had finally let go, I grabbed him back, then remarked that I would have to tell him sometime about my thesis which is [about gender and touching behavior]. He expressed interest, so I began telling him about it, and he found it plausible; at this moment the Chancellor approached, the only man on campus with higher authority, laid his hand on the arm of the Vice Chancellor, and urged him to accompany him to the next meeting. The V.C. and I were both struck by the aptness of this action and I think I made my point.

This story also illustrates the point that higher-status people are relatively free to interrupt lower-status people.

Research shows that dominance–deference relations are displayed even in touching behavior between male and female intimates. Among couples, it is still expected that sexual contact will be initiated by the male. One study (Borden and Homlied, 1978) of heterosexual couples walking together holding hands found that if one member of the couple is left-handed and the other is right-handed, they walk with their dominant hands clasped together. If they are both either left- or right-handed, however, the man tends to hold the woman's weaker hand with his dominant hand.

Gender norms and status also influence eye contact. Even the initiation of contact with another person is sometimes called "catching the person's eye." Initiation of eye contact, especially staring, is the prerogative of higher-status people, and once again, both research and common experience suggest that this contact is also the prerogative of men. When a woman and man who do not know each other pass on a street and catch each other's eyes, the woman ordinarily drops her gaze first. If the woman holds her gaze, it may be interpreted as an invitation to sexual pursuit.[10] Men are supposed to approach women or initiate relationships, not the reverse (Green and Sanders, 1983).

What happens when women violate the traffic rules of space? Think of a woman who sits with her arms and legs spread out and who stares at, touches, and drapes herself on strange men. What message will a man receive from such a woman? Most women are fully aware that if they sit with their arms spread back, rather than in front of them, men are likely to become distracted and stare at their chests. (It is difficult to have a serious conversation with someone who is staring at your chest.) Thus, when a woman behaves the same way men do in their use of space, she communicates a very different message.

Some research has examined gender differences in the relationship between the use of public space and status. It seems natural, for example, that in groups, the leader or other person of highest status should sit at the head of the table or alone in the front of the room. When husband and wife sit at opposite ends of the family dinner table, the man's place is usually called the "head" of the table, and the woman's the "foot." This arrangement helps the higher-status person control the situation and be the focal point of communication.

Natalie Porter and Florence Geis (1981) did some interesting research showing that the differentiated status rankings of women and men are strong enough to overcome the convention that the person of highest status occupies the authoritative position. They showed subjects pictures of a group of people sitting around a table. Some of the groups were all male or all female, and some were mixed. Each showed one person at the short end of the table and three people down each side. Whenever a man was shown sitting at the head of the table, most observers perceived him to be the leader of the group. In all-female groups, the woman at the head of the table was also perceived to be the leader of the group. In mixed groups, however, when a woman occupied the head of the table, many people chose one of the men at the sides of the table as the leader. Thus, the use of space and positioning are important indicators of status, but gender may be even more important.

This study is similar in implication to another in which students were given diagrams of a rectangular table and told they were going to meet either Professor Susan Smith or Professor Henry Smith there. When asked where they would seat themselves, most placed the professor at the head of the table. This was not true in all cases, however. The students were more likely to choose the head of the table for themselves when meeting Professor Susan Smith than when meeting Professor Henry Smith (Lott and Sommer, 1967).

Right-of-Way in Conversation. According to the old stereotype, women talk so much that men "can't get a word in edgewise." If so, it seems that women must have the right-of-way in conversation. Research shows, however, that in mixed-sex discussions, not only do men both talk more and take stronger leads in discussions, but also they employ techniques, often unconsciously, that silence women and diminish women's abilities to influence the group. Where, then, do people get the idea that women talk too much? Consider this pattern found by linguists: Higher-status people often think that people of lower status talk and interrupt more than they do, even though research shows that it is higher-status people who talk and interrupt more.

Men employ a number of techniques that curb and limit women's speech. The most important is that men interrupt women considerably more often than they interrupt other men or than women interrupt anyone else. One study found that over 90% of all interruptions in conversation were instigated by men (Zimmerman and West, 1975; see also Smith-Lovin and Brody, 1989). Men are more likely to overlap women's speech or to begin talking after women have begun and continue to talk at the same time. These speech challenges may be sustained by one person either forcibly holding his or her ground and continuing to speak or even by saying something such as, "I'm not finished yet." Men are more likely to sustain challenges than women are (Smith-Lovin and Brody, 1989).

Despite the assumed right to interrupt and overlap that higher-status people (men) have, there are some variations in the pattern. A study of sex and race differences showed that White males and black females were particularly likely to hold their ground during verbal challenges (Adams, 1980), suggesting that White females are especially susceptible to being silenced by men's challenges. Another point that Deborah Tannen has made is that in some ethnic groups, overlap and interruption are signs of solidarity in speech; once again, translating the meanings of communication behavior requires sensitivity to the specific context (Tannen, 1994, 53–73).

One of the intriguing aspects of studying communication behavior is its complexity and subtlety. A person's speech may be stopped by a verbal challenge, but it may also be stopped by silence. Speakers tend to require some indication that the other person is paying attention in conversation. Listeners demonstrate attentiveness through verbal conventions (e.g., adding the occasional *mm-hmm, uh-huh, oh, yeah,* or laughing appropriately) or, in face-to-face conversations, through nonverbal behavior (nodding, gesturing, making some facial response, etc.). If the listener does not use these verbal conventions during a telephone conversation, the speaker is likely to elicit a response purposely, or even to ask, "Are you still there?" Showing no response tends to distract the speaker and eventually to kill the conversation. Men tend to show no response to women more often than women do it to men.

Other patterns emerge in discussions among women and men. Men initiate new topics more than women do, but this is partly because a man is especially likely to introduce a topic other than the one a woman is discussing. A higher proportion of men's sentences are statements, and a higher proportion of women's are questions. Some observers even suggest that in a discussion in which a woman has made a valuable point, it is often attributed by others to a male in the group.[11]

These differences in verbal behavior are reinforced in day-to-day life by the different positions males and females who interact are likely to hold. In cases involving a male boss and a female secretary or other subordinate or a male doctor and a female patient, part of the man's right-of-way is derived from the higher status of his position. Males, however, tend to take a right-of-way reflecting higher status, regardless of their occupational positions. Even when women hold high-status positions, they do not gain, or do not use, the same privileges in communication traffic. Female doctors, for example, are much less likely than male doctors to use their positions to dominate verbal interactions with patients. Patients, moreover, interrupt female doctors more than they interrupt male doctors (West, 1984).[12] Because gender differences in the possession of formal authority and power positions are so great, it is easy to overlook the fact that formal authority and power are much more important than gender in determining the roles people play in social interaction (Johnson, 1994). But gender still has an impact, as well.

The Right-of-Way: Conclusion. Thus far, this chapter has shown that the traffic rules of communication and interaction are governed in part by a hierarchical relationship between women and men, by patterns of dominance and deference, and by a male right-of-way. Victor A. Thompson's work (1961) on communication and hierarchy offers an instructive way of looking at this relationship and its impact on communication behavior. Although he was specifically considering the relationship between manager and subordinate in a bureaucratic organization, Thompson's analysis is appropriate for other kinds of hierarchies, as well, including the one between women and men.

Thompson argued that status and hierarchy rankings are reflected in the rights and duties individuals have, with regard to transmitting and accepting information and directives. Superiors have communication rights, and subordinates have communication duties or obligations. Many of these rights and duties are left unstated, even in formal organizations, because the rules are obvious to everyone.

Thompson (1961, 60–66) listed the communication rights of the superior in a hierarchical relationship:

1. The right to veto or affirm the goals or proposals of subordinates
2. The right to expect obedience and loyalty
3. The right to monopolize communication both within the organizational unit and between the unit and the outside world (especially the latter)
4. The right to expect deference from subordinates
5. The right to be "somewhat insensitive as to subordinates' personal needs"

Thompson further argued that there is a "halo effect of status" that "requires high-status persons to speak out on all sort of matters from a position of almost complete ignorance" (1961, 67). Subordinates in a hierarchical relationship have a series of obligations that are the inverse of the superior's rights. Subordinates are expected to leave the final word to superiors, to defer to superiors, to be obedient and loyal, and to be aware of and responsive to superiors' needs and desires.

These descriptions characterize the communication behavior between women and men well, partly because in most occupations and organizations, women remain segregated in the lower-status subordinate positions. Even within the institution of the family, women are traditionally supposed to be obedient, loyal, and deferential. The double standard of loyalty is illustrated by the double standard of sexual morality, in which women are expected to be more sexually loyal than men. Family communication is also structured by status relationships. Although women are central to communication within the family (particularly in the absence of the husband/father) and between the family and outsiders, many of the most important communications between the family and other institutions are expected to be carried out either by the husband or under his supervision. The different responses women and men evince toward each other's needs may be seen in the trite (and not always true) image of the unequal degree of sensitivity that husbands and wives show toward each other's needs and feelings at the end of a hard day of work.

Does the interaction between women and men follow hierarchical patterns of communication only because women and men occupy different formal positions in organizations, or do these hierarchical patterns exist between women and men as such? Is gender in and of itself a status marker that leads to hierarchical patterns of interaction? Much of the answer is known already: Evidence of the male right-of-way is exhibited in many day-to-day informal interactions. Gender-based communication patterns conform remarkably well to Thompson's analysis of organizations. The male right-of-way allows men to monopolize communication, to veto or affirm subordinates' goals or proposals, to gain deference, and to be insensitive to subordinates' personal needs. When women use patterns of interaction that show hesitation and self-deprecation, they become parties to this dominance–deference system.

Women appear to be better equipped than men to respond to the needs of others. A review of 75 studies shows that women are better able than men to decode other people's nonverbal cues (Hall, 1978; see also Briton and Hall, 1995). The ability to read people's behavior can be interpreted as a defensive skill developed by low-status people; African-Americans have also been found to be particularly skillful at behavior decoding. For both women and African-American men, these skills are especially strong in detecting negative feelings and reactions. Women also look at people with whom they interact more than men do, which can be interpreted as part of this reading of behavior. Consider these findings in relation to two characteristics often attributed to women: intuition and oversensitivity.

The one observation by Thompson not yet discussed is that high status "requires" a person to "speak out on all sorts of matters from a standpoint of almost complete ignorance." As mentioned previously, women speak more hesitantly than men. At least one study also suggests that men may indeed be more willing to speak on the basis of little knowledge. Ronald Rapoport (1981) studied people who voiced political opinions in public-opinion surveys. He divided his sample into three groups: those who seemed very, moderately, or not at all knowledgeable about politics, and then he compared the first and last groups. Rapoport found that knowledgeable men and women were equally willing or able to offer opinions on political issues to the interviewer. In contrast, unknowledgeable men continued to voice opinions, while unknowledgeable women tended either to acknowledge their ignorance or to offer no opinion. Rapoport's work suggests that, at least in the male-dominated field of politics, men may be more willing to discuss things about which they know very little, perhaps because of gender-role pressure not to appear ignorant.

One of the most important features of the relationship between gender and communication is that people expect women to exhibit the communication and interaction patterns characteristic of subordinates. Consider some of the standard stereotypical traits people define as feminine: yielding, loyal, sympathetic, sensitive to the needs of others, understanding, and soft-spoken (Bem, 1975). In contrast, stereotypic male traits include defending one's own beliefs, taking a stand, and acting as a leader (Bem, 1975). As this book has shown many times, if people expect women and men to conform to gender-stereotyped norms, they will perceive and treat women and men as though they are actually doing so.

It might seem that the principle "ladies before gentlemen" contradicts the argument about the male right-of-way. Men are supposed to open doors for women and to allow women to enter rooms first, to help them put on and remove their coats, to pull out chairs for them, to rise when they enter rooms, and to remove hats in their presence. Men are also supposed to refrain from swearing in women's presence and, in the past, to save their talk about aggressive topics such as sports, business, and politics until the ladies left the room. Many a woman has voiced her objection to feminism by saying, "I believe in equal pay for equal work, but I still like a man to open doors for me." What are the implications of these social customs for questions of gender and the right-of-way?

As early as two centuries ago, Mary Wollstonecraft ([1792] 1975) argued that male chivalry was a ruse, albeit an unconscious one. Since that time, feminists have continued to ask *which* doors men open for women and why they do so. As with other behaviors and interactions, understanding these acts requires examining the circumstances under which they are done, why they are done, and how they relate to other acts. Most feminists argue that men who take the right-of-way when it really counts but continue to open doors for women or help them put on their coats are showing paternalistic power, symbolically reinforcing the ideas of men as stronger and in control and women as delicate and dependent. Such chivalry sometimes interferes with women's work, as when a businesswoman meets chivalrous resistance to picking up the luncheon check for her client. What would be wrong with a system of politeness in which people hold doors for each other? After all, the woman who can manage to carry the laundry or a toddler without male help can surely manage a door.

Strategies of Power and Influence

Thus far, we have been discussing research that reconfirms the existence of a hierarchical sex/gender system, both in structures of social institutions and in people's everyday behavior. We now turn directly to questions of power and influence in social interaction. When women and men are trying to influence others or achieve their own goals in a social setting, do they behave differently? We certainly find a widespread view that women and men use different strategies of influence and use and react to power differently. As usual, however, we can much more readily find evidence that people *think* there are gender differences than evidence that women and men actually act differently in similar circumstances. Studies of women and men who hold formal positions of power in business, for example, generally find substantial similarity between women's and men's exercise of authority (Colwill, 1982).

Despite the fact that leadership is stereotypically regarded as a male attribute, a meta-analysis of many empirical studies shows that men and women are equally effective at leadership, controlling for the situation. However, men are more effective than women in roles that are defined as masculine, and women are more effective than men in roles that are defined as feminine. The one setting that was most different from all others was the military, where women were systematically rated lower than men in leadership (Eagly, Karau, and Makhijani, 1995).

Many theorists have argued that men and women do use different styles of influence, although surprisingly few theorists have attempted to provide convincing and systematic empirical evidence. One line of thinking suggests that women's and men's communication goals, and therefore behavior, are different. The sociologist Talcott Parsons (1951) led his field for a long time in arguing that men

Women have been learning to use forceful language for their own purposes. This woman's coat hanger is a reminder of the results of antiabortion policies.

emphasize *instrumental values* (getting things done), while women emphasize *expressive values* (creating group harmony and good feelings).[13] Others have offered variations on this theme, including those who suggest that men emphasize *agentic values* (concern for the impact of the individual on decisions and activities), and women emphasize *communal values* (concern for the group, group values, and group activities).

There is some evidence for these theories, but it is not strong and consistent. David Buss (1981) found, for example, that when people were asked about the desirability of 100 different acts of dominance, the ones found less desirable by women than by men were acts of "unmitigated agency" (variations of selfishness). The ones found more desirable by women were more mixed and communal acts. Likewise, the acts Buss's subjects thought were less desirable when performed by women than by men were the highly agentic acts. (One of these was "She/he refused to cook or clean the house.") Overall, however, when the subjects were asked which acts they themselves had ever performed, the men claimed to have performed more acts of dominance of almost all sorts.

Other theorists leave aside overall goals and look specifically at strategies of influence. Paula Johnson (1976), for example, argued that the style a person uses to exert influence may fall along three different continua: direct–indirect, personal–concrete, and helplessness–competence. Johnson claimed that women's and men's attempts to exert influence can be distinguished along all three lines. Women display a more indirect, and even manipulative, style than men; tend to rely on personal appeals; and use a style that rests on helplessness ("I need your help"), rather than on arguments or displays of competence. What causes these differences? For a long time, feminist theorists have argued that women use whatever strategies of influence are open to them. If they are not allowed to be direct and forthright, they will find devious means to achieve their objectives. If this is true, it is easy to see how women might be trapped into fulfilling the stereotype of the sneaky, manipulative woman.

Johnson and others have found evidence that people do consider these different styles particularly masculine or feminine and that they react more positively to someone who uses the "gender-appropriate" style. One study, for example, asked subjects to react to speeches by a man and a woman who used either the "male" power base of expertise or the "female" power base of helplessness. The subjects responded more positively to the male speaker than to the female when both used the power base of expertise, and they responded more positively to the female speaker than to the male when they both used the power base of helplessness. When the investigators compared the subjects' attitudes toward speakers of a single sex according to the style of speech used, they found that the subjects preferred the speakers who used "gender-appropriate" speech, regardless of sex (Falbo, Hazen, and Linimon, 1982).

In another study, participants viewed a videotape of a woman or man delivering a persuasive message, using one of four different types of nonverbal styles of emphasis: task performance, social relations, submissiveness, or dominance. The participants both liked and were influenced by the task and social styles more than the others. Participants tended especially to *like* the person who used a social-relations style, and to find the one who used the task-performance style *competent*. Both likeability and competence made the message more influential, but likeability was an especially important determinant of the influence of a woman in a male audience. This would suggest that a woman gets better results from men if she seems likeable than if she seems competent (Carli, LaFleur, and Loeber, 1995).

Evidence of actual *behavioral* differences between men and women are not as easy to find as differences in the *perceptions and reception* of men and women. Certainly, men are more likely than women to employ physical violence to get their way, as crime statistics show, but what of more peaceful means? In one study (Instone, Major, and Bunker, 1983), men made more attempts to influence others than women did in similar situations, and the men used a wider variety of types of influence. At the same time, these small gender differences in the types of influence strategies all but disappeared when the researchers took the subjects' levels of self-confidence into account. In other words, women used different strategies of influence because they had less self-confidence than men. In the same study, both women and men had lower expectations of success when trying to influence the opposite sex than when they were trying to influence members of their own sex.

A number of studies have looked at the use of direct and coercive techniques of influence, such as using threats. Not surprisingly, people are more likely to use coercive techniques when they think they have little chance of influencing others otherwise. One study found that men and women trying to influence people of the other sex used more coercive strategies than those trying to influence people of their own sex (Instone, Major, and Bunker, 1983). People think more about their self-presentation with people of the other sex or with people of their own whom they do not know very well (Leary, Nezlek, and Downs, 1994).

A study of business managers found no overall gender differences in how direct or polite they were in their efforts to influence others (Hirokawa, Mickey, and Miura, 1991). Instead, communication behavior was related to the managers' positions. Those with high *request legitimacy*—that is, whose positions gave them more right to seek compliance of others—tended to use more direct and less polite means of influencing others than those with less request legitimacy. In real life, of course, men occupy most of the business positions of high request legitimacy. The same study did find one important gender difference, however. Among those who had high request legitimacy, men used more direct and less polite means of influence than women did. This finding can be interpreted in two different ways: (1) Men might be more likely than women to forget about politeness and consideration of subordinates when they reach high positions; or (2) even when women reach high positions, they may still perceive themselves as having less request legitimacy. This study does not reveal which reason is true.

Gender differences in interaction have been detected relatively early in childhood. Miller, Danaher, and Forbes (1986) observed children's interactions on a playground and found that girls and boys both used a range of strategies to deal with conflict, but the researchers also noted some differences. Boys were more likely than girls to start with heavy-handed behavior (aggression) whether they were interacting with girls or boys. Girls were also heavy-handed at times, but only with boys and not as quickly in the interactions as boys were. The strategies girls used more often included acknowledging the feelings of others, changing the topic, and indirect displays of anger.

Overall, there is considerable evidence that women and men are expected to use different types of influence and are viewed more favorably when they do so. Some evidence also shows that there are gender differences in strategies for exerting social influence. As usual, in the world of stereotypes, we cannot always trust our eyes. Men are perceived as using more controlling or forceful strategies of influence than women, even when they are not actually doing so (Burrell, Donahue, and Allen, 1988). The interesting question is why these differences occur. Here are three possible answers:

1. Women and men occupy different positions in social institutions, and they use the forms appropriate to their positions.
2. Strategies for exerting social influence depend in part on self-confidence and expectations of success, and women and men do not experience similar levels of self-confidence or anticipation of success in similar situations.

3. Social pressure is exerted on individuals to make their behavior conform to appropriate gender norms. People are not liked or accepted as much when they deviate from the norm.

Perhaps the most difficult aspect of communication to study is not what people communicate but what they do *not* communicate. Subordinates have to be careful of how they act in front of those who are more powerful, and there is plenty of evidence that women use their knowledge of gender norms to protect themselves. Women learn to mask their abilities in "masculine" areas in order to avoid the possibility of punishment or rejection. Women have variously hidden their sexuality or faked orgasms (as Sally delightfully illustrated in the movie *When Harry Met Sally*) in order to avoid the dangers of offending men's sexual sensibilities. Women often expend considerable effort controlling their reactions to sexual harassment. It is also more important for women than men to keep smiling, no matter how they are feeling (Deutsch, LeBaron, and Fryer, 1987). Indeed, the one kind of communication behavior that seems to be more determined by gender than by formal authority position is smiling and laughing (Johnson, 1994).

If gender subordination creates a special need to be strategic about self-presentation, women who face additional problems of social subordination face a multiplied need for care. For example, in a homophobic society, lesbian women cannot avoid having to confront issues of whether to mask their sexuality. Darlene Clark Hine has written very powerfully about the culture of dissemblance among black women, or "the behavior and attitudes of Black women that created the appearance of openness and disclosure but actually shielded the truth of their inner lives and selves from their oppressors" (1989, 912).

Hine has argued that the effort to appear open while hiding one's persona was an imperative of the conditions of oppression and sexual violence:

> A secret, undisclosed persona allowed the individual Black woman to function, to work effectively as a domestic in White households, to bear and rear children, to endure the frustration-born violence of frequently under- or unemployed mates, to support churches, to found institutions, and to engage in social service activities, all while living within a clearly hostile White, patriarchal, middle-class America. (1989, 916)

A study of African-American domestic workers and their employers shows how the relations of dominance and subordination can trick those in a position of power into thinking that they know their subordinates, when in fact they do not (Rollins, 1983). The exact substance of what one reveals and fears revealing differs from one context of social subordination to another, but close inspection reveals elements of a culture of dissemblance by any group of people with experience of reprisals from a more powerful group. Women are no exception. Hine (1989) recognized the trap of dissemblance, however: It serves as an important strategy of self-protection, but at the same time, it also buttresses the system that provoked the dissemblance. It is not a trap of the victim's making, but if one plays stupid, one looks stupid.

The structure of communication has been the subject of heated controversy in recent decades. On one side are feminist activists and scholars who claim that the ways in which people express themselves and behave in social situations are determined and restricted by a gender ideology that grants men higher status and more power to control their own and other people's lives than it grants to women. Moreover, feminists argue, the language used for referring to men and women captures this androcentric and sexist ideology, thereby limiting the ways women can speak about and express themselves.

These foreclosures on women's options are particularly powerful for three reasons:

1. Among the first skills learned in infancy are how to communicate and how to interact with others. Learning how to express thoughts and feelings to other people and how to understand and react to others is in many ways the central task of learning to be human. If the structure of communication is determined by gender, the process of learning to be human is at the same time a process of learning how to be male or female, masculine or feminine.
2. Many of the patterns discussed in this chapter become unconscious and automatic once they are learned. Many of the male behaviors described earlier, which render women silent or ineffective, are done unconsciously; men are unaware of what they are doing. Although people may speak of choosing their words carefully, anyone who considered all the implications of every word, gesture, facial expression, posture, and reaction would quickly become immobilized.
3. The limitations imposed by language and communication patterns are so powerful because they are so ubiquitous, and their effects can be felt in so many ways. This chapter has emphasized everyday communication, but earlier discussions of the structure and impact of important social institutions showed numerous practical applications of these patterns of communication. Consider the languages of health, theology, or politics, and the gender-based patterns of interaction within health, religious, and political institutions. Any single instance of sexist communication—for example, a married woman's difficulty in getting people to address letters to her under her own name rather than her husband's—may seem trivial. Together, however, such instances form a comprehensive and enveloping system with enormous impact.

On the other side of the debate about gender and communication are people who attack any effort to analyze and change the style and structure of communication. Most of these efforts focus on attempts to eliminate sexist language. Following are some of the arguments against such efforts: Some people argue that the movement to use gender-neutral or inclusive language strips our language of its richness and renders it awkward, ungrammatical, and odd sounding. In most cases, these perceptions occur simply because people are unaccustomed to nonsexist forms. Unfamiliar forms often sound awkward, and it feels awkward to have to think about terms that were previously used automatically. Many people worry about the difficulty of pronouncing *Ms.,* for example, when they have done perfectly well with the rhyming words *fizz, 'tis,* and, certainly, *his.* When used fluently, nonsexist language is no more likely to be ungrammatical than is sexist language; people certainly make grammatical mistakes in both forms.[14] Why do some people consider language that excludes women more rich and vivid than language that includes them? Some opponents of language change claim to find language that includes women less authoritative and weaker than traditional male forms. (See, for example, the discussion of male God language in Chapter 7.) This is precisely the point: Language reflects and supports the values and power structure of the surrounding society.

Some people object to language change on the grounds that language is a valuable cultural possession with which no one must tamper. They warn against the horrors of "Newspeak," the language used in the fictional world created by George Orwell in his novel *1984.* In that frightening world, the government dictated that language conform to politically correct principles laid down by its Ministry of Truth. In the 1990s, many people attacked language reform for exerting a regime of political correctness. Language is indeed a valuable cultural possession, and Orwell was no doubt correct that language can be used to control the thoughts and lives of individuals and groups in society. This is precisely the point at hand. Who possesses language? Whom shall it serve? Who determines the uses to which it is put? Can a serious argument be made that people should continue to use a language that denigrates the majority of humanity? Can women and men, instead, choose to speak in a way that connotes respect for themselves?

Language changes over time because human experience changes. Just as those who view women in ways that are defined by androcentric gender ideology find nonsexist language awkward and irritating, those who view women as complete beings and full members of society find androcentric language awkward and irritating. It is perhaps true that, at times, feminists and antifeminists do not understand each other; they speak different languages. The difference is that most feminists now alive have been, at least at some point in their lives, bilingual: They grew up with the old androcentric language and have learned the new inclusive language.

Changing the language we speak is not as easy as it might appear. Eliminating the most obvious signs of androcentrism is not difficult with a little thought, and numerous guides offer assistance. Some examples of the types of changes people might make can be found in the list in Box 10-2, compiled by Barbara and Gene Eakins. Nonsexist language cannot flow naturally, however, if people do not experience the world in a nonsexist way. As discussed earlier, sexist language is not simply a matter of how one uses the word *man* or whether one retains *man and wife* and the asymmetrical *obey* in a marriage ceremony. If apparently gender-neutral words such as *love, selfishness, strength,* and *consent* are applied in different ways to men and women, language remains gender laden. Concerns about language require considering not only the words we utter but also the way we think and see.

Changing the patterns of social interaction is even more difficult and requires even more self-consciousness and will than changing the language. Men and women who try to break free of the gender-based structure of interaction

BOX 10-2 Nonsexist Treatment of Women and Men

1. Avoid typecasting in careers and activities.
   a. Avoid typecasting women in traditional roles.
   b. Avoid showing men as subject to the "masculine mystique" in interests, attitudes, and careers.
   c. Attempt to break job stereotypes for women and men.
   d. Show married women who work outside the home, and emphasize the point that women have choices about their marital status.
   e. Address course materials to students of both sexes.
   f. Portray women and girls as active participants the same as men and boys, and not only in connection with cooking, sewing, and shopping.

2. Represent members of both sexes as whole human beings.
   a. Represent women and men with human (not just feminine or masculine) strengths and weaknesses. Characteristics praised in males should also be praised in females.
   b. As in portraying men and boys, show women and girls as active, logical, accomplishing.
   c. Sometimes show men as quiet and passive, fearful and indecisive, just as women are sometimes portrayed.

3. Accord women and men the same respect, and avoid either trivializing women or describing them by physical attributes when men are described by mental attributes.
   a. Avoid (1) girl-watching tone and sexual innuendoes; (2) focusing on physical appearance; (3) using female-gender word forms, such as "poetess"; (4) treating women as sex objects or as weak and helpless; (5) making women figures of fun or scorn (not "the weaker sex," but "women"; not "libber," but "feminist").
   b. Avoid references to general ineptness of males in the home or to their dependence on women for meals.
   c. Treat women as part of the rule, not the exception (not "woman doctor," but "doctor"). Avoid gee-whiz attitudes toward women who perform competently.
   d. Represent women as participants in the action, not as possessions of men. (Not, "Pioneers moved west, taking their wives and children," but "Pioneer women and men moved west, taking their children.")
   e. Avoid portraying women as needing male permission to act.

4. Recognize women for their own achievements.

encounter resistance, frustration, and even pain. Some tasks are relatively easy, such as extending common courtesies to both sexes, rather than maintaining them as acts of male chivalry toward delicate females. Research on communication and interaction behavior suggests, however, that women find acceptance or respect difficult to obtain, and women may be seen as loud, harsh, demanding, and overly

5. In references to humanity at large, use inclusive language.
    a. Avoid the generic word *man,* because it is often not interpreted broadly. (Not "mankind" but "humanity"; not "manmade" but "artificial"; not "primitive man" but "primitive peoples.")
    b. Avoid the generic pronouns *he, him, his* in reference to a hypothetical person or humanity in general.
        • Reword sentences. (Not "The average American drinks his coffee black," but "The average American drinks black coffee.")
        • Recast into plural. ("Most Americans drink their coffee black.")
        • Replace the male pronoun with "one," "you," "he or she," and so forth.
        • Alternate male and female expressions and examples: "I've often heard supervisors say, 'She's not the right person for the job,' or 'He lacks the qualifications.'"
        • If the generic *he* is used, explain in the preface and in the text that the reference is to both females and males.
    c. Replace occupational terms ending in *-man* with inclusive terms. (Not "businessman," but "businessperson"; not "fireman," but "firefighter.")
    d. Avoid language assuming that all readers are male. (Not "you and your wife," but "you and your spouse.")

6. Use language that designates and describes the sexes equally.
    a. Use parallel language for women and men. (Not "man and wife," but "husband and wife" or "man and woman.")
    b. Identify women by their own names, not in terms of their roles as wife, mother, and so forth. (Not "Nehru's daughter," but "Indira Gandhi.") Avoid unnecessary reference to marital status.
    c. Use terms that include both sexes; avoid unnecessary references to gender.
    d. Use nonsexist job titles. (Not "maid" and "houseboy" but "housekeeper" or "office cleaner.")
    e. Avoid linking certain pronouns with certain work or occupations. Pluralize or else use "he or she" or "she and he." (Not "the shopper . . . she," but "shoppers . . . they"; not "the breadwinner . . . his earnings," but "the breadwinner . . . her or his earnings.")
    f. Do not always mention males first. Alternate the order: "women and men," "gentlemen and ladies," "she or he."

Source: Adapted from Eakins and Eakins (1978, 186–197).

masculine if they do not automatically yield the right-of-way to men or they carry and present themselves with confidence. Men may be regarded as weak if they choose to share ground with women more equally and treat women as more equal partners. Many feminists claim that the primary reason they seem to lack a sense of humor is that they do not find demeaning treatment amusing.

Feminist organizations have often experimented with different types of group interactions to try to achieve more open and participatory styles and to encourage the shy to assert themselves. Some feminist groups, for example, used to pass out chips or markers at the beginning of meetings. Each time a woman spoke, she gave up a marker, and she could speak no more when she ran out. This technique seems a very artificial way of managing interpersonal relations, but it can provide a lasting lesson about the nature of power, self-expression, and interaction. Feminist therapists have tied the issue of styles of communication to the question of mental health. They not only work on clients' communication skills and abilities but also try to restructure the process of therapy to reflect a less hierarchical structure in the therapeutic relationship itself. Their argument is that therapists cannot meet the needs of clients if therapy takes place within a hierarchical environment.

One of the issues to which feminists have paid increasing attention in recent years is the degree to which networks of communication have been used by women. Women and men have always had networks within their separate spheres through which they sought and gave support and information and exerted social control. The system of old-boy networks has long been recognized as important to men's lives. Unfortunately, although women's networks have been equally important to their lives, the value of these channels of communication has not been recognized until recently, and in the past, they have been dismissed as "kaffeeklatsches," "hen sessions," and "ladies clubs."[15] Women now take their communication networks more seriously, partly because they find themselves excluded and isolated as they enter male-dominated occupations. Most recently, the growth of electronic communication has encouraged the growth of feminist electronic mail and bulletin boards. Throughout this book are references to the communication networks that women have established in almost all domains of life. Women are beginning literally to give voice (or print) to their needs and experiences.

Notes

1. When I use the terms *language* and *communication,* they include both verbal and nonverbal dimensions, unless otherwise specified.

2. Simone de Beauvoir made a similar argument elegantly in *The Second Sex* (1952).

3. This is also one case among many in which the connotations are also shaped and elaborated differently within different ethnic, class, or other socially defined groups. Among African-Americans, for example, *girl* is an epithet of familiarity.

4. Interestingly, some people seem to think that the only people who use *Ms.* are single women, perhaps those who are somewhat embarrassed about being single. Some businesses include only the following options in check-off boxes on application forms: Ms., Mrs., Mr.

5. Recall the discussion of gendered and inclusive language in religion, Chapter 7.

6. Good reviews of this research can be found in Eakins and Eakins (1978).

7. Research also shows, however, that males are more likely than females to have speech impediments and defects (Eakins and Eakins, 1978, 92–94).

8. A very good review of the research offering evidence for the points raised in the following discussion can be found in Henley (1977).

9. I know this from personal experience.

10. Try this as an experiment: The next time you are walking in a safe, crowded area, pick a stranger out of the crowd, and try to hold that person's eye. Use only your eyes. Observe what happens, how you feel, and how you think the other person feels.

11. This is related to the tendency for people to see women's work in the arts as derivative of men's (see Chapter 8).

12. For an excellent bibliography on women, language, and health care, see Treichler (1984).

13. For more discussion of Talcott Parsons, see Chapter 2.

14. Sounding awkward and speaking incorrectly do not always go together. Most Americans seem to feel more comfortable with the split infinitive ("we need to carefully explore the gender implications of language") than they do with proper construction ("we need to explore the gender implications of language carefully"). Similarly, many people find it less awkward to say that "many surgeon generals have warned us against smoking" (which is incorrect) than that "many surgeons general have warned us against smoking" (which is correct).

15. For an influential historical view of women's networks, see Smith-Rosenberg (1975).

11

❧❧❧

Consenting Adults?
Personal and Sexual Relationships

As he spoke, enormous tears formed in his rather prominent eyes and ran
down the sandy tracts of his long and lanky cheeks.

That men cry as frequently and as unreasonably as women, Orlando
knew from her own experience as a man; but she was beginning to be aware
that women should be shocked when men display emotion in their presence,
and so, shocked she was.

Virginia Woolf, Orlando ([1928] 1995, 88)

WE HUMANS ARE SOCIAL ANIMALS; few of us can live secluded from human contact. However, conventional wisdom and stereotypes tell us that women and men are very different in how we approach, manage, and use personal relations of all sorts. Our friendships are different, we are told, as are the ways we relate to our family, lovers, and children. Some people (such as Sigmund Freud) say that women cannot get along with each other because of their jealousy. Most people believe that men need sex more than women do. Women are supposedly fickle, although they are also thought to be less promiscuous and to need marriage more than men. Some people say that women are more enmeshed in social relationships than men, that their lives are more bound by their relationships. Our task here is to look beyond conventional wisdom and even theory, to see what evidence we have about gender and personal relationships.

We begin with the role that gender plays in defining personal relationships, and then we turn to sexuality and sexual relationships. Finally, we examine the social institution of marriage, both to understand its structure and dynamics in relation to gender and to probe its significance as the primary organization through which societies institutionalize sexual and personal relationships. Above all, in this chapter, we are concerned with the degree to which women and men have been able to be consenting adults in their own lives—that is, to make their own choices about their relationships with other people.

Gender and Personal Relationships

357

Chapter 11:
Consenting Adults?
Personal and Sexual
Relationships

Many philosophers and social scientists have pondered the question of whether there are important differences between women and men in how central their social relationships are to them and what role those relationships play. It is interesting to compare the claims of two influential researchers from very different scholarly traditions: the anthropologist Lionel Tiger (1969), whose approach is based in sociobiology; and the psychologist Carol Gilligan (1982), whose work is based in developmental psychology.

Lionel Tiger argued that men's dominance in society stems largely from their greater "bonding instincts," evidenced especially in their forging of the alliances they have formed from the dawn of history, in hunting bands, defense networks, and ultimately governmental, military, and economic organizations. These bonding instincts are natural mechanisms that have been essential not just for the formation of human communities, but also for men's dominance in governance, defense, and the provision of sustenance. Human societies were established on the basis of bands of men defending themselves. Women lack these instincts (they do not even have as much propensity as men to play team sports), and thus, they are dominated by those people who have these instincts.

Contrast Tiger's view with Carol Gilligan's; Gilligan claims that women define themselves more in terms of the web of social relationships and obligations in which they are enmeshed than men do. She bases her views partly on Nancy Chodorow's (1978) more psychoanalytic work noting that connection is a special problem for men because of the gender and sexual dynamics between sons and mothers. Gilligan has underscored the importance of relationships in women's lives, forged first by the connection between mother and daughter, and then maintained through the importance of the people orientation that women learn. Given that part of woman's central life work is to nurture and to be oriented toward the needs of husband and children, it should be no surprise if women's sense of ethics and morality is based on the significance of human behavior and events for relationships among people.

In a sense, this conflict of views is based on different views of what constitutes the basic, primary social relationship that governs society: the hunting band or the mother and child. The fact is that whatever we might say about these relationships theoretically, historically, they were both central to the way that societies developed.

Some systematic research speaks to the question of gender differences in social relationships. Men generally report having more same-sex friends than women. At the same time, they seem to define friendship differently, defining as "friends" those with whom they are not as emotionally close or intimate as is true for women's "friends." While men often view their special male friends as people with whom they go in groups to drink or play sports, women are more likely to define their special friends as the people with whom they can share confidences and to whom they can turn when they feel vulnerable.

Robert Lewis (1978) speculated that the relative distance between male friends is the result both of men's fears of appearing vulnerable and of *homophobia* (the fear of homosexuality). He pointed out that men often discover their most intimate and close male relationships in two special activities: sports and war. Lewis suggested that American men are especially likely to avoid touching each other "unless it is roughly done as in a game of football or other contact sport" (1978, 112). On these occasions, ritual greetings such as slaps on the back or handshakes might be added. In recent years, part of the men's movement has focused on developing closer relationships among men.

A study of working- and middle-class men and women found that although they both get together with others to engage in activities such as sports, women are more likely to use these occasions as an opportunity for wide-ranging conversation, while men stick to the activity at hand (Walker, 1994). This observation adds support to other studies, which have found that conversation and talk are especially central in the dynamics of women's friendships (Johnson, 1996). Men are more likely to see their friendships as an "unspoken bond" (Inman, 1996). Some studies show that the network of women's friendships depends on their class background; working-class women's friendships are more tied to their families and local geographic area, while middle-class women's are more dispersed and various, probably because of their educational and occupational backgrounds and greater mobility (O'Connor, 1992).

Of course, many aspects of social relationships are enacted dependent on *culture* and are shaped *historically*. For example, heterosexual American men generally do not kiss each other or dance with each other, but men in some other countries are more physically expressive; many, for example, have dances in which only men participate with other men. The culture-based enactment of social relations is also conditioned by the *institutional organization* of people's lives. Thus, because women's and men's lives are institutionally different, their social relations should be expected to differ. A very large proportion of men in industrialized societies spend much of their time in formal organizations with explicit lines of communication and procedures for dealing with problems. Women, on the other hand, have relied on more informal networks of female relatives, friends, neighbors, and others in their communities. Certainly, men face social pressure to avoid showing dependence or weakness, which in turn prevents them from using friendships the way women do. As Virginia Woolf's gender-bending character Orlando noted (in the chapter-opening quotation), it is not that men *cannot* cry, but that under certain circumstances, it is not considered as appropriate for a man to do so as it might be for a woman.

Social scientists have observed some important gender differences in the types of relationships people have and the way they deal with relationships. Women, for example, are more likely to rate lying within a friendship or romantic relationship as a significant act and unacceptable, and it provokes a more emotional reaction than is true for men (Levine, McCormack, and Avery, 1991). As noted in Chapter 10, there are important differences between men's and women's modes of communication and in the way they interpret other people. These differences have serious implications for their relationships. Among other things, these patterns provide considerable scope for misunderstanding between men and women, as a normal part of their interaction. This issue is discussed further later in this chapter, in regard to sexual cues and perceptions.

359

Chapter 11:
Consenting Adults?
Personal and Sexual
Relationships

Discussion of women's relationships probably brings to most people's minds women's connections with men and children. Contemporary emphasis on *gender integration* (the increasing tendency for women and men to share interests, activities, and roles) sometimes leads to overlooking how rich women's social networks can be. Modern ideas of personal networks often scorn the old-fashioned idea of segregated social life and sometimes dismiss women's traditional relationships and activities as impoverished and limited, compared with men's. In contrast, historian Carroll Smith-Rosenberg's research on relationships among women in the 19th century led her to conclude that "women . . . did not form an isolated and oppressed subcategory in male society. . . . Women's sphere had an essential integrity and dignity that grew out of women's shared experiences and mutual affection" (1975, 9–10). As Smith-Rosenberg pointed out, it is no wonder: In a world that is highly sex segregated, to whom would women turn? Women turned to each other for solace and aid. They were each other's teachers; they helped each other give birth; and they helped each other die. Many historians are now investigating the importance of female friendships in women's lives (Freedman, 1979; Leavitt, 1983; Ryan, 1979).

By researching women's letters and other available documents, Smith-Rosenberg and others have found evidence that women have long depended throughout their lives on the constancy and intimacy of their female friendships and kin. These historians are now correcting the problems Smith-Rosenberg identified in the early 1970s: "The female friendship of the nineteenth century, the long-lived, intimate, loving friendship between two women, is an excellent example of the type of phenomena which most historians know something about, which few have thought much about, and which virtually no one has written about" (1975, 1).

Research on contemporary women's lives has captured some of the same sense of closeness and interdependence among women, including, for example, Carol Stack's (1974) work on Black women in urban ghettos and Mirra Komarovsky's (1967) study of married working-class women. Circumstances make it likely that female friendships have changed over time; for instance, male and female domains are more integrated than they once were, and sexual mores have changed. Women can socialize with men more freely today, without their relationships being regarded as sexual. Now, women, too, are enmeshed in bureaucratic workplaces. Ironically, the intimacy of some female friendships of the 19th century would today be interpreted as explicitly sexual and therefore might be inhibited.

Sexuality and Sexual Relationships

Studying the social and cultural construction of sexuality is a crucial part of understanding sex/gender systems because women have been defined largely as sexual objects of men within androcentric societies. As workplaces and other parts of society, such as the military, become more gender integrated, the sexual implications of women and men working together emerge as stumbling blocks in the reorganization of society. It appears that to introduce women other than those in auxiliary positions, such as nurses and secretaries, into male-dominated workplaces is to introduce misplaced sexuality. An understanding of gender relations requires an understanding of sexual relations.

Defining Sexuality and Sexual Relationships

What is the difference between a sexual and a nonsexual relationship? This question might seem odd at first. Isn't the answer obvious? "No," as the difficulties of trying to develop effective and reasonable sexual harassment policies demonstrate. What is the essential difference between a sexual and a nonsexual caress? What is the fundamental difference between platonic and nonplatonic love and affection? Is the difference merely where and how people touch one another, or whether people consciously initiate genital contact for the purpose of giving or receiving pleasure? Why does there seem to be such a strong link between sexuality and aggression or dominance behavior?

As Susan Brownmiller (1975) pointed out, rape has often been used as an instrument of war and domination. One fast walk through an adult bookstore reveals how much of what some people consider erotic involves aggression, violence, and domination. It can, at times, be difficult to distinguish between physical struggle and sexual passion. For that matter, most people have had specific relationships in which they were not at all sure whether there was a sexual or romantic element involved, or to what degree. It is often difficult to distinguish between sexual and other types of intimacy on the one hand, and between sexuality and violence on the other. These confusions are created partly by the relationship between sexual and gender norms.

Sigmund Freud was the theorist most responsible for calling attention to the difficulties of distinguishing between sexual and other relationships and feelings. Freud's views on the matter were quite radical, but it is worth reviewing those views to see some of the most important questions and controversies.[1] Freud argued that the instincts or unconscious drives are undifferentiated formless energy. The *libido* is a generalized drive for stimulation and pleasure, similar in men and women. There is no instinctual difference between seeking one or another kind of pleasure, and the libido knows nothing of morality or guilt. Freud, in fact, labeled platonic love and attachment "aim-inhibited eroticism"—in other words, an erotic or pleasure-seeking relationship in which the sexuality is repressed.

Only through socialization, *repression* (the process of excluding these drives from consciousness), *sublimation* (transforming basic erotic drives into less threatening or more acceptable forms), and even direct coercion do people channel their pleasure seeking into acceptable forms and make conscious distinctions among feelings and actions they might describe as sexual and nonsexual, aggressive and nonaggressive, good and bad, normal and perverted. Shame, guilt, and morality are alien to infants and remain alien to the adult unconscious. Unconscious drives threaten people's conscious senses of self and morality, so the psyche works to reduce the resulting tension by transforming or reinterpreting the meaning of these drives.

Hot flashes. Tingles. Shakes. Dizziness. A need to cling to someone. What is this experience? Fear? A fever? Or sexual arousal? It could be any of these. The early phases of sexual arousal resemble other states of emotional arousal. How do we interpret and *know* what we are feeling? Cognitive psychologists argue that we interpret sensations by taking cues from the situation and our beliefs, as well as from our feelings (Rook and Hammer, 1977). Certain aspects of the situation make individuals label an instance of emotional arousal as sexual, rather than something else. Both cognitive psychology and psychoanalytic theory, then, argue that we have both motive and capability to understand similar feelings in different ways. If our upbringing tells us that we should not be sexually aroused in a given situation or by a particular stimulus, we are likely to label our emotional responses in these situations as nonsexual. Experimental research shows that it is even possible to change our minds about the appropriate label for a particular emotional reaction (White, Fishbein, and Rutstein, 1981). Most of us have probably heard someone say, "I thought I felt like it—but then I realized I really didn't. It was all a mistake." Of course, the implication here is not that the speaker has changed his or her mind, but that the original feeling was misunderstood.

Our understanding and interpretation of our own arousal depends, then, not just on the particular context and situation, but on the values and beliefs we have learned. We learn these, in turn, at least partly from the social and cultural norms of our societies, communities, and families. A rich historical literature traces the development of sexual norms and customs. Human sexuality is, of course, based in many ways in physiological phenomena, but to understand sexuality as a whole, we need also to understand that it is socially and historically constructed. As with many other aspects of life, we *learn* how to think about the natural (and certainly, the moral), and these ideas are not the same from one historical period to the next.[2]

Sexual Identity and Orientation

One important aspect of human sexual life is *sexual orientation,* the overall framework of a person's erotic attractions, identity, and practices toward members of one's own or the other sex. Human sexuality is very complex and composed of many parts. Sexual norms, tastes, and practices vary across cultures, through history, and across the course of an individual's lifetime.[3] As this chapter discusses further, sexuality is inseparable from general problems of human interaction and communication, and it is fundamentally tied to the construction of gender in society. Sexuality is a crucial component of a sex/gender system.

To understand sexuality and especially how it is related to gender, it is useful to remember that sexuality is not just a composite of physiologically based "feelings" or "urges" but is also shaped by the way we think about ourselves, our character, our relations with others and with the larger society and its values, and the perspectives we have accumulated through experience. Some scholars find the concept of *sexual self-schemas* useful for summarizing this package. (Recall the discussion of self-schemas and gender schemas in Chapter 3.) One interesting study defined *sexual self-schemas* as "cognitive generalizations about sexual aspects of oneself. . . . derived from past experience, manifest in current experience, influential in the processing of sexually relevant social information, and they guide sexual behavior" (Andersen and Cyranowski, 1994, 1079). Our sexual self-schemas are

361

Chapter 11:
Consenting Adults?
Personal and Sexual
Relationships

derived from our past feelings and experiences and serve as frameworks for the present and future. In their study of sexual self-schemas, Andersen and Cyranowski (1994) found that people's self-schemas varied along three dimensions: how passionate/romantic they define sexuality, how open, and how embarrassed/conservative.

Analysis of sexual orientation—heterosexual, bisexual, or homosexual—shows very clearly that people's ideas about sexuality and gender are not just related but also interdependent; people's views of gender depend on their views of sexuality, and people's views of sexuality depend on their views of gender. Indeed, Letitia Anne Peplau and Steven Gordon (1983) have argued that people often confuse three different components of individuals' identities: (1) *gender identity*, a person's understanding of being male or female; (2) *gender-role behavior*, a person's repertoire of "masculine" and "feminine" behaviors; and (3) *sexual orientation*, attraction to or preference for people of a given sex.

Masculinity and femininity are both judged according to how well people conform not just to traditionally prescribed gender divisions of labor but also to traditionally prescribed heterosexual behavior. Indeed, masculinity and femininity depend not just on appropriate sexual behavior but also on whether a person possesses the characteristics that are sexually attractive to members of the other sex. Indeed, most sociobiologists and much of the public believe that gender differences in personality and divisions of labor are caused by—and gain their logic from—heterosexuality of a very specific sort: Men are the pursuers and possessors, and women are the pursued and possessed. Many sociobiologists believe that the construction of gender and gender roles inevitably follows from this supposed fact of sexual life. Feminist theorists who analyze sex/gender systems argue that although gender and gender roles have been so constructed as to serve and maintain this sexual system, neither is inevitable.

As Peplau and Gordon (1983) have pointed out, this cultural view of the linkages between the human sexual and gender personae means that to be masculine (a "real man"), a person must possess the characteristics appropriate to being heterosexually aggressive, and to be feminine (a "real woman"), a person must possess the characteristics appropriate to being attractive to men, but only as the more passive, at most receptive, partner. According to this view, women who are sexually oriented toward women, and men who are sexually oriented toward men, cannot be appropriately feminine or masculine and further, they must experience confusion in their identities. (How could a real man love another man?)

Some common myths and stereotypes illustrate the widespread belief that heterosexuality is both the most natural sexual orientation and the primary determinant of people's personalities and behaviors as men and women. Most people think it is easy to distinguish between heterosexuals and homosexuals. This is why people often suspect men with stereotypically feminine characteristics and women with stereotypically masculine characteristics of being homosexual and why they often are disbelieving when they hear that a typically masculine man or feminine woman is actually gay or lesbian.

Consider some myths specifically about lesbians, that demonstrate the relationship between sexual and gender ideology. One commonplace idea is that lesbians do not really prefer women as sexual partners; instead, some trauma in their relationships with men made them hate and reject men and turn to women by default. Gays and lesbians are often thought to hate people of the other sex. It is often said that if they could just experience a good heterosexual relationship, they would be able to change their sexual orientation. Many people cannot believe that homosexuals can be as happy with themselves as heterosexuals are.

In fact, there is no evidence that homosexuals experience any more confusion about their gender identities than anyone else. It is not even clear how much homosexuals and heterosexuals differ from each other in the degree to which they have masculine and feminine traits. One study of women from the ages of 20 to 54, for example, compared lesbians and heterosexual women, using the Bem Sex Role Inventory (BSRI). The result was that lesbians scored as no less feminine than other women did. They were, however, more androgynous, because they scored higher on "masculine" characteristics than the heterosexual women (Oldham, Farmill, and Bell, 1982).

It is not surprising that people are confused and ignorant about sexual orientation. Until recently, homosexuality was seldom discussed, except as a sort of illness. Although American children receive more sex education in school now than they did a generation ago, topics such as homosexuality are not well covered (Trudell, 1993); traditionally, sex-education classes have often limited lessons about homosexuality simply to saying that it is wrong (Levitt and Klassen, 1974).

What do the labels *heterosexual, bisexual,* and *homosexual* mean? What is a sexual orientation? What might serve as evidence that someone has one sexual orientation or another? Among the clues to sexual orientation are *feelings and fantasies, behavior,* and *identity.*

A common belief is that if a person feels—or has felt—any desire for sexual contact with someone of the same sex, he or she is really a homosexual, despite any behavioral proof to the contrary. Philip Blumstein and Pepper Schwartz, who have done very important studies of sexuality and sexual practices, argue that the reason for this view is ideological (1977, 39): "Our cultural logic holds that it is almost impossible to have only some homosexual feelings. The idea is seldom questioned that a single homosexual act or strong homosexual feelings reveal the 'true person.'" Also, according to this definition, there can be no such thing as a bisexual; a person must be either heterosexual or homosexual. Why is there no culturally parallel view that if someone who normally prefers homosexual sex has a heterosexual fantasy or encounter, that person is really a heterosexual?

Other people take their cues more specifically from a person's sexual behavior, rather than the person's desires or fantasies. From this perspective, someone who has had sexual relations with a member of his or her own sex is homosexual. The problem is that it is common for individuals to engage in homosexual relationships, even quite regularly, and still think of themselves as heterosexuals (Blumstein and Schwartz, 1977). Some amount of sexual play with members of one's own sex is very common among children, especially during late childhood and early adolescence. Likewise, some people are married or live as heterosexuals yet understand their own preferences to be homosexual. Sexual behavior, then, is not as clear a clue as might be expected. Moreover, *how much* sexual activity of one or another type is required to make the label *homosexual* or *heterosexual* appropriate? In their work on bisexuality, Blumstein and Schwartz wrote,

363

Chapter 11:
Consenting Adults?
Personal and Sexual
Relationships

The inescapable—but often escaped—conclusions from Kinsey, et al.'s findings are that a mix of homosexual and heterosexual behaviors in a person's erotic biography is a common occurrence, and that it is entirely possible to engage in anywhere from a little to a great deal of homosexual behavior without adopting a homosexual life-style. (1977, 32)

People's sexual orientations often vary a lot over a lifetime.

Sexual orientation may also be defined by the way people identify themselves. In a four-city survey, Blumstein and Schwartz (1977) found that just as people with extensive homosexual experience often identify themselves as heterosexuals, many people adopt homosexual or bisexual identities without having had any homosexual experiences. Sexual self-definition does not require any sexual experience at all. People, of course, face tremendous pressure to reject any idea that they might be homosexual. The social sanctions have been so severe that people are often afraid to admit their feelings, even to themselves.

Carmen de Monteflores and Stephen Schultz (1978) studied the process of *coming out,* acquiring and expressing a homosexual social identity, through interviews among women and men. They concluded that coming out is a psychological process that takes place over time, and that the process is typically not the same for women as for men. The men they talked to often had their first homosexual experiences before they really understood the meaning of homosexuality or thought of themselves as having any preference for men. In explaining their earlier encounters, they tended to emphasize sexual gratification and to deny responsibility for their choices (to say, for example, "I was drunk"). The women tended to act on their preferences only after they had recognized them and to emphasize the emotional bonds they had with their first female partners before having sexual relations with them. The men focused on the special circumstances of their first homosexual encounters, and the women emphasized their special partners. Men also report more difficulty in identifying themselves as homosexual (Blumstein and Schwartz, 1977), for reasons discussed later in this chapter.

The process of coming out involves a number of stages. Individuals first grapple with their own sense of identity and personal choice. Next, they reveal this new identity to others, generally people in the gay community. Because of the likely negative repercussions, it continues to be difficult for gays and lesbians to express their sexual identity to people in the "straight" world, including family, friends, and employers. Since the issue of sexual orientation has become increasingly politicized, and because gay communities are much more active and cohesive than they once were, for many people, coming out also involves becoming a member of an identifiable social and political community.[4]

In Sheila Kitzinger and Sue Wilkinson's (1995) study of lesbians who had spent at least 10 years of their adult lives active as heterosexuals and identifying unequivocally as heterosexuals, the researchers found distinctive patterns of stages the women went through in their transition from one orientation to the other. For these adults, the first stage was dealing with their new feelings or behavior in the context of a society that devalues homosexuality. Once they broke through those barriers, which often necessitated ending a period of denial, the women described different paths through which they acquired their new identities.

365

Chapter 11:
Consenting Adults?
Personal and Sexual
Relationships

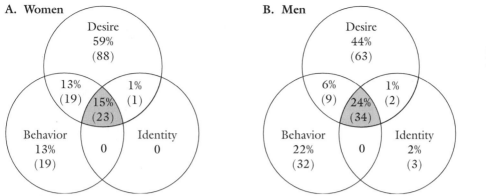

A. Women
B. Men

FIGURE 11-1 Interrelation of components of homosexuality. A. For 150 women (8.6% of the total 1,749) who report any adult same-gender sexuality. B. For 143 men (10.1% of the total 1,410) who report any adult same-gender sexuality.

The process of developing self-identity is not easy for heterosexual people, either. Freud, for example, thought that the process of becoming heterosexual was especially difficult for females, who have to learn to suppress themselves and become relatively passive. Young heterosexual men certainly devote considerable effort to proving themselves healthy, masculine heterosexuals, so adolescence is a period of great sexual anxiety for them. Nevertheless, because of social constraints, the problems of developing a comfortable sexual identity are different for those leaning toward a heterosexual orientation and those leaning toward a gay or bisexual orientation. It is precisely the fear of not being heterosexual enough and the fear of homosexuality that motivate some of the struggles of heterosexuals. Young people usually receive more social support from parents, friends, and other important people in their lives as they face the difficulties of developing heterosexuality; young people who are developing their homosexuality are more often isolated. Bisexuals face unique problems because they are often not trusted by either the homosexual or the heterosexual community (Blumstein and Schwartz, 1977).

A major national study of sexual practices in the early 1990s asked a series of questions that touched on the different elements of sexual orientation. The researchers found that among 18- to 44-year-olds, for example, 5% of White men, 6% of White women, 4% of Black men, and 6% of Black women found the idea of same-gender sex "very" or "somewhat" appealing; 90% of White men, 84% of White women, 91% of Black men, and 85% of Black women found it "not at all appealing" (Laumann, Michael, Gagnon, and Michaels, 1994, 162–165). It is more informative, however, to look at the combinations and overlap of desire, behavior, and identity. As Figure 11-1 shows, of those men and women who report *any* aspect of same-gender sexuality, the largest proportion (59% of women and 44% of men) claim that they have felt only some desire. A sizable minority (13% of women and 22% of men) claim to have participated in some same-gender sexual activity without having either felt desire or identified as homosexual. At the center of the figures, we see the 15% of women and 24% of men who have any same-gender sexuality, who feel desire, have acted on it, and self-identify as homosexual.

These definitional problems are matched by controversies over the causes of sexual orientation. By far the majority of scholarly theories understand homosexuality as developing from social causes, and many theories see all sexual orientation as socially caused and constructed.[5] Until the 1970s, the predominant view among scholars was the *medical model,* which defined heterosexuality as normal, and homosexuality and bisexuality as a mental disturbance, usually rooted in the relationship with the mother (or the mother's character) and in a lack of a strong father figure. In this view, homosexuality had to be cured. The American Psychological Association declassified homosexuality as a sign of mental illness in 1973.

As described previously, Sigmund Freud's version of the *psychoanalytic model* poses no particular natural form for sexuality. For Freud, there are reasons why the majority of people eventually take on a relatively stable heterosexual orientation, but he also believed that people whose orientation developed as homosexual or bisexual could be just as healthy and contented, even though he also believed that these orientations were less mature than heterosexuality. Freud himself thought that people devoted too much effort to making homosexuals become heterosexual. Many of his followers, however, accepted a view much closer to the medical model. Irving Bieber (1962) and Charlotte Wolff (1971), for example, used psychoanalytic approaches in their studies of (respectively) gay men and lesbians to conclude that mothers—dominant mothers of men, and inattentive mothers of women—cause their children's homosexuality. In recent decades, psychologists, sociologists, and others have increasingly considered other factors in a person's *development and life experiences* that contribute to homosexuality.

Since the late 1970s, scholarship has revitalized biological approaches to explaining the sources of sexual orientation. A Kinsey Institute study (Bell, Weinberg, and Hammersmith, 1981) tested a series of hypotheses about the sources of homosexuality, through lengthy interviews with samples of gay men, lesbians, and heterosexual men and women. They found little evidence for the most popular theories of homosexuality—that it is caused by parental relations, traumatic heterosexual experiences, seduction, or labeling. The authors argued that because sexual orientation generally seems to be developed relatively early, and because these social and environmental causes did not seem to offer much explanatory power, there must be some strong basis of sexual orientation in a person's biological makeup.

Biological explanations were bolstered in the 1990s by research showing that among twins, if one sibling was a gay male, the male twin was more likely also to be gay among identical twins than among fraternal twins (Bailey and Pillard, 1991). Even more influential is the work of Simon LeVay (1991), who studied the brains of a small sample of gay men and heterosexual men and women. He found certain cells in the hypothalmus of gay men that were different from those in the heterosexual men's brains and, indeed, more like those in the women's brains. Both of these studies have problems, however. For example, identical twins may be raised differently than fraternal twins, and, in any case, if sexual orientation is purely genetic, the identical twins should have *identical* sexuality. In LeVay's study, the men identified as "heterosexual" were labeled as heterosexual only because they had not been identified as homosexual. Also, the gay men in the study had all died of AIDS, so the biological marker may have been linked to AIDS, rather than to sexual orientation. Nevertheless, these studies have attracted a lot of attention, including in parts of the gay and lesbian community, where many activists argued that if sexuality is biologically determined, then it is natural and therefore should not be persecuted.

Whether or not sexual orientation has a biological base, and no matter how strong that basis is, no serious scholar rules out the importance of culture and social construction in shaping the people's experiences of their sexual orientation. Historians note that although people have varied in their sexual orientations since the beginning of recorded history, the designation of a "homosexual role" or of specific individuals as homosexuals is of recent vintage, going back only to the 19th century (Weeks, 1977). In considering the variability both across individuals and within individuals' lifetimes, it can seem futile to try to classify people. Shere Hite, for example, has argued that "the terms *heterosexual* and *homosexual* should be used not as nouns but as adjectives, and . . . should be used to describe activities, not people. Other than that, these words have no meaning. And even used as adjectives referring to activities, the words are vague" (1981, 809). On the other hand, if these words are used not just as descriptions of sexual relations but also in the more political and sociological senses to refer to communities and lifestyles, Hite's suggestion may not be adequate.

One thing is certain. A large number of people are homosexual. In the 1940s, Alfred Kinsey and his associates found that 28% of their sample of almost 8,000 women had had some homosexual experience (Kinsey, Pomeroy, and Martin, 1948). In Shere Hite's (1981) study of over 7,000 men, 11% said that they preferred to have sex with another man rather than with a woman. In her earlier study of women (1976), Hite found that 8% said they preferred sex with another woman, and 4% said they were bisexual. Some 1990s surveys seem to identify fewer people who identify themselves as either homosexual or sexually experienced with someone of their own sex, sparking a controversy of how adequate any of these social-science surveys are for identifying how many people in the population have what kind of sexual orientation (Laumann, Michael, Gagnon, and Michaels, 1994).[6]

Many scholars have studied attitudes toward homosexuality, especially *homophobia,* the fear or hatred of homosexuality. Homophobia is a form of prejudice, like sexism or racism. Table 11-1 shows that although most Americans are somewhat tolerant of homosexuality, a large proportion would place great limits on the lives of homosexuals and, especially, would try to shield their children from any exposure to homosexuals. When research uncovers gender differences in attitudes, the difference is usually that men are more hostile to and threatened by homosexuality than are women. A survey of new undergraduates in 1995–1996, for example, found that 46% of the men and only 24% of the women agreed that "it is important to have laws prohibiting homosexual relationships."[7]

After looking at a range of possible explanations for male homophobia, including age, education, religion, and various attitudes, one study found that the single best predictor of homophobia was whether a person accepted traditional family ideology. The more strongly men believe that a family should consist of a dominant father, submissive mother, and obedient children, the more likely they

367

Chapter 11:
Consenting Adults?
Personal and Sexual
Relationships

TABLE 11-1
Attitudes Toward Homosexuality

Homosexuality should be considered an acceptable alternative lifestyle.	36
Homosexual relations between adults are morally wrong.	55
Homosexuals should have equal rights in terms of job opportunities.	78
Would object to having an airline pilot who is homosexual.	11
Would object to having a homosexual as Representative in Congress.	38
Would object to having a homosexual as their child's elementary school teacher.	55
Would not permit their child to read a book that contains a story about a homosexual couple.	59
Would not permit their child to watch a prime time television situation comedy show with homosexual characters.	36
Would not permit their child to play at the home of a friend who lives with a homosexual parent.	58
Would be very upset if their college-age son or daughter revealed that they were homosexual.	49
Think that being homosexual is something people choose to be.	44
Think that being homosexual is something people cannot change.	43

Source: New York Times / CBS News Poll, February 9–11, 1993.

are to show signs of homophobia (Morin and Garfinkle, 1978). The second best predictor of homophobia is gender ideology. The more strongly the men believe in traditional women's roles and character, the more homophobic they are likely to be.

Several experimental studies show how homophobia and stereotypes affect the way people think. In one study, psychologists provided subjects with a vignette of an individual. Later, they gave the subjects information indicating that the individual in the vignette was either a homosexual or a heterosexual, then asked them what they remembered about the individual. As the researchers expected, the subjects mentally reconstructed the facts of the story to fit their stereotypes of the sexual orientation assigned to the individual (Snyder and Uranowitz, 1978). It is interesting to compare these findings with those of Carmen de Monteflores and Stephen Schultz (1978), who found the same process of reconstruction in the process of coming out among gay men and women. As newly self-identified homosexuals go through the process of labeling themselves, they also tend to reconstruct their past by remembering events and feelings they had forgotten, or reinterpreting the meanings of different events and relationships in their lives.

Homosexuality has always been suppressed in the United States. Leadership in the suppression of homosexuality has come especially from organized religion and government. Government, following from religious views, labeled sodomy or "homosexual acts" (especially by men) as criminal activities punishable by death in certain circumstances in the past. As recently as 1986, the Supreme Court declared that private intimate acts between consenting adults are not protected under the constitutional right to privacy, which means that state laws on sodomy, used primarily against homosexuals, are perfectly legal (*Bowers* v. *Hardwick*).[8]

In 1991, a national debate erupted about whether homosexuality should continue to disqualify men and women from serving in the military and should be grounds for discharge. A policy of "don't ask, don't tell" (i.e., everyone should agree not to talk about the question) was instituted, much to the ire of both people who defined this as an unacceptable continuation of the old discrimination policies and people who believed that this policy would undermine order in the military. Just when many gay activists thought that the military could enter an era of nondiscrimination, Air Force major Debra L. Meeks was court marshaled for sodomy and conduct unbecoming an officer—for being a lesbian. She had already served 22 years in the Air Force. She was acquitted.[9]

Nevertheless, some legal progress has occurred. Civil rights groups have pushed for legislation to protect the rights of gays and lesbians. When Congress passed the Hate Crimes Statistics Act of 1991, aimed at collecting information about hate crimes in order to reduce their frequency, gay women and men constituted one of the categories of people who needed this type of protection. Many towns around the country passed ordinances banning discrimination based on sexual orientation in housing, employment, education, public accommodation, and services. As part of the backlash to these changes, Colorado voters passed an amendment to the state constitution forbidding any legislative, judicial, or executive action that would protect people on the basis of their "homosexual, lesbian, or bisexual orientation, conduct, practices, or relationships." The Supreme Court ultimately found this part of the Colorado state constitution in violation of the U.S. Constitution, on a 6–3 decision. The Court stated that this "general announcement that gays and lesbians shall not have any particular protections from the law" seems "born of animosity toward the class that it affects" and is a "status-based classification of persons undertaken for its own sake, something the Equal Protection Clause does not permit" (*Romer* v. *Evans*, 1996).

Why is sexual orientation, especially homosexuality, a key issue in feminist research and activism? The primary explanation is so obvious that it is often neglected: Lesbians are women who defy the stereotypes of womanhood and femininity in very important ways. At the same time, the fact that a woman is a lesbian increases the likelihood that she will experience the effects of androcentric values and women's lack of freedom. For example, gender discrimination in employment affects women regardless of their sexual orientation, but lesbians are less likely than others to be sharing a higher-paid male's salary. Moreover, lesbians are subject to employment discrimination, both as women and as homosexuals (Levine and Leonard, 1984). Lesbians with children also have the problems of single motherhood, with the additional problem that much of society is antagonistic to the idea that lesbians should raise children. All women are justified in fearing the violence of rape, but lesbians cannot rely on male protectors as they go about their business.

369

Chapter 11:
Consenting Adults?
Personal and Sexual
Relationships

If women in general suffer from constricting stereotypes of femininity, so do lesbians. However, because they deviate from the stereotypes in an obvious respect, lesbians face the further problem of being defined as unhealthy and as not real women. Women are subtly and not so subtly directed to make their lives revolve around a man's. For this reason, some feminists, such as Adrienne Rich, have argued that one of the most rebellious things a woman can do is to defy the norm of *compulsory heterosexuality* (1980), a term widely used to refer to the norms reinforcing heterosexuality as the only healthy, normal, acceptable sexual orientation.

Many feminists have argued that homophobia and *heterosexism* (prejudice against homosexuality) oppress women, regardless of their sexual orientations. Charlotte Bunch (1979, 1981) made this point especially effectively. She has argued that heterosexism and sexism assume that "each woman exists for a man— her body, her children, and her services are his property. If a woman does not accept that definition of heterosexuality and of herself, she is queer—no matter who she sleeps with" (Bunch, 1979, 554). Women are given marginal status in the workforce and in education, partly because of the assumption that they will ultimately depend on men. Women also gain much of their social status and privileges through their relationships with men. "One of the things that keeps heterosexual domination going is heterosexual privilege; those actual or promised benefits for a woman who stays in line: legitimacy, economic security, social acceptance, legal and physical protection" (Bunch, 1979, 554).

Heterosexual women who do not recognize heterosexism and heterosexist privilege, Bunch has argued, cannot see how much they depend on men for their rights and privileges and how easily they can lose those rights and privileges by not conforming to heterosexual practices. In this one respect, radical feminists and right-wing antifeminists are in substantial agreement. Both see increasing equality for women as threatening to traditional sexual mores, and both see the breakdown of traditional sexual mores as threatening to the life of the patriarchal family.

Feminists such as Charlotte Bunch and Adrienne Rich also argue that heterosexism is a powerful force limiting the ability of women to respect themselves and to organize socially and politically. Homophobia certainly decreases personal intimacy among men (Lewis, 1978). Although there appears to be somewhat more intimacy among women, heterosexism defines women as incomplete without men, and it defines their relationships with men as more important than their relationships with other women. (For example, many women unhesitatingly renege on a commitment to go out with another woman if a man later asks them for a date at the same time.) To turn away from heterosexism implies the ability to imagine limitless love and respect for women as independent and complete people.

The issue here is not necessarily whom one chooses as a sexual partner, but the degree to which one accepts or rejects androcentric sexual and gender ideologies at the most personal level. This is the reason that Adrienne Rich (1979) has chosen to define *lesbianism* not by people's habits of sexual behavior but by the way people understand and identify with women. Antifeminists may be right that the women's movement has encouraged more women to choose to be lesbian, but it can also be argued that the women's movement has meant that more women could choose to be heterosexual without having to devalue themselves.

371

Chapter 11:
Consenting Adults?
Personal and Sexual
Relationships

Sexuality, Love, and Power

What are some of the gender differences in sexuality and love? Certainly, conventional wisdom sees men and women very differently in this regard. What does research say?

Many studies have examined male–female differences in sexual attitudes and behavior. It is sometimes difficult to compare these studies because the methods of research are so different. Research methodology is an especially important problem for studying sensitive topics such as sexuality.[10] Studies vary in whether they use direct observation or self-reports obtained in interviews or via self-administered questionnaires; they vary in whether they focus on attitudes or behavior; and they vary in how obtrusive (that is, direct) the methods are.

As in other fields of study, researchers in this field find more similarities than differences between women and men. In addition, similarity has increased as time has passed, through the 20th century. A review of 177 studies of sexual behavior from the 1960s to the 1980s found that women tend to be less favorable toward casual sex than men, and they masturbate less, but few other differences appear (Oliver and Hyde, 1993).

A major new empirical study by four researchers in the early 1990s looked at sexual practices across the United States. Edward Laumann, Robert Michael, John Gagnon, and Stuart Michaels (1994) used a series of surveys to study both attitudes and behavior. Their work offers good insights into gender comparisons (as well as comparisons by race, ethnicity, education, age, marital status, and religion). As usual, they present a picture of striking similarity and overlap between women and men in sexual practices and preferences. Nevertheless, they found some differences, some of which are reviewed here.

Laumann et al. (1994) asked their respondents about 14 different sexual practices to find out how appealing their respondents found these practices (p.152). In many cases, some practices appeared so unpopular—or at least people were not willing to admit to finding them very appealing—that any gender differences that emerge are probably not trustworthy as data. Of the 5 sex practices that at least 10% of men or women found appealing, however, men were much more likely to find watching a partner undress and receiving or giving oral sex "very appealing." (The other options were "somewhat," "not," and "not at all" appealing.) Also, men were somewhat more likely to find vaginal intercourse very appealing.

Men were also more likely to find group sex very appealing; 13% of men and only 1% of women found this idea very appealing. Additional analysis from their study helps elaborate on some of these findings, with respect to group sex, for example. Of the younger people, ages 18–44 years, 31% of White men and 39% of Black men found group sex not at all appealing. Women were much more likely to fall into the "not at all" category: 77% of White women and 75% of Black women. The rejection of this practice is higher in each race–gender group among 44- to

59-year-olds, especially among Black men. It is likely that fear, especially women's fear of sexual violence, accounts for some of the gender difference.

Other data from the Laumann et al. (1994) study reveal some gender differences often suggested by other research. The researchers asked people (a) whether they always had an orgasm when they had sex with their primary partner in the past year (that is, for those who had a primary partner), and (b) whether their primary partner always had an orgasm when they had sex in the past year (pp. 116–117). About 75% of men and 29% of women said they always had an orgasm with their primary partner. About 80% of women said their partner always had an orgasm, and a very optimistic 44% of men said their partner always had an orgasm. What explains these differences? Some earlier research offers insights.

Shere Hite's well-known work on sexuality (1976, 1981) shows how little heterosexual couples understand each other's sexuality, especially how little men understand and pay attention to women's sexuality. Hite's male respondents sometimes displayed an amazing ignorance about women's bodies and how they work. Many did not know about the clitoris or its role in women's sexuality. Many men could not tell whether their partners had orgasms, and many thought the question not particularly important anyway. Numerous men equated sexual intimacy with genital penetration and considered that women's orgasms should happen during penetration if they happened at all.

Men have greater control in sexual relations, and sexual encounters are structured more by their desires and needs. Thus, a combination of widespread ignorance and a gender ideology that places men in the central role and women as supporting cast helps explain men's and women's different attitudes toward and understanding of heterosexual relations. This pattern also explains the finding that women in lesbian relationships experience more orgasms than those in heterosexual relationships, even though lesbians have sex less often: Women understand how their own bodies work (Blumstein and Schwartz, 1983).

Men also have more sexual partners than women do, and they claim to engage in sexual relations more often, to masturbate more often, and to use autoerotic materials more (Laumann et al., 1994). Interestingly, men also feel more guilty about masturbating than women do (something about wasting seed?) except among the least educated and oldest respondents, where men seem to feel a little more at ease with this practice. How big the gender differences are with respect to sexual practices depends on the age, race, and educational background of the women and men; nevertheless, the differences exist at some level among all of these groups. In a survey of the entering university class of 1995–1996, for example, 54% of the men and 32% of the women thought that "if two people really like each other, it's all right for them to have sex even if they've known each other for only a very short time."[11]

The concept of sexual schemas underscores the idea that an understanding of sexual practices requires an understanding of how people think about what they are doing. A fascinating study of 19- and 20-year-old Scotswomen's views of having a sexual reputation offers a good example (Kitzinger, 1995). These young women, with very different sexual experiences, were asked what it means to be called a "slag," which is roughly equivalent to the American term *slut*. The women generally rejected the term for themselves, no matter how sexually experienced

373

Chapter 11:
Consenting Adults?
Personal and Sexual
Relationships

they were, although all of them had been called a slag at some time, and all thought they knew one who deserved the term. Although many of them began their conversation with the researcher by saying that they did not care what people called them, as the conversation progressed, it became clear that they did care about their reputations. Their rejection of identifying themselves as slags, however, was not solely to avoid being seen as promiscuous. Rather, the crucial undesirable element of being a slag from their point of view was being *used* or *exploited* by men. Being sexually active or even promiscuous was not necessarily bad in and of itself for these young women, but being used or out of control was.

Another study of adolescent sexual behavior also shows the importance of understanding the frameworks through which people enact their sexuality. Catherine Sanderson and Nancy Cantor (1995) found that adolescents pursued social and sexual relationships through either of two different kinds of goals: (1) *intimacy goals,* in which they were oriented toward the actual relationship and development of connections with others; or (2) *identity goals,* in which they were oriented toward exploration, trying out different things, and establishing their autonomy and individual sense of self. Those who sought intimacy goals were more likely both to restrict their sexual activities to committed relationships and to prefer communication and mutual dependence, while those who pursued identity goals were more inclined toward casual relationships and the more hedonistic aspects of sex. There were no sex differences in terms of which teens pursued which goals.

A further phase of this study clearly showed the implications of these different sexual schemas. The researchers wanted to know whether they could design programs to encourage condom use in order to reduce sexually transmitted diseases by shaping the message of the program according to whether the audience had more intimacy or more identity goals. They designed one program for the intimacy-goals group, which emphasized communication skills and the importance of knowledge and protection for maintaining relationships. Their alternative program for adolescents with identity goals emphasized technical skills for protection while having a good time. The experiment worked. Even a year later, the young people were more likely to be using condoms if the message of the program in which they participated matched their own dating goals.

This study also emphasizes the importance of understanding sexuality and sexual practices within the context of human relationships and the dynamics of establishing and maintaining couples relationships. The following discussion turns to some of the issues involved in these relationships. Many people may be surprised to read that men tend to fall in love more quickly than women do (Hill, Rubin, and Peplau, 1976). Love and the initiation of intimate relationships mean different things to women and men. Sex appears to be more central and important to men in a relationship than it is to women, and men describe their love in slightly more passionate terms than women do (Hatfield, 1983; Peplau, Rubin, and Hill, 1977). Women are slightly more likely to feel a *companionate* love for their partners, or a love that emphasizes friendship and sharing. Some research suggests that a woman more carefully considers whether to live with a man because deciding to do so commits her to undertaking domestic labor and responsibility for the two of them. Men still generally expect the women they live with to do most of the cooking and cleaning.

Philip Blumstein and Pepper Schwartz's (1983) study of American couples reveals some interesting characteristics of attachment in relationships. Their study (which I discuss often in this chapter) focused on married couples, heterosexual cohabiting couples, and gay cohabiting couples.[12] The researchers found widespread division of emotional labor within the relationships, which generally included one partner who was more oriented toward the relationship than the other was. "The majority of couples, heterosexual and homosexual, have at least one partner who is relationship-centered. Couples without a relationship-centered partner are less satisfied and less committed" (p. 170). The traditional division of labor assigns women this role, although women by no means constitute all of the relationship-centered partners. Of course, among same-sex partners, such a division of labor could not be gender based.

Blumstein and Schwartz found some interesting differences in how people managed and felt about their relationships. "Among heterosexual couples, young men have less desire for their partner's companionship than do young women, but the tables are turned as the couple ages" (p. 176). The early stages of marriage can be difficult for women, who expected constant sharing and companionship with their new husbands, only to find that the husbands turned much of their attention to their jobs and other interests. With the birth of children, wives often withdraw some of their attention from their husbands as they devote themselves to care of the children (Sarrel and Sarrel, 1984). This is one reason why the early stages of parenthood can be so very stressful for husbands. For the relatively few remaining employed-husband-with-homemaker-wife couples, the husband's retirement can again pose a problem. The men may now be ready for companionship with their wives, but the women's well-established lives and routines may not fit their husbands' new needs.

Same-sex couples appear to share more of their leisure activities and their time than heterosexual couples do (Blumstein and Schwartz, 1983, 180). Part of the reason is that just as the economic world is segregated by sex, so are many leisure and social activities. This barrier does not divide homosexual couples. Private time away from one's partner is also important to a relationship. Of the types of couples that Blumstein and Schwartz studied, "Cohabitors feel most strongly about having time away from their partners" (1983, 186), a characteristic consistent with the generally higher levels of independence that mark these couples. Perhaps a more surprising finding, given women's desire for companionship in relationships, is that women express a stronger wish than do men for more time to themselves. The need for private time does not necessarily indicate a lack of love for one's partner. As mentioned previously, women have less control over their time and space than men do, and women with young children often feel cloistered by their families.

Blumstein and Schwartz (1983) also examined the role of possessiveness in relationships and found women to be slightly more possessive than men. Further analysis revealed the reason: Men tend to have more power and control within their relationships, and women's possessiveness is partly a reaction to insecurity. Only among wives in the study did possessiveness seem to be related to the degree of commitment to a relationship; the more they wanted the relationship to last, the more possessive they were. Men's degree of commitment did not affect how possessive they were of their wives, and—perhaps even more important—their level of possessiveness did not indicate how committed they were.

The issue of possessiveness raises a related topic: sexual fidelity and monogamy. Public-opinion polls generally show that women are more conservative than men in their attitudes toward extramarital sex and divorce. One possible reason is that women actually gain protection by safeguarding a traditional sexual morality because they are generally in a weaker position. In addition, Blumstein and Schwartz's (1983) study suggests that women simply are more likely to define commitment to monogamy as part of a stable relationship. The heterosexual women and lesbians were about equally likely to value monogamy. This finding is also consistent with others showing that for women, personal commitment and affection more often precedes the initiation of sexual relations. Another study of couples in the 1970s also concluded that lesbian and heterosexual women are very similar in their desires for close, permanent, and loving relationships (Peplau et al., 1978; Peplau and Gordon, 1983).

Shere Hite's study (1981) of male sexuality provides more insight into men's views of extramarital sex. About two thirds of the married men in her sample claimed to have had at least one extramarital affair. Most did not view this activity as having anything to do with their marital relationships, and most did not think that it detracted from their love for their wives. They were searching for sex in their affairs, often because they thought they did not have enough with their wives. Most thought that sex within marriage eventually becomes boring. However, most of the men strongly disliked the idea of their wives having affairs.

What is known about patterns of sexual intimacy within relationships? The frequency of sexual intercourse decreases over the life of a relationship. It is difficult to determine how much of the decrease is the result of habituation and how much the result of aging. Sexual activity tends to decrease after midlife because of physiological aging, but not nearly to the degree that young people suspect. Men's physiological capacities for sex begin decreasing at an earlier age and to a greater extent than women's do. However, as A. R. Allgeier concluded in his discussion of aging and sexuality, "The North American stereotype of the sexless older person is inaccurate. Sexy young people mature into sexy middle-aged and elderly people. The sexually disinterested elderly person was probably not very enthusiastic about sex in youth" (1983, 144).

Blumstein and Schwartz's (1983) couples study also shows that the traditional sexual division of labor is alive and well among heterosexual couples. The majority of people—53% according to female cohabitors and 67% according to husbands—thought that one partner in the couple tended to initiate sex. In heterosexual couples, this partner is more often the man, especially among married, as compared with cohabiting, couples.

Power is an important issue in relationships. One of the major findings in Blumstein and Schwartz's research on couples (1983, 53) is that "money established the balance of power in relationships, except among lesbians." The balance of power is more even in households with employed wives than in those of other married women, perhaps because these women earn money of their own. Feminists have long maintained that married homemakers' lack of financial

375

Chapter 11:
Consenting Adults?
Personal and Sexual
Relationships

resources makes them dependent and reduces their leverage in a marriage. The couples study shows that a woman gains additional respect from her husband if she is employed.

On the other hand, the employment of wives can introduce strains in marriages, especially given the lingering gender-role traditions in which women retain responsibility for most of the domestic labor. Blumstein and Schwartz found that although cohabiting couples are somewhat more egalitarian about the division of domestic labor, even in those couples, women do most of the domestic labor. Both heterosexual and homosexual men feel that a successful partner should not have to do housework unless that partner is female (Blumstein and Schwartz, 1983, 151). Men in general do not demonstrate that they are ready to share domestic labor; the more housework a husband does, the more conflict the couple has (p. 146).

In addition to *financial* dependency, *psychological* dependency is an important factor in relationships. Traditional gender ideology encourages psychological dependency in women by defining women's purpose as to please their mates; therefore women's self-esteem is dependent on their pleasing their partners. Traditional gender ideology also encourages a form of psychological dependency in men. That is, in order to feel masculine and to have a strong sense of self-esteem, a man must be needed by the woman he cares most about. She must be weak and economically dependent on him, so he is psychologically dependent on her dependence and has a strong motivation to keep her that way. Women's dependency in marriage has other effects as well. Blumstein and Schwartz (1983) discovered that in a heterosexual relationship, the more the power balance tips toward the man, the more the couple's sexual activity will be limited to intercourse in the missionary position, which tends to tilt sexual satisfaction toward the male.

Women's economic and psychological dependency appears to give men the power to abuse women. One study found women's subjective or psychological dependency related to relatively minor acts of abuse, while economic dependency seems to provide a breeding ground for more major acts of abuse (Kalmuss and Strauss, 1982). Another study showed that among abused wives, women who were not employed (and were therefore financially dependent) were less likely to leave the relationship than were employed women (Strube and Barbour, 1983). Experts on partner abuse have long been aware that one of the dynamics of an abusive relationship is that the abuser acts to isolate the abused partner and to make her or him dependent.

The double standard, which essentially validates different rules and degrees of power for men than for women, has been weakened and widely questioned, but it has by no means disappeared. Men are still more likely to initiate sexual relationships. Women retain their power to say "no," although they are pressured to use that power less often than they once were because of misguided interpretations of what constitutes a liberated woman. Another problem is that men and women do not even understand how to say "yes" and "no" in the same way (this problem is elaborated further in the next section).

Men expect to take the lead during sex, and many women are reluctant to press their own demands. Men are more resistant to condom use than women are (Campbell, Peplau, and DeBro, 1992). Inequality and male dominance in sexual

377

Chapter 11:
Consenting Adults?
Personal and Sexual
Relationships

BOX 11-1 This Letter Could Save Your Life

To the Editor:

Magic Johnson, the basketball great, produced unforgettable numbers. Let him, as a spokesman for HIV . . . , continue to talk the numbers and tell every 14-year-old in the world:

Suppose you started having sex when you were 15 and had one new partner each year until you were 23.

Suppose that your partners at 16, 17, 18, had followed the same pattern.

Now suppose also, as the AIDS epidemic makes plain, that when you have sex with one person you also come inevitably into contact with the biochemicals of all that person's previous partners—now your "phantom" partners. At 15, your number of actual and phantom partners was merely 1 plus 0 for a total of 1. At 16, your number of actual partners was 2, and phantom partners, 1, for a total of 3. At 17, 3 actual and 4 phantoms gave you a total of 7: your partner at 17 joined you with 2 actuals and 1 phantom of her or his own; and add the single phantom associated with last year's partner.

Please get out your ballpoint and calculator because at 18, 19, 20, and onward, up you went into the wild blue yonder. Result: at the still tender age of 23, with only 9 actual partners, your still-tender membranes and your still-tender bloodstream were potentially serving as fairgrounds for the entertainment and nourishment of active viruses and other bacterial fellow travelers from no fewer than 502 phantoms!

No one should bet that not one of those hundreds of phantoms had the HIV virus. Play it safe or don't play at all!

Timothy C. Brock
Laura A. Brannon

Source: Letter to the Editor, *New York Times,* November 23, 1991.

relationships are clearly not healthy for women, and these characteristics have become less healthy in the era of AIDS. If the sexual right-of-way means that women are coerced into having more sexual partners than they might otherwise have, and they are prevented from protecting themselves during sexual relations, then this double standard is potentially fatal to them. To see how much risk women face, see Box 11-1. The persistence of a gender division of labor means that women are held more responsible if conception occurs. One fact of life will never change: It is the woman who becomes pregnant.

In the 1960s, the press and other experts announced that the "sexual revolution" had begun. Men and women would now be freer to express themselves sexually and to make their own decisions about their sexuality. Of course, some people thought that a "sexual revolution" is merely a matter of having *more* sex. Feminists argued at the time that the real revolution would be to attain equality in sexuality. Gender equality and sexual equality must be attained in tandem.

Sex, Coercion, and Violence Against Women

Despite changes, our sexual culture continues to define male and female sexuality differently. In the words of romance novels, men "take" women, while women "give" themselves or at least are "swept away." Young men are under pressure to conform and to view women as their sexual objects. The ideology supporting male sexual dominance often makes it difficult for men to cope with more independent and self-assured women, and the pressure to conform to the standard of the conquering sexual hero creates strains of its own for men.

Societies differ in their sexual ideologies, and comparative research indicates that the sexual double standard tends to be more apparent in cultures in which women lack power relative to men. As Naomi McCormick and Clinton Jesser wrote,

> Male-dominated societies seem to permit men to use power to have sex while women are allowed to exercise power only to avoid sex with unsuitable partners. In such a society, a woman who uses power to seduce a man openly is regarded as "bad" and possibly dangerous. A man who uses power to avoid sex with a "turned on" woman is regarded as "religious" at best, and inept, stupid, and unmanly at worst. (1983, 68–69)

A male *sexual right-of-way* parallels and is related to the *communication right-of-way* discussed in Chapter 10. That right-of-way is an everyday problem for women. Women can easily lose their rights of control over themselves; a 1992 study of entering college students found that 17% of men and 6% of women thought a man is *entitled* to have sex with a woman if he *thinks* she "led him on."[13]

If, as discussed earlier, people have difficulty interpreting *their own* feelings, they certainly must have difficulty interpreting those of *others*. This problem is particularly acute for sexual relations between men and women for two reasons:

1. Males and females communicate differently (see Chapter 10) and therefore can misunderstand each other. This misunderstanding may be especially great on the part of men, who tend to be less able to read nonverbal signals than women.
2. Sexual norms tend to define women as sexual objects and men as sexual pursuers with a right-of-way in sexuality and communication.

Consider first the finding of a national study of sexuality (Laumann et al., 1994, 336): While only 3% of men say they have ever forced a woman to engage in a sexual act she did not want to do, 23% of women say they have been forced by a man to do something sexual they did not want to do. Other studies also show large numbers of women who feel that they have experienced sexual coercion, and small numbers of men who believe that they have coerced any women. An even larger number of women did not end up being coerced successfully but nevertheless experienced a man's insistence on doing things she was trying to resist.

What is going on? Research by Michael Motley and Heidi Reeder underscores the implications of sexual miscommunication. They ask, "If *she* indicates unwillingness to increase physical intimacy, why does *he* attempt to escalate the intimacy?" (Motley and Reeder, 1995, 355). Their perspectives from the field of communications led them to ask a further question: Do men even *understand* women's resistance messages?

In the first phase of their research, Motley and Reeder (1995) studied the ways in which women express their resistance to engaging in sexual acts they do not want to do. These ranged from the very direct ("Please don't do this"; "I don't want to do this"; "Let's stop this") through the somewhat less direct ("I'm confused about this"; "I can't do this unless you're committed to me"; "I don't think I know you well enough for this") to the indirect ("Let's be friends"; "I'm seeing someone else"; "Hey, what are you doing?"). They found that women have a large repertoire of resistance messages they use in different circumstances. They use the more direct forms if they do not plan on seeing someone again; they use the less direct form if they want to continue to see the man. Why do women use less direct means of saying "no" to someone they like and want to continue a relationship with? Women do so because they believe that more direct methods will make the man hurt or angry or will make him think badly of her.

The problem is that men do not perceive the less direct resistance messages as resistance. Motley and Reeder (1995) gave men the list of women's resistance messages and asked them what they thought each of these messages meant. In some cases, they simply took the words literally and did not draw the implications. In other cases, they translated the message in a way that simply did not mean "no." For example, the resistance message "I don't think I know you well enough" means "She wants to go further but wants me to know that she usually only does this with people she has known longer." "I'm seeing someone else" means "She wants to go further but wants me to be discreet so that the other guy doesn't find out." In this study, men claimed they would not be angry or act negatively if women were more direct about saying no.[14] Other experimental research provides additional evidence that men read sexual messages into women's behavior that neither the women themselves nor other female observers see (Abbey, 1982). Indeed, men perceive greater sexuality than women in the behavior of both women and men (Shotland and Craig, 1988). Of course, there are also circumstances in which women read sexual cues into other women's behavior that men claim not to see.

These studies might merely help explain the small dramas of crossed signals between men and women, were it not for three points. First, the situations involving conflicting definitions of sexuality are neither random nor merely occasional; they constitute a widespread pattern that reflects a gender-based and androcentric sexual ideology. Women find they have to be on guard constantly to avoid being misinterpreted by men. Second, conflicts in the definition of sexuality play an important role in two serious problems that confront most women at least indirectly: sexual harassment and rape. Third, violence occurs all too readily within sexual relationships, even from an early age. A 1995 poll found that 40% of girls ages 14–17 years said they had a friend their own age who had been hit or beaten by a boyfriend.[15]

379

Chapter 11:
Consenting Adults?
Personal and Sexual
Relationships

Demonstrations at the 1968 Miss America contest protested the definition of women as sex objects. This poster of a woman as suitable for meat carving was a well-known restaurant advertisement.

Sexual Harassment

A professor repeatedly suggests that rather than meeting during office hours, it might be better to discuss the student's directed reading work in the evening over drinks; during these sessions, the professor sits uncomfortably close and keeps turning the conversation to personal issues. A secretary finds herself constantly distracted at work by her boss, who usually gets her attention by putting his hands on her neck or back, and he often makes comments about her dress. An anatomy instructor mixes pinups from *Playboy* among the slides he shows in lecture, making "just us boys" cracks that both embarrass the women students and encourage the men to laugh at the women's comments and to laugh even more when the women blush. A woman is walking down the street, trying to get her shopping done, when she passes a group of men, who stare pointedly at her and make sotto voce comments about her; one whistles softly. An employer indicates to an employee that unless they have sexual relations together, the next evaluation will not be a good one.

Sexual harassment involves the use of sexuality as a tool of power or dominance. Most women have been victimized by it at some time or another, although many believe that "being hassled" is a normal part of life; they do not identify it by

381

Chapter 11:
Consenting Adults?
Personal and Sexual
Relationships

name. This omnipresence became clear in 1991 when a law professor, Anita Hill, testified to a Senate committee that a nominee for Supreme Court justice, Clarence Thomas, had sexually harassed her on the job years before. This case caught the nation's attention and became the subject of tremendous debate, in part because of the issues it raised about what constitutes sexual harassment, who the perpetrators are, who the victims are, and what should be done about it. Could a lawyer and high official in charge of equal-opportunity policy have engaged in harassment? Could a lawyer actually have been a victim, continued to work for a man who was harassing her, and remained silent for 10 years, as Hill claimed she had done? Whichever of these two people was telling whatever kind of truth or falsehood, it seemed that millions of women across the country learned the name of the problem that had afflicted them for years, and they told journalists and public-opinion pollsters—and probably in some cases, their bosses, teachers, doctors, and colleagues—that they had had enough.[16]

Although most of the public attention to sexual harassment has focused on specific relations within workplaces and schools, Carol Brooks Gardner's study of "public harassment"—that is, harassment that takes place in public places among strangers—shows how commonly women are subjected to "abuses, harryings, and annoyances" on the basis of their gender, in spaces that are supposed to be open to everyone (Gardner, 1995, 4). Gardner's study, based on observation and interviews, examines the way that people's ability to travel freely and comfortably through public space is restricted by harassment on the basis of gender, race, sexual orientation, disability, and age.

She has outlined three types of public harassment. Those subjected to *exclusionary* practices of harassment are barred or discouraged from entering specific places. I might be made too uncomfortable to visit a particular store or part of a beach because people act menacingly toward me or stare at me when I try to go there. I am excluded from public spaces with no wheelchair access if I must use a wheelchair to get around. Those subjected to *exploitative* practices of harassment have their freedom or privacy violated. Women experience this frequently when men follow them or feel free to invade their privacy in other ways. Finally, those subjected to *evaluative* practices of harassment receive unsolicited, unwanted, unnecessary, and intrusive or threatening evaluations of, for example, their bodies, hair, clothing, behavior, buying habits, or whatever else the harasser cares to comment on.

As Gardner found, these acts of harassment are facilitated by unequal power relations between different groups in society. These acts are often trivialized as minor annoyances, people "just playing around" or "just trying to be nice" or "just trying to be helpful." Victims of public harassment are required to be submissive recipients. Consider the woman who makes it clear that she does not want to hear comments about her breasts or to be stared at or to hear people making kissing noises at her. If she were to say politely that she did not like the situation, the laughter and remarks would probably only increase. If she were to react angrily, the remarks would probably become more aggressive and abusive, often making the undercurrent of sexual dominance and violence more explicit. Some victims of public harassment are likely to suffer from more vicious or violent attacks in the first place, as occurs to those people singled out for gay bashing.

Most women are probably aware enough of the gender basis of public harassment they experience to know that they are less subject to psychological assault on the basis of their gender if they are accompanied by a male protector.

Sexual harassment has taken on a more specific legal meaning because of increasing awareness of its role as an instrument of domination in workplaces and educational institutions. Sexual harassment has very serious consequences for women's ability to gain an education and to earn a living. Research repeatedly shows that most employed women experience at least some sexual harassment. Women who have been victims of sexual harassment overwhelmingly report that they feel embarrassed, demeaned, intimidated, angry, or upset. Many are frightened or suffer physiological symptoms (such as headaches, tiredness, and nervousness) brought on by stress (Backhouse and Cohen, 1981). Thus, the pressures of harassment may make it difficult to work effectively, which in turn has a negative impact on the quality of a woman's work and decreases her employment opportunities. Indeed, a federal government study has estimated that the amount of job turnover, medical insurance claims, absenteeism, and reduced productivity due to sexual harassment may cost the economy $189 million over a 2-year period (Livingston, 1982).

For a long time, no legal remedies were available to victims of harassment. Most people, including judges, thought that sexual harassment was really a personal matter, based on sexual attraction, which had little, if anything, to do with the job. Men, who predominate as judges, are still not as convinced as women that harassment is a problem, as shown by large-scale studies of federal employees (U.S. Merit Systems Protection Board, 1981) and of business executives (Collins and Blodget, 1981).

Catherine Mackinnon, one of the first legal theorists of harassment (1979), argued that there are two types of sexual harassment. The first is the *quid pro quo type,* in which sexual favors are required for a raise, promotion, or good evaluation or simply to retain one's job. The second is the *condition of work type,* in which there may be no explicit demand for exchange of sexual acts for goods, but in which being subjected to harassment is a regular part of the work environment; it is simply part of a person's working conditions, like the decor, the presence or absence of Muzak, or the number of breaks available during the workday. Consider the secretary who is never asked directly or indirectly to trade sexual services for job benefits but is subjected to a constant flow of sexual remarks and nonverbal innuendos while she does her work. Until the early 1980s, a woman in this situation had no legal recourse because unless she could show specific harm—mere constant stress was not enough—general harassment was not covered by the law.

The legal turning point came in 1981, when a circuit court redefined systematic sexual harassment as a form of sex discrimination:

The relevance of these "discriminatory environment" cases to sexual harassment is beyond serious dispute. Racial or ethnic discrimination against a company's minority clients may reflect no intent to discriminate directly against the company's minority employees, but in poisoning the atmosphere of employment it violates Title VII. . . . How . . . can sexual harassment, which injects the most demeaning sexual stereotypes into the general work environment and which always represents an intentional assault on an individual's innermost privacy, not be illegal? (*Bundy* v. *Jackson*, 1981)[17]

383

Chapter 11:
Consenting Adults?
Personal and Sexual
Relationships

The first sexual-harassment case to reach the Supreme Court was the definitive legal turning point for women nationwide. In 1986, the Court formally recognized the quid pro quo and work conditions forms of harassment, declaring that (a) sexual harassment is a violation of equal-employment law because it poisons the work environment selectively on the basis of sex, and (b) employers can be held responsible for harassment in their workplace (*Meritor Savings Bank* v. *Vinson*). These two points were crucial because they put governmental mechanisms designed to fight employment discrimination at the disposal of those fighting harassment.

There is a curious problem in sex-discrimination law. Here is an often-cited and very influential passage from a 1977 U.S. Court of Appeals case showing how courts justify claiming that sexual harassment is sex discrimination:

> *But for her womanhood* . . . her participation in sexual activity would never have been solicited. To say, then, that she was victimized in her employment simply because she declined the invitation is to ignore the asserted fact that *she was invited only because she was a woman* subordinate to the inviter in the hierarchy of agency personnel. Put another way, she became the target of her superior's sexual desires because she was a woman and was asked to bow to his demands as the price for holding her job. (*Barnes* v. *Costle*, emphasis added)

This logic raises an interesting problem. Its logic clearly applies when a heterosexual male harasses a woman or when a heterosexual woman harasses a man. Courts have found somewhat more contentious whether the law applies when a homosexual man or woman harasses someone of his or her own sex. In each case, the rule applies: But for the victim's sex he or she would not have been victimized. What about a bisexual perpetrator, however? Bisexual harassers are exempt from the logic of this decision. Many people argue that this legal tolerance of bisexual harassment shows that the underlying logic of anti-sexual-harassment policy is misguided.

A further question: Does the victim have to prove harm to charge sexual harassment successfully? In 1993, the Supreme Court decided a case that involved a woman who was harassed by her employer. She was subjected to sexual innuendos; the boss repeatedly said such things to her as, "You're a woman, what do you know," in front of other employers. The company's lawyers said basically that he was obnoxious, but she had not displayed any real psychological damage. The Court set an important precedent by replying,

> Title VII comes into play before the harassing conduct leads to a nervous breakdown. A discriminatorily abusive work environment, even one that does not seriously affect employees' psychological well-being, can and often will detract from employees' job performance, discourage employees from

remaining on the job, or keep them from advancing in their careers. More-over, even without regard to these tangible effects, the very fact that the discriminatory conduct was so severe or pervasive that it created a work environment abusive to employees because of their race, gender, religion, or national origin offends Title VII's broad rule of workplace equality. (*Harris* v. *Forklift Systems, Inc.,* 1993)

Although the law on sexual harassment has become stricter, most women still do not complain about harassment, either because they do not think that anything (or anything serious) would be done to the perpetrator, or because they think they would be penalized for complaining. Indeed, men—who are likely to be the supervisors women would need to address—tend to think that harassment is not a serious problem and that women who claim to be harassed are actually misinterpreting men's friendly behaviors. The women, they say, should feel complimented that men pay such attention to them. Many men believe that charges of harassment are phony, and that what is really occurring is normal sexual interplay between men and women.

Perceptions of victims' precipitation are involved in sexual-harassment cases, much as they are in cases of rape and domestic violence.[18] As in those cases, traditional sexual and gender ideology shapes the view of women as temptresses likely to make irrational and false charges of harm against men. Consider the evidence provided by a study of more than 1,200 people, in which men were more likely than women to blame women for being sexually harassed (Jensen and Gutek, 1982). Gender ideology shapes even women's views of harassment; the more they believed in traditional divisions of labor and power between men and women, the more they believed that it is a woman's own fault if she is the victim of sexual harassment.

It is not always easy to tell the difference between sexual harassment and mutual but difficult relations or mere miscommunication. How can people distinguish between sexual harassment and legitimate attraction of one person to another that happens to occur in the workplace or at school? Most people argue that the test is whether the activity is persistent and continues despite lack of encouragement on the part of the victim. The legal interpretation usually requires that the harasser be in a clear position of organizational power over the victim. However, who is to judge what constitutes persistence and lack of encouragement? Do policies restricting any intimate relations between employers and employees or students and faculty members violate their own freedom of choice? What constitutes insulting or demeaning remarks that might poison the work atmosphere? Who should be the judge? The argument feminists have made is that unequal gender relations in social institutions such as workplaces and schools interact with the gender basis of sexual relations that give men the sexual right-of-way, leading women to be especially vulnerable.

Rape

The traditional wisdom on rape is that men are at the mercy of their sexual drives and therefore rape when they are overly frustrated or when the opportunity arises.[19] Contemporary sociobiologists often use this argument to show why sex

385

Chapter 11:
Consenting Adults?
Personal and Sexual
Relationships

equality can never occur. Social science research, on the other hand, shows that the proclivity to rape and attitudes toward rape depend considerably on culture and ideology. Peggy Sanday's analysis of societies around the world (1981b) indicates that rape is by no means universal. In some societies, rape is virtually unknown; in others, it is a normal, ritualized part of men's and women's lives. American society falls somewhere in between (see also Gordon and Riger, 1989).

Feminists argue that rape is a logical outcome of an androcentric sex/gender system and its supporting ideology, which grants men a sexual right-of-way. If men are assumed to be sexually demanding by nature and women to be submissive, there is no strong barrier to rape, other than men's mutual agreement not to rape because this protects "their own" women from other men. American sexual ideology says that rape is wrong, but it gives men who do rape an excuse. For this reason, at least one author has called the laws about rape a "male protection racket" (Peterson, 1977).

Traditional treatment of rape in the legal and criminal justice systems provided considerable evidence of such a racket. Penalties assessed against a rapist used to be higher when the rape victim was married than when she was unmarried, and it was often the husband of the married victim, rather than the married victim herself, who could sue for damages—of his property. Rape has often been a weapon of war because the ability of the men of one nation to rape the women who "belong" to the men of another is an important symbol of domination and humiliation. Conquerors rape for much the same reason that they confiscate or damage other property of the vanquished. Although rape has been used on a massive scale in many wars, only in 1996, when a UN tribunal indicted 8 Bosnian Serb military officers in connection with a campaign of rape during the Bosnian war, was rape ever treated separately as a war crime by a legal body. Until then, rape had only been treated as part of soldiers' abusive behavior.[20]

Research by Stephanie Gordon and Margaret Riger (1989) has revealed that women and men define rape differently. Almost all the women and men they surveyed thought that "unwanted sexual intercourse with someone when physically forced or overpowered" was rape. About 95% also thought that "sexual intercourse with someone without their consent" was rape. In addition, however, the study showed examples of important gender differences in the definitions of rape. About 91% of women and 83% of men defined "a relative having sexual intercourse with a child" as rape. About 80% of women and 64% of men defined "a relative having sexual intercourse with a teenager under age 18" as rape. About 63% of women and 44% of men defined "unwanted sexual intercourse between a husband and wife" as rape. Finally, 23% of women and 10% of men defined "a stranger pinching or grabbing in a sexually suggestive way" as rape (1989, 61).

Martha Burt (1980) did an important empirical study of the role of gender and sexual stereotypes in people's beliefs about rape. She has pointed out that widely accepted cultural rape myths maintain that women are at least in part responsible for their own victimization, that rape is not as common as women believe, and that rapists are in large part not responsible for their own actions. People who accept traditional gender-role stereotypes or who believe that heterosexual relationships are necessarily adversarial are more likely to accept rape myths. Also, the more that people accept interpersonal violence in general, the more they

BOX 11-2   Sexual Ideology: Adversarial Sexual Beliefs, Sexual Conservatism, and Rape-Myth Acceptance

Following are three lists of statements that indicate three different but related aspects of sexual ideology. Do you agree or disagree with each of these statements? Do you think most of your friends would agree or disagree? How about the police? Most people? What difference does it make whether someone agrees or disagrees with these statements?

Adversarial Sexual Beliefs

Greater *agreement* with these statements indicated greater belief that heterosexual relationships are adversarial relationships.

A woman will only respect a man who will lay down the law to her.

Many women are so demanding sexually that men just can't satisfy them.

A man's got to show the woman who's boss right from the start or he'll end up henpecked.

A woman is usually sweet until she's caught a man; then she lets her true self show.

A lot of men talk big, but when it comes down to it, they can't perform well sexually.

In dating relationships, women take advantage of men.

Men only want one thing.

Most women are sly and manipulative when they want to attract men.

Many women seem to get pleasure in putting men down.

Sexual Conservatism

Greater *agreement* with these statements indicates greater sexual conservatism.

A woman who initiates a sexual encounter will probably have sex with anybody.

A woman shouldn't give in sexually to a man too easily or he'll think she's loose.

Men have a biologically stronger sex drive than women.

A nice woman will be offended or embarrassed by dirty jokes.

Masturbation is not a normal form of sexual activity.

People should not have oral sex.

accept rape myths. In other words, acceptance of the predominant rape myths is part of a package of ideas that include belief in men's social and sexual superiority and acceptance of the inevitability of male power and violence. An adaptation of Burt's survey is shown in Box 11-2.

Neil M. Malamuth (1981) pursued this line of inquiry further by investigating the links between rape and people's beliefs and attitudes. Like most other investigators of rape, he has noted that research consistently fails to reveal many psychological differences between men who have raped and men who have not. In other words, rapists are psychologically similar to normal (nonraping) men. Malamuth has discussed several studies asking samples of normal men whether they would

387

Chapter 11:
Consenting Adults?
Personal and Sexual
Relationships

I have no respect for a woman who engages in sexual relationships without any emotional involvement.

Having sex during the menstrual period is embarrassing.

The primary goal of sexual intercourse should be to have children.

Rape-Myth Acceptance

Greater *agreement* with *unstarred* statements and greater *disagreement* with *starred* statements indicate greater acceptance of rape myths.

A woman who goes to the home or apartment of a man on their first date implies that she is willing to have sex.

* Any female can get raped.

One reason that women falsely report a rape is that they frequently have a need to call attention to themselves.

Any healthy woman can successfully resist a rapist if she wants to.

Women who go braless or wear short skirts and tight tops are asking for trouble.

In most rapes, the victim is promiscuous or has a bad reputation.

If a girl engages in necking or petting and she lets things get out of hand, it is her own fault if her partner forces sex on her.

Women who get raped while hitchhiking get what they deserve.

A woman who is stuck-up and thinks she is too good to talk to men on the street deserves to be taught a lesson.

Many women have an unconscious wish to be raped and may unconsciously set up a situation in which they are likely to be attacked.

If a woman gets drunk at a party and has intercourse with a man she's just met there, she should be considered fair game to other males at the party who want to have sex with her, too, whether she wants to or not.

Many women who report rapes are lying because they are angry and want to get back at the man they accuse.

Source: Adapted from Burt (1980).

rape if they thought they could get away with it. In a typical study, 35% said that there was at least some chance they would, and 20% said it was fairly likely that they would. In a study of nearly 4,000 college students, 23% of the men said that they had been in a situation in which they had been so aroused that they "couldn't" stop, even though they knew that the woman did not want to continue. Only 3% of the men in the sample reported that they had actually used physical force, however. (At the same time, 8% of the women in the study said that a man had used physical force against them.) A proclivity toward rape appears to be widespread.

What psychological differences distinguish rapists from other men? Malamuth (1981, 139) has said that two differences show up in the literature on rape: the tendencies "to hold callous attitudes about rape and to believe in rape myths" and "to show relatively high levels of sexual arousal to depictions of rape." Malamuth further investigated these observations in his own research. He found that, compared with other men, those who said they were likely to rape if they could get away with it were more accepting of rape myths, more tolerant of interpersonal violence against women, and more readily aroused by depictions of rape.

Are the men's statements about their own proclivity to rape any indication of their real tendency to be violent toward women? Malamuth (1981) investigated this question by conducting an experiment in which men were told they could choose to punish another person for incorrect responses in solving a problem. The problem solver was a female confederate. Malamuth arranged for the woman either to insult mildly or to reject each man before the experiment. In the course of the experiment, the men who had reported that they had a higher likelihood of raping were angrier and more aggressive toward the woman and reported a greater desire to hurt her than did other men.

These results are consistent with studies of men who have been convicted of rape. Rapists often report not on their feelings of sexual arousal or attraction to their victims but on their desire to hurt or dominate them. Even when rapists admit what they have done, they often feel their actions were justified under the circumstances (Scully, 1990). For this reason, many people classify rape as a crime of aggression or violence, rather than as a sexual crime. Sexual organs are involved (in part as weapons), and the act of rape resembles other sexual acts in some outward respects. However, the main point of the encounter is not fulfillment of sexual or erotic desires, unless one accepts violence as an erotic act.

The tie between sexuality and aggression—and especially the definition of aggression against women as erotic and sexual—seems a logical result of an androcentric and even misogynist gender ideology. The research reviewed here shows that (a) an inegalitarian and androcentric gender ideology is associated with an androcentric sexual ideology; (b) these ideologies are associated with a belief that aggression against women is justifiable and necessary, at least in some circumstances; and (c) these values help support the existence of actual violence against women.

Men who accept traditional sexual and gender ideologies may find it difficult to understand, at least in the abstract, what is so horrifying about rape. They may wonder why women do not just "lie back and enjoy it." Frances Cherry reports on how she sees this problem and how she tackles it in her teaching (1983, 247):

> When I have introduced the topic of rape in my classes, students often snicker when I raise the possibility that a man can be raped by a woman. Some of the men have sat back in their desks, opened their arms, and sighed, "rape me." When I further suggest we consider that men are raped by men, the men's chortles and sighs abruptly turn to nervous laughter, downward turning of the head and closing of the legs and arms.

It is reasonable to guess that this reaction is not just because of the men's fear of homosexuality, although that undoubtedly plays a part. Through this example, the men are probably realizing that rape can be violent, aggressive, and truly

389

Chapter 11:
Consenting Adults?
Personal and Sexual
Relationships

against one's will, and that there may be no recourse if the rapist is at least the victim's physical match in size and strength. It is important to note, however, that whereas men are taught to fight off attackers, women are often counseled to avoid further harm by submitting. These issues became important in the debate over integrating gays into the military. Many feminists suspected that the vehement resistance of many men was based in their fear that they might be treated by other men as men have so often treated women.

Rape myths do not just support men's proclivity to rape; they are also important mechanisms for controlling and limiting women's activities and movements and decreasing their abilities to defend themselves and to make appropriate responses to rape. Conventional wisdom is that potential victims—women—can help decrease the incidence of rape by limiting their activities. This is a logical outcome of the view that women are in large part responsible when rape occurs. Such social control over women is made effective by women's fear of rape and their knowledge that there is a very small likelihood that a rapist will be caught, let alone convicted.

Women's lives are indeed limited by a fear of rape; one study of three major cities showed that while 18% of the male residents expressed some fear about being out in their own neighborhoods at night, 40% of the female residents had such fears. Those who felt most vulnerable were old people, low-income people, African-Americans, and Hispanics (Gordon and Riger, 1989).

Many women accept the idea that women are responsible for their own victimization, so much so that rape victims commonly report feeling guilty for their own victimization. This also happens because so many rapes do not resemble the stereotype. The myth says that rapes occur on dark deserted streets between strangers, but in reality, a majority of victims and perpetrators know each other (not even counting rapes of wives by their husbands), and rapes often occur in the home. Likewise, many women experience date rape or acquaintance rape. Many men on university campuses admit that they use a variety of tactics to try to coerce or trick women into having sexual relations with them; it is a crass game in which affection plays little part.[21] Because these attempts take place in a circumstance in which women have willingly gone out with a man or spent time with him, self-doubt on the part of the victim is a special problem. Also, because women blame themselves so often, and they know that others will be suspicious of their claims, many women hesitate to report these rapes to the police.

Women who accept the traditional adversarial ideology of sexuality—that normal heterosexual sex involves an active pursuing male and a reluctant female—may not even interpret their own experiences of rape and near rape for what they are. Women who enter shelters for battered wives often report that for a long time they had not recognized their own experiences of rape in situations when their husbands forced them, sometimes violently, to have sexual relations. As in other forms of wife battery, a woman who is dependent on her husband is relatively unlikely to leave home until the situation becomes intolerable.

As a group, women are no longer the passive victims they might once have been. Public awareness is rising, and hundreds of organizations are involved in educating people about the facts of rape and giving psychological and legal assistance to those who have or might become victims. Research by Pauline Bart and

Patricia O'Brien (1984) indicates that those who successfully avoid rape attempts have a larger range of preventive actions at their disposal than do other women. Among other things, they are able to respond aggressively to their attackers. If nothing else, women who defend themselves successfully know how to kick off their heeled shoes, if necessary, and to run. In many towns, women have organized to establish women's transit systems to help women avoid rape without having to lock themselves away.

Above all, however, the fight against rape involves a struggle against sexual and gender norms, the ideology that increases the likelihood of rape and that justifies the crime. Women have given the symbolic message that they intend to do something in "Take Back the Night" demonstrations, in which large numbers of people march through often notoriously dangerous parts of towns at night, in a show of strength.

Marriage: Family, Property, and State

At the center of our sex/gender system lies a relationship institutionalized by acts of government and religion: marriage. Adult women's status, roles, rights, and obligations historically have been governed by marriage and the norms that underlie it. Female children have been taught to think of marriage as the single most important goal in their lives. Experimental research shows that women who have never married are evaluated more negatively than other women and more negatively than either single or married men (Etaugh and Foresman, 1983). Hardly a woman who has reached age 30 without marrying has avoided being barraged with, "So when are you getting married?" or the whispered, "Don't worry, your time will come." After age 30, these comments come less frequently; indeed, a woman who has not married by then is often viewed with pity. In the end, most people marry at least once in their lives.

The institution of marriage is created and defined by law. In the United States, the level of government responsible for ruling marriage is the state; only a representative of the state can marry people. Even if two people are married by a member of the clergy, it is the state that grants the cleric the right to officiate. The only *enforceable* terms of marriage are those established by governmental law and policy. The state decides who may marry, at what age they may marry, and under what circumstances they may marry. Only the state may declare a marriage ended. Sexual relations outside of marriage are illegal in many places. Children born outside of marriage are designated *illegitimate*, outside the bounds of law.

The Marriage Contract

When two people marry, they agree to live under the terms of a marriage contract. This contract is much like others in one respect: It defines the rights and duties of the contracting parties. Beyond this, the marriage contract is very different from most others in three ways:

1. Most contracts are *written,* and people are generally advised to "read the fine print" carefully and possibly consult a lawyer before they sign on the dotted line. They may even negotiate amendments or alterations to the contract. In contrast, the terms of the marriage contract are not written in any single place, and they are not made available for review. Instead, they are scattered throughout laws and court decisions that have been handed down over time. Most people have very little idea about what is in the marriage contract, and very few consider consulting an attorney before they marry, to learn about their rights and obligations; it just does not seem very romantic.

2. The terms of most contracts *cannot be changed while they are in force without the knowledge and consent* of the signing parties. In contrast, because the terms of the marriage contract are defined by legislators, judges, and other policy-makers, the only way to find out what changes have been made is to read newspapers and law reports regularly. When marriage laws change, they affect all married people, but no one sends couples notification that the rules governing their marriages have changed. Some important marriage laws are state laws, which cover only the residents of a particular state, only while they live in that state. If a couple marry in one state and settle there, they are covered by that state's law. If the same couple move to another state, they are covered by the laws of the new state in which they reside. The contractual terms for marriage in that state may be very different from the terms they originally agreed to.

3. The fact that marriage contracts are defined by state law means that generally *no private agreement by husband and wife can contradict the terms set out in those laws.* When a man and woman say "I do," they are agreeing to accept these definitions, rights, and obligations, although they may make separate agreements respecting property rights. Of course, all legally binding contracts must stay within the law.

What values do states attempt to support through the regulation of marriage? The original English common law on which most American marital law is based was designed to maintain the patriarchal gender divisions of roles and power, regarded as the moral basis of a stable society.[22] To what degree does the law continue to define a wife's identity as incorporated and consolidated into that of the husband? The answer to this question requires a look at the legal definition of marriage, the content of the marriage contract.[23]

Names and Places

One of the most obvious and immediate outward signs of marriage used to be that a couple would begin to live together. Of course, in a large proportion of cases, couples do not *start* to live together after they marry; they are already cohabiting. In fact, the law grants the husband the right to choose his place of residence, and it imposes on the wife an obligation to be domiciled in her husband's choice of residence. Even if the members of a couple actually have different residences, in most states, they are assumed to be domiciled at the husband's residence. If a wife

391

Chapter 11:
Consenting Adults?
Personal and Sexual
Relationships

refuses to move with her husband to another city, she is assumed by law to have abandoned him; if a husband refuses to move with his wife to another city, she is still assumed to have abandoned him. In many states, a woman may now establish a separate domicile for a specific purpose, but the assumption remains that the head of the household—the husband, whenever he is present—determines where a family lives.

The traditional norms about domicile embedded in law are not just remnants of the past, but remain part of American cultural values. A 1985 survey showed that the majority of people—72% of women and 62% of men—said that a woman should quit her job and move to another city if her husband got a job there, even if she had a good job where they already lived. Ten percent of women and 19% of men said that the husband should turn down the job (Simon and Landis, 1989, 272).

Another outward sign of marriage is that the wife usually changes her surname to her husband's. Contrary to what most people believe, this practice is derived from custom, rather than law. The legal requirement that a woman use her husband's name is of relatively recent vintage. Most states now give women full rights to retain their birth names, although some still require them to use the husband's surname for specific legal purposes, such as obtaining a driver's license. Federal courts have declared that such laws do *not* violate a woman's constitutional rights. Many women do not take their husband's name, although keeping separate names is more common among highly educated, professional couples. About 5% of high-school-educated wives, 15% of those with bachelor degrees, and 20% of those with postgraduate degrees use a surname other than their husband's.[24] Many couples face problems when they maintain separate names, usually amounting to confusion on the part of strangers because the culture is still not used to independent names for husbands and wives. Consider this result: In 1993, a study concluded that 35% of all babies born in California that year had unmarried parents. Eventually, it was discovered that because the forms from which the information was taken did not actually include marital status, the researchers decided whether the parents were married or unmarried on the basis of whether they shared a surname. As Assemblywoman Martha Escutia said when she found out how she was counted, "I can't wait to tell my mother-in-law I am an unmarried woman and my child was born out of wedlock."[25]

Rights and Obligations

The heart of marital law is the relative rights and obligations of husband and wife. In fact, the marriage contract bears a striking resemblance to a (nonnegotiable) labor contract. According to law, until recently, the marital relationship is simply this: The wife owes the husband household, domestic, and companionship services, and the husband, in return, has the duty to support the wife. To what degree and in what ways are these principles enforceable by law?

The husband's right to his wife's services is largely unenforceable by law in any direct sense. There are, however, some extremely important consequences of this aspect of the marriage contract. Because of the notion of "conjugal rights," in most states, until recently, a wife could not have charged her husband with rape.

This is known as the *marital exemption,* which means that a man is exempt from rape charges if the victim is his wife. This has begun to change. Many states—at least 23 by 1996—had no marital exemption in their rape laws. Others have some type of exemption; for example, a spouse may be immune to prosecution for raping a "mentally defective" spouse, immune for certain acts (such as plain old "sexual intercourse"), or immune unless the victim uses extreme resistance or shows bodily injury. A few states (e.g., New York, North Carolina, South Dakota) have full marital exemptions (Posner and Silbaugh, 1996).

393

Chapter 11:
Consenting Adults?
Personal and Sexual
Relationships

Because the wife is obliged to perform domestic labor and therefore is not entitled to any direct compensation for it, until the 1980s, a wife's contribution to the family's economic welfare through her labor was almost never considered in adjudication of property division—for example, during divorce proceedings. This labor is now sometimes taken into account. Because the wife's obligations are unspecified and can cover any work she does in her home or any assistance she gives her husband as a helpmate, if a third party injures her, her husband may sue for the value of the household service he has lost, even though he has no legal obligation to pay his wife. Further, if he owns a farm or business and the wife performs duties associated with these ventures, she is not entitled to compensation.

The wife's rights to support by her husband are also largely unenforceable. Court cases concerning the husband's duty point to a single conclusion: As long as a husband and wife live together, whatever support he chooses to give her is sufficient. A woman who feels that her husband is not providing for her has virtually no legal recourse.

Property

If this book had been written before the middle of the 19th century, this section would be very short. Following the common-law tradition accepted in most states, wives could not own property (with a few exceptions). All property a woman owned when she married, all income earned by her labor, and all property acquired by other means during the marriage belonged to her husband and could be managed by him without her knowledge or consent. If he wished, he could use her income to fulfill his obligation of support for her.

By 1993, 41 states had marital property systems based in the common law, in which the basic rule for determining who owns what is "property follows title." In *common-law property states,* as states following this rule are called, the husband and wife are treated as individuals with independent rights to own and manage property. Whoever has proof of title to specific assets owns them. If no one has specific proof of title, however, most courts assume that the husband is the owner, especially if the wife has been a homemaker. Homemakers are assumed to have no income with which to acquire assets. Even joint bank accounts have sometimes been viewed as the husband's property if the wife was a homemaker, on the assumption that she had simply been allowed access to her husband's account.

Assuming that most husbands earn more than their wives, and that in a substantial minority of marriages women earn virtually no income, common-law property states give great leverage to husbands. Even if the husband and wife are both income earners, they have to pay attention to how they divide the payment of expenses. If a couple divides its expenses equally, but the husband pays for investment and durable goods and the wife for immediate-consumption expenses, the husband ends up with the property, and the wife does not.

A second type of marital property regime—*community property*—is found in 9 states, primarily in the Southwest and West, as well as Louisiana and Wisconsin. In community-property states, assets acquired during a marriage, with certain exceptions, are assumed by law to be jointly and equally owned by husband and wife, regardless of their employment status. Because the married couple is treated as an economic unit, such laws make it difficult for either partner to maintain any separate assets.

Property laws affect people most directly when divorce or the death of one partner occurs. Common-law property states traditionally compensated widows to some extent for what could be the cruelty of the situation by the principle of the "widow's share," which granted a minimum proportion of the husband's property to the widow. Nevertheless, the property that widows have inherited has been subject to inheritance taxes, even if it is the house or the only car in the family. If she does not have the added money to pay the taxes on this property, she has to sell it. In community property states, this cannot happen. The distinctions between these two different kinds of marital property laws have been blurred more in the 1980s and 1990s, partly in response to claims that women's economic contributions to marriage should be taken into account and partly because of a desire to protect the economic situation of children of divorced and widowed parents.

The State's View of Marriage

What do marital law and policy tell us about the state's definition of marriage? Marriage is viewed in part as a couple's commitment to carry on their lineage by conceiving and raising children. As the Minnesota Supreme Court argued in 1971, when explaining why homosexuals could not be legally married, "The institution of marriage as a union of man and woman, uniquely involving the procreation and rearing of children within a family, is as old as the book of Genesis" (*Baker* v. *Nelson*).

Marital property laws are also the state's primary means of regulating the distribution of property within and across generations. Many conservatives have argued that an important reason why so much public money is spent on social-welfare programs is that women are not doing their jobs properly. If women would stay at home and take care of children and old people, less money would have to be spent to replace their labor.

The laws that help maintain women in a dependent position do not affect everyone equally. If a husband and wife continue to love each other and are kind and generous with each other, the law has little effect on them, especially if they die at the same moment. Nonetheless, the law continues to render women dependent on their husbands' goodwill.

Many people have pointed to a cruel irony in marital law and policy. The women who fulfill their traditional roles most completely are most hurt by these laws and policies. Full-time homemakers have few assets of their own and are most vulnerable during and after marriage. Despite years of labor and service, the "displaced homemaker" has few marketable skills that can earn her a living. At the turn of the century, Charlotte Perkins Gilman ([1898] 1966) pointed out the inequity of the familial services–support relationship. The woman from a poor family has the hardest labor as a homemaker and is supported at only the most meager levels by even the most generous husband; the woman from a wealthy family does relatively little strenuous labor but is handsomely supported.

395

Chapter 11:
Consenting Adults?
Personal and Sexual
Relationships

Poverty policy in the late 1990s weighed especially heavily against unmarried mothers, supporting different social norms about their relationship to their children than those regarding married mothers. During the 1990s, the media reported increasing numbers of stories speaking approvingly of married mothers leaving the workforce and becoming financially dependent (on their husbands) in order to stay home with their children. The Welfare Reform Act, on the other hand, mandated a different fate for unmarried mothers who could not support themselves, with respect to caring for their children. In order to receive welfare assistance, these mothers had to work outside the home; after an established time period, they and their children were denied further benefits, regardless of whether they found adequate work.

Changes in marital law and related policies have been substantial. There are more choices available to people, especially women, than there ever have been before. Young women have changed their expectations about marriage over recent decades, but especially in the 1960s and 1970s (Weeks and Botkin, 1987).

Marriage, Gender, and Day-to-Day Life

We have already discussed many aspects of the everyday gendered dynamics of marriage, including the idea of his and hers marriages and the implications for health and stress (Chapter 6) and the role of wives in health and religious institutions (Chapters 6 and 7). In this chapter, we have focused on some aspects of sexual life and the power dynamics of couples. In the next two chapters (Chapters 12 and 13), we examine parenthood and divisions of labor between husbands and wives.

In regard to the gender dynamics of marriage, the marital dynamics and expectations that people bring to marriage vary widely across time and culture and even across the course of a single marriage. Observers can easily be trapped into overemphasizing gender differences and conflict. Research repeatedly shows that, in the United States at least, likes tend to marry likes. Contrary to the conventional wisdom about complementarity of wives' and husbands' lives and interests, people tend to be attracted and to form couples on the basis of similarity in basic attitudes and approaches to life (Aube and Koestner, 1995; Saint 1994).

Compatibility—or even mutual attraction—is not the norm in all cultures or times, however. Where marriages are arranged, for example, a different pattern appears. Likewise, where marriage is not regarded as a particularly romantic institution—in Japan, for example—husbands and wives are not expected to be very similar to each other or to spend a lot of time together (especially because of the work pressures on the Japanese "salaryman"), and women are supposed to tolerate their husband's affairs. Some claim that Japanese divorce rates are low at least partly because of the low expectations that many Japanese couples have for their marriages. A study of the similarity of husbands and wives in 37 countries found that Japan ranked last. The United States ranked well above average in similarity between husbands and wives but lower than Turkey, Spain, Nigeria, and Ireland, for example. Another study found that only about one third of Japanese say that they would marry the same person if they had another chance.[26]

Many factors affect marital relationships among different couples within one country, including people's backgrounds, such as their race/ethnicity, class, or education and their attitudes toward marriage, gender, and related issues. People of higher social class and education tend to marry later, in general, as do women with higher English proficiency among non-native-born women. Education and language proficiency help to provide independence to women, decreasing their need to be married. Chinese- and Japanese-American women tend to marry later than women of other race/ethnic groups, and native-born, non-Latina White women marry the youngest. As the author of one study wrote, "In spite of the influences of feminism and advances in women's educational attainment and labor force participation rates, the dominant culture still tells White women to marry" (Ferguson, 1995, 335).

Gender ideology and feminism make a difference in marital relations, as well. In a national sample of married people interviewed in 1980, 1983, and 1988, husbands and wives developed more egalitarian gender attitudes over time, but women remained more egalitarian than men (Amato and Booth, 1995). These changes had different effects on men and women's marital satisfaction over time, however. When men became more egalitarian during the course of the study, their reports of negative aspects of their marriages *decreased;* when women became more egalitarian over the course of the study, their reports of negative qualities of their marriage *increased.* Why? Consider the source of increased gender-role egalitarianism. Given that the women tended to be more egalitarian in the first place, when men became more egalitarian, they were likely to be moving in the direction of their wives, perhaps influenced by the women's movement. Their changes may have helped make their marriages more compatible.

In contrast, research suggests that women who change their gender attitudes after marriage often do so after entering the labor force or having a daughter (Warner, 1991). Their increased feminism may come from increasing discontent with the inequality they experience, and it may increase the differences between themselves and their husbands. Indeed, other research finds that wives' employment has different effects on marriages, depending on the gender-role attitudes of the women. For women with more traditional, inegalitarian views, the amount of paid labor they do has no impact on their marital stability. For these women, the increasing double burden they feel does not offend their sense of fairness in household divisions of labor. For women with less traditional, more egalitarian gender ideology, the more hours of employment they have, the more their marital stability seems threatened, probably because they grow more discontented with the double burden (Greenstein, 1995). Of course, it should not be surprising that there is not a one-to-one fit between the gender ideology and beliefs of couples and how they actually act in their marriages (Blaisure and Allen, 1995).

397

Chapter 11:
Consenting Adults?
Personal and Sexual
Relationships

Divorce

The divorce rate has been rising steeply throughout the population in the second half of the 20th century, but it is especially high among people who marry young. Nearly half of women who marry before age 18 are divorced within 10 years, compared with 19% who marry later.[27] Using divorce to end a marriage was not always as possible as it is today. Throughout most of American history, the marriage contract had few escape clauses. To sue for divorce, one partner had to prove that the other partner had provided the grounds (i.e., violated the marriage contract) by, for example, committing adultery. Of course, there have been debates about divorce throughout American history; at the end of the 19th century, there was much worry about "divorce mills," especially in godless places such as Sioux Falls, South Dakota; Fargo, North Dakota; and Guthrie, Oklahoma (Riley, 1991).

Divorce procedures were not designed to try to achieve amicable agreement. After all, if the partners were amicable, there could not be much reason for divorce. Indeed, a divorce suit could be turned down if it appeared there was collusion between the divorcing partners in an effort to get a divorce. Property division depended in part on the assignment of fault or innocence. Because the guilty party had committed a crime against state law in violating the marriage contract, he or she could not profit by divorce.

Since the 1970s, most states have moved toward *no-fault divorce*, in which one partner does not have to charge the other with a crime. Instead, the couple seek divorce on grounds of "irretrievable breakdown" or "irreconcilable differences." Although this change has made divorces easier to obtain, these procedures have pitfalls. Consider the homemaker who has been the victim of cruelty or who finds out that her husband has been having affairs. In earlier days, she could have charged her husband with the fault and then sought a divorce. As the innocent party, she would probably have been awarded a considerable proportion of the couple's property. Under the current system, if that same woman and her husband divorce on no-fault grounds, there is no reason for the court to award her any more than her basic share. Most states are trying to relieve this problem by giving courts the power to redistribute property, particularly where children are involved.[28]

A major source of contention and controversy in recent years has been the awarding of alimony. The practice of forcing a husband to pay alimony dates from the time when divorce was not possible except under conditions of fault. Under early laws, following church rules, divorced people could not remarry. In effect, a divorce meant that a couple were still husband and wife and could not remarry, but they could no longer live together. Alimony was originally "a judicial order entered during the existence of marriage fixing a husband's duty to support his wife while they were living apart due to his fault." Legal scholar Herma Hill Kay calls this a "functional substitute" for the duty of the husband to support his wife (Kay, 1996, 317).

By the middle of the 20th century, alimony was granted to wives in only a minority of cases, and usually the wives never actually received payments. In 1979, the Supreme Court declared unconstitutional an Alabama law restricting alimony to payments by husbands to wives (*Orr* v. *Orr*) because of its discriminatory nature. The Court argued that alimony is awarded on the basis of need, and "there is no reason . . . to use sex as a proxy for need." Most states now allow courts discretion to apportion marital property according to the merits of the case. As attorney Martha Davis has pointed out, this change results from changes in the views of gender roles in marriage: "This modification of the common law system reflects changed ideas of economic fairness which dictate that the homemaker's nonmonetary contributions to the marriage be recognized and acknowledges that title is an inaccurate indicator of participation in marriage" (1983, 1092–1093). It also allows courts the flexibility to decide what is best for each case individually, especially where children are involved.

The Law on "Living in Sin"

Most states had done away with common-law marriage by the 1920s. A *common-law marriage* was one in which two people were declared married after 7 years of living together—that is, after the statute of limitations had run out on the crime of having fornicated outside of marriage. Such a definition makes it clear that common-law marriages were not favored practice, but merely tolerated.

Many couples now live together and run households without getting married. If marriages are not always made in heaven, however, neither are the relationships of unmarried couples. If a couple has established a household and perhaps have children and the relationship breaks up, what happens to the property and the children? Can such a couple choose to be treated like a married couple?

The law remains in a state of confusion. Unmarried individuals are in a better position than married people to have their private contracts enforced, although there are limitations. If it seems that the couple is exchanging sex for support, the contract is not enforceable because it is, in effect, a criminal agreement for prostitution. Of course, when people simply move in together, their agreements are usually implied and informal and rarely written down.

The most famous court case on cohabitation is *Marvin* v. *Marvin,* which was decided in the California Supreme Court in 1976. Actor Lee Marvin and Michelle Triola (who used Marvin's surname) lived together for 7 years. After breaking up, Triola claimed that he had reneged on an agreement that she would provide household services, he would support her, and they would share their property, just like a married couple. The court declared that this agreement had to be honored. At the same time, the court made its view of marriage clear:

> We take this occasion to point out that the structure of society itself largely depends on the institution of marriage; and nothing we have said in this opinion should be taken to derogate that institution. The joining of the man and woman in marriage is at once the most socially productive and individually fulfilling relationship that one can enjoy in the course of a lifetime.

In the end, Triola received very little. Most other states have refused to enforce marriagelike norms for the dissolution of nonmarital arrangements, largely because of fears of weakening the institution of marriage.

399

Chapter 11:
Consenting Adults?
Personal and Sexual
Relationships

Thus far, this chapter has looked at the law covering couples composed of a man and a woman. What if the couple entering into a relationship is composed of two men or two women? What if they wish to marry or to be covered by marriagelike protections? Many gay and lesbian couples have participated in public ceremonies of marriage; these are not yet legal relations, and they are not covered by marital law. In some cities and states, same-sex partners have won some of the benefits accorded to married couples; for example, some employers allow gay and lesbian partners to include each other in health benefits, just as husbands and wives cover each other.

Some people argue that enlightened law would respect people's choices and treat the unmarried as though they are married and would allow any couple desiring to do so to commit themselves to a marital relationship. Would this change in the law eliminate the problems discussed here, however, or would it just allow more people to share the same old problems, plus create some new ones? Consider the problems with marital law itself. What fundamental principles governing people's personal relationships should be enforced? The question cannot be dismissed by saying simply that people should make their own choices. These personal choices affect the community as a whole and are sometimes mere reflections of the larger, androcentric sex/gender system.

Politics of Personal Life

One of the reasons that feminism is so threatening to many people and creates so much contention is that it questions our personal lives—our friendships, intimacies, and sexual relationships—in unaccustomed ways. The structure of sex/gender systems affects the most private aspects of our lives, not just because our private relationships are in part governed by law, but also because the gender ideologies we have learned affect the ways in which we interact with others. Social institutions are based to some degree on our expectations about the nature of relationships among people. Most of us do not want to think about intimacy in political terms, as matters involving struggles over power, but research supports feminist arguments that our personal lives, particularly our sexual lives, constitute a key arena for both oppression and liberation.

This analysis suggests why change in sex/gender systems is both difficult and frightening. Sexuality is central to our sense of identity, and—at least in American culture—it is also a source of tremendous anxiety. To question our sexuality and the patterns it takes is to question our very sense of self. Men who have learned that masculinity requires them to be the successful pursuer and to dominate women in sexual and other intimate relations are threatened by women who either demand equality in their personal relationships or do not see their relationships with men as sexual.

Increasing numbers of women and men are thinking carefully about the significance of their intimate behavior and the choices they make in their private lives.

Awareness is not sufficient, however. In can hurt to make choices in the face of ingrained ideology and personal feelings and even state enforcement. Nonetheless, feminists argue that the reward for facing these challenges is great: a chance for friendship, love, and intimacy that are not based on domination and coercion.

Over a century ago, the feminist Margaret Fuller summed up her ideal of a personal relationship between a husband and wife, not as a couple in which two were merged into one and thus lost their individual autonomy or equality, but as the progress of "two pilgrims toward a common shrine" (Fuller, [1845] 1971, 80–81). As Fuller's words show, the application of feminist theory and the pursuit of autonomy for women does not mean having to abandon all sense of mystery and romance in life.

Notes

1. See the earlier discussion of Freud in Chapters 2 and 3.

2. A superb study showing not just the history of sexuality but that of many aspects of private life is the multivolume *A History of Private Life,* edited by Ariès and Duby (1987).

3. An excellent basic text on human sexuality is Hyde (1994).

4. See also Penelope and Wolfe (1989) and Phelan (1989).

5. This discussion basically follows the outline in Hyde (1994).

6. Felicity Berringer, "Measuring Sexuality Through Polls Can Be Shaky," *New York Times,* April 25, 1993.

7. "Freshman Survey: Their Opinions, Activities, and Goals," *Chronicle of Higher Education,* http://chronicle.com/che-data.

8. For a full discussion of privacy and gay rights, see Samar (1991).

9. "Court Acquits Major Accused of Being Lesbian," *New York Times,* August 17, 1996.

10. For the more introductory reader, Hyde (1994, Chapter 3) has a good discussion of sex-research methodology. For a more advanced reader, Laumann et al. (1994) provide good discussions of methodology in Part I and the Appendices.

11. See Note 7.

12. This study surveyed more than 12,000 people, including 4,314 heterosexual couples, 969 gay male couples, and 788 lesbian couples. More recent research suggests that the findings of this study probably remain valid, with the exception of certain changes in sexual behavior that resulted from the AIDS epidemic, which occurred after Blumstein and Schwartz did their research.

13. "Fact File: This Year's Freshman: A Statistical Profile," *Chronicle of Higher Education,* January 13, 1993. See also Oliver and Hyde (1993).

14. In a completely unscientific study, I told various female acquaintances about this finding, and all laughed and reported experiences they had of being direct and then receiving angry or other negative reactions.

15. Tamar Lewin, "Parents Poll Finds Child Abuse to Be More Common," *New York Times,* December 7, 1995.

16. There are many fascinating readings on this event. See, for example Morrison (1992). For one of the few major accounts that is completely unsympathetic to Anita Hill, see Brock (1993).

401

Chapter 11:
Consenting Adults?
Personal and Sexual
Relationships

17. Title VII (of the 1964 Civil Rights Act), which is discussed in Chapter 13, is the federal law barring sex discrimination in employment.

18. See the discussion of victim precipitation in Chapter 9.

19. See, for example, the discussion of sex-war theories in Chapter 2.

20. Marlise Simons, "For First Time, Court Defines Rape as War Crime," *New York Times,* June 28, 1996.

21. Michele N-K Collson, "'A Sure-Fire Winner Is to Tell Her You Love Her; Women Fall for It All the Time': Men Talk Frankly with Counselor to Assess Harassment and Acquaintance Rape," *Chronicle of Higher Education,* November 13, 1991.

22. This was discussed in Chapter 9.

23. During this discussion, remember that because marriage is generally governed by state law, it varies to some degree across states.

24. Laura Pederson-Pietersen, "To Have and to Hyphenate: The Marriage Name Game," *New York Times,* March 16, 1997.

25. "California Unwed-Mother Tally Includes Many Married Women," *New York Times,* May 5, 1996.

26. Nicholas D. Kristof, "Who Needs Love? In Japan, Many Couples Don't," *New York Times,* February 11, 1996.

27. Laura Meckler, "Less Sex, More Condoms Equal Less Teen Pregnancy," *Wisconsin State Journal,* May 2, 1997.

28. For an influential discussion of the faults of no-fault divorce, see Weitzman (1985).

12

⚜

Reproduction, Parenthood, and Child Care

> *"Motherhood means to us something which I cannot yet discover in any of the countries of which you tell us. You have spoken . . . of Human Brotherhood as a great idea among you, but even that I judge is far from a practical expression?"*
>
> *Jeff nodded rather sadly. "Very far—" he said.*
>
> *"Here we have Human Motherhood—in full working use. . . . Nothing else except the literal sisterhood of our origin, and the far higher and deeper union of our social growth. The children in this country are the one center and focus of all our thoughts. Every step of our advance is always considered in its effect on them—on the race. You see, we are Mothers," she repeated, as if in that she had said it all.*
>
> Gilman, [1915] 1992, 67

CHARLOTTE PERKINS GILMAN'S fictional account of this confrontation between an early-20th-century American man and a woman he met in the women's paradise Herland represents two conflicting views of motherhood: the version familiar to those living in most modern, Western industrialized societies until now, where motherhood is a woman's life work, and Gilman's version, shared by many feminists of her day and later, in which motherhood is—a woman's life work. The different versions were very distinct, but among the many different visions of womanhood observable over time, motherhood is usually still a central element. Law, theology, and medicine each have their special perspectives on womanhood, but historically, when authorities in these areas have thought about women, their attentions have focused on women as mothers and potential mothers.

In the 20th century, scholarly activity has paid increasing attention to motherhood and reproduction for at least five reasons:

1. Childhood is a historical invention. The idea that childhood is a special time of life when people are supposed to be nurtured and protected from adult concerns evolved over recent centuries (Ariès, 1942). If, as historians now believe, *childhood* is a changing historical concept, *motherhood* must also have changed over time. Certainly, the tasks, roles, and duties of mothers have changed. In colonial America, as in Europe at that time, not even the suckling of infants was a necessary task of the biological mother's work (Matthaei, 1982). Those who could afford to do so hired wet nurses. Raising children meant introducing children to their adult work as soon as possible. Because women and men had different work to do, childrearing was done by mothers, fathers, and other family and nonfamily members who were gender appropriate for the job. Thus, fathers played an important role in childrearing.

2. The growth of industrialization separated production from the home. As a distinct sphere of family life emerged, so did distinct roles within that sphere. As Matthaei wrote, "Family relationships—between husband and wife, between parents and children—began to gain a content of their own" (1982, 110). Homemaking, including motherhood, became a vocation.

3. Motherhood was transformed into an activity regarded as having great social importance. New psychological theories focused on the impact of children's socialization on the societies around them. From attempts to invent the American character in the early 19th century to worries about the impact of immigrant children in the early 20th century, to the concerns about the impact of urban blight, poverty, the new immigration, and broken families and family values in the late 20th century, the welfare of children and the quality of their caregivers has long been a focus of national debate.

4. Underlying much of the debate was the growing belief that people could actually control and make choices about whether and when to reproduce and about the ways to raise children. The perception of choice grew with the development and spread of (a) technologies for controlling conception and birth, and (b) knowledge about reproduction and child development. As more people realized that choices *could* be made, they evaluated and weighed alternatives in terms of their benefits both to themselves and to the society as a whole.

5. Feminism and related social movements increasingly offered critiques and alternative visions of motherhood, childhood, and the role of reproduction in women's lives.

Many debates flow from this new consciousness of motherhood and reproduction. Should control be exerted over the number of children people have? How much control should individual men and women have over reproduction? What type of mother would produce the best children? What would be the best way to raise children? What responsibilities does society as a whole (especially through the force of government and law) have for the production and care of children? This chapter looks more closely at these issues, beginning with choices about whether to become a parent, and under what circumstances, then turning to parenthood itself, and finally to the question of the responsibilities and roles of the larger society for reproduction and the care of children.

To Be or Not to Be a Parent

> If the right of privacy means anything, it is the right of the individual, married or single, to be free of unwarranted governmental intrusion into matters so fundamentally affecting a person as the decision whether to bear or beget a child.

This was the view taken by the U.S. Supreme Court in 1972, when it declared that laws barring single people from purchasing contraceptives were unconstitutional (*Eisenstadt* v. *Baird*). The major breakthrough in giving individuals more control over their own reproductive decisions had come in 1965, when (in *Griswold* v. *Connecticut*) the Supreme Court first declared that there is a constitutional right to privacy and indicated that this right meant that married people could not be barred from purchasing contraceptives. The Court later restated and extended this point further when it declared that even an unmarried minor should be able to obtain contraceptives: "The Constitution protects individual decisions in matters of childbearing from unjustified intrusion by the State" (*Carey* v. *Population Services International*, 1977). How well protected is this constitutional right? How free are people, especially women, to make their own decisions over whether and when to become a parent?

Reproduction and Choice

A woman is about as likely nowadays to have at least one child as she ever was, but when she will have a child, how many she will have, and under what circumstances is substantially shaped by historical conditions. Socialization and social pressure play important roles in people's thinking about reproduction and parenthood. Women without children are generally regarded negatively, sometimes viewed as though they are not quite adult themselves (Morell, 1994). Adults without children are described according to what they *lack:* There are mothers, fathers, parents, and *childless* people. Lucia Valeska (1975) has asked what would be people's reaction if more women without children described themselves as "child free." The term sounds jarring because it suggests that not having children might be a good choice for some people.

For most people, having children seems a natural, probably inevitable part of being an adult. A 1994 survey of teenagers found that only 7% of girls and 4% of boys thought it was "not at all likely" they would have children when they grew up. For some people, parenting is one of the most central features of their adult lives; 23% of the girls and 16% of the boys said that having children is the thing they look forward to the most in their adult lives. At the same time, roughly half the boys and girls thought they could still live a happy life if they could not have

The right and ability to choose how many children to have has been the privilege of very few women until recently.

children.[1] When the first-year undergraduates of 1995–1996 were polled about which of many life objectives they considered "essential" or "very important," 72% of both men and women said "raising a family"—the largest category among women, and the second largest (following "being very well-off financially") among men.[2]

There are many reasons why people choose not to have children. As discussed more fully later in this chapter, people who are single face special burdens in having and raising children. People who are married may reject parenthood because childrearing does not fit their goals and interests, they do not have the financial resources to care for children adequately, they feel they would not be good parents, or they worry about overpopulation.

Why *do* people have children? Few parents ever have to think of their reasons. For most, it is probably not as much a matter of *reasons* as *emotions* (Grewal and Urschel, 1994). Many people, of course, do not regard reproduction as a choice; it is simply what adults do. Also, for some people, without access to appropriate information or the means or opportunity to prevent or terminate a pregnancy, bearing children is not a choice.

In certain kinds of economies, such as preindustrial and non-welfare-state industrial societies (as existed in the United States in the 19th and early 20th centuries), children are an important economic resource to adults by providing both added labor for the family and a means of support for parents in old age. In advanced industrial economies with welfare states, people may choose to have children because they like the idea of having children, think they would be good parents, view having children as fulfilling in their marital relationship, believe having children will provide personal fulfillment, or feel that in having children, one can leave a mark on the world. Some ethnic minorities and religious groups even urge their members to have children to preserve or expand the group itself. At various times in history, governments have established policies to encourage people to have children to fill *national* goals and needs, especially in countries worried about not having a large enough labor force or worried about some classes within the population producing too many or too few children. Throughout much of the 20th century, the Soviet Union, which had suffered tremendous population depletion during the two world wars, had programs to encourage reproduction. Modern states try to affect birth rates by increasing or decreasing benefits to parents who have children, including tax breaks, cash bonuses, child care, and parental leave.[3]

The *timing* of births changes historically and differs from one social group to another. In the late 1960s and early 1970s, the press began to worry that women were giving up having babies (often blaming the women's movement). Later, it became clear that the primary change was not in *whether* women were having children, but in *when* they did so. Women have children at an older age now than they did throughout most of the 20th century. In 1970, about 36% of mothers had had their first child before they were 20 years old, and most had had their first child by age 25 years. In 1987, about 23% had had their first child before age 20. The age distribution among *all* women giving birth in a single year also reveals changes in the age structure of births. Among the births reported in 1970, 18% were to women under age 20, 82% were to women under age 30, and only 6% were to women at least 35 years old. In contrast, among all births in 1993, 13% were to women under 20, 67% were to women under 30, and 11% were to women at least 35 years old (U.S. Bureau of the Census, 1997, 75).

There are at least three reasons for the trend toward later births. First, the availability of contraception and abortion makes choice possible. Second, because of changing health-care technology and research, health experts now view pregnancy at older ages as being more safe than they once believed it to be. Third, women's increased education and workforce participation make later childbearing more attractive to women who want to complete their education or become established in a career prior to having children. Life-course paths are more variable now than they used to be. Most women once believed that motherhood necessarily came first and could perhaps be followed by a career. More women now establish themselves in careers first.

Even though the birth rate among teenagers is relatively low in historical perspective, it is nevertheless alarming, given that women who become mothers while they are still teenagers, rather than later, tend to curtail their education, face dimmer occupational prospects, and have higher poverty rates. A related change that has been greeted with alarm, partly also because of the implications for poverty, is the rising proportion of births to single women.[4] In 1950, 4% of all births involved single women, in 1970, the figure was almost 11%, and in 1992, it was 30%. The race differences in births among the young and unmarried are striking,

TABLE 12-1
Teens and Unmarried Mothers: Births and Prenatal Care, by Race, 1992

	African-American	American Indian	Asian-American	Hispanic	White
Births to teenage mothers (%)	23	20	6	17	11
Births to unmarried mothers (%)	68	55	15	39	23
Mothers beginning prenatal care in 1st trimester (%)	64	62	77	64	81
Mothers beginning prenatal care in 3rd trimester or never (%)	10	11	5	10	4
Births with low birth weight (%)	13	6	7	6	6
Number of maternal deaths per 1,000 births	21	NA	NA	NA	5

Note: NA = not available.

Source: Adapted from U.S. Bureau of the Census (1987a, 78).

as Table 12-1 shows. A majority of the African-American and Native American women giving birth in 1992 were unmarried; at least 20% were teenagers. The rates of teen and unmarried pregnancy are also high among Latinas. The rates are very low among Asian-American women, especially Chinese- and Japanese-Americans.

Another sign of the problems faced by many impoverished and young pregnant women is the high proportion of women receiving inadequate prenatal health care. The health of mothers and babies depends on receiving adequate health care early on; as Table 12-1 shows, a shockingly high proportion of women, especially African-American, Native American, and Hispanic women, do not receive prenatal health care in the first trimester. At least one tenth do not receive prenatal care until very late—or not at all. The results can have lasting ill effects on the child. Low birth weight, which is especially high among African-American babies, is one important sign of health problems.

Many of these births among the very young do not result from considered decisions. For the young and poor, lack of adequate knowledge about contraception and access to medical care hurts an increasingly sexually active population. A 1990 study of pregnant teens, for example, found that many of them thought that abortion causes sterility or that it is illegal (Stone and Waszak, 1992). Governmental decisions allowing states to refuse public funding for abortions also mean that poor women do not have the same options that wealthier women have. Young motherhood is especially prevalent in communities in which young women do not stay in school much longer than they have to and have no careers for which they are likely to be making long-term plans. A large proportion of teenage mothers became pregnant by adult men.[5]

Of course many single and young women have *chosen* to become pregnant. Between 16% and 25% of teenagers say they intended to become pregnant (Resnick, 1984; Stone and Waszak, 1992). For many of these young women, however, this choice is based on misunderstanding. Many teens who choose to have children believe that having children will make them more adult, will make others treat them more like adults, or at least will give them a way to leave home and their family. Tragically, childhood abuse is often a contributing factor to adolescents' pregnancies. One study of pregnant and parenting teens found that at least half had experienced rape, and many had been abused by their own caregiver and subjected to other forms of violence (Boyer and Fine, 1992). Some adolescents do not feel that they can seek help from their parents if they become pregnant, even if they have not experienced abuse, because of the teens' expectations about their parents' reactions. A study of pregnant African-American teens found that those who were more likely to tell a parent about their pregnancy were younger, lived farther from the clinic, did not attend religious services very often, had generally good communication with their mothers, and anticipated a supportive reaction (Zabin, Hirsch, Emerson, and Raymond, 1992).[6]

The rise in births among unmarried women does not just reflect births among the very young. A large proportion of African-American women have learned not to expect to be married when they have children. Many relatively wealthy professional women who have the financial means to provide a home for a child are choosing to have children, regardless of their marriage prospects. For some of these women, the reason for their choice is age. As they move into and through their 30s, they worry that their biological aging will take away the choice to have a child they may want. These women face important moral dilemmas: Is it right to marry a man just because a woman wants a child? Some people argue that it is fairer to children to provide them with two parents, but if the marriage was really only an expedient, how long will it last? Other women have children without being married because they want a child but do not want a husband.

Reproductive choice has been debated for well over a century. Choice, however, means more than whether to have children. Many 19th-century feminists fought for what they called "voluntary motherhood," by which they meant not just birth control, but also strategies to manage reproduction to bolster the dignity of mothers and their abilities to carry out their important social functions and be the best mothers they could be (Gordon, 1982). Charlotte Perkins Gilman, in her utopian novel *Herland* ([1915] 1979, a passage of which opened this chapter), envisioned a society of women who had evolved the skill of parthenogenesis and decided that only women with the right temperament and skills for motherhood would conceive. Only babies who were wanted could be conceived; in Herland, the idea of abortion was considered utterly appalling. In the real world, however, to consider control over reproduction, the questions of both contraception and abortion must be investigated.

Contraception

Most of the forms of birth control now available have been around for a very long time in one form or another. Of course, technological advances have changed many of them, with the exception of the safest and most effective form of birth control known to woman: abstinence.[7] In the 19th century, changes in the process of manufacturing rubber produced more effective and comfortable condoms and led, in the latter part of the century, to the development of the diaphragm as we know it. The vaginal condom was approved for use in the 1990s. The cervical cap, approved by the Food and Drug Administration (FDA) in 1988, is similar to the diaphragm in the way it works, but it fits more snugly over the cervix. The design of intrauterine devices (IUDs) has changed radically in recent years. Spermicidal agents and douches are chemically different from the ones used for centuries, and they are applied in different ways, most recently by using the contraceptive sponge, approved by the FDA in 1983. Methods of sterilization for men and women have changed in recent decades. Even the rhythm method has changed in technique, with the use of basal temperature charting, although the principle and the results are the same.

The one major family of contraceptives that are truly recent developments in human history is the type based on hormonal regulation of the reproductive system to avoid ovulation. The *birth-control pill*, approved in its original form by the FDA in 1960, was regarded as the harbinger of a new revolution. In 1990, the FDA approved a contraceptive implant, called "Norplant," which involved implanting capsules inside the upper arm. Depo-Provera is another form, taken by injection.

Contraceptive use can be explained at two levels. One is to look at *societal-level patterns* of contraceptive use and its response to such factors as the state of the economy, population size, demographic changes, and cultural and legal pressures. The other is to look at *individual-level patterns* of contraceptive use, which emphasizes what determines the behavior of particular individuals and social groups. This section looks first at the societal-level patterns, then at the individual-level ones.

The use of various birth-control methods grew in the 19th century. Indeed, a governmental onslaught against birth control in the 1870s and 1880s suggests how widespread and threatening the use of birth control seemed (Gordon, 1990; Petchesky, 1984). The governmental response came in the form of the Comstock Laws, inspired and promoted by a self-proclaimed emissary of God, Anthony Comstock. These laws were intended to control pornography. The following quotation from the most famous law reveals its definition of pornography:

Whoever (within the United States) shall sell . . . or shall offer to sell, or to lend, or to give away, or in any manner to exhibit, or shall otherwise publish or offer to publish in any manner, or shall have in his possession, for any such purpose or purposes, any obscene book, pamphlet, paper, writing, advertisement, circular, print, picture, drawing or other representation, figure, or image on or of paper or other material, or any cast, instrument, or other article or any drug or medicine, or any article whatever, for the *prevention of conception,* or for causing unlawful *abortion,* or shall advertise the same for sale, or shall write or print, or cause to be written or printed, any card, circular, book, pamphlet, advertisement, or notice of any kind, stating when, where, how, or of whom, or by what means any of the articles . . . can be purchased or obtained, or shall manufacture, draw, or print, or in any wise make any of such articles, shall be deemed guilty of a misdemeanor. (Quoted in Kerber and Mathews, 1982, 438)

In other words, the means to control reproduction was defined as pornography. The punishment was between 6 months' and 5 years' imprisonment at hard labor, or a prohibitively large fine.

The first important birth-control battle was over access to information about reproductive biology and birth-control techniques. Poor and uneducated women —those most affected by the repression of such information—were especially vulnerable to anticontraception or pronatalist policies suppressing information. Birth-control activists such as Margaret Sanger and Emma Goldman worked especially among poor, working-class, and immigrant women, and both were arrested under the Comstock laws for their efforts.

A historical irony is that although, in effect, poor and minority community women have often had difficulty gaining access to contraception, contraception has sometimes been forced on them. Early in the 20th century, the *eugenics movement* argued that reproduction of the so-called unfit should be controlled in order to improve the quality of human life. Margaret Sanger was associated with this movement. As part of this movement, sterilization of the "feeble-minded" and certain convicted criminals was a widely respected practice.

In 1942, the U.S. Supreme Court, declaring a right to parenthood, showed a realization of what sterilization could mean if it was guided by the wrong rules and practices:

> We are dealing here with legislation which involves one of the basic civil rights of man. Marriage and procreation are fundamental to the very existence and survival of the race. The power to sterilize . . . may have subtle, far-reaching and devastating effects. In evil or reckless hands it can cause races or types which are inimical to the dominant group to wither and disappear. There is no redemption for the individual whom the law touches. (*Skinner* v. *Oklahoma*)

In the 1970s, it became widely known that many poor women, especially poor African-American, Latina, and American Indian women, were forced to undergo sterilization, sometimes without their consent, sometimes under considerable pressure to consent, and sometimes without their knowledge. This often happened when doctors or hospitals argued that women who have too many children depend on welfare programs and cannot afford medical treatment, so these women should be stopped from having more children. Although the government has issued guidelines to eliminate abuse of this kind, problems remain. As recently as 1977, a U.S. Court of Appeals decided in favor of a doctor who refused to treat any pregnant patient who already had two children if she could not pay her own medical bills (for example, those on Medicaid), unless she underwent sterilization (*Walker* v. *Pierce,* 1977). Control over reproduction is a question not simply of whether the means to avoid pregnancy or childbirth is available but also of whether the means to choose parenthood is available (Reilly, 1991).

Comstock-style contraception policy remained largely intact until 1965. Many different advocates fought for legalization of birth control, but it was a U.S.

Supreme Court decision that made the difference. In *Griswold* v. *Connecticut,* one of the most historically important Supreme Court cases, the Court declared that a state law prohibiting contraceptive use by married people was unconstitutional. In this case, the Court argued for the first time that Americans have a constitutional right to privacy, and, further, that this right includes the right to keep the state from invading the privacy of the marriage bed. This case served as the precedent on which further expansions of the right to contraception and, eventually, abortion, were based. The Supreme Court expanded its application of the right to privacy to single people in 1972 (*Eisenstadt* v. *Baird*) and to minors in 1977 (*Carey* v. *Population Services International*). The Court noted that barring single people from obtaining contraceptives does not keep them from fornicating, and in any case, it would be unreasonable to make "the birth of an unwanted child [a] punishment for fornication."

Even with the legalization of birth control, however, many people—especially young people—end up with unwanted pregnancies. What determines whether people use birth control, and use it effectively? Legalization of contraception does not automatically give people the knowledge and information necessary to make decisions about birth control. Adolescents in particular often lack a clear understanding of their reproductive systems (Koff and Rierdan, 1995). Young men are certainly under no greater pressure to understand reproduction than women are.

Traditional sexual ideology and guilt also play a role in guiding people's behavior. Women who have learned to feel guilty about having sexual relations are less likely to understand and to use contraception than people who do not feel guilty (Rohrbaugh, 1980). This difference appears, in part, because women who use birth control must admit to themselves that they are preparing to have sexual relations. Alternatively, they could think, "I couldn't have *meant* to do this because, after all, I wasn't prepared." Traditional ideology, which holds men to be the pursuers, may also lead women to assume that men will take care of contraception (an assumption showing more trust than wisdom) while it makes men believe that it is women's business to avoid getting pregnant.

Traditional sexual ideology and guilt about sex may keep partners from discussing contraception and may make the actual process of donning a condom or inserting a diaphragm more distasteful and sexually inhibiting than it is for people who are more comfortable with themselves and each other. Thus, traditional sexual ideology and guilt allow people only two choices: abstinence or unwanted pregnancy. One study of women ages 18 to 34 years found that regular contraception users differed from women who took more risks when they had sex. The users were more likely (a) to initiate sex, (b) to report having more orgasms, (c) to be living with their partners and for a longer time, and (d) to be from non-Catholic backgrounds (Harvey and Scrimshaw, 1988).

Even for people who seek contraception, good means and complete knowledge are sometimes difficult to obtain. Each available method has drawbacks, such as relatively high failure rates (rhythm, withdrawal, vaginal foam alone), aesthetic or erotic disadvantages for some people (condom, diaphragm with antispermicide, abstinence), possible health drawbacks (the birth-control pill, the IUD), or expense (Norplant, the pill).

After it became widely available in the 1960s, the birth-control pill quickly became the most popular means of contraception used in the United States, particularly among young people. Doubts about the safety of the pill, especially for cigarette smokers and women over age 35 years, led to greater caution on the part of many women. Many doctors had special worries about young women's reactions to information about side effects, because for them, going off the pill often meant not using any birth-control method. The pill is the easiest method of birth control to use, next to Norplant, and a young woman is especially likely to neglect more interventionist alternatives because she might still be more concerned with not putting off her boyfriend than she is with protecting herself.

Nevertheless, the popularity of the pill increased until the late 1980s, when 76% of women had positive attitudes toward it. The condom was not a very popular form of birth control until the 1980s, when women's attitudes became increasingly positive, partly because of the fear of AIDS. Luckily, teenagers are now much more likely to use condoms if they are sexually active than they once were, although the figure is still lower than it should be: 54%, compared with 18% in the early 1970s.[8] On the other hand, IUDs became less widely used because of safety issues and failure rates (Forrest and Fordyce, 1988). Of women between menarche and menopause, about 35% rely on their own or their partner's sterilization; 28% take the pill; 13% use condoms; 10% use no contraceptive method; 5% use diaphragms; 4% use withdrawal, abstinence, or rhythm; and less than 2% use an IUD.[9]

One point is clear: In the sexual division of labor, contraception is still women's responsibility. Only two relatively effective means of contraception are available to heterosexually active men: condoms and vasectomies. Condoms are not as reliable as some other methods (although more reliable than some), and many men object to them on aesthetic grounds. AIDS makes the aesthetic excuse tragic. *Vasectomies,* male sterilization, are reversible in most cases, but doctors generally will not perform this operation on very young men or on men who have not yet had children. Many men find the idea of sterilization scary because of mistaken notions that their masculinity or sex drive will be decreased; however, sterilization has become more widely used by men who have had children.

Work on effective male forms of contraception has progressed very slowly. Scientists argue that because the male reproductive system is more complex, intervention is more difficult. Moreover, the safety standards now observed in developing a male birth-control pill appear to be higher than those used in the development of the female birth-control pill, partly because safety standards in general have become more stringent over the past quarter of a century. In any case, contraception will probably remain primarily women's responsibility for the foreseeable future. Even if most people agree that greater sharing of responsibility is desirable, many women wonder whether they want to entrust contraception to the partner who cannot get pregnant.

Abortion: Legal Status

When the early Americans adopted the English common law, they adopted the legal view that abortion is not a crime until *quickening*—that is, until the fetus's movements can be felt by the mother. The first law in the United States that explicitly discussed abortion was an 1821 Connecticut statute reinforcing the common law. The first statute dealing with what would now be called a first-trimester fetus was New York's 1828 statute making abortion of an unquickened fetus a misdemeanor and abortion of a quickened fetus second-degree manslaughter unless the abortion was necessary to preserve the life of the mother.

Abortion rates rose in the 1840s. Soon, more states began to pass restrictive legislation that abolished distinctions among kinds of abortions and increased the penalties for violations. In the late 1860s, the Roman Catholic Church condemned most abortions. By the beginning of the 20th century, abortion was illegal throughout the United States. The option of a legal abortion was all but foreclosed until the 1960s unless a woman could afford to go to a country that allowed them.

Why did abortion law become more restrictive? The Supreme Court asked itself precisely this question in 1973, when it was trying to decide what to do about the question in the case of *Roe* v. *Wade*. Justice Harry Blackmun, who wrote the Court's opinion, found three reasons:

1. The new abortion laws helped support the morality of the time, which defined any control over reproduction, including abortion, as pornographic and obscene.
2. Abortion was hazardous when not performed properly, and the medical field was filled with quacks. The restrictive laws, therefore, were sometimes forwarded in an effort to protect women's health.
3. These laws were viewed (relatively rarely) as ways to protect the life of the unborn from the time of conception. This became much more important to the prevailing public view in the 20th century than it had been previously.

The 1960s saw a rise in the agitation for abortion rights, and some states began to reform their laws. Once again, however, the real change was forged by the Supreme Court, which in January 1973 tore down much of the edifice of antiabortion laws in its decisions on two cases, *Roe* v. *Wade* and *Doe* v. *Bolton*. The Court relied on its right to privacy doctrine enunciated in *Griswold* v. *Connecticut*, arguing that abortion must be considered as part of the right to decide whether to have a child. It also said, however, that "a State may properly assert important interests in safeguarding health, in maintaining medical standards, and in protecting potential life." At some point in pregnancy, these respective interests—the mother's right to privacy, the state's interest in safeguarding health and medical practices, and the baby's right to life—become rebalanced, so that the state may begin to regulate "the factors that govern the abortion decision." But at what point?

The Court decided that it was in no position to argue the theological or philosophical question of when life begins, although it did agree that under the law, a fetus is not treated as a legal person with civil rights. It therefore divided pregnancy into three stages, distinguished by the relative claims a state could make in intervening in a woman's decision.

In the first stage, covering roughly the first trimester, the claims of the woman are strongest when weighed against other factors, and therefore the state may not interfere with her right to choose abortion by making restrictive policies. At this stage, the Court reasoned, the state does not have sufficiently strong grounds to restrict a woman's constitutional right to privacy. In this first trimester, "mortality in abortion may be less than mortality in normal childbirth." During the second trimester, however, abortion becomes riskier for women. At that point, therefore, "the state, in promoting its interest in the health of the mother, may, if it chooses, regulate the abortion procedure in ways that are reasonably related to maternal health."

Finally, "For the stage subsequent to viability, the state in promoting its interest in the potentiality of human life may, if it chooses, regulate, and even proscribe, abortion except where it is necessary, in appropriate medical judgment, for the preservation of the life or health of the mother." In the final stages of pregnancy, the government has almost full latitude to ban abortion.

This Supreme Court decision effected a compromise between those who speak unilaterally about the rights of the fetus and those who speak unilaterally about the rights of the woman. Thus, while many people regard this case as having attained a delicate balance among conflicting and essentially irresolvable claims, many others—especially those who regard abortion as murder, were unhappy and even outraged by the decision. Instead of settling the question, the decision increased public debate over abortion and intensified the political debate surrounding abortion. A large antiabortion movement organized to fight back.

The contenders over abortion have fought many court battles since 1973. *Roe* v. *Wade* left many finer points of legal interpretation unarticulated, as is usually the case when a court issues an important decision. In addition, the antiabortion movement found many new fronts on which to chip away at the right to abortion and hem it in.

One of the most important later Supreme Court decisions that expanded abortion rights was *Planned Parenthood* v. *Danforth* (1976), which dealt with the constitutionality of several provisions of a Missouri law limiting abortion. Its conclusions demonstrate some of the ways in which states attempted to narrow *Roe* v. *Wade*'s impact, and they raise some interesting questions about the nature of choice and justice in abortion decisions. Following are some of the Court's conclusions:

1. States may use a *flexible definition of viability* in deciding when abortion should be forbidden, rather than adhering to a strict trimester rule. Given advances in medicine, this enables states to restrict abortion for a longer portion of pregnancy.

2. A woman *may be required to give written consent* before undergoing first-trimester abortion. Some states used this provision to require that women review graphic descriptions of even minutely possible risks before having an abortion, as well as pictures of aborted fetuses and fetal development in order to deter them from having abortions.

3. It is unconstitutional to require a *spouse's consent* for a first-trimester abortion because this would constitute granting the spouse a veto over the woman's decision. As the Court said, "Ideally, the decision to [abort] should be one concurred in by both the wife and her husband. . . . But it is difficult to believe

that the goal of fostering mutuality and trust in a marriage and of strengthening the marital relationship and the marriage institution will be achieved by giving the husband (an unlimited) veto power."

4. It is *unconstitutional to require parents' consent* for a first-trimester abortion for an unmarried minor. "Minors, as well as adults, are protected by the Constitution." The Court further argued, "It is difficult . . . to conclude that providing a parent with absolute (veto power) will serve to strengthen the family unit. Neither is it likely that such veto power will enhance parental authority or control." In 1990, the Court allowed states to require that parents be *notified* of a minor's intention to have an abortion, as long as the child can alternatively notify a judge (*Hodgson* v. *Minnesota, Ohio* v. *Akron Center for Reproductive Health*).

5. It is *unconstitutional to make amniocentesis illegal.* Some states attempted to do this on the grounds that the primary purpose of amniocentesis was to screen the fetus for certain defects, which, if found, might end in the woman's choosing to abort.

6. States may *require hospitals to keep records* of every abortion performed in a state.

7. It is *unconstitutional to require doctors to make every effort to save the fetus's life* without specifying the stage of fetal development at which this must take place. In an effort to dissuade doctors and hospitals from performing abortions, Missouri's law had made a blanket statement that doctors were required to try to save the life of the aborted fetus.

Despite internal disagreement, later Supreme Court cases have underscored the key idea concerning the decision over whether to have a child: "These matters, involving the most intimate and personal choices a person may make in a lifetime, choices central to personal dignity and autonomy, are central to the liberty protected by the Fourteenth Amendment" (*Planned Parenthood of Southeastern Pennsylvania* v. *Casey,* 1992). The Court also hemmed in the original decision somewhat, however. In 1992, although it kept the viability standard for judging how strong the rights of the potential newborn would be, it abandoned the idea of trimesters as a guide to the balancing act among rights. In a sense, it shifted from an image of a seesaw (as one set of rights grows and is raised to the forefront, the other is reduced and declines to the background) to a more constant negotiation among the rights, in which none is absolute. The state may regulate abortion at any point for good reason (such as protection of the health and safety of the woman), and it may engage in actions for which their "purpose is to persuade the woman to choose childbirth over abortion," as long as they do not place "an undue burden on the right" of the woman (*Planned Parenthood of Southeastern Pennsylvania* v. *Casey,* 1992).

As with many major precedent-setting Supreme Court decisions, a number of unanticipated consequences followed from the *Roe* decision and its offspring. Because the case opened up the legal possibility of the state asserting the rights of the fetus in the later stages of pregnancy, *Roe* paved the way for court-ordered cesarean sections and other interventions on behalf of the child in the womb.

Public Funding for Abortion

One of the most successful strategies used by antiabortion forces falls particularly heavily on the poor: the refusal of public funding for abortions. There are basically two ways that patients use public funds for health care and medical treatment such as abortion. One involves those whose health care is covered by antipoverty programs such as Medicaid. The other is, simply, to seek treatment in a public hospital or clinic. Regardless of how one covers the charges for treatment (e.g., cash, health insurance, subscription to a health-maintenance organization), by using a public health facility, one has used public funds. This section probes these two forms of funding in relation to abortion.

Congress established the Medicaid program in the 1960s as part of the "Great Society" antipoverty programs, by amending the Social Security Act of 1935 (Title XIX). Medicaid provides federal funding to states for medical services rendered to the poor. Participation in the program by any state is voluntary, but all states choosing to participate must accept certain federal regulations. One is that Medicaid coverage cannot be denied for services that are medically necessary. All 50 states have chosen to participate in the Medicaid program.

Beginning in the 1970s, both individual states and the U.S. Congress passed laws that would deny Medicaid funds for abortions. The Supreme Court decided that states could refuse to use Medicaid funds to pay for abortions (*Beal* v. *Doe*, 1977); that Congress could forbid states to use federal funds (including Medicaid) to pay for abortions, even including for pregnancies caused by rape (*Harris* v. *McRae*, 1980); and that Congress could pass a law allowing states to refuse to use public funds *even for medically necessary abortions* (*Harris* v. *McRae*, 1980). When some cities began to refuse to allow abortions for nontherapeutic purposes in public hospitals, the Court also decided that this refusal was legally acceptable (*Poelker* v. *Doe*, 1977). Nevertheless, some state supreme courts, including New Jersey, Massachusetts, and California, decided that to deny funding for abortions to poor women was to deny these women's rights.

It is important to understand the rationale used in these cases. As the Supreme Court said in *Harris* v. *McRae*, "Although government may not place obstacles in the path of a woman's exercise of her freedom of choice, it need not remove those not of its own creation. Indigency falls in the latter category." The law does not require the government to remedy the fact that poverty makes it difficult or even impossible for some women to have abortions. What about Congress allowing states to refuse funding for *medically* necessary abortions? The Court answered, "The fact remains that [this law] leaves an indigent woman with at least the same range of choice in deciding whether to obtain a medically necessary abortion as she would have had if Congress had chosen to subsidize no health costs at all" (*Harris* v. *McRae*). Congress created the Medicaid program, and if it wanted to allow states to favor childbearing over abortion, it is perfectly free to do so. Government has a right to offer incentives to make childbirth more attractive than abortion, ignoring the plight of women whose health is threatened by pregnancy and childbirth.

These court cases, of course, all decrease the likelihood that a poor woman can obtain a safe abortion; the exclusion of abortion from many public hospitals also affects a much wider group of women, especially given that a large proportion of hospitals that are *not* public are run by religious organizations opposed to abortion. As dissenting Justice Thurgood Marshall pointed out in the *Harris* case, the sponsors of these pieces of legislation specifically and openly wished to interfere with women's choices to have abortions, and such intention was specifically declared unconstitutional in the original (*Roe* v. *Wade*) abortion case.

One study calculates that the cost to the public of an unwanted birth averages 100 times the cost to the public of the abortion it turned down (Sommers and Thomas, 1983). It is also the case that the availability of abortion dramatically decreases the rate of infanticide in the first hour of human life ("*Roe* and Neonatal Homicide," 1992). Of course, these arguments carry no weight with people who define abortion as murder.

Abortion Politics and the Current Situation

Abortion rights and access have been hotly contested ever since the original *Roe* v. *Wade* case in 1973. Although the balance of public opinion has not shifted much over that time (Wiederman and Sensibaugh, 1995), the intensity of the debate grew, and the political organization became more active, sophisticated, and even violent over time. The majority of the public has consistently favored allowing abortions in cases in which the pregnancy was caused by rape or incest, a woman's health is endangered by pregnancy and childbirth, or the baby would be born with severe defects.

A typical *New York Times* Poll/CBS News Poll from late 1995 showed that 35% of the population thought that abortion should be "generally available to those who want it," 22% thought that "abortion should be available but under stricter limits than it is now," 36% thought it "should be against the law except in cases of rape, incest, and to save the woman's life," and 6% thought "abortion should not be permitted at all."[10] In July 1996, 53% of registered voters in a Gallup poll called themselves "prochoice" and 36% called themselves "prolife." Men's answers were not affected by their education, but women's were. While women with less than a high school education split in favor of the prolife position 47–37, college-educated women split in favor of the prochoice side 73–24.[11] In a national sample of the college entering class of 1995–1996, 56% of the men and 57% of the women thought "abortion should be legal."[12] That same lack of a gender difference usually appears in public opinion polls.

Of course, different social groups view abortion differently. Research generally shows more prochoice attitudes among young, unmarried, higher educated, less religious, and more liberal people, while more prolife attitudes are more common among older, married, less educated, more religious, and more conservative people. Even in the group where the most widespread antiabortion feeling might be expected, however—religious Roman Catholics—a 1989 poll found only 22% in favor of banning abortion entirely. Indeed, that poll found less religious Catholics to be *more* prochoice than less religious Protestants.[13]

Earlier research shows other attitudes that distinguish prochoice from prolife supporters. Abortion opponents tend to have more traditional gender ideology, to believe it is good to have larger families, and to be less committed to protection of a range of civil liberties (Baker, Epstein, and Forth, 1981; Granberg and Granberg, 1981). Overall, however, prolife advocates are not very different from prochoice advocates on other "life" issues, such as capital punishment, gun control, government spending and programs on health, or military spending, although abortion opponents tend to oppose right-to-die practices and to condemn suicide more strongly than prochoice advocates.

These differences of opinion do not capture the depth of the political divisions over abortion. These divisions became more evident in the 1980s and 1990s, as parts of the antiabortion movement became more militant and violent. Groups such as Operation Rescue (founded by Randall Terry in 1987, with the slogan, "If you think abortion is murder, act like it")[14] organized demonstrations near abortion clinics and the homes of clinic staff, and they organized general harassment campaigns for abortion providers. Many demonstrations were violent.

Abortion providers report that most of them receive harassing and threatening phone calls and mail. A survey of facilities performing at least 400 abortions a year reported in 1988 that 81% had experienced picketing, including 46% that experienced picketing involving physical contact or blocking of patients' entry to clinics; 36% had received bomb threats; 34% had been vandalized; and for 17% of the facilities, the homes of the staff members were picketed (Henshaw, 1991). During 1992 alone, there were at least 43 chemical attacks on abortion clinics, in which foul-smelling chemicals such as butyric acid were sprayed into the clinics, making it impossible for the buildings to be occupied.[15]

From 1993 to 1995, the harassment and attacks escalated; there were at least 9 attempted murders on clinic workers, and 5 successful murders. The majority of leaders of the antiabortion movement disassociated themselves from this violence and often bitterly attacked it. Nevertheless, the harassment, threats, and other tactics continued. In 1991, a U.S. congressional report found that about 2,000 antiabortion centers were advertising themselves as abortion clinics. These offices, which usually had no medical personnel, were set up only to give an antiabortion message to women who were seeking pregnancy testing or pregnancy or abortion counseling and services.[16]

Supporters of abortion rights countered with lawsuits and legislation. Courts have barred antiabortion centers from presenting themselves falsely as clinics. In 1994, the Supreme Court allowed a limited buffer zone to be established around abortion clinics, to allow patients and staff members to enter and leave in an orderly fashion, and to control noise around the premises used for surgery and recovery (*Madsen et al.* v. *Women's Health Center, Inc., et al.,* 1994). That same year, the Freedom of Access to Clinic Entrances (FACE) Act made it a federal crime to block access to an abortion clinic or to use force or threats against clinic patients or employees, and mandating a life sentence for anyone using violence resulting in the death of a provider or a patient.[17] In 1991, an abortion clinic won a large award from antiabortion organizations that had prevented it from carrying out its business, and in 1995, a jury in a federal court in Texas awarded $8.6 million in damages to an obstetrician who was driven from his practice and his home by the constant threats of violence and stalking he and his family received.[18] The more violent wing of the prolife movement has been weakened by these laws, but groups remain that believe that the cause of stopping abortion is important—even sacred—enough that they still pursue legal and illegal means of harassing doctors and patients.[19] There were 110 incidents of anticlinic violence in 1996, 2 years after the passage of FACE. In 1994, there had been 160.[20] About 30% of clinics experienced some form of severe violence in 1996.[21]

Regardless of these legal changes, however, the antiabortion movement has been very successful in reducing access to abortion. By the early 1990s, a substantial proportion of women who wanted abortions could not get them. In the year of the *Roe* and *Doe* cases, 52% of abortions took place in hospitals and 46% in clinics. By 1988, 86% took place in clinics and 10% in hospitals, partly because of the limits on public funding.[22] Doctors are not now being trained to perform abortions; whereas in 1985, 23% of residency programs in obstetrics and gynecology included abortion training, in 1992, only 12% included routine training in abortion, and 31% included no such training. The antiabortion movement had other effects on women's choices regarding reproduction. For example, a drug invented in France in the 1960s and used throughout Europe as a "morning-after pill," RU 486 (mifepristone), faced unusual delays in being tested in the United States because of political pressure applied by the antiabortion movement, and President Bush placed a ban on it, so no individuals who were taking RU 486 could bring it into the country. The FDA finally moved toward approval in the late 1990s.

Who undergoes abortions? Taking account only of women who have become pregnant, girls under 15 years old are most likely to have abortions by far. The next most likely group is women who are 15 to 19 years old, followed by those who are over 40 years old. Unmarried women are more likely than married women to abort, by a ratio of almost six to one (U.S. Bureau of the Census, 1987a, 86). Abortion providers report that their clients include women of all sorts, including, occasionally, women they have seen demonstrating against abortion. Even if the battle over abortion is intense, however, the battle lines are complicated. The leaders and members of Operation Rescue were thrilled, in 1995, when Norma Leah McCovey, known more famously as "Jane Roe" in *Roe* v. *Wade,* quit her job with an abortion clinic and announced that she now believed that abortion is murder and is wrong—*after* the first trimester, that is.[23]

As might be expected, the abortion rate rose after the procedure was legalized and then began to decline somewhat in the 1980s. In 1980, there were 24.3 abortions for every 1,000 White women in the United States and 56.5 abortions for every 1,000 nonWhite U.S. women. By 1991, the figure was 20.3 abortions for every 1,000 White women and 53.8 for every 1,000 nonWhite women. Decreasing the abortion rate is regarded as a good thing by prochoice advocates if the decrease is due to fewer women having unwanted pregnancies in the first place; for prolife advocates, a decrease for any reason is a step in the right direction.

Parenthood

Most people become parents at some point in their lives. What choices and decisions do people have to make as parents, and how are these shaped by gender? What are the differences between mothering and fathering? What are some of the questions about parenting raised by changes in gender roles and sexuality?

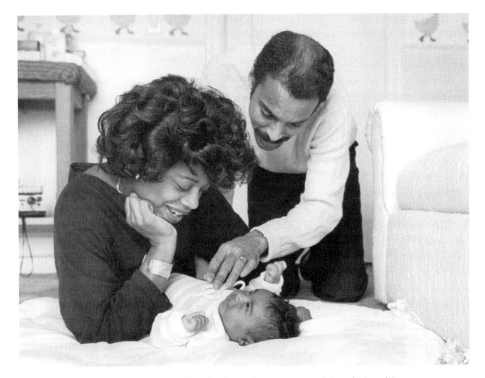

The birth of a child can bring joy, but it also refocuses a couple's relationship.

Motherhood and Fatherhood

When young people contemplate growing up, getting married, and having babies, few understand just how much having children will affect their lives and especially their marriages. Couples know to prepare the baby's space at home and that their time and their movements will not be as free as they were. However, the new baby will bring additional shocks to family life, some of which are related to gender roles and ideology. This section begins with a discussion of the impact of children in two-parent families.

Conventional wisdom says that having a child brings couples together and fulfills and cements marriages. This can be true, and the joy of new parents who wanted children can be immense, but a first child's birth changes the marriage relationship. Partners have less time and energy for themselves as a couple and as individuals. Women experience a comparatively large reduction in their free time because of the persistence of traditional divisions of labor. Men often feel that they are being cared for less than they were before their wives became mothers. The effects of parenthood on marital satisfaction and happiness are generally negative, at least early on, partly because people who are not prepared for what will happen to them experience stress when children arrive (Glenn and McLanahan, 1982). If women leave employment to become full-time mothers, husbands and wives may find that their lives become increasingly dissimilar. The most egalitarian marriage may quickly begin to conform to traditional norms once children arrive.

The degree and type of change a woman experiences seem to depend on whether her motherhood is structured as an exclusive and isolating relationship—that is, whether it becomes her sole occupation.[24] The effects of motherhood on women are most negative when it cuts them off from the outside world. Being a full-time mother may be more difficult now than it was when women were more likely to be able to count on their mothers, grandmothers, and other female family members, as well as the women with whom they had grown up, to share their experiences, provide a support group, and ease the transition to and through motherhood. Americans' geographic mobility has changed this pattern. Young people move to seek education and job opportunities, and their parents move to seek pleasant locales for retirement. The relatively small number of women who leave the labor force entirely for more than a short time also increases the isolation of those who do stay home.

The post–World War II development of suburbs also increased the homemakers' isolation. Suburbs are designed to provide space and privacy and to make very clear distinctions between private and public space, residence and commerce. On the whole, suburbs are also designed with the private automobile in mind. As more women seek employment, the remaining suburban housewives face more loneliness than ever, certainly more than their mothers or grandmothers faced.

The last generation in which full-time mothering was the predominant style was also the first generation to enter motherhood in the post–World War II era. In 1950, about 28% of married women with school-age children were in the labor force. A decade later, the figure was 39%; in 1970, it was 49%; in 1980, it was 62%; and in 1990, 74% of married mothers of school-age children and 59% of married mothers of children less than 6 years old were in the workforce (U.S. Bureau of the Census, 1992, 388). Women are continuing to choose motherhood, but that choice no longer forecloses other choices.

As though the issues raised by parenthood were not already complicated enough, the very definition of motherhood was thrown open in the late 1980s, as more people chose to enter parenthood through *surrogate* arrangements, in which a woman is impregnated by a man whose wife cannot conceive or carry a child. The woman then gives the baby up for adoption by the wife of the father. In these arrangements, the biological mother contracts out the use of her womb, not to mention her genes, and is called a "surrogate mother."

Public discussion became heated during the trial about "Baby M," in which the biological/surrogate mother sued for custody of her child and lost. The contract she had made to have a baby and then give it up was viewed as unbreakable. Up through the middle of 1992, about 4,000 babies were born in the United States through surrogate arrangements, which involve very large financial payments to the birth mother—the "surrogate." These cases raise many crucial questions: Should women be allowed to make unbreakable contracts to conceive, carry, and give birth to a child and then relinquish the child to the father and his partner? If it is illegal for women to rent their bodies for sex, why is it legal to rent them for baby making? Above all, what is a mother? More states are regulating surrogacy more strictly in order to avoid the appearance or practice of baby selling. (For more discussion, see Macklin, 1994.)

422

Part 3:
Choice and Control
in Personal Life,
the Family, and Work

Mothering and Fathering

He fathered that child. She mothered that child. The connotations of these two sentences are different. *Fathering* generally refers to the act of conception, while *mothering* refers not only to conception but also to birthing and caring for a child and to the style of care given. The commonsense differences between mothering and fathering are also illustrated in these two sentences: Don't mother me! Don't father me! The first means, stop treating me as though I need to have someone take care of me; the second makes no sense at all.

The mother is at the same time one of the most revered and one of the most denigrated of American cultural figures. One could hardly begin to describe the feelings of love, tenderness, and reverence that people have for their own mothers and that are expressed through the cultural media. The relationship is a deeply ambivalent one, however. The child, young or otherwise, wants to be nurtured but also wants to be autonomous. The mother who wants to nurture and care for her children also needs that care herself; a mother is also a daughter. The tremendous responsibility accorded to motherhood is double edged. The ties that bind can be interpreted as both supportive and restrictive.

This unequal responsibility for parenting also means that mothers, rather than fathers, receive the blame for their children's problems. Numerous popular books and studies explore the ill effects of mothers on society. Philip Wylie's book *A Generation of Vipers* (1942) for example, told people how stultifying to young people, especially young men, mothers and "momism" are. Wylie blamed many of society's problems on the selfish overprotectiveness of women.

In a provocative article, Nancy Chodorow and Susan Contratto (1982) discussed the problem of both blaming and idealizing mothers as a central theme in our cultural ideology. They argue that good scholarly analysis of motherhood is especially difficult because of our emotional ties to a particular version of reality: the child's-eye view of our own mothers.

> [The ideology of both blaming and idealizing mothers] gains meaning from and is partially produced by infantile fantasies that are themselves the outcome of being mothered exclusively by one woman. If mothers have exclusive responsibility for infants who are totally dependent then to the infant [mothers] are the sources of all good and evil. Times of closeness, oneness and joy are the quintessence of perfect understanding; times of distress, frustration, discomfort, and too great separation are entirely the mother's fault. For the infant, the mother is not someone with her own life, wants, needs, history, other social relationships, work. She is known only in her capacity as mother. (p. 651)

In the process of growing up, we are likely to discover that our mothers are indeed human—thus, the rage of disillusionment—and blame.

Chodorow and Contratto (1982) have pointed out that some feminist writing seeming to suggest that the only problem with women's mothering is the oppression of women also suffers from these infantile fantasies. If liberated from this oppression, all mothers, like those in Gilman's ([1915] 1979) *Herland*, would be eternally rich, warm, loving, and not only all-giving to their children but also active and fulfilled by their rewarding outside lives. Indeed, many women (and men) may be trying to live up to this ideal in their own lives, with the frequent result of guilt over their own human limitations and emotional and physical stress. Chodorow and Contratto have suggested that this pursuit is merely a continuation of the fantasy of the ideal mother.

Like motherhood, fatherhood has changed over time. When parenting meant introducing children to their adult roles as soon as possible, men with sons had very important parental roles to perform. Men also used to be regarded as the moral heads of the family, responsible for safeguarding the morals of wife and children. With the separation of production from the home and the extension of schooling and childhood, however, men became more separate from their children than ever before.

Men also lost some of their parental authority through the course of the 19th century. Until then, all legal rights over children rested with the father. Under the common law (although to a lesser degree in the United States than in England), a man had an unquestioned right to the custody of his children in cases of separation or divorce, and he could even turn custody over to someone other than the mother after his own death. Today, some vestiges of patriarchal authority over children remain, even though the power of mothers over their children has become greater. "Wait until your father gets home" is a token of this authority. Many fathers became absentee landlords who crammed their fathering into weekends and holidays.

There has been a growing movement of men trying to build or restore the place of fathers in their children's lives. This movement is diverse, incorporating many different groups of men, with sometimes conflicting and often overlapping understandings of what their task should be. For some groups, often defining themselves in terms of "fathers' rights," the issue is one of power that has been lost, in part at the instigation of the women's movement. Others, such as the "Promise Keepers," emerged from a conservative Christian perspective, aimed at restoring a moral order, with men more at the center than they are now and, for many, a more traditional division of roles between women and men. Indeed, many men from these first two branches of the fatherhood movement would agree with a leader of the National Fatherhood Initiative, who said, "We're trying to counter this sense in our culture that the mother and father do the same thing."[25] Others define the task as evolving a new approach to fatherhood that would lead to a more central role for men in their children's lives, often in close alliance with women's movement aims. For many men in the African-American community, working to enhance men's relationships to their children and families is a means toward saving the lives of men and their children, especially their sons.

At present, the tasks of childrearing are divided very unevenly. The dominant gender ideology still assumes that those who are naturally fitted to bear children are also naturally fitted to raise them, even if both mother and father are also employed outside the home. Women are responsible for more child care, and women and men continue to believe that most child-care activities are better or more appropriately done by women. Couples sometimes find it difficult to share parenthood. Women learn to feel guilty when they are not doing the job, and men

Charles Dana Gibson's 1897 painting, *His First Love,* depicts a romantic ideal
of motherhood.

often lack the confidence to assume roles that have previously been women's.
Some women feel reluctant to give up control or to trust fathers to be competent.
Sharing would require that men and women reorganize their time and commitments. In the end, people often follow the traditional division of roles simply
because it is the path of least resistance. Sharing requires discussion and negotiation, which can take more effort and energy than simply doing what needs to be
done. Role sharing may be healthier and more just, but it is not necessarily easier.

A large child-development literature examines the different impacts of mothers and fathers on sons and daughters. Most of it finds that mothers and fathers
tend to interact with their children differently and to have different effects on
them. One study observing mothers and fathers in middle- and working-class
White families rearing firstborn sons from age 10 months to 21 months found that
"whereas men functioned principally as playmates and, in fact, were often the
child's preference as play partner, women functioned as basic care providers, comforting their children when distressed, responding to most of their expressed
needs, and being affectionate with them" (Belsky, Crnic, and Woodworth, 1995,
925). A study of the emotional relations between adolescents and their parents
over time found that fathers and daughters were especially reactive to each other's
distress over time, and mothers and sons were especially reactive to each other's
distress (Ge, Conger, and Lorenz, 1995). Another study (of small children)
demonstrated a gender-based interaction between marital and parent–child relationships. The father–daughter relationship seemed especially vulnerable to the
effects of unsatisfying marriages (Kerig, Cowan, and Cowan, 1993).

Fathers tend to do more than mothers to reinforce traditional gender ideology in children, and they are more rigid in expecting their children to conform to traditional gender norms (Johnson, 1982). Children recognize at a fairly early age that men have more social power than women, and if boys especially see that part of that power means being able to expect the wife–mother to do most of the work around the house, they would be odd indeed not to try to take on that role themselves. On the other hand, child-development experts suspect that one of the important aspects of a successful woman's upbringing is a close and encouraging relationship with her father.

While there remains disagreement in this literature about exactly what the gender-based differences are between fathers and mothers, the important points are that parent–child and marital relationships interact and shape each other, and that the social and emotional dynamics among the various partners to a family relationship—parents and children—are partly gender based.

Single and Separated Parents

The classic image of a family with children includes a mother and father living under the same roof with each other and the children. This image is far from reality. If we consider all family households in the United States that include at least one parent with a child under 18 years old, we find that 75% of White families, 64% of Hispanic families, and 32% of African-American families are maintained by two parents living together. In contrast, 21% of White families, 31% of Hispanic families, and 58% of African-American families are maintained by the mother alone. Also, 4% of White families, 5% of Hispanic families, and 6% of African-American families are maintained by the father alone. These figures represent a substantial shift even from 1970, when 90% of White families and 64% of African-American families were maintained by the mother and father (U.S. Bureau of the Census, 1987a, 62). In this section, we look first at the gender issues raised by divorce and then turn to questions raised by unmarried women and their children.

When a Marriage Breaks Up. Over a century ago, when the great 19th-century political theorist and politician John Stuart Mill (quoted in Rossi, 1970) was advocating liberalization of England's very strict divorce laws, he reacted to an idea still heard very commonly today: Married couples should stay together "for the sake of the children." He believed that people should think more *before* they got married or became parents. He was not impressed with the idea that couples should stay together merely because they had children. Of course, the divorce rate today is massively higher than it was in Mill's day, but experts still debate about the impact of divorce on children.

The answer must have something to do with the impact of the parents' relationship on the children. Certainly, in the case of spousal violence, it is difficult to imagine that keeping a family intact has many benefits for the children. In addition, given what we know about the impact of marital relationships on parent–child dynamics, there must be a degree of tension that counterbalances the beneficial effects of having two parents close at hand. It is probably no wonder that in a poll of teenagers asked, "In general are children better off if their parents remain married even if they fight a lot, or are children better off if their parents get divorced?" the majority—66%—picked the divorce option. Perhaps more interesting is that the girls and boys reacted differently. More of the girls (76%) than boys (57%) said children of parents who fight a lot are better off divorced.[26] This may reflect the idea that if parents are fighting a lot, the mother is more likely to get hurt.

Treatment of children during divorce has changed dramatically over the years. As mentioned previously, under traditional English common law, which formed the core of much of the American legal system, fathers had absolute rights of custody over their children. Before the late 19th century, this idea was often reflected in proceedings that awarded children to their fathers. In a sense, the mother was related to her children only by marriage; when the marriage ended, so did her motherhood if that was what the head of the family wanted. Toward the beginning of the 20th century, a new principle weakened patriarchal authority: the *maternal* or *tender-years presumption,* widely supported by both jurists and psychologists until recently. The tender-years presumption is that children require their mother's care in particular during their tender years of childhood; all else being equal, child custody should be awarded to mothers following divorce. As a typical court decision stated in 1948, "The mother is the natural custodian of her child in tender years, and . . . if she is a fit and proper person, other things being equal, she should be given custody" (*Muller* v. *Muller*).

What could a mother do to prove herself not "fit and proper"? Certainly, evidence that mothers abused their children or were alcoholics affected custody. Mothers could also be accused of other moral faults judged to create an unhealthy environment for children. Sexual activity outside of marriage often served as grounds on which to deny women custody of their children. In 1979, for example, the Illinois Supreme Court threatened to deny custody to a mother for immoral conduct (*Jarrett* v. *Jarrett*). The mother, who divorced her husband because of his cruelty to her, originally had been awarded custody of the child, but when she announced that her boyfriend was going to move in with her, the father then sought custody. The court concluded that it was the policy of the state to "safeguard the moral well-being of children" and that the mother's "conduct offends prevailing public policy." Although a moral indiscretion was not sufficient grounds for denial of custody, the court feared that if the boyfriend moved in and lived with the mother, the children "may learn to disregard existing standards" of morality. Therefore, the boyfriend could not reside in the house if the woman wanted to keep her children.

Lesbian activity has also been used as grounds to deny a woman custody of her children, although mere proof of lesbian inclinations is not treated as negatively by courts as it once was, and lesbian activity is coming to be treated similarly to heterosexual activity. One reason is that courts are becoming aware of research showing that the upbringing children receive from lesbian and gay parents is not very different from the upbringing they receive from heterosexual parents. It appears that children of lesbian mothers even learn conventional gender norms about as well as other children do (Patterson, 1992). A study of 15 lesbian couples with 3- to 9-year-old children (born as a result of artificial insemination) and 15 heterosexual couples with children the same age found no difference between the two groups of children in cognitive functioning or behavior, and no difference between the two sets of parents in parenting, except that the lesbian parents showed more parenting-awareness skills (Flaks, Ficher, and Masterpasqua, 1995).

Consider a state supreme court decision, which illustrates the conflicting views about homosexuality and child custody found in current law (*Schuster* v. *Schuster*, 1978). Two women separated from their husbands to live together. The fathers filed for divorce in a lower court, and the mothers were given custody of their children but were ordered to live apart, which they refused to do. The fathers then sued to obtain custody of the children. The court not only refused to change the custodial arrangements but also lifted the ban on the women's living together.

The court was not unanimous, however. One dissenting opinion included a quotation from a law article that illustrates the classic objections to allowing lesbians custody of their own children:

> In seeking to regulate homosexuality, the state takes as a basic premise that social and legal attitudes play an important and interdependent role in the individual's formation of his or her sexual destiny. A shift on the part of the law from opposition to neutrality arguably makes homosexuality appear a more acceptable lifestyle, particularly to younger persons whose sexual preferences are as yet unformed. . . . If homosexual behavior is legalized, and thus partly legitimized, an adolescent may question whether he or she should "choose" heterosexuality. . . . If society accorded more legitimacy to expressions of homosexual attraction, attachment to the opposite sex might be postponed or diverted for some time, perhaps until after the establishment of sexual patterns that would hamper development of traditional heterosexual family relationships. For those persons who eventually choose the heterosexual model, the existence of conflicting models might provide further sexual tension destructive to the traditional marital unit.

In this view, allowing lesbians custody of their children may not hurt the children themselves, but it could perpetuate marital instability from one generation to the next.

These cases raise important issues. Few people would object to judges' attempts to act in the interests of children, especially to protect them where the parents have conflicting interests. Exactly how should the courts protect children, though? How far should public bodies go in deciding what is morally and socially good for a child? As the cases cited here show, safeguarding the child can mean quite profound regulation of the parents' lives and the parents' understanding of what is good for the child, including regulation on the basis of gender and sexual ideology.

States have now generally abolished the maternal presumption. More fathers are now contesting for custody. Some men's rights groups offer assistance to men considering such a contest. Courts now tend to focus more squarely on the "best interests of the child," taking many different factors into account, such as the resources available to the children in their maternal and paternal homes. However, the more *financial* resources are taken into account, the more disadvantaged the mother will be. The facts of economic life would almost certainly point to the father more often than not.

Women still gain custody of children in the majority of divorce cases because men do not seek custody as often as women do. When men do seek custody, however, they are increasingly likely to win. More divorcing couples are also seeking *joint* custody, in which children live part-time with one parent and part-time with the other. This arrangement requires that the parents be able to coordinate schedules and that they live in close proximity to each other.

Another common issue for the impact of divorce on parenting is what, if any, child-support payments the noncustodial parent is ordered to make and whether the court order will be enforced. Because even in joint-custody cases the children usually reside more with the mother, and fathers are most often the parties charged with contributing support payments to the other parent. In most cases, divorced mothers are in a weak financial position. They are likely to have considerably less earning power than the father, particularly if they have been full-time mothers and homemakers. If they gain custody, they have the added financial burden of children, including child-care costs when they must be absent from home. A study of child-support awards in simple cases found that although decisions weighed the postdivorce welfare of mother, father, and children, the combined welfare of the custodial mother and the child were given significantly less weight in the outcome than the father's welfare (Del Boca and Flinn, 1995).

In the late 1960s, public-policy makers became aware of a growing social problem with major policy implications: Fathers were not paying court-ordered child support. Within a very short time after divorce, many mothers assume full responsibility for the financial support of their children. Because this situation was one of the most important contributing factors to a growing problem of poverty among women and children—and therefore an issue for the welfare system—by the late 1970s, states were computerizing their records and coordinating efforts to catch delinquent fathers. By the middle of the 1980s, the federal government was actively involved in trying to help enforce child-support payments, especially against men who had left their home state and thus avoided the enforcement agents from that state.

Divorce involving children, then, creates a very complex web of choices that have important implications for women's and men's lives *as* women and men.

Single Parenthood.   About 30% of the babies born in 1992 were born to unmarried women. Regardless of whether a father lives with the mother and child or whether he assists in the support and care of the child, unless he marries the mother or follows the formal legal procedure to acknowledge paternity, the child is regarded by law as having only one parent, the mother, and is designated illegitimate. At one time, this meant that although mother and child had full legal claims on each other, as far as the law was concerned father and child were strangers to each other. No claims could be made by or on behalf of the child for support, inheritance, or any other rights of the parent–child relationship.

Lawsuits involving illegitimate children and their parents raise questions about gender and sexual ideology and the influence these have on the choices people make. Part of the reason the law distinguishes between children born in and out of wedlock is that these distinctions help governments *enforce certain sexual morals*. However, these distinctions punish the children, who obviously cannot choose the circumstances of their births, for their parents' violation of social norms. Although the United States has not abandoned the classification of illegitimacy as some other countries have, American law is increasingly regarding discrimination between legitimate and illegitimate children as illegal and even unconstitutional under the equal protection clause of the Fourteenth Amendment. As the Supreme Court said, "it is unjust and ineffective for society to express its condemnation of procreation outside the marital relationship by punishing the illegitimate child who is in no way responsible for his situation and is unable to change it" (*Parnham v. Hughes*, 1979). New laws are likely to do away with the distinction over the coming years.

Legitimacy laws do not discriminate among *children* as much as they once did, but they still discriminate against *men*. A Supreme Court case decision, for example, ruled that an unwed father had no right to sue for the wrongful death of his child after the child and mother were killed in an automobile accident. The majority decided that because the father had never bothered to make the child legitimate, he could not benefit by the child's death (*Parnham v. Hughes*).

A second purpose of legitimacy laws is to *discourage people from having children out of wedlock*. Policies that pursue this goal tend to place different burdens on men and women. For instance, some policies have made it difficult for men to claim their children and care for them. More often, however, they simply place burdens on the child and on the caregiving parent—in the vast majority of cases, the mother. These problems came to the fore once again following passage of the Welfare Reform Act of 1996. The changes to the system were intended to encourage the poor to seek work and stop being dependent on public-welfare programs for support. The people who depend on those programs are disproportionately children and their single mothers, and part of the program is designed to discourage women from having children out of wedlock. There is no question that women who have children when they are not married are disproportionately young and poor, have relatively low levels of education, and have—or at least regard themselves as having—few prospects. The question that will be important to answer as the effects of the new system and its revisions become clear is whether the children involved and their mothers become better off after all. (For more on single motherhood, see Polakow, 1993.)

A Case Study of African-American Families

One of the most interesting scholarly and policy debates over the issue of gender and family structure revolves around the history of African-American families. These debates highlight related questions important not just for studying African-American families, but also for studying gender and the family more generally:

1. How do researchers explain the evolution of particular family structures in particular communities? Anthropologists and historians have long studied variation in the family across different cultures and societies and across time. Even within one country at a single time, a rich variety in family forms exists.

2. What difference does the basic family household composition make for its members and for the larger society? Imagine three of the many possible variations of family households in which children might be raised: two parents, one parent (either mother or father), or a three-generation household including at least one grandparent and an extended family with uncles or aunts, cousins, or more distant relatives. (Of course, there are many other variations.) Does this variation have systematic effects on children and their development? Does this variation have specific implications for the role of *gender* in family relationships?

3. What difference do variations in the structure and culture of families make for their members and for the larger society? Consider especially differences in power and resources across *gender* and across *generation*. What difference does it make if a family is more *patriarchal* (ruled by the father), *matriarchal* (ruled by the mother), or egalitarian? What difference does it make if the oldest family generation holds the most power and resources in a family or actually *loses* power and resources as it ages, especially given that the power of a generation is often gender specific (i.e., it is the grand*mother* or grand*father* that rules the family)?

These questions all come together in scholarly and policy discussions of African-American families.

Three characteristics have long distinguished the structure of African-American and White households and families: In the African-American community, single-parent families are more common, children are less likely to live with a parent, and households are more likely to be composed of extended families. Some observers have defined African-American family culture as more matriarchal because of the large proportion of children raised by only their mothers for a significant period of their childhood. Of course, comparing African-American and White families gives only crude generalizations; there is a lot of variation within the African-American community, for example across class, urban–rural, and recent–early immigrants; and also across the different ethnic and religious groups classified as White families (Glenn, Chang, and Forcey, 1994).

For the first two centuries of American history following the settlement of colonies populated by Europeans and Africans in the early 17th century, the forces shaping the family life of Black Americans were vastly different from those exerted on Whites. The vast majority of Black people were owned *individually* as slaves. Slave owners were under no pressure to respect the integrity of the family relationships of the people they owned, and even when the members of a Black family were owned by the same person, their first duties were to their master. Despite their anguish when husbands, wives, or children were sold to other masters, generations of Black Americans learned to survive with a family reality that differed substantially from both the kinds their ancestors experienced in Africa and the ones the Whites who lived around them took for granted.

The development of family structures and culture among African-Americans both during the slave period and after was further influenced by an ideology at odds with the predominant beliefs of patriarchal societies that women are the weaker sex and men are the primary breadwinners. African cultures were very diverse and defy generalization at least as much as European cultures did. Nonetheless, the gender norms regarding sexuality and divisions of labor in the societies from which African-Americans came were different from those that sent Europeans to America. In many African societies, women were more economically active than was true in European cultures, and in some societies, sexual norms were freer, or at least patriarchal norms were less dominant. To the degree that African-Americans preserved any of the values of their forebears, their cultures were not necessarily consistent with European-American patriarchal values.

Moreover, the experience of Black women in the United States was inconsistent with the ideology that women were weak. Of course, White people applied this ideology of frail womanhood to White women only. As slaves, Black women were expected to do hard labor. After emancipation, Black women continued to be regarded as workhorses, and they found employment primarily in the hardest of the jobs classified as women's work, including domestic service, unskilled service work, and farmwork. Black women had little opportunity to learn to see themselves as the weaker sex.

Even following the end of slavery, life remained harder for the average African-American than it was for the average White person. Poverty and worse job opportunities, a profoundly racist and discriminatory society, and—toward the end of the 19th century—systematic violence against African-American men in the form of lynching all took their toll on African-Americans as individuals, as families, and as a community. In the 20th century, poverty, migration, and continued job discrimination against African-American women and men continue to mitigate against the existence of stable two-parent homes, let alone the patriarchal family. In addition, Black men tend to die young, partly because of the likelihood that they will be the object of violence, so there is a large demographic imbalance between Black women and men.

As a result, the structure of the average African-American family was different from that of the average White family after emancipation, and the differences became even wider in the late 20th century. As Table 12-2 shows, there was a lot of variation in both White and Black households in the late 19th century, but White households were more likely to consist of a married couple and children, and Black children were more likely to live with only their mothers or without a parent. The latter occurred for two reasons: (1) Because of the higher death rate among African-Americans, the parents of Black children were more likely to be deceased; and (2) in the late 19th century Black children were more likely to be placed in other families to work, a practice also true in many White families earlier in American history. African-American households were consistently more likely to involve extended families, but up to 1940, the difference was almost completely due to the higher rates of single parenthood and parentless children among African-Americans. After controlling for single parenthood and parentless children, White and Black households were equally likely to contain extended families up to 1940. A simple economic explanation does not fully tell why this is the case; evidence suggests, for example, that "blacks in 1880 who faced the worst conditions—illiteracy and residence in the poorest districts—had the highest odds of residing in a two-parent family" (Ruggles, 1994, 148). Among White families illiteracy and poverty were associated with being *less* likely to reside in a two-parent family.

TABLE 12-2
The Changing Structure of Black and White Families, 1880–1980

	1880		1960		1980	
			Percentages			
	Black	*White*	*Black*	*White*	*Black*	*White*
Households consisting of						
Primary individuals	9	5	18	15	27	27
Single parents with children	12	8	10	5	21	7
Married couple with children	46	56	31	47	25	35
Vertically extended families	13	11	14	7	10	4
Other extended families	9	9	11	5	7	3
Children living with						
Both parents	70	87	68	91	47	84
Mother only	13	6	18	6	37	12
Father only	5	3	3	1	4	2
No parent	12	4	11	2	12	2

Note: "Primary individuals" are unrelated individuals. "Vertically extended families" contain children-in-law or more than two generations. "Other extended families" contain other relatives.

Source: Adapted from Ruggles (1994, 138, 140).

By 1960, many things had changed for American families, especially among African-Americans, but even more change took place within the following 20 years. By 1980, the rate of single-parent and extended households was much higher among African-Americans, and African-American children were twice as likely to live with only their fathers, three times more likely to live with only their mothers, and six times more likely to live with neither parent—either with another relative, an unrelated individual, or in an institutionalized setting.

By the middle of the 1960s, many social scientists and policy analysts began to worry about the potential impact of the changing family structure on the Black community. As a result, public attention in the 1960s was drawn increasingly to the Black "matriarchal family." Elizabeth Almquist (1984) has pointed out that the usual description of Black families contains some gross inaccuracies, but the image that became seared into public perception was of families dominated by women who, because of their strength, "emasculated" the men in their families and therefore further weakened the family. The strength of women in the family was often blamed for juvenile delinquency, failure in school, and lack of achievement motivation, especially among sons. In 1965, a government report entitled "The Negro Family: The Case for National Attention" (the "Moynihan Report") based its assessment of the situation of American blacks on this kind of analysis.

The discussion and critique of the "Black matriarchy" is of theoretical and political importance in a discussion of motherhood and fatherhood, regardless of race. Aside from the important fact that the Black matriarchy theories tend to undervalue discrimination as a source of the problems of blacks, these theories reveal some important and continuing assumptions about gender and parenting. The analysis does not simply point to broken or single-parent families as the reasons for difficulty in the Black community; it underscores *female dominance* and strength. These theories assert that Black families (and, it follows, White families as well) would be better off if the male would take "his rightful place" as the *dominant* authority figure in the family. Women again are the scapegoats, this time for being strong and showing a remarkable ability to cope with oppressive circumstances. Male dominance is posed as the center of gravity for a stable society. (For more discussion, see Collins, 1989b; Zinn, 1989). These theories reflect a double standard in parenting. Most people are not concerned about the effects of unequal power and authority of parents when the dominant parent is the father. There is much greater concern about mother dominance, however, just as a marriage in which a wife is particularly strong tends to be ridiculed (the poor henpecked husband).

Both cultural and economic factors rooted in early American history created different kinds of family structures and cultures evident since emancipation. Something further happened in the 20th century, however, that drove the structures of Black and White families further apart, especially in the last part of the 20th century. The multiplying effects of economics and culture drive a situation where a substantial proportion of Black women undertake the entire burden for having and raising children. Many diverse groups within the Black community are today searching for ways of reconnecting Black men with their families. While some, like the organizers of the "Million Man March" in the late 1990s, picked up the theme of readjusting relations between men and women to have women stand back a bit, most others are searching for other ways to strengthen Black men's connections with their families.

Parents Without Children

Sooner or later, most mothers find themselves with children who no longer need or want their daily care and who no longer help them fulfill the child-centered role for which they were trained. These mothers' children have grown up and may even have children of their own. On the problem of mothers with grown children, Pauline Bart has written,

> Nowhere is [the inadequacy of traditional female roles] more apparent than when studying the super mothers suffering from Portnoy's Mother's Complaint, middle-aged depression, coming not from the hormonal changes of the menopause, but from the life cycle changes, when the children from whom the woman drew her identity depart and she has nothing to replace them with. (1975, 12)

Many writers have investigated the "empty nest syndrome," or maternal role loss, in middle-aged women. Bart has argued, "It is true that we all lose roles throughout our lives; but when we are young there are new roles to replace the old ones, and rites of passage to ease the transition. But as we age, there are usually not such new roles . . . and there are few rites of passage. There is no Bar Mitzvah for menopause" (1975, 12). The next major section of this chapter addresses whether there are new roles for the "long-distance mother" to adopt, but the remainder of this section focuses on the serious problem of loneliness and depression among some women at this stage in life.

Bart studied more than 500 women between the ages of 40 and 59 who had been diagnosed as depressed at mental hospitals and had had no previous hospitalization for mental illness. In looking at the relationship between depression and marital, maternal, and occupational role loss, she found that maternal role loss was the most important predictor of these women's depression. The relationship between depression and maternal role loss was even stronger among middle-class homemakers, or women who had had "an overprotective or overinvolved relationship" with their children. Her findings seem consistent with common sense: The more a woman's life revolves exclusively around her children, the more she will suffer when they are no longer children. Gender-role norms that prescribe full-time motherhood for women throughout their younger years may lay a treacherous path for them as they age.

The problems of maternal role loss are magnified by other changes in women's situation as they age. There are different standards of beauty and attractiveness in women and men, and in American society, aging is viewed as less attractive in women than in men. Many women also find that their marriages indeed endured only for the sake of the children when their husbands leave them for younger women around the time the children become independent. In addition, many women take on the new role of mother-in-law when their children leave home, a role that is itself the subject of painful stereotypes. In this role, women become one of the most ridiculed and resented of American cultural figures.

One of the factors that causes problems for women with older children is the view that a woman loses her meaning when her children grow up. Critics of society's treatment of older women should not focus too long on the emptiness of life without young children. As Bart's study shows, depression due to maternal role loss afflicts a very special group of women, and the majority of women are now protected from it to some degree by employment, especially after their last child has entered school. In poor and working-class families, grandmothers are still relatively likely to be part of the day-to-day lives of families, at least to a greater extent than tends to be true of wealthier, more mobile families.

Changing attitudes toward aging also mitigate the effects of maternal role loss, and preventive medicine and improved health care mean that women are even more likely to be able to begin new lives and activities when their children leave home. The popularity of new towns designed mainly for the postparental stage of life testify to the increased tendency for parents to launch new lives. Parents do not want to be cast off by their children, but increasing numbers also do not want to give up their new—or renewed—independence to adult children in need of babysitters.

Eventually, in many families, the roles of parent and child come to be reversed in many respects. Elderly mothers and fathers depend on care and attention from their grown children. This role, too, is gender based; just as women do most of the caregiving for children, they also do so for elderly parents.

Beyond the Family: Who Cares for Children?

American society, especially through the instruments of law and public policy, often makes great claims about the high value it places on families and about its intention to protect the family and children. Ever since the end of the 1970s, however, many critics from left to right have charged that American public policies are, in effect, antichild, antimother, and antifamily. Feminists and others on the left have argued that public policy regarding the family is based on and reinforces traditional gender and sexual values, placing the primary burden for child care and domestic labor on women without giving them much help in performing these important tasks. They charge that public policy has not fully recognized the facts of life of modern society. Men are not the sole breadwinners in families; most women now do and will continue to seek employment to support themselves and their dependents. In fact, a growing proportion of women are the sole heads of families.

The androcentric structure of education and the job market means that women have fewer of the financial resources to provide for their children, and in too many cases, the promise that fathers will provide these resources is empty. Social-welfare assistance to provide for children is inadequate and is dispensed so reluctantly as to make recipients feel degraded for turning to the government for help in raising what is claimed to be society's "most valuable resource." Public debate about welfare policy in the late 1990s made clear that women who depend on public assistance are regarded as second-class citizens. In 1995, when asked, "Do you think unmarried mothers who are 18 years old or younger and have no way of supporting themselves should or should not be able to receive welfare," a majority of the population thought the mothers should, but nearly one third— 31%—thought they should not.[27]

U.S. policy now mandates the availability of parental leave for new parents, but it is the stingiest such program among the leading industrialized nations, as Chapter 1 showed. Policymakers and the public know that families have trouble managing without high-quality affordable child care, but they regard public provision of care as an unaffordable luxury. Women who take traditional gender norms at face value and become full-time mothers and homemakers are rewarded by being the most economically and psychologically vulnerable of all women. Carolyn Adams and Kathryn Winston's comparative research led them to conclude in 1980, "The United States has the distinction of being the only major industrialized country in the world that lacks a national insurance plan covering medical expenses for childbirth and is one of few governments in industrialized nations that does not provide any cash benefits to working women to compensate for lost benefits" (1980, 33). This statement continues to be true.

There has been inadequate effort to provide care for the children of working mothers. Mothers once relied on other women, such as their own mothers, to help them, but this reliance is less possible now.[28] Relatively few people take seriously the idea that fathers and mothers should share the responsibility for childrearing equally. Jobs, particularly men's jobs, are so structured as to make sharing difficult.

Child care is not a new idea in American history.[29] Early in the 19th century, some private nurseries were set up for poor and working-class women. These were merely custodial, compared with the kindergartens developed later in the century, which were intended to foster child development. Limited numbers of publicly funded child-care centers were established during the Depression. There were also publicly funded child-care centers during World War II, when the nation had a specific interest in enabling women to enter the workforce while men were at war. When the men came home, the funding for this relatively small program stopped. Repeated proposals to start a new program have been defeated. In 1971, a bill that would have instituted a network of federally funded and locally run child-care centers that would have been available to all children who needed them passed in Congress, but President Nixon vetoed it on the grounds that he thought it would weaken the family.

Since the mid-1970s, a series of new and increasingly popular efforts have been aimed at trying to make the provision of healthy and high-quality child care a part of public policy. Although there have been efforts to expand public programs, most of what has been available is private. Both businesses and local communities are beginning to sponsor child care for children, although the available spaces make only a small dent in the need.

What arrangements do parents make for their children while they are at work? A study of child-care provisions for children less than 5 years old with mothers who are employed full-time shows that only a minority (28%) attend a child-care center, nursery school, or preschool. Another 24% are cared for in the *child's own home,* by the father (11%), a grandparent, another relative, or a nonrelative. The largest proportion (42%) are cared for in *someone else's home,* by a nonrelative (28%), a grandparent (11%), or another relative (3%) (U.S. Bureau of the Census, 1989). This means that one of the most common ways of obtaining child care is to send the child to the home of a nonrelative, who is often running the equivalent of a small, unregulated, and uninspected child-care center. Child care is also expensive, especially for the less well off. Families with incomes below the poverty line spend about 21% of their income on child care; families with incomes above the poverty line spend about 7%.[30]

The public is becoming increasingly discontented with the current situation. By the mid-1980s, about 55% of Americans agreed that companies should share responsibility for providing child care, rather than leaving it up to individual employees to work out, and 63% thought that companies should make child care available to employees as part of benefits packages. This provision is available more widely now. There is also growing support for public provision of child care. By 1985, 43% of the public thought that child care should be made available to all preschool children as part of the public school system and supported through taxes. This has not happened to date.

There are other problems with public support of the family, from the progressive point of view. In many cities, families have difficulty finding a place to live because landlords refuse to rent to families with children, and city governments refuse to intervene. Assistance to women and children who have been victims of abuse in the family is minimal because the public is reluctant to interfere in the private life of the family. Government and business often have very limited understanding of the definition of "the family," sometimes restricting it to married couples with children. In summary, feminists argue that American policy seems most supportive of motherhood and children when the husband–wife family unit is intact, the women gets pregnant only when she wants to be pregnant, the woman is a full-time homemaker, and the husband can and does provide for the family. In other words, the American system is not supportive of the family or motherhood per se, but of a particular type of family and motherhood.

Conservatives and antifeminists see the world differently than progressives do. They focus on how much the patriarchal family has been weakened and worry about the eventual collapse of the family order. To them, sexuality and morality have become unconstrained by traditional morality and family values. Adults have become individualistic and self-serving, putting themselves before the interests of their families. Women have given up devoting themselves to caring for home and children, which leaves men without incentives to be good husbands and fathers and leaves children without primary caregivers who are personally motivated. As a result, husbands abandon their families.

Conservatives further argue that the incentive for individuals to provide for their own families was stripped away by tax-supported public programs, especially those supporting the poor. Government intrudes in the family by telling parents how to care for and discipline children and how husbands and wives should treat each other (e.g., by forbidding parents and husbands to beat their children and wives). Government policy makes it too easy for families to break apart. The law is moving in the direction of treating heterosexuals and homosexuals, married couples and cohabiting couples all the same, thus encouraging immorality and instability. Power over children is being taken away from parents, especially in education policies. In some places, at some times, a fetus is as likely to be killed as to be nurtured to birth, and more marriages are ending than beginning.

Despite the vast differences between the progressive and the conservative perspectives, both groups claim to be profamily, and these different positions should be taken seriously and understood as reflecting different conceptions of the family. Feminists emphasize the degree to which patriarchal principles still underlie family policy, and antifeminists emphasize how much that order has broken down. The red herring in the debate is the question of whether there should be government interference in the family. Both sides want the government to do something about the family to support the values they are pursuing. Both sides understand that the values that shape and define the family in its various forms have profound effects on all aspects of our lives. That is why the debate is so rancorous.

One of the core issues in the continuing debate is whether or to what extent child care and the raising of children should be the work of an isolated family unit. More specifically, because of the persistence of gender divisions of labor, the issue is whether and to what degree child care and the raising of children should be the work of *women* in isolated family units. The rise of public education means that some of that duty has long since become a shared societal task. Nonetheless, the history of child-care provisions reveals the continuing assumption that whatever else they do, when their children are not in school, women should be with them.

Reproduction and the care of children are among the most important tasks we have as individuals and as a society. Are children, our future generation, indeed a national resource, or are they private property? Given the current structure of society, behind this question is another: What are the relative roles, responsibilities, and options of women and men in creating and caring for those future generations?

Notes

1. *New York Times* Poll/CBS News Poll, "National Teenagers Survey, May 26–June 1, 1994," n.d.

2. "Freshman Survey: Their Opinions, Activities, and Goals," *Chronicle of Higher Education,* http//chronicle.com/che-data.

3. For example, because of a decline in the birth rate in the former East Germany, some German states instituted cash payments to encourage parenthood. Steven Kinzer, "$650 a Baby: Germany to Pay to Stem Decline in Births," *New York Times,* November 25, 1994.

4. For more on teenage mothers, see Horowitz (1995) and Luker (1996).

5. Mireya Navarro, "Teen-Age Mothers Viewed as Abused Prey of Older Men," *New York Times,* May 19, 1996.

6. For two very interesting studies of the politics of teen pregnancy, see Horowitz (1995) and Luker (1996).

7. For clear and helpful information on the various forms of contraception, see Boston Women's Health Book Collective (1992) and Hyde (1994, Chapter 8).

8. Laura Meckler, "Less Sex, More Condoms Equal Less Teen Pregnancy," *Wisconsin State Journal,* May 2, 1997.

9. Philip Hilts, "Birth Control Safer Than Unprotected Sex," *New York Times,* April 23, 1991.

10. "*New York Times* Poll/CBS News Poll, October 22–25, 1995," n.d.

11. David Moore, Frank Newport, and Lydia Saad, "Public Generally Supports a Woman's Right to Abortion," Gallup Organization, http://www.gallup.com/news/960815.html/.

12. "Freshman Survey."

13. *New York Times,* April 26, 1989.

14. Timothy Egan, "Conspiracy Is an Elusive Target in Prosecuting Foes of Abortion," *New York Times,* June 18, 1995.

15. Tamar Lewin, "Abortion-Rights Groups See a Rise in Attacks on Clinics," *New York Times,* January 4, 1993.

16. Tamar Lewin, "Anti-abortion Center's Ads Ruled Misleading," *New York Times,* April 22, 1994.

17. Ronald Smothers, "Protester Is Arrested in Pensacola's 2d Clinic Killing," *New York Times,* July 30, 1994.

18. Allen R. Myerson, "Jury Assesses Abortion Foes $8.6 Million," *New York Times,* September 26, 1995.

19. For a description of these groups, see "Who's Who on the Anti-choice Front," http://205.177.10.1/agm/main/whoswho.htm#ACLA/.

20. National Abortion Federation, http://www.cais.com/naf/violence/analysis97. htm.

21. This figure is from the most complete annual study of anticlinic violence, distributed by the Feminist Majority Foundation; see http://www.feminist.org/research/ cvsurveys/.

22. Tamar Lewin, "Hurdles Increasing for Women Seeking Abortion," *New York Times,* March 15, 1992.

23. Sam Howe Verhovek, "New Twist for a Landmark Case: Roe v. Wade Becomes Roe v. Roe," *New York Times,* August 12, 1995.

24. Recall the discussion of health issues in Chapter 6.

25. Susan Chira, "Push to Revamp Ideal for American Fathers," *New York Times,* June 19, 1994.

26. "*New York Times* Poll/CBS News Poll, National Teenagers Survey."

27. "*New York Times* Poll/CBS News Poll, December 9–11, 1995," n.d.

28. At the same time, it should be remembered that the vast majority of paid child-care workers are women.

29. Much of the following is from Norgren (1989).

30. "Weekly Child Care Costs Paid by Families with Employed Mothers, 1985–1993," http://www.census.gov/population/socdemo/child/cctab2.txt/.

13

❧

Work, Employment,
and the Economics of Gender

Look at me! Look at my arm! I have ploughed, and planted, and gathered
into barns, and no man could head me! And ar'n't I a woman? I could
work as much and eat as much as a man (when I could get it) and bear de
lash as well! And ar'n't I a woman? I have borne thirteen children, and
seen 'em mos' all sold off to slavery, and when I cried out with my mother's
grief, none but Jesus heard—and ar'n't I a woman?

Sojourner Truth ([1851], quoted in White, 1985, 14)

WOMEN HAVE ALWAYS WORKED. They may not always have been paid for
it, and their work has not always been recognized. In fact, cultural beliefs have
often claimed women can't work—but they have and always will. Consider
Sojourner Truth's 1851 speech, as reported by Frances Gage, printed in this chapter's opener. Her experience is often cited as extraordinary; in many ways, it was.
Her speech was not just about her own life, however; it was also about the lives of
thousands of other women whose occupation was slavery. Much of her labor,
including fieldwork and mother work, has been shared to some extent by millions
of women in many communities, both before and after her time. Her speech
describes the specific experience of an African-American woman held in slavery,
but it was also about women more generally.

In this chapter, we look at women and work in the broadest sense of that
term, encompassing what Evelyn Nakano Glenn has called *social reproduction:* not
just the act of earning money, but the "array of activities and relationships involved
in maintaining people both on a daily basis and intergenerationally" (Glenn, 1992,
1). This concept offers us a better handle on understanding the relationship of
gender to human labor and economics, and to economic institutions. Many feminist scholars have criticized traditional economics and economic history scholarship for not adequately incorporating women and women's work into its models

and explanations (Ferber and Nelson, 1993; Nelson, 1996). Let us look at these claims more closely.

Roslyn Feldberg and Evelyn Nakano Glenn (1979) have argued that sociologists tend to use two entirely different models (i.e., sets of assumptions and questions), depending on whether they are focusing on men or women. For men, there is the *job* model, which assumes that men's social relations and identities are determined by their jobs, their sociopolitical attitudes and behavior are derived from their occupational roles and status, and their central interests and motivations in life are their employment and earnings. Men's primary connection with their families is in their role as economic providers. Thus, the job model leads us to assume that the most important thing to know about a man is his occupation.

In contrast, Feldberg and Glenn argue, women are analyzed according to a gender or (probably more appropriately) a *family* model.[1] Social scientists assume that women's basic social relations are determined by their relationship to the family; their sociopolitical attitudes and behavior are derived from their family roles, status, and gender-role socialization. Women's central interests and motivations in life revolve around the internal dynamics of family life. Women's place is the family, which is supposedly not where work happens. Women have only a tentative and marginal relationship with the outside occupational world. The family model leads us to assume that the most important things to know about a woman are whether she is married and if she has children.

The worlds of work and the family are culturally defined as two distinct places that are complementary and often in conflict. In the work world, people are (supposed to be) ambitious, competitive, and aggressive and are valued in the currency of money. In the family world, people are (supposed to be) nurturant and relatively peaceful and are valued in the currency of love and loyalty. Historically, women were assigned to one and men to the other, and their characters were defined by the worlds they were supposed to occupy.

As useful as these models are for understanding how culture and scholarship alike comprehend women and men in their everyday activities, Glenn, among others, has urged us to refine our understanding even further by incorporating race and ethnicity into these models (1992). The mutual isolation of these two aspects of social structure—race/ethnicity and gender—has resulted in our understanding White women through a primarily gender-based model, as though race and gender do not interact in creating their experience, and in our understanding women of other races through a primarily race-based and secondarily gender-based model.[2] By using a complex model of gender (including both the jobs and the family models) and race, we can more adequately trace the dynamics of who does what social-reproduction labor under what circumstances, and it is more possible to see change over time. Glenn's own research on gender, race, and domestic service offers good examples (Glenn, 1986, 1992).

In this chapter, we explore women's work lives, gender divisions of labor, and the resulting economic situation of women. We focus especially on the opportunities women have for making choices in their work and economic lives, and the effects of these choices, or the lack of them, on other aspects of their lives.

Making a Living Versus Making a Home: Defining Differences

If we stopped people on the street and asked them whether their mothers worked when they were children, a large proportion would say "no." What they would mean, of course, is that their mothers were not employed for pay. Their mothers probably spent long hours shopping, cleaning, cooking, and performing the numerous other tasks involved in managing family life, but that is not seen as real work. They might have contributed many hours of labor to voluntary organizations, but that, too, is not considered real work. Only if a woman has done any of these activities for pay is she likely to be viewed as having worked. Otherwise, she is "just a housewife."

The distinctions between work and family, breadwinning and homemaking, seem so obvious today that many people are surprised to learn that these distinctions are relatively new and make sense only in certain kinds of economies. In subsistence economies, where all members of a household labor most of their waking hours to provide themselves with the necessities of life, there is little difference between making a home and making a living. In small-farm agricultural societies and urban societies of craftspeople, the workplace or market is not entirely distinct from the home. In these societies, there are gender divisions of labor, but describing one person as a "worker" and one as "just a housewife" does not make sense, especially when many of the goods required in the home are produced there by women. Certainly, before the 20th century, relatively few women worked outside the home, but relatively few men worked outside the home then, either.

The Rise and Fall of Homemaking

When did the distinction between making a living and making a home emerge? How and when did the distinct role of homemaker arise? Historians point to the rise of industrial capitalism, which increasingly moved production outside the home and provided opportunities (for men) to seek wage labor there. This does not mean that capitalism *created* gender divisions of labor or gender inequality. Women in preindustrial American society were already governed by feudal laws denying married women the opportunity to own property and to make contracts. Indeed, women in almost all preindustrial societies suffered from tremendous gender inequality and domination. If the new jobs that developing industrial capitalism made available outside the home provided opportunities primarily to men, it was partly because these jobs, as they were created, were *already* regarded as masculine.[3]

What the rise of capitalism did do was to elaborate on gender divisions of labor, create some new ones, and make men's and women's spheres of activity more spatially separate and socially distinct. The value of labor was increasingly assessed in the currency of money, and productivity began to be defined as the amount of monetary profit one's labor returned *to one's employer*, rather than just how much work one did. Women's domestic sphere of labor did not involve wage labor, so it could not be assigned a monetary value, and it was no longer seen as productive. The key point here is not just whether women and men do different work, but how this different work is valued. As industrial development occurred, women continued to engage in many of the tasks they had done before, but either they were excluded from the wage and profit sector of the economy (e.g., domestic labor), or their labor became routinized, deskilled, and devalued (e.g., mass-market textile production). An interesting example of this process is the shift in Navajo women's production of rugs and blankets over the late 19th and early 20th centuries. Before the development of a cash economy, women wove for both personal use and trade, but with the United States policy of incorporation of Navajo society and the development of a capitalist economy (even if a peripheral one), women lost control over their weaving and became wage-labor weavers with reduced status (Harris, 1990).

The nature of households and families—and therefore the labor of its members—also changed. Early in American history, children were expected to contribute their labor as soon as they could, and they were often apprenticed to other families to learn their work. When even breastfeeding could be done by a wet nurse, motherhood did not provide a central core to the meaning of homemaking (Matthaei, 1982). There was a division of labor, but roles often overlapped. At harvest time, people did not preserve gender roles at the risk of letting crops rot. The harvest season signaled not only the work of getting the crops out of the ground but also the work of preserving the food for later use. Women married to men whose work took them away from home for long periods of time (e.g., sailors and some salesmen) had to carry on all the tasks necessary to keep a household running.

The development of production and wage labor outside the household changed both women's and men's lives and the ways people thought about work. Men's lives became fragmented into specific segments defined as work, family, and leisure, each associated with particular times, places, and activities. The new structure of work literally and figuratively distanced men from their families. As it also provided more men with some opportunity to enter the labor market as individuals to "make something of themselves," American culture began to promote the idea of the "self-made man." "Under capitalism, men's striving in the economy became, literally, a seeking of their selves, a struggle to establish their own identities by economically competing with other men" (Matthaei, 1982, 105). The measure of men's success was the wealth they were able to accumulate; one important measure of masculinity became the ability to provide financially for the family. The need for a wife to seek employment began to represent the husband's failure as a man. Because of the tie between men's work and earnings and their masculinity, men came under great pressure to deny that their wives worked.

The movement of men and production out of the home did not strip either the home or women of meaning and significance; rather, it transformed them.

> When the development of industrial capitalism separated commodity production from the household, the family was freed from the function of organizing this production, and it was freed from the presence of strangers in the family. The household became a home, a private family place. Family relationships . . . began to gain a content of their own. (Matthaei, 1982, 110)

Running the private family place became a distinct role with distinct content. That role, homemaking, belonged to women.

The most important change in women's homemaking roles was not as much what specific tasks women did, although those did change; rather, it was the significance and social meaning of homemaking. Homemaking was raised to the status of a vocation embedded in an ideology historians call the "cult of domesticity." Even if homemakers were not valued in wages, that role slowly came to be seen as the one that held together the very fabric of society. Contrary to what many feminists seem to argue, taking on this new homemaking role was not a passive process. "It demanded the active self-seeking of women as homemakers, their creative and individual responses to the needs of their families" (Matthaei, 1982, 112).

Women's success at home became the measure of their femininity. "Femininity began to involve as much self-expression and choice as masculinity—but whereas a man's self-seeking meant striving to subordinate other selves, a woman's self-seeking meant striving to subordinate herself to the self-advancement of her husband and children" (Matthaei, 1982, 113). Thus, the economy became an important site in which the sex/gender system was developed and maintained, where domestic labor demanded and produced "femininity," and paid employment demanded and produced "masculinity." Women who worked outside their own homes, including especially immigrant women from around the world, African-Americans, and Native Americans, could not be considered fully feminine by the dominant society because they were engaged in labor that neither reflected nor produced femininity.

The next stage came late in the 19th century, when people began to conceive of homemaking not just as what women did, but as a vocation that could and should be professionalized. Homemaking was introduced as a subject of study at school, eventually even at universities. At the turn of the century, experts urged homemakers to apply in their homes management techniques that had been developed in business and industry. Like other jobs, homemaking should become more scientific and efficient.[4] Scientific homemaking would help women enter the 20th century, as a 1912 article from the *Ladies' Home Journal* demonstrated:

> I know that any woman who has once felt the comfort, satisfaction, and pride that come from the use of a systematic filing method will never return to the slipshod ways of the past. She will feel that it is just as commendable to have her home run in such a manner that a stranger can run it in the same grooves as herself as it is desirable to have the cogs in the wheels of a great railway sys-

tem go right on moving, even though the fingers of the president of the road cease to write his dictates. (Quoted in Matthaei, 1982, 161)

The image of homemaking had risen to new heights, but lurking behind this image was the hint of its fall. If homemaking could be done so scientifically and with such a set routine that a homemaker became a replaceable part, what did the homemaker gain from her task? If homemaking really did use the same principles as business and industry, why couldn't women go into business and industry? This question became even more pressing as Americans came to accept education, including college education, as an appropriate and even necessary part of the training of homemakers who could afford it.

Homemaking became the prototype for women's work outside the home in the larger community. Married women who had the resources to do so engaged in "social homemaking," which meant applying their concerns and skills as homemakers to the community at large. Women's clubs and organizations worked to offset the "masculine" hardness of the outside world by protecting mothers, children, consumers, and others who fell through the cracks of an industrialized society and by working to contain alcoholism and other largely male excesses that hurt the family. As Matthaei argued,

> Their feminine morality—a concern that the needs of particular individuals be filled—was a perfect complement to capitalism's masculinity. Capitalism gave all men a chance to compete; the existence of low-wage and unemployed workers was simply a part of the game. Social homemakers, progressives, and eventually the welfare state charitably "mothered" the losers; they did not try to change the game. (1982, 177)

The movement called "social homemaking" has also been called "social feminism," and it included many of the best-known suffragists. Single women increasingly took on paid jobs—such as nursing, teaching, and social work—that were regarded as consistent with domestic roles.

Homemaking has remained a mandatory occupation for adult women, including those who are also employed for pay, throughout the 20th century. Despite their protests to the contrary, most men still do little domestic labor. With the majority of women in the labor force, and economic changes making it difficult for most families to survive on only one adult income, homemaking has lost the status it once had. Many full-time homemakers now view themselves as "just housewives," devaluing the role that society regards as especially theirs. Homemaking is, in many respects, invisible. Those who do not do it do not know what women do with their days.

The Political Economy of Homemaking

What is the relationship of homemaking to the larger economy? What does homemaking look like if we examine it as a job? Given the substantial amount of labor performed in the economy through homemaking, anyone who does not understand the economic functions of homemaking has only a partial understanding of the economy as a whole.

Problems of Definition: Housework as Work.   Homemaking does not easily fit into our common definitions of work for three reasons.

1. *Pay.* If work is something people do to earn a living (i.e., *for pay*), homemaking must be something other than work. Few have argued that homemakers should be paid for their work, although divorce settlements occasionally now recognize the economic value of homemaking by taking account of a homemaker's contribution to her husband's career and earnings. Until recently, the law implied that women's household labor was required as part of the marriage contract, and therefore women could not expect direct compensation in property or salary for it.

    Some people have argued that marriage is a "business partnership," in which women's contribution is their homemaking. Recognizing the economic value and contribution of homemaking raises some tricky questions. If women perform the role of homemaker solely for financial support, marriage seems to be reduced to a purely economic relationship, and, as Emma Goldman pointed out at the turn into the 20th century, it resembles an insurance pact or prostitution (cited in Shulman, 1983). Women are supposed to do their homemaking for the love of their families and from nurturant, altruistic, even self-sacrificing natures, not out of economic interests. This argument, however, leads back to saying that women's work in the home (if work is a paid occupation) is not really work.

2. *Location.* Homemaking takes place not in the impersonal world of strangers and acquaintances in the marketplace, but in the intimate, personal, and closely bonded structure of the family. Much of the motivation for homemaking is based on the personal relations of the members of the family and not on economic interests per se; the work and the personal relationships are inseparable. Raising a child is indeed work, but it is difficult to imagine a parent who, having just helped a child walk for the first time, turns to someone else, shrugs, and says, "Well, it's a job." Even someone who argued that household labor is an economic function and therefore is work would not say that homemaking is *only* that.

3. *Work Versus Leisure.* In the 19th century, the home came to be defined as a "haven in a heartless world" (Lasch, 1977). The home is the place a person goes to rest, relax, and be "rehumanized" after leaving work; it is a site for leisure, not labor. This understanding assumes that someone else has cleaned the house and made it comfortable, done the grocery shopping, and cooked the meals; in other words, it is based on men's experiences and renders women's work invisible, as something other than work. It is also consistent with the idea that the household and the work done in it are distinct and distant from the economic system.

There is not as great a difference between women's domestic labor and other kinds of work as it might seem. Most people do not work solely to make a living;

they have many motivations for doing what they do. Many people claim they would continue to work even if they did not need money. People choose their specific work for many reasons other than financial questions. People also develop personal relationships with and loyalties to their coworkers and occupational organizations, and these relationships can provide some of the motivation for doing a task particularly well. For many people, a job is not just a job, although some are more fortunate than others in being paid for activities they truly enjoy. The fact that people do housework for motivations other than financial reward, or that housework is regarded as part of a personal relationship, does not mean that it is not work.

In any case, there is tremendous variation in how people define *work*. A survey conducted by the U.S. Census Bureau shows that women and men define *work* differently. In another study, people read a series of vignettes in which the gender of the person described was varied; it showed men were more influenced than women by the gender of the person in the vignette in determining whether that person was working. For men more than women, whether a person is male or female helps to determine whether what they are doing is work.[5] Men were also more likely to describe marginal activities as work, such as preparing for a task, or doing casual labor for a few hours. Presumably, women are used to doing lots of those kinds of tasks without being told they are working.

Economic Functions of Homemaking. Homemakers provide necessary goods and services that would otherwise have to be supplied by someone else's labor. The homemaker's job responds to changes in the wealth of a family. The wealthier a family, the more a homemaker can replace some of her labor by paying someone else to do it. This process of replacement does not necessarily mean that there is a proportionate decrease in the overall amount of work she does. A wealthier homemaker can decrease the amount of certain kinds of work she does, including physical labor, but to do this, she will probably increase her management and purchasing tasks.

Homemakers have at least four important economic roles: They (1) manage household resources, (2) create and maintain the labor force, (3) serve as an auxiliary unpaid labor force, and (4) serve as an auxiliary paid labor force. This section looks at each role a little more closely. First, women *manage household resources* and are in charge of day-to-day household consumption. They respond to the financial situation of a family, but they also help create wealth and raise the standard of living. Because homemakers are responsible for managing the day-to-day consumption habits of the family, their skills and choices determine what proportion of family income is depleted by day-to-day needs and what proportion can be saved or put to other uses. In a sense, a full-time homemaker determines the real value of her husband's income. "Labor-saving devices" help in this endeavor. They transform labor by increasing productivity, where *productivity* is defined as the amount of return for a given amount of time or effort. Labor-saving devices in the home serve the same function as new technology in industry: such devices increase the productivity of workers, who experience no change in the length of their work.

Consumption has become an increasingly important aspect of homemaking over the 20th century. Women link the family to the rest of the economy through

An early "labor-saving" vacuum cleaner.

their roles as chief consumers. Women's consumption roles are especially important in market-based economies, such as the United States, in which production
depends on advertising-stimulated consumption. Nevertheless, it is fascinating
that women's potential power as the nation's consumers is not always realized, and
women face discriminatory pricing. For example, women's haircuts are traditionally more expensive than men's (regardless of current types, and despite the fact
that licensing standards have often been higher for barbers than for hairdressers),
and clothing manufacturers and distributors charge more—even by 50%—for the
same item when it is labeled as women's wear, rather than men's wear.[6] A study of
new-car dealerships showed that dealers quoted significantly lower prices to White
males than to Black or any female test buyers who used identical bargaining strategies, despite the fact that Black males and all females are likely to be less well-off
than White male customers. This practice could occur because car salespeople
assess White men as tougher bargainers (Ayres and Siegelman, 1995).

Despite these discriminatory pricing practices, many women have recognized their potential power as consumers. At the turn into the 20th century, the consumer movement, composed largely of women, "attempted to constitute consumption as a productive vocation through which woman as homemaker could realize her individuality and social importance. It therefore demanded that women's work of consumption be professionalized and valued" (Matthaei, 1982, 165). Among the groups women organized to pursue their interests as consumers were the National Housewives League, the National Consumer's League, and the Pure Food Association. Women continue to use their economic and political power as consumers to organize or threaten boycotts of specific products and producers.

Homemakers also *reproduce the labor force* on an intergenerational and daily basis. Women have the primary responsibility for raising children and thereby contribute to the character of the future labor force. They also provide essential life services to the members of the current labor force in their families (including themselves), so they can return to work each day.

Homemakers are an *auxiliary labor force of unpaid labor.* Because the homemaker has been defined through law and custom as a helper to her husband, she often makes direct contributions to his work, depending, of course, on the nature of his job and the family's economic situation. Wives of farmers, clergymen, politicians, businessmen, and writers ("I'd like to thank my wife" for typing, editorial comments, etc.) often assist in their husbands' work. Whenever entertaining clients, business colleagues, or parishioners at home is considered part of the job, homemakers have traditionally contributed the bulk of that work or, if they are wealthy enough, its management.

Homemakers also provide the economy with vital labor that would otherwise have to be paid. Communities have long depended on women's volunteer labor for providing many services, especially to the elderly, poor, and ill. As Nona Glazer (1993) has pointed out, however, in the recent era of "downsizing," both public and private businesses and industries have saved money by shifting some work to consumers, especially women. In fact, a number of forces have come together to cause this to happen. First, the reinvigoration of consumer movements and demands in the 1960s and 1970s led to a greater willingness for consumers to become involved in the provisions of goods and services to themselves, especially in cases in which a little added labor on the part of the consumer—for example, in self-service filling stations or in unprepared foods—could lead to apparent savings on their part. Second, there has been a widespread feeling on the part of the public that the provision of goods and services had become *too* commercial, impersonal, mass produced, and distant to the family. Thus, for example, supermarkets caught on to the profit they could earn by presenting bulk food, such as bins of rice, beans, and herbs, instead of offering only prepackaged food. Third, in the 1990s, the mass media became more filled with stories about families that felt guilty or should have felt guilty about using public services such as child-care centers, homes for the elderly, poverty benefits, and other social services, rather than providing for themselves. Finally, as the economy generally weakened, families themselves sought ways of saving money, often by replacing purchased goods and services with their own labor.

All of these trends tended to lead to a replacement of paid labor in the market with women's unpaid domestic labor. Glazer investigated case studies of health care (especially the move toward home health care) and retailing. As she concluded, "The postindustrial economy has not curtailed service work for the public. Instead, it has depended on the free labor of women as members of households" (1993, 219). This analysis underscores the importance of incorporating the many different forms of labor into analysis at the same time, especially in studies of women and the economy. "I hope that my analysis shows the boundary between *work* in the so-called private sphere and the so-called public sphere is nonexistent or, at most, highly permeable and that the relationship between unpaid and paid work is one of interdependence and reciprocal influence" (1993, 205; emphasis in original).

Homemakers also serve as an *auxiliary labor force of paid workers*. Many businesses and industries have relied on a flexible workforce of homemakers who are willing and able to do paid labor, often in their own homes. The auxiliary labor force of homemakers can be called into action and discarded, as it suits the needs of companies. These jobs have been especially important in families that need the woman's income but either cannot spare her for a regular outside job or consider it improper to do so. Indeed, women's paid work at home can help the family preserve the impression that the husband does not depend on his wife's labor. Women have long found ways to earn incomes without appearing to abandon their feminine, home-based roles. In the 19th century, many women rented spare rooms to boarders. Farmwomen still earn their "chicken and egg" money, although they participate in many more ways than this (Gasson, 1992). Other women take in sewing or do babysitting in their homes.

In the 1980s, the spread of home computers and other developments in information-processing technology gave the "putting out" system (now often labeled "outsourcing") new life as a means of satisfying businesses' clerical needs with home workers. Other businesses using this system extensively are textile and electronics manufacturers because it allows employers to avoid many of the costs associated with labor: relatively expensive union or salaried employees; overhead expenses such as providing workers with utilities, furniture, equipment, and a place to work; employee benefits; and the necessity of using proper procedures for hiring, training, and firing employees. Many companies, in fact, depend on the image of the homemaker as their public face for conducting business. Many have done this literally in their advertising, by employing models *posing* as homemakers to sell their products; perhaps the most interesting case is Betty Crocker, whose face has literally changed over the years as cultural images of the ideal homemaker have changed.[7] Companies such as Tupperware and Avon, which depend on telephone canvassing and sales or at-home and door-to-door sales, also rely on homemakers for their workforces.

One company, Welcome Wagon, depends not just on "homemakers" for their sales staff, but also on customers' belief that these people are just homemakers, volunteering to be nice to new neighbors. In fact, Welcome Wagon representatives serve as points of contact between local businesses and families, and they can earn about $40,000 in commissions through their apparent altruism. The vice president of the large corporation that now owns Welcome Wagon said, "People don't think it is a company. We're playing on the strength of that nonthreatening whole-someness."[8] A historian has argued that in the early 20th century, the largest telephone company, American Telephone & Telegraph Company (AT&T), could have saved money by replacing telephone operators with automatic switching devices many years before they did so, but they put off making the change because AT&T managers saw women operators as crucial to their competitive strategy (Lipartito, 1994). These examples offer added evidence that there is not a radical unbreachable divide between public and private, the family and the market.

This auxiliary labor force of women can substitute for men, especially their husbands, when necessary. Since colonial times, widowhood has allowed women to perform work generally considered unfit for women in the abstract. Julie Matthaei has correctly noted that

> such women were not destroying the sexual division of labor, or even challenging it; as widows, daughters, or sisters, they were fulfilling their womanly obligation of replacing an absent or deceased male family member at the helm of a family business. In such cases it was within their duties as women to enter into men's work, and their actions were understood as such. (1982, 191–192)

This same framework may be used to understand women's war work. Sometimes, women explicitly substituted for their absent husbands. During World War II, automobile companies that had turned to war production sometimes deliberately hired the wives of men who had worked in the same plant before going off to war. It then seemed natural to the companies to fire these women at the end of the war, in favor of the returning GIs (Milkman, 1982). Historically, women's work was often regarded as auxiliary because of a gender identity that required men but not women to support their families.

Homemakers' role as an auxiliary labor force has limits, however. Traditional gender ideology, especially among White people, resisted having a woman replace an involuntarily unemployed husband in the labor force or entering the labor force because the husband's income was insufficient to meet the family's basic needs. Women could work as auxiliaries but not as breadwinners because that would threaten both the wife's sense of femininity and her husband's sense of masculinity. Until the last quarter of the 20th century, an employed wife was still a sign of failure for most men. Indeed, earlier in the 20th century, before the advent of child-labor laws, children (especially daughters) in poor families (especially White families) were often pulled out of schools and sent to work instead of the adult woman. Black families were less likely to do this than White families because female employment was less stigmatized for them, and they were especially eager to gain more education for their children, to give their children more life chances.

Attitudes toward the employment of wives have changed dramatically, especially since the majority of women entered the labor force. Nevertheless, many people continue to regard wives' income as supplementary to their husbands'. Certainly, many people are uncomfortable with the idea of a woman earning more money than her husband. Men's sense of masculinity still tends to be tied in part

TABLE 13-1

Attitudes Toward the Employment of Married Women, 1938–1986

Proportion approving of a married woman earning money in
business or industry if she has a husband capable of supporting her:

Year	Women (% approving)	Men (% approving)	Married Women in Labor Force (%)
1938	25	19	15[a]
1972	66	62	42
1975	71	69	45
1982	75	73	52
1986	76	78	55

[a] This figure is from 1940.
Source: Hesse (1979, 53), Simon and Landis (1989, 270), and U.S. Bureau
of the Census (1989, 385).

to their roles as breadwinners. Nonetheless, as each generation has faced an economic system in which two incomes are increasingly required to maintain desired
standards of living, men's expectations about breadwinning are responding to economic reality and changing (Wilkie, 1993).

Making a Living Versus Making a Home: Choices

Even as recently as 1985, although 57% of women and 50% of men thought that
the most satisfying and interesting marriage would be one in which the husband
and wife share responsibilities, such as housekeeping and child care, 37% of
women and 43% of men thought that the most interesting and satisfying marriage
would be a traditional one in which the husband assumes responsibility for providing for the family and the wife runs the house and takes care of children
(Simon and Landis, 1989). Most married women are still responsible for housework, regardless of their employment status, suggesting that they have more
choice over whether to seek employment than whether to do housework. Moreover, women of some classes and races have had little choice about paid employment, other than domestic service—that is, to do housework, but for pay. Even if
there has been less change than might be expected in attitudes toward the division of domestic labor, the majority of Americans believe that married women
should be able to work for wages. Yet as Table 13-1 shows, a sizable minority still
disapproved until recently.

Why have some women sought employment? Why have others been homemakers? This section probes these questions by (a) taking a historical perspective
to see when women as a group have moved in and out of the labor force, and (b)
viewing women's life cycles and personal situations to see patterns of employment
in women's individual life histories.

The proportion of women who are employed rose dramatically throughout the 20th century, as Table 13-1 shows. At the same time, because of changes in education and retirement patterns, the proportion of men who were employed declined. As a result, women now constitute more than 40% of the civilian labor force, and 56% of women are employed. Why did patterns of women's labor-force participation change over time?

Economist Claudia Goldin has pointed out that while people tend to pay attention to the rising female employment rate of the 20th century, it is also important to note the falling rate in the 19th century, when work other than unpaid family domestic labor came to be discouraged and ignored (Goldin, 1990). By the turn into the 20th century, relatively few women entered the labor market. Even when they were employed, they tended toward work consistent with familial and gender norms. This trend helped create the race difference in women's employment, which later decreased as employment became less stigmatized among whites. At the beginning of the 20th century, the average female worker in the United States was young, unmarried, and from a working-class family. Most ended their employment careers by their early 20s, when they married.

The trade-off between employment and marriage is well illustrated by the lives of the growing population of college-educated women who entered professions at the beginning of the century. Relatively few of them married; marriage would have ended their careers. This trade-off was enforced by employers, who would not hire married women or would fire female employees who married. A study of female college graduates done in 1900 showed that by the age of 50 years, only about half had married (Matthaei, 1982, 181).

The ideology that barred married women, especially middle-class White women, from employment began to fray with the growth of jobs that seemed compatible with women's roles as social homemakers. As the nation needed more nurses, teachers, and social workers, women filled these jobs, partly because these occupations were regarded as incompatible with masculinity. The invention of the typewriter and the telephone created other jobs defined as feminine. The position of secretary, once an entry-level male job in business, was transformed into the more familiar dead-end female job of today. Many factory owners favored using a labor force of compliant, nonunionized females who, their stereotypes told them, would be good at light, repetitive work requiring dexterity.

The major boosts to female employment came in the middle of the 20th century. By 1940, the majority of households had electricity, refrigerators, stoves, washing machines, and automobiles, and women could make time for employment. During World War II, employers, the government, and the mass media urged women to join the labor force. Female employment rose dramatically; in the auto industry, for example, it rose by 600% (Milkman, 1982).

Although women were later pushed out of their war work, the expansion of the female labor force picked up steam again in the 1950s and 1960s for various reasons:

1. Many women never lost their taste for the independence of employment, even if they left the workforce temporarily to have children.

2. After the war, both males and females began to stay in school longer, providing women with greater motivation and qualification for employment.

3. The economy grew tremendously for the three decades following World War II and could accommodate—indeed it demanded—massive growth in the labor force. Some of this expansion was very specifically in the female sectors of the job market. The need for clerical and sales workers ballooned. As baby-boom babies reached school age in the 1950s and early 1960s, there was an even greater need for teachers. The increased wealth of the time sparked the growth of service industries such as restaurants, which call for female labor. The expansion of the welfare state and the growth of the public sector created other jobs, such as clerical work, nursing, and teaching, which also called for women. Millions of women entered the labor market without ever competing directly with men.

Other social and policy changes also affected women's entry into the labor market: The rising divorce rate caused more women to find themselves in need of jobs. Women's increased control over reproduction through birth control also afforded them more choice and ability to plan when and whether to have children. The new enforcement of antidiscrimination legislation of the 1960s and the beginning of its real enforcement in the 1970s also gave women greater employment opportunities.

The ideology barring wives and mothers from seeking employment weakened throughout the last quarter of the 20th century. Evidence for change appears not simply in public-opinion polls but also in people's behavior. In 1970, half of the mothers of 12-year-olds were in the workforce, and by 1975, half the mothers of 7-year-olds had joined them. In 1980, half the mothers of 3-year-olds were in the labor force, and by 1983, half the mothers of 2-year-olds were there, too (Waldman, 1983). In 1988, half the mothers of 1-year-olds were in the labor force (U.S. Bureau of the Census, 1989). Now, half the mothers of babies under 1 year old are employed.[9] The "tipping point," as Jessie Bernard (1975) put it, was finally reached: Regardless of marital or maternal status, more women enter the labor force than stay out of it.

These patterns also point to another change in women's work habits. Until recently, most employed women stayed in the labor force for a relatively short period of their lives, which was one of the excuses employers used for excluding women from job categories for which they desired a stable, permanent workforce. This excuse is no longer valid. Women now have fewer children; they drop out of the labor force for only short periods, if at all (and many men now also demand the right to take leave from the labor force to care for children); and they seek to remain employed for most of their adult lives. Although many mothers seek part-time work when their children are young, the majority are employed full-time.

Will these trends persist in the future? To answer this question, we must make some educated guesses about the future of the forces that affect women's employment. Surely, women's levels of education will not decrease relative to men's. Likewise, although fertility rates fluctuate over time, unless abortion becomes illegal—still a possibility—women will probably not lose their current control over reproduction. Barring a major war that humanity manages to survive, we have little reason to expect a dramatic rise in birthrates. It is unlikely that we will return to a time when women expect to marry at a young age and be supported by their husbands for the rest of their lives. Men will probably decreasingly tie their senses of masculinity to their abilities to be the sole financial supporters of their families. Women increasingly seem to feel they need excuses to stay *out* of the labor force rather than to stay *in* it.

Labor-force participation of women may be most affected by the gender division of labor in the family and the balance of burdens women face. Will women continue to accept a double burden? Will men come to accept not just women's integration into the workforce but also their own responsibilities in the family? Women's employment decisions are likely to depend in part on whether they can keep their jobs and seniority through the maternity period and on the availability of affordable child care. This section explores some of the factors that facilitate or inhibit achieving this balance while examining women's employment patterns through the life course. Given the current average birthrate of two closely spaced children per woman, and the view that women do not need to be home past their children's infancy, the average woman will probably continue to leave the workforce for only a tiny fraction of the 50 years or more between the time she leaves school and the time she retires.

A final influence on the future of women's employment rates is the structure of the job market and the gender division of labor in the workforce. Although we may see economic growth again, massive economic expansion like that experienced from about the end of World War II to 1973 seems unlikely. As long as the job market remains relatively gender segregated, knowing what will happen to women's employment requires knowing *which* sectors of the market are likely to expand or contract. At one point in the 1970s, for example, men's jobs were particularly hard hit by layoffs in the construction and automobile industries. Later, cutbacks in social services and new developments in information technology caused women's jobs to suffer.

Consider the example of AT&T. In 1971, the Equal Employment Opportunity Commission (EEOC) launched an investigation of sex discrimination at AT&T and filed suit against the company after concluding that it was "the largest discriminator against women in the United States." When AT&T was ordered to draw up affirmative-action goals for future hiring and promotion of women, it drew up a document targeting a decline in the number of women to be hired in the future. The reason: Expected technological changes would eliminate the jobs of thousands of women. Because the company could not reasonably expect to hire a compensating number of women in other job categories, there was nothing the government could do (Hacker, 1979).

Like men, many women who seek work do not find it. Unemployment rates have generally been higher for women than for men, and economists suspect that unemployment figures are underestimated even more for women than for men. After a period of unemployment, men and women often become "discouraged workers"—that is, people who are so pessimistic about their job prospects that they no longer try to find work. At that point, many women probably begin to call themselves "homemakers" and are therefore classified as such in government figures, even though they would rather be employed. This label, then, hides their real employment status.

Women's Employment Experiences Through Life

Having looked at the historical trends in women's employment, we now examine the situation women face today. How can we explain women's participation in the labor force? Because work patterns are so shaped by individuals' life courses, from childhood through old age, we organize our investigation that way.

Childhood and Adolescence. Attitudes and beliefs that underlie people's economic choices develop during childhood. Girls now grow up knowing they will be employed, and most boys also know that employment is a part of women's lives. A 1994 survey of 13- to 17-year-olds found that 86% of the girls thought they would work outside the home when they got married, while 7% said they would stay home. In contrast, 58% of the boys thought their wives would work outside the home, 19% said their wives would stay home, and 19% said they could not predict the future.[10] These data reveal that young people—boys especially—do not regard men's and women's employment the same way. For another example, a 1996 survey of entering college students found that 19% of women and 31% of men thought that "married women's activities are best confined to home and family."[11]

Despite young women's assumption that they will be employed, their expectations still reflect that they are born of a society structured by gender. Girls' career planning takes account of marriage and family more than boys' does, and girls plan to marry and have children younger than boys do (Flanagan, 1993; Machung, 1989). Families' treatment of girls' preparation also seems more contingent; families that face constraining financial situations are less likely to invest in a daughter's education than in a son's (Flanagan, 1993).

Anne Machung's (1989) study of a race-diverse group of college seniors found that the men expected to help out at home when they got married, where "helping out" fell far short of full sharing and equality. When probed further, the men defined their notion of an equal situation as one in which the partners respect each other and the women take more responsibility at home. The women defined equality differently; as one African-American woman put it, "I'll be damned if I do a double shift" (Machung, 1989, 45).

Beginning in 1993, the Ms. Foundation organized a nationwide campaign to encourage young women to explore their options in the labor market by running "Take Our Daughters to Work Day" each spring. A large proportion of companies across the country participate, but the event has sparked annual controversy, largely because of the exclusion of boys. Some people have made a feminist case for including boys, suggesting that it is good for all children to think about their occupational futures, and it is wise to avoid having boys resent being excluded. In addition, it might be especially important for boys to be taken to work with their mothers so they become less likely to think about the workplace as male. Nevertheless, when a representative from the Ms. Foundation was asked about the statement of a major corporative executive, who said his company would not discriminate on the basis of gender and have a girls-only event, she responded, "It bothers me when companies where all the high officers are men say they're making it Take Our Children Day because they don't want to discriminate against boys. Executives with glass ceilings shouldn't throw stones."[12]

Girls and boys indeed grow up with many of the same attitudes toward work. A study of high school students in 1976 and 1991 showed that young men and women attached the same importance to the extrinsic or external rewards of work, such as earning money or having influence over others. They also attached the same importance to some intrinsic rewards, such as being able to make decisions on the job and finding challenging work. But there are differences. Girls attached more importance to other intrinsic, altruistic, and social aspects of their work and they were less concerned than boys about leisure-related aspects (Marini, Fan, and Finley, 1996). These gender differences depend on culture, however. A study of employment attitudes in Hungary, Israel, and the Netherlands found that men tended to rank influence, independence, responsibility, and pay as more important to them than women did (Elizur, 1994). A cross-national study of university students in 20 countries found that men placed a higher value on competitiveness and valuation of money (Lynn, 1993).

These attitudes, and the planning they entail, make a difference for later work experiences. Young women planning to be employed throughout their adulthood make different choices about investing time, energy, and money in training, and they choose their work differently than women who plan to work sporadically. They also respond to the market forces they are likely to face. One study found that high school girls with high aspirations and similar personalities emphasizing curiosity and interest in subjects at school made different career-path choices, depending on their social class: Girls with higher-class backgrounds emphasized academic achievement, which could ultimately lead to higher-status jobs; and girls of lower-class backgrounds made more investment in work and occupational training (Poole, Langan-Fox, and Omodei, 1990). The latter choice is also more likely to lead to gender-stereotyped work. In general, however, women who maintain consistent plans to be employed from their adolescence on tend to have higher wages by their mid-30s than women who had had at least some plans to be homemakers (Shaw and Shapiro, 1987).

Paid work experience usually begins for both girls and boys before they finish their schooling. Although there is little available research on patterns of work among children, it appears that boys tend to begin paid work earlier and to work longer hours than girls (Greenberger and Steinberg, 1983). Young unmarried men and women enter the labor force at roughly similar rates.

Early and Middle Adulthood. For most men and women, the end of education signals the real beginning of adult labor-market participation, and that participation is highly structured by the amount of education a worker has received, perhaps even more for women than for men, as Table 13-2 shows. While slightly under half of women with less than a high school education are employed, almost three fourths of men with similar education are employed; therefore, this education group has the largest gender difference in employment. Among women with

TABLE 13-2
Labor Force Participation, 1995

	Women	Men	Women–Men
Race			
African-American	60	69	−9
Hispanic	53	79	−26
White	59	76	−17
Education			
< High school	47	72	−25
High school graduate	69	87	−18
Some college	77	90	−13
College graduate	83	94	−11
Age			
16–19	52	55	−3
20–24	70	83	−13
25–34	75	93	−18
35–44	77	92	−15
45–54	74	89	−15
55–64	49	66	−17
65+	9	17	−8
Marital Status			
Single	67	74	−7
Married	61	78	−17
Age of Children			
< 1 yr. old	59	NA	
2 yrs.	67	NA	
3–5 yrs.	67	NA	
6–13 yrs.	75	NA	
14–17 yrs.	80	NA	
No children < 18	81	NA	

Note: NA = not available.

Source: U.S. Bureau of the Census (1997, 393, 395, 396, 399).

some college education, and especially among college graduates, the vast majority of women are employed.

Discussing the life-course factors related to women's employment inevitably raises questions about the relationship between family and work lives and commitments. Marriage slightly depresses women's employment rates, especially among less educated people, although not nearly as much as was once true. In fact, some women are pushed *into* the labor market by marriage. These women (who might otherwise have continued their education or training) take low-paid, low-status, and usually gender-typed jobs while their husbands increase their earning potential. Relatively few husbands do the same for their wives. Given the continuing centrality of men's work, when a woman's husband disapproves of female employment, she is likely to do volunteer work instead of paid work (Schram and Dunsing, 1981). Nonetheless, most married women—61% in 1995—are in the labor force. In only 19% of married couple families in 1996 was the husband the sole breadwinner.

Some women, especially those who marry young, delay their entry into the labor force until after they have had children. They face some special problems in obtaining jobs. Of course, some former homemakers seek employment because of an emergency—they find themselves in need of a job suddenly and unexpectedly because of divorce or widowhood. They then have little opportunity for undertaking necessary training.

A significant portion of the female unemployment rate consists of older women trying to enter or reenter the labor market. The biggest problem is that employers expect good job candidates to follow the male pattern of beginning careers relatively young, and they are often reluctant to take on people who are over 30 years old, much less over 40. Some employers argue that it is not worthwhile to invest in "late starters" who will have relatively short careers. Thus, many women have been ruled out of "male" occupations, not because of their gender but because of their age.

Another problem "late entry" women face is the lack of "prior relevant experience" that employers will consider seriously. Most employers expect to see a listing of the applicant's prior work experience. The skills and experiences women have gained through homemaking or volunteer work usually do not count, even if the volunteer work can amount to a nearly full-time job, with considerable responsibility. Employers are now being urged to look at these experiences more seriously and carefully. Many communities have programs designed to help former homemakers entering the labor market. Also, the Age Discrimination Act of 1967, which bars discrimination against people between 40 and 70 years old, provides some relief for women but does not cover all the problems.

Although many women leave the labor force temporarily when they have children, they do so for a shorter time period than used to be the case. For most women, the main task of early and middle adulthood is balancing the demands and commitments of work and of family, not to mention self. Chapter 6 has already discussed health implications of this balancing act, especially the creation of stress.

Women find many different ways of coping. Some seek jobs that appear to afford more time flexibility, including not just part-time work, but also work that can be flexibly scheduled or that can be done at home. Of course, the degree of difficulty also depends on what commitments and obligations a woman has at home—for example, how much of the domestic labor she is expected to undertake. A husband's participation in housework and child care is partly determined by how many hours his wife works, but it is also affected by other factors less directly related to who is how busy: the degree to which the husband has feminist attitudes, the relative salaries of the husband and wife, the occupational prestige of the wife, and the general dynamics of the relationship between the husband and wife (Deutsch, Lussier, and Servis, 1993). A study of men and women in six different living circumstances (never married and living with parents, never married and living independently, cohabiting, married, divorced, and widowed) found that women spend more time doing housework in every situation, but the gender gap is widest among married people. Factors such as the number of children at home or the number of hours the wife worked have more impact on women's time spent at housework than on men's. Gender roles in housework are so clear (and trump generational effects) that having an adult son living at home increases women's housework noticeably, but having an adult daughter living at home decreases it (South and Spitze, 1994).

The balancing act may have become more difficult in important ways; as economist Juliet Schor has written, the productivity demands on American workers has increased so much during the last quarter of the 20th century that it is hard to extract the flexibility out of work life to balance family demands unless there are explicit policies facilitating this flexibility (Schor, 1992). The policies and practices that may assist this balance are as follows:

1. *Flextime,* policies that allow workers to arrange the hours they work in a flexible way to accommodate other time commitments—This might involve working unusual hours or varying the times at which one works.

2. *Parental leave*—As of 1993, companies with 50 or more employees must allow employees to take up to 12 weeks of unpaid leave for birth or adoption or to care for seriously ill family members.[13] In fact, many companies offered at least that level already,[14] and the number that offer more generous benefits than the law requires has expanded. Despite this law, the United States still falls far behind what has been offered in most other industrialized countries. For example, in Italy, women are required to take off from work the last 2 months of pregnancy and the first 3 months after the birth, but they receive full pay (80% paid by the state), and they can take another 6 months off at 30% salary, paid by the state. Although many other countries have trimmed some of these policies somewhat because of economic pressures, they still offer more than the United States requires.[15] Nevertheless, in the 1990s, nearly half of all U.S. employed women who had children took maternity leave. College-educated mothers and women over age 30 were more likely to take advantage of maternity leave, probably partly because they knew more about the policy, and partly because their job situations made it more possible.[16]

3. *Home work*—Some employers have become more flexible about allowing parts of a job to be done off the premises. The development of electronic mail and the World Wide Web, among other technological changes, has made this more possible since the mid-1990s.

4. *Dependent care*—Although the United States does not provide publicly funded child care to the degree that, for example, France has for a long time, many companies provide child-care benefits or even have facilities on site. Some companies are now also offering help with care for elderly parents.

5. *Women's networks at work*—Social networks are crucial to relieving stress, and they are especially important for women and other social groups who are entering into new positions, as women in nontraditional jobs are. Mechanisms to facilitate social support may be especially important for minority women, such as African-Americans, who may be especially likely to lack social supports *outside* of work from people who are familiar with what they are facing at work

(Bailey, Wolfe, and Wolfe, 1996). Women in jobs in which they are recent entrants often form groups to assist each other to break down their isolation, but also to work on developing their own ways of doing the job.[17]

In fact, both men and women make career trade-offs now for their families. A study of 6,000 employees of the Du Pont Company in professional and manufacturing jobs found that roughly the same number of women and men told their bosses they were not available for relocation or had turned down a promotion. In the professional group, 32% of women and 19% of men said they had told their bosses they would not take a job that required extensive travel, and in the manufacturing group, 45% of women and 39% of men had refused to work overtime. Du Pont, like many other companies, has found that it makes good business sense to provide benefits that facilitate combining family and work. The Du Pont study found that employees who had used the company's programs designed to help out were especially likely to say they would "go the extra mile" for the company.[18] As a partner in the investment firm of Goldman, Sachs & Company said, "If people have trouble finding child care, they will be absent, late, or worrying about their arrangements. If we can alleviate that pressure, people will be more effective."[19]

Despite the increasing availability of these resources, and the increasing number of workers who are using them, sociologist Arlie Russell Hochschild shocked readers with her study of worker attitudes and behavior. Her study revealed that not only do large numbers of workers not take advantage of these benefits, but also they are actively participating in the "overworking" practices Juliet Schor (1992) described. Hochschild's research on workers at a major corporation showed that many people are working longer hours because they feel more "at home" at work than at home, and feel more "at work" at home than at work (Hochschild, 1997).

Overall, the majority of women of every category except the least educated are now in the labor force. As Table 13-2 shows, the *gap* between women and men depends on their social situation. For example, the labor-force participation rates of men and women are closest among African-Americans and farthest apart among Latinos. The gap is also greatest among the least educated, among married people, and among those in the prime childbearing ages of 25–34 years.

Women's life-course experience of employment has changed historically. Table 13-3 shows the proportion of married men and women of four different age groups in the labor force from 1960 to 1995. As would be expected, the gap between men and women of all age groups was extremely large in 1960 and has been narrowing ever since. This table shows one important pattern that is not very related to gender: The stagnation of the economy since the late 1970s means that 45- to 64-year-olds have been increasingly disadvantaged in the labor market. Among women, the growth of employment in the main childbearing ages has not kept up with growth in employment among 35- to 44-year-olds, but the increase has nevertheless been impressive.

Later Adulthood. As more women enter and stay in the labor force, more also face the experience of retirement. It is incorrect to assume that women fit right back into the home after retirement without any difficulty. A woman who has been

TABLE 13-3
Labor Force Participation of Married Men and Women
by Age, 1960–1995

	Age			
	20–24	*25–34*	*35–44*	*45–64*
1960				
Men	97	99	99	94
Women	32	29	37	36
1970				
Men	95	98	98	91
Women	48	39	47	44
1975				
Men	95	97	97	87
Women	57	48	52	44
1980				
Men	97	98	97	84
Women	61	59	62	47
1985				
Men	96	97	97	82
Women	66	66	68	49
1990				
Men	96	97	97	83
Women	66	70	74	57
1995				
Men	95	96	95	82
Women	65	72	76	63

Note: Entries show the percentage of men and women of each age group in each year who were in the workforce.

Source: U.S. Bureau of the Census (1997, 399).

employed for much of her adult life has lived a very different life from that of a full-time homemaker. The retiree may have done most of the housework as she went along, but becoming a homemaker means taking on a new role. Like retired men, women change their daily lives dramatically when they no longer spend their days on the job. Because of differences in male and female life expectancy, as well as in divorce and remarriage rates, a woman who retires is considerably more likely than a man to go home to an empty house. In 1990, 34% of women 65 to 74 years old lived alone, compared with 13% of men of a similar age; for people over 75 years old, the figures rise to 53% of women and 21% of men (U.S. Bureau of the Census, 1992, 51). A retired woman is not the same as an older homemaker.

Women's retirement experiences are somewhat different from men's. Men are more likely than women to have done financial planning (Kroeger, 1982). Only 13% of women, compared with 33% of men, have private pensions (including only 10% of African-American women and 8% of Hispanic women). This results in an increasing poverty gap between men and women as they age.[20] On the other hand, retiring women tend to draw on larger support networks of people who are close to them. Retired women also tend to belong to a relatively large number of organizations through which they can remain active and socialize with people. They are thus also more active than homemakers of their own age (Depner and Ingersoll, 1982; Keith, 1982).

No matter what aspect of women's work life is being considered, it is necessary to remember why women seek employment in the first place. Like men, women seek employment to support themselves and, if they have them, their families. They work because they must. They cannot always arrange their work and family roles as they wish; they often find roadblocks in their private lives and in the world around them. The process of making choices is difficult, and unfortunately, in the process of coming to grips with the choices they have made, women sometimes denigrate the choices of other women. Some employed women belittle those choosing the domestic route; some who base themselves in the family decry the selfishness of women in the workforce. These conflicts are encouraged in part by a social and economic structure that militates against combined roles (Gerson, 1985).

Gender Divisions of Labor in Employment

Thus far, we have discussed whether and under what circumstances women work for pay. We now turn to the substance of their work. We begin with a theoretical and historical look at the definitions of women's and men's work. Although there has been tremendous change in women's employment *rates* over the past century, there has not been equivalent change in the *kinds* of work women and men do. In this discussion, we turn first to *horizontal segregation,* the separation of women and men into different job categories, and then to *vertical segregation,* their differentiation into higher and lower positions. We then consider major developments in antidiscrimination law and policy since the 1960s designed to eliminate discrimination based on these cultural understandings of women's and men's work. Finally, we look at the social and social-psychological dynamics of gender-based discrimination in the workplace, to see how it occurs and, especially, why it persists despite the development of powerful antidiscrimination law.

What Is the Difference Between Women's and Men's Work? Horizontal Segregation

When women first moved into the labor market, they had few skills to take with them other than the homemaking skills they had been taught since childhood. What was called "women's work," therefore, had the dual advantage of being at least somewhat familiar and seeming gender appropriate; it allowed women to work for pay without too radically violating norms of femininity. Of course, employers would usually hire women only for work that required what they saw as women's natural skills. Much of this "women's work" has been labeled "pink-collar" work, which is an obvious extension of women's roles at home, particularly work involving service to other people (Howe, 1978).

The history of clerical work is a good example of how the content and structure of jobs are related to their gender composition and how changes in the structure of the economy affect women's work and work opportunities. Until the late 19th century, clerical work was the bottom rung of the male business ladder. In 1870, 3 years before the invention of the typewriter, women constituted about 2% of America's clerical workers. By 1890, they were about 17%; by 1900, they were 27%; and by 1910, they were 36% of U.S. clerical workers. The feminization of clerical work occurred by mid-20th century; women were 45% of clerical workers in 1920, and 52% in 1930. By 1970, three quarters of all clerical workers were women, and in 1980, over 80% were women. From 1950 on, secretarial work employed more women than any other single job (Glenn and Feldberg, 1989, 288).

Why did employers begin to prefer women for clerical work? As businesses began to grow in size and complexity, employers saw a need for maintaining larger, more specialized staffs. One way to achieve this was to separate the increasingly important but routine tasks of clerical work from those of lower-level managers. After some initial resistance, they began to see women as well suited to these now dead-end clerical jobs for various reasons, including the following: (1) Women have constituted a large pool of literate workers with few job opportunities, who could be hired cheaply; (2) it seemed natural that women would willingly accept jobs that did not lead to higher positions, which were left for men; and (3) after a promotion campaign by early manufacturers of typewriters, using women to demonstrate their use, typewriting came to be seen as a woman's job.

Why did women flock to clerical work? The most obvious reason is that the jobs were available and expanding, and they fit very comfortably within the definition of feminine work. Glenn and Feldberg (1989) have also shown that clerical work offered women advantages over blue-collar work. The work itself and the work environment are relatively clean, the work involves little physical exertion, and it offers women more opportunities to use their education and literacy. Clerical workers were traditionally more likely than blue-collar workers to be paid a fixed and secure salary, rather than hourly and fluctuating wages; their hours were more regular; and they had greater job security and greater opportunities for advancement. Further, clerical jobs usually involved working with people.

Clerical work has undergone more changes over time, including three in particular: (1) The more feminized the job has become, the greater the gap between women's clerical salaries and men's blue-collar salaries, also caused by the greater unionization of male blue-collar work. (2) Secretaries have come to be seen as personal assistants to the boss. In the conventional situation, many female secretaries faced with male bosses were even regarded as the "office wife," expected to perform a wide range of personal services for him, such as making coffee, picking up the boss's laundry, or buying presents for his wife. (3) As the need for clerical labor has increased and having a personal secretary has increasingly become the prerogative only of high-ranking people, secretarial work has become more specialized, routine, and unskilled (see Davies, 1983).

Many women have broken out of female job classifications throughout women's employment history, even before integration of the labor market expanded at the end of the 20th century. One example is the women who have taken over their absent or deceased husbands' work. Women also took over men's work while the men were away at war. "Rosie the Riveter," the symbolic representation of women who worked in heavy industry during World War II, is often cited, but this image is misleading. Ruth Milkman concluded from her study of women in the automobile industry that "Rosie the Riveter did a 'man's job,' but more often than not she worked in a predominantly female department or job classification" (Milkman, 1982, 338). Both the automobile industry and the United Auto Workers (UAW), a generally progressive union, fought against integrating women into the plants. The industry preferred to import male workers from the South until the War Production Board forced them to stop causing migration and start hiring women. In 1943, women were 25% of the automobile industry's workers. Following World War II, automobile companies used every means at their disposal to push women out, and within a year of the end of the war, women constituted only 8% of the automobile company workforce. The women did not go quietly, but they did go, often to other jobs (Gabin, 1982).

Since the late 1970s, women have entered new kinds of jobs, although the degree of change should not be overestimated. First, especially in the professions, women had to regain the ground they had lost earlier. The proportion of professors, doctors, and lawyers who are women, for example, fell after 1930 and returned to the 1930 level only around 1970. In addition, women's entry into new job classifications does not always signal growth in equality with men. Apparent progress may be an illusion. Many of these jobs are either (a) in industries that have undergone substantial growth and are in need of a new labor force, or (b) in industries that are in decline, which men are abandoning. Some of the professions in which women have most increased their proportions are those that have become more routine, are relatively low paying, and are undergoing a loss of power and status (Carter and Carter, 1981). In some cases, such as the traditionally male steel industry, women made gains only to see some progress lost during a recession in which layoffs took place in order of seniority, thus hurting women's new jobs especially (Deaux and Ullman, 1983).

There has been remarkable continuity in the types of jobs women have held during the 20th century. Table 13-4 lists the 10 jobs employing the largest number of women for each decade from 1890 to 1990. Jobs shift position on the list from decade to decade, but overall, the lists look remarkably similar year after year. Women clean, cook and serve food, sew, teach, and do clerical and sales work; in other words, much of the work women do for pay is the same they are expected to do as wives and mothers at home. When moving farther down the list, past the top 10 jobs in 1990, many of the same occupations (or related work) continue to appear, similar to those on earlier lists: The jobs that held 11th through 15th place in 1990 were sewing-machine operators, assemblers, cooks, typists, and child-care workers.

TABLE 13-4
The Ten Largest Occupations of Women, 1890–1990

1890	1900	1910	1920	1930	1940
Servants	Servants	Other servants	Other servants	Other servants	Servants (private family)
Agricultural laborers	Farm laborers (family members)	Farm laborers (home farm)	Teachers (school)	Teachers (school)	Stenographers, typists, and secretaries
Dressmakers	Dressmakers	Laundresses (not in laundry)	Farm laborers (home farm)	Stenographers and typists	Teachers (n.e.c.)
Teachers	Teachers	Teachers (school)	Stenographers and typists	Other clerks (except in stores)	Clerical and kindred workers (n.e.c.)
Farmers, planters, and overseers	Laundry work (hand)	Dressmakers and seamstresses (not in factory)	Other clerks (except in stores)	Saleswomen	Saleswomen (n.e.c.)
Laundresses	Farmers and planters	Farm laborers (working out)	Laundresses (not in laundy)	Farm laborers (unpaid family workers)	Operators and kindred workers, apparel and accessories
Seamstresses	Farm and plantation laborers	Cooks	Saleswomen (stores)	Bookkeepers and cashiers	Bookkeepers, accountants, and cashiers
Cotton mill operators	Saleswomen	Stenographers and typists	Bookkeepers and cashiers	Laundresses (not in laundry)	Waitresses (except private family)
Housekeepers and stewards	Housekeepers and stewards	Farmers	Cooks	Trained nurses	Housekeepers (private family)
Clerks and copyists	Seamstresses	Saleswomen (stores)	Farmers (general farms)	Other cooks	Trained nurses and student nurses

Note: Categories within each year show the ten jobs that employed the largest number of women in descending order, according to the U.S. Census Bureau. "n.e.c.": not elsewhere classified. Note that census classifications are not exactly comparable from one decade to the next.

Source: For 1890–1970, Berch (1982, 12–13), for 1980, calculated by the author from U.S. Bureau of the Census (1982), for 1990 calculated by the author from U.S. Bureau of the Census (1992, 392–394).

TABLE 13-4
The Ten Largest Occupations of Women, 1890–1990 (*continued*)

1950	1960	1970	1980	1990
Stenographers, typists, and secretaries	Stenographers, typists, and secretaries	Secretaries	Secretaries	Secretaries
Other clerical workers	Other clerical workers	Sales clerks (retail trade)	Teachers (elementary school)	Cashiers
Saleswomen	Private household workers	Bookkeepers	Bookkeepers	Bookkeepers
Private household workers	Saleswomen	Teachers (elementary school)	Cashiers	Nurses, registered
Teachers (elementary school)	Teachers (elementary school)	Typists	Office clerks	Information clerks
Waitresses	Bookkeepers	Waitresses	Managers (n.e.c.)	Nursing aides, orderlies, attendants
Bookkeepers	Waitresses	Sewers and stitchers	Waitresses	Teachers (elementary school)
Sewers and stitchers, manufacturing	Misc. and not specified operators	Nurses, registered	Salesworkers	Sales, supervisors and proprietor
Nurses, registered	Nurses, registered	Cashiers	Nurses, registered	Health technologists, technicians
Telephone operators	Other service workers (except private household)	Private household cleaners and servants	Nursing aides	Waitresses

There is still substantial occupational gender segregation in the United States. Women are concentrated into many fewer occupations than men, and the jobs in which there is a high proportion of female workers are the same ones in which the vast majority of workers are women. Women and men in the same general job classifications or sectors are segregated into different types of work. Not only are people aware of gender segregation in employment, but they also tend to exaggerate the amount of segregation that exists by overestimating the number of women in "women's" jobs, underestimating the proportion of women in integrated jobs, and underestimating even more strikingly the number of women in "men's" jobs (Cooper, Doverspike, and Barrett, 1985). Table 13-5 shows some of the most and least gender-segregated jobs in the current U.S. labor market.

Some of the increase in women's employment in traditionally male jobs is due to their entry into new specialties within those jobs, creating new female ghettos. Family law or medicine, residential (as opposed to commercial) real estate, and "women's" fields in university education are some examples (Patterson and Engleberg, 1978). Consider the example of bakers. Although the proportion of women in baking shifted from 25% in 1970 to 48% in 1988, much of that is accounted for by the rise of bakeries inside supermarkets, usually staffed by women who appear to do home baking, but in fact only heat prepackaged dough. A baker in these establishments is a lower-status, lower-paid worker than other bakers, who remain predominantly male (Reskin, 1988). At the same time, there are many areas, including business management, in which research shows there has been considerable progress in gender integration (Jacobs, 1992). Also, although there are female ghettos in professions such as law and medicine, this does not account for the shift toward a more even balance of women and men entering those professions since the mid-1970s.

A study of women's employment in 25 countries helps explain the degree of gender segregation in different economic systems. Maria Charles (1992) found that some of the same features of an economy that promoted women's entry into the labor market in the first place also tends to lead toward a relatively high degree of segregation. This is largely because the economies with the highest numbers of employed women have the larger service sectors and employee classes, arenas that welcomed women into gender-typed jobs. Countries without large job sectors specializing in women's labor have less gender segregation, but also fewer employed women.

What Is the Difference Between Women's and Men's Work? Vertical Segregation

Women's work and men's work do not just entail different jobs; they also sort men and women into jobs that are valued differently and that have different levels of power and prestige. Men's jobs generally have more authority and higher status, and they are better paid. Where women work in the same sectors, men are more concentrated in the positions of higher status and authority than women. This is true in "women's" jobs as well as in "men's." Observers have often called this the rule of "the higher the fewer": the higher the value or power of a position, the fewer the women occupying it.

TABLE 13-5
Most- and Least-Segregated Occupations, 1996

Most Segregated: Female	*Most Integrated*	*Most Segregated: Male*
Dental hygienists (99)	Bartenders (54)	Aerospace engineers (5)
Secretaries (99)	Dispatchers (54)	Material moving equipment operators (5)
Dental assistants (99)	Technical writers (54)	Mechanical engineers (5)
Family child-care providers (98)	Advertising and related sales (53)	Truck drivers (5)
Prekindergarten and kindergarten teachers (98)	Editors and reporters (53)	Extractive occupations (4)
Receptionists (97)	Physicians' assistants (53)	Forestry and logging (4)
Private household child-care workers (97)	Social, recreation, and religious workers (53)	Mechanics and repairers (4)
Private household cleaners and servants (95)	Accountants, auditors (52)	Water and sewage plant operators (4)
Practical nurses (95)	Production inspectors, testers (52)	Airplane pilots and navigators (3)
Typists (94)	Real estate sales (51)	Pest-control occupations (3)
Registered nurses (93)	Biological technicians (50)	Transport occupations, excluding motor vehicles (3)
Dietitians (93)	Economists (50)	Aircraft engine mechanics (2)
Bookkeepers, accountants (93)	Financial managers (50)	Construction trades (2)
Hairdressers (92)	Painters, sculptors, craft artists (50)	Firefighters (2)
Speech therapists (92)	Property and real estate managers (50)	Telephone installers (2)
Teacher aides (91)	Public officials and administrators (50)	Auto mechanics (1)
	Sales supervisors and proprietors (50)	Carpenters (1)
		Vehicle and mobile-equipment mechanics (1)

Note: Figures show the percentage of women in each occupation.
Source: U.S. Bureau of the Census (1997, 405–407).

A study of women's employment in authoritative positions in seven countries found that the barriers to higher-level jobs are especially low in the United States and Australia, compared with those in many others, including especially Japan (Wright, Baxter, and Birkelund, 1995). It found that women's attainment of high-level positions was related to a combination of having a lot of managerial positions available in the system *and* the existence of a relatively strong women's movement that could challenge the barriers.

Although the barriers have certainly been challenged in the United States, they are still there. There is still discrimination against women in leadership positions; some research suggests that even women sometimes trust female bosses less than they trust male bosses (Jeanquart-Barone and Sekaran, 1994). In occupation after occupation, research continues to find that women are not promoted as much as men, and women face higher barriers in entering the more prestigious, higher-paid specialties.

Some of the most extensive research has investigated women's success in business and corporations. The Federal Glass Ceiling Commission found that White men hold 95% of the nation's senior management positions.[21] A study done by Catalyst, an organization devoted to promoting women in the corporate world, found that no matter how one defines what constitutes power positions—whether pay, title, or responsibility—women hold about 2% of these positions.[22] Nearly one fifth of Fortune 500 companies have no women directors. Companies that exclude women from their top ranks may suffer when they try to recruit good new employees; the top women students at the leading business schools know which corporations have women in their leadership and which have good policies for women.[23]

Sometimes, jobs are accorded lower status and pay *because* they are women's jobs; in other words, the fact that a job is seen as something women can and should do makes it worth less than something regarded as a man's job. Gender segregation creates what Claudia Goldin has called an "aura of gender," a cultural meaning that goes beyond who happens to do the job (Goldin, 1990, 81). The business world provides one of the clearest examples of the principle of "the higher, the fewer" with regard to women's work. In 1990, almost 99% of all secretaries and typists were women, while more than 99% of the highest-paid officers and directors of the 799 largest industrial and service companies (Jacobs, 1992, 282) and 97% of the people holding the top five jobs at Fortune 500 companies were men.[24] No one expects secretaries to rise to the top, although most secretaries know that their bosses would be lost in the office without them.

Gender is only one of many factors that structure inequality in the labor market. Race is another. Gender and race also interact to determine women's employment experience. Gender inequality in the labor market exists across racial and ethnic groups; for all groups, women and men are segregated from each other in the work force, and women tend to be concentrated in lower-paying, lower-status jobs. The *degree* of gender inequality is not constant across groups, however. A study of gender effects among the 11 largest non-European racial and ethnic minorities found that there was greater gender inequality in the more affluent groups and among those with lower fertility rates—in other words, among those with more resources (Almquist, 1987).

Women have often worked together—even in competitive industries and jobs —to promote women's entrance into the higher levels, sometimes through professional organizations and caucuses; sometimes through interest groups such as Catalyst, Inc.; sometimes through government-sponsored efforts, such as those coordinated through the Small Business Bureau; and sometimes in informal friendship groups. One of the most interesting examples of the latter category is the "A Team," a group of about a dozen Boston health-care professionals in their 30s who, having met together for 7 years, decided in 1984 that at least three of them had to become health-care executives. At the time, when not a single hospital in the Boston area was run by a woman, some of them were worried about fulfilling the image of the pushy woman, but they set to work developing strategies for promotion. The group grew and changed, but by the 1990s, about half a dozen of the active members had reached the health-care executive suite.[25] Having more women at the senior levels is important for the advancement of women in general. Women leaders tend to hire more women than men do, and some research suggests that the higher the percentage of women in top positions, the better the job performance of women lower down on the scale (Perkins, 1994).

More women than ever are seeking their own way to becoming leaders by starting their own businesses, a route that takes a tremendous willingness to take risks and sometimes—but not always—financial resources. An investigation of why many women executives and professionals leave large companies in order to start their own companies finds that many are seeking (a) more control over their abilities to balance family and work, and (b) means to escape the discrimination and other roadblocks they face in large companies (Buttner and Moore, 1997; Green and Cohen, 1995). Women-owned businesses outnumbered businesses owned by men in both services and retail trade, and women own about the same number as men in finance, insurance, and real estate.[26] Of course, a large proportion of these businesses are small (and, of course, a large proportion of all businesses are small), but small businesses add up. Estimates are that in 1994, there were 7.7 million women-owned businesses, employing more workers in the United States than all of the Fortune 500 companies employed worldwide.[27] A large proportion of these firms—perhaps 12%—are owned by African-American, Hispanic, Asian-American, or Native American women, who generated more than $184 billion in sales in 1996.[28] Women-owned businesses employ 20% of U.S. workers, and women seem to stay in business longer than the national average.[29]

Employment Discrimination

Gender divisions of labor begin at a very young age. Male and female children are given different jobs at home, which correspond to adult divisions of labor. The first paid work done by children and adolescents also corresponds to these divisions; boys do more manual labor, and girls do more child care and clerical, sales, and service work. Even when their work is similar, girls tend to work with people and boys with things (Greenberger and Steinberg, 1983; White and Brinkerhoff, 1981). Parents and employers thus help to perpetuate gender-based divisions of labor in childhood. Educational and training institutions help sort workers into gender-appropriate jobs and into jobs defined as appropriate for women of a particular race/ethnicity (Glenn, 1992).[30]

Conventional wisdom says that gender segregation results partly from women choosing jobs that are especially compatible with their family responsibilities. In this view, women's choices cause gender segregation, and gender segregation is good for women. Research using national employment data calls this assumption into question. In fact, as research shows, "exactly the opposite was found in professional and blue-collar jobs where female concentration was negatively related to compatibility" (Glass and Camarigg, 1992, 148). Women are concentrated into positions with low levels of authority, low flexibility, and high levels of supervision, in part so that their employers can make sure they are not distracted from their work. "The very job characteristics that would reduce stress and job–family tension among employed mothers are difficult for them to obtain because these rewards are linked to an authority and reward structure that places women in marginalized 'women's jobs' outside central lines of authority" (Glass and Camarigg, 1992, 1148). Gender segregation, as it is currently structured, makes women's lives worse, not better.

Women, of course, are not just shoved around the job market like passive game pieces; they also make choices all along the way. However, as women make their job choices, they use what they have learned about themselves and their society to assess their chances in the labor market and in specific jobs. Most women who know that very few women succeed in one particular career, but many are successful in another, will choose the path of less resistance. People are aware of the gender, racial/ethnic, and class compositions of many jobs, and they are aware of the likelihood that they will be relatively welcome or unwelcome in jobs because of some combination of their own gender, race/ethnicity, or class background. As the discussion of women in many walks of life throughout this book has shown, discrimination occurs in many subtle and not-so-subtle ways. Most of the most explicit barriers are long gone, but research in many areas continues to show that women's credentials may count for less when they are up for promotion, and they are subject to nonconscious discrimination.

Certainly, a lot of discrimination also takes place consciously, when employers believe that members of a particular group of people, defined for example by gender or race/ethnicity, are unsuitable for a job or when an employer simply does not want people from that group around. These are the relatively easy cases of discrimination to detect, even if many employers go to great lengths to disguise their prejudice. In addition, however, employers are not always aware that they are discriminating against women. Personnel assessment is not an exact science, and there is much room for bias in perception and judgment by employers and employees who may act on gender-related cues. This book has cited numerous experimental studies that show evidence of nonconscious gender bias in evaluations of men and women.[31] Some of these studies apply specifically to employment, and some use businesspeople as subjects.

The most telling studies are those in which people are asked to evaluate men and women who have exactly the same credentials or characteristics, to see whether they treat men and women differently. Consider the stereotype that women are not as assertive or do not exert the same leadership characteristics as men. Research suggests that employers often see women and men through stereotypes that make them look different, even when they are not. One study showed that when managers evaluated reports about a fictitious man or woman, they evaluated men who used power strategies at work more favorably and as more effective than women who used similar strategies. They were also more likely to believe that a woman, rather than a man, was a subordinate (Wiley and Eskilson, 1982). Another experimental study of managers in a large corporation investigated hiring for two different kinds of engineering jobs, one of which also involved some managerial duties. For the job involving managerial duties, women were rated lower than men with the same qualifications; these women were even rated lower than women applying for the technical engineering job without the management component. Women are also expected to hold their jobs for briefer periods than men (Gerdes and Garber, 1983).

Not all discrimination is nonconscious, and some occurs so early in the hiring process that employers avoid even considering women or men for nontraditional jobs. Muriel Siebert, who became the first woman member of the New York Stock Exchange in 1967, offers many examples from her own career. When she first sent out her résumé in the late 1950s, she received no offers; but she received many when she sent her résumé under the name of "M. Siebert." Early on, she could not attend many important company meetings because they were held in country clubs that excluded women.[32] This practice was common, and women have sued for entrance into males-only social clubs on the grounds that this exclusion has ramifications for women's employment opportunities. Many men in these clubs claim that the clubs are only social and cannot see why they do not have a right to "freedom of association"—without women.

No law or policy can cancel all the effects of nonconscious discrimination. It is often difficult, or sometimes even impossible, for a person to know when she has been the victim of such discrimination. This is of particularly great significance in light of other research suggesting that women tend to attribute their failure in "masculine" areas to their own lack of skill. Nonconscious discrimination can depress the aspirations of women who have no ready explanation for their lack of success, other than their own abilities. Men who have acted in a discriminatory manner often deny that they have engaged in wrongdoing because they are not aware of it, and they may even be shocked at the suggestion that they would do such a thing.

There is evidence that nonconscious discrimination has even been activated by attempts to end sex discrimination. Reminding personnel departments that they are obliged to consider women and men equally for jobs, they may feel resentment or may be stimulated to believe that women are people with special, and inferior, characteristics. In his experimental study, William Siegfried (1982) found that when men were given standard equal-opportunity warnings, they tended to find male candidates more likable than females and to hire them more often. Rosen and Mericle (1979) found that strong warnings had no effect on whether men or women were hired but did result in women being hired at lower starting salaries than men.

Such evidence makes it clear that job equity will evolve only when sexist beliefs and attitudes disappear. Many people have come to believe that policy changes now mean that unqualified women are given jobs, so their assumption is that the women they see in nontraditional jobs must be unqualified. After all, if they had been qualified, all these women would have had jobs earlier, wouldn't they? In order to understand the changes, one has to understand that the system has been fundamentally discriminatory, and this is difficult for many people to believe. The implication of accepting the idea that the system has been discriminatory is to accept the idea that many White men did not, in the past, obtain their jobs solely through merit.

Recent attention to sexual harassment points to the lingering problem of hostility toward women in some workplaces, especially women in traditionally masculine jobs (e.g., Swerdlow, 1989). Many women have experienced harassment based in male hostility toward the female invader. Sometimes, the hostility takes apparently sexual forms. Women may be subject to hazing or initiation processes by their male colleagues when they enter very male-dominated jobs, and some of the hazing takes dangerous forms. Female police officers, for example, report cases in which male colleagues have refused to answer their calls for assistance or have cut the wires to their radios. When women object to these actions, they are often accused of being oversensitive and not having a sense of humor.

Studies of women in nontraditional blue-collar jobs reveal that more than 25% feel hostility directed against them by male coworkers. Such disapproval poisons the work environment for women, who then experience less job satisfaction than those who are not exposed to coworker hostility (O'Farrell and Harlan, 1982). This problem is not limited to blue-collar workers. Female professionals in traditionally male occupations also find a significant number of male colleagues who, if not openly hostile and harassing, show obvious discomfort in their presence and confusion about how to deal with them. Often, the burden is on the newcomer to make those around her feel comfortable, a responsibility that cannot ease her integration into a new job. In traditional male fields, even a few women can feel like a wholesale invasion to the men who formerly enjoyed sole proprietorship.

The Law on Discrimination

The first and most important federal law affecting gender discrimination in employment is Title VII of the 1964 Civil Rights Act.[33] It declares illegal discrimination on the basis of sex in hiring, firing, "compensation, terms, conditions, or privileges of employment," or "to limit, segregate, or classify employees or applicants . . . in any way which would deprive or tend to deprive any individual of employment opportunities." Most employers, employment agencies, and labor organizations are covered by this law.

Title VII states that sex *may* be used as a criterion in employment, but only in "those certain instances where . . . sex . . . is a bona fide occupational qualification reasonably necessary to the normal operation of that particular business or enterprise." This phrase, the *bona fide occupational qualification,* or *bfoq,* is crucial to lawsuits over gender discrimination. The point is that gender cannot be used as a basis of judgment unless an employer can prove that gender is crucial to job performance. What, exactly, constitutes a bfoq? Under what circumstances can an employer say that being male or being female is necessary to get the job done? These questions have been answered by courts as the result of lawsuits. Among the very few cases that stand are jobs for actors and actresses, sopranos and basses, bathroom attendants, and prison guards under certain circumstances.

The 1964 Civil Rights Act went into effect in 1965, but it had very little real impact until the early 1970s, when (a) a federal agency (the EEOC) was created to enforce the law, and (b) courts began to interpret the law in a way that attacked discrimination. In 1972, Congress gave the EEOC the power to sue employers under Title VII. Before the EEOC had this power, victims of discrimination themselves had to assume the burden of suing. The EEOC cannot take every case that comes to it, even if a case seems to have merit; given that the agency deals with complaints about discrimination on the basis of gender, race, age, and disability, it watches for cases that might have far-reaching effects to stop specific types of discriminatory behavior for other people, and cases in which delay could be perilous, such as those in which violent harassment or retaliation is likely. A 1995 report asserted that there were 97,000 unresolved cases at one time. The agency received 54,908 complaints about sexual harassment from 1990 to 1995.[34] Because of the overload, and the cuts in the federal budget, the EEOC hears many fewer cases now than it did in the past; for example, it filed 643 cases in fiscal year (FY) 1990, and 160 in FY 1996.[35]

The courts have extended and refined the meaning of Title VII considerably. In the first Supreme Court case that dealt with Title VII, the Court concluded that a policy of refusing employment to mothers of preschool children but not to fathers of preschool children violated Title VII (*Phillips* v. *Martin Marietta*, 1971). The Martin Marietta Corporation claimed that it was not discriminating against women, but rather against a certain classification of women: mothers. The company thought that because mothers but not fathers of small children are likely to take time off from work because of children's illnesses and holidays, it would be fair to say that mothers (but not fathers) were bad risks as employees. The Court rejected this argument, observing that the company had "one hiring policy for women and another for men—each having preschool aged children." The company had failed to show that *not* being a mother of preschool children was a bfoq. Discrimination of the "sex plus" type (in this case, sex plus parenthood) is illegal, a decision reinforced in later cases, including one that condemned a company that discriminated against married women, but not married men (*Sprogis* v. *United Airlines*, 1971).

It is important to remember that Title VII applies to men, as well as to women. In *Diaz* v. *Pan American Airways*, a 1971 case involving discrimination against a man, a federal court found that Pan Am violated Title VII by refusing to hire men as cabin attendants, despite the company's evidence that passengers prefer female attendants. The court said that a company cannot justify discrimination on the grounds that it pleases clients.

If an employer discriminates against pregnant women, does this violate the law against sex discrimination? At first, the answer was no because, as the Supreme Court reasoned, there is no such thing as a pregnant man, and therefore there is no sex discrimination. For pregnancy discrimination to be *sex* discrimination, the Court reasoned, there would have to be different treatment of women and men in a similar condition: pregnant (*General Electric Co.* v. *Gilbert*, 1976). Congress tried to take care of this problem by passing the Pregnancy Discrimination Act, which amended Title VII of the 1964 Civil Rights Act to say that discrimination on the basis of pregnancy is sex discrimination. Nevertheless, bias against pregnant workers and new mothers still shows up. As a staff member for the NOW Legal Defense and Education Fund said, "Word is out that [the law] prohibits pregnancy discrimination. So employers are typically more devious and couch discrimination in other terms. During an economic downturn, employers can mask pregnancy discrimination as layoffs and downsizing, which makes it harder to prove the underlying discriminatory motivation."[36]

The Civil Rights Act of 1991 helped people who think they are victims of discrimination by making it easier (a) to launch *class-action suits* (lawsuits on behalf of a whole class of workers, not just particular, named parties), (b) to sue for *punitive damages* (i.e., not just restoring lost pay, but, in cases of intentional discrimination, making the defendant pay extra as a form of punishment), (c) to allow discrimination cases to be heard by juries rather than just by judges, and (d) to prove patterns of bias. As a result, the number of large class-action discrimination suits brought against companies is increasing, from 30 in 1992 to around 70 by 1995.[37]

Perhaps the most well known and most controversial legal mechanism used to combat discrimination is *affirmative action*, first applied to women as a federal policy mechanism in 1967. Its purpose was to enforce the spirit of Title VII of the 1964 Civil Rights Act. Affirmative action was first ordered by President Kennedy in 1961, to apply to alleviating race discrimination, declaring that certain employers must "take affirmative action to ensure that applicants are employed, and that employers are treated equally during employment, without regard to race, creed, color, or national origin." Prior to affirmative action, all antidiscrimination policy had been couched in *negative* terms, concentrating on telling employers what they should not do. Affirmative-action policy, in contrast, tells employers what positive (affirmative) steps they must take to eliminate discrimination.

Under affirmative-action guidelines, employers were required to figure out how many women were being used in each major job classification and to compare that number with an estimate of how many women available locally either had or could in a reasonable time be given the appropriate skills needed to do the job. Then the employers could assess where they should have more women and develop a time frame and strategy for hiring them, taking account of the available workforce and the probable future vacancies. These "goals and timetables" have been the focus of attack on affirmative action. The original program declared that "goals may not be rigid and inflexible quotas which must be met, but must be targets reasonably attainable by means of applying every good faith effort to make all aspects of the entire affirmative action program work." A company that seemed earnest in its efforts could not be punished, even if it had made no real changes at all. All the company needed to prove were "good faith efforts." In fact, most organizations under investigation passed this test satisfactorily. The worst punishment available under the policy is withdrawal of all government contracts from that institution. This threat is obviously more serious to some institutions than to others, but it was rarely carried out.

Employers who attempted to use quotas, rather than goals, or who made being a woman or a member of a minority a requirement for a job were sued, usually by White men arguing that these programs discriminated against them. In most cases, the courts agreed that using gender or race as a qualification for hiring, except where gender or race is a bfoq, violated the Title VII ban on discrimination in employment. The Supreme Court did, however, allow employers to take gender and race into account as one of the characteristics employers are looking for in order to pursue more equality in the workforce (*Johnson* v. *Transportation Agency, Santa Clara County,* 1987). Stricter nondiscrimination standards are used with public employers than with private employers.

One result of the widespread misunderstanding of affirmative-action policies is that many people believe that it is difficult for White males to get jobs and that the women and minorities who are being hired are unqualified. This misperception of affirmative-action policies reinforces the tendency for people to see women and minorities as less competent than White men because of the belief that the women and minorities have their jobs not because they deserve them but because of preferential treatment. Indeed, research has suggested that gender-based preferential treatment incurs social-psychological costs for women, whose sense of competence is undermined by the perceptions created by these programs. It is not clear that race-based affirmative-action programs have the same effect on African-Americans (Doverspike and Arthur, 1995). At the same time, it is only since the early 1970s, when antidiscrimination and affirmative-action policies were first really implemented, that women have become more integrated into a wider range of workplaces.

As Chapter 12 discussed, in 1986 the Supreme Court expanded its interpretation of Title VII of the 1964 Civil Rights Act, to declare sexual harassment a form of sex discrimination (*Meritor Savings Bank* v. *Vinson,* 1986). The Court said that in barring sex discrimination, the 1964 Civil Rights Act did not just disallow "economic" or "tangible" discrimination, but also forbid making some people work in a discriminatorily hostile or abusive environment. This was a crucial change. Without this explicit definition of harassment as discrimination, sexual harassment remains a normal part of the working conditions of a very large proportion of women workers; women are told that harassment is normal, and they should live with it.

The legal assault on sexual harassment was extended in 1993, when the Supreme Court unanimously elaborated its position further and said that plaintiffs do not have to prove they have suffered "concrete psychological harm" to win their cases. As Sandra Day O'Connor wrote for the majority,

> Title VII comes into play before the harassing conduct leads to a nervous breakdown. A discriminatorily abusive work environment, even one that does not seriously affect employees' psychological well-being, can and often will detract from employees' job performance, discourage employees from remaining on the job, or keep them from advancing in their careers. Moreover, even without regard to these tangible effects, the very fact that the discriminatory conduct was so severe or pervasive that it created a work environment abusive to employees because of their race, gender, religion, or national origin offends Title VII's broad rule of workplace equality. (*Harris* v. *Forklift Systems, Inc.,* 1993)

Thus, if a woman's work environment is poisoned by intimidation or demeaning treatment just because she is a woman, she has suffered from illegal discrimination.

Income, Worth, and Poverty

Thus far, we have looked at the work women and men do. We now turn to the financial situation of women and their families, beginning with job-related pay and benefits issues, then other problems of financial support and poverty.

TABLE 13-6
Women's Wages as a Proportion of Men's Wages, 1990

	1–3 Years of High School	4 Years of High School	1–3 Years of College	4+ Years of College
All Women				
as % of all men	.55	.55	.60	.64
Hispanic				
as % of Hispanic men	.61	.65	.60	.68
as % of White men	.54	.50	.57	.57
Black				
as % of Black men	.70	.74	.75	.85
as % of White men	.51	.54	.58	.68
White				
as % of White men	.53	.53	.57	.62

Note: These figures can be read as "cents on the dollar"; e.g., the least-educated White women earn 53 cents for every dollar earned by the least-educated White men.

Source: Adapted from U.S. Census Bureau figures presented in Ms. Foundation for Women (1992, 6).

Women's Pay

Women may be increasing the amount of time they spend in employment, but they continue to earn considerably less than men do. As Table 13-6 shows, women in full-time year-round employment earn less than men at every education level. It also shows the interaction of gender and race by showing how many cents on the male dollar females earn compared within each educational level among Hispanics, African-Americans, and whites. The table also shows how many cents on the White male dollar Hispanic and African-American females earn. These figures do not take account of the difference between full- and part-time work or work lasting only part of the year, compared with all year. They do, however, show the situation experienced by women across the country: Women earn considerably less than men of their own educational level and race/ethnic group. The gender gap among White people is greater than the gender gap in every other racial group; this is because of the depressing effects of race on both men's and women's wages among Hispanics and African-Americans.

Race makes remarkably little difference, however, in how far behind White men's women's wages are, regardless of race. For all groups except the most educated African-Americans and whites women's wages are less than 60% of men's, and among the least educated, they are less than 55%. The gender gap in wages is also largest among the least educated, largely because of the difference between wages for blue-collar and pink-collar unskilled and semiskilled jobs. The gender gap in pay is not simply due to differences in the positions held by women and men or differences in their levels of experience. There are also differences in the pay received by women and men in similar jobs.

Sex discrimination in pay has been illegal since the Equal Pay Act of 1963. That law states, "No employer . . . shall discriminate . . . between employees on the basis of sex by paying wages to employees . . . at a rate less than the rate at which he pays wages to employees of the opposite sex . . . for equal work on jobs the performance of which requires equal skill, effort, and responsibility, and which are performed under similar working conditions." Labor unions were also covered by the law.

Employers reacted quickly to this law. Realizing that "equal pay for equal work" could be costly, especially because employers could not reduce anyone's salary to comply with the Equal Pay Act, many gave male and female employees different job titles in order to pay them differently. Some employers also made sure there was something slightly different about the actual work that men and women did so that their work could be proven to be of unequal value. A turning point came in 1970, when a federal court decided that in ordering equal pay for equal work, Congress "did not require that the jobs be identical, but only that they must be substantially equal. Any other interpretation would destroy the remedial purposes of the Act" (*Schultz* v. *Wheaton Glass Co.*). Thus, women and men are supposed to be paid the same for doing *substantially similar* work.

Nonetheless, women and men continue to be paid somewhat differently for the same work. In most jobs, pay is based partly on subjective evaluations of the worker by a supervisor, which allows conscious and nonconscious discrimination to take its toll. Many studies show that difference in credentials and training, time at work, or other characteristics of the employee does not fully account for the pay gap between men and women; some of the difference still has to do with discrimination (Bellas, 1994; Brett and Reilly, 1992; Wellington, 1994). A study of the United States and five other industrialized countries found that the gender gap in wages in the United States is high compared to that in the other countries, largely because wage inequality in the United States is high, compared to that in other nations (Blau and Kahn, 1992). One study found that women in the United States receive more promotions than men, but their promotions do not net them as much salary increase as men's do. Further investigation showed that women earn more promotions because they tend to start jobs at lower levels than they otherwise might, in order to follow a husband who has moved positions. Starting at a lower level gives more scope for promotions, but it keeps women's salaries lower (Hersch and Viscusi, 1996). Women also work at or below the minimum wage at much higher rates than men do (U.S. Bureau of the Census, 1997, 429). Nevertheless, as women's and men's education, training, and experience are converging, and some male-dominated blue-collar sectors of the economy are in decline, the gender-related wage differential has been decreasing (O'Neill and Polachek, 1993).

The greater problem for salary equity is labor-market segregation. As long as women and men occupy different jobs, equal pay for equal work is, practically speaking, meaningless unless *equal* is defined to mean something other than similarity in the substance of the job. This observation led many experts in the 1980s to look to the principal of *comparable worth* or *pay equity* as the standard for identifying sex discrimination in pay. A comparable-worth policy requires assessment of the relative amounts of skill, training, experience, and other valued characteristics required to do different jobs, to determine the relative worth of different jobs in terms of pay. Without comparable worth, the only way to determine whether there is gender bias in pay is to compare women and men holding substantially similar jobs, but there may not be any such similarity. The implementation of comparable worth would transform the process of determining pay and would cost businesses considerable sums of money. Although there was some movement toward these principles, the movement has stalled (Hartmann, 1985; Steinberg, 1987).

The dominant school of economics teaches that the wage market, if left to its own devices, will provide workers with the appropriate pay for their jobs. According to this view of economics, the unseen hand of the marketplace works out the best negotiated compromise among employers seeking employees and workers seeking jobs. This school of thought vehemently opposes pay-equity policies as disruptive to the market. It may be, they argue, that women take jobs that pay less than the jobs that men take, but this is only due to the mutual choices of workers and employers. Feminist scholars point out that the unseen hand may help work out a position of economic equilibrium in a market, but the values accorded to workers are shaped not by any essential value, but by many features of the culture, including the values the culture places on people of one gender or race or another.

Historian Alice Kessler-Harris (1990) has shown how, throughout the 20th century, wages have been shaped by the cultural values defining the sex/gender system in which the wages are developed. Cultural pressures urge employers to think of men's wages (and thus fair wages for the kinds of work men do) as those that will help support a family, while viewing women's wages (and thus fair wages for the kinds of work women do) as extra wages. Thus, Kessler-Harris has concluded, "The market, as it functions in the daily lives of people, is not independent of the values and customs of those who participate in it" (Kessler-Harris, 1990, 117–118; see also Goldin, 1990). Customary ideas of wage fairness may unfairly keep women's wages relatively low.

Women make many compromises in their work lives, which reduce their pay. Many women seek part-time work in order to balance family and economic responsibilities or because it is more consistent with cultural conceptions of women's roles. Part-time employees are paid on a lower scale than full-time employees and often do not receive fringe benefits, including valuable health and other insurance coverage. Part-time employees do not usually have the same opportunities for promotion that full-time employees have. When women delay their entry into the labor market or take time out for raising children, they also face decreased wages when they return. These choices do not account for all of the wage gap, however, and more men are beginning to make job compromises in favor of their families. Moreover, many women who might not otherwise enter the labor market at all take low-paying, temporary jobs because economic hard times are making it harder for their husbands' pay to cover family needs.[38]

Of course, most women do a considerable amount of valuable work for which they receive no pay: household labor. What is *this* work worth in money? Experts generally agree there are two methods to estimate a dollar value for women's household labor: opportunity cost and replacement value (Berch, 1982). Using the *opportunity-cost* approach, the value of the household labor is calculated according to what a woman could be earning if, instead, she held a paid job. In this case, housework's value is calculated in the lost opportunity to earn income. Estimates are that the average opportunity cost of homemaking in 1991 was about $17,000 per homemaker per year.[39] Opportunity-cost figures, which are sometimes used in divorce proceedings, have two drawbacks. First, the *value* of the labor is not an assessment of the *labor itself;* domestic work remains essentially valueless. Second, unpaid domestic labor is not an alternative to employed labor for married women. Women do domestic labor, regardless of their employment status.

As an alternative, using the *replacement-cost* approach entails calculating the cost of paying someone else to do the housework. Insurance companies use this method to calculate how much to compensate widowers who insured their wives' value as housewives. In the early 1990s, the average replacement cost of a housewife was calculated to be more than $16,000 per housewife per year.[40] Another study calculated the work of housework, taking account of the differential wage rates of men and women. The authors concluded that women's housework was worth about $5.50 per hour after taxes, or about $10,000 take-home pay, while men's housework was worth $9.60 per hour (because of the higher pay men usually receive), but their contributions amount to about $6,600 per year because they do so much less housework.[41]

Many policymakers around the world have argued that even if housework is not financially reimbursed, its value should be incorporated into government figures such as the calculation of gross national product (GNP), in order to raise the status of the women who do this work, and also to make the value and the needs of these workers more apparent to the system as a whole. This proposal was made through the United Nations Women's Decade conference in Nairobi, and a bill calling for this action was endorsed by the Congressional Women's Caucus and proposed to the U.S. Congress.[42]

Jobs do not provide just money wages, but also many other often extremely valuable benefits, such as pensions and health insurance. As mentioned previously, many of these benefits help facilitate the balance between employment and family. As sociologist Arlie Hochschild has said, "We have to acknowledge that the majority of American women will work for the majority of their lives through their childbearing years and we have to adapt the work place. Don't pretend they're men who have wives at home to do this."[43] Also, given that the United States is one of the few nations historically lacking comprehensive government-sponsored health care, benefits can be crucial.

Other Means of Support: Social Welfare

Salaries are not the only sources of income for men or women. The poor, disabled, unemployed, and retired, for instance, may depend on various types of public benefits. Similarly, the wealthy may receive income from investments. In analyzing the economic situations of women and men, it is necessary to look at all the different sources of financial support for individuals and families.

Assistance to the poor is a woman's issue because women appear in disproportionately large numbers among the poor. Numerous social scientists point to the *feminization of poverty,* the increasing tendency for poor populations in the United States to be composed of women. The poverty rates for female-headed families is substantial, especially among African-Americans and Hispanics, for whom at least half the female-headed families are below the poverty line. Regardless of race, people living in families headed by single women are much more likely to be impoverished than other people are.

Poverty has become a more widespread U.S. problem since the early 1980s. Young families with children have significantly less money than their counterparts did a generation ago, and they suffer from child poverty rates that are twice as high.[44] Although the rise in single-parent families accounts for some of that increase, both decreasing wages and government policies in that era that cut welfare and unemployment benefits account for about half the increase in child poverty rates. If we consider only families with parents less than 30 years old, between 1972 and 1990, incomes of those who completed a college education rose by 3%; among those with some college education, income fell by 15%; among those who completed only high school, incomes fell by 30%; and among those who never finished high school, income fell by 46%.[45]

Poverty, and specifically the feminization of poverty, stems from a number of sources. In the 1980s and 1990s, changes in the global economy created greater financial pressure, which led to widespread job loss and decreases in wages and benefits for the jobs that remained. Public policies eliminated some of the means of support that had existed earlier, as welfare programs came under greater attack.

For single women with children, these problems compound the economic burdens they already face. Although courts usually charge fathers with the obligation of remaining financially responsible for their children following divorce from the mother, the fact is that a large proportion of those without custody do not fulfill their responsibility to their children. A 1987 study showed, for example, that of the divorced women who had custody of their children, 59% had been awarded some child support due them from the father, and of those, 51% received the full amount, 25% received part of it, and 24% received none of it, amounting to billions of dollars accumulated over time that should have gone to mothers to support their children. It is very difficult to collect from delinquent fathers who have left the state, even though governmental mechanisms to do this now exist.[46]

Women of *all* classes experience a decline in their economic standing as a result of divorce, although the decline is steepest for those whose marital income had been the highest. In other words, divorce has a leveling effect on women, reducing the financial differences among them (Weiss, 1984). In the first year after divorce, 71% of women who had had lower marital income used welfare payments such as Aid to Families with Dependent Children or food stamps to help, as did 25% of middle-income and 4% of higher-income divorcées. Even more shocking is the fact that in the first year after divorce, welfare payments and food stamps constituted 60% of the income of lower-income women, 37% of the income of middle-income women, and 26% of the income of higher-income women (Weiss, 1984).

Poverty has many self-perpetuating effects that harm women in particular, through their roles as mothers. Low-income women are much less likely to receive health care during the terms of their pregnancy, which is part of the reason that infant and maternal mortality rates are higher in the United States than in most other industrialized nations. Numerous public programs have been established over the course of the 20th century to assist the poor. Exactly how these worked, whom they helped, and under what circumstances varied as public assessments of the causes of poverty changed. Among the most important were Aid to Families of Dependent Children (AFDC, begun in 1935), Medicaid (health-care aid for the poor, begun in 1965), and food stamps. Unfortunately, these programs were remarkably ineffective in helping people move out of poverty.

The federal program AFDC is a case in point. AFDC began in 1935 as a program to aid impoverished children cared for by one-parent families. It is estimated that about 25% of all American children receive AFDC at some time in their lives, and the vast majority of these children live with their mothers. The AFDC program slowly grew until the Reagan administration began cutting it in 1981. The welfare system has been under increasing attack since then, culminating in the "Welfare Reform Bill" of 1996, which severely limited (a) the types of people who may seek assistance, (b) the types of assistance available, and (c) the amount of time people may continue to receive welfare payments.

A persistent charge aimed at poor women is that they have children in order to obtain or to stay on welfare. A study of recipients of AFDC, food stamps, and Medicaid proves that this charge is baseless. After controlling for factors such as race, education, and age, analysis showed that women on welfare had a substantially lower fertility rate than other women, and the longer they remained on welfare, the lower their fertility rate became (Rank, 1988).

These cuts in the support systems available to the poor, and especially to poor women, stem from increasing public feeling, especially among men, that the welfare state costs too much and that most people who have depended on it would not have to do so if they were only better motivated either to look for work or to stop having children. A series of responses to a national public opinion poll taken in 1995 shows the problem: "Do you think there are jobs available for most welfare recipients who really want to work, or not?" the survey asked. "Yes, jobs are available," said 76% of the American population. "Do you think most of these jobs pay enough to support a family?" asked the survey. "No," answered 63% of the population. "Do you think that women with young children who receive welfare should be required to work or should they stay at home and take care of their young children?" The answers were divided. Most respondents thought the mothers should be required to work; 32% thought the mothers should work for pay while the government should provide child care, and 24% thought the mothers should work and should pay for the child care themselves. In any case, the majority of the population favored stopping welfare payments to recipients regardless of their financial situation after 2 years. That is what the Welfare Reform Bill provided.

Organization of Women in the Workforce

Women entered the labor force in large numbers at the same time that male labor was organizing and was seeking recognition and the power to fight for its growing union membership. Although the proportion of the U.S. labor force that is unionized is one of the smallest among Western democracies, unions have been successful in improving working conditions and benefits (including pay) in the workplace through collective bargaining and by lobbying the government. What has been women's relationship to labor organizations? What role have such organizations played in the history of gender segregation and equity in the workplace?[47]

Most labor organizations were male dominated and androcentric from their inception. Before its official founding in 1886, for example, the American Federation of Labor (AFL) had approved the organization of working women and policies of equal pay. Union members and leaders, however, were skeptical of women as workers. In fact, women were sometimes used as strikebreakers to replace men whose unions excluded women from membership. Union leadership was often opposed to women workers on the grounds that women took jobs from men, reduced men's wages, and destroyed the family. Samuel Gompers, the influential head of the AFL, unsuccessfully urged the government to place an outright ban on the employment of women in government in 1898. The female membership of unions declined from 4.6% in 1895 to 2.9% in 1908 (Berch, 1982). Women have remained weak within the union movement throughout the 20th century. Unions did not work very hard to organize workers in "women's" jobs (with certain important exceptions, such as those in the textile trade) until recently, and unions were often slow to support the special interests of women workers.

Despite considerable opposition, many women tried to organize workers and force labor unions to consider women's needs and interests. One of the best-known efforts was the founding of the National Women's Trade Union League (NWTUL) in 1903 at an AFL meeting. The NWTUL involved working union members and their allies, such as wealthy women who were sympathetic to the plight of working women. Indeed, it was the wealthy women who had the time to contribute to the NWTUL, so the policies of that group did not reflect the interests of the workers themselves as much as they might have. Therefore, the women of the NWTUL fell in behind the cause of protective labor legislation for women.

Women's union participation expanded in the post–World War II era, especially as union leaders began to see arenas for bolstering the embattled union movement in formerly unorganized areas of women's work. In 1960, women were 18% of union members; by 1980, they were 30%; and in 1987, they were 35% (U.S. Department of Labor, 1989, 225).

The proportion of American workers in labor unions has always been small, compared with that in other industrialized countries, and that proportion has fallen further still over recent decades. In 1995, 17% of employed men and 12% of employed women were union members. Union memberships include a higher proportion of African-American women (19%) than White or Hispanic women (14% each) (U.S. Bureau of the Census, 1997, 438). Women are an even smaller proportion of national union leadership. Some people argue that women would not have made even this much progress, were it not for the founding in 1974 of the Coalition of Labor Union Women (CLUW), a women's caucus in the AFL-CIO.[48]

Despite these problems, women have made gains through the unions. Although men earn more than women in all occupational sectors, the gap is generally smaller between Black and White unionized men and women than between nonunionized men and women (U.S. Bureau of the Census, 1997, 438). Regardless of sex, workers earn more if they are unionized than if they are not.

There are also other workers' organizations that help the quality of women's treatment in the labor market. Some of the largest are employee associations, such as the American Nurse's Association and the National Educational Association. These associations are female dominated in membership, and some, such as the two just mentioned, also have a preponderance of women leaders. A more recent trend is toward organizations composed specifically of women workers. Among the best known of these are 9 to 5 (an organization of secretaries) and Women Office Workers (WOW). Another is La Mujer Obrera (The Working Woman), an organization of Chicana garment workers. Women also organize at their workplaces and within many occupations and professions. Women are no longer waiting for other people to organize them or tell them what is in their best interests.

The Uneasy Balance

People have long been worried about conflicts between work and family in the lives of women. Many of these fears were unfounded. Work, as such, need not conflict with women's traditional family roles or senses of femininity, because, first, women's family roles constitute much of their work. Moreover, as women have expanded their work to locations outside the home and have begun to receive pay, they have done so in ways that have stretched, rather than disregarded, the meaning of femininity. Eventually, the main issue has not been whether women worked for pay, but how they did so. Women's employment has not destroyed the family, as some people thought might happen. Nor does employment mark a straight path to liberation.

For many experts now, the issue is to accept an important fact of life—that women need their jobs—and to focus on how to develop high-quality alternatives for caring for children. "Whatever their views of the evidence, child-development experts . . . are virtually unanimous in their calls for generous parental-leave policies, improved availability and quality of day care and greater flexibility in the workplace to allow, for example, more part-time work."[49]

The amount of time women spend working for pay has greatly increased, but women spend only slightly less time doing free domestic labor now than they did formerly (especially if they are also employed). Women have increasing incentives to enter the labor force, but it is less clear what will motivate men to do more domestic labor. Many employed women find it easier to avoid conflicts by simply continuing to do the housework themselves. But is this wise, especially in the long run?

Notes

1. Although Feldberg and Glenn talked about the *job model* for men and *gender model* for women, in fact both are gender models because both are determined by gender. The family model, like the job model, is used by scholars primarily for *White* women.

2. This concept was discussed more thoroughly in Chapter 4.

3. An excellent book on gender and economic development today is Kabeer (1994).

4. For more on the development of scientific homemaking, see Cowan (1983).

5. Elizabeth A. Martin, Jennifer Hess, and Paul M. Siegel, "Some Effects of Gender on the Meaning of 'Work': An Empirical Example," U.S. Census Bureau, 1997. http://www.census.gov/srd/www/abstract/mhs95.html.

6. Cathy Horyn, "Clothes Carry 'Sexist' Prices," *Capitol Times* (Madison, WI), October 4, 1994.

7. "More Than Just Another Pretty Face," *Wisconsin State Journal*, September 13, 1995.

8. Barbara Whitaker, "Just Neighbors or Being Friendly? Not Exactly," *New York Times*, November 1994.

9. U.S. Bureau of Labor Statistics, "Labor Force Statistics from the Current Population Survey: Table 6," http://stats.bls.gov/news.release/famee.t06.htm.

10. "*New York Times* Poll/CBS Poll National Teenagers Survey, May 26–June 1, 1994," n.d.

11. "Freshman Survey: Their Opinions, Activities, and Goals," *Chronicle of Higher Education*, http://chronicle.com/che-data/infobank.dir/students.dir/freshmen.dir/97/97opin.htm.

12. Tamar Lewin, "Daughters' Workplace Visits Stir Issue: What About Boys?" *New York Times*, April 26, 1996.

13. Vivian Marino, "Impact of Leave Law? Experts Say Little Need for Businesses to Worry," *Wisconsin State Journal*, February 6, 1993.

14. Marino, "Impact of Leave Law?"

15. Celestine Bohlen, "Where Every Day Is Mother's Day," *New York Times*, May 12, 1996.

16. "Maternity Leaves Double," Women's Connection Online, http://www.womenconnect.com/news/jun10-1997.htm.

17. Leonard Sloane, "Brokerage Building Women's Strengths," *New York Times*, November 27, 1994.

18. Tamar Lewin, "Workers of Both Sexes Make Trade-offs for Family, Study Shows," *New York Times*, October 29, 1995.

19. Carol Lawson, "On-the-Job Child Care Comes to the Rescue," *New York Times*, April 22, 1993.

20. Tamar Lewin, "Income Gap Between Sexes to Widen in Retirement," *New York Times*, April 26, 1995.

21. Judith H. Dobrzynski, "Some Action, Little Talk: Companies Embrace Diversity but Are Reluctant to Discuss It," *New York Times*, April 20, 1995.

22. Judith H. Dobrzynski, "Some News for Women on Corporate Ladder," *New York Times*, November 6, 1996.

23. Maggie Jackson, "Women Are Joining America's Boardrooms at a Slower Rate," *Wisconsin State Journal*, December 12, 1996.

24. "Daughters Already at Work, and Succeeding," *New York Times*, April 28, 1993.

25. Andrea Gavor, "Crashing the 'Old Boy' Party," *New York Times*, January 8, 1995.

26. U.S. Bureau of the Census, "Percentage of Gender-Based Firm Ownership in Major Business Sectors," http://www.census.gov/agfs/gender/gend_tbl.html.

27. Jennifer S. Thomas, "Businesses Owned by Women Multiplying," *Wisconsin State Journal*, February 4, 1996.

28. "Minority Women–Owned Firms Boom," *Women's Connection Online*, http://womenconnect.com.

29. U.S. Small Business Administration, "Statistics on Women Business Ownership," http://www.sbaonline.sba.ogv/womeninbusiness/stats96.html.

30. See a more complete discussion in Chapter 5.

31. For a review of experimental research on sexism in personnel decision making, see Cash, Gillen, and Burns (1977); also, see the discussion in Chapter 3.

32. Patrick Harverson, "Women Take Stock of Wall Street," *Financial Times,* January 6, 1993.

33. "Title VII" refers to the *section* of the law.

34. Peter T. Kilborn, "In a Rare Move, Agency Acts Swiftly in a Sexual Harassment Case," *New York Times,* January 10, 1995.

35. Allan R. Myerson, "As U.S. Bias Cases Drop, Employees Take Up Fight," *New York Times,* January 12, 1997. *FY* refers to "fiscal year," the unit of time used in government reports of its activities; an FY is 12 months but does not begin in January.

36. Barbara Presley Noble, "An Increase in Bias Is Seen Against Pregnant Workers," *New York Times,* January 2, 1993.

37. Myerson, "As U.S. Bias Cases Drop."

38. Peter T. Kilborn, "More Women Take Low-Wage Jobs Just So Their Families Can Get By," *New York Times,* March 13, 1994.

39. Maria Odum, "If the G.N.P. Counted Housework, Would Women Count for More?" *New York Times,* April 5, 1992.

40. Odum, "If the G.N.P. Counted Housework."

41. "Housework Done by a Married Woman Is Worth $5.50 an Hour," *Chronicle of Higher Education,* January 20, 1993, A6.

42. Odum, "If the G.N.P. Counted Housework."

43. Susan Chira, "New Realities Fight Old Images of Mothers," *New York Times,* October 4, 1992.

44. Jason DeParle, "Incomes in Young Families Drop 32% in 17 Years, Study Finds," *New York Times,* April 15, 1992.

45. DeParle, "Incomes in Young Families Drop 32% in 17 Years."

46. Tamar Lewin, "New Tools Are Helping the States in Collecting Child-Support Funds," *New York Times,* June 15, 1991.

47. To read more on the history of women in labor unions, see Foner (1982); Cook, Lorwin, and Daniels (1984); and Cobble (1993).

48. The AFL-CIO, formed by a unification of the American Federation of Labor and the Congress of Industrial Organizations, is the largest federation of labor unions in the United States.

49. Eric Eckholm, "Finding Out What Happens When Mothers Go to Work," *New York Times,* October 6, 1992.

PART FOUR

Feminism and the Global Context

THUS FAR, each chapter of this book has considered some of the ways in which women have acted individually and together to try to improve both the life options open to them and the quality of their lives as women. This final section turns specifically to the questions of feminism and united action among women.

Reflect *Before* You Read

1. What changes in the status and roles of women and of men do you think need to be made in the future? How can these best be accomplished? What role will you play? Why?
2. You are probably aware of the many different strategies women use to become involved in questions raised by feminism. Some women actively oppose feminist organizations. Some try to do the best they can individually in their own lives. Some become involved in organizations that work through conventional political means. Some become involved in radical kinds of action. Why do you think people choose each of these different paths? Which path are you following? Why? If you have remained aloof from them all, why?
3. Do you think of yourself as a feminist? Why or why not? How would you describe feminists and feminism? Where did you get your ideas about feminism?

14

❧

Feminism and the Future

A group of people are standing together in a room. Over there is Abigail Adams, wife of a revolutionary who will later become the second president of the United States. Adams is telling her husband (half-jokingly) that the ladies are bound to foment a revolution of their own if they are not remembered in the design of the new government. Standing nearby is Elizabeth Cady Stanton, who spent half a century pushing for expansion of women's rights. She is arguing with Ida B. Wells, who exposed the prevalence of lynching at the turn of the century and also pointed out the special sexual oppression of Black women. Wells is angry with Stanton for her racist remarks and belief that it is more important for White women than for Black men to have the vote.

There is a young Jewish immigrant who has spent the past 14 hours at a factory sewing machine working to support her family. She is about to strike in support of higher wages and a 10-hour working day. She is gazing at a wealthy patron of the arts who has helped build a concert hall where women's music can be heard. A curious conversation is taking place between Valerie Solanas of the Society for Cutting Up Men (SCUM) and Phyllis Schlafley, who vigorously opposes the Equal Rights Amendment (ERA) and supports policies she thinks will maintain the dignity of women's roles in the family. Catharine Beecher, looking on, is partly sympathetic to Schlafley and points out that she devoted considerable effort to the task of improving the status of women, although she saw no need for women to vote.

One woman is walking away from one of the few men in the room because she cannot imagine what he would have to say to her about women's rights that would be useful. She has argued that the only way to seek freedom for women is by working with other women to figure out what they need. John Stuart Mill shakes his head sadly, thinking about the hours he spent trying to convince his colleagues in Parliament to support giving women the franchise.

Three women stand at the edge of the room. One is thinking that she certainly is not a feminist, but she does believe women should have a better chance to earn a living and do the things they want to do. Another impatiently thinks she has no time for these arguments because she is too busy working with her welfare-rights organization fighting for higher benefits for single mothers. The third woman impatiently thinks she has no time for feminism because she works 15 hours a day as the first female head of a corporation in her industry.[1]

Which of these people are feminists? More than 200 years separate their birth-dates; they are of different sexes, races, religions, and classes; and they would find few points of agreement. They all, however, worked for what they saw as improvements in the status of women, did things that might have direct and special benefits for women, or lived in defiance of stereotypes of women. After all is said and done, what is feminism? Who are feminists? When and how do feminist movements happen, and what is their social significance? These are the questions this chapter explores.

Ever since the word *feminism* was coined near the end of the 19th century, those attached to it and those antagonistic toward it have struggled among and between themselves to define it (Cott, 1987; Offen, 1988). Why would people who are not bookish academics struggle over the meaning of a word? The answer to this question begins to point toward the nature of feminism. Feminism has an inseparably dual character, involving both theory and practice. Feminism is both a way of thinking about the world and a way of acting in it.

The meaning of feminism is derived not just from footnote-dotted books but also from the decisions and actions of generations of people around the world claiming to act on its behalf. So disagreement over the definition of *feminism* is a disagreement over how people should act and interact. This debate is conditioned in part by the historical eras in which it has taken place. It is also an international and cross-cultural argument, involving women (and some men) from around the world and from different social groups, each with a different experience and, therefore, with a different view on the needs of women.

In this chapter, we start with a general working definition and then turn briefly to some alternative contemporary feminist theories to investigate some of the disagreements. If we sort through all these different perspectives, we can find a core of characteristics about which most agree. *Feminism* is a perspective that views gender as one of the most important bases of the structure and organization of the social world. Feminists argue that in most known societies, this structure gives women lower status and value than men, more limited access to valuable resources, and less autonomy and opportunity to make choices about their lives. To say that gender structures social life, of course, does not deny that other social classifications, such as race, class, or religion, are important. Indeed, many feminists argue that we cannot clearly understand the significance of gender without setting it in these contexts. However, the point is that whatever else we take into account to whatever degree, feminists regard gender as a central fact of life.

Feminists further believe that although this gender-based world may be organized around certain biological facts—such as the exclusive capacity of men to create sperm and the exclusive capacity of women to bear children—gender inequality is rooted in the social construction of human experience, which means that societies with a will to do so can eliminate gender inequality. Feminists may not differ much over *inequality*, but they do vary a lot over questions of *difference* because these are not exactly the same things. For some feminists, it is neither possible nor desirable for all differences between men and women to be eliminated, while for others, any difference in treatment, roles, activities, or cultural constructions of male and female is bound to buttress unacceptable inequality.

Most feminists also share the belief that inequality will not be eliminated simply by having women work individually to do the best they can in their individual lives because inequality is embedded in the larger culture, social practices, and institutions. Women must also work together to change the structure of the social world. Any other action means making the best of an unjust situation.

This general working definition provides only the common denominator in definitions of feminism. Further refinement requires examining various traditions and types of feminism. To understand the meaning of feminism in more depth, it is important to undertake two tasks. The first is to survey the history of feminism to understand how it has developed over time and to ground an understanding of feminism in the historical conditions in which it has been created. From the point of view of social science research, feminist movements constitute a case study of the wider phenomenon of social movements. This chapter begins, therefore, with a discussion about the knowledge of social movements developed by sociologists, political scientists, and historians, among others, then it uses that knowledge as a framework to examine the history of feminist movements in the United States. The second task is to explore the body of thought loosely known as feminist theory, in which feminist scholars and activists have experimented with frameworks for understanding women's situation and sex/gender systems and worked to create new visions of the future and strategies to achieve these visions.

The Development of Feminism and Women's Movements in the United States

Like most social movements, feminist movements are not spontaneous uprisings that occur randomly. A *social movement* is a collective effort by a large group of people to solve a set of problems they think they share. Participants in social movements generally do not have the political power to achieve the changes they desire through regular governmental channels and procedures, which is why they turn to collective action.

How do these groups of people come together in the first place? Why do they come together when they do? What makes them decide that they share common problems and that they can solve these problems through collective action? How do they choose the particular strategies for action? How and why do they succeed or fail? Historians and social scientists disagree about the details, but their study of past social movements offers broad suggestions.[2]

Social-Movement Theory

Social movements do not necessarily begin because a group faces a new problem. They begin when some portion of the larger group (who will serve as initiators and early leaders) arrives at a new perception of the group's problems and the possibilities for change. In fact, many specialists in the study of social movements argue that they are most likely to take off when a group's situation is already starting to improve, and people's hopes and expectations for change outstrip the reality. The women's movement of the 1960s did not arise because inequality in employment or education or marital law and policy were just developing. Instead, it arose because enough women came to a special awareness of these inequities, largely because their expectations were growing and because they became more aware of the roadblocks because they *were already* entering higher education and employment in larger numbers.

A social movement is often incited by a *precipitating event* that both sparks a special awareness or new consciousness on the part of a relatively small group of people and becomes a symbol of problems and possibilities. This early core of people, in turn, organizes and attempts to *mobilize* others whom the core people think should share this consciousness. The success of organization and mobilization generally seems to depend on three factors:[3]

1. The early leaders must be able to draw on some prior *frustration or discontent* experienced by their potential followers, even if that discontent has not yet been expressed in the specific form the new social movement will give it. In the 1950s, for example, Betty Friedan witnessed the "problem that had no name," a feeling of personal discontent on the part of middle-class women, which no one seemed to understand.
2. Social movements generally do not start from scratch but develop from and build on *existing networks and organizations.* Jo Freeman (1975) shows how the contemporary women's movement was built from earlier networks, and many historians of 19th-century feminism show the same pattern in the suffrage movement.
3. Social movements also tend to arise when there is a favorable configuration of *political opportunities*—for example, (a) a facilitative political climate or a set of national leaders who are supportive of political change; (b) other social conflicts going on at the same time, from which the new movement can draw tangible or intangible resources or organizational strategies; or (c) new laws, policies, or governmental programs that in fact aid the development of the social movement. Political opportunities were crucial in the development of the 1960s women's movement (Costain, 1992).

The task of mobilizing recruits is the most crucial and difficult aspect of social movements. Early in any movement's history—when they are most likely to fail—mobilization is even more important than attempting to influence the powerful. Unlike most interest groups, which may rely on money or contacts or special forms of power, social movements rely largely on numbers. It is hard to make a credible case or credible threats to power holders if the movement contains only a tiny proportion of the group that it claims to represent. Mobilization of potential members of a social movement involves identifying the people who are most likely to develop a sense of *group consciousness* or shared political identity with the group, convincing them that they have a shared problem with a shared solution.

The already converted often underestimate the difficulty of mobilizing a base of supporters. They, after all, have already developed a consciousness that redefines the nature of their situation, its problems, and potential solutions. The problem, they believe, is *gender* (or for other social movements, race or class or "the government" or secular people). But consciousness does not flow automatically from one's demographic characteristics (such as gender or race); consciousness is the complicated *subjective* phenomenon of self-perceptions and -definitions. The more socially complex is the target group for mobilization, the harder it will be to stir up the group consciousness and motivation for action required to get people into the social movement. The diversity among women serves as a case in point.

Successful mobilization is only the first difficult step in the process of maintaining a strong social movement. Indeed, successful movements can become threatening to themselves because they are susceptible to change and fragmentation as they grow. Consider these three tendencies:

1. The *methods and strategies* appropriate to a large movement are different from those appropriate to a small new movement. A large group has different resources, is more diverse, and does not need to devote as much effort to consciousness raising among potential members. Sometimes, the initial group of organizers cannot adapt to—or certainly lead—these changes.

2. As a movement grows, its actions must adjust to the changing reactions of outsiders and to changes in *historical circumstances*. The suffrage movement, for example, used different strategies and approaches at the close of the Civil War than it did on the eve of World War I, just as the contemporary women's movement—born in a time of prosperity, optimism, and a general push toward progressive politics in the 1960s—had to adjust to the economic and political hard times of the 1980s and early 1990s. Even the technological context of political activism changed dramatically for both movements. The early 20th-century suffragists had modes of transportation and communication not available to their predecessors in the mid-19th century, and the current feminist movement depends heavily on computers and computer technology that were not available in the late 1960s and early 1970s.

3. The characteristics of the people involved change; a different *generation* moves into play. Early participants gain experience, learn, and are sometimes left behind by the changes that take place within their own organizations. Elizabeth Cady Stanton was 33 years old when she organized the Seneca Falls Convention; she was 75 years old when she served her last term as president of a national suffrage organization. Many of the women who first came together at the beginning of the contemporary women's movement are still active, but they are now decades older and changed by their experiences.[4] New women with new experiences, motivations, and skills enter a movement in its later stages. They bring with them fresh ideas of what is to be done and how, and they sometimes feel considerable frustration with the old guard, who may deal with them skeptically.

American feminism's long history exemplifies these patterns. Even the brief sketch provided here points out how varied and continuous the history of feminism in America has been. This section examines four phases in this history: the period before the Civil War, often characterized as the era of the women's rights movement; the period from the Civil War to the ratification of the Nineteenth Amendment in 1920, most remembered for the suffrage movement; the period from 1920 to the establishment of presidential commissions on women's status in 1961, when there was no unified national women's movement; and the era from the early 1960s to the present, when the contemporary women's movement grew, gained force, and came to be regarded as part of the old politics by the new movements of the 1990s.

Before the Civil War

If feminism is a self-conscious, collective effort to improve the condition of women, there was little feminism as such before the Civil War.[5] No mass movement attacked the oppression of women as a group, although many individuals and organizations worked to alleviate certain specific problems that particular groups of women faced. By the middle of the 19th century, however, advocates of women's rights had laid the groundwork for the post–Civil War surge in feminism and had contributed to a change in the consciousness of many women, which provided the breeding ground for a more comprehensive feminist ideology and action.

In the first decades of the American republic, discussion of the roles and status of women was part of the more general attempt by intellectuals and other leaders to define the nature of the new nation and its members (Evans, 1989; Kerber, 1986). Mary Wollstonecraft's ([1792] 1975) *Vindication* made the rounds in these circles, and an American, Judith Sargent Murray, wrote a series of newspaper essays (using the "Constantia" pen name) that explained the need for better education for women (see Rossi, 1988). Newspapers often served as a forum for discussion of needed societal improvements.

Even if there was not a large social movement, there was some agitation for women's rights before the rise of 19th-century women's movements, especially in the early 19th century. Activists' predominant focus of attention was female education, and it was often promoted by one person or a small group of people working to establish schools for females. Emma Willard (1787–1870), for example, established the Troy Female Seminary in 1821 and managed to get some public funding for it. Her success is particularly notable because the idea of *public* schools was still in its infancy. People such as Willard and Mary Lyon (1797–1849), who founded Mount Holyoke in 1837, pursued the principle of women's rights by spreading their ideas and attempting to fulfill their own dreams in individual ways.

Although these women had no notion of founding a mass movement, they inspired those who later led the feminist movement. Lucy Stone (1818–1893), for example, seems to have awakened to feminist ideas as she sat in a sewing circle working to provide the income for a young man to pursue his studies (as many young women did). While she sewed, she listened to Mary Lyon speaking of women's education. Stone apparently left her sewing thinking, "Let these men with broader shoulders and stronger arms earn their own education while we use our scantier opportunities to educate ourselves" (quoted in Flexner, 1975, 34). Stone went on to become one of the first female graduates from Oberlin College and a moving force in American feminism.

The early 19th century was a time of great social and religious activism. At the same time, women's roles became more restricted in many ways with the development of the American nation, its economy, and the resulting cult of true womanhood. Not surprisingly, many women chafed at the change and resisted. Historians usually discuss this change with respect to White society, but it affected the women of many communities. As pressures from both White society and Cherokee men began to introduce the cult of domesticity into Cherokee society in the early 19th century, for example, Cherokee women tried to protest their loss of rights and reduced status (Perdue, 1989). As early as the 1820s, free African-American women began organizing mutual aid societies (Shaw, 1991).

Women became involved in two widespread social movements that transformed their ideas about the condition of women and thus provided the country with a core of feminist leaders and organizers: the *moral-reform movement* and the *abolition movement*. Barbara Berg (1978) has provided an account of the growth of female moral-reform societies during the first half of the 19th century and of their evolutionary role in transforming many women's views of their own conditions. Like other historians, Berg has offered a reminder that the growth of female social activism and feminine—and ultimately, feminist—consciousness occurred during a time of widespread social change and redefinition. On one hand, there was the growth of an urban culture and pressures for democratization; on the other, there was a groping for security best exemplified by the pursuit of a romantic, orderly, pastoral ideal. That ideal included the cult of domesticity and the belief that woman's place was in the home. The home came to be seen as a place distinct from the public world of politics and markets, and woman, the guardian and symbol of the home, came to be seen as having a character distinct from that of man.

Berg has argued that not just the home but also this emerging perception of woman's character provided a base of security to White urban men in a confusing and dynamic world.

> Woman's nature, then, perceived as the opposite of man's, gave clear expression to the elusive male identity. Moreover, the alleged and exaggerated difference between the sexes substituted for the absence of rigid class distinctions in the first part of the nineteenth century. Because masculine security depended so heavily on the distance man set between himself and woman, every effort had to be made to indicate vast differences in the nature of the two sexes. (Berg, 1978, 73–74)

The result was the creation of a relatively rigid theory of sex distinction, as well as a class of women with very little to do.

Many women turned their attentions to social activities that seemed appropriate for ladies. In some cases, these were clubs and literary societies; in many cases, these were benevolent and moral-reform societies (Ginzberg, 1990; Scott, 1990, 1992; Shaw, 1991). Because these women had no intention of defying social mores, most of their good works involved helping other women. The result, however, was a growing awareness that there was something especially oppressive about women's lives. As Berg has written (1978, 170),

Voluntarism exposed many facets of woman's oppression. It brought into sharp focus those abuses that generally had the greatest impact on the lives of poorer women. Whether they distributed firewood to widows, shelter to orphans, medicine to the sick, Bibles to the unconverted or education to young girls, the women in philanthropic organizations visited with and listened to hundreds of thousands of destitute females in cities across the country. Their collective experiences vivified the depth and extent of feminine suffering.

The two aspects of women's lives underscored most clearly by this experience with different groups of women were economic inequality and women's "subjugation to masculine brutality." Berg (1978) has further argued that as the volunteer women began to work more closely with those less fortunate—such as poor women, widows, prostitutes, imprisoned women, and the wives of drunkards—many began to see considerable similarity between themselves and these other women. Because the ideology of the time was that men and women have distinct and opposite natures, it was a small step for these early social workers to feel a certain unity with women in apparently very different circumstances.

Some activists began to speak and act in ways that would seem very familiar to feminists today. In New York, for example, members of the Moral Reform Society kept vigil at brothels and reported their findings in their journal. They publicly identified some patrons of the brothels and threatened to do the same to others (Berg, 1978, 185). The writing in moral-reform periodicals could be very biting:

> Women have so long been called "angels" that men seem to have come to the conclusion that they have no persons to protect; and as for property, they say women do not know enough to take care of it, and therefore the laws and customs of society virtually say they shall have none to protect . . . the law in its kind care for women . . . takes away every cent from her. This is not exactly burning a woman on the funeral pile of her husband, but is rather a refinement on the Asiatic cruelty. (Quoted in Berg, 1978, 209)

Above all, the reformers came to believe that women had to take responsibility for themselves and, as they said repeatedly, to think for themselves. Their work in women's organizations gave many women a new respect and affection for women and their abilities (Degler, 1980, 301).

Women in moral-reform and related organizations focused on several specific issues. Some concentrated on marital-property reform, especially in the 1830s and 1840s. Others concentrated on the conditions of working women. A large proportion focused on the poor, widows, and orphans. Many of their efforts were aimed at protecting women from male exploitation and brutality, through, for example, temperance and birth control (women's right to refrain from sex), and helping "fallen women," who had already been prey to such exploitation and brutality. Finally, many women became active in the abolition movement.

The abolition movement gave many African-American and White women their first real taste of collective social and political action. As in the moral-reform movement, these women did not simply talk, but also engaged in action, which in this case could be mortally dangerous, especially when the women served as conductors or provided stations on the Underground Railway. As White women worked toward the emancipation of Black slaves, they began to see more clearly some aspects of their own condition as women. For example, Sarah (1792–1873) and Angelina (1805–1879) Grimké argued that women had a special role to perform in emancipation work and began to talk more broadly about women's roles, as well (Lerner, 1971; Rossi, 1988). In 1870, more than 30 years after Angelina's "Appeal to Christian Women of the South," both sisters cast symbolic ballots in special ballot boxes in Massachusetts to demonstrate their support for the female vote.

It is often said that 19th-century feminism, especially the suffrage movement, was born of the abolition movement (DuBois, 1978). Although more of the White women who became involved in the later feminist movements probably came through moral-reform organizations, abolition provided the original cadre of suffrage leaders, and it gave shape to midcentury feminist organizations. The early link between abolition and feminism is direct and well known. In 1833, the "men only" American Anti-Slavery Society was founded in Philadelphia. Undaunted by the fact that they were not allowed to join, interested women founded the Philadelphia Female Anti-Slavery Society. Their separatism was foisted upon them; unwilling to pick a leader from their midst, they chose a Black freedman as the head of their organization. In 1837, at the first convention of the National Female Anti-Slavery Society, however, the members made it clear that women were quite capable of managing without male leaders such as Theodore Weld (the man whom Angelina Grimké later married).

In 1840, the World Anti-Slavery Convention in London excluded women, including abolition activists Lucretia Mott (1793–1880; one of the founders of the Female Anti-Slavery Society) and Elizabeth Cady Stanton (1815–1902). The two women walked around London angrily discussing their plight, but they then went their separate ways for the next 8 years, although they stayed in contact. Eventually, Stanton and her husband settled in the small town of Seneca Falls, New York, where she found herself growing increasingly discontented with her own limited domestic roles and with the roles assigned to women in general.

> The general discontent I felt with woman's portion . . . impressed me with the strong feeling that some active measures should be taken to remedy the wrongs of society in general and of women in particular. My experience at the World Anti-Slavery Convention, all I had read of the legal status of women, and the oppression I saw everywhere, together swept across my soul, intensified now by many personal experiences. It seemed as if all the elements had conspired to impel me to some onward step. I could not see what to do, or where to begin—my only thought was a public meeting for protest and discussion. (Quoted in Flexner, 1975, 73–74)

The same pattern occurred repeatedly both at that time and later: A woman or group of women is struck by a combination of personal experiences and events that demand action. But what action? The first step for Stanton, as for others, was to call a meeting to share observations with other women and to figure out what needed to be done.

In the summer of 1848, Stanton met with Mott and four other women and "poured out, that day, the torrent of my long accumulating discontent, with such vehemence and indignation that I stirred myself, as well as the rest of the party, to do and dare anything" (quoted in Flexner, 1975, 74). The meeting they planned came to be known as the Seneca Falls Convention, which ended in the signing of the Declaration of Sentiments and Resolutions. Elizabeth Cady Stanton's feelings at that time kept her active for more than half a century more. Only one woman present at the meeting, which issued the first tentative call for women's suffrage, lived to vote as a result of the Nineteenth Amendment to the U.S. Constitution.

Activists continued their abolitionist work until the Civil War, adding their commitment to the rights of women to their abolition efforts. In 1850, an important women's rights convention held in Worcester, Massachusetts, gained international fame through the writings of Harriet Taylor in England (see Rossi, 1988). Conventions then were held nearly every year until 1861. The overlap between the abolitionist and women's rights movements is well illustrated by the names of the key leaders who spoke and acted for both. Although Elizabeth Cady Stanton, Susan B. Anthony (who joined Stanton in 1851), Lucretia Mott, and Lucy Stone are usually associated with women's rights, and Sojourner Truth (1797?–1883), Theodore Weld, Wendell Phillips, and William Lloyd Garrison are generally associated with abolitionism, in fact all of these people devoted their efforts to both causes. Sojourner Truth's most famous speech ("Ain't I a Woman?") was delivered to a woman's rights convention in Akron, Ohio, in 1851.

The women's movement was not yet a very large social movement. It consisted of various groups of political activists pursuing different, discrete goals, often tied to other concerns, such as moral reform or abolition. As small as the women's movement was, however, the group was criticized for doing nothing but talk. The historian Eleanor Flexner has answered that charge as follows:

> At this stage, there was not much else they could do. Having stated their dissatisfaction with things as they were, they had to agree on what they wanted to achieve, and to develop an ideology which would serve to refute their critics and win them new adherents. What was the proper condition of married women? What should be women's place in the church, the community, the professions, the state? On what basis should divorce be permitted . . . ? From the gatherings where these issues were thrashed out there emerged a body of thought, new and dedicated leadership, wide publicity, and new recruits. (1975, 81–82)

Many of the feminists began to write about these issues, and some started their own periodicals. There was some attempt to coordinate feminist activity nationally. A central committee was formed in the 1850s, with delegates from any state in which there was women's rights activity. Flexner has noted that at that time, activists had little desire for greater organization, for much the same reasons that later feminists were wary of too much organization: They feared that it would stultify growth and would inhibit rather than promote action (1975, 83). The intentional building of a strong movement had to wait until after the Civil War.

Fifty Years and More: From Civil War to Suffrage

The Civil War offered women new avenues for their social concern and activism.[6] Many social activists turned their attention to new organizations such as the Sanitary Commission, which did war relief and nursing work. The more politically minded put their efforts to a new task: fighting in Congress for passage of a constitutional amendment that would forever ban slavery in the United States. Elizabeth Cady Stanton and Susan B. Anthony gained their national political organizing skills through their positions as officers in the National Women's Loyal League, which in 1864 presented to Congress a petition with more than 300,000 signatures supporting an amendment to ban slavery.

The text that eventually became the Fourteenth Amendment to the U.S. Constitution both sparked the organization of a full-blown women's suffrage movement and deeply divided it as it was forming. That amendment, which was to become critical in defining citizenship, contained the first and only use of the word *male* in the U.S. Constitution; it levied a punishment against states that interfered with the voting rights of "male citizens." Activists such as Stanton and Anthony were infuriated and wanted, at least, that the word *male* be removed. But they went further and added their voices to the discussion of another proposed amendment (eventually the Fifteenth Amendment), which would guarantee the right to vote regardless of race. They wanted that amendment also to guarantee the right to vote regardless of sex.

The rift that ensued broke up the Equal Rights Association, which had been organized at the end of the war to pursue the rights of women and Black men. The rift focused on two related questions: First, should the Association fight to get what it could, which might mean legal guarantees of rights for blacks (or at least Black men) and not women, or should it press for rights for women as well? Second, which was the more pressing need: legal guarantees for Black men or for women? This insidious type of question is often faced by different oppressed groups attempting to work in coalition.

In fact, the question makes no sense at all with respect to a large group of women: those oppressed by both race and gender. Consider Sojourner Truth's argument,

> I feel that I have a right to have just as much as a man. There is a great stir about colored men getting their rights, but not a word about the colored women; and if colored men get their rights, and not colored women theirs, the colored men will be masters over the women, and it will be just as bad as it was before. So I am for keeping the thing going while things are stirring; because if we wait till it is still, it will take a great while to get it going again. (Sterling, 1984, 411–412)

The Equal Rights Association chose race rights as its primary goal. In 1869, Stanton and Anthony broke away to form the National Woman Suffrage

Association (NWSA), open to any interested women but only women, on the belief that the men of the Equal Rights Association were selling out and duping the women of that organization. The NWSA became dedicated to a constitutional amendment for women's suffrage. Later that year, Lucy Stone and others formed the American Woman Suffrage Association (AWSA), including both women and men, but restricting its membership to delegates. It preferred the more conservative strategy of pursuing women's rights on a state-by-state basis. The national organization for the late-19th-century women's movement was in place, but it remained divided for the next 20 years.

The breakup of the Equal Rights Association caused unforgettable tension between Black and White leaders. Stanton and Anthony embellished their break with many racist remarks, just as many later suffragists pitted "native women" (native-born Americans of European stock) against immigrants. Although these events are often discussed as if they involved only Black men and White women, they also involved White men and Black women. The White men of the Equal Rights Association by and large stuck with the argument "this is the Negro's hour," and Black women faced a most difficult dilemma. An amendment that barred discrimination on the basis of race alone would not give Black women the vote. However, if clear incursions into racism were not made, no amount of women's rights legislation would help them.

The ambivalence of Black women lasted throughout the 19th century because they were "placed in a double bind; to support women's suffrage would imply that they were allying themselves with White women activists who had publicly revealed their racism, but to support Black male suffrage was to endorse a patriarchal social order that would grant them no political voice" (hooks, 1981, 3). Despite the number of times White suffragists made racist statements and discriminated against Black suffragists, many Black women fought for women's rights throughout the end of the 19th century and into the beginning of the 20th, sometimes in their own organizations, and sometimes in integrated organizations. In the split between the NWSA and AWSA, most Black suffrage leaders, including Sojourner Truth and Harriet Tubman (1820?–1913), chose to stay with Stanton and Anthony in the NWSA.

The suffrage movement remained active throughout the rest of the 19th century, but it was by no means the only activist women's movement. The suffrage movement mobilized women by drawing on those involved in other kinds of women's organizations. Women's organizations in the postwar period were even more active than they had been before the war. Social activists, including many of the leading suffragists, increased their efforts to influence the morals and social life of the nation, especially as they affected women and children. These efforts in the last decades of the 19th century are often called the "social purity" movement.

One of the best known of the social-purity organizations was the Women's Christian Temperance Union (WCTU), which was founded in 1874 and became the largest single women's organization in the nation. Under the leadership of Frances Willard (1839–1898), it was also linked to the suffragist cause, although many people worried about whether the two issues should be mixed. Willard herself took care not to be associated with so-called radicals such as Stanton and Anthony. To most other temperance suffragists (such as Anthony herself), the reason for mixing temperance and suffrage seemed obvious. If men would stop spending their wages on drink and coming home to be useless fathers and husbands or worse, women would be better able to provide themselves and their children with good and healthful lives. If women had the vote, they would also have the political leverage to provide themselves and their children with good and healthful lives, as well as a means to spread their own moral influence.

By the end of the 19th century, the suffrage movement was also drawing from other sources: women who were receiving advanced degrees and were becoming professionals, some of the women of the new labor movement, and some of the women of the American West who had become involved in the labor movement and in populist uprisings and organizations, such as the Grange clubs. Even if the suffragist movement began as an alliance primarily of homemakers who had the time to devote to social housekeeping and reform causes, by the end of the 19th century, it included many working women who were drawn in not as individuals but as members of work-related groups.

The late-19th-century suffragists used many strategies to pursue their goals. They lobbied, spoke, organized petitions, and got involved in state referendum campaigns. The NWSA worked on increasing congressional support for a constitutional amendment. Suffragists also engaged in protest and direct actions, such as attempting to cast ballots in elections, as they did across the country in the early 1870s. They also tried to use the courts: Two famous cases, those of Susan Anthony in a New York state court and Virginia Minor (1824–1894) in the U.S. Supreme Court, made it clear that the judicial system could not be used to gain women the vote. Both women attempted to vote and sued unsuccessfully when they were barred from doing so. Other participants in the protest, such as Sojourner Truth, were turned away before they could obtain ballots.[7] By the end of the 19th century, only a handful of states and local areas had given women the right to vote, and Congress did not seem to be moving toward support for a suffrage amendment. The differences between the two major suffragist organizations (the NWSA and the AWSA) blurred, and in 1890, they merged, forming the National American Woman Suffrage Association (NAWSA).

By the turn of the century, the early suffrage activists were very old. The last of the original leaders, Stanton and Anthony, died in the early 1900s. The new leaders and activists differed from their predecessors. Carrie Chapman Catt (1859–1947) did not fear organization as earlier feminists had. Catt, who engineered the final successful stage of the campaign, brought with her a modern sense of political organization. Elizabeth Cady Stanton's daughter, Harriot Stanton Blatch (1856–1940), had spent 20 years in England and imported to America some of the techniques she had witnessed there. She formed a new organization and tried new strategies, such as holding open-air meetings and marches and working with trade unions. She captured for suffrage work some of the brightest and eventually best-known women of that era, including Charlotte Perkins Gilman (1860–1935) and Florence Kelley (1859–1932) (Flexner, 1975, 261). The movement drew women of all types and classes, from trade-union women of the garment district to wealthy wives of bankers and industrialists. Women of all political parties—Democrats, Republicans, Socialists, and Progressives (a new party that endorsed women's suffrage in 1912)—were involved. At the same time, the size

Alice Paul, a suffragist and activist.

and complexity of the movement meant that agreement on a single plan was diffi-cult to achieve, and the movement was often torn by disagreements about tactics.

One woman who both breathed new life into the movement and fostered a schism within it was Alice Paul (1885–1977), who had spent some time in England before coming home to the United States to complete her Ph.D. She had been greatly impressed with the radical activities of the Pankhursts (a woman and her two daughters, who led the English suffrage movement) and thought she could use the same techniques to call attention to women's plight in America. When she became head of the Congressional Committee of NAWSA, one of her first acts was to organize a parade of 5,000 women in Washington the day before Woodrow Wilson's inauguration, sparking a near riot (Flexner, 1975, 272–273).

Alice Paul's radicalism led to a separation of her group from NAWSA. Paul wanted to hold whichever political party happened to be in power responsible for the lack of a federal amendment granting suffrage to women. NAWSA opposed this position because this would mean working against some prosuffragist candi-dates. Paul's group, the Congressional Union (CU), worked in the 1914 election campaigns to punish the party in power at that time, the Democrats. The group's activities succeeded in bringing the suffrage amendment to a vote, but it was defeated, at first.

Paul and her organization then became more militant. In 1917, the Congressional Union picketed the White House, the first time any political group had done so. The CU changed its name to the National Women's Party and added antiwar slogans to its rhetoric. These demonstrations provoked violence by onlookers, and the women demonstrators (not the violent onlookers) were arrested. Eventually, the women held a new kind of protest inspired by the English feminists. They demanded to be called political prisoners and went on a hunger strike in prison. Prison officials reacted by force-feeding them, which caused a public outcry that eventually led to the women's release.

Many people argued that these radical actions hurt more than they helped and made people unwilling to join the suffragists. This argument is still used to oppose militancy in contemporary social movements. The criticism, however, is often launched by people who have not been drawn into the movement by more conservative strategies, either. Analysis of the effects of different wings of the suffrage and other feminist movements suggests that the combined or parallel actions of the moderate and radical wings allow more widespread participation and more varied strategies.

Alice Paul's actions called attention to the resolve of the feminists in a way that other strategies did not; these actions showed that women were willing to risk their lives and careers for suffrage. Many people would have been unaware of the suffrage movement had it not been for the headlines that Alice Paul and her group provoked, and the public was appalled by the violence with which the state fought against them. Meanwhile Carrie Chapman Catt's "Winning Plan," as she labeled her strategy of intense but more conventional political campaigning, achieved passage and ratification of the Nineteenth Amendment. The irony is that in large part, people like Alice Paul made Catt's strategies appear conventional, conservative, and reasonable. Until that time, the political tactics that NAWSA was using may have been conventional for men, but they were very unconventional for women.

An interesting perspective on this question of moderation versus radicalism in strategy has been offered by Arvonne Fraser, an activist who became a leader in mainstream feminist groups in the 1960s and 1970s, including the Women's Equity Action League (WEAL):

> Radical feminists identified and publicized "the system's" oppression of women. They also made it respectable for women to work on women's issues. Eventually, establishment women began to work within the system to change laws and regulations and their task was made easier by these earlier efforts. Our group and others like it would never have been formed if the women's liberation groups had not staked out a more extreme position. (Fraser, 1983, 122)

It is difficult to ascertain whether success would have come if only one strategy had been used, and it is even more difficult to know the effects of any strategy while in the middle of the battle.

Many casual observers paint the suffrage amendment and the feminist movement that supported it as failures for two reasons: (1) feminist goals were too narrowly focused on getting the vote, and (2) the feminist movement disappeared after 1920. The remainder of this section examines the first of these two points more carefully. The subsequent section addresses the second of these points. The vote was no small goal to achieve. It is the symbol of citizenship, without which women could not be seen as free citizens. Before suffrage, political leaders argued that women's rights did not matter because, after all, women could not vote. In addition, some rights are contingent on voting, either by law or by custom, including the right to hold certain types of political offices and to sit on juries. The vote is an instrument to be used to pursue other goals, and this is how most suffragists saw it.

Although suffrage is the best-known goal of feminists of this period, it was not the only one. As mentioned previously, the social-purity movement was based on the belief that women should have increased control over their destinies. The specific goals of this movement may seem conservative to today's feminists, but they were nonetheless intended to free women from various unfair constraints. A new and more radical birth-control movement developed after the turn of the century, as women such as Margaret Sanger (1883–1966) and Emma Goldman (1869–1940) fought to make contraception more widely available.

The same era witnessed the rise of organizations oriented toward alleviating the plight of working women. The Women's Trade Union League (WTUL) was formed in 1903 because of the failure of male-dominated unions to work for the rights of women. A related effort was the National Consumer's League, established in 1899, which originally worked to alert consumers about whether the products they were buying were made in shops with proper working conditions. Meanwhile, women who had entered various professions formed organizations to fight for women's rights within their own groups.

It is difficult to identify an area of life that was not in some way touched by feminism in the late 19th and early 20th centuries. There were attempts at dress reform for women and continuing debates over women's health and education. Amelia Bloomer, after whom the bloomer was named, was only one of the many women who organized the dress-reform movement of the 1840s and 1850s. There is a rich feminist literature from the late 19th century, produced by feminists in the social sciences, journalism, and the literary arts. Women's groups intensified their efforts to help immigrants and the poor. Women's organizations within various racial, religious, and ethnic groups focused on some of the special problems these groups faced. These groups were as diverse as the San Francisco–based Korean Women's Patriotic Society, focusing on educating and developing social awareness among the picture brides from Korea (Yang, 1984), and the New York women who used the Yiddish language *Jewish Daily Forward*'s women's page to formulate a Jewish socialist view of women and feminism (Seller, 1987). Increasingly, after the turn of the century, the various feminist organizations also threw their support behind suffrage, much as the widely divergent feminist groups in the 1970s added their voices and efforts to support of the Equal Rights Amendment. Thus, suffrage was not the only goal of turn-of-the-century feminism; it was not even the only goal of most suffragists. It was only the most widely accepted one, and the only one that many people now remember.

The Quiet Time: From Suffrage to Presidential Commissions

Did feminism disappear after 1920, as so many people charge?[8] If the question is whether a large, well-coordinated movement of women persisted after the vote was won, feminism indeed disappeared. However, if the question is whether all the feminists packed their intellectual and activist bags and went home, feminism did not disappear, at least not immediately.

To explain these answers, it is necessary to analyze the 40-year period following 1920 by asking two questions: (1) What happened to the large suffrage organizations? (2) What other forms did feminism take during the postsuffrage period? The presuffrage feminists certainly did not think their war would be over when they won the suffrage battle. An understanding of what happened to them and their movement requires an examination of the events that followed in the context of the sociology of social movements.

As this chapter has emphasized, mass social movements are fragile coalitions of different types of people with different motivations, pursuing similar goals. The suffrage movement was a carefully constructed coalition of people who agreed that women should have a basic right of citizens: the vote. They disagreed considerably over what other issues they should pursue. Should they work for temperance, for birth control, for equal pay, for protective legislation, or for marital and divorce reform? How should they structure their organizations? Should whites and blacks work together, even if such integration alienated a large block of legislators and White suffragists? Should they work in as "ladylike" a manner as possible, or should they display their anger and frustration and use threats and coercion to achieve their ends? Should they focus on the national or the state and local levels? Should they center their work on politics or culture or personal life? It is often more surprising when the coalitions in social movements hang together than it would be if they fell apart. Feminism is one of the largest and longest-lived movements in American history, and although it had its share of failures, its longevity is an indication of its relative strength and success, compared with other American movements. As the suffrage battle was won, an intense and active rethinking of the terms of feminism and feminist action occurred (Cott, 1987).

The suffrage coalition weakened and eventually fell apart after the vote was gained because there was no consensus on the next major goal or the primary strategy. The goals of different individuals and organizations overlapped, but that was not enough, and other events of the period put obstacles in their path. Nonetheless, leaders of the suffrage movement did not wait for ratification to begin planning for the future. Alice Paul and Carrie Chapman Catt, assuming that they should be prepared for the inevitable time when their constituents would be voters, began transforming their respective organizations before the Nineteenth Amendment was in place. The differences between these two new organizations reflect feminism's important disagreements over the definitions of feminist goals and strategies.

Alice Paul's Congressional Union became the National Women's Party (NWP), the offices of which still stand two blocks from the national Capitol. As the name implies, Paul had visions of an explicitly feminist political party that would continue its battle for women's rights at the highest levels of government. Still believing in the most direct and vigorous route to equality, Alice Paul proposed in the early 1920s that the U.S. Constitution should be amended to make discrimination on the basis of sex unconstitutional. The wording of the amendment has changed only slightly over time. The most recent version states simply, "Equality of rights under the law shall not be denied or abridged by the United States or by any state on account of sex." This proposal has been the main goal of the NWP since 1923 (Cott, 1987; Rupp, 1985).

For most of its history, the NWP has stood relatively isolated in its support of an equal rights amendment, although other important organizations eventually joined in support. In 1935, the National Association of Women Lawyers endorsed the amendment, and 2 years later, the 90,000-member National Federation of Business and Professional Women's Clubs added their support. The NWP gained important allies in the 1940s, when the amendment was endorsed by the General Federation of Women's Clubs (GFWC), the National Educational Association, five national women's service organizations, and the Republican and Democratic Parties (Rawalt, 1983). Although the Equal Rights Amendment was introduced in Congress in 1923 and in every successive Congress, it did not pass until nearly 50 years later, in 1972. Ten years later, the necessary number of states had not ratified it, and the proposal died—for the time being.

This amendment was not the only focus of the NWP's attention, however. The post–World War I period was a time of international conferences on law and human rights, and Alice Paul fought to make equality of the sexes part of international law, as well. The NWP took a leading role in the fight to allow women their own citizenship, distinct from their husbands', and to pass their nationality on to their children. As they pointed out, gaining the right to vote in 1920 did not make women full citizens because if an American woman married a foreigner, she was stripped of her citizenship, and if she had a child by an alien, the child was an alien. Members of the NWP, many of them also members of the feminist National Association of Women Lawyers, continuously lobbied and testified to Congress until their demands were met in 1934 (Becker, 1981, 1983; Sapiro, 1984).

The NWP met opposition in the feminist community, primarily because their goals were incompatible with protective labor legislation. This opposition reflects a fundamental disagreement within feminist theory at the time. Alice Paul and her group wanted equal opportunity and equal treatment for women and men. Most other feminists thought that equal treatment, especially in the labor market, would maintain a system of laissez-faire economics in which women were a cheap and exploited labor force and in which no extra care was given to mothers and children.

Most feminists also continued to see Paul's goals and strategies as too radical and militant, and most rejected a separate women's party on two grounds: First, they preferred a more integrated system in which women and men worked together as responsible citizens for the betterment of all. Second, if women wanted power in the political system, many argued, they would do better to make inroads into the main political system than to form a party of their own.

As head of NAWSA, Carrie Chapman Catt was the leader of the more widely accepted brand of feminism. She transformed NAWSA into the League of Women Voters (LWV). Catt's idea was that the LWV would be a nonpartisan training ground for female political activities and citizenship. It would be a place where women could develop their own political agenda. They could then fight for their goals through the regular political parties and processes as equals. The LWV was intended to promote women in politics, much as the National Women's Political Caucus (NWPC) is today. In its first few years, the LWV drew up an impressive agenda of policy goals covering democratization in government; improvements in health, education, consumer, and welfare policy; better care for children and mothers; and protective labor legislation for women.

The LWV was strengthened when it initiated an even wider coalition of feminist groups. In 1920, the LWV became aware that it might be stepping on the toes of other women's groups, such as the GFWC and the WTUL, because its program and leadership overlapped with theirs. Under the leadership of Maud Wood Park (1871–1955) the LWV negotiated the formation of the Women's Joint Congressional Committee (WJCC). Any federal bill supported by at least three of the member organizations was backed by the financial and labor resources of the WJCC.

The greatest early victory of the WJCC was passage of the Sheppard Towner Act in 1921, which was drafted by Julia Lathrop (1858–1932), a League of Women Voters member and director of the Children's Bureau, and introduced into Congress by Senator Jeanette Rankin (1880–1973) in 1917. The Sheppard Towner Act, which provided federal funding for child and maternal health care, was an early breakthrough in the development of federal welfare policies. This early success, however, also contributed to the eventual weakening of the coalition responsible for it. The women's groups were caught in the middle of the first "red scare" of this century and in the subsequent wave of anticommunism.

Feminists had long been accused of being socialists or communists; indeed, some feminist leaders were socialists. Such accusations became very serious matters after the 1917 Russian Revolution, when many radicals, including Emma Goldman, were deported. In the 1920s, anti-Communism and xenophobia in general played important roles in American politics. The Sheppard Towner Act, widely regarded as the first step toward socialism in America, signified to many people that feminists were insidious Bolshevik radicals. Different scare tactics were used against the WJCC, including the drawing of a spiderweb showing the connections among feminism, socialism, and Moscow (Cott, 1987; Lemons, 1972). This spiderweb suggested a dangerous conspiracy that could trap the innocent. The resulting backlash helped weaken the coalition and forced many of the women's groups, including the LWV, to put their heads down to survive.

Other factors aided the demise of widespread, united feminism. The political parties were resentful of groups such as the LWV, arguing that they were trying to compete with the parties. Women party activists found their loyalties tested, and the LWV's hold on many of its members was strained by the greater power of the political parties. Many members were also overstretched and had to reevaluate their commitments.

The feminist activists of the 1920s and 1930s were different from their 19th-century predecessors in one important respect. They were, for the most part, employed as professionals or as blue- or white-collar workers. Some worked in government. These women had limited time for activism, and many devoted this time to the organizations most relevant to their work. The specific political goals that dominated their interests diverged—many goals were compatible but different—and the feminist movement became more fragmented. Unfortunately, the breakdown of a coalition can also weaken its constituent parts.

In the 1920s, feminists had difficulty attracting young women to their cause. The young women, especially those who were college educated, believed that there really was no battle left to fight, or at least not one that was significant enough to join. They could vote, drink, smoke, and, it seemed, dress as they liked. Many believed that women had gained their freedom, and the public press agreed with them. Flappers and movie stars were more glamorous than tiresome, serious-minded feminists. The feminist movement thus lost an important pool of new recruits. Finally, the stock-market crash of 1929 and the ensuing economic depression overshadowed the demands of feminists.

Between the two world wars, some women continued to fight for feminist change through their jobs or through women's organizations or religious and ethnic associations. Many women in government and journalism pushed for reforms. The New Deal programs of President Franklin Roosevelt offered a special opportunity for women to gain some of the types of programs they supported and to participate in their administration. Eleanor Roosevelt (1884–1962) associated herself with women's interests and organizations and, in her position as the first activist First Lady, provided an important support for women. People such as Margaret Sanger continued their work on birth control, and trade-union women continued to organize women workers. Women in groups such as the International League for Peace and Freedom, many of whom also had been active in other feminist groups, continued their efforts to avert war. At the same time, women began to take their places in formerly male domains of economic and social life. The early 1930s also saw a peak in the proportion of higher degrees and some professional jobs held by women. That record was not matched again until the 1970s.

The story of World War II and its effects on women has been told throughout this book. Women plunged into war work at home and abroad, and many gained a new consciousness of their potential and the social inhibitions placed on it. Surveys showed that most women did not want to "go home" after the war, and in some industries, women struggled together to keep their jobs (Gabin, 1982). The systematic attempt to demobilize women, or at least to bump them down into lower-paying and more traditionally gender-appropriate jobs, proved too strong for them, however (Tobias and Anderson, 1982). By the 1950s, *feminism* was associated with what seemed to be ancient history, and as Betty Friedan suggested, women did not even have a name for the problems they faced (Friedan, 1963).

Events of the early 1960s, however, provide evidence that feminism never entirely disappeared. The NWP and some other women's groups had continued to push for an equal rights amendment, which the Senate had passed in 1950 and 1953, and both major parties had supported the ERA in their platforms since 1944. As a liberal Democrat, President John F. Kennedy could not ignore the issue of women's rights, and he established a presidential commission on the status of women to look into the matter. He also urged the states to establish their own commissions, which all had done by 1967. This series of study commissions set the stage for the rise of the new women's movement in the late 1960s.

Rebirth of Feminism: Emma Said It in 1910/ Now We're Going to Say It Again[9]

If the birth of social movements generally depends on changing perceptions of a group's situation, an established network among potential leaders, and an event that precipitates action, the women's liberation movement fits the pattern very well. The post–World War II economic boom drew women into education and jobs at an unprecedented rate in the late 1950s and 1960s. Divorce rates began to rise in the early 1960s, following a decline from a postwar peak. Finally, although America was increasingly affluent, and its growth potential seemed unlimited, new social movements were asking people to question whether life was as good as it could be. The Black civil rights movement, the ban-the-bomb and antiwar movements, and the early 1960s Free Speech Movement (which sparked student activism nationwide) were all part of the new social ferment of the times and provided the training ground for many social activists who went on to lead the women's liberation movement.

The first real bubblings of the new women's movement came in the mid-1960s. As usual, there were women involved in various political activities on behalf of women. A large number participated in government-sponsored events, such as the Commissions on the Status of Women, urged on by President Kennedy, and the EEOC, established to implement the 1964 Civil Rights Act. Betty Friedan published the widely read *The Feminine Mystique* in 1963.

The turning-point events in the rise of a new mass movement occurred between 1964 and 1966. These events involved very different women, participating in very different activities, but the events incited what began as parallel developments and ultimately a large and complex social movement, first known as the Women's Liberation Movement and later, simply the women's movement or the feminist movement. One part of the parallel strand originated in the South, during the 1964 "Freedom Summer," a concentrated effort to register African-Americans to vote, organized by the Student Nonviolent Coordinating Committee (SNCC), an organization founded by African-American students in 1960. That summer, many Northern White women and men joined the SNCC efforts, in a remarkable biracial political effort organized by African-Americans. Among the many debates that erupted that summer were those involving not just issues of strategy and organization and the relations between White and Black activists, but also the treatment of women in the movement, and the tensions that arose from the sexual relations and suspect motives among African-American men, White men, African-American women, and White women.

In the course of that summer, women began to raise questions and debate about the position of women in the civil rights movement and the implications for their politics in general. Ultimately, two White women activists, Casey Hayden and Mary King, wrote a paper on the "sexual caste system" they saw. This paper gained wide circulation and an even wider reputation. The frustration on the part of women in the main organizations of the movement—SNCC and the Students for a Democratic Society (SDS)—grew and developed over the next couple of years. By 1968–1969, women associated with various factions of the New Left had formed small groups, such as the Chicago westside group, the Redstockings in New York, and Bread and Roses in Boston, which formed a first core of what came to be known as the "younger" or "radical" branch of the women's movement.

Meanwhile, at the annual meeting of the National Conference of State Commissions, some of the delegates became angry when they found that they would not be allowed to do anything to correct the problems they had been assigned to study. These women were older and more established political figures (after all, they came together as delegates to this particular conference), but contrary to common belief, they could be characterized as "conservative" only in comparison to the young radicals. In the context of the times, these women's concern for the status of women, plus the background many of them had in the civil-rights movement and the labor-union movement, certainly put them clearly to the left of the political mainstream. A group of angry and frustrated women met in the hotel room of Betty Friedan, one of the delegates, to decide what to do. After this and a series of later meetings, in October 1966, they decided that the solution was to form a distinct organization aimed at women's rights, which they called the National Organization for Women (NOW), with 300 members and Betty Friedan as president.

Two groups of women thus emerged: Both groups were already involved in politics, indeed both were involved in different versions of the politics of the left, and both were meeting the frustration that led them to strike out on their own politically and to organize women on the basis of their gender. As Jo Freeman, a scholar and member of one of the earliest of the radical feminist groups, has argued, the differences between the two kinds of feminist organizations were at least as much of style as of substance (Freeman, 1975). NOW has always had a formal organizational structure and paid officers. It has concentrated on legal and policy changes and has become one of the foremost lobbyists for the women's movement. NOW may have been criticized as conservative by more radical feminists, but this is not how the larger society viewed it. In fact, some of the first women to break away from NOW formed their own feminist groups because they thought NOW was too radical for having supported the ERA and abortion rights.

These patterns created by the early radical feminists and the women of NOW were followed many times over the subsequent years in other New Left, traditional left, and antiwar organizations across the country. Like Elizabeth Cady Stanton, over a century earlier in the antislavery movement, many women reacted with rage, confusion, and the desire to meet separately to plan a course of action. The result was the formation of small feminist groups across the country, based on the politics of the New Left and many caucuses and committees formed from other types of political, professional, and trade organizations.

The contemporary women's movement therefore began not as a single organization, but as a complex network of very different groups, much as the women's suffrage movement had developed from parallel and sometimes conflicting organizations. At times, the differences have seemed to overshadow the similarities. The more radical groups' antipathy toward formal structure and hierarchy has led them to experiment with leaderless structures, in an attempt to create a more thoroughly consensual democracy. The radical feminist groups in the early days emphasized consciousness-raising sessions to awaken women to their situations and help them translate their discontent into political action. As women in consciousness-raising sessions discussed their own personal problems, they became aware that these same problems were commonly faced by other women, and this helped mobilize many women to action. Other groups assumed the task of providing services, such as child-care centers and counseling and assistance services for victims of rape and of wife battery.

Feminists quickly began to organize demonstrations to attract national attention to their demands. One of the most infamous was a protest staged at the 1968 Miss America contest, where a Freedom Trash Can was set up to dispose of "women's garbage," and a sheep was crowned Miss America. Despite the fact that no one recalls the burning of any bra, from that date forward, feminists were given the trivializing name "bra burners," thanks to the mass media who heard that this was going to happen. The next major demonstration—on the 50th anniversary of women's suffrage, August 26, 1970—was the Women's Strike for Equality, which involved feminists of all views.

As the feminist movement grew, it developed the rifts and fragmentation common to most social movements. These rifts were apparent both within and across organizations. Because of the growth in the membership of the movement, feminists could specialize in particular concerns—abortion, child care, employment discrimination, sexuality—which made the movement more comprehensive and effective but also made coordination and consensus more difficult to attain. Some women felt that their concerns were being neglected, and some argued that concentration on such issues as professional employment, higher education, and women's studies was elitist and of little relevance to most women. From its earliest days, debates swirled around (a) the relationship of Black women to the women's movement (especially because of the role of the civil rights and early Black Power movements in the founding of feminism and the lives of those who identified with it) and (b) the relationship of working-class and poor women to the women's movement. Many argued that the women's movement was too conservative and ignored the interests of women who were not White, middle class, and heterosexual. Others argued that the tactics of such radical women as the lesbian separatists would scare off the more conservative women who most needed the movement. By 1970, sexual politics and homophobia were the focus of great dissent and bitterness in both major branches of the movement.

It is one thing for a social movement to appear united when it consists of a relatively small group of people with an apparently simple demand, such as "equality" or "equal pay for equal work"; it is quite another when the movement is large and increasingly precise in its identification of problems and solutions. Because many people mistakenly think that disagreement within a social movement is necessarily a sign of failure, many assumed that the women's movement was about to fall apart, even as it was growing larger.

The history of NOW is a microcosm of the larger movement. As some of its associates moved away because they feared issues such as abortion, others grew dissatisfied because they thought NOW too conservative. The arguments, which at times threatened the organization's existence, revolved around NOW's hierarchical structure, the distribution of power in the organization, and the low priority given to lesbian issues. In the early 1970s, the battle between lesbian activists and the NOW leadership reached its height and caused what many described as a purge of the lesbian leaders. Although NOW later added support for lesbian women to its platform, scars remained. Despite these disagreements, NOW's membership and the membership of the thousands of other women's groups across the country continued to grow tremendously into the middle of the 1980s, and the number of groups multiplied until it is now impossible to list all that exist. It is probably safe to say that a feminist group exists for every social category or interest.

The movement developed other discernible branches over time. The early radical feminists were, as Alice Echols (1989) has argued, "politicos," whose politics were framed by the Marxist and socialist politics of the left, and whose focus was on organization, power, and political economy, even if they also introduced the women's movement to consciousness raising (which was borrowed from the Chinese "speaking bitterness" groups). As Echols also has argued, this branch faded in the face of a different radical feminism, a feminism based more in cultural politics—for example, the emphasis on developing a distinct women's culture. Where the early politico radical feminists turned their backs on conventional electoral politics, the cultural-politics framework led many feminists to concentrate on the politics of the personal, eschewing political mobilizing altogether (unless music festivals count). The women's spirituality movement went even further in this direction.

Lesbian politics and ultimately multicultural politics became more central themes in U.S. feminism. The growing gay and lesbian movement (and ultimately "queer politics") breathed new life into the women's movement, even if it also renewed tensions. Multiculturalism permeated all branches of the women's movement (as the following section shows) but also helped restore some of the connections to women in poorer communities, which had been the starting place of the contemporary women's movement.

Feminism and the Women's Movement Today

Despite differences in views and strategies, the feminist movement has been remarkably cohesive. It is no longer a young movement, and it has been through many trials. The different branches and organizations have learned much from each other, to the point where some earlier differences have become obscured. During its development, a lot of change has occurred. The young feminists of the late 1960s are mostly in their 50s now. By the time the current young women of the women's movement were born, the Women's Strike for Equality had come and gone, as had Betty Friedan's early 1970s antilesbian speech about the Lavendar Menace, the first national Chicana conference (La Conferencia de Mujeres por la Raza) in 1971, the founding of the National Black Feminist Organization in 1973, the 1973 *Roe* v. *Wade* abortion decision and the founding of the first battered women's shelters in the same year. Indeed, many of today's young feminists were born during the time in which the backlash was setting in during the Reagan administration.

Of course, much of the agenda and style of the women's movement is different now from what it was in its early days. Nonetheless, the general themes pick up the threads from the many different traditions and organizations that have fed into it since the late 1960s. What follows is a brief list of these themes.

Women's Rights. The inclusion of women in all of the basic civil, political, and human rights remains central to the agenda of feminism. Women still face employment and education discrimination; their pay is still not equivalent to men's for the same amount and type of work. The points of discrimination are as trivial as being barred from using the golf greens of country clubs at the prime hours and as major as being subject to dangerous, even life-threatening sexual harassment, merely for being a woman in the U.S. military.

Sexual Politics. The women's movement continues to contend with what Adrienne Rich called "compulsory heterosexuality," including problems of both gay and lesbian rights, and of women's ability to take control over their sexuality, regardless of their sexual orientation. Central within this theme are issues concerning sexual harassment, pornography, and violence against women.

Violence Against Women. Feminists have achieved many inroads in policies dealing with rape and woman battery, the incidence of these crimes against women remains far too high, women still blame themselves too often, and the justice, therapeutic, and health-care systems still have a long way to go in helping women who are victims.

Reproductive Issues. Despite the existence of groups such as "Feminists for Life," the majority of feminists and women's movement organizations remain committed to giving women the rights of choice over reproduction, including at least some rights to abortion. Sterilization abuse also remains an issue, as do important questions regarding the use of different reproductive technologies. Questions about surrogacy also raise tough issues for feminists. The women's movement also focuses on the special reproductive issues of particular groups of women, including especially teen pregnancy.

Women's Health. One of the most important foci of the contemporary women's movement is the wide range of issues relating to women's health. Of special interest is support for more research on women's health and for devoting more effort to solving the problems that are the greatest health afflictions for women: cardiovascular disease and breast cancer. Women's health takes on a special importance in the United States, where large numbers of women have little or no access to affordable high-quality health care, especially as compared with women in other industrialized nations.

Child and Family Issues. This category includes a multitude of issues, including especially the division of labor within the family between husbands and wives, the availability of high-quality affordable child care and other arrangements—such as parental leave and dependent care—that make it possible for people to combine caring for their families with earning a living and supporting their family financially.

Social-Welfare Policies.   This theme includes a wide range of issues that affect a large portion of the population, especially the poor. As the social-welfare safety net became more threatened during the 1990s, social-welfare policy became increasingly central on the feminist agenda, a concern that certainly stretches back to the Progressive era at the turn of the 20th century. Considering the disproportionate share of poverty that afflicts women and their children, the particular health-care needs for women who are reproductively active, and the fact that women are a high proportion of the aged, the shrinking of the welfare state has hurt women more than it has hurt men.

Women's Culture.   The early 1970s witnessed a dramatic growth in attention to women's graphic and performing arts, crafts, publications, periodicals, bookstores, and other modes of cultural expression. These continue to be a primary focus of the women's movement.

Multicultural Feminism.   One of the most important changes in feminism and feminist politics in the 1980s was a shift toward a *multicultural* feminism.[10] Although more recent participants in the women's movement sometimes mistakenly suggest that race, ethnicity, class, and globalism were not seriously considered in the women's movement until very recently (a sign of how fast the historical consciousness of a movement can fade), for many years, the search for, or emphasis on, *commonality* among women made it difficult for feminist theory and practice to take full account of the *differences* among women.

Two developments effected a shift in the frame and terms of feminist discussion and debate. First, *international contact* among women concerned with the condition of women increased. The United Nations International Women's Decade (1975–1985) was only the largest and best known of many efforts to bring together women from around the world. Feminism organized most quickly in the United States in the 1960s and 1970s, but by the 1970s and 1980s, there were many large or well-organized feminist movements around the world. Feminism began to have a major impact on theory and scholarship in different countries. The feminist practice and theory that developed around the globe was different across countries because of their distinctive histories, cultures, social structures, and problems. As the growth of feminist organization and influence within different countries facilitated contact across countries, the debates among feminists, which highlighted the distinctions among women's situations, became important. Increased contact between First and Third World feminists enriched feminism considerably.

Second, increased *feminist activism and involvement of women of color, poor women, and others whose experiences had been marginalized* forced feminists to take account of the differences among women's social circumstances. Although many of the early activists in the contemporary women's movement—in both of the major original branches—had been involved *first* in movements focusing on race or class, the growing strength of organization among African-American and Hispanic women and those in the battered-women's movement, for example, became important forces within feminism and demanded greater reckoning with the diversity of women's lives from everyone involved.

Thus, multicultural feminism does more than simply recognize that women live in many different kinds of situations. Such recognition forms a core part of multicultural feminism, which not only looks for the obvious similarities in women's lives, but also analyzes the varying effects of androcentric sex/gender systems, as Chapter 4 suggested. The idea of differences among women is central to multicultural feminism, not something that is ignored or explained away. According to this view, we cannot really understand the role of gender in people's lives without also understanding its relationship to such other aspects of social life as race and class.

Multicultural feminism itself is necessarily various, drawing from arguments of the liberal, socialist, or radical traditions in feminist theory. In highlighting diversity, multicultural feminism also recognizes conflict among women, even those who consider themselves feminists. This recognition is unusual in social movements, which usually emphasize a kind of solidarity among their members, attempting to minimize difference and conflict. In multicultural feminism, the recognition of diversity and the acceptance of some conflict is interpreted as part of a healthy political process.

It is important to note that a piece of feminist writing about women of different cultures or social groups is not necessarily multicultural, and a piece of writing about women of one culture or social group is not necessarily *non*multicultural feminism. Merely adding some focus on women of color to thinking that is otherwise dominated by the experience of whites is not sufficient to make it multicultural, just as it is not sufficient simply to add some focus on women to otherwise androcentric thinking to make it feminist. Multiculturalism depends on a distinctive framework and method of analysis. Patricia Hill Collins's effort to construct an Afrocentric or Black feminist thought incorporates different and conflicting ways of understanding Black women without "trying to synthesize competing worldviews that . . . may defy reconciliation" (Collins, 1989a, 773). She has not tried to make single what is multiple.

Similarly, bell hooks has emphasized the importance of understanding the differing relationships to domination each individual can have:

> I understand that in many places in the world oppressed and oppressor share the same color. I understand that right here in this room, oppressed and oppressor share the same gender. Right now as I speak, a man who is himself victimized, wounded, hurt by racism and class exploitation is actively dominating a woman in his life—that even as I speak, women who are ourselves exploited, victimized, are dominating children. (1989, 20–21)

She has argued that "to understand domination, we must understand that our capacity as women and men to be either dominated or dominating is a point of connection, of commonality" (1989, 20). Her argument is part of a multicultural feminism (a) because it is her awareness of differences among women that helps her understand gender relations, and (b) because she shifts the center of her focus and tries to take account of the multiple standpoints and experiences of the people she talks about.

Oppositions

In 1991, a best-selling book became the focus of great discussion across the United States and, indeed, in many other countries: Susan Faludi's *Backlash: The Undeclared War Against American Women*. This book, written by a Pulitzer Prize–winning journalist, argues that following some of the early successes of the new women's movement, a vehement backlash developed in almost all walks of life during the 1980s, which sought to restore women to a more traditional and sub-ordinate place. The power of the book—probably more widely known than any feminist book since Betty Friedan's *The Feminine Mystique* (1963)—was enhanced by the vicious attacks on feminism and prominent women activists launched soon after its publication by the right wing of the Republican Party during the 1992 presidential campaign.

As Faludi documented, there has been tremendous resistance to feminism. It grew through the 1990s from many directions, but especially from two sources: (1) the strengthening conservative politics that had grown angry at the legacies of 1960s politics and blamed these policies for the economic problems the country faced, and (2) the burgeoning religious fundamentalist right, found most strongly first among Protestant evangelicals, but then among fundamentalists of many religions and denominations.

To understand that resistance, it is necessary to look not just at the events of the contemporary era, but also at the history of oppositions to feminisms and women's movements, which reveals considerable continuity over the course of American history. Some of the attacks made on today's feminists were also made against the suffragists. The current and past antifeminist arguments are as varied as feminist arguments.

One of the chief arguments against feminism has been that if women are given equal treatment and opportunities in society, they will lose their protection and become more overburdened than they already are. Antisuffragist women and men used this argument in the 19th and early 20th centuries, and antifeminists continue to use it today. They claim that equality will, in fact, result in injustice for women.

Another argument against feminism has had religious origins. In fact, much opposition throughout the history of feminism has come from religious groups and leaders. These groups are distressed by feminist attacks on what they see as the moral order of male and female difference and changes in familial, sexual, and reproductive mores.[11]

Some opposition is based on economic arguments. Various business interests, including railroads and liquor producers, opposed suffrage because they feared what women would do with their votes (Flexner, 1975). The National Association of Manufacturers (NAM), which opposes any governmental restraint on business, opposed feminist demands that employers prove that they treat employees fairly and equitably.

Some opponents to feminism have worried about the domino effect of social change: If changes are accepted for women, who will want changes next? During the later years of the suffrage movement, many political leaders worried that if women were granted new rights, there would be little justification for denying the same rights to blacks or immigrants.

Sometimes, the opposition has framed its argument not in terms of feminism or women's roles per se, but in terms of the effects any changes might have on the larger society. Because feminists have tended to look to the federal government for assistance, supporters of state rights have tended to be antagonistic to feminism. Feminist proposals support government interference with husbands' traditional abilities to overpower their wives financially and physically. Many opponents see these proposals as demands for big government to expand still further and thus to interfere with private rights of commerce and personal relations. Feminist proposals have also tended to call for the expansion of social services, which stirs up opposition on the part of those who see these proposals as socialist or as too costly.

Opposition also comes from those who quite simply think that society has been well structured in the past, has worked well, and has had no need of tampering. Those who believe that American social institutions have operated in a fair and open way in the past regard any effort to change their gender composition as an attack on "merit" systems. They argue that women are underrepresented or receive less reward because they have not wanted—or been good enough—to do better. Conservative critics of feminist efforts to alter the emphasis of research and education argue that these efforts will result in research agendas and curricula based on political decisions, rather than merit decisions. They believe that an objective market of ideas (not men raised in androcentric cultures, even if well educated) has determined that women and their creations are not worth much attention.

Explicit antifeminist activity tends to emanate from the most conservative sectors of society. Throughout the 20th century, antifeminists have accused feminists of being socialist and anti-American, particularly because feminists support both social programs to help the needy and governmental regulation of industry to benefit the consumer and the worker. Studies in the 1970s showed that antifeminist activists tended to be particularly fearful about the spread of communism in the United States.

The argument between feminists and antifeminists has generally not been a battle of equal and opposing parties appealing to the government for change. The battle has usually been between groups of mostly women (generally led by women) on the one hand and the mostly male leaders of government, business, and religion on the other. Of course, many women are opposed to feminism, including members of such women's organizations as Phyllis Schlafley's Stop-ERA, and Women Who Want to Be Women (WWWW). In the 19th century, many of the most active female opponents were wives of men in government or business who had power to maintain the old system of discrimination and oppression. The most effective opposition then and now is from those who already have power. It is generally easy to see why these institutional leaders want to forestall change: It is costly to those already in power. Although men can derive many benefits from feminism, women who argue that men can only benefit by equality for women are naïve, and most men know it.

The contemporary women's movement may be the first in American history to face the opposition of an organized antifeminist social movement. From the mid-1970s to the 1990s, a coalition of groups calling themselves profamily and prolife emerged. These groups, which drew from right-wing political organizations and the Moral Majority, were formed in reaction to feminist successes in reproductive, family, and antidiscrimination policies. These antifeminists have used all the opposition arguments already mentioned, but they have focused on the presumed protection of women and the preservation of what they define as traditional Christian moral values.

Antifeminist women are not generally opposed to women holding jobs or engaging in political activity; many of them do the former and all, by their involvement in the antifeminist movement, are doing the latter. They are willing to use all of the political rights won for them by earlier feminists: they organize, demonstrate, petition, lobby, litigate, vote, and hold office. Some even use violence—for example, firebombing abortion clinics or physically harassing women going in and out of these clinics. Antifeminist women use these means to defend what they define as women's interests, just as feminists use most of these tactics (except violence against women) to defend what they define as women's interests. How can antifeminist women reconcile their opposition to demands for equality and liberation with their claims that they are fighting for women?

A clue to the answer lies in 19th-century feminism, in which women's-rights activists and moral- and social-purity campaigners were often one and the same because these were seen as two sides of the same equation. Moral and social purity, they claimed, could give women the dignity and protection they needed from the brutal masculine world and the men in it. Men, they argued, are not trustworthy. They will exploit, neglect, and hurt their families if left to their own devices. Women need protection from men, and men need protection from themselves. The key to the solution was seen as strengthening women to spread their influence as nurturers and preservers of traditional values.

Contemporary antifeminists often use much the same argument, but they also argue that contemporary feminists have gone too far in the wrong direction. Today's antifeminists say that by emphasizing a social structure of genderless individuals with precisely the same rights, roles, and characters, and by destroying the foundations of familial morality, the feminists are taking away men's motivation to remain loyal to their families and women's motivation to be anything but self-seeking, individually competitive people, just like men. If feminist goals are achieved, they argue, women, children, old people, and others will be left without any protection or with caregiving by sterile, bureaucratic public institutions.

An important question for contemporary feminism is how women come to define themselves as feminist, or as linked to other women in some common set of experiences, problems, or strategies for change (Sapiro, 1989, 1991). The sources of feminism—and of opposition to it—are as varied as women's experiences themselves, lodged both in the facts of individuals' lives and in the historical and cultural situation in which women find themselves. There are many ways of thinking about why people are feminists or antifeminists, why people join one movement or the other or simply remain aloof. Probably the least useful way is to regard the opposition (be it feminist or antifeminist) as evil or ignorant. One of the most important writings along these lines was contributed by Robyn Rowland (1984). Rowland wrote to many different women around the world, feminist and antifeminist, and asked them to write about their understanding of and attitudes toward feminism. These essays, collected under the title *Women Who Do and Women Who Don't Join the Women's Movement*, offer an unparalleled opportunity to hear many different women speak for themselves. The number of different paths they took to reach their conclusions is striking.

Despite the disagreements and the different paths, research shows that a substantial proportion of the American population shares some of the feminist critique of society as it has been structured and sees room for change. In the early 1990s, about 62% of Americans thought that men have more power than they should relative to women *in government and politics,* and 65% thought that men had more power than they should relative to women *in business and industry.* Americans were more divided about the balance of power *in the family.* About 25% thought that men had too much power relative to women, 24% thought that women have too much power relative to men, and 51% thought that the balance of power between women and men is just right as it is. The vast majority of those people (86%) thought that women and men currently have equal power in the family.[12] Nevertheless, although only a minority of people call themselves *feminists,* a majority still see a need for a women's movement.

Global Feminisms

Feminism is a worldwide movement, and American feminism must therefore be understood in this context. American feminists have often learned from their sisters abroad, and they have often influenced the feminists of other nations. Feminism has long crossed national borders as women from different nations have worked together for their common cause.

American feminists have been influenced by those from other nations since the 18th century. They found their intellectual roots, for example, in the writings of people such as Mary Wollstonecraft, an Englishwoman. Late-19th- and early-20th-century feminists such as Margaret Sanger, Harriot Stanton Blatch, and Alice Paul gained considerable training and inspiration from European activists during their travels abroad. American feminists have also been effective in exporting their ideas and strategies to the outside world through their travels, their publications, and the impressions they have made on foreign women who have traveled in the United States.

The turn of the 20th century witnessed the rise of international organizations of feminists, including the International Woman Suffrage Alliance (IWSA) and international meetings of trade unionists. At these meetings, women exchanged ideas about goals and strategies to support each other in their struggles at home. Carrie Chapman Catt was particularly active in these efforts, and, through her, the NAWSA agreed to contribute to the IWSA. The 1930s were a time of heightened feminist international activity. Governments and international lawyers made numerous efforts to construct a more coherent and enlightened system of international law, particularly as it concerned human rights. Women quickly seized the

A soldier hugs her son before she leaves for duty during the Gulf War. International politics
has profound impacts on women and their families.

opportunity to advocate women's rights, as they did at an international conference
specifically on women's rights held in Montevideo in 1933. The NWP was particularly active in this regard. The United Nations and its agencies have continued to
promote international agreements and conventions on women's rights, as have the
Organization for Economic Cooperation and Development (OECD), of which
the United States is a member, and the European Community, a confederation of
western European nations.

Changes in transportation and communications technology have facilitated
the coordination of international feminist organizations. International women's
conferences are held yearly around the world, women's caucuses meet in the context of larger international meetings and organizations, and thousands of feminists

around the world communicate with each other daily through the medium of electronic-mail networks. These international efforts are important not just because they offer an opportunity for feminists to compare notes but also because it has become increasingly obvious that women's problems are not local in origin and sometimes arise from countries' foreign policies.

Sometimes, the collective action among feminists globally is very specific. For example, some dangerous birth-control drugs or devices banned by the U.S. Food and Drug Administration (FDA) have been channeled to women in countries without such strong consumer protections. American feminists have fought such policies and have also sought less sexist and discriminatory administration of American foreign-aid programs (Jaquette and Staudt, 1985; Staudt, 1985). During 1992, when mass rape and so-called ethnic cleansing became an instrument of war used by the Serbians in the former Yugoslavia, the news traveled fast by electronic means among feminists.

International feminism has its own special problems. The four international conferences held in 1975, 1980, and 1985 as part of International Women's Decade and then in 1995 as the Fourth World Conference made some of these problems rise painfully to the surface. In 1975, the United Nations sponsored an International Women's Year Conference in Mexico City. When it became clear that some women delegates were being used to foster their governments' own aims, an alternative meeting, called the Tribune, was convened. Most of the feminist activists went to this other meeting, rather than the official meeting. In 1980, a meeting was held in Copenhagen to evaluate progress since 1975. That meeting was also disrupted by official delegates less concerned with feminism than with their countries' nationalistic goals. Some delegates went so far as to try to bar and censure women from other countries, simply because of their nationalities. Many feminist delegates left bitter and skeptical about the potential of international efforts, especially those organized through official governmental bodies.

Despite these difficulties, feminists of different nations met again in Nairobi in 1985—more successfully this time—and again in Beijing in 1995, and they continue to cooperate where they can.[13] The United Nations (UN) organized and served as the primary instigator for these meetings and, in fact, many other international efforts. Although women in the United States tend to ignore the UN efforts, these efforts are, in fact, very important for leveraging rights and better conditions around the globe, both directly through the committees on women and indirectly through major world initiatives on such things as literacy, health care, banning of female genital mutilation, and human rights. The United Nations Convention on the Elimination of All Forms of Discrimination Against Women is a major world initiative that has been ratified by most UN members—but not the United States.[14]

One of the hardest lessons for feminists in the United States to learn is that they are part of a global system in which there are many different societies and cultures, each with their own subjectivities. In the 20th century, Americans have become used to thinking of themselves as the leaders and the central players on the world scene. This parochialism extends to feminism, to the extent that Americans define their situation as the standard for women's situation and their feminism as the global model of feminism. Even the particular character of American diversity is different from other forms, so a United States–based understanding of social structure—of how race/ethnicity or class works—is limited. Feminisms are shaped by the historical and cultural experiences of specific societies. One nation's or one culture's feminism is as limited as any other. There are vital and active women's movements in many countries around the globe, and although they influence each other, each is also, in its own way, a local feminism (Basu, 1995).

Feminists around the world are beginning to realize how central sex/gender systems are, not just to domestic societies, but to the international system, as well. Defense and foreign policies often depend on gendered assumptions, and they certainly have gendered effects.[15] In this highly economically interdependent world, feminism must look beyond national borders.

One of the most exciting developments is the fall of many authoritarian governments that took place in the late 1980s and early 1990s. After a first euphoria, women in those and other countries began to realize what women should have known anyway: The fall of an authoritarian system does not necessarily usher in the rise of a democratic one, and in the course of struggling toward democracy, women's interests may be left behind. This story has been played out in the older democracies such as the United States, and it is playing out again in the newer ones.

Feminism and the Future

During the 19th and 20th centuries, there seem always to have been at least some people thinking about and working to improve the status of women. At some times, there have been large mass movements, and at others, there have been only isolated actions by individuals and small groups. In each generation, people have continued the debate over what equality or liberation would mean and how it could best be achieved. In each generation, there have been many women who were frightened by the changes proposed, or who thought that they had all the choice and freedom they needed. In each generation, there have been masses of people who have remained ignorant both about their own history and about the turmoil of the present.

As feminism has achieved some goals and failed to meet others, its agenda for the future has grown longer, rather than shorter. The solutions to one set of problems always seem to reveal many other problems. Each turning point in feminist history has revealed the degree to which gender continues to be used to restrict people's options. Moreover, as human societies change over time and develop new ways of making women's lives better and worse, their situation changes.

Anyone who needs confirmation that there is still much to be done need only consider that many people regard feminism and women's studies as frivolous and of only peripheral importance. Women who take an interest in their own status and roles in society are seen as selfish or divisive, and men who take an interest in women's status and roles in society are seen as odd or even pitiable. Nevertheless, many women and men persevere.

There has been much change in the definition of female and male gender in recent centuries. As this book has shown, many of the changes have been liberating, and some have not. What is left to be done? This book is filled with suggestions that come from today's feminism and social analysis. Beyond this, future generations will have to decide for themselves.

Notes

1. My thanks to Sarah Slavin, who suggested this approach to the differences and commonalities among different thinkers (see Schramm, 1979).

2. For works on social movements, see McAdam, McCarthy, and Zald (1996); and Morris and Mueller (1992).

3. Those knowledgeable in the social-movements literature will notice that these factors correspond to some of the major alternative theories of social movements.

4. The author of this book was a 19-year-old college sophomore when she first became involved in feminism in 1970.

5. For more reading on feminism in this period, see Berg (1978), DuBois (1978), Evans (1989), and Flexner (1975).

6. The literature on this period of feminism is voluminous. For some different approaches, see DuBois (1978); Flexner (1975); Kraditor (1965); Sochen (1972); and Stanton, Anthony, and Gage ([1881] 1969).

7. For further discussion, see Chapter 9.

8. For further reading on this period, see Becker (1981), Hartmann (1983), Higgonet et al. (1987), Honey (1984), Kaledin (1984), Lemons (1972), Scharf and Jensen (1983), Sochen (1973), and Ware (1981, 1983).

9. "Emma said it in 1910. Now we're going to say it again" was a chant used in women's movement marches in the late 1960s. "Emma" was Emma Goldman. For further reading on this period, see Boles (1979), Costain (1992), Echols (1989), Evans (1979), Freeman (1975), Hole and Levine (1971), and Klein (1984).

10. *Multicultural feminism* is a name I have chosen for this new turn in feminist theory. It is important to note that, contrary to common perceptions, even at the beginning of this century, many feminists were struggling with questions of diversity (Cott, 1987). For some examples of multicultural feminism, see Aptheker (1982), Collins (1989a), hooks (1981, 1984, 1989), Hurtado (1989), Minh-ha (1989), Moraga and Anzaldúa (1981), Spelman (1988), and Spivak (1987).

11. At the same time, many religious organizations have worked as part of the feminist coalition. Among the principal supporters of the ERA were the American Association of Women Ministers, the American Jewish Committee, Disciples of Christ, Lutheran Church in America, National Council of Churches, Union of American Hebrew Congregations, United Church of Christ, United Jewish Congress, United Methodist Church, and United Presbyterian Church, plus a number of Catholic organizations and many women's organizations of numerous demoninations.

12. Analysis by the author of the 1991 American National Election Study Pilot Study.

13. For readings on international feminism, see Alvarez (1990); Basu (1995); Eisenstein (1992); Gelb (1989); Jaquette (1989); Jayawardena (1986); Mohanty, Russo, and Torres (1991); Nelson and Chowdhury (1994); and Rowland (1984).

14. An excellent source of information on the UN's work on women is their "Women Watch" website, http://www.un.org/womenwatch/un.htm/.

15. Works on women and international politics include Afshar and Dennis (1992), Enloe (1983, 1989), Jaquette and Staudt (1985), Peterson (1992), and Staudt (1985).

References

Abbey, Antonia. 1982. "Sex differences in attributions for friendly behavior: Do males misperceive females' friendliness?" *Journal of Personality and Social Psychology* 42: 830–38.

Abbott, Pamela, & Roger Sapsford. 1988. *Women and Social Class*. New York: Routledge.

Abel, Emily. 1981. "Collective protest and the meritocracy: Faculty women and sex discrimination lawsuits." *Feminist Studies* 7:505–38.

Abramson, Phyllis. 1990. *Sob Sister Journalism*. Westport, CT: Greenwood.

Adams, Carolyn Teich, & Kathryn T. Winston. 1980. *Mothers at Work*. New York: Longman.

Adams, Karen L., & Norma C. Ware. 1989. "Sexism and the English language: The linguistic implications of being a woman." In *Women: A Feminist Perspective*, edited by Jo Freeman, pp. 470–84. Mountain View, CA: Mayfield.

Adams, Kathryn A. 1980. "Who has the final word? Sex, race, and dominance behavior." *Journal of Personality and Social Psychology* 38:1–8.

Afshar, Haleh, & Carolyn Dennis, eds. 1992. *Women, Recession and Adjustment in the Third World*. New York: St. Martin's.

Allen, Ann M., Daniel N. Allen, & Gary Sigler. 1993. "Changes in sex-role stereotyping in Caldecott Medal Award picture books 1938–1988." *Journal of Research in Childhood Education* 7:67–73.

Allen, Mike, Dave D'Alessio, & Keri Brezgel. 1995. "A meta-analysis summarizing the effects of pornography II: Aggression after exposure." *Human Communication Research* 22:258–83.

Allgeier, A. R. 1983. "Sexuality and gender roles in the second half of life." In *Changing Boundaries: Gender Roles and Sexual Behavior*, edited by Elizabeth Rice Allgeier & Naomi B. McCormick, pp. 135–57. Palo Alto, CA: Mayfield.

Almquist, Elizabeth. 1984. "Race and ethnicity in the lives of minority women." In *Women: A Feminist Perspective*, edited by Jo Freeman, pp. 423–53. Palo Alto, CA: Mayfield.

———. 1987. "Labor market gender inequality in minority groups." *Gender and Society* 1:400–414.

Alonso, Harriet Hyman. 1993. *Peace as a Women's Issue: A History of the U.S. Movement for World Peace and Women's Rights*. Syracuse, NY: Syracuse University Press.

Alvarez, Sonia E. 1990. *Engendering Democracy: Women's Movements in Transition Politics*. Princeton, NJ: Princeton University Press.

Amato, Paul R., & Alan Booth. 1995. "Changes in gender role attitudes and perceived marital quality." *American Sociological Review* 60:58–66.

American Association of University Women. 1992. *How Schools Shortchange Girls*. Washington, DC: AAUW Educational Foundation.

American Psychiatric Association. 1987. *Diagnostic and Statistical Manual of Mental Disorders-III-R*. Washington, DC: American Psychiatric Association.

Ammerman, Nancy Tatom, & Wade Clark Roof, eds. 1995. *Work, Family, and Religion in Contemporary Society*. New York: Routledge.

Andelin, Helen. 1974. *Fascinating Womanhood*. New York: Bantam.

Andersen, Barbara L., & Jill M. Cyranowski. 1994. "Women's sexual self-schema." *Journal of Personality and Social Psychology* 67:1079–1100.

Andrade, Vibiana M. 1981. "The toxic workplace: Title VII protection for the potentially pregnant woman." *Harvard Women's Law Journal* 4:71–104.

Aneshensel, Carol S., Carolyn M. Rutter, & Peter A. Lachenbruch. 1991. "Social structure, stress, and mental health: Competing conceptual and analytic models." *American Sociological Review* 56:166–78.

Aptheker, Bettina. 1982. *Woman's Legacy: Essays in Race, Sex, and Class*. Amherst: University of Massachusetts Press.

Aquinas, Saint Thomas. 1945. "Question XCII: the production of women." In *Basic Writings of Saint Thomas Aquinas*, edited by Anton C. Pegis, pp. 879–84. New York: Random House.

Arbuckle, Justin, et al. 1996. "Safe at home? Domestic violence and other homicides among women in New Mexico." *Annals of Emergency Medicine* 27:210–15.

Ariès, Philippe. 1942. *Centuries of Childhood*. London: Jonathan Cape.

Ariès, Philippe, & Georges Duby, eds. 1987. *A History of Private Life*. Cambridge, MA: Harvard University Press.

Ashby, Marylee Stoll, & Bruce C. Whittmaier. 1978. "Attitude changes in children after exposure to stories about women in traditional or nontraditional occupations." *Journal of Educational Psychology* 70:945–49.

Aslin, Alice. 1977. "Feminist and community mental health center psychotherapists' expectations of mental health for women." *Sex Roles* 3:537–44.

Aube, Jennifer, & Richard Koestner. 1995. "Gender characteristics and relationship adjustment: Another look at similarity-complementarity hypotheses." *Journal of Personality* 63:879–904.

Ayres, Ian & Peter Siegelman. 1995. "Race and gender discrimination in bargaining for a new car." *The American Economic Review* 85:304–21.

Backhouse, Constance, & Lea Cohen. 1981. *Sexual Harassment on the Job*. Englewood Cliffs, NJ: Prentice-Hall.

Bailey, Darlyne, Donald Wolfe, & Christopher R. Wolfe. 1996. "The contextual impact of social support across race and gender: Implications for African American women in the workplace." *Journal of Black Studies* 26: 287–307.

Bailey, J. Michael, & Richard C. Pillard. 1991. "A genetic study of male sexual orientation." *Archives of General Psychiatry* 48:1089–96.

Bailey, Susan McGee. 1993. "The current status of gender equity research in American schools." *Educational Psychologist* 28:321–39.

Baker, David P., & Deborah Perkins Jones. 1993. "Creating gender equality: Cross-national gender stratification and mathematical performance." *Sociology of Education* 66:91–103.

Baker, Ross K., Laurily K. Epstein, & Rodney D. Forth. 1981. "Matters of life and death: Social, political, and religious correlates of attitudes on abortion." *American Politics Quarterly* 9:89–102.

Bank, Barbara J., Bruce J. Biddle, & Thomas L. Good. 1980. "Sex roles, classroom instruction, and reading achievement." *Journal of Educational Psychology* 72: 119–32.

Banks, Taunya Lovell. 1997. "Two life stories: Reflections of one black woman law professor." In *Critical Race Feminisms*, edited by Adrien Katherine Wing, pp. 96–100. New York: New York University Press.

Banton, Michael. 1983. *Racial and Ethnic Competition*. New York: Cambridge University Press.

Barker-Plummer, Bernadette. 1995. "News as a political resource: Media strategies and political identity in the U.S. women's movement, 1966–1975." *Critical Studies in Mass Communication* 12:306–24.

Bart, Pauline B. 1975. "Emotional and social status in the older woman." In *No Longer Young: The Older Woman in America*, pp. 3–22. Ann Arbor: Institute for Gerontology, University of Michigan.

Bart, Pauline B., & Patricia H. O'Brien. 1984. "Stopping rape: Effective avoidance strategies." *Signs* 10:83–101.

Basow, Susan A., & Nancy T. Silberg. 1987. "Student evaluations of college professors: Are female and male professors rated differently?" *Journal of Education Psychology* 79:308–14.

Basu, Amrita, ed. 1995. *The Challenges of Local Feminisms: Women's Movements in Global Perspectives*.

Beasley, Maurine H., & Sheila J. Gibbons. 1993. *Taking Their Place: A Documentary History of Women and Journalism*. Washington, DC: American University Press.

Bebel, August. [1910] 1970. *Women and Socialism*. New York: Schocken.

Becker, Susan D. 1981. *The Origins of the Equal Rights Amendment: American Feminism Between the Wars*. Westport, CT: Greenwood.

———. 1983. "International feminism between the wars: The National Women's Party versus the League of Women Voters." In *Decades of Discontent*, edited by Lois Scharf & Joan M. Jensen, pp. 223–43. Westport, CT: Greenwood.

Beecher, Catharine. [1841] 1977. *A Treatise on Domestic Economy*. New York: Schocken.

Bell, Alan P., Martin S. Weinberg, & S. K. Hammersmith. 1981. *Sexual Preference*. Bloomington: Indiana University Press.

Bellas, Marcia L. 1994. "Comparable worth in academia: The effects on faculty salaries of the sex composition and labor-market conditions of academic disciplines." *American Sociological Review* 59:807–21.

Belsky, Jay, Keith Crnic, & Sharon Woodworth. 1995. "Personality and parenting: Exploring the mediating role of transient mood and daily hassles." *Journal of Personality* 63:905–29.

Bem, Sandra L. 1974. "The measurement of psychological androgyny." *Journal of Consulting and Clinical Psychology* 42:155–62.

Bem, Sandra Lipsitz. 1975. "Sex role adaptability: One consequence of psychological androgyny." *Journal of Personality and Social Psychology* 31:634–43.

———. 1983. "Gender schema theory and its implications for child development: Raising gender-aschematic children in a gender-schematic society." *Signs* 8:596–616.

Bensing, J. M., A. Van den Brink-Muinen, & D. H. de Bakker. 1993. "Gender differences in practice style: A

Dutch study of general practitioners." *Medical Care* 31:219–29.

Benson, John M. 1981. "The polls: A rebirth of religion?" *Public Opinion Quarterly* 45:576–85.

Berch, Bettina. 1982. *The Endless Day: The Political Economy of Women and Work.* New York: Harcourt, Brace, Jovanovich.

Berg, Barbara. 1978. *The Remembered Gate: Origins of American Feminism: The Woman and the City, 1800–60.* New York: Oxford University Press.

Berlage, Gai Ingham. 1994. *Women in Baseball: The Forgotten History.* Westport, CT: Greenwood.

Berlo, Janet Catherine. 1976. "The Cambridge School: Women in architecture." *Feminist Art Journal* 5:27–32.

Bernard, Jessie. 1972. *The Future of Marriage.* New York: Bantam.

———. 1975. *Women, Wives, Mothers: Values and Options.* Chicago: Aldine.

Bernstein, Barbara, & Robert Kane. 1981. "Physicians' attitudes toward female patients." *Medical Care* 19:600–608.

Bethune, Mary McLeod. [1941] 1982. "How the Bethune-Cookman College campus started." In *Women's America,* edited by Linda K. Kerber & Jane De Hart Mathews, pp. 260–62. New York: Oxford University Press.

Bieber, Irving. 1962. *Homosexuality: A Psychoanalytic Study.* New York: Basic Books.

Bigler, Rebecca S., & Lynn S. Liben. 1992. "Cognitive mechanisms in children's gender stereotyping: Theoretical and educational implications of a cognitive-based intervention." *Child Development* 63:1351–63.

Blaisure, Karen R., & Katherine R. Allen. 1995. "Feminists and the ideology and practice of marital equality." *Journal of Marriage and the Family* 57:5–19.

Blau, Francine D., & Lawrence M. Kahn. 1992. "The gender earnings gap: Learning from international comparisons." *The American Economic Review* 82:533–38.

Blee, Kathleen M. 1991. *Women of the Klan: Racism and Gender in the 1920s.* Berkeley: University of California Press.

Bleier, Ruth. 1984. *Science and Gender: A Critique of Biology and Its Theories on Women.* New York: Pergamon.

Blumstein, Philip W., & Pepper Schwartz. 1977. "Bisexuality: Some social psychological issues." *Journal of Social Issues* 33:30–45.

———. 1983. *American Couples: Money, Work, Sex.* New York: William Morrow.

Boles, Janet. 1979. *The Politics of the Equal Rights Amendment.* New York: Longman.

Bond, Selena, & Thomas F. Cash. "Black beauty: Skin color and body images among African-American col-

lege women." *Journal of Applied Social Psychology* 22:874–88.

Bonvillain, Nancy. 1989. "Gender relations in native North America." *American Indian Culture and Research Journal* 13:1–28.

Borden, Richard J., & Gorden M. Homleid. 1978. "Handedness and lateral positioning in heterosexual couples: Are men still strongarming women?" *Sex Roles* 4:67–73.

Bordin, Ruth. 1990. *Women and Temperance: The Quest for Power and Liberty, 1873–1900.* New Brunswick, NJ: Rutgers University Press.

Boston Women's Health Book Collective. 1992. *The New Our Bodies, Ourselves: A Book by and for Women.* New York: Simon & Schuster.

Boyer, Debra, & David Fine. 1992. "Sexual abuse as a factor in adolescent pregnancy and child maltreatment." *Family Planning Perspectives* 24:4–11.

Brabeck, M. 1983. "Moral judgment: Theory and research on differences between males and females." *Developmental Review* 3:274–91.

Breines, Wini, & Linda Gordon. 1983. "New scholarship on family violence." *Signs* 8:490–531.

Brett, Jeanne M., & Anne H. Reilly. 1992. "All the right stuff: A comparison of female and male managers' career progression." *Journal of Applied Psychology* 77:251–60.

Briggs, Kenneth A. 1983. "Women and the church." *New York Times Magazine,* November 6.

Briton, Nancy J., & Judith A. Hall. 1995. "Beliefs about female and male nonverbal communication." *Sex Roles* 32:79–90.

Brock, David. 1993. *The Real Anita Hill: The Untold Story.* New York: The Free Press.

Brooks-Gunn, Jeanne, & Diane K. Ruble. 1982. "The development of menstrual-related beliefs and behaviors during early adolescence." *Child Development* 53:1567–77.

Broverman, Inge K., Donald M. Broverman, Frank E. Clarkson, Paul S. Rosencrantz, & Susan R. Vogel. 1970. "Sex role stereotypes and clinical judgments of mental health." *Journal of Consulting and Clinical Psychology* 34:1–7.

Brownmiller, Susan. 1975. *Against Our Will: Men, Women, and Rape.* New York: Simon & Schuster.

Buckley, Thomas, & Alma Gottlieb, eds. 1988. *Blood Magic: The Anthropology of Menstruation.* Berkeley: University of California Press.

Buczek, Teresa A. 1981. "Sex biases in counseling: Counselor retention of the concerns of a female and male client." *Journal of Counseling Psychology* 28:13–21.

Budgeon, Shelley, & Dawn H. Currie. 1995. "From feminism to postfeminism: Women's liberation in fashion magazines." *Women's Studies International Forum* 18: 173–86.

Bunch, Charlotte. 1979. "Learning from lesbian separatism." In *Issues in Feminism: A First Course in Women's Studies,* edited by Sheila Ruth, pp. 551–56. Boston: Houghton Mifflin.

———. 1981. "Not for lesbians only." In *Building Feminist Theory: Essays from Quest,* pp. 67–73. New York: Longman.

Burg, Mary Ann. 1995. "Health problems of sheltered homeless women and their dependent children." *Health & Social Work* 19:125–31.

Burns, Nancy, Kay Lehman Schlozman, & Sidney Verba. 1997. "The public consequences of private inequality: Family life and citizen participation." *American Political Science Review* 91:373–89.

Burrell, Nancy A., William A. Donahue, & Mike Allen. 1988. "Gender-based perceptual biases in mediation." *Communication Research* 15:447–69.

Burris, Val. 1983. "Who opposed the ERA? An analysis of the social bases of anti-feminism." *Social Science Quarterly* 64:305–17.

Burstyn, Varda, ed. 1985. *Women Against Censorship.* Vancouver: Douglas and McIntyre.

Burt, Martha R. 1980. "Cultural myths and supports for rape." *Journal of Personality and Social Psychology* 38:217–30.

Busby, Linda J., & Greg Leichty. 1993. "Feminism and advertising in traditional and nontraditional women's magazines 1950s-1980s." *Journalism Quarterly* 70: 247–64.

Buss, David M. 1981. "Sex differences in the evaluation and performance of dominant acts." *Journal of Personality and Social Psychology* 40:147–54.

Butsch, Richard. 1992. "Class and gender in four decades of television situation comedy: Plus ça change." *Critical Studies in Mass Communication* 9:387–99.

Buttner, E. Holly, & Dorothy P. Moore. 1997. "Women's organizational exodus to entrepreneurship: Self-reported motivations and correlates with success." *Journal of Small Business Management* 35:34–46.

Cahn, Susan K. 1994. *Coming on Strong: Gender and Sexuality in Twentieth Century Women's Sport.* New York: Free Press.

Campbell, Anne, Steven Muncer, Alison Guy, & Maura Banim. 1996. "Social representations of aggression: Crossing the sex barrier." *European Journal of Social Psychology* 26:135–47.

Campbell, Susan Miller, Letitia Anne Peplau, & Sherrine Chapman DeBro. 1992. "Women, men, condoms: Attitudes and experiences of heterosexual college students." *Psychology of Women Quarterly* 16:273–88.

Canada, Katherine, & Richard Pringle. 1995. "The role of gender in college classroom interactions: A social context approach." *Sociology of Education* 68:161–86.

Caplan, Paula J., & Jeremy B. Caplan. 1994. *Thinking Critically About Research on Sex and Gender.* New York: HarperCollins.

Caplan, Paula J., Joan McCurdy-Myers, & Maureen Gans. 1992. "Should 'premenstrual syndrome' be called a psychiatric abnormality?" *Feminism and Psychology* 2: 27–44.

Caplow, Theodore, & Bruce A. Chadwick. 1979. "Inequality and life-styles in Middletown, 1920–78." *Social Science Quarterly* 60:367–86.

Carli, Linda L., Suzanne J. LaFleur, & Christopher C. Loeber. 1995. "Nonverbal behavior, gender, and influence." *Journal of Personality and Social Psychology* 68: 1030–41.

Carlsson, Marianne, & Pia Jaderquist. 1983. "Note on sex role opinions as conceptual schemata." *British Journal of Social Psychology* 22:65–68.

Carpenter, Eugenia S. 1980. "Children's health care and the changing role of women." *Medical Care* 18:1208–18.

Carpenter, Linda Jean, & R. Vivian Acosta. 1991. "Back to the future: Reform with a woman's voice." *Academe: Bulletin of the Association of University Professors* (January-February): 23–27.

Carroll, Jackson W., Barbara Hargrove, & Adair T. Lummis. 1981. *Women of the Cloth: A New Opportunity for the Churches.* New York: Harper & Row.

Carroll, Susan J., & Ronnee Schreiber. 1997. "Media coverage of women in the 103rd Congress." In *Women, Media, and Politics,* edited by Pippa Norris, pp. 131–48. New York: Oxford University Press.

Carter, Michael J., & Susan Boslego Carter. 1981. "Women's recent progress in the professions, or women get a ticket to ride after the gravy train has left the station." *Feminist Studies* 7:477–504.

Cash, Thomas F., Barry Gillen, & D. Steven Burns. 1977. "Sexism and beautyism in personnel consultant decision making." *Journal of Applied Psychology* 62:301–10.

Cassell, Joan. 1996. "The woman in the surgeon's body: Understanding difference." *American Anthropologist* 98:41–53.

Catsambis, Sophia. 1994. "The path to math: gender and racial-ethnic differences in mathematics participation from middle school to high school." *Sociology of Education* 67:199–215.

Chadwick, Whitney. 1990. *Women, Art, and Society.* London: Thames and Hudson.

Charles, Maria. 1992. "Cross-national variation in occupational sex segregation." *American Sociological Review* 57:483–502.

Chavkin, Wendy, ed. 1984. *Double Exposure: Women's Health Hazards on the Job and at Home.* New York: Monthly Review Press.

Cherry, Frances. 1983. "Gender roles and sexual violence." In *Changing Boundaries: Gender Roles and Sexual Behavior,* edited by Elizabeth Rice Allgeier & Naomi B. McCormick, pp. 245–60. Palo Alto, CA: Mayfield.

Chesler, Phyllis. 1971. "Patient and patriarch: Women in the psychotherapeutic relationship." In *Women in Sexist Society,* edited by Vivian Gornick & Barbara K. Moran, pp. 251–75. New York: Basic Books.

Chesney-Lind, Meda, & Randall G. Shelden. 1992. *Girls, Delinquency, and Juvenile Justice.* Pacific Grove, CA: Brooks/Cole.

Chmielewski, Wendy E., Louise J. Kern, & Marilyn Klee-Hartzell, eds. 1993. *Women in Spiritual and Communitarian Societies in the United States.* Syracuse, NY: Syracuse University Press.

Cho, Sumi K. 1997. "Converging stereotypes in racialized sexual harassment: Where the model minority meets Suzie Wong." In *Critical Race Feminism,* edited by Adrien Katherine Wing, pp. 203–20. New York: New York University Press.

Chodorow, Nancy. 1978. *The Reproduction of Mothering: Psychoanalysis and the Sociology of Gender.* Berkeley and Los Angeles: University of California Press.

Chodorow, Nancy, & Susan Contratto. 1982. "The fantasy of the perfect mother." In *Rethinking the Family: Some Feminist Questions,* edited by Barrie Thorne & Marilyn Yalom, pp. 54–72. New York: Longman.

Chow, Esther Ngan-Ling. 1987. "The development of feminist consciousness among Asian-American women." *Gender and Society* 1:284–99.

Chrisler, Joan C., & Karen B. Levy. 1990. "The media construct a menstrual monster: A content analysis of PMS articles in the popular press." *Women and Health* 16:89–104.

Christ, Carol. 1987. *Laughter of Aphrodite: Reflections on a Journey to the Goddess.* San Francisco: Harper & Row.

Christ, Carol, & Judith Plaskow, eds. 1979. *Womanspirit Rising: A Feminist Reader in Religion.* New York: Harper & Row.

Christensen, Dana, & Robert Rosenthal. 1982. "Gender and nonverbal decoding skill as determinants of interpersonal expectancy effects." *Journal of Personality and Social Psychology* 42:75–87.

Christoplos, Florence, & JoAnn Borden. 1978. "Sexism in elementary school mathematics." *The Elementary School Journal* 78:275–77.

Cixous, Hélène. 1976. "The laugh of the Medusa." *Signs* 1:875–94.

Clark, Roger, Rachel Lennon, & Leanna Morris. 1993. "Of Caldecotts and kinds: Gendered images in recent American children's books by black and non-black illustrators." *Gender and Society* 7 (June): 227–45.

Clarke, Cheryl. 1981. "Lesbianism: An act of resistance." In *This Bridge Called My Back: Writings by Radical Women of Color,* edited by Cherrie Morága and Gloria Anzaldúa, pp. 128–37. Watertown, MA: Persephone Press.

Clinton, Catherine. 1985. "Women and southern history: Images and reflections." *Perspectives on the American South* 3:45–62.

Cobb, Nancy J., Judith Stevens-Long, & Steven Goldstein. 1982. "The influence of televised models in toy preference in children." *Sex Roles* (October): 1075–80.

Cobble, Dorothy Sue, ed. 1993. *Women and Unions: Forging a Partnership.* Ithaca, NY: ILR Press.

Cohen, Claudia. 1981. "Person categories and social perception: Testing some boundaries of the processing effects of prior knowledge." *Journal of Personality and Social Psychology* (March): 441–52.

Cole, C. Maureen, Frances A. Hill, & Leland J. Daly. 1983. "Do masculine pronouns used generically lead to thoughts of men?" *Sex Roles* 9:737–50.

Collins, Eliza G. C., & Timothy Blodget. 1981. "Sexual harassment . . . some see it . . . some won't." *Business Review* 59:76–94.

Collins, Patricia Hill. 1989a. "The social construction of black feminist thought." *Signs* 14:745–73.

———. 1989b. "A comparison of two works on black family life." *Signs* 14:875–84.

Colwill, Nina. 1982. *The New Partnership: Women and Men in Organizations.* Palo Alto, CA: Mayfield.

Conover, Pamela, & Virginia Gray. 1983. *Feminism and the New Right: Conflict Over the American Family.* New York: Praeger.

Conover, Pamela Johnston, & Virginia Sapiro. 1993. "Gender, feminist consciousness, and war." *American Journal of Political Science* 37.

Cook, Alice H., Val R. Lorwin, & Arlene Kaplan Daniels, eds. 1984. *Women and Trade Unions in Eleven Industrialized Countries.* Philadelphia: Temple University Press.

Cook, Deborah J., et al. 1996. "Residents' experiences of abuse, discrimination, and sexual harassment during residency training." *Canadian Medical Association Journal* 154:1657–65.

Cook, Ellen Piel. 1985. *Psychological Androgyny.* New York: Pergamon.

Cooper, Elizabeth A., Dennis Doverspike, & Gerald V. Barrett. 1985. "Comparison of different methods of determining the sex type of American occupations." *Psychological Reports* 57:747–50.

Costain, Anne N. 1992. *Inviting Women's Rebellion: A Political Process Interpretation of the Women's Movement.* Baltimore: Johns Hopkins University Press.

Cott, Nancy F. 1987. *The Grounding of American Feminism.* New Haven, CT: Yale University Press.

Couture, Pamela D. 1991. *Blessed Are the Poor? Women's Poverty, Family Policy, and Practical Theology.* Nashville, TN: Abingdon.

Cowan, Gloria, Carole Lee, Danielle Levy, & Debra Snyder. 1988. "Dominance and inequality in x-rated videocassettes." *Psychology of Women Quarterly* 12:299–311.

Cowan, Ruth Schwartz. 1983. *More Work for Mother: The Ironies of Household Technology from the Open Hearth to the Microwave.* New York: Basic.

Crouter, Ann C., Beth A. Manke, & Susan M. McHale. 1995. "The family context of gender intensification in early adolescence." *Child Development* 66:317–29.

Daddario, Gia. 1992. "Swimming against the tide: *Sports Illustrated*'s imagery of female athletes in a swimsuit world." *Women's Studies in Communication* 15:49–64.

Dalton, Katarina. 1964. *The Premenstrual Syndrome.* Springfield, IL: Thomas.

Daly, Mary. 1973. *Beyond God the Father: Toward a Philosophy of Women's Liberation.* Boston: Beacon.

———. 1975. *The Church and the Second Sex.* New York: Harper & Row.

———. 1978. *Gyn/Ecology: The Metaethics of Radical Feminism.* Boston: Beacon.

Daniels, Arlene Kaplan. 1988. *Invisible Careers: Women Civic Leaders from the Volunteer World.* Chicago: University of Chicago Press.

Darcy, R., Susan Welch, & Janet Clark. 1994. *Women's Elections, and Representation.* New York: Longman.

Das Gupta, Monica. 1995. "Life course perspectives on women's autonomy and health outcomes." *American Anthropologist* 97 (September): 481–91.

Davies, Margery. 1983. *Woman's Place Is at the Typewriter: Office Work and Office Workers: 1870–1930.* Philadelphia: Temple University Press.

Davis, Martha F. 1983. "The marital home: Equal or equitable distribution?" *The University of Chicago Law Review* 50:1089–1115.

Dawson, Debra L. A. 1988. "Ethnic differences in female overweight: Data from the 1985 National Health Interview Study." *American Journal of Public Health* 78: 1326–29.

Dayhoff, Signe. 1983. "Sexist language and person perception: Evaluation of candidates from newspaper articles." *Sex Roles* 9:527–40.

de Beauvoir, Simone. 1952. *The Second Sex.* New York: Knopf.

de Monteflores, Carmen, & Stephen J. Schultz. 1978. "Coming out: Similarities and differences for lesbians and gay men." *Journal of Social Issues* 34:59–72.

de Pauw, Linda Grant. 1975. *Founding Mothers: Women of America in the Revolutionary Era.* Boston: Houghton Mifflin.

Deaux, Kay. 1976. *The Behavior of Women and Men.* Monterey, CA: Brooks/Cole.

Deaux, Kay, & Joseph C. Ullman. 1983. *Women of Steel: Female Blue-Collar Workers in the Basic Steel Industry.* New York: Praeger.

Degler, Carl N. 1980. *At Odds: Women and the Family in America from the Revolution to the Present.* New York: Oxford University Press.

Del Boca, Daniela, & Christopher J. Flinn. 1995. "Rationalizing child-support decisions." *The American Economic Review* 85:1241–62.

Delaney, Janice, Mary Jane Lupton, & Emily Toth, eds. 1988. *The Curse: A Cultural History of Menstruation.* Urbana: University of Illinois Press.

Delgado, A., L. A. Lopez-Fernandez, & J. De Dios Luna. 1993. "Influence of the doctor's gender in the satisfaction of the users." *Medical Care* 31:795–800.

Dellmann-Jenkins, Mary, Lisa Florjancic, & Elizabeth Blue Swadener. 1993. "Sex roles and cultural diversity in recent award winning picture books for young children." *Journal of Research in Childhood Education* 7: 74–82.

DeLoache, Judy S., Deborah J. Cassidy, & C. Jan Carpenter. 1987. "The three bears are all boys: Mothers' gender labeling of neutral picture book characters." *Sex Roles* 17:163–78.

Demarest, Jack, & Jeanette Garner. 1992. "The representation of women's roles in women's magazines over the past 30 years." *The Journal of Psychology* 126:357–68.

Depner, Charlene, & Berit Ingersoll. 1982. "Employment status and social support: The experience of mature women." In *Women's Retirement: Policy Implications of Recent Research,* edited by Maximiliane Szinovacz, pp. 77–91. Beverly Hills, CA: Sage.

Deutsch, Francine M., Dorothy LeBaron, & Maury March Fryer. 1987. "What's in a smile?" *Psychology of Women Quarterly* 11:341–52.

Deutsch, Francine M., Julianne B. Lussier, & Laura J. Servis. 1993. "Husbands at home: Predictors of paternal participation in childcare and housework." *Journal of Personality and Social Psychology* 65:1154–66.

Dibble, Ursula, & Murray Straus. 1980. "Some social structure determinants of inconsistency between attitudes and behavior: The case of family violence." *Journal of Marriage and the Family* 42:71–82.

Dodson, Debra L., & Susan J. Carroll. 1991. *Reshaping the Agenda: Women in State Legislatures.* New Brunswick, NJ: Center for the American Woman and Politics.

Doering, Charles H., H. K. H. Brodie, H. Kramer, H. Becker, & D. A. Hamburg. 1974. "Plasma testosterone levels and psychologic measures in men over a two month period." In *Sex Differences in Behavior,* edited by R. Friedman, R. Richart, & R. Vande Wiele, pp. 413–31. New York: Wiley.

Doner, Kalia. 1993. "Women's magazines: Slouching towards feminism." *Social Policy* 23:37–43.

Donnerstein, Edward, Daniel Linz, & Steven Penrod. 1987. *The Question of Pornography: Research Findings and Policy Implications.* New York: Free Press.

Douglas, Ann. 1977. *The Feminization of American Culture.* New York: Knopf.

Doverspike, Dennis, & Winfred Arthur, Jr. 1995. "Race and sex differences in reactions to a simulated selection decision involving race-based affirmative action." *Journal of Black Psychology* 21:181–200.

Downs, Donald Alexander. 1989. *The New Politics of Pornography.* Chicago: University of Chicago Press.

Dresler, Carolyn, et al. 1996. "Experiences of women in cardiothoracic surgery." *Archives of Surgery* 131:1128–34.

DuBois, Ellen Carol. 1978. *Feminism and Suffrage: The Emergence of an Independent Women's Movement in America, 1848–69.* Ithaca, NY: Cornell University Press.

Duncan, Carol. 1992. "The MoMA's hot mamas." In *The Expanding Discourse: Feminism and Art History,* edited by Norma Broude and Mary D. Garrard, pp. 347–58. New York: HarperCollins.

Duncan, Kevin C. 1996. "Gender differences in the effect of education on the slope of experience-earnings profiles: National Longitudinal Survey of Youth, 1979–1988." *The American Journal of Economics and Sociology* 55:457–71.

Duncan, Lauren E., & Gail S. Agronick. 1995. "The intersection of life stage and social events: Personality and life outcomes." *Journal of Personality and Social Psychology* 69:558–68.

Durio, Helen F., & Cheryl A. Kildow. 1980. "The Nonretention of Capable Engineering Students." *Research in Higher Education* 13:61–71.

Durndell, Alan, & K. Thomson. 1997. "Gender and computing: A decade of change?" *Computers & Education* 28:1–9.

Dweck, Carol S., William Davidson, Sharon Nelson, & Bradley Enna. 1978. "Sex differences in learned helplessness." *Developmental Psychology* 14:268–76.

Dworkin, Andrea. 1979. *Pornography: Men Possessing Women.* New York: G. P. Putnam's Sons.

Dwyer, Carol A. 1974. "Influence of children's sex role standards on reading and arithmetic achievement." *Journal of Educational Psychology* 66:811–16.

Eagly, Alice H., & L. L. Carli. 1981. "Sex of researchers and sex-typed communications as determinants of sex differences in influenceability: A meta-analysis of social influence studies." *Psychological Bulletin* 90:1–20.

Eagly, Alice H., & Maureen Crowley. 1986. "Gender and helping behavior: A meta-analytic review of the social psychological literature." *Psychological Bulletin* 100:283–308.

Eagly, Alice H., Steven J. Karau, & Mona G. Makhijani. 1995. "Gender and the effectiveness of leaders: A meta-analysis." *Psychological Bulletin* 117:125–45.

Eakins, Barbara Westbrook, & R. Gene Eakins. 1978. *Sex Differences in Human Communication.* Boston: Houghton Mifflin.

Eaton, W. O., & L. R. Enns. 1986. "Sex differences in human motor activity." *Psychological Bulletin* 100:19–28.

Eccles, Jacquelyn S. 1989. "Bringing young women to math and science." In *Gender and Thought: Psychological Perspectives,* edited by M. Crawford & M. Gentry, pp. 36–58. New York: Springer-Verlag.

Echols, Alice. 1989. *Daring to Be Bad: Radical Feminism in America, 1967–1975.* Minneapolis: University of Minnesota Press.

Eckert, Penelope, & Sally McConnell-Ginet. 1994. "Think practically and look locally: Language and gender as community-based practice." In *The Women and Language Debate: A Sourcebook,* edited by Camille Roman, Suzanne Jugasz, & Chistanne Miller, pp. 432–55. New Brunswick, NJ: Rutgers University Press.

Edwards, Julia, & Linda McKie. 1996. "Women's public toilets: A serious issue for the body politic." *European Journal of Women's Studies* 3:215–30.

Ehrenreich, Barbara, & Dierdre English. 1979. *For Her Own Good: One Hundred Fifty Years of the Experts' Advice to Women.* Garden City, NY: Doubleday.

Eichler, Margrit. 1980. *The Double Standard: A Feminist Critique of Feminist Social Science.* New York: St. Martin's.

Eisenberg, N., & R. Lennon. 1983. "Sex differences in empathy and related capacities." *Psychological Bulletin* 94:100–131.

Eisenstein, Hester. 1992. *Gender Shock: Practicing Feminism on Two Continents.* Boston: Beacon.

Eisenstein, Zillah. 1981. *The Radical Future of Liberal Feminism.* New York: Longman.

Elder, Ruth Gale, Winnefred Humphreys, & Cheryl Laskowski. 1988. "Sexism in gynecology textbooks: Gender stereotypes and paternalism, 1978–1983." *Health Care for Women International* 9:1–17.

Elizur, Dov. 1994. "Gender and work values: A comparative analysis." *The Journal of Social Psychology* 134:201–12.

Elstad, John Ivar. 1994. "Women's priorities regarding physicians' behavior and their preference for a female physician." *Women and Health* 21:1–19.

Engels, Friedrich. [1884] 1972. *The Origin of the Family, Private Property, and the State.* New York: Pathfinder.

Enloe, Cynthia. 1983. *Does Khaki Become You? The Militarization of Women's Lives*. Boston: South End.

———. 1989. *Bananas, Beaches, and Bases: Making Feminist Sense of International Politics*. London: Pandora.

Entwisle, Doris R., Kail L. Alexander, & Linda Steffel Olson. 1994. "The gender gap in math: Its possible origins in neighborhood effects." *American Sociological Review* 59:822–38.

Erickson, Deborah. 1995. "Work and health: Are women and men that different?" *Harvard Business Review* 73 (September/October): 12–14.

Estler, Suzanne. 1975. "Women as leaders in public education." *Signs* 1:363–85.

Etaugh, Claire, & Ethel Foresman. 1983. "Evaluations of competence as a function of sex and marital status." *Sex Roles* 9:759–65.

Evans, Sara M. 1979. *Personal Politics: The Roots of Women's Liberation in the Civil Rights Movement and the New Left*. New York: Vintage.

———. 1989. *Born for Liberty: A History of Women in America*. New York: Free Press.

Ewen, Elizabeth. 1980. "City lights: Immigrant women and the rise of movies." *Signs* 5:45–66.

Ewen, Stuart. 1976. *Captains of Consciousness: Advertising and the Social Roots of Consumer Culture*. New York: McGraw-Hill.

Faderman, Lillian. 1991. *Odd Girls and Twilight Lovers: A History of Lesbian Life in Twentieth-Century America*. New York: Penguin.

Fagot, Beverly I., & Mary D. Leinbach. 1989. "The young child's gender schema: Environmental input, internal organization." *Child Development* 60:663–72.

Fagot, Beverly I., Mary D. Leinbach, & Cherie O'Boyle. 1992. "Gender labeling, gender stereotyping, and parenting behaviors." *Developmental Psychology* 28:225–30.

Falbo, Toni, Michael D. Hazen, & Diane Linimon. 1982. "The costs of selecting power bases or messages associated with the opposite sex." *Sex Roles* 9:147–57.

Faludi, Susan. 1991. *Backlash: The Undeclared War Against American Women*. New York: Crown Publishers.

Faust, Drew Gilpin. 1992. "'Trying to do a man's business': Slavery, violence, and gender in the American Civil War." *Gender and History* 4:197–214.

"Female athletic triad risk for women." 1993. *Journal of the American Medical Association* 270:921.

Feingold, Alan. 1994. "Gender differences in personality: A meta-analysis." *Psychological Bulletin* 116:429–56.

Feldberg, Roslyn K., & Evelyn Nakano Glenn. 1979. "Male and female: Job versus gender models in the sociology of work." *Social Problems* 26:524–38.

Fenster, Laura, et al. 1997. "A prospective study of work-related physical exertion and spontaneous abortion." *Epidemiology* 8:66–74.

Ferber, Marianne A., & Julie A. Nelson, eds. 1993. *Beyond Economic Man: Feminist Theory and Economics*. Chicago: University of Chicago Press.

Ferguson, Susan J. 1995. "Marriage timing of Chinese American and Japanese American women." *Journal of Family Issues* 16:314–43.

Ferrante, Carol L., Andrew M. Haynes, & Sarah M. Kingsley. 1988. "Images of women in television advertising." *Journal of Broadcasting and Electronic Media* 32:231–37.

Fiorenza, Elizabeth Schüssler. 1984. *Bread Not Stone: The Challenge of Feminist Biblical Criticism*. Boston: Beacon Press.

———. 1992. *But SHE Said: Feminist Practices of Biblical Interpretation*. Boston: Beacon Press.

Firestone, Shulamith. 1970. *The Dialectic of Sex*. New York: Bantam.

Fishman, Sylvia Barack. 1995. *A Breath of Life: Feminism in the American Jewish Community*. Waltham, MA: Brandeis University Press.

Flaks, David K., Ilda Ficher, & Frank Masterpasqua. 1995. "Lesbians choosing motherhood: A comparative study of lesbian and heterosexual parents and their children." *Developmental Psychology* 31:105–14.

Flanagan, Constance. 1993. "Gender and social class: Intersecting issues in women's achievement." *Educational Psychologist* 28:357–78.

Flexner, Eleanor. 1975. *Century of Struggle: The Women's Rights Movement in the United States*. Cambridge, MA: Harvard University Press.

Foner, Philip S. 1982. *Women and the American Labor Movement: From the First Trade Unions to the Present*. New York: Free Press.

Ford, M. R., & C. R. Lowery. 1986. "Gender differences in moral reasoning: A comparison of the justice and care orientations." *Journal of Personality and Social Psychology* 50:777–83.

Foreit, Karen G., et al. 1980. "Sex bias in the newspaper treatment of male-centered and female-centered news stories." *Sex Roles* 6:475–80.

Forrest, Jacqueline Darroch, & Richard R. Fordyce. 1988. "U.S. women's contraceptive attitudes and practice: How have they changed in the 1980s?" *Family Planning Perspectives* 20:112–18.

Foster, D. C., D. S. Guzick, & R. P. Pulliam. 1992. "The impact of prenatal care on fetal and neonatal death rates for uninsured patients: A 'natural experiment' in West Virginia." *Obstetrics and Gynecology* 7:40.

Foster, Martha A., Barbara Strudlar Wallston, & Michael Berger. 1980. "Feminist orientation and job seeking behavior among dual career couples." *Sex Roles* 6:59–65.

Fournier, Janice E., & Samuel S. Wineburg. 1997. "Picturing the past: Gender differences in the depiction of historical figures." *American Journal of Education* 105: 160–85.

Frable, Deborah E. S., & Sandra Lipsitz Bem. 1985. "If you are gender schematic, all members of the opposite sex look alike." *Journal of Personality and Social Psychology* 49:459–68.

Frank, Dana. 1985. "Housewives, socialists, and the politics of food: The 1917 New York cost-of-living protests." *Feminist Studies* 11:255–86.

Frank, Erica, & Lynn K. Harvey. 1996. "Prevention advice rates of women and men physicians." *Archives of Family Medicine* 5:215–19.

Fraser, Arvonne S. 1983. "Insiders and outsiders." In *Women in Washington: Advocates for Public Policy,* edited by Irene Tinker, pp. 120–39. Beverly Hills, CA: Sage.

Freedman, Estelle. 1979. "Separatism as strategy: Female institution building and American feminism, 1870–1930." *Feminist Studies* 5:512–29.

Freeman, Jo. 1975. *The Politics of Women's Liberation.* New York: Longman.

Freud, Sigmund. [1930] 1961. *Civilization and Its Discontents.* New York: Norton.

———. [1933] 1965. "Femininity." In Sigmund Freud, *New Introductory Lectures in Psychoanalysis,* pp. 112–35. New York: Norton.

Friedan, Betty. 1963. *The Feminine Mystique.* New York: Dell.

Fritz, Kathlyn Ann, & Natalie Kaufman Hevener. 1979. "An unsuitable job for a woman: Female protagonists in the detective novel." *International Journal of Women's Studies* 2:105–29.

Frost, J. William. 1973. *The Quaker Family in Colonial America.* New York: St. Martin's.

Fuller, Margaret. [1845] 1971. *Women in the Nineteenth Century.* New York: Norton. Also excerpted in Rossi (1988).

Gabin, Nancy. 1982. "They have placed a penalty on womanhood: The protest actions of women auto workers in Detroit area UAW locals, 1945–47." *Feminist Studies* 8: 373–98.

Gage, Matilda Joslyn. [1900] 1972. *Women, Church, and State: A Historical Account of the Status of Women Through the Christian Ages, With Reminiscences of the Matriarchate.* New York: Arno Press.

Gardner, Carol Brooks. 1995. *Passing By: Gender and Public Harassment.* Berkeley: University of California Press.

Garrard, Mary D. 1982. "Artemisia and Susanna." In *The Expanding Discourse: Feminism and Art History,* edited by Norma Broude & Mary D. Garrard, pp. 147–72. New York: HarperCollins.

Garvey, Ellen Gruber. 1995. "Reframing the bicycle: Magazines and scorching women." *American Quarterly* 47: 66–101.

Gasson, Ruth. 1992. "Farmers' wives: Their contribution to the farm business." *Journal of Agricultural Economics* 43 (January): 74–87.

Ge, Xiaojia, Rand D. Conger, & Frederick O. Lorenz. 1995. "Mutual influences in parent and adolescent psychological distress." *Developmental Psychology* 31: 406–19.

Gelb, Joyce. 1989. *Feminism and Politics: A Comparative Perspective.* Berkeley: University of California Press.

Gelb, Joyce, & Marian Palley. 1987. *Women and Public Policies.* Princeton, NJ: Princeton University Press.

Geller, Laura. 1983. "Reactions to a woman rabbi." In *On Being a Jewish Feminist,* edited by Susannah Heschel, pp. 210–13. New York: Schocken.

Gelles, Richard J. 1980. "Violence in the family: A review of research in the 1970's." *Journal of Marriage and the Family* 42:873–76.

Gerbner, George. 1978. "The dynamics of cultural resistance." In *Hearth and Home: Images of Women in the Mass Media,* edited by Gaye Tuchman, Arlene Kaplan Daniels, & James Benet, pp. 46–50. New York: Oxford University Press.

Gerdes, Eugenia Proctor, & Douglas M. Garber. 1983. "Sex bias in hiring: Effects of job demands and applicant competence." *Sex Roles* 7:307–19.

Gerson, Kathleen. 1985. *Hard Choices: How Women Decide About Work, Career, and Motherhood.* Berkeley: University of California Press.

Gertzog, Irwin, & Michele Simard. 1980. "Women and 'hopeless' congressional candidates: Nomination frequency 1916–78." *American Politics Quarterly* 9: 449–66.

Giddings, Paula. 1984. *When and Where I Enter: The Impact of Black Women on Race and Sex in America.* New York: Bantam.

Gilkes, Cheryl Townsend. 1987. "Some mother's son and some father's daughter: Gender and biblical language in Afro-Christian worship tradition." In *Shaping New Visions: Gender and Values in American Culture,* edited by Clarissa W. Atkinson, Constance H. Buchanan, & Margaret Miles. Ann Arbor, MI: UMI Research Press.

Gilligan, Carol. 1982. *In a Different Voice: Psychological Theory and Women's Development.* Cambridge, MA: Harvard University Press.

Gilligan, Carol, Nona P. Lyons, & Trudy J. Hanmer. 1990. *Making Connections: The Relational Worlds of Adolescent Girls at Emma Willard School.* Cambridge, MA: Harvard University Press.

Gilligan, Carol, Janie Victoria Ward, & Jill McLean Taylor, eds. 1988. *Mapping the Moral Domain: A Contribution of Women's Thinking to Psychological Theory and Education.* Cambridge, MA: Harvard University Press.

Gilman, Charlotte Perkins. [1898] 1966. *Women and Economics.* New York: Harper & Row.

———. [1903] 1972. *The Home.* Urbana: University of Illinois Press.

———. [1911] 1970. *The Man-Made World: Our Androcentric Culture.* New York: Charlton.

———. [1915] 1979. *Herland.* New York: Pantheon.

———. [1915] 1992. *Herland.* In *Herland and Selected Stories by Charlotte Perkins Gilman,* edited by Barbara H. Solomon, pp. 1–146. New York: Penguin.

Ginsburg, Faye D. 1989. *Contested Lives: The Abortion Debate in an American Community.* Berkeley: University of California Press.

Ginzberg, Lori D. 1990. *Women and the Work of Benevolence: Morality, Politics, and Class in the Nineteenth-Century United States.* New Haven, CT: Yale University Press.

Glass, Jennifer, & Valerie Camarigg. 1992. "Gender, parenthood, and job-family compatibility." *American Journal of Sociology* 98:131–51.

Glazer, Nona Y. 1993. *Women's Paid and Unpaid Labor: The Work Transfer in Health Care and Retailing.* Philadelphia: Temple University Press.

Glenn, Evelyn Nakano. 1986. *Issei, Nisei, Warbride: Three Generations of Japanese-American Women in Domestic Service.* Philadelphia: Temple University Press.

———. 1992. "From servitude to service work: Historical continuities in the racial division of paid reproductive labor." *Signs* 18:1–43.

Glenn, Evelyn Nakano, Grace Chang, & Linda Rennie Forcey, eds. 1994. *Mothering: Ideology, Experience, and Agency.* New York: Routledge.

Glenn, Evelyn Nakano, & Roslyn L. Feldberg. 1989. "Clerical work: The female occupation." In *Women: A Feminist Perspective,* edited by Jo Freeman, pp. 287–312. Mountain View, CA: Mayfield.

Glenn, Norval D., & Sara McLanahan. 1982. "Children and marital happiness: A further specification of the relationship." *Journal of Marriage and the Family* 44:63–72.

Glick, Peter, Cari Zion, & Cynthia Nelson. 1988. "What mediates sex discrimination in hiring decisions?" *Journal of Personality and Social Psychology* 55:178–86.

Goldberg, Philip. 1968. "Are women prejudiced against women?" *Transaction* 4:28–30.

Goldin, Claudia. 1990. *Understanding the Gender Gap: An Economic History of American Women.* New York: Oxford University Press.

Goldstein, Leslie Friedman. 1988. *The Constitutional Rights of Women: Cases in Law and Social Change.* Madison: University of Wisconsin Press.

Gordon, Linda. 1982. "Why nineteenth century feminists did not support 'birth control' and twentieth century feminists do: Feminism, reproduction, and the family." In *Rethinking the Family: Some Feminist Questions,* edited by Barrie Thorne & Marilyn Yalom, pp. 40–53. New York: Longman.

———. 1991. "On 'Difference.'" *Genders* 10:91–111.

———, ed. 1990. *Women, the State, and Welfare.* Madison: University of Wisconsin Press.

Gordon, Margaret T., & Stephanie Riger. 1989. *The Female Fear.* New York: Free Press.

Gove, Walter R., Corlynn Briggs Style, & Michael Hughes. 1990. "The effect of marriage on the well-being of adults." *Journal of Family Issues* 11:4–35.

Granberg, Donald, & Beth Wellman Granberg. 1981. "Pro-life versus pro-choice: Another look at the abortion controversy in the United States." *Sociology and Social Research* 65:424–33.

Grant, Jacqueline. 1989. *White Women's Christ and Black Women's Jesus: Feminist Christology and Womanist Response.* Atlanta: Scholar's Press.

Green, Eileen, & Laurie Cohen. 1995. "'Women's business': Are women entrepreneurs breaking new ground or simply balancing the demands of 'women's work' in a new way?" *Journal of Gender Studies* 4:297–316.

Green, Susan K., & Philip Sanders. 1983. "Perceptions of male and female initiators of relationships." *Sex Roles* 9:849–52.

Greenberger, Ellen, & Laurence D. Steinberg. 1983. "Sex differences in early labor force experience: Harbinger of things to come." *Social Forces* 62:467–86.

Greenstein, Theodore N. 1995. "Gender ideology, marital disruption, and the employment of married women." *Journal of Marriage and Family* 57:31–42.

Grewal, Raji P., & John D. Urschel. 1994. "Why women want children: A study during phases of parenthood." *The Journal of Social Psychology* 134:453–5.

Griffin, John Howard. 1961. *Black Like Me.* Boston: Houghton Mifflin.

Griffin, Susan. 1981. *Pornography and Silence: Culture's Revenge Against Nature.* New York: Harper & Row.

Grossman, Michele, & Wendy Wood. 1993. "Sex differences in intensity of emotional experience: A social role interpretation." *Journal of Personality and Social Psychology* 65:1010–22.

Gruhl, John, Cassia Spohn, & Susan Welch. 1981. "Women as policy makers: The case of trial judges." *American Journal of Political Science* 25:308–22.

Hacker, Sally L. 1979. "Sex stratification, technology, and organizational change: A longitudinal case study of AT&T." *Social Problems* 26:539–57.

Hafkin, Nancy J., & Edna G. Bay, eds. 1976. *Women in Africa: Studies in Social and Economic Change.* Stanford, CA: Stanford University Press.

Hagler, D. Harland. 1980. "The ideal woman in the antebellum south: Lady or farmwife?" *Journal of Southern History* 46:405–18.

Hall, Elaine J. 1988. "One week for women? The structure of inclusion of gender issues in introductory textbooks." *Teaching Sociology* 16:431–42.

Hall, Jacquelyn Dowd. 1989. "Partial truths." *Signs* 14:902–11.

Hall, Judith A. 1978. "Gender differences in decoding nonverbal cues in conversation." *Psychological Bulletin* 85:845–57.

Hamilton, Mykol C. 1988. "Masculine generic terms and misperception of AIDS risk." *Journal of Applied Social Psychology* 18:122–24.

Hamilton, Mykol C., Barbara Hunter, & Shannon Stuart Smith. 1994. "Jury instructions worded in the masculine generic." In *The Women and Language Debate: A Sourcebook,* edited by Camille Roman, Suzanne Jugasz, & Chistanne Miller, pp. 340–47. New Brunswick, NJ: Rutgers University Press.

Hamington, Maurice. 1995. *Hail Mary? The Struggle for Ultimate Womanhood in Catholicism.* New York: Routledge.

Hansen, Finy Josephine, & Dawn Osborne. 1995. "Psychopharmacology from a feminist perspective." *Women and Therapy* 16:129–50.

Harding, Sandra. 1991. *Whose Science? Whose Knowledge? Thinking from Women's Lives.* Ithaca: Cornell University Press.

Hare-Mustin, Rachel T., Sheila Kaiser Bennett, & Patricia C. Broderick. 1983. "Attitudes toward motherhood: Gender, generational and religious comparisons." *Sex Roles* 9:643–61.

Harris, Betty J. 1990. "Ethnicity and gender in the global periphery: A comparison of Basotho and Navajo women." *American Indian Culture and Research Journal* 14:15–38.

Harris, Shanette M. 1994. "Racial differences in predictors of college women's body image attitudes." *Women & Health* 21(4): 89–104.

Hartmann, Heidi, ed. 1985. *Comparable Worth: New Directions for Research.* Washington, DC: National Academy Press.

Hartmann, Susan M. 1983. *The Home Front and Beyond: American Women in the 1940's.* Boston: Twayne.

Hartz, Louis. 1955. *The Liberal Tradition in America.* New York: Harcourt, Brace, and World.

Harvey, S. Marie, & Susan C. M. Scrimshaw. 1988. "Coitus-dependent contraceptives: Factors associated with effective use." *Journal of Sex Research* 25:364–78.

Hatfield, Elaine. 1983. "What do women and men want from love and sex?" In *Changing Boundaries: Gender Roles and Sexual Behavior,* edited by Elizabeth Rice Allgeier & Naomi B. McCormick, pp. 106–34. Mountain View, CA: Mayfield.

Hayden, Dolores. 1981. *The Grand Domestic Revolution: A History of Feminist Designs for American Homes, Neighborhoods, and Cities.* Cambridge, MA: MIT Press.

Hayes, Charles B., Alice Ryan, & Elaine B. Zseller. 1994. "The middle school child's perceptions of caring teachers." *American Journal of Education* 103:1–19.

Hayes, Kathryn E., & Patricia L. Wolleat. 1978. "Effect of sex in judgments of a simulated counseling interview." *Journal of Counseling Psychology* 25:164–68.

Hedges, Elaine, & Ingrid Wendt, eds. 1980. *In Her Own Image: Women Working in the Arts.* New York: McGraw Hill.

Heinemann, Sue. 1996. *Timelines of American Women's History.* New York: Roundtable Press.

Helfand, Mark, & Melanie J. Zimmer-Gembeck. 1997. "Practice variation and the risk of low birth weight in a public prenatal care program." *Medical Care* 35:16–31.

Henley, Nancy M. 1977. *Body Politics: Power, Sex, and Nonverbal Communication.* Englewood Cliffs, NJ: Prentice-Hall.

Henshaw, Stanley K. 1991. "The accessibility of abortion services in the United States." *Family Planning Perspectives* 23:246–52.

Hersch, Joni, & Viscusi, W. Kip. 1996. "Gender differences in promotions and wages." *Industrial Relations* 35:461–72.

Heschel, Susannah, ed. 1983. *On Being a Jewish Feminist.* New York: Schocken.

Hesse, Sharlene. 1979. "Women working: Historical trends." In *Working Women and Families,* edited by Karen Wolk Feinstein, pp. 35–62. Beverly Hills, CA: Sage.

Higginbotham, Evelyn Brooks. 1992. "African-American women's history and the metalanguage of race." *Signs* 17:251–74.

Higgonet, Margaret Randolph, et al., eds. 1987. *Behind the Lines: Gender and the Two World Wars.* New Haven, CT: Yale University Press.

Hill, Charles T., Zick Rubin, & Letitia Anne Peplau. 1976. "Breakups before marriage: The end of one hundred three affairs." *Journal of Social Issues* 32:147–68.

Hine, Darlene Clark. 1989. "Rape and the inner lives of black women in the Middle West: Preliminary thoughts on the culture of dissemblance." *Signs* 14:912–20.

Hirokawa, Randy Y., Jeffrey Mickey, & Steven Miura. 1991. "Effects of request legitimacy on the compliance-gaining tactics of male and female managers." *Communication Monographs* 58:421–36.

Hite, Shere. 1976. *The Hite Report: A Nationwide Study of Female Sexuality.* New York: Macmillan.

———. 1981. *The Hite Report on Male Sexuality.* New York: Alfred Knopf.

Hochschild, Arlie Russell. 1989. *The Second Shift.* New York: Avon.

———. 1997. *The Time Bind: When Work Becomes Home and Home Becomes Work.* New York: Metropolitan Books.

Hole, Judith, & Ellen Levine. 1971. *Rebirth of Feminism.* New York: Quadrangle.

Holmes, Douglas S., & Bruce Jorgensen. 1971. "Do personality and social psychologists study men more than women?" *Representative Research in Social Psychology* 2:71–76.

Holsti, Ole, & James N. Rosenau. 1981. "The foreign policy beliefs of women in leadership positions." *Journal of Politics* 43:326–47.

Holtgraves, Thomas, & Joong-Nam Yang. 1992. "Interpersonal underpinnings of request strategies: General principles and differences due to culture and gender." *Journal of Personality and Social Psychology* 62:246–56.

Honey, Maureen. 1984. *Creating Rosie the Riveter: Class, Gender, and Propaganda During World War II.* Boston: Northeastern University Press.

hooks, bell. 1981. *Ain't I a Woman: Black Women and Feminism.* Boston: South End Press.

———. 1984. *Feminist Theory: From Margin to Center.* Boston: South End Press.

———. 1989. *Talking Back: Thinking Feminist, Thinking Black.* Boston: South End Press.

Horgan, Dianne. 1983. "The pregnant woman's place and where to find it." *Sex Roles* 9:333–39.

Horney, Karen. 1967. *Feminine Psychology.* New York: Norton.

Hornung, Carlton A., Claire McCullough, & Taichi Sugimoto. 1981. "Status relationships in marriage: Risk factors in spouse abuse." *Journal of Marriage and the Family* 42:71–82.

Horowitz, Ruth. 1995. *Teen Mothers: Citizens or Dependents?* Chicago: University of Chicago Press.

Hoseley, David H., & Gayle K. Yamada. 1987. *Hard News: Women in Broadcast Journalism.* Westport, CT: Greenwood.

Houston, B. Kent, David S. Cates, & Karen E. Kelly. 1992. "Job stress, psychosocial strain, and physical health problems in women employed full-time outside the home and homemakers." *Women and Health* 19:1–26.

Howe, Lucy Kapp. 1978. *Pink Collar Workers.* New York: Avon.

Hrdy, Sarah Blaffer. 1981. *The Woman That Never Evolved.* Cambridge, MA: Harvard University Press.

Hubbell, F. A., et al. 1996. "Differing beliefs about breast cancer among Latinas and Anglo women." *Western Journal of Medicine* 164:405–9.

Huddy, Leonie. 1997. "Feminists and feminism in the news." In *Women, Media, and Politics,* edited by Pippa Norris, pp. 183–204. New York: Oxford University Press.

Hull, Gloria T., Patricia Bell Scott, & Barbara Smith, eds. 1982. *All the Women Are White, All the Blacks Are Men, But Some of Us Are Brave: Black Women's Studies.* Old Westbury, NY: The Feminist Press.

Humphries, Drew. 1993. "Mothers and children, drugs and crack: Reactions to maternal drug dependency." In *It's a Crime: Women and Justice,* edited by Roslyn Muraskin & Ted Alleman, pp. 130–45. Englewood Cliffs, NJ: Prentice-Hall.

Hurtado, Ada. 1989. "Relating to privilege: Seduction and rejection in the subordination of white women and women of color." *Signs* 14:833–55.

Huttenlocher, Janellen, Wendy Haight, & Anthony Bryk. 1991. "Early vocabulary growth: Relation to language input and gender." *Developmental Psychology* 27: 236–48.

Hyde, Janet Shibley. 1984. "How large are gender differences in aggression? A developmental meta-analysis." *Developmental Psychology* 20:722–36.

———. 1991. *Half the Human Experience: The Psychology of Women.* Lexington, MA: D. C. Heath.

———. 1994. *Understanding Human Sexuality.* New York: McGraw Hill.

Hyde, Janet Shibley, Elizabeth Fennema, & Susan J. Lamon. 1990. "Gender differences in mathematic performance: A meta-analysis." *Psychological Bulletin* 107: 139–55.

Hyde, Janet Shibley, & Marcia C. Linn. 1988. "Gender differences in verbal ability: A meta-analysis." *Psychological Bulletin* 104:53–69.

Ilknoian, Therese. 1993. "What ails women athletes?" *American Health* 12:55.

Immarigeon, Russ, & Meda Chesney-Lind. 1993. "Women's prisons: Overcrowded and overused." In *It's a Crime: Women and Justice,* edited by Roslyn Muraskin & Ted Alleman, pp. 242–59. Englewood Cliffs, NJ: Prentice-Hall.

Inman, Chris. 1996. "Friendships among men: Closeness in the doing." In *Gendered Relationships,* edited by Julia T. Wood, pp. 95–110. Mountain View, CA: Mayfield.

Instone, Debra, Brenda Major, & Barbara A. Bunker. 1983. "Gender, self-confidence, and social influence strategies: An organizational simulation." *Journal of Personality and Social Psychology* 44:322–33.

Inter-Parliamentary Union. 1997. *Men and Women in Politics: Democracy Still in the Making-A World Comparative Study.* Geneva: Inter-Parliamentary Union.

Irvine, Jacqueline Jordan. 1986. "Teacher-student interactions: Effects of student race, sex, and grade level." *Journal of Educational Psychology* 78:14–21.

Iyengar, Shanto, Nicholas A. Valentino, Stephen Ansolabehere, & Adam F. Simon. 1997. "Running as a woman: Gender stereotyping in political campaigns." In *Women, Media, and Politics,* edited by Pippa Norris, pp. 77–98. New York: Oxford University Press.

Jackson, Linda A. 1992. *Physical Appearance and Gender: Sociobiological and Sociocultural Perspectives.* Albany: State University of New York Press.

Jacobs, Jerry A. 1992. "Women's entry into management: Trends in earnings, authority, and values among salaried managers." *Administrative Science Quarterly* 37:282–301.

Jaggar, Alison M. 1983. *Feminist Politics and Human Nature.* Totowa, NJ: Littlefield, Adams.

Jaquette, Jane S., ed. 1989. *The Women's Movement in Latin America: Feminism and the Transition to Democracy.* Boston: Unwin Hyman.

Jaquette, Jane S., & Kathleen A. Staudt. 1985. "Women as 'at risk' reproducers: Biology, science, and population in U.S. foreign policy." In *Women, Biology, and Public Policy,* edited by Virginia Sapiro, pp. 235–68. Beverly Hills, CA: Sage.

Jaskoski, Helen. 1981. "'My heart will go out': Healing songs of Native American women." *International Journal of Women's Studies* 4:118–34.

Jayawardena, Kumari. 1986. *Feminism and Nationalism in the Third World.* London: Zed Books.

Jeanquart-Barone, Sandy, & Uma Sekaran. 1994. "Effects of supervisor's gender on American women's trust." *The Journal of Social Psychology* 134:253–55.

Jeffrey, Julie Roy. 1979. *Frontier Women: The Trans-Mississippi West, 1840–1880.* New York: Hill & Wang.

Jennings, M. Kent. 1979. "Another look at the life cycle and political participation." *American Journal of Political Science* 23:755–71.

Jennings, M. Kent, & Barbara G. Farah. 1981. "Social roles and political resources: An over-time study of men and women in party elites." *American Journal of Political Science* 25:462–82.

Jennings, Thelma. 1990. "'Us colored women had to go through a plenty': Sexual exploitation of African-American slave women." *Journal of Women's History* 1:45–74.

Jensen, Inger W., & Barbara A. Gutek. 1982. "Attributions and assignment of responsibility in sexual harassment." *Journal of Social Issues* 38:121–36.

Jepson, Barbara. 1975–1976. "American women in conducting." *Feminist Art Journal* 4:13–18.

Jessell, John C., & Lawrence Beymer. 1992. "The effects of job title vs job description on occupational sex typing." *Sex Roles* 27:73–83.

Johnson, Cathryn. 1994. "Gender, legitimate authority, and leader-subordinate conversations." *American Sociological Review* 59:122–35.

Johnson, Fern L. 1996. "Friendships among women: Closeness in dialogue." In *Gendered Relationships,* edited by Julia T. Wood, pp. 79–94. Mountain View, CA: Mayfield.

Johnson, Miriam M. 1982. "Fathers and 'femininity' in daughters: A review of the research." *Sociology and Social Research* 67:1–17.

Johnson, Paula. 1976. "Women and power: Toward a theory of effectiveness." *Journal of Social Issues* 32:99–110.

Jolliffe, Lee. 1994. "Women's magazines in the 19th century." *Journal of Popular Culture* 27:125–40.

Jones, Jacqueline. 1980. "Women who were more than men: Sex and status in Freedman's teaching." *History of Education Quarterly* 19:47–60.

Jones, W. T. 1963. *Masters of Political Thought,* Vol. 3. London: George Harrap.

Jones, Warren H., Mary Ellen Chernovetz, & Robert O. Hansson. 1978. "The enigma of androgyny: Differential implications for males and females?" *Journal of Consulting and Clinical Psychology* 46:298–313.

Kabeer, Naila. 1994. *Reversed Realities: Gender Hierarchies in Development Thought.* New York: Routledge.

Kahn, Kim Fridkin, & Ann Gordon. 1997. "How women campaign for the U.S. Senate: Substance and strategy." In *Women, Media, and Politics,* edited by Pippa Norris, pp. 59–76. New York: Oxford University Press.

Kaledin, Eugenia. 1984. *Mothers and More: American Women in the 1950's.* Boston: Twayne.

Kalmuss, Debra S., & Murray A Strauss. 1982. "Wife's marital dependency and wife abuse." *Journal of Marriage and the Family* 44:277–86.

Kandiyoti, Deniz, ed. 1991. *Women, Islam, and the State.* Philadelphia: Temple University Press.

Kaplan, Laura. 1995. *The Story of Jane: The Legendary Underground Feminist Abortion Service.* Chicago: University of Chicago Press.

Karraker, Katherine Hildebrant, Dena Ann Vogel, & Margaret Ann Lake. 1995. "'Parents' gender-stereotyped perceptions of newborns: The eye of the beholder revisited." *Sex Roles* 33:687.

Kay, Herma Hill. 1996. *Sex Based Discrimination.* St. Paul, MN: West.

Keith, Pat M. 1982. "Working women versus homemakers: Retirement resources and correlates of well being." In *Women's Retirement: Policy Implications of Recent*

Research, edited by Maximiliane Szinovacz, pp. 77–91. Beverly Hills, CA: Sage.

Keller, Evelyn Fox. 1985. *Reflections on Gender and Science.* New Haven, CT: Yale University Press.

Kellerman, Jonathan. 1974. "Sex role stereotypes and attitudes toward parental blame for the psychological problems of children." *Journal of Consulting and Clinical Psychology* 42:153–54.

Kendrick, Walter. 1987. *The Secret Museum: Pornography in Modern Culture.* New York: Viking.

Kerber, Linda K. 1982. "The daughters of Columbia: Educating women for the republic, 1787–1805." In *Women's America,* edited by Linda K. Kerber & Jane de Hart Mathews, pp. 82–94. New York: Oxford University Press.

———. 1986. *Women of the Republic: Intellect and Ideology in Revolutionary America.* New York: Norton.

Kerber, Linda K., & Jane de Hart Mathews. 1982. *Women's America: Refocusing the Past.* New York: Oxford University Press.

Kerber, Linda K., et al. 1986. "On *In a Different Voice:* An interdisciplinary forum." *Signs* 11:304–33.

Kerig, Patricia K., Philip A. Cowan, & Carolyn Pape Cowan. 1993. "Marital quality and gender differences in parent-child interaction." *Developmental Psychology* 29:931–39.

Kessler-Harris, Alice. 1982. *Out to Work: A History of Wage-Earning Women in the United States.* New York: Oxford University Press.

———. 1990. *A Woman's Wage: Historical Meanings and Social Consequences.* Lexington: University of Kentucky Press.

Kidwasser, Alfred P., & Michelle A. Wolf. 1992. "Mainstream television, adolescent homosexuality, and significant silence." *Critical Studies in Mass Communication* 9:350–73.

Kierstead, Diane, Patti D'Agostino, & Heidi Dill. 1988. "Sex role stereotyping of college professors: Bias in students' ratings of instructors." *Journal of Educational Psychology* 80:342–44.

Kinsey, Alfred C., Wardell B. Pomeroy, & Clyde E. Martin. 1948. *Sexual Behavior in the Human Male.* Philadelphia: Saunders.

Kitzinger, Celia, & Sue Wilkinson. 1995. "Transitions from heterosexuality to lesbianism: The discursive production of lesbian identities." *Developmental Psychology* 31:95–104.

Kitzinger, Jenny. 1995. "'I'm sexually attractive but I'm powerful': Young women negotiating sexual reputation." *Women's Studies International Forum* 18: 187–96.

Klebanov, Pamela Kato, & John B. Jemmett III. 1992. "Effects of expectations and bodily sensations on self-reports of premenstrual symptoms." *Psychology of Women Quarterly* 16:289–310.

Klein, Ethel. 1984. *Gender Politics.* Cambridge, MA: Harvard University Press.

Klein, M. C., et al. 1994. "Relationship of episiotomy to perineal trauma and morbidity, sexual dysfunction, and pelvic floor relaxation." *American Journal of Obstetrical Gynecology* 171:591–98.

Knupfer, Anne Meis. 1995. "Toward a tenderer humanity and a nobler womanhood: African-American women's clubs in Chicago, 1890–1920." *Journal of Women's History* 7:58–76.

Koehler, Lyle. 1982. "The case of the American Jezebels: Anne Hutchinson and female agitation during the years of antinomian turmoil, 1636–40." In *Women's America,* edited by Linda K. Kerber & Jane De Hart Mathews, pp. 36–51. New York: Oxford University Press.

Koff, Elissa, & Jill Rierdan. 1995. "Early adolescent girls' understanding of menstruation." *Women & Health* 22:1–19.

Kohlberg, Lawrence. 1966. "A cognitive-developmental analysis of children's sex role concepts and attitudes." In *The Development of Sex Differences,* edited by Eleanor Maccoby, pp. 82–173. Stanford, CA: Stanford University Press.

Komarovsky, Mirra. 1967. *Blue Collar Marriage.* New York: Vintage.

Kraditor, Aileen S. 1965. *The Ideas of the Woman Suffrage Movement, 1890–1920.* New York: Columbia University Press.

———, ed. 1968. *Up from the Pedestal: Selected Writings in the History of Feminism.* New York: Quadrangle.

Kramer, Heinrich, & James Sprenger. 1928. *Malleus Maleficarum.* London: Arrow.

Kramer, Pamela E., & Sheila Lehman. 1990. "Mismeasuring women: A critique of research on computer ability and avoidance." *Signs* 16:158–72.

Kravetz, Diane, & Linda E. Jones. 1981. "Androgyny as a standard of mental health." *American Journal of Orthopsychiatry* 51:502–509.

Kroeger, Naomi. 1982. "Preretirement preparation: Sex differences in access, sources, and use." In *Women's Retirement: Policy Implications of Recent Research,* edited by Maximiliane Szinovacz, pp. 95–112. Beverly Hills, CA: Sage.

Kumanyika, Shiriki, Judy F. Wilson, & Marsha Guilford-Davenport. 1993. "Weight-related attitudes and behaviors of black women." *Journal of the American Dietetic Association* 93:416–22 and discussion, v93:125.

Lakoff, Robin. 1975. *Language and Women's Place.* New York: Harper & Row.

Lamb, Sharon, & Susan Keon. 1995. "Blaming the perpetrator: Language that distorts reality in newspaper articles on men battering women." *Psychology of Women Quarterly* 19:209–20.

Lamke, Leanne K. 1982. "The impact of sex role orientations on self-esteem in early adolescence." *Child Development* 53:1530–35.

Lander, Louise. 1988. *Images of Bleeding: Menstruation as Ideology.* New York: Orlando Press.

Lasch, Christopher. 1977. *Haven in a Heartless World: The Family Besieged.* New York: Basic.

Laumann, Edward O., Robert T. Michael, John H. Gagnon, & Stuart Michaels. 1994. *The Social Organization of Sexuality: Sexual Practices in the United States.* Chicago: University of Chicago Press.

Leach, William. 1980. *True Love and Perfect Union: The Feminist Reform of Sex and Society.* New York: Basic.

Leary, Mark R., John B. Nezlek, & Deborah Downs. 1994. "Self-presentation in everyday interactions: Effects of target familiarity and gender composition." *Journal of Personality and Social Psychology* 67:664–73.

Leavitt, Judith Walzer. 1980. "Birthing and anesthesia: The debate over twilight sleep." *Signs* 6:147–64. Also in Leavitt (1984).

———. 1983. "'Science' enters the birthing room: Obstetrics in America since the eighteenth century." *Journal of American History* 70:281–304.

———. 1986. *Brought to Bed: Childbearing in America, 1750–1950.* New York: Oxford University Press.

Leavitt, Judith Walzer, & Whitney Walton. 1982. "Down to death's door: Women's perceptions of childbirth in America." In *Proceedings of the Second Motherhood Symposium: Childbirth: The Beginning of Motherhood,* edited by Sophie Colleau, pp. 113–36. Madison, WI: Women's Studies Program.

Lederer, Laura, ed. 1980. *Take Back the Night.* New York: William Morrow.

Lee, Valerie E., & David T. Burkam. 1996. "Gender differences in middle grade science achievement: Subject domain, ability level, and course emphasis." *Science Education* 80:613–50.

Lee, Valerie E., Susanna Loeb, & Helen M. Marks. 1995. "Gender differences in secondary school teachers' control over classroom and school policy." *American Journal of Education* 103:259–301.

Lee, Valerie E., Helen M. Marks, & Tina Byrd. 1994. "Sexism in single-sex and coeducational independent secondary school classrooms." *Sociology of Education* 67:92–120.

Lehman, Edward C., Jr. 1993. *Gender and Work: The Case of the Clergy.* Albany: State University of New York Press.

Leinhardt, Gaea, Andrea Mar Seewald, & Mary Engel. 1979. "Learning what's taught: Sex differences in

instruction." *Journal of Educational Psychology* 71: 432–39.

Lemons, Stanley. 1972. *The Woman Citizen: Social Feminism in the 1920's.* Urbana: University of Illinois Press.

Lerner, Gerda. 1971. *The Grimké Sisters from South Carolina: Pioneers for Women's Rights and Abolition.* New York: Schocken.

LeVay, Simon. 1991. "A difference in hypothalamic structure between heterosexual and homosexual men." *Science* 253:1034–37.

Levine, Gavrielle. 1995. "Closing the gender gap: Focus on mathematics anxiety." *Contemporary Education* 67: 42–45.

Levine, Martine P., & Robin Leonard. 1984. "Discrimination against lesbians in the workforce." *Signs* 9:700–710.

Levine, Timothy R., Steven A. McCormack, & Penny Baldwin Avery. 1992. "Sex differences in emotional reactions to discovered deception." *Communication Quarterly* 40:289–96.

Levitt, Eugene E., & Albert D. Klassen. 1974. "Public attitudes toward homosexuality." *Journal of Homosexuality* 1:29–47.

Levy, A. H. 1983. "Double-bars and double standards: Women composers in America, 1880–1920." *International Journal of Women's Studies* 6:162–74.

Levy, Gary D. 1994. "Aspects of preschoolers' comprehension of indoor and outdoor gender-typed toys." *Sex Roles* 30:391–406.

Lewis, Charles, & Neville, John. 1995. "Images of Rosie: A content analysis of women workers in American magazine advertising, 1940–1946." *Journalism and Mass Communication Quarterly* 72:216–27.

Lewis, Robert A. 1978. "Emotional Intimacy Among Men." *Journal of Social Issues* 34:108–21.

Liben, Lynn S., & Margaret L. Signorella. 1993. "Gender-schematic processing in children: The role of initial interpretations of stimuli." *Developmental Psychology* 29: 141–49.

Lifton, P. D. 1985. "Individual differences in moral development: The relation of sex, gender, and personality to morality." *Journal of Personality* 53:306–34.

Lillard, Lee A. & Linda J. Waite. 1995. "'Til death do us part: Marital disruption and mortality." *American Journal of Sociology* 100 (March): 1131–56.

Linn, M. C., & A. C. Peterson. 1985. "Emergence and characterization of gender differences in spatial ability: A meta-analysis." *Child Development* 56:1479–98.

Lipartito, Kenneth. 1994. "When women were switches: Technology, work, and gender in the telephone industry, 1890–1920." *The American Historical Review* 99: 1075–1111.

Lips, Hilary. 1993. *Sex and Gender: An Introduction.* Mountain View, CA: Mayfield.

Lirgg, Cathy, Ro DiBrezz, & Angie Smith. 1994. "Influence of gender of coach on perceptions of basketball and coaching self-efficacy and aspirations of high school female basketball players." *Women in Sport and Physical Activity Journal* 3:1–14.

Livingston, Joy A. 1982. "Responses to sexual harassment on the job: Legal, organizational, and individual actions." *Journal of Social Issues* 38:5–22.

Lobel, Thalma E. 1994. "Sex typing and the social perception of gender stereotypic and nonstereotypic behavior: The uniqueness of feminine males." *Journal of Personality and Social Psychology* 66:379–85.

Lorde, Audrey. 1984. "Man child." In *Sister Outsider.* Trumansburg, NY: Crossing Press.

Lorentzen, Robin. 1991. *Women in the Sanctuary Movement.* Philadelphia: Temple University Press.

Loring, Marti, & Brian Powell. 1988. "Gender, race, and DSM-III: A study of the objectivity of psychiatric diagnostic behavior." *Journal of Health and Social Behavior* 29:1–22.

Lott, Dale F., & Robert Sommer. 1967. "Seating arrangements and status." *Journal of Personality and Social Psychology* 7:90–95.

Luecke-Aleksa, Diane, Daniel R. Anderson, & Patricia A. Collins. 1995. "Gender constancy and television viewing." *Developmental Psychology* 3:773–80.

Luker, Kristin. 1996. *Dubious Conceptions: The Politics of Teenage Pregnancy.* Cambridge, MA: Harvard University Press.

Lundeberg, Mary Anna. 1997. "You guys are overreacting: Teaching prospective teachers about subtle gender bias." *Journal of Teacher Education* 48:55–61.

Lynd, Robert S., & Helen Merrell Lynd. 1929. *Middletown: A Study of American Culture.* New York: Harcourt & Brace.

———. 1937. *Middletown in Transition: A Study in Cultural Conflict.* New York: Harcourt & Brace.

Lynn, Richard. 1993. "Sex differences in competitiveness and the valuation of money in twenty countries." *Journal of Social Psychology* 133:507–11.

Lyons, Judith A., & Lisa A. Serbin. 1986. "Observer bias in scoring boys' and girls' aggression." *Sex Roles* 14:301–13.

Maccoby, Eleanor, & Carol Jacklin. 1974. *The Psychology of Sex Differences.* Stanford, CA: Stanford University Press.

Machung, Anne. 1989. "Talking career, thinking job: Gender differences in career and family expectations of Berkeley seniors." *Feminist Studies* 15:35–58.

Mackinnon, Catharine. 1979. *The Sexual Harassment of Working Women.* New Haven, CT: Yale University Press.

Macklin, M. Carole, & Richard G. Kolbe. 1984. "Sex role stereotyping in children's advertising." *Journal of Advertising* 13:34–42.

Macklin, Ruth. 1994. *Surrogates and Other Mothers: The Debates Over Assisted Reproduction.* Philadelphia: Temple University Press.

MacLeod, Arlene Elowe. 1991. *Accommodating Protest: Working Women, the New Veiling, and Change in Cairo.* New York: Columbia University Press.

Macleod, Beth Abelson. 1993. "'Whence comes the lady tympanist?' Gender and instrumental musicians in America, 1853–1990." *Journal of Social History* 27: 291–308.

Mainardi, Patricia. 1982. "Quilts: The great American art." In *The Expanding Discourse: Feminism and Art History,* edited by Norma Broude & Mary D. Garrard, pp. 331–46. New York: HarperCollins.

Major, Brenda. 1981. "Gender patterns in touching behavior." In *Gender and Nonverbal Behavior,* edited by Clara Mayo & Nancy Henley, pp. 15–38. New York: Springer-Verlag.

Malamuth, Neil M. 1981. "Rape proclivity among males." *Journal of Social Issues* 37:138–57.

Mamay, Patricia D., & Richard L. Simpson. 1981. "Three female roles in television commercials." *Sex Roles* 7:1223–32.

Mandelbaum, Dorothy Rosenthal. 1978. "Women in medicine." *Signs* 4:136–45.

Mann, Susan A. 1989. "Slavery, sharecropping, and sexual inequality." *Signs* 14:774–98.

Marini, Margaret Mooney, Pi-ling Fan, & Erica Finley. 1996. "Gender and job values." *Sociology of Education* 69:49–65.

Markens, Susan. 1996. "The problematic of 'experience': A political and cultural critique of PMS." *Gender and Society* 10 (February): 42–58.

Markus, H., M. Crane, S. Bernstein, & M. Siladi. 1982. "Self-schemas and gender." *Journal of Personality and Social Psychology* 42:38–50.

Martin, Elaine. 1984. "Power and authority in the classroom: Sexist stereotypes in teaching evaluations." *Signs* 9:482–92.

Martinez, James C. 1995. "Risk taking on gender-typed tasks following an assignment based on sex." *The Journal of Social Psychology* 135:573–79.

Marx, Karl, & Friedrich Engels. [1845–1846] 1947. *The German Ideology.* New York: International.

Marzolf, Marion. 1977. *Up From the Footnote: A History of Women Journalists.* New York: Hastings House.

Matheson, Kimberly, & Connie M. Kristensen. 1987. "The effect of sexist attitudes and social structures on the use of sex-biased pronouns." *Journal of Social Psychology* 127:395–401.

Mathews, Alice E. 1987. "Tall women and mountain belles: Fact and fiction in Appalachia." In *Perspectives on the American South: An Annual Review of Society, Politics, and Culture,* edited by James C. Cobb & Charles R. Wilson, pp. 39–54. New York: Gordon and Breach Science Publishers.

Matthaei, Julie A. 1982. *An Economic History of Women in America: Women's Work, The Sexual Division of Labor, and the Development of Capitalism.* New York: Schocken.

McAdam, Doug, John D. McCarthy, & Mayer N. Zald, eds. 1996. *Comparative Perspectives on Social Movements.* New York: Cambridge University Press.

McClintock, Martha K. 1971. "Menstrual synchrony and suppression." *Nature* 229:244–45.

McCormick, Naomi B., & Clinton J. Jesser. 1983. "The courtship game: Power in the sexual encounter." In *Changing Boundaries: Gender Roles and Sexual Behavior,* edited by Elizabeth Rice Allgeier & Naomi B. McCormick, pp. 64–86. Palo Alto, CA: Mayfield.

McCracken, Ellen. 1993. *Decoding Women's Magazines: From Mademoiselle to Ms.* New York: St. Martin's.

McDonough, Eileen. 1982. "To work or not to work: The differential aspect of achieved and derived status upon the political participation of women, 1956–76." *American Journal of Political Science* 26:280–97.

McGhee, Paul E., & Terry Frueh. 1980. "Television viewing and the learning of sex role stereotypes." *Sex Roles* 6:179–88.

McLanahan, Sara, & Julia Adams. 1987. "Parenthood and psychological well-being." *Annual Review of Psychology* 5:237–57.

McManus, Karen A., Yvonne Brackbill, Lynn Woodward, Paul Doering, & David Robinson. 1982. "Consumer information about prenatal and obstetric drugs." *Women and Health* 7:15–29.

McNamara, Jo Ann Kay. 1996. *Sisters in Arms: Catholic Nuns Through Two Millennia.* Cambridge, MA: Harvard University Press.

Mechanic, David. 1978. *Medical Sociology.* New York: Free Press.

Melosh, Barbara. 1991. *Engendering Culture: Manhood and Womanhood in New Deal Public Art and Theater.* Washington, DC: Smithsonian Institution Press.

Merlo, Alida V. 1993. "Pregnant substance abusers: The new female offender." In *It's a Crime: Women and Justice,* edited by Roslyn Muraskin & Ted Alleman, pp. 146–60. Englewood Cliffs, NJ: Prentice-Hall.

Milkman, Ruth. 1982. "Redefining 'women's work': The sexual division of labor in the auto industry during World War II." *Feminist Studies* 8:337–72.

Miller, Judith Harmon. 1997. "Gender issues embedded in the experience of student teaching: being treated like a sex object." *Journal of Teacher Education* 48:19–28.

Miller, Patrice M., Dorothy L. Danaher, & David Forbes. 1986. "Sex-related strategies for coping with interpersonal conflict in children aged 5 to 7." *Developmental Psychology* 22:543–48.

Millett, Kate. 1970. *Sexual Politics.* Garden City, NY: Doubleday.

Mills, Kay. 1993. *This Little Light of Mine: The Life of Fannie Lou Hamer.* New York: NAL/Dutton.

Milman, Barbara. 1980. "New rules for the oldest profession: Should we change our prostitution laws?" *Harvard Women's Law Journal* 3:1–82.

Minh-ha, Trinh T. 1989. *Woman, Native, Other: Writing Postcoloniality and Feminism.* Bloomington: Indiana University Press.

Mirandé, Alfredo, & Evangelina Enríquez. 1979. *La Chicana: The Mexican-American Woman.* Chicago: University of Chicago Press.

Mitchell, Juliet. 1974. *Psychoanalysis and Feminism.* New York: Pantheon.

Mohanty, Chandra Talpade, Ann Russo, & Lourdes Torres, eds. 1991. *Third World Women and the Politics of Feminism.* Bloomington: Indiana University Press.

Morága, Cherrie, & Gloria Anzaldúa, eds. 1981. *This Bridge Called My Back: Writings by Radical Women of Color.* Watertown, MA: Persephone.

Morell, Carolyn M. 1994. *Unwomanly Conduct: The Challenges of Intentional Childlessness.* New York: Routledge.

Moresque, John, & Catherine E. Ross. 1995. "Sex differences in distress: Real or artifact?" *American Sociological Review* 60:449–68.

Morgan, Edmund S. [1944] 1978. "The Puritans and sex." In *The American Family in Historical Perspective,* edited by Michael Gordon, pp. 363–73. New York: St. Martin's.

Morin, Stephen F., & Ellen M. Garfinkle. 1978. "Male homophobia." *Journal of Social Issues* 34:29–47.

Morisset, Colleen E., Kathryn E. Barnard, & Cathryn L. Booth. 1995. "Toddlers' language development: Sex differences within social risk." *Developmental Psychology* 31:851–65.

Morris, Aldon D., & Carol McClung Mueller, eds. 1992. *Frontiers in Social Movement Theory.* New Haven, CT: Yale University Press.

Morrison, Toni, ed. 1992. *Race-ing, Justice, En-gendering Power: Essays on Anita Hill, Clarence Thomas, and the Construction of Social Reality.* New York: Pantheon.

Motley, Michael T., & Heidi M. Reeder. 1995. "Unwanted escalation of sexual intimacy: Male and female perceptions of connotations and relational consequences of resistance messages." *Communication Monographs* 62: 355–82.

Motluk, Alison. 1997. "Sex bias study shocks world." *New Scientist Archive,* http://newscientist.com/ns/970524/women_nf.html/

Moyer, Imogene L. 1993. "Women's prisons: Issues and controversies." In *It's a Crime: Women and Justice,* edited by Roslyn Muraskin & Ted Alleman, pp. 193–210. Englewood Cliffs, NJ: Prentice-Hall.

Ms. Foundation for Women. 1992. *A Policy Guide: Women's Choices: A Joint Project.* New York: Ms. Foundation for Women.

Mueller, Carol. 1991. "The gender gap and women's political influence." *The Annals: American Feminism: New Issues for a Mature Movement* 515:23–37.

Mueller, Carol, & Thomas Dimieri. 1982. "The structure of belief systems among contending ERA activists." *Social Forces* 60:657–75.

Mueller, Claus. 1973. *The Politics of Communication: A Study in the Political Sociology of Language, Socialization, and Legitimation.* New York: Oxford University Press.

Mulac, Anthony, & Torborg Louisa Lundell. 1986. "Linguistic contributors to the gender-linked language effect." *Journal of Language and Social Psychology* 5: 81–101.

Muller, Charlotte F. 1990. *Health Care and Gender.* New York: Russell Sage Foundation.

Muraskin, Roslyn. 1993. "Disparate treatment in correction facilities." In *It's a Crime: Women and Justice,* edited by Roslyn Muraskin & Ted Alleman, pp. 211–25. Englewood Cliffs, NJ: Prentice-Hall.

Nead, Lynda. 1992. "The female nude: Pornography, art, and sexuality." In *Sex Exposed: Sexuality and the Pornography Debate,* edited by Lynne Segal & Mary McIntosh, pp. 280–94. New Brunswick, NJ: Rutgers University Press.

Nelson, Barbara J., & Najma Chowdhury, eds. 1994. *Women and Politics Worldwide.* New Haven, CT: Yale University Press.

Nelson, Julie A. 1996. *Feminism, Objectivity and Economics.* New York: Routledge.

New Jersey Supreme Court Task Force. 1986. "The first year report of the New Jersey Supreme Court Task Force on Women in the Courts-June 1984." *Women's Rights Law Reporter* 9:129–75.

Nichols, Patricia C. 1978. "Black women in the rural South: Conservative and innovative." *International Journal of the Sociology of Language* 17:45–54.

Nicol-Smith, Louise. 1996. "Causality, menopause, and depression: A critical review of the literature." *British Medical Journal* 313:1229–32.

Nicolson, Paula. 1995. "The menstrual cycle, science and femininity: Assumptions underlying menstrual cycle research." *Social Science & Medicine* 4:779–84.

Nochlin, Linda. 1971. "Why are there no great women artists?" In *Women in Sexist Society,* edited by Vivian Gornick & Barbara K. Moran, pp. 480–510. New York: New American Library.

Nolen-Hoeksema, Susan. 1987. "Sex differences in unipolar depression." *Psychological Bulletin* 101:259–82.

Norgren, Jill. 1989. "Child care." In *Women: A Feminist Perspective,* edited by Jo Freeman, pp. 176–96. Mountain View, CA: Mayfield.

Norris, Pippa. 1997. "Women leaders worldwide: A splash of color in the photo opportunity." In *Women, Media, and Politics,* edited by Pippa Norris, pp. 149–65. New York: Oxford University Press.

O'Connor, P. 1992. *Friendships Between Women: A Critical Review.* New York: Guilford Press.

O'Farrell, Brigid, & Sharon L. Harlan. 1982. "Craft workers and clerks: The effects of male co-worker hostility on women's satisfaction with non-traditional jobs." *Social Problems* 23:252–65.

Offen, Karen. 1988. "Defining feminism: A comparative historical approach." *Signs* 14:119–57.

Oldham, Sue, Doug Farmill, & Ian Bell. 1982. "Sex role identity of female homosexuals." *Journal of Homosexuality* 8:41–46.

Olivardia, Roberto, Harrison G. Pope, Jr., Barbara Mangweth, & James I. Hudson. 1995. "Eating disorders in college men." *American Journal of Psychiatry* 152: 1279–85.

Oliver, Mary Beth, & Janet Shibley Hyde. 1993. "Gender differences in sexuality: A meta-analysis." *Psychological Bulletin* 114:29–51.

———. 1995. "Gender differences in attitudes toward homosexuality: A reply to Whitley and Kite." *Psychological Bulletin* 117:155–58.

O'Malley, K. M., & S. Richardson. 1985. "Sex bias in counseling: Have things changed?" *Journal of Counseling and Development* 63:294–99.

O'Neill, June, & Solomon Polachek. 1993. "Why the gender gap in wages narrowed in the 1980s." *Journal of Labor Economics* 11:205–28.

Owen, Diana, & Jack Dennis. 1988. "Gender differences in the politicization of American children." *Women and Politics* 8:23–44.

Paige, Karen E., & Jeffrey M. Paige. 1981. *Politics of the Reproductive Rituals.* Berkeley: University of California Press.

Paisner, Daniel. 1989. *The Imperfect Mirror: Inside Stories of Television Women*. New York: Morrow.

Parisi, Nicolette. 1982a. "Exploring female crime patterns: Problems and prospects." In *Judge, Lawyer, Victim, Thief: Women, Gender Roles, and Criminal Justice,* edited by Nicole Hahn Rafter & Elizabeth Anne Stanko, pp. 111–30. Boston: Northeastern University Press.

———. 1982b. "Are females treated differently? A review of the theories and evidence on sentencing and parole decisions." In *Judge, Lawyer, Victim, Thief: Women, Gender Roles, and Criminal Justice,* edited by Nicole Hahn Rafter & Elizabeth Anne Stanko, pp. 205–29. Boston: Northeastern University Press.

Parker, Dorothy. 1944. "Words of comfort to be scratched on a mirror." In *The Viking Portable Dorothy Parker,* p. 173. New York: Viking Press.

Parlee, Mary Brown. 1992. "On PMS and psychiatric abnormality." *Feminism and Psychology* 2:105–19.

Parsons, Jacqueline Eccles. 1983. "Sexual socialization and gender roles in childhood." In *Changing Boundaries: Gender Roles and Sexual Behavior,* edited by Elizabeth Rice Allgeier & Naomi B. McCormick, pp. 19–48. Mountain View, CA: Mayfield.

Parsons, Talcott. 1951. *The Social System.* New York: Free Press.

———. 1954. "Age and sex in the social structure of the United States." In *Essays in Sociological Theory,* edited by Talcott Parsons, pp. 89–103. New York: Free Press.

Parsons, Talcott, & Robert F. Bales. 1955. *Family, Socialization and Interaction Process.* Glencoe, IL: Free Press.

Patterson, Charlotte J. 1992. "Children of lesbian and gay parents." *Child Development* 63:1025–62.

Patterson, Michelle, & Laurie Engleberg. 1978. "Women in male dominated professions." In *Women Working: Theories and Facts in Perspective,* edited by Anne H. Stromberg & Shirley Harkness, pp. 266–92. Mountain View, CA: Mayfield.

Pedersen, Darhl M., Martin M. Schinedling, & Dee L. Johnson. 1968. "Effects of sex of examiner and subject taught on children's quantitative test performance." *Journal of Personality and Social Psychology* 10:251–54.

Penelope, Julia, & Susan J. Wolfe. 1989. *The Original Coming Out Stories.* Freedom, CA: The Crossing Press.

Penn, Donna. 1991. "The meanings of lesbianism in postwar America." *Gender and History* 3:190–203.

Peplau, Letitia Anne, Susan Cochran, Karen Rook, & Christine Padesky. 1978. "Loving women: Attachment and autonomy in lesbian relationships." *Journal of Social Issues* 34:7–27.

Peplau, Letitia Anne, & Steven Gordon. 1983. "The intimate relationships of lesbian and gay men." In *Changing Boundaries: Gender Roles and Sexual Behavior,* edited by Elizabeth Rice Allgeier & Naomi B. McCormick, pp. 226–44. Palo Alto, CA: Mayfield.

Peplau, Letitia Anne, Zick Rubin, & Charles Hill. 1977. "Sex intimacy in dating relationships." *Journal of Social Issues* 33:96–109.

Perdue, Theda. 1989. "Cherokee women and the Trail of Tears." *Journal of Women's History* 1:14–30.

Perkins, Anne G. 1994. "Women in the workplace: The ripple effect." *Harvard Business Review* 72:15.

Perkins, Linda M. 1983. "The impact of the 'cult of true womanhood' on the education of black women." *Journal of Social Issues* 39:17–28.

Petchesky, Roslyn P. 1984. *Abortion and Women's Choice: The State, Sexuality, and Reproductive Freedom.* New York: Longman.

Peterson, Susan Rae. 1977. "Coercion and rape: The state as a male protection racket." In *Feminism and Philosophy,* edited by Mary Vetterling-Braggin, Frederick A. Elliston, & Jane English, pp. 313–32. Totowa, NJ: Littlefield, Adams.

Peterson, V. Spike, ed. 1992. *Gendered States: Feminist (Re)Visions of International Relations Theory.* Boulder, CO: Lynne Reinner.

Phelan, Shane. 1989. *Identity Politics: Lesbian Feminism and the Limits of Community.* Philadelphia: Temple University Press.

Pistrang, Nancy. 1984. "Women's work involvement and experience of new motherhood." *Journal of Marriage and the Family* 46:433–47.

Plaskow, Judith. 1990. *Standing Again at Sinai.* San Francisco: HarperCollins.

Polakow, Valerie. 1993. *Lives on the Edge: Single Mothers and Their Children in the Other America.* Chicago: University of Chicago Press.

Pollard, Diane S. 1993. "Gender, achievement, and African-American students' perceptions of their school experience." *Educational Psychologist* 28:341–56.

Poole, Debra A., & Anne E. Tapley. 1988. "Sex roles, social roles, and clinical judgments of mental health." *Sex Roles* 19:265–72.

Poole, Millicent, Janice Langan-Fox, & Mary Omodei. 1990. "Determining career orientations in women from different social-class backgrounds." *Sex Roles* 23: 471–90.

Pope, Jacqueline. 1989. *Biting the Hand That Feeds Them: Organizing Women on Welfare at the Grass Roots Level.* Westport, CT: Greenwood.

Porter, Natalie, & Florence Geis. 1981. "Women and nonverbal leadership cues: When seeing is not believing." In *Gender and Nonverbal Behavior,* edited by Clara Mayo & Nancy Henley, pp. 39–62. New York: Springer-Verlag.

Posner, Richard A., & Katharine B. Silbaugh. 1996. *A Guide to America's Sex Laws.* Chicago: University of Chicago Press.

Prather, J., & Linda S. Fidell. 1975. "Sex differences in the control and style of medical ads." *Social Science and Medicine* 9:23–26.

Purvis, Sally B. 1995. *The Stained-Glass Ceiling: Churches and Their Women Pastors.* Louisville, KY: Westminster.

Rafter, Nicole Hahn. 1982. "Hard times: Custodial prisons for women and the example of the New York State Prison for Women at Auburn, 1893–1933." In *Judge, Lawyer, Victim, Thief: Women, Gender Roles, and Criminal Justice,* edited by Nicole Hahn Rafter & Elizabeth Anne Stanko, pp. 237–60. Boston: Northeastern University Press.

Rafter, Nicole Hahn, & Elizabeth Anne Stanko, eds. 1982. *Judge, Lawyer, Victim, Thief: Women, Gender Roles, and Criminal Justice.* Boston: Northeastern University Press.

Rank, Mark R. 1988. "Fertility among women on welfare: Incidence and determinants." *American Sociological Review* 54:296–304.

Rapoport, Ronald B. 1981. "The sex gap in political persuading: Where the 'structuring principle' works." *American Journal of Political Science* 25:32–48.

Rawalt, Marguerite. 1983. "The Equal Rights Amendment." In *Women in Washington: Advocates for Public Policy,* edited by Irene Tinker, pp. 49–78. Beverly Hills, CA: Sage.

Reed, Susan O. 1993. "The criminalization of pregnancy: Drugs, alcohol, and AIDS." In *It's a Crime: Women and Justice,* edited by Roslyn Muraskin & Ted Alleman, pp. 93–117. Englewood Cliffs, NJ: Prentice-Hall.

Reid, Leonard N., Karen Whitehall King, & Peggy J. Kreshel. 1994. "Black and white models and their activities in modern cigarette and alcohol ads." *Journalism Quarterly* 71:873–86.

Reid, Penny, & Gilliam Finchilescu. 1995. "The disempowering effects of media violence against women on college women." *Psychology of Women Quarterly* 19:397–412.

Reilly, Philip. 1991. *The Surgical Solution: A History of Involuntary Sterilization in the United States.* Baltimore, MD: Johns Hopkins University Press.

Reinharz, Shulamith. 1992. *Feminist Methods in Social Research.* New York: Oxford University Press.

Reskin, Barbara F. 1988. "Bringing the men back in: Sex differentiation and the devaluation of women's work." *Gender and Society* 2:58–81.

Resnick, Michael D. 1984. "Studying adolescent mothers' decision making about adoption and parenting." *Social Work* 29:5–10.

Rhodes, Jane. 1991. "Television's realist portrayal of African-American women and the case of 'L.A. Law.'" *Women and Language* 14:29–34.

Rich, Adrienne. 1979. *On Lies, Secrets, and Silence.* New York: Norton.

———. 1980. "Compulsory heterosexuality and lesbian existence." *Signs* 5:631–60.

Richards, Lynne, & Laurie McAlister. 1994. "Female submissiveness, nonverbal behavior, and body boundary definition." *Journal of Psychology* 128:419–24.

Richardson, J. T. 1989. "Student learning and the menstrual cycle: Premenstrual symptoms and approaches to studying." *Educational Psychology* 9:215–38.

Richardson, John T. E. 1995. "The premenstrual syndrome: A brief history." *Social Science & Medicine* 41: 761–67.

Rickel, Annette U., & Linda M. Grant. 1979. "Sex role stereotypes in the mass media and schools: Five consistent themes." *International Journal of Women's Studies* 2:164–79.

Riley, Glenda. 1991. *Divorce: An American Tradition.* New York: Oxford University Press.

Rix, Sara E. 1988. *The American Woman, 1988–89: A Status Report.* New York: Norton.

Robbins, James. 1980. "Religious involvement, asceticism, and abortion among low income black women." *Sociological Analysis* 41:365–74.

Robertson, Nan. 1992. *The Girls in the Balcony: Women, Men and the New York Times.* New York: Random House.

Robinson, John P. 1980. "Household technology and household work." In *Women and Household Labor,* edited by Sara F. Berk, pp. 29–52. Beverly Hills, CA: Sage.

"*Roe* and neonatal homicide." 1992. *Family Planning Perspectives* 24:146.

Rohrbaugh, Joanna Bunker. 1980. *Women: Psychology's Puzzle.* Brighton, England: Harvester Press.

Rollins, Judith. 1983. *Between Women: Domestics and Their Employers.* Philadelphia: Temple University Press.

Rong, Xue Lan. 1996. "Effects of race and gender on teachers' perception of the social behavior of elementary students." *Urban Education* 31:261–90.

Rook, Karen S., & Constance Hammer. 1977. "A cognitive perspective on the experience of sexual arousal." *Journal of Social Issues* 33:7–29.

Rosen, Bernard, & M. F. Mericle. 1979. "Influence of strong versus weak fair employment policies and applicant's sex on selection decisions and salary recommendations in a management simulation." *Journal of Applied Psychology* 64:435–39.

Rosenberg, Dorothy J. 1991. "Shock therapy: GDR women in transition from a socialist welfare state to a social market economy." *Signs* 17:129–51.

Ross, Catherine E., & John Mirowsky. 1988. "Child care and emotional adjustment to wives' employment." *Journal of Health and Social Behavior* 29:127–38.

Ross, Laurie, Daniel R. Anderson, & Patricia A. Wisocki. 1982. "Television viewing and adult sex-role attitudes." *Sex Roles* 8:589–92.

Rossi, Alice, ed. 1970. *Essays in Sex Equality: John Stuart Mill and Harriet Taylor Mill.* Chicago: University of Chicago Press.

———. 1988. *The Feminist Papers: From Adams to de Beauvoir.* Boston: Northeastern University Press.

Rothblum, Esther· D. 1992. "The stigma of women's weight: Social and economic realities." *Feminism and Psychology* 2:61–74.

Rothman, Barbara Katz. 1982. *In Labor: Women and Power in the Birthplace.* New York: Norton.

Rowland, Robyn, ed. 1984. *Women Who Do and Women Who Don't Join the Women's Movement.* Boston: Routledge & Kegan Paul.

Rubin, Gayle. 1974. "The traffic in women: Notes on the 'political economy' of sex." In *Toward an Anthropology of Women,* edited by Rayna Reiter, pp. 157–210. New York: Monthly Review Press.

Rubin, Jeffrey Z., Frank J. Provenzano, & Zella Luria. 1974. "The eye of the beholder: Parents' views on sex of newborns." *American Journal of Orthopsychiatry* 44:512–19.

Ruddick, Sara. 1982. "Maternal thinking." In *Rethinking the Family: Some Feminist Questions,* edited by Barrie Thorne & Marilyn Yalom, pp. 76–94. New York: Longman.

Ruddick, Sara, & Pamela Daniels, ed. 1977. *Working It Out: Twenty-Three Women Writers, Artists, Scientists, and Scholars Talk About Their Lives and Work.* New York: Pantheon.

Ruether, Rosemary. 1983. *Sexism and God-Talk: Toward a Feminist Theology.* Boston: Beacon.

———, ed. 1974. *Religion and Sexism: Images of Women in the Jewish and Christian Traditions.* New York: Simon & Schuster.

Ruggiero, Karen M., & Donald M. Taylor. 1995. "Coping with discrimination: How disadvantaged group members perceive the discrimination that confronts them." *Journal of Personality and Social Psychology* 68:826–38.

Ruggles, Steven. 1994. "The origins of African-American family structure." *American Sociological Review* 59:136–51.

Rupp, Leila. 1985. "The woman's community in the National Woman's Party, 1945 to the 1960's." *Signs* 10:715–40.

Russo, Ann, & Cheris Kramarae, ed. 1991. *The Radical Women's Press of the 1850s.* New York: Routledge.

Ryan, Mary P. 1979. "The power of women's networks: A case study of female moral reform in antebellum America." *Feminist Studies* 5:66–85.

Sadker, Myra Pollack, & David Miller Sadker. 1980. "Sexism in teacher education texts." *Harvard Education Review* 50:36–46.

Sagatun, Inger J. 1993. "Babies born with drug addiction: Background and legal responses." In *It's a Crime: Women and Justice,* edited by Roslyn Muraskin & Ted Alleman, pp. 118–29. Englewood Cliffs, NJ: Prentice Hall.

Saint, David J. 1994. "Complementarity in marital relationships." *Journal of Social Psychology* 134:701–3.

Salem, Dorothy. 1990. *To Better Our World: Black Women in Organized Reform, 1890–1920.* New York: Carlson Publishing.

Salzinger, Suzanne, Sandra Kaplan, & Connie Artmeyeff. 1983. "Mothers' personal social networks and child maltreatment." *Journal of Abnormal Psychology* 92:68–76.

Samar, Vincent. 1991. *The Right to Privacy: Gays, Lesbians, and the Constitution.* Philadelphia: Temple University Press.

Sanday, Peggy Reeves. 1981a. *Female Power and Male Dominance: On the Origins of Sexual Inequality.* New York: Cambridge University Press.

———. 1981b. "The socio-cultural context of rape: A cross-cultural study." *Journal of Social Issues* 37:5–27.

Sanders, Marlene, & Marcia Rock. 1988. *Waiting for Prime Time: The Women of Television News.* Urbana: University of Illinois Press.

Sanderson, Catherine A., & Nancy Cantor. 1995. "Social dating goals in late adolescence: Implications for safer sexual activity." *Journal of Personality and Social Psychology* 68:121–34.

Sapiro, Virginia. 1982a. "Public costs of private commitments or private costs of public commitments: Family roles versus political ambition." *American Journal of Political Science* 26:265–79.

———. 1982b. "If U.S. Senator Baker were a woman: An experimental study of candidate images." *Political Psychology* 3:61–83.

———. 1983. *The Political Integration of Women: Roles, Socialization, and Politics.* Urbana: University of Illinois Press.

———. 1984. "Women, citizenship, and nationality: Immigration and nationalization policies in the United States." *Politics and Society* 13:1–26.

———. 1989. "The women's movement and the creation of gender consciousness: Social movements as socialization agents." In *Political Socialization for Democracy,* edited by Orit Ichilov, pp. 266–80. New York: Teachers' College Press.

———. 1991. "Feminism: A generation later." *The Annals of the American Academy of Political and Social Science* 515:10–22.

———. 1992. *A Vindication of Political Virtue: The Political Theory of Mary Wollstonecraft.* Chicago: University of Chicago Press.

———. 1993a. "Engendering cultural differences." In *The Rising Tide of Cultural Pluralism: The Nation State at Bay?*, edited by M. Crawford Young, pp. 36–54. Madison: University of Wisconsin Press.

———. 1993b. "'Private' coercion and democratic theory." In *Reconsidering the Democratic Public,* edited by George E. Marcus & Russell Hansen. University Park: Pennsylvania State University Press.

Sapiro, Virginia, & Pamela Johnston Conover. 1997. "The variable nature of gender in elections." *British Journal of Political Science* 27:497–524.

Sapiro, Virginia, & Barbara G. Farah. 1980. "New pride and old prejudice: Political ambitions and role orientations among female partisan elites." *Women and Politics* 1:13–36.

Sarrel, Lorna, & Philip Sarrel. 1984. *Sexual Turning Points: The Seven Stages of Adult Sexuality.* New York: Macmillan.

Sayers, Janet. 1982. *Biological Politics: Feminist and Anti-Feminist Perspectives.* New York: Tavistock.

Scanlon, Jennifer. 1995. *Inarticulate Longings:* The Ladies Home Journal, *Gender, and the Promises of Consumer Culture.* New York: Routledge.

Scharf, Lois, & Joan M. Jensen, eds. 1983. *Decades of Discontent.* Westport, CT: Greenwood.

Schneider, Alison. 1997. "Proportion of minority professors inches up to about 10%." *The Chronicle of Higher Education,* June 20, 1997.

Schneider, Joseph W., & Sally L. Hacker. 1973. "Sex role imagery and the use of generic 'man' in introductory texts." *American Sociologist* 8:12–18.

Schor, Juliet B. 1992. *The Overworked American: The Unexpected Decline of Leisure.* New York: Basic Books.

Schram, Vicki R., & Marilyn M. Dunsing. 1981. "Influences on married women's volunteer work participation." *Journal of Consumer Research* 7:373–79.

Schramm, Sarah Slavin. 1979. *Plow Women Rather Than Reapers: An Intellectual History of Feminism in the United States.* Metuchen, NJ: Scarecrow Press.

Schwendinger, Loren. 1990. "Property-owning free African-American women in the South, 1880–1970." *Journal of Women's History* 1:13–44.

Scott, Anne Firor. 1970. *The Southern Lady: From Pedestal to Politics.* Chicago: University of Chicago Press.

———. 1990. "Most invisible of all: Black women's voluntary associations." *Journal of Southern History* 56:3–22.

———. 1992. *Natural Allies: Women's Associations in American History.* Urbana: University of Illinois Press.

Scott-Jones, D., & M. Clark. 1986. "The school experiences of black girls: The interaction of gender, race, and socioeconomic status." *Phi Delta Kappan* 67:520–26.

Scully, Diana. 1990. *Understanding Sexual Violence: A Study of Convicted Rapists.* Cambridge, MA: Unwin Hyman.

Segal, Lynne, & Mary McIntosh, eds. 1992. *Sex Exposed: Sexuality and the Pornography Debate.* New Brunswick, NJ: Rutgers University Press.

Seiden, Ann M. 1976. "Overview: Research on the psychology of women: Gender differences in sexual and reproductive life." *American Journal of Psychiatry* 133:995–1007.

Seidenberg, Robert. 1971. "Advertising and abuse of drugs." *New England Journal of Medicine* 284:789–90.

Seidman, Steven A. 1992. "An investigation of sex-role stereotyping in music videos." *Journal of Broadcasting and Electronic Media* 36:209–16.

Seller, Maxine S. 1982. "The education of immigrant women, 1900–35." In *Women's America,* edited by Linda K. Kerber & Jane de Hart Mathews, pp. 242–56. New York: Oxford University Press.

———. 1987. "Defining socialist womanhood: The women's page of the *Jewish Daily Forward* in 1919." *American Jewish History* 76:416–38.

Serbin, Lisa A., Daniel K. O'Leary, Ronald M. Kent, & Ilene J. Tonick. 1973. "A comparison of teacher response to the preacademic and problem behavior of boys and girls." *Child Development* 44:796–884.

Seto, Todd B., et al. 1996. "Effect of physician gender on the prescription of estrogen replacement therapy." *Journal of General Internal Medicine* 11:197–203.

Settin, Joan M., & Dana Bramel. 1981. "Interaction of client class and gender biasing in clinical judgment." *American Journal of Orthopsychiatry* 51:510–20.

Shapiro, Robert Y., & Harpreet Mahajan. 1986. "Gender differences in policy preferences: A summary of trends from the 1960's to the 1980's. *Public Opinion Quarterly* 50:42–61.

Sharpe, Patricia A. 1995. "Older women and health services: Moving from ageism toward empowerment." *Women & Health* 22:9–23.

Shaver, Philip, & Jonathan Freedman. 1976. "Your pursuit of happiness." *Psychology Today* 10:26–32.

Shaw, Lois B., & David Shapiro. 1987. "Women's work expectations and actual experience." *Monthly Labor Review* 110:7–13.

Shaw, Stephanie J. 1991. "Black club women and the creation of the National Association of Colored Women." *Journal of Women's History* 3:10–25.

Sherman, Julia. 1980. "Mathematics, spatial visualization, and related factors: Changes in boys and girls, grades 8–11." *Journal of Educational Psychology* 72:476–82.

Shevelow, Kathryn. 1989. *Women and Print Culture: The Construction of Femininity in the Early Periodical.* New York: Routledge.

Shoemaker, Nancy, ed. 1994. *Negotiators of Change: Historical Perspectives on Native American Women.* New York: Routledge.

Shorter, Edward. 1982. *A History of Women's Bodies.* New York: Basic.

Shotland, R. Lance, & Jane M. Craig. 1988. "Can men and women differentiate between friendly and sexually interested behavior?" *Social Psychology Quarterly* 51:66–73.

Shulman, Alix Kates. 1983. *Red Emma Speaks.* New York: Schocken.

Shumaker, Sally A., Teresa Rust Smith. 1994. "The politics of women's health." *The Journal of Social Issues* 50: 189–202.

Siegfried, William D. 1982. "The effects of specifying job requirements and using explicit warnings to decrease sex discrimination in employment interviews." *Sex Roles* 8:73–82.

Signorielli, Nancy, & Margaret Lears. 1992. "Children, television and conceptions about chores: Attitudes and behaviors." *Sex Roles* 27:157–70.

Silber, Nina. 1989. "Intemperate men, spiteful women, and Jefferson Davis: Northern views of the defeated South." *American Quarterly* 41:614–35.

Simon, Rita J., & Jean M. Landis. 1989. "Report: Women's and men's attitudes about a woman's place and role." *Public Opinion Quarterly* 53:265–76.

Sinkoff, Nancy B. 1988. "Educating for 'proper' Jewish womanhood: A case study in domesticity and vocational training, 1897–1926." *American Jewish History* 77: 572–99.

Sklar, Kathryn Kish. 1982. "Catharine Beecher: Transforming the teaching profession." In *Women's America,* edited by Linda K. Kerber & Jane de Hart Mathews, pp. 140–48. New York: Oxford University Press.

Skocpol, Theda. 1992. *Protecting Soldiers and Mothers: The Political Origins of Social Policy in the United States.* Cambridge, MA: Harvard University Press.

Sloane, Ethel. 1993. *Biology of Women,* 3rd ed. New York: Delmar Publishers.

Smart, Charles R., R. Edward Henrick, James H. Rutledge, & Robert A. Smith. 1995. "Benefit of mammography screening in women ages 40 to 49 years: Current evidence from randomized controlled trials." *Cancer* 75: 1619–26.

Smith, Lois J. 1994. "A content analysis of gender differences in children's advertising." *Journal of Broadcasting & Electronic Media* 38:323–37.

Smith, M. 1980. "Sex bias in counseling and psychotherapy." *Psychological Bulletin* 87:392–407.

Smith, Tom W. 1987. "That which we call welfare by any other name would smell sweeter: An analysis of the impact of question wording on response patterns." *Public Opinion Quarterly* 51:75–83.

Smith-Lovin, Lynn, & Charles Brody. 1989. "Interruptions in group discussions: The effects of gender and group composition." *American Sociological Review* 54: 424–35.

Smith-Rosenberg, Carroll. 1975. "The female world of love and ritual: Relations between women in nineteenth century America." *Signs* 1:1–29.

Sniezek, Janet A., & Christine H. Jazwinski. 1986. "Gender bias in English: In search of fair language." *Journal of Applied Social Psychology* 16:642–62.

Snyder, Mark, & Seymour W. Uranowitz. 1978. "Reconstructing the past: Some cognitive consequences of person perception." *Journal of Personality and Social Psychology* 36:941–50.

Snyder, Paula. 1992. *The European Women's Almanac.* New York: Columbia University Press.

Sochen, June. 1972. *The New Woman: Feminism in Greenwich Village, 1910–20.* New York: Quadrangle.

———. 1973. *Movers and Shakers: American Women Thinkers and Activists, 1900–70.* New York: Quadrangle.

———. 1981. *Herstory: A Record of the American Woman's Past.* Sherman Oaks, CA: Alfred.

Sommer, Barbara, & Robert Sommer. 1997. *A Practical Guide to Behavioral Research: Tools and Techniques.* New York: Oxford University Press.

Sommers, Paul M., & Laura S. Thomas. 1983. "Restricting federal funds for abortion: Another look." *Social Science Quarterly* 6:40–46.

Sonnert, Gerhard, & Gerald Holton. 1996. "Career patterns of women and men in the sciences." *American Scientist* 84:63–71.

South, Scott J., & Glenna Spitze. 1994. "Housework in marital and nonmarital households." *American Sociological Review* 59:327–47.

Spelman, Elizabeth V. 1988. *Inessential Woman: Problems of Exclusion in Feminist Thought.* Boston: Beacon Press.

Sperling, Susan. 1991. "Baboons with briefcases: Feminism, functionalism, and sociobiology in the evolution of primate gender." *Signs* 17:1–27.

Spiegel, David. 1982. "Mothering, fathering, and mental illness." In *Rethinking the Family: Some Feminist Questions,* edited by Barrie Thorne, pp. 95–110. New York: Longman.

Spivak, Gayatri Chakravorty. 1987. *In Other Worlds: Essays in Cultural Politics.* New York: Routledge.

Sprafkin, Joyce N., & Robert M. Liebert. 1978. "Sex typing and children's television preferences." In *Hearth and Home,* edited by Gaye Tuchman, Arlene Kaplan Daniels, & James Benet, pp. 228–39. New York: Oxford University Press.

Stack, Carol B. 1974. *All Our Kin: Strategies for Survival in a Black Community.* New York: Harper & Row.

Stake, Jayne, & Charles R. Granger. 1978. "Same sex and opposite sex teacher model influences on science career commitment among high school students." *Journal of Educational Psychology* 70:180–86.

Stanko, Elizabeth Anne. 1982. "Would you believe this woman? Prosecutorial screening for 'credible' witnesses and a problem of justice." In *Judge, Lawyer, Victim, Thief: Women, Gender Roles, and Criminal Justice,* edited by Nicole Hahn Rafter & Elizabeth Anne Stanko, pp. 63–82. Boston: Northeastern University Press.

Stanton, Elizabeth Cady. [1895] 1974. *The Woman's Bible.* New York: Arno Press.

Stanton, Elizabeth Cady, Susan B. Anthony, & Mathilda J. Gage. [1881] 1969. *History of Women's Suffrage.* New York: Arno.

Stanworth, Michelle. 1983. *Gender and Schooling.* London: Hutchison.

Starhawk. 1979. *The Spiral Dance: A Rebirth of the Ancient Religion of the Great Goddess.* San Francisco: Harper & Row.

Staudt, Kathleen A. 1985. *Women, Foreign Assistance, and Advocacy Administration.* New York: Praeger.

Steichen, Donna. 1991. *Ungodly Rage: The Hidden Face of Catholic Feminism.* San Francisco: Ignatius Press.

Steinberg, Ronnie. 1987. "Radical challenges in a liberal world: The mixed success of comparable worth." *Gender and Society* 1:466–75.

Sterling, Dorothy, ed. 1984. *We Are Your Sisters: Black Women in the Nineteenth Century.* New York: Norton.

Stipek, Deborah J., & J. Heidi Gralinski. 1991. "Gender differences in children's achievement-related beliefs and emotional responses to success and failure in mathematics." *Journal of Educational Psychology* 83:361–71.

Stone, Rebecca, & Cynthia Waszak. 1992. "Adolescent knowledge and attitudes about abortion." *Family Planning Perspectives* 24:52–57.

Strober, Myra H., & David Tyack. 1980. "Why do women teach and men manage? A report on research on schools." *Signs* 5:494–503.

Strube, Michael J., & Linda S. Barbour. 1983. "The decision to leave an abusive relationship: Economic dependence and psychological commitment." *Journal of Marriage and the Family* 45:785–93.

Sullivan, Patrick F. 1995. "Mortality in anorexia nervosa." *The American Journal of Psychiatry* 152 (July): 1073–74.

Swerdlow, Marian. 1989. "Men's accommodations to women entering a nontraditional occupation: A case of rapid transit operatives." *Gender and Society* 3:373–87.

Swim, Janet. 1994. "Perceived versus meta-analytic effect sizes: An assessment of the accuracy of gender stereotypes." *Journal of Personality and Social Psychology* 66: 21–36.

Swim, Janet K., Kathryn J. Aikin, Wayne S. Hall, & Barbara A. Hunter. 1995. "Sexism and racism: Old-fashioned and modern prejudices." *Journal of Personality and Social Psychology* 68:199–214.

Swim, Janet, Eugene Borgida, Geoffrey Maruyama, & David G. Myers. 1989. "Joan McKay versus John McKay: Do gender stereotypes bias evaluations?" *Psychological Bulletin* 105:409–29.

Tannen, Deborah. 1990. *You Just Don't Understand: Women and Men in Conversation.* New York: William Morrow.

———. 1994. *Gender and Discourse.* New York: Oxford University Press.

Tanney, Mary Faith, & Janice M. Birk. 1976. "Women counselors for women clients? A review of the research." *Counseling Psychologist* 6:28–32.

Thistlethwaite, Susan. 1989. *Sex, Race, and God: Christian Feminism in Black and White.* New York: Crossroad.

Thomas, Claire Sherman. 1991. *Sex Discrimination in a Nutshell.* St. Paul, MN: West Publishing.

Thomas, Sue. 1994. *How Women Legislate.* New York: Oxford University Press.

Thomas, V. G., & M. D. James. 1988. "Body image, dieting tendencies, and sex role traits in urban black women." *Sex Roles* 18:523–29.

Thompson, Becky Wangsgaard. 1992. "'A way outa no way': Eating problems among African-American, Latina, and white women." *Gender and Society* 6:546–61.

Thompson, Victor A. 1961. *Modern Organization.* New York: Alfred A. Knopf.

Tidball, M. Elizabeth. 1980. "Women's colleges and women achievers revisited." *Signs* 5:504–17.

Tiger, Lionel. 1969. *Men in Groups.* New York: Vintage.

Tobias, Sheila, & Lisa Anderson. 1982. "What really happened to Rosie the Riveter? Demobilization and the female labor force, 1944–47." In *Women's America: Refocusing the Past,* edited by Linda K. Kerber & Jane de Hart Mathews, pp. 354–73. New York: Oxford University Press.

Toth, Emily. 1980. "The fouler sex: Women's bodies in advertising." In *Issues in Feminism: A First Course in Women's Studies,* edited by Sheila Ruth, pp. 107–14. Boston: Houghton Mifflin.

Treichler, Paula A. 1984. "Women, language, and health care: An annotated bibliography." *Women and Language News* 7:7–19.

Trennert, Robert A. 1988. "Victorian morality and the supervision of Indian women working in Phoenix, 1906–30." *Journal of Social History* 22:113–28.

Trudell, Bonnie Nelson. 1993. *Doing Sex Education: Gender Politics and Schooling*. New York: Routledge.

Tsosie, Rebecca. 1988. "Changing women: The cross-currents of American Indian feminine identity." *American Indian Culture and Research Journal* 12:1–38.

Tuchman, Gaye. 1978. "Introduction." In *Hearth and Home: Images of Women in the Mass Media*, edited by Gaye Tuchman, Arlene Kaplan Daniels, & James Benet, pp. 3–38. New York: Oxford University Press.

Tuchman, Gaye, Arlene Kaplan Daniels, & James Benet, eds. 1978. *Hearth and Home: Images of Women in the Mass Media*. New York: Oxford University Press.

Tudor, William, Jeanette F. Tudor, & Walter R. Gove. 1977. "The effects of sex role differences on the social control of mental illness." *Journal of Health and Social Behavior* 18:98–112.

Turkel, Sherry, & Seymour Papert. 1990. "Epistemological pluralism: Styles and voices within the computer culture." *Signs* 16:128–57.

Ulbrich, Patricia, & Joan Huber. 1981. "Observing parental violence: Distribution effect." *Journal of Marriage and the Family* 43:623–32.

Unger, Rhoda K. 1979. *Female and Male: Psychological Perspectives*. New York: Harper & Row.

United Nations. 1995a. *Women and Men in Europe and North America, 1995*. Geneva, Switzerland: United Nations.

———. 1995b. *The World's Women, 1995:Trends and Statistics*. New York: United Nations.

U.S. Bureau of the Census. 1982. *Statistical Abstract of the United States*. Washington, DC: Government Printing Office.

———. 1987a. *Statistical Abstract of the United States*. Washington, DC: Government Printing Office.

———. 1987b. *Current Population Reports Series P-70, No. 10: Male-Female Differences in Work Experience, Occupation, and Earnings, 1984*. Washington, DC: Government Printing Office.

———. 1989. *Statistical Abstract of the United States*. Washington, DC: Government Printing Office.

———. 1992. *Statistical Abstract of the United States*. Washington, DC: Government Printing Office.

———. 1997. *Statistical Abstract of the United States*. Washington, DC: Government Printing Office. Also available at http://www.census.gov/prod/www/abs/cc97stab.html/.

U.S. Commission on Civil Rights. 1979. *Window Dressing on the Set: An Update*. Washington, DC: Government Printing Office.

U.S. Congress, House of Representatives Committee on Immigration and Naturalization. 1930. "Supreme Court decision, citations, comment, etc. *In re* Rosika Schwimmer and Martha Jane Graber." 71st Congress, 2d Session, 6 March.

U.S. Department of Education, Office of Educational Research and Improvement. 1992. *Digest of Education Statistics*. Washington, DC: U.S. Government Printing Office.

U.S. Department of Labor. 1989. *Employment and Earnings* (January 1989). Washington, DC: Government Printing Office.

———. 1992. *Monthly Labor Review* (November 1992). Washington, DC: Government Printing Office.

U.S. Merit Systems Protection Board. 1981. *Sexual Harassment in the Federal Workplace: Is It a Problem?* Washington, DC: Government Printing Office.

Valeska, Lucia. 1975. "If all else fails, I'm still a mother." *Quest* 1:52–63.

Vance, Carole S., ed. 1984. *Pleasure and Danger: Exploring Female Sexuality*. New York: Routledge.

Vande Berg, Leah R., & Diane Streckfuss. 1992. "Primetime television's portrayal of women and the world of work: A demographic profile." *Journal of Broadcasting and Electronic Media* 36:195–208.

Vanek, Joann. 1980. "Household work, wage work, and sexual equality." In *Women and Household Labor*, edited by Sarah Fenstermaker Berk, pp. 275–92. Beverly Hills, CA: Sage.

Vest, David. 1992. "Prime-time pilots: A content analysis of changes in gender representation." *Journal of Broadcasting and Electronic Media* 36:25–43.

Vladeck, Judith P. 1981. "Sex discrimination in higher education." *Women's Rights Law Reporter* 7:27–38.

Voyer, Daniel, Susan Voyer, & M. P. Bryden. 1995. "Magnitude of sex differences in spatial abilities: A meta-analysis and consideration of critical variables." *Psychological Bulletin* 117:250–70.

Waelti-Walters, Jennifer. 1979. "On princesses: Fairy tales, sex roles, and loss of self." *International Journal of Women's Studies* 2:180–88.

Wagner, Lilya. 1989. *Women War Correspondents of World War II*. Westport, CT: Greenwood.

Waldman, Elizabeth. 1983. "Labor force statistics from a family perspective." *Monthly Labor Review* 106:16–20.

Walker, Anne. 1995. "Theory and methodology in premenstrual syndrome research." *Social Science and Medicine* 41:793–800.

Walker, K. 1994. "Men, women, and friendship: What they say, what they do." *Gender and Society* 8:246–65.

Walker, Lawrence. 1984. "Sex differences in the development of moral reasoning: A critical review." *Child Development* 55:667–91.

Walsh, Mary Roth. 1979. "The rediscovery of the need for a feminist medical education." *Harvard Education Review* 49:447–66.

Ware, Susan. 1981. *Beyond Suffrage: Women in the New Deal.* Cambridge, MA: Harvard University Press.

———. 1983. *Holding Their Own: American Women in the 1930's.* Boston: Twayne.

Warner, Marina. 1976. *Alone of All Her Sex: The Myth and the Cult of Mary.* New York: Random House.

Warner, Rebecca L. 1991. "Does the sex of your child matter? Support for feminism among women and men in the U.S. and Canada." *Journal of Marriage and the Family* 53:1951–56.

Weeks, Jeffrey. 1977. *Coming Out: Homosexual Politics in Britain, from the Nineteenth Century to the Present.* London: Quartet.

Weeks, M. O'Neal, & Darla R. Botkin. 1987. "A longitudinal study of the marriage role expectations of college women: 1961–84." *Sex Roles* 17:49–58.

Weinraub, M., L. P. Clements, A. Sockloff, E. Gracely, & B. Myers. 1984. "The development of sex role stereotypes in the third year: Relationship to gender labeling, gender identity, sex-typed toy preferences." *Child Development* 55:1493–1503.

Weisfeld, Carol C., Glenn E. Weisfeld, & John W. Callaghan. 1982. "Female inhibition in mixed sex competition among young adolescents." *Ethnology and Sociobiology* 3:29–42.

Weiss, Robert S. 1984. "The impact of marital dissolution on income and consumption in single-parent households." *Journal of Marriage and the Family* 46:115–28.

Weissinger, Catherine, ed. 1993. *Women's Leadership in Marginal Religions: Explorations Outside the Mainstream.* Urbana: University of Illinois Press.

Weitzman, Leonore J. 1979. *Sex Role Socialization.* Mountain View, CA: Mayfield.

———. 1985. *The Divorce Revolution: The Unexpected Social and Economic Consequences for Women and Children in America.* New York: Free Press.

Welch, Susan. 1978. "Recruitment of women to public office: A discriminant analysis." *Western Political Quarterly* 31:372–80.

Wellington, Alison J. 1994. "Accounting for the male/female wage gap among whites: 1976 and 1985." *American Sociological Review* 59:839–48.

Welter, Barbara. 1966. "The cult of true womanhood, 1830–1860." *American Quarterly* 18:151–74.

West, Candace. 1984. "When the doctor is a 'lady': Power, status, and gender in physician-patient encounters." *Symbolic Interaction* 7:87–106.

West, Candace, & Don H. Zimmerman. 1987. "Doing gender." *Gender and Society* 1:125–51.

Wheeless, Virginia Eman, & Paul F. Potorti. 1989. "Student assessment of teacher masculinity and femininity: A test of the sex role congruency hypothesis on student attitudes toward learning." *Journal of Educational Psychology* 81:259–62.

White, Deborah Gray. 1985. *"Ar'n't I a Woman?" Female Slaves in the Plantation South.* New York: Norton.

White, E. Frances. 1990. "Africa on my mind: Gender, counter discourse and African-American nationalism." *Journal of Women's History* 2:73–97.

White, Evelyn C. 1990. *The Black Women's Health Book: Speaking for Ourselves.* Seattle, WA: Seal Press.

White, Gregory L., Sanford Fishbein, & Jeffrey Rutstein. 1981. "Passionate love and misattribution of arousal." *Journal of Personality and Social Psychology* 41:56–62.

White, Lynn K., & David B. Brinkerhoff. 1981. "The sexual division of labor: Evidence from childhood." *Social Forces* 60:170–81.

Whitley, Bernard E., Jr., & Mary E. Kite. 1995. "Sex differences in attitudes toward homosexuality: A comment on Oliver and Hyde (1993)." *Psychological Bulletin* 117:146–54.

Whittaker, Susan, & Ron Whittaker. 1976. "Relative effectiveness of male and female newscasters." *Journal of Broadcasting* 20:177–84.

Wiederman, Michael W., & Christine Cregan Sensibaugh. 1995. "The acceptance of legalized abortion." *The Journal of Social Psychology* 135:785–87.

Wiegers, T. A., et al. 1996. "Outcome of planned home and planned hospital births in low risk pregnancies." *British Medical Journal* 313:1309–13.

Wilbanks, William. 1982. "Murdered women and women who murder: A critique of the literature." In *Judge, Lawyer, Victim, Thief: Women, Gender Roles, and Criminal Justice,* edited by Nicole Hahn Rafter & Elizabeth Anne Stanko, pp. 151–80. Boston: Northeastern University Press.

Wiley, Mary G., & Arlene Eskilson. 1982. "The interaction of sex and power based on perceptions of managerial effectiveness." *Academy of Management Journal* 25:671–77.

Wilkie, Jane Riblett. 1993. "Changes in U.S. men's attitudes toward the family provider role, 1972–1989." *Gender and Society* 7:261–79.

Wilson, E. O. 1975. *Sociobiology: A New Synthesis.* Cambridge, MA: Harvard University Press.

Wing, Adrien Katherine. 1997. "Brief reflections toward a multiplicative theory and praxis of being." In *Critical Race Feminism,* edited by Adrien Katherine Wing, pp. 27–34. New York: New York University Press.

Wise, Erica, & Janet Rafferty. 1982. "Sex bias and language." *Sex Roles* 8:1189–96.

Wolff, Charlotte. 1971. *Love Between Women.* New York: Harper & Row.

Wollstonecraft, Mary. [1792] 1975. *A Vindication of the Rights of Woman.* Baltimore: Penguin. Excerpted in Rossi (1988).

"Women drinking alcohol: When less is more." 1995. *Science News* 146:324.

Women on Words and Images. 1972. *Dick and Jane as Victims.* Princeton, NJ: Know, Inc.

Woods, Laurie. 1981. "Litigation on behalf of battered women." *Women's Rights Law Reporter* 7:39–46.

Woolf, Virginia. 1995. *Orlando.* Ware, England: Wordsworth Editions, Ltd.

Wright, Erik Olin, Janeen Baxter, J., & Gunn Elizabeth Birkelund. 1995. "The gender gap in workplace authority: A cross-national study." *American Sociological Review* 60:407–35.

Wylie, Philip. 1942. *A Generation of Vipers.* New York: Farrar and Rinehart.

Yang, Eun Sik. 1984. "Korean women of America: From subordination to partnership, 1903–1930." *Amerasia Journal* 11:1–28.

Yee, Doris K., & Jacquelynne S. Eccles. 1988. "Parent perceptions and attributions for children's math achievement." *Sex Roles* 19:317–33.

Zabin, Laurie S., Marilyn B. Hirsch, Mark R. Emerson, & Elizabeth Raymond. 1992. "To whom do inner city minors talk about their pregnancies? Adolescents' communication with parents and parent surrogates." *Family Planning Perspectives* 24:148–54.

Zeldow, Peter B. 1976. "Effects of nonpathological sex role stereotypes on student evaluations of psychiatric patients." *Journal of Consulting and Clinical Psychology* 44:304.

Zellman, Gail L., & Jacqueline D. Goodchilds. 1983. "Becoming sexual in adolescence." In *Changing Boundaries: Gender Roles and Sexual Behavior,* edited by Elizabeth Rice Allgeier & Naomi B. McCormick, pp. 49–63. Mountain View, CA: Mayfield.

Zimmerman, Don H., & Candace West. 1975. "Sex roles, interruptions, and silences in conversation." In *Language and Sex,* edited by Barrie Thorne & Nancy Henley, pp. 105–29. Rowley, MA: Newbury House.

Zinn, Maxine Baca. 1989. "Family, race, and poverty in the eighties." *Signs* 14:856–74.

Zucker, Kenneth J., Debra N. Wilson-Smith, & Janice A. Kurita. 1995. "Children's appraisals of sex-typed behavior in their peers." *Sex Roles* 33:703–25.

Credits

Photographs

Chapter 1 p. 8, New York State Historical Association, Cooperstown; p. 23, © Elizabeth Crews; **Chapter 2** p. 44(l), © AP/Wide World Photos; p. 44(c), © AP/Wide World Photos; p. 44(r), © Reuters/Corbis-Bettmann; p. 57, © Culver Pictures; p. 61, Courtesy Wyoming Division of Cultural Resources; **Chapter 3** p. 109, © Reuters/Mike Theiler/Archive Photos; **Chapter 4** p. 122, © Zigy Kaluzny/Tony Stone Images; p. 134, © Bettye Lane/Photo Researchers, Inc.; **Chapter 5** p. 150, Courtesy Bethune-Cookman College, Office of Public Relations; p. 157, © Andrea Mohin/NYT Permissions; p. 170, Photo by A.J. Schillare, Northampton, MA. Smith College, Sophia Smith Collection; **Chapter 6** p. 185, © Brown Brothers; p. 195, © Brown Brothers; p. 198, © David Levinthal; p. 200, © NYT Pictures/NYT Permissions; **Chapter 7** p. 223, © Kevin Horan/Picture Group; p. 236, © Corbis; p. 237, © UPI/Corbis-Bettmann; **Chapter 8** p. 251, © 1997 ABC, Inc.; **Chapter 9** p. 289, © AP/Wide World Photos; p. 297, © AP/Wide World Photos; p. 307, © Brown Brothers; **Chapter 10** p. 337, © Reuters/Archive Photos; p. 346, © Patsy Davidson/The Image Works; **Chapter 11** p. 380, © AP/Wide World Photos; **Chapter 12** p. 405, Courtesy The Staten Island Historical Society; p. 420, © Elizabeth Crews; p. 424, © The Granger Collection, New York; **Chapter 13** p. 448, © Brown Brothers; **Chapter 14** p. 504, © Brown Brothers; p. 522, © AP/Wide World Photos

Text and Illustrations

Chapter 2 p. 42 Fig. 2-1 *From Women and Men in Europe and North America*, 1995, p. 30. Reprinted by permission of The United Nations. **Chapter 3** p. 77 "Words of Comfort to Be Scratched on a Mirror" by Dorothy Parker, from *The Portable Dorothy Parker* by Dorothy Parker, Introduction by Brendan Gill. Copyright ©1928, renewed © 1956 by Dorothy Parker. Used by permission of Viking Penguin, a division of Penguin Putnam Inc. p. 79 By permission. From *Merriam-Webster's Collegiate® Dictionary*, Tenth Edition. Copyright © 1996 by Merriam-Webster, Incorporated. p. 79 From *Concise Oxford Dictionary*. Reprinted by permission of Oxford University Press. p. 81 Table 3-1 Reproduced by special permission of the Distributor, Mind Garden, Inc., P.O. Box 60669, Palo Alto, CA 94306, from the Bem Sex Role Inventory by Sandra Lipsitz Bem. Copyright

Chapter 5 p. 168 Table 5-5 From "Characteristics of Full-Time Faculty Members with Teaching Duties" in *Chronicle of Higher Education,* Fall 1992. Copyright © 1992 The Chronicle of Higher Education. Excerpted and adapted with permission. **Chapter 8** p. 253 Table 8-1 From Media Report to Women 20 (Fall 1992), pp. 4–5. Reprinted by permission. p. 261 From Katarina Bjarvall, "Women Pack Swedish Parliament," Associated Press, September 20, 1994. Used with permission. **Chapter 9** p. 317 Table 9-3 From *Women and Men in Europe and North America,* 1995, p. 30. Reprinted by permission of the United Nations. **Chapter 10** p. 333 From *The Oxford English Dictionary.* Reprinted by permission of Oxford University Press. p. 352 Box 10-2 From B.W. Eakins and R.G. Eakins, *Sex Differences in Human Communication.* Copyright ©1978 Harper & Row Publishers. Reprinted by permission of Addison Wesley Educational Publishers Inc. **Chapter 11** p. 365 Fig. 11-1 From Edward O. Laumann, Robert T. Michael, John H. Gagnon, Stuart Michaels, *The Social Organization of Sexuality: Sexual Practices in the United States,* University of Chicago Press, 1994. Reprinted with permission of the publisher. p. 368 Table 11-1 From NYT/CBS News Poll, February 9–11, 1993. Copyright ©1993 by The New York Times Company. Reprinted by permission. p. 377 Box 11-1 Letter to the Editor by Timothy C. Brock and Laura A. Brannon from *The New York Times,* 11/23/91. p. 386 Box 11-2 From "Cultural Myths and Supports for Rape" by Martha R. Burt in *Journal of Personality and Social Psychology* 38:217-30. Copyright © 1980 by the American Psychological Association. Adapted with permission from the American Psychological Association and the author. **Chapter 12** p. 432 Table 12-2 Adapted from Ruggles 1994, #1, February, pp. 138, 140. American Sociological Association. Copyright ©1994 American Sociological Association. Used with permission of the publisher. **Chapter 13** p. 466 Table 13-4 From Bettina Berch, *The Endless Day: The Political Economy of Women and Work.* Orlando, FL: Harcourt Brace & Company, 1982, pp. 12–13. With permission from the publisher.

Name Index

Subject Index

American Indian Healthcare Association, 181
American Indians. *See* Native American women
American Medical Association, 207
American Nurse's Association, 485
American Sign Language, 324
American Social Science Association, 151
American Telephone & Telegraph Company, 451, 455
American Transcendentalists, 148
American Woman Suffrage Association, 502
Amniocentesis, 415
Anal phase, of psychosexual development, 89
Androcentrism, 4–5, 63
Androgyny, 80, 81
Anglican Church, 219
Anorexia nervosa, 197–198
Anthropocentric, 4
Anthropomorphism, 219
Antiabortion movement, 418–419
Antidiscrimination laws, 44–46
Antifeminism, 55, 520
  sex-war theories, 73
Antiwar Movement, 511
"Appeal to the Christian Women of the South" (Grimké), 228
Archival research, 20–21
Arranged marriages, 395–396
Arts
  bias against special domains of women, 271
  bias against women in arts management, 269–270
  bias against women in film and television direction, 269
  bias against women musicians, 268–269
  bias in judgments of women artists, 270
  and censorship, 275–276
  distinctions between crafts and art, 271–272
  emphasis of modern art on female body, 276–277
  gender-typed images in, 267, 272–277

women in dance, 270
Asian American women
  dominant-society stereotypes of, 120
  unmarried mothers among, 407
Associated Press, 247
"A Team," 471
Athletes, women, and disordered eating patterns, 200
Athletics
  discrimination against women on college level, 173–174
  institutionalized as a male domain, 199–200
Athletic skills, gender differences, 87–88
Atrributional measures, of personality, 84
Automobile workers, women as, 465
Avon, 450

Backlash: The Undeclared War Against American Women (Faludi), 70, 518
Baker v. *Nelson*, 394
Ballard v. *U.S.*, 288
Bar mitzvah, 229
Barnard College, 149
Barnes v. *Costle*, 383
Bat mitzvah, 229
Bazaarr, 255
Beal v. *Doe*, 416
Beauty, gender-based standards of
  based upon various body parts, 195–196
  ideal image of in early 20th century, 195
  ideal image of in 19th century, 194–195
  physical and mental health effects of, 201
  relation to other forms of inequality, 202
Behavioral measures, of personality, 84
Bem Sex-Role Inventory, 81
Bethune-Cookman College, 149
Better Homes and Gardens, 255
Betty Crocker, 450
Bible

feminist interpretations of stories, 220–221
  interpretation of by various denominations, 218, 220–221
Biological research, on gender differences, 86–88
Birth control. *See* Contraception
Birth-control movement, 506
Birth-control pill, 409, 411, 412
Birthrate, teenage, 37–38, 406–407
Bisexuality, 363
Black matriarchal theories, 432–433
Blacks. *See* African American men; African Americans; African American women
Blind auditions, 269
Boda fide occupational qualification, 474, 475, 476
Body image, of African American women, 196–197
Body language and posture, gender differences in, 337–338
Bosnian war, 385
Boston's Women's Health Book Collective, 210
Bowers v. *Hardwick*, 369
Bradwell v. *Illinois*, 284–285
Brain lateralization, 53–54
Bread and Roses, 512
Breasts
  debate about cancer rates, 180
  historical view of, 180–181
  implants, 196
  self-examination, 180, 213 n.5
Bulimia, 197
Bundy v. *Jackson*, 383

Capitol Press Gallery, 247
Carey v. *Population Services International*, 404, 411
Case studies, 19–20
Castration complex, 90, 91
Catalyst, Inc., 470
Catholic Church. *See* Roman Catholic Church
Catholic Worker, The, 247
Censorship, and the arts, 275–277
Center for the American Woman and Politics, 315

controversy over causes of, 366–367

development of self-identity, 363–365

incidence of, 367

and military service, 292–293

religious suppression of, 225–226

repression of in U.S., 368–369

same-sex couples and the law, 399

Horizontal segregation, of employment by gender, 463–468

Hormone-replacement therapy, 184

Hormones, and sex differences, 51–53

Hourglass figure, 195

Household energy sources, in developing nations, 40–41

How Schools Shortchange Girls (AAUW), 153, 155–156, 164

Hoyt v. *Florida*, 288

Hull House, 209

Human evolution *vs.* human history, 64

Hunger strikes, 505

Hunter-gatherer societies, 63–64

Hypothesis testing, 12

Hysterectomy, 179–180

Hysteria, 50, 179

Iceland

maternal mortality rates, 187

Id, 89, 90

Illegitimate children, 390, 428–429

Illiteracy, 32–34

Immigrant women

educational efforts for, 151

organization for community action, 313

In a Different Voice (Gilligan), 85, 99

Inclusive language, 331

Inclusive Language Lectionary, 229

Industrialization, effect on power relations between men and women, 67

Inequality, and gender differences, 28–29

Infant mortality rates, 187, 482

Infibulation, 178–179

Influence styles, 345–349

Innate *vs.* developed skills, 54

Instincts, 88–89

Institutional theories, of gender differences, 108–112

Instrumental values, 346

Interdisciplinary studies, 10

International Association of Women Police, 306

International feminism, 516

International Ladies Garment Workers Union, 151

International League for Peace and Freedom, 510

International politics, and women, 316–317

International Woman Suffrage Alliance, 521

International Women's Decade, 481, 516, 523

International Women's Year Conferences, 523

Intersubjectivity, 14–15

Interviewing, depth, 19

Intrauterine devices, 409, 411, 412

Islam, separation of women, 220

Ivy League schools, 164

Jane (Kaplan), 16

Japan

marriage dynamics in, 395–396

state-sponsored rape by occupation forces, 47

Japanese American women, 396

Jarrett v. *Jarrett,* 426

Jesus, gender images of in Christian tradition, 219

Jewish Americans, 218

and conflicts in women's spirituality movement, 241

dominant-society stereotypes of women, 120

feminist interpretations of biblical stories, 220–221

gender in religious language, 220

integration of formerly gender-segregated rituals, 229

position on birth control, 226

position on divorce, 231

responsibility of women in creating Jewish home, 231

Sabbath meal, 231

views on gender, 220

Jewish Daily Forward, 506

Jewish socialist feminism, 506

Job model, 441, 485 n.1

Johnson v. *Transportation Agency, Santa Clara County,* 476

Joint custody, 428

Journalism. *See* Print media

Journal of the American Medical Association, 200

Judges, women as, 306, 314

Judicial interpretations, of rights of women, 284–285, 286–287

Judicial review, 284

Julia, 255

Jury duty, women and, 287–288

Justice *vs.* caring modes, of moral reasoning, 99

Kalliope: A Journal of Women's Art, 256

Kashruth, 231

Koran, 218

Korean Presbyterian Church, 226

Korean Women's Patriotic Society, 506

Ku Klux Klan, 116

Labor. *See* Domestic labor; Employment, of women

Labor force

auxiliary paid, 450–451

auxiliary unpaid, 449–450

Labor-saving devices, 265, 447

Labor unions, women in, 313, 483–484

La Conferencia de Mujeres por la Raza, 514

Ladder, The, 248

Ladies' Home Journal, 248, 255, 256, 257

Ladies Waist Makers Union, 151

Lamarckian principle, 64, 75 n.21

Lamaze classes, 206

La Mujer Obrera (The Working Woman), 485

Language. *See* Communication/ language

Late luteal phase dysphoric disorder (LLPDD), 183

Rape *(continued)*
  underreporting of, 298
  women's fear of, 389
Rape shield laws, 299, 300
Reader's Digest, 247
Redbook, 255
Red Scare, 509
Redstockings, 512
Reed v. *Reed,* 287
Regression, 95
Reliability, 14
Religion, organized
  forbidden marriages, 226
  fostering of women's activism, 224
  ordination of women, 235–236
  patriarchal images and language, 219
  position on birth control and abortion, 226
  position on divorce, 226
  power of in shaping American culture, 217
  promotion of inequality between men and women, 240
  punishment of politically and socially active women, 223–224
  regulation of sexual morality, 225–228
  resistance to feminism, 222, 518
  role in defining male and female, 219–225
  separation of church and state, 217
  and society, 239–241
  suppression of homosexuality, 225–226, 227, 368–369
  See also specific religions
Religious activities, of women
  charity and servicework, 232–235
  in everyday life, 230–231
  feminist alternatives to orthodoxy, 228–230, 240
  and ideal of female benevolence, 233–234
  linking of spirituality and political action, 234–235
  in the ministry, 236–239
  in nonministerial roles, 239
  as religious authorities and leaders, 235–239

as wives of clergy and missionaries, 231–232
Religious fundamentalist right, 518
Religious orientation
  and attitudes toward gender equality, 224
  effect on sexual views and behavior, 227–228
  by gender, 217, 218
Replacement-cost approach, of evaluating value of domestic labor, 480–481
Replicability, 14
Repression, 360
Reproduction and choice, 404–408
  abortion law, 412–416
  contraception, 408–412
  cross-national fertility, abortion, and contraception rates, 37–40
  as feminist issue, 515
  public funding for abortion, 416–417
  reasons for having children, 405–406
  teenage births, 37–38, 406–408
  timing of having children, 406
  unmarried-mother births, 406–407
Reproductive health, 181–187
Republican Wish List, 309
Request legitimacy, 348
Research methods. *See* Social science research; Women's studies, research methods
Restoration comedies, 272
Retirement experiences, of women, 461–463
Revolution, The, 246
Rhythm method, 409, 411
Rights of women, government view of
  founding ideas, 283–284
  judicial interpretations, 284–285
  in the late 20th century, 286–287
  legislative changes, 285–286
Ringwood's Afro-American Journal of Fashion, 245
Roe v. *Wade,* 413, 414, 415, 417, 419
Role. *See* Gender roles
Role conflict
  of employed women, 459–461

of women faculty, 170–171
Role loss, maternal, 433–434
Role models, importance to identity development, 159
Roman Catholic Church, 219
  celibacy rules, 227
  cult of the Virgin, 220
  notion of reproduction as sole reason for sexual activity, 225
  opposition to abortion, 226
  opposition to birth control, 226
  role of nuns, 227, 239
  sanctions against activist women, 223–224
Romer v. *Evans,* 369
Rosencrantz and Guildenstern Are Dead (Stoppard), 4
"Rosie the Riveter," 465
Rotsker v. *Goldberg,* 290–291
RU 486 (mifepristone), 419
Russian Revolution, 509

Same-sex couples, 399
Sample, 18
Sanctuary movement, 234
Sanitary Commission, 501
Schultz v. *Wheaton Glass Co.,* 479
Science, discrimination against women in, 160
Second Shift, The (Hochschild), 188
Selective exposure, 262
Selective perception, 262
Self-denial, in psychosexual development, 89
"Selfish gene," 72
Self-schemas, sexual, 361–362, 372–373
Seneca Falls Convention, 216, 282, 495, 500
Serial bonding, 37
Seven Sisters colleges, 149, 164
Seventeen, 256
Seventh Day Adventist Church, 235
Sex, defined, 54–56
Sex, extramarital, 375
Sex differences. *See* Gender differences
Sex education
  early campaigns for, 151
  gender-segregation in, 165